AF519663

HANDBOOK OF TELEVISION AND RADIO BROADCASTING

HANDBOOK OF TELEVISION AND RADIO BROADCASTING

Components, Tools and Techniques

VED PRAKASH GANDHI

KANISHKA PUBLISHERS, DISTRIBUTORS
NEW DELHI-110 002

KANISHKA PUBLISHERS, DISTRIBUTORS
4697/5-21A, Ansari Road, Daryaganj
New Delhi-110 002
Phones : 2327 0497, 2328 8285
Fax : 011-2328 8285
e-mail: kanishka_publishing@yahoo.co.in

First Published 2009

ISBN 978-81-8457-153-0

PRINTED IN INDIA

Published by Madan Sachdeva for Kanishka Publishers, Distributors, 4697/5-21A, Ansari Road, Daryaganj, New Delhi-110 002; Typeset by Sunshine Graphics, Delhi, and Printed at Rajdhani Printers, Delhi.

Preface

This book titled "Handbook of Television and Radio Broadcasting: Components, Tools and Techniques" provides readers with an overview of programming, networking and licensing aspects of broadcasting, broadcasting programme and broadcast programming. It also provides an exhaustive list of legal resources and regulatory notifications issued by Government of India as far as Indian broadcasting system and industry are concerned. An introduction to television broadcasting in India is provided, so is the details about the Indian Broadcasting Regulations Forum. Context of the report of the task force on introduction of Conditional Access System in India is outlined in detail. An overview of broadcasting content regulation is given with details of Ministry of Information and Broadcasting notifications in this regard. Also, presented is the text of the draft of the proposed broadcasting services regulation bill. The guidelines issued by the Ministry of Law and Justice, its legislative department, is also documented in detail. Similarly, the guidelines issued by the Ministry of Information and Broadcasting's Plan Co-ordination Cell is presented. Also, a list heads of all media units and organization is appended.

This handbook also makes sincere efforts towards creating an in-depth understanding of audio broadcasting systems, sound recording and reproduction and provides readers with details of basic and advanced tools, techniques and components. The focus here lies on digital sound recording and broadcasting. This reference book attempts to create a better understanding of video broadcast systems, both basic and additional types. Also, it makes efforts towards analyzing various audio-visual equipments being used by professionals towards broadcasting production and programming. The educational aspects of this issue are also covered briefly. The multiple types, components and standards of television and TV systems, such as NTSC, PAL, SECAM etc., are discussed in detail. This handbook also takes necessary initiatives to reflect briefly on various modulation principles, types and techniques, with special focus on keying and multiplexing. An overview of television programme production, organization and studies is given, with special mention of ways and means of getting a professional degree in this sector. In addition, this book also provides readers with an overview of radio, radio programming and radio production, with focus again of its educational aspects. All necessary details about camera types, materials and processes are provided herein. Similarly, knowledge required for effective lighting tools, techniques is outlined in brief. To further make this handbook user friendly and knowledge oriented, bibliography and Index are provided.

Ved Prakash Gandhi

Contents

Preface v

1. **Broadcasting: An Overview of Programming, Networking and Licensing** 1
   - ❑ Broadcasting
   - ❑ Broadcasting Programme
   - ❑ Broadcast Programming

2. **Indian Broadcasting: Legal Resources and Regulatory Notifications** 8
   - ❑ An Introduction to Television Broadcasting in India
   - ❑ Indian Broadcasting Regulations Forum
   - ❑ Report of the Task Force on Introduction of Conditional Access System
   - ❑ Broadcasting Content Regulation: An Overview
   - ❑ Ministry of Information and Broadcasting Notifications
   - ❑ Text of the Draft of the Proposed Broadcasting Services Regulation Bill
   - ❑ Guidelines by Law Ministry
   - ❑ Sports Broadcasting Signals (Mandatory Sharing with Prasar Bharti) Ordinance
   - ❑ Guidelines by Ministry of Information & Broadcasting, Plan Coordination Cell
   - ❑ List of Heads of All Media Units/Organisations

3. **Towards Understanding the Audio Broadcast System, Sound Recording and Reproduction: Basic and Advanced Tools and Techniques** 64
   - ❑ Audio
   - ❑ Audio Frequency
   - ❑ Basic Audio
   - ❑ Sound Recording and Reproduction
   - ❑ Manual of Sound Recording
   - ❑ Tape Recorder
   - ❑ Digital Audio Broadcasting

4. **Towards Understanding the Video Broadcast System: Basic and Additional Types** **89**
- Video
- Basic Video
- Video Clip
- Getting the Word Out
- Additional Video

5. **Understanding Various Audiovisual Equipments: An Overview** **118**
- Audiovisual
- Professional Audiovisual Industry
- Audiovisual Education
- Diorama
- Magic Lantern
- Planetarium
- Projector
- Film Projector
- Movie Projector
- Slide Projector
- Video Projector
- Overhead Projector
- Opaque Projector
- Camera Obscura
- Ceiling Projector
- Enlarger
- Interactive Whiteboard

6. **Television and Television Systems: Types, Components and Standards** **171**
- Television
- Terrestrial Television
- Digital Television
- National Television System Committee (NTSC)
- Phase Alternating Line (PAL)
- SECAM
- Field-Sequential Colour System
- Multiplexed Analogue Components
- Multiple Sub-Nyquist Sampling Encoding System
- EIA Standards

7. Towards Better Understanding of Modulation: Principles, Types and Techniques **220**

- Modulation
- Amplitude Modulation
- Single-Sideband Modulation
- Frequency Modulation
- Phase Modulation
- Space Modulation
- Frequency-Shift Keying
- On-Off Keying
- Amplitude-Shift Keying
- Phase-Shift Keying
- Quadrature Amplitude Modulation
- Minimum-Shift Keying
- Continuous Phase Modulation
- Pulse-Position Modulation
- Trellis Modulation
- Orthogonal Frequency-Division Multiplexing
- Frequency-Hopping Spread Spectrum
- Direct-Sequence Spread Spectrum

8. Television Programme Production, Organization and Studies: An Overview **295**

- Television Programme
- Introduction to TV Production: An Overview
- Television Production Tips
- Organization of Materials
- Rights and Responsibilities
- TV Production Shots
- Storyboarding
- Storyboard Artwork Project
- Using Cutaways in Interviews
- Case Study: Degree in Associate of Applied Science in Television Production
- Television Studies

9. Radio, Radio Programming and Radio Production: An Overview **325**

- Radio
- All India Radio
- Pirate Radio
- Radio Commercial
- Radio Propagation
- Radio Programming
- Producing Radio Programmes
- Radio Production
- Radio Software
- Radio Format
- Radio Documentary
- Case Study: Associate of Applied Science Degree

10. Camera: Types, Materials and Processes **358**

- Camera
- Digital Single-Lens Reflex Camera
- Twin-Lens Reflex Camera
- Photographic Film
- Camcorder
- Cinematography
- Manual of Stills Photography
- Manual of Shooting Styles
- Photo Imaging

11. Lights: Process and Power Sources **400**

- Manual of Lighting
- Lighting Tools and Techniques
- Manual of Power Sources
- Television Lighting

Bibliography 410

Index 418

1

Broadcasting: An Overview of Programming, Networking and Licensing

BROADCASTING

Broadcasting is the distribution of audio and/or video signals which transmit programmes to an audience. The audience may be the general public or a relatively large sub-audience, such as children or young adults.

There is a wide variety of broadcasting systems, all of which have different capabilities. The smallest broadcasting systems are institutional public address systems, which transmit spoken messages and music within, for example, a school or hospital, and low-powered radio or television stations transmitting programmes to a small local area. National radio and television broadcasters have nationwide coverage, using retransmitter towers, satellite systems, and cable distribution. Satellite radio and television broadcasting can cover areas as wide as entire continents, while internet channels can distribute text or streamed music and speech worldwide. Individuals can also use make use of internet services to stream or podcast sound or video.

The sequencing of content in a broadcast is called a schedule. As with all technological endeavours, a number of technical terms and slang have developed. A list of these terms can be found at list of broadcasting terms. Television and radio programmes are distributed through radio broadcasting or cable, often both simultaneously. By coding signals and having decoding equipment in homes, the latter also enables subscription-based channels and pay-per-view services.

The term "broadcast" originally referred to the sowing of seeds by scattering them over a wide field. It was adopted by early radio engineers from the midwestern United States to refer to the analogous dissemination of radio signals. Broadcasting forms a very large segment of the mass media. Broadcasting to a very narrow range of audience is called narrowcasting.

Economically there are a few ways in which stations are able to continually broadcast. Each differs in the method by which stations are funded:

- In-kind donations of time and skills by volunteers (common with community broadcasters)
- Direct government payments or operation of public broadcasters
- Indirect government payments, such as radio and television licenses
- Grants from foundations or business entities

- ❑ Selling advertising or sponsorships, and
- ❑ Public subscription or membership.

Broadcasters may rely on a combination of these business models. For example, National Public Radio, a non-commercial network within the United States, receives grants from the Corporation for Public Broadcasting (which in turn receives funding from the U.S. government), by public membership, and by selling "extended credits" to corporations.

Recorded Broadcasts and Live Broadcasts

One can record and produce live broadcasts. The former allows correcting errors, and removing superfluous or undesired material, rearranging it, applying slow-motion and repetitions, and other techniques to enhance the programme. However some live events like sports telecasts can include some of the aspects including slow motion clips of important goals/hits etc. in between the live telecast.

American radio network broadcasters habitually forbade prerecorded broadcasts in the 1930s and 1940s requiring radio programmes played for the Eastern and Central time zones to be repeated three hours later for the Pacific time zone. This restriction was dropped for special occasions, as in the case of the German dirigible airship *Hindenburg* at Lakehurst, New Jersey in 1937. During World War II, prerecorded broadcasts from war correspondents were allowed on U.S. radio. In addition, American radio programmes were recorded for playback by Armed Forces Radio stations around the world.

A disadvantage of recording first is that the public may know the outcome of an event from another source, which may be a spoiler. In addition, prerecording prevents live announcers from deviating from an officially-approved script, as occurred with propaganda broadcasts from Germany in the 1940s and with Radio Moscow in the 1980s.

Many events are advertised as being live, although they are often "recorded live" (sometimes called "live-to-tape"). This is particularly true of performances of musical artists on radio when they visit for an in-studio concert performance. This intentional blurring of the distinction between live and recorded media is viewed with chagrin among many music lovers. Similar situations have sometimes appeared in television ("*The Cosby Show* is recorded in front of a live studio audience").

A broadcast may be distributed through several physical means. If coming directly from the studio at a single radio or TV station, it is simply sent through the air chain to the transmitter and thence from the antenna on the tower out to the world. Programming may also come through a communications satellite, played either live or recorded for later transmission. Networks of stations may simulcast the same programming at the same time, originally via microwave link, now usually by satellite.

Distribution to stations or networks may also be through physical media, such as analog or digital videotape, CD, DVD, and sometimes other formats. Usually these are included in another broadcast, such as when electronic news gathering returns a story to the station for inclusion on a news programme.

The final leg of broadcast distribution is how the signal gets to the listener or viewer. It may come over the air as with a radio station or TV station to an antenna and receiver, or may come through cable TV or cable radio (or wireless cable) via the station or directly from a network. The Internet may also bring either radio or TV to the recipient, especially with multicasting allowing the signal and bandwidth to be shared.

The term "broadcast network" is often used to distinguish networks that broadcast an over-the-air television signal that can be received using a television antenna from so-called networks that are broadcast only via cable or satellite television. The term "broadcast television" can refer to the programming of such networks.

Legal Definitions

UK

- The Copyright, Designs and Patents Act 1988 defines a broadcast as *a transmission by wireless telegraphy of visual images, sounds, or other information which is capable of lawful reception by the public or which is made for presentation to the public.* It thus covers radio, television, teletext etc.

BROADCASTING PROGRAMME

Students in the Broadcasting programme study digital audio and video production techniques, including nonlinear editing, post-production, animation, web and multimedia graphics, and sports. WIUS-FM gives students the opportunity to put into practice learned skills.

They also examine the impact of history, law, and programming on broadcasting, cable, and satellite operations. Graduates of the programme enter various careers in television, radio, cable, satellite, and post-production operations including directing, producing, reporting, on-air talent programming, sales, advertising, sports, and post-production.

All students taking a broadcasting class that requires writing or a lab of any sort must adhere to our attendance policy.

Bachelor of Arts—Broadcasting

CORE (15)—All Students must Take these Core Courses

BC 100	Introduction to Broadcasting
BC 101	Introduction to Broadcast Production
BC 102	Introduction to Broadcast Research and Writing
BC 323	Broadcasting and Society
BC 425 WID	Broadcast/Cable Law and Ethics

There are two sequences to choose from. Students may choose News and Performance or Production. Classes from the sequence not chosen may be taken as elective credit.

News and Performance Sequence (19)

BC 200	Broadcast Reporting I
BC 222	Broadcast Performance

BC 310	Advanced Broadcast Performance
BC 312	Broadcast Sports Performance
BC 315	Broadcast News I
BC 415	Broadcast News II
BC 419	Online Writing, Design and Production
BC 431	Special News/Sports Projects
BC 385	Production Practicum I
BC 386	Production Practicum II
BC 485	Production Practicum III
BC 486	Production Practicum IV

Production Sequence (19)

BC 250	Audio Production I
BC 260	Video Production I
BC 302	Broadcast Research and Writing II
BC 350	Audio Production II
BC 361	Video Production II
BC 402	Advanced Broadcast Writing
BC 385	Production Practicum I
BC 386	Production Practicum II
BC 485	Production Practicum III
BC 486	Production Practicum IV
BC 490	Senior Workshop in Production

Broadcast Electives (6)

BC 325	Comparative Broadcast Systems
BC 328W	Mass Media and Minorities
BC 400	Senior Honors Thesis Research
BC 401	Honors Thesis
BC 418	Independent Research
BC 420	Television Graphics
BC 426	Sports Broadcasting
BC 430	Multimedia Design for Mass Media

BROADCAST PROGRAMMING

Broadcast programming, or scheduling, is the practice of organising television or radio programmes in a daily, weekly, or season-long schedule. Modern broadcasters regularly change the scheduling of their programmes to build an audience for a new show, retain that audience, or compete with other broadcasters' programmes.

Television scheduling strategies are employed to give programmes the best possible chance of attracting and retaining an audience. They are used to deliver programmes to audiences when they are most likely to want to watch them and deliver audiences to advertisers in the composition that makes their advertising most likely to be effective (Ellis 2000).

At a micro level, scheduling is the minute planning of the transmission; what to broadcast and when, ensuring that every second of airtime is covered.

Scheduling Strategies

Dayparting

In broadcasting, dayparting is the practice of dividing the day into several parts, during each of which a different type of radio programming or television programming appropriate for that time is aired. Programmes are most often geared toward a particular demographic, and what the target audience typically engages in at that time.

Theming

Having a special theme-night.

Stripping

Running a syndicated television series every day of the week. It is commonly restricted to describing the airing of shows which were weekly in their first run; *The West Wing* could be stripped, but not *Jeopardy!*, as daily is the schedule for which it is intended.

Stacking

Stacking is a technique used to develop audience flow by grouping together programmes with similar appeals to "sweep" the viewer along from one programme to the next (Vane and Gross, 1994).

Counterprogramming

Counterprogramming is used when a time period is filled with a programme whose appeal is different from the opponent programme because it is a different genre or appeals to a different demographic.

Bridging

Bridging is being used when a station tries to prevent the audience from changing channels during a junction point—the main evening breaks where all channels stop programmes and shift gear (Ellis, 2000). This is achieved in a number of ways including: having a programme already underway and something compelling happening at a junction point, running a programme late so that people 'hang around' and miss the start of other programmes, or advertising the next programme during the credits of the previous.

Tentpoling

In tent pole programming the programmers bank on a well-known series having so much audience appeal that they can place two unknown series on either side, and it is the strength of the central programme that will bring the others along to victory.

Hammocking

A technique used by broadcasters whereby an unpopular programme is scheduled between two popular ones in the hope that viewers will watch it. Public-service broadcasters use this as a way of promoting serious but valuable content.

Crossprogramming

Cross-programming involves the interconnection of two shows. This is achieved by dragging a storyline over two episodes of two different programmes.

Broadcast Network

A broadcast network is an organisation, such as a corporation or other association, that provides live or recorded content, such as movies, newscasts, sports, and public affairs programmes for broadcast over a group of radio or television stations. They are generally primarily either a *television network* or a *radio network,* although some organizations run both types of networks.

Broadcast License

A broadcast license is a specific type of spectrum licence that grants the licensee the right to use a portion of the radio frequency spectrum in a given geographical area for broadcasting purposes. Licensing is typically performed by government agencies, providing a mechanism both for managing the limited resource of radio frequency spectrum and for implementing prevailing public policy, such as policies regarding concentration of media ownership. Management of technical specifications, such as those implemented in broadcast television systems, is normally undertaken as a part of broadcast licensing in each country.

Economics

Originally, broadcast licences were issued for only a nominal payment, but work by economist Ronald Coase developed a theory that broadcast licences in a spectrum that was limited had high economic value, which could and should be paid for on the open market. Increasingly, spectrum licences are offered via spectrum auctions.

School of Broadcasting

Richard and Helen Brown started the School of Broadcasting in 1946 to train young men and women for careers in the emerging field of Radio Broadcasting. In the 1950s, television changed communication forever. Brown responded with the addition of the Television Production Programme in 1954. Today, technology—including the Internet, streaming audio, on-demand video, satellite radio and podcasts—is fueling a communications revolution. And this revolution is creating opportunities for people who can produce the audio and video messages to feed an information-hungry world.

The Twin Cities of Minneapolis and St. Paul comprise one of the nation's largest media markets. You'll find Brown alumni on the air and behind the scenes at a number of radio and television station in both towns. In fact, Brown grads from our Television Production Programme are helping produce news and entertainment everyday, for stations from New York to LA, from small-town radio shows to CNN.

The School of Broadcasting offers three programmes:

Communication Studies. *Bachelor of Science.*

Radio Broadcasting. *Applied Associate of Science.*

Television Broadcasting. *Applied Associate of Science.*

2

Indian Broadcasting: Legal Resources and Regulatory Notifications

AN INTRODUCTION TO TELEVISION BROADCASTING IN INDIA

A huge industry by itself, the Indian silver screen has thousands of programmes in all the states of India. The small screen has produced numerous celebrities of their own kind some even attaining national fame. TV soaps are extremely popular with housewives as well as working women. Some small time actors have made it big in Bollywood.

History

Post-Independence Television

Television first came to India (named as Doordarshan or DD) as the National Television Network of India. The first telecast started on September 15, 1959 in New Delhi. After a gap of about 13 years, second television station was established in Mumbai (Maharashtra) in 1972 and by 1975 there were five more television stations at Srinagar (Kashmir), Amritsar (Punjab), Calcutta (West Bengal), Madras (Chennai) (Tamil Nadu) and Lucknow (Uttar Pradesh). For many years the transmission was mainly in black and white. Television industry got the necessary boost in the eighties when Doordarshan introduced colour TV during the 1982 Asian Games.

1980s

Indian small screen programming started off in the early 1980s. At that time there was only one national channel Doordarshan, which was government owned. The Ramayana and Mahabharata was the first major television series produced. This serial notched up the world record in viewership numbers for a single programme. By the late 1980s more and more people started to own television sets. Though there was a single channel, television programming had reached saturation. Hence the government opened up another channel which had part national programming and part regional. This channel was known as DD 2 later DD Metro. Both channels were broadcast terrestrially.

Post Liberalization Television

The central government launched a series of economic and social reforms in 1991 under Prime Minister Narasimha Rao. Under the new policies the government allowed private and foreign broadcasters to engage in limited operations in India. This process has been pursued consistently by all subsequent federal administrations. Foreign channels like CNN, Star TV and domestic channels such as Zee TV and Sun TV started satellite broadcasts. Starting with 41 sets in 1962 and one channel (Audience Research Unit, 1991) at present TV in India covers more than 70 million homes giving a viewing population more than 400 million individuals through more than 100 channels. A large relatively untapped market, easy accessibility of relevant technology and a variety of programmes are the main reasons for rapid expansion of Television in India.

Cable Television

In 1992, the government liberated its markets, opening them up to cable television. Five new channels belonging to the Hong Kong based STAR TV gave Indians a fresh breath of life. MTV, STAR Plus, BBC, Prime Sports and STAR Chinese Channel were the 5 channels. Zee TV was the first private owned Indian channel to broadcast over cable. A few years later CNN, Discovery Channel, National Geographic Channel made its foray into India. Star expanded its bouquet introducing STAR World, STAR Sports, ESPN and STAR Gold. Regional channels flourished along with a multitude of Hindi channels and a few English channels. By 2001 HBO and History Channel were the other international channels to enter India. By 2001-03, other international channels such as Nickelodeon, Cartoon Network, VH1, Disney and Toon Disney came into foray. In 2003 news channels started to boom.

Government Rules and Policies

The New Telecom Policy [NTP 1999] announced by the government.	New Telecom Policy
The Media Policy announced by the BJP government as a part of their Election manifesto for the forthcoming Lok Sabha elections.	Media Policy
National Task Force on Information Technology and Software Development Information Technology Action Plan.	Information Technology Action Plan

Acts and Regulations for Cable and Television in India

The Cable Television Networks Rules, 1994	The Cable Television Networks Rules, 1994
The National Security Act, 1980	The National Security Act, 1980
Almost everybody in the country is familiar with the cable television. It has been spreading its wings from the initial urban cities, right to the remote villages. There has been a haphazard mushrooming of cable television networks all over the country due to the availability of signals of foreign television networks via satellites. To check the screening of undesirable programmes and advertisements which are screened on these channels and to regulate the operation of the cable television networks in the country, so as to bring uniformity in their functioning, the Cable Television Networks (Regulation) Act was passed in both the Houses of the Parliament.	The Cable Television Networks (Regulation) Act

(Contd.)

The Prasar Bharati Act,1990 was passed to provide for the establishment of a Broadcasting Corporation for India, to be known as Prasar Bharati. It says that it shall be the primary duty of the Corporation to organize and conduct public broadcasting services to inform, educate and entertain the public and to ensure a balanced development of broadcasting on radio and television.	The Prasar Bharati Act,1990
The Bill is to provide for an independent authority to be known as the Broadcasting Authority of India which is for the purpose of facilitating and regulating broadcasting services in India.	The Broadcasting Bill, 1997
The Indian Telegraph Act, 1885 came into force on 1st October 1885. "Telegraph" means any appliance, instrument, material or apparatus used or capable of use for transmission or reception of signs, signals, writing, images, and sounds or intelligence of any nature by wire, visual or other electro-magnetic emissions, Radio waves or Hertzian waves, galvanic, electric or magnetic means. The Indian Telegraphic Act, 1885 was an Act to amend the law relating to Telegraphs in India.	The Indian Telegraph Act 1885
The importance of copyright was recognized after the invention of the printing press which enabled the reproduction of books in large quantity. The Indian Copyright Act was thus passed in 1914. But, during the last four decades, modern and advanced means of communications like broadcasting, litho-photography, television, etc. made inroads in the Indian economy. It necessitated the fulfillment of international obligations in the field of Copyright. A comprehensive legislation had to be introduced to completely revise the Copyright law. This was achieved by the introduction of a Copyright Bill, 1957 in the Parliament.	The Copyright Act 1914
The Union Government has taken a decision on 25th July 2000 to further liberalise its Uplinking Policy and permit the Indian private companies to set up uplinking hub/teleports for licensing/hiring out to other broadcasters. The new policy also permits uplinking of any television channel from India. It also allows the Indian news agencies to have their own uplinking facilities for the purposes of newsgathering and its further distribution.	Guidelines for uplinking from India
THE CABLE TELEVISION NETWORKS (REGULATION) AMENDMENT BILL, 2002 A BILL further to amend the Cable Television Networks (Regulation) Act, 1995.	Latest CAS amedments of the Cable Television Act
The proceedings in the Rajya Sabha regarding the passage of THE CABLE TELEVISION NETWORKS (REGULATION) AMENDMENT BILL 2002.	What the speakers had to say

Important Judgements and Committee Reports

Excerpts from the historic judgement in 1995 which stated that the Air Waves are not the monopoly of the Indian government.	Judgement for ownership of Air Waves
The Nitesh Sengupta Committee was set up to review the provisions of Prasar Bharati (Broadcasting Corporation of India) Act, 1990 and to make recommendations regarding the restructuring of Prasar Bharati. Read the contents of the report submitted by The Nitesh Sengupta Committee.	The Nitesh Sengupta Committee Report

(Contd.)

Excerpts from 'Major Recommendations' of Shri B.G. Verghese Working Group on Autonomy for Akashvani and Doordarshan, February 1978. "*We envisage an autonomous national trust as the authority under which Akashvani and Doordarshan should grow.* This we are naming *Akash Bharati - the National Broadcast Trust.*"	Recommendations of Verghese Working Group
Summary of the recommendations given by the Ram Vilas Paswan Consultative Committee on National Media Policy for the Information and Broadcasting Ministry, 1996. "9.1 - *The broadcasting should observe a greater degree of responsibility and sensitivity to Indian culture and ethos and cater to the developmental requirement of the country. It should achieve an Indian personality in telecasting/ broadcasting.*" (Para 6.4.1.1)	Recommendations by Ram Vilas Paswan Consultative Comittee
Summary of the recommendations of the interdepartmental committee on electronic media under the chairmanship of Shri K.A. Varadan, Additional Secretary in the Ministry of Information and broadcasting.	Varadan Committee Report
India's dream of becoming a super-power in Information Technology. India is in a competitive race for investment and it is believed that investment in this new millenium will flow to countries where there is visible evidence of a strong policy framework, supported by clear and precise laws facilitating growth of business in a converged environment.	Interim Report of the Sub-Group on convergence
A complete report presented by Fali Nariman Committee to Cabinet.	Final Report of the Sub-Group on convergence
Draft Communication Convergence Bill, 2000	Draft Communication Convergence Bill, 2000
Incorporating Comments/suggestions received from interested organisations and individuals on the Draft Bill prepared by the Sub-Group on Convergence in January 2001.	Revised Draft Communication Convergence Bill, 2001
The Communication Convergence Bill 2001 which was introduced in Parliament on 31 August 2001 by Former Communications Minister Ram Vilas Paswan.	Communication Convergence Bill 2001

Policies for Doordarshan

The DD Notice	The DD Notice
The DD Advertising Code The Code for commercial advertising on Doordarshan.	The DD Advertising Code
Guidelines for Commissioning of Programmes in Doordarshan	DD Press release

INDIAN BROADCASTING REGULATIONS FORUM

The Indian government has announced that it wants a Broadcasting Act enacted within the next six months. It has the old broadcasting bill draft and the report of the Sharad Pawar Committee which reviewed the draft as reference points. But it is seeking the opinion of the satellite channels and cable TV industry once again later this month. You, as a television or media executive, can share your opinions on what shape Indian broadcasting regulations should take by posting them in indiantelevision.com's Indian Broadcasting Regulations Forum. Feel free-to-air your views on:

- The limits for foreign equity in Indian broadcasting and on cross-media holdings. On what should these restrictions be based.
- Whether DTH television should be allowed and in what form.
- Whether a broadcasting regulator is needed or not and what shape should it take, what powers should it have.
- Whether a television license fee is needed.
- Whether a Prasar Bharti is needed and should it be autonomous or government-controlled.
- Whether the current unorganised nature of the cable TV business should be allowed to continue or whether licensing should be brought in and in what form.
- Whether uplinking from India should be made mandatory for all channels including foreign ones.
- Whether wireless cable should be permitted.
- Whether private firms should be allowed to enter terrestrial television broadcasting.

INCLUSION OF COMMUNITY BROADCASTING IN THE BROADCASTING BILL 1997. Recommendations to the Ministry of Information and Broadcasting on non-profit community broadcasting. Prepared by VOICES in consultation with broadcasting and development professionals and the National Law School of India, Bangalore. VOICES is a development communication organization. One of our key thrust area is Community Radio and we have been working in this issue for the past four years. This includes, Bangalore Declaration on Radio, Airing community related programmes from AIRs Chitradurga FM station, and lobbying for promotion of CR at ministerial and local level. Respected H'nble Minister with the ongoing technological revolution, information plays a crucial role in bringing people together and enables them to make informed choices. The right of free speech and expression includes the right to receive and impart information. For ensuring the Indian citizens? right to free speech and information, it is necessary that they have the benefit of plurality of views and access to range of options to public issues. The national goals of an Indian broadcasting policy have to be unique keeping in mind the diverse citizenry and the need for the peoples participation in a democracy. The Joshi Commission (1982) recommended a decentralized system of broadcasting, stressing upon the need for access, participation, local autonomy and control training and public service as the basis for broadcasting future of India. Thus any broadcasting policy must carry with it the onus to safeguard the citizen's right be informed, transmit varied programmes to awaken, inform, enlighten, educate, enrich and entertain all sections of the people and serve the rural and urban illiterate and underprivileged populations, keeping in mind the special needs and interests of the young women, social and cultural minorities, the tribal populations and those residing in the backward areas. The Broadcasting Bill, 1997 must be analyzed in this light to see if it fulfils these national objectives. Analysis of the Provisions of the Broadcasting Bill Section 16(2) talks about granting licensee to institutions which provide, education, environment protection and community service under a restricted bid system as notified by the regulations. There is some ambiguity in the terms used here: What type of institutes can be considered eligible? Private institutions, non-profit institutions or community broadcasting services? The South African Independent Broadcasting Authority Act 153 of 1993 defines a community broadcasting service as—one which is fully controlled by non-profit entity and operated for non-profitable purposes: serves a particular community: encourages members of the community served by it to participate in the selection and provisions of the programmes to be broadcast: may be funded by donations, grants, sponsorship or advertising or membership fees. This kind of clarity of definition is required. There must be cogent differentiation between a private broadcasting service operated for profit and non-profit community broadcasting which can fall under Section 16(2) Suggested Amendments To Clauses DEFINITIONS Section 2 of the Bill should therefore include of both running thus: 2(zt) "Private Broadcasting Service" means a broadcasting service operated for profit and controlled by an entity which is not a public broadcasting licensee. 2(zu) "Community Broadcasting Service" means a non-profit broadcasting service which caters to the needs of geographically bounded group of persons having a definite ascertainable common interest, subject to Section 25(2) and which is permitted to raise funds to meet operational costs through donations, grants, sponsorships, membership fees, advertising or a combination of aforementioned. FUNCTIONS OF THE AUTHORITY Section 7 of the Bill deals with the Functions of the Authority. This section lays no positive obligation on the Authority to promote a diverse range of services on national, local, and regional level which would cater to the different cultural language groups and communities. It must be seen that a healthy balance is maintained between the different electronic media so that it does not lead to the marginalization of radio which is the only medium of information for 70 per cent of rural India and covers 90 per cent of the geographical area. Promotion of community-based non-profit developmental radio, which is characterized by active participation of the community the process of creating news, information, entertainment, and culturally relevant material with emphasis on local issues and concerns, should be one of the responsibilities of the Authority. An addition should be included under Section 7, to come after 7(iii) to read as: 7(iv) To promote broadcasting through low cost terrestrial radio and protect the interests and concerns of local communities. GRANT OF LICENSES Section 16(2) may read as: Notwithstanding anything contained in Sub-section (1), the Authority may grant licenses to such institutions as may be notified for terrestrial broadcasting services through restricted bids or on payment of nominal fee that may be determined by the regulations. The proviso 16(2) should be broadened in the public interest, to read: Provided that no institution shall be notified under this sub-section unless the object of such institutions is to promote education, community service, environment protection, health awareness, women's empowerment or cultural expression. RESTRICTIONS ON HOLDING LICENSES Part I, Clause 4 of the schedule disqualifies publicly funded bodies from obtaining license. This brings under its purview universities and other educational institutions as well as co-operatives. These should be exempt, bearing in mind the need for youth participation in media and deployment of media for promoting education. The Varadan Report (1991) had in fact enunciated that preference to be given to public bodies like universities, co-operative institutions etc., if they apply for licenses. The proviso to Clause 4 here should read as: Provided that this disqualification does not apply to the universities and other educational institutions and co-operatives. Provided that the disqualified under this clause shall not apply to the a community broadcasting service. STATEMENT OF OBJECTS AND REASONS One of the objects of this Bill is to meet the challenges proposed by the invasion of the skies by direct satellite broadcasting by foreign entities and it has addressed this issue. However, the main object remains to keep India's democratic traditions alive and keep its diverse citizens well informed and this issue needs a closer look. For instance deregulation in the USA is not synonymous with the total abrogation of government regulation: media laws can liberate this neo-liberal communication policy initiative by not ignoring matters vital to public interest and community participation in India. The last sentence of the statement number 3 of this section should read as: This can be provided by facilitating private broadcasting and broadcasting services which enable access and participation by the citizens of the country. The role of broadcasting is all the more important in providing information and access to media so that people can participate in the process of nation building. In the unique conditions of India, terrestrial radio has the widest audience. Thus the Bill seeks to encourage and create conditions for the development of community radio. SIGNATORIES Ms Sucharita Eashwar Ex Director-VOICES, Bangalore Dr. K.E. Eapen International communication expert and Scholar Mr. N. Kalayan Raman ASC Enterprises, New Delhi Dr. Michael Traber United Theological College, Bangalore. Mr. A.R. Pasha Cinematics, Bangalore Ms Ammu Joseph Freelance journalist, Bangalore Ms M.T. Rukhmini Family Planning Association of India, Bangalore Ms N. Lakshmi Concerned for Working Children, Bangalore Ms N. Bhatia Indian Express, Bangalore Ms Amula Seethanaman, Indian Express, Bangalore Ms Raji Reddy Bangalore Ms. Vijayashree Rajaram, Jyothi Nivas College, Bangalore Ms Preetha Mount Carmel College, Bangalore Ms Udaya Mount Carmel, Bangalore Ms Vinaya Mount Carmel, Bangalore Ms Puja Mount Carmel, Bangalore Ms Bhavana Thakur National Law School of India, Bangalore Mr. M.A.S. Rajan IAS (Retd.) Formerly Add. Chief Secretary, Karnataka, Ms Indubai Ramesh Director of Commercial Broadcasting (Retd.), AIR Bangalore Ms K.E. Eapen Bangalore Mr. Chandra Mouli, AIR, Bangalore Mr. Sam Emmanuel Media Center, Bangalore Mr. T.N. Munniswamy FPAI, Gauribidanur Mr. Prem James FEBA, Bangalore Mr. Simon Verghese Deccan Herald, Bangalore Ms Prachi Bhuchar Indian Express, Bangalore Mr. Sowmya Bharadwaj Jyothi Nivas College, Bangalore Ms Neerja Mount Carmel College, Bangalore Ms Shalini Mount Carmel College, Bangalore Ms Winnie Mount Carmel College, Bangalore Ms Mayura Mount Carmel College, Bangalore VOICES is Bangalore based non-profit development communication organization. One of our key thrust area is promoting community radio and have been into it for the past 4 and half years now. We came up with Bangalore Declaration on radio in 1996. We also aired programmes exclusively on local issues on FM in Chitradurga, courtesy AIR, in 1999 and plan to set up a CR in Kolar. Our address is VOICES, 165, 9th CROSS, STAGE-I, INDIRANAGAR, BANGALORE-650 038 TEL# 080-521 3902-3 FAX# 080-521 3901 EMAIL voices@vsnl.com

Mahesh Acharya <voices@vsnl.com>
Bangalore, Karnataka, India
—Thursday, February 24, 2000 at 22:36:56 (PST)

I AM A CABLE OPERATOR. THERE IS AN ACT TO REGULATE THE CABLE TV NETWORKS. BUT IT IS NOT SUFFICIENT. THERE ARE MANY YOUTHS WHO MAY BE UNEMPLOYED AND HAVE INVESTED HUGE AMOUNT OF MONEY IN THIS BUSINESS. THEY ARE EARNING THEIR LIVELIHOOD OUT OF THIS. CABLE TV NETWORKS REGULATIONS ACT-1995 DOES NOT PROTECT ANY CABLE OPERATORS FROM BEING HARASSED BY THE SUBSCRIBERS, PAY CHANNELS AND THE BAD COMPETITORS (FELLOW CABLE OPERATORS). MAJOR PROBLEM WE ARE FACING EVERY DAY IS ABOUT OUR AREA OF OPERATION. I think the unregulated Cable TV industry should be regulated. In most of the places only GOONDAs, Thugs and Dirty Politicians are having ownership of these and they try everything possible to wipe out their law abiding good competitors. NEW BROADCAST BILL SHOULD INCLUDE THE AREA OF OPERATION AND CONTROL OVER PAY CHANNELS AND THE BAD PAY MASTER SUBSCRIBERS. BROADCAST BILL SHOULD PROTECT THE LAW ABIDING CABLE OPERATORS AND MEANWHILE CABLE TV SUBSCRIBERS ALSO.

R.S. Patilkulkarni <rspk@satyam.net.in>
Dharwad, Karnataka, India
—Saturday, January 22, 2000 at 04:07:59 (PST)

To Whom Ever May Concern: One of the main concern regarding growth of broadcasting is the separation of Broadcasting and Distribution. World over in its infancy stage all the progressing countries have not allowed the Cross Ownership of Broadcasting and Distribution. If allowed, a monopolistic distributor can and will restrict the upstart Broadcasters in their tracks. Take the US as example, it is after over 30 years the cross ownership of two streams is allowed only in last 5 years. One should study these and formulate any policies regarding this. Even the DTH, if not licensed and not made neutral will surely affect the growth of the Broadcast Media. I think DTH should be looked at in tandem with Cable laws. Once again, one needs to really look at the issue of cross ownership of Broadcasting and Distribution. I encourage the policy-makers to study the developments in some of the developed markets. Thank you for the opportunity to voice of my opinion.

Vishnu Patel <vishnupatel>
Mumbai, Maharashtra, India
—Monday, November 22, 1999 at 23:31:38 (PST)

I represent an organization in Bangalore called VOICES. This is a non-profit organization working towards decentralised communication and citizen's access to the media. VOICES has been actively involved in a community radio programme for the last three years. In 1998 VOICES launched it's first community radio show called Namma Dhwani (our Voices) in Holalkere, a village in Karnataka. Since then VOICES has conducted projects in Kolar and Chitradurga in Karnataka. Our request to the Minister is for a separate provision in the Broadcast Bill for Community Radio. We think that a separate provision is necessary since a clear distinction must be made between commercial broadcasting services and community radio. In this respect there should be a separate nominal license fee for community radio broadcasters. Institutions and groups working with developmental and organisational goals must also be made eligible for licenses to set up community radio stations. We hope that the Minister will look into this matter and ensure that Community radio is duly represented in the Broadcast Bill.

Shilpa Jacobie<voices@vsnl.com>
Bangalore, Karnataka, India
—Sunday, November 21, 1999 at 22:03:33 (PST)

Prasar Bharti is of no use to the government or the people today. Let us remember that it was thought of, when only AIR and DD were in existence and they were really misused by the then Government. After all the government as everywhere else in the world, needs a vehicle for propagating its views. Let AIR and DD be with the Government. Let the private operators be given a chance to have their say on their own channels. In a poor country like India, it is essential to have private radio as much as private TV. How come nobody is thinking of that? Small radio stations, owned by communities, to reflect the language, aspirations and music of the community are essential today. The top down pattern of even the private TV operators will be disliked after a while. Let us have small private radio stations.

Indu Ramesh <ramind@vsnl.com>
Bangalore, Karnataka, India
—Wednesday, November 17, 1999 at 06:33:37 (PST)

I would like cable TV operators to sort out their operations and give me a box which will allow me to watch what I want to watch. The government should make cable operators responsible for this rather than just waiting for the winds of change take it in that direction. I have heard there is this box called an addressable box which can allow us to watch what I want to. This is the box I'm referring to. There should be DTH restrictions excepting pornography should be allowed on the service late into the night and with parental control systems in place. Foreigners should be allowed to come in as partners of Indian companies to upgrade our technology in television. We have very skilled people here but we need the direction which the government and foreigners can give. Let's catch up with the US and UK markets now and get digital television in place, why keep reinventing the wheel every time; that's the advantage we have of beginning late. We can catch up that much faster. I hope the authorities are listening. Thanks Anirudh Chatterjee

Anirudh Chatterjee <tvlover@mailindia.com>
Calcutta, West Bengal, India
—Thursday, November 11, 1999 at 20:32:12 (PST)

I would like to see foreign and Indian broadcasters having some controls on the programming and advertising side. Nobody is really selecting programming responsibly, the basic idea is to broadcast programmes that make pots of money or that hopefully will. A regulator like the TRAI would help TV broadcasters to be less adventurous. But please give it muscle unlike the TRAI is. Thank you Road skater

Road skater <rs@indiamail.com>
Delhi, Delhi, India
—Monday, November 08, 1999 at 08:30:46 (PST)

The foreign equity in Indian broadcasting can be allowed upto 49 per cent without any hesitation, since Broadcasting segment also require huge funds as other sector for its growth. There is no relevance in restricting the foreign equity less than 49 per cent for investment proposal. DTH must be allowed immediately in India. Politicians play dirty game in DTH without understanding the nature of technology, since DTH is already operating in India in c-band for the past 7-8 years. Then, what is the point in banning it in the Ku-band alone. DTH must be allowed in PROPERITARY TECHNOLOGY format with a license to two to three operators nationally, since the nature of investment is very high and returns will take not less than 5 years to reach break-even. DTH operator must be able to provide Hardware like off-set small dish, LNB and decoders at free of cost to customers along with INTERNET service as value-added service. So that, they can expect to cover good number of customers, otherwise DTH will not be successful in present Indian scenario. Totally, DD is unfit to provide DTH service in any form, it is irrelevant to allow DD for 5 years as monopoly. It will destroy the entire concept of DTH in Indian market. Cable TV must be regulated to avoid unhealthy competition in the sector. The license to two operator per telecom circle can be a ideal solution to bring down the present controversy. Even though wireless cable losts its relevance now, it can be allowed on trial basis, since DTH will destroy MMDS sector, if it is opened alogwith DTH operations. It is like, MOBILE PHONE segment has now, reduced the importance of PAGERS everywhere in India.

R. Manoharan <sharcstar@vsnl.com>www.sharcstar.com
COIMBATORE, Tamil Nadu, India
—Saturday, November 06, 1999 at 21:54:08 (PST)

Prasar Bharti is needed and should it be autonomous. We have to give freedom to Broadcasting sector by getting rid of bloody politician and goondas. Learn something which are good in US than always find bad thing with them. Government has no business in business.

Indian <indian2@hotmail.com>
India
—Friday, November 5, 1999 at 09:53:29 (PST)

I think the unregulated Cable TV industry should be regulated. In most of the places only GOONDAs, Thugs and Dirty Politicians are having ownership of these and they try everything possible to wipe out their law abiding good competitors.

Rick Janarthanam <Alert_bodyshoper@hotmail.com>
Chennai, Tamil Nadu, India
—Friday, November 5, 1999 at 07:01:20 (PST)

REPORT OF THE TASK FORCE ON INTRODUCTION OF CONDITIONAL ACCESS SYSTEM

Introduction

The issue of introduction of an addressability system has been engaging the attention of the Government for some time, keeping in view the problems being highlighted by sections of the broadcasting industry, including Cable operators, MSO's and Content Providers. A large number of complaints had also been received from subscribers, protesting unwarranted and frequent increase in subscription rates by Cable operators. With almost 38 million cable and satellite households in the country and with a household paying on an average Rs. 125 per month, as subscription charges, the revenue generated in the sector is close to Rs. 5,700 crores. Of this, there have been reports of substantial under reporting by different sections depriving the different players of the industry of their entitled revenue/collection and reportage of transparent viewership figures and the Government of tax.

To deliberate and decide upon various issues on this topic, it was decided to set up a Task Force, under Joint Secretary (Broadcasting) in the Ministry of Information and Broadcasting, with representations from the cross-section of the industry. The objective, *inter alia,* was to deliberate in the need for introducing a Conditional Access System for viewing channels through the cable network and to determine the modalities for doing so.

Constitution of Task Force and Terms of Reference

The Task Force was constituted by an order dated 25th September, 2001 and it consists of representatives from Indian Broadcasting Federation, MSOs Content Creators, Cable

Operators, Broadcasters, Infrastructure Providers, nominee from the Ministry of Consumer Affairs, representative of Consumer activists and technical experts. The order constituting the committee, with its Terms of Reference, is annexed.

The Committee was empowered to invite experts and to broadbase the representation on the Task Force, technical experts were co-opted from the industry. Other participants who desired to contribute were also invited to attend. The primary issue of concern for the Committee was to establish the need for introducing Conditional Access System in order to provide a choice to the consumer and to examine the feasibility of doing so, to protect the interests of the consumer from additional costs on replacement of the TV receiver or on purchase of the Conditional Access System, and to debate technology issues relating to standardization and performance.

Meetings

The Task Force held three meetings, one each in the month of October, November and December 2001. At each meeting specific issues were identified for discussion and deliberation and decisions were taken there on, at the same meeting. Since the technology issues were more complex and required extensive consultations, a Subcommittee was constituted under Director (BD), I&B with representations from the industry, equipment manufacturers and technical experts to go into those aspects. This Subcommittee held separate meetings and their recommendations were considered by the Task Force in its last meeting held on 26th December 2001. At each stage the members were encouraged to send further comments/observations in writing for the consideration of the Task Force.

After each meeting of the Task Force, the minutes were circulated to the members by post as well as over Internet. Members of the Task Force as well as other representatives of the industry have provided inputs, which were also considered by the Task Force. This included comments, which were received from National Cable and Telecommunications Associations, Cable Operators etc.

Summary of Discussions

It was acknowledged that Cable Television in India was a technology, which had entered in an unbridled manner and had become a reality totally through private investment. A connectivity of over 35 million homes had been achieved in this syndrome. The MSOs were later entrants. Cable and Satellite Television had gradually become an irresistible force in the process of transformation of communication technology and the perceived potential of Cable TV, DTH, DTT etc. was immense. The Cable Operators observed that since demand of content was driving ad revenue and viewership, the Broadcasters and the Content Creators were whimsically levying exorbitant charges for programmes, channels and for bouquets. Arbitrary increases in subscription rates were creating a problem because Cable Operators were left with no option but to pass on this burden frequently to the subscribers.

The Group discussed the problems and alternatives available and was of the view that the consumer needed to exercise a choice of watching what he chose, and that the viewer should be made aware of what it would cost to view 'Pay' Channels.

Addressability is a technique, where signals are sent in an encoded from and an equipment, placed at the subscriber's end, decodes the signals, in accordance with the choice exercised by the consumer and authorized by the Service Provider, specifically on the subscriber's request. The Task Force considered it desirable that the Conditional Access System should be introduced to provide the consumer choice of viewing and an option to pay for what he chose to watch. The consumer should also not be expected to pay unreasonably for the 'Free-to-Air' channels and must be able to receive the 'Free-to-Air' channels without any Set Top Box or any need to change the existing receiver

The Task Force acknowledged the existence of the value chain starting from the Content Maker, to the Content Provider (Broadcaster) to the main Content Distributor, to the last mile Content Distributor (Cable Operator) and finally the consumer household. In the existing arrangement the consumer was paying for all the channels, irrespective of what he actually watched or desired to watch. There was now need to make the system transparent in respect of the Pay Channels/Pay programmes, which can be watched by selective subscribers. The subscribership of all 'Pay' channels should be fully determinable. This transparency would allow entitled revenue to accrue to the different links in the chain, permit the consumer to have programming of his choice and watch channels according to their affordability, hopefully at a lower cost, and provide realistic and authentic viewership data. The Task Force was unanimous that the Conditional Access System is necessary to bring transparency at different levels, but that it should not add to the financial burden of the consumer. It was decided that the Government should mandate it by law. The Set Top Box, allowing addressability, should be required only for 'Pay' channels; for subscribers who opt to view only 'Free-to-Air' channels, there would be no requirement of a Set Top Box. The Set Top Box shall be supported by the MSOs/Cable Operators through installation of necessary infrastructure like Subscriber Management System etc. It was considered desirable that the Government must be empowered to enter and inspect the premises and operations of the MSOs and Cable Operators to ensure enforcement of the requirements of the Set Top Box, of transparent recording of viewership figures, display of channel rates etc.

The Task Force saw a presentation on the system introduced by M/s Ortel Communications, in Bhubaneshwar, on experimental basis. It is using 'Dalvi', a low cost conditional access scrambling system, which combines security and multi-tiered addressability. It encrypts analogue signals and the system is compatible with any video transmission system. The system has the potential to address 80,000 customers with a subscriber Management System. A total of 4 channels—mix of 'Free-to-Air' and 'Pay' 1 m are presently being routed through the Set Top Box. The cost of the Set Top Box is approximately Rs. 3,500. The system is one way and not interactive. It was informed that the start up costs, for investment in equipment at Head-end Level, was approximately Rs. 50,000 for each channel. The financial implications of introducing the Set Top Box and addressability system, at each level, were discussed against this background. The need to keep the present system intact, at least for those viewers who prefer to watch only 'Free-to-Air' channels, was favoured.

The Task Force felt that the Set Top Box should be mandated only for " Premium Tier"; 'Free-to-Air' channels being taken in a "Basic Tier", receivable by all viewers at a standard subscription rate. The Task Force debated other issues emerging out of the presentation and felt that the price of channels/content for the Cable Operators should be fixed in a transparent manner, by Content Providers and Channel owners, for all operators.

The Task Force was unanimous in its view that there was need for an enabling provision in the legislation for Government to prescribe certain basic minimum standards for the equipment and its performance. In order to consider all issues relating to prescriptions of Standards and Performance Parameters, for the Set Top Box/ Conditional Access System, a Sub-Committee made recommendations on the standards and the specifications for Digital Cable TV and Analogue Cable TV, as well as for Digital/Analogue Set Top Boxes. It also recommended that the Cable Operator/ Equipment Provider should declare, in a transparent manner, the capability of the Set Top Box and its inter-operability with other networks. It also recommended that unauthorized viewing/redistribution of the signal should be made a cognizable offence. The packaging of services, including Value Added Services, should be left to the Operators who should be free to choose the middleware/software/hardware provided that it conformed to basic minimum performance standards. It further recommended that the subscriber management system should provide transparent information to all the players.

The Task Force was of a strong view that there was urgent need to educate the subscribers, by all the stake holders, on the operation of Cable Television and the cost of various services, including the operation and cost of Set Top Boxes. The Task Force accepted the recommendation of the Sub-Committee, for an enabling provision in the Act to prescribe basic minimum technical standards and performance parameters, through the Bureau of Indian Standards (BIS). The manufacturers of the equipment must provide full information on the capability of the hardware. It was also considered desirable that BIS may invite comments from the industry and examine internationally acceptable standards before prescribing standards for India. The Task Force was of the view that eventually the Set Top Box would permit migration, by the subscriber, across various delivery media-Satellite, Cable and Terrestrial. The user will thus have the capability to migrate to various delivery media, simply by changing the "Network Interface Module".

The members of the Task Force debated the need for a Conditional Access System base on DVB simulcrypt technology or any other currently acceptable technology but eventually felt it appropriate to leave the issue of technological specifications to the Bureau of Indian Standards, who would ensure that the technology is not proprietary in nature. In order to ensure transparency in the interface between MSOs and the Cable operators, it was decided that the Government be empowered to obtain monthly reports from the MSOs, Broadcasters and Cable operators in the manner prescribed.

The Task Force also debated the issue of "must carry" provision for the content of the Public Service Broadcaster and the pricing of the "Basic Tier" of service and the Set Top Box. The Group felt that the consumer should not be burdened with the cost of changing his television sets on purchasing a Set Top Box, if he wanted to view only Free-to-Air channels. The Subscriber should exercise choice of viewing the 'Pay' channels through a Set Top Box. However there was no need to prescribe the cost price of either the Set Top Box. However there was no need to prescribe the cost price of either the Set Top Box or the 'Pay' channels. It was however, considered desirable that the pricing of various channel bouquets, by the Broadcasters, MSOs should be done in a transparent manner. The Group was unanimous that the Government should fix the price of the 'Basic Tier' and therefore legislation should enable the determination of the 'Basic Tier' price, from time to time by the Government. The Pricing/subsidy of the Set Top Boxes, by any player should be left to market forces, as long as the consumer was made fully aware of the availability and capability of the equipment. The equipment suppliers were confident that with larger volume, market forces would drive down the price of Set Top Boxes. The Group also felt that the Broadcasters, MSOs and Cable Operators should be allowed the freedom to work out their individual business plans to subsidies the Set Top Boxes, in accordance with their own marketing strategy.

The Group acknowledged the fact that with progressive introduction of Digital Video Broadcasting technology, its combination with interactive return path, between the user and the Service operator, will pave the way for other Services, for which the Subscriber should be prepared to pay on the basis of charges fixed.

Recommendations

(*a*) The Conditional Access System and the supportive Subscriber Management System should be mandated under the Cable Television Networks (Regulation) Act, 1995.

(*b*) The Set Top Box shall be required only for "Pay" Channels and the "Free-to-Air" channels shall be receivable by the subscribers in the current mode, without Set Top Box. The encrypted channel should be defined as "Subscription based Channel".

(*c*) The Technical parameters of the Set Top Box shall conform to the Indian standards, to be prescribed by the Bureau of Indian Standards, in accordance with the provisions of the Bureau of Indian Standards Act, 1986. While doing so, the Bureau of Indian Standards may take into account the internationally acceptable standards and obtain recommendations from technologists and manufacturers of equipment.

(*d*) It shall be mandatory for the Equipment Provider/Manufacturer to declare, in a transparent manner, the capability of the Set Top Box and its interoperability on other networks.

(*e*) In order to ensure transparency in the operations between MSOs, Cable Operators etc., the Government must be empowered to obtain detailed information, on regular basis, from each level of operation. This may include information on total subscriber base, on individual programmers, viewership of independence channels, subscription rates, charges fixed by the Broadcasters, Content Creators for each channel etc. Each subscriber shall be keep informed in a transparent manner of the subscription rates for each individual 'Pay' channel.

(*f*) Unauthorised viewing/distribution/redistribution of the broadcast signal should be made a cognizable offence.

(*g*) The Government should regulate the price of 'Basic Tier' of the 'Free-to-Air' channels. The Government should also be enabled to revise the cost of the 'Basic Tier', from time to time. The Government will also make a special provision for the channels of the Public Services Broadcaster. No government intervention was considered necessary with regard to the cost of the Set Top Box or the rates of the individual 'Pay' channel.

(*h*) There should be no requirement for change of the receiving set, irrespective of whether the consumer chooses to watch 'Free-to-Air' channels and/or 'Pay' channels.

(*i*) There was an immediate need to educate the consumer on the operation of cable television, on the cost of content creation and its distribution up to the households. The Broadcasters, Content Creators and MSOs should not enhance the charges of the 'Pay ' channels arbitrarily, it should be done in a transparent manner.

(*j*) The packaging of services, includes Value Added Services, as well as the pricing of the paid bouquets would be left to market forces. However, consumer interest needed to be protected by providing efficient and responsive service and through a transparent and accurate billing and collection system. This will also ensure that the revenue accruable to the Government is determined in a fair manner.

BROADCASTING CONTENT REGULATION: AN OVERVIEW

A. Violation of Advertising Code

Ministry of I&B has issued show cause notices to various satellite channels for telecasting the following objectionable advertisements for the year 2005-06. All the Satellite television Channels are requested not to telecast/retelecast these advertisements and they are directed to strictly adhere to the Advertising Code prescribed under the Cable Television Networks (Regulation) Act, 1995 and Rules framed there under.

S. No.	*Name of the Advertisement/Product*	*S. No.*	*Name of the Advertisement/Product*
1.	Roope Amrit	14	Day Night Soda
2.	Gen-X	15.	Royal Stag Cup Ind/Zim 05
3.	Franchise-X	16.	Royal Challenge Premium Sparkling Water
4.	Gilbeys Green Label Pure Aqua	17.	Kingfisher Mineral Water
5.	Hayward 5000 Soda	18.	White Mischief Holidays
6.	McDowell's No. 1 Soda	19.	100 Pipers Cassettes and CDs
7.	Seagram's Fling Wicked	20.	Sand Piper NA Mald Beverage
8.	Mason Summer's Royal Crown Ca	21.	Kingfisher Model Hunt
9.	Seagram's 100 Pipers Pure Music	22.	Paan Parag Paan Masala
10.	Smirnoff's Cassettes/CD's	23.	Seagram's Imperial Blue
11.	Officer's Choice Premium Soda	24.	Mahak Chaini Chaini
12.	Old Tavern Mineral Water	25.	Gopal Zarda 132
13.	Bacardi Blast Cassettes and CD's		

B. Violation of Programme Code

Similarly, the Ministry has also issued Show Cause Notices to the various satellite Television Channels for telecasting objectionable programmes for the year 2004-06. They are:

S. No.	Name of the Programme
1.	Final orders giving warning issued to MH1, ETC, Channel [V], B4U, Balle Balle, iTV, MTV for telecasting songs "Bin Tere Sanam", "Chadati Jawani", "Kabhi Aar Kabhi Paar", "Leke Pehla Pehla Pyar", "Meri Beri Ke Ber."
2.	SCN issued to Zee News Channel for telecasting a programme titled "Kal Kapal Mahakal".
3.	Final Order giving warning issued to India TV for telecasting a programme on private activities of MPs and MLAs.
4.	Final Order giving warning issued to India TV for telecasting news item on sexual involvement of priest of the Swaminarayan Temple.
5.	Final Order giving warning issued to FTV for telecasting several programmes, which are violative of the Programme Code.
6.	SCN issued to Zoom TV for telecasting a programme titled "Dangerous" telecast from Monday to Thursday at 11:00 p.m.
7.	SCN issued Trends TV for telecasting programmes namely 'Lingerie Show' etc.
8.	SCN issued to In Digital Channel for telecasting an adult film, *i.e.* 'A' certified film by CBFC titled "Khawahish".
9.	SCN issued to Teja TV for telecasting a programme "Kamasutra".
10.	SCN issued to Zee TV for telecasting programme "Item Bomb".
11.	SCN issued to FTV for telecasting obscene programme on 09.12.05.
12.	SCN issued to Maa TV for telecasting programmes titled "Kamasutra", "Manmadha Samrajyam", "Samaram Samayam" and "Sarasm".
13.	SCN issued to Zoom TV for telecasting trailers of films titled "Fun, Sheesha, Shabd and Chahat" which are certified as 'A' by CBFC.
14.	SCN issued to ETC for telecasting trailers of films titled "Fun, Sheesha, Shabd and Chahat" which are certified as ' A' by CBFC.
15.	SCN issued to Zee TV for telecast of a news item regarding alleged phone tapping of Justice (Retd.) S.N. Variava.
16.	SCN issued to MTV for telecast of objectionable songs from Hindi films "Ashiq Banaya Aapne" and "Zeher".
17.	SCN issued to Zee News for telecast of programme "Deshdroh".

असाधारण
EXTRAORDINARY
भाग II– खण्ड 3–उपखण्ड (i)
Part II—Section 3—Sub-section (i)
प्राधिकार से प्रकाशित
Published by Authority

[सं. 201] नई दिल्ली, बृहस्पतिवार, मई 11, 2006/वैशाख 21, 1928
[No. 201] NEW DELHI, THURSDAY, MAY 11, 2006/VAISAKHA 21, 1928

सूचना और प्रसारण मंत्रालय

अधिसूचना

नई दिल्ली, 11 मई, 2006

सा.का.नि. 282(अ).–केन्द्रीय सरकार, केबल टेलीविजन नेटवर्क (विनियमन) अधिनियम, 1995 (1995 का 7) की धारा 22 की उप-धारा (1) द्वारा प्रदत्त शक्तियों का प्रयोग करते हुए, केबल टेलीविजन नेटवर्क नियम, 1994 का और संशोधन करने के लिए निम्नलिखित नियम बनाती है, अर्थात्:–

1. (1) इन नियमों का संक्षिप्त नाम केबल टेलीविजन नेटवर्क (संशोधन) नियम, 2006 है ।

(2) ये राजपत्र में इनके प्रकाशन की तारीख को प्रवृत्त होंगे ।

2. केबल टेलीविजन नेटवर्क नियम, 1994 के नियम 6 में उप-नियम (5) के पश्चात्, निम्नलिखित अंत:स्थापित किया जाएगा, अर्थात्–

"(6) कोई भी केबल ऑपरेटर अपनी केबल सेवा में किसी भी ऐसे टेलीविजन प्रसारण या चैनल को प्रसारित या शामिल नहीं करेगा जिसको भारत के राज्य क्षेत्र के भीतर देखे जाने के लिए केन्द्रीय सरकार द्वारा रजिस्ट्रीकृत न किया गया हो":

परन्तु, कोई भी केबल ऑपरेटर जिसने इस अधिसूचना के प्रारम्भ की तारीख को या उसके पूर्व केन्द्रीय सरकार को रजिस्ट्रीकरण के लिए आवेदन किया है, किसी भी टेलीविजन प्रसारण या चैनल को, अधिसूचना के प्रारंभ की तारीख से छह मास की अवधि तक अथवा ऐसे रजिस्ट्रीकरण के मंजूर या अस्वीकृत होने तक इनमें से जो भी पहले हो, अपनी केबल सेवा में प्रसारित या शामिल करना जारी रख सकेगा ।

परन्तु, यह और कि् 2 दिसंबर, 2005 से पूर्व अपलिंकिंग हेतु प्रदान की गई अनुमति के अनुसार भारत से अपलिंक किए जाने वाले चैनलों को "रजिस्ट्रीकृत" टेलीविजन चैनल माना जाएगा और उनको केबल सेवा में प्रसारित या शामिल किया जा सकता है ।

[फा. सं. 2302/1/2004 बी.सी.-III]

प्रवीण कुमार त्रिपाठी, संयुक्त सचिव

पाद टिप्पण: मूल नियम सं. सा.का.नि. 729(अ) तारीख 29 सितम्बर, 1994 के तहत प्रकाशित किए गए थे और सं. सा.का.नि. 459(अ), तारीख 8 अक्तूबर, 1996 और सं. सा.का.नि. 710(अ), तारीख 8 सितम्बर, 2000 द्वारा संशोधित किए गए थे ।

MINISTRY OF INFORMATION AND BROADCASTING NOTIFICATIONS

New Delhi, the 11th May, 2006

G.S.R.282(E).— In exercise of the powers conferred by Sub-section (1) of Section 22 of the Cable Television Networks (Regulation) Act, 1995 (7 of 1995), the Central Government hereby makes the following rules further to amend the Cable Television Networks Rules, 1994, namely:

1. (1) These rules may be called Cable Television Networks (Amendment) Rules, 2006.
   (2) They shall come into force on the date of their publication in the Official Gazette.
2. In the Cable Television Networks Rules, 1994, in rule 6 in Sub-rule (5) for the following shall be inserted, namely:

"(6) No cable operator shall carry or include in his cable service any television broadcast or channel, which has not been registered by the Central Government for being viewed within the territory of India":

Provided that a cable operator may continue to carry or include in his cable service any Television broadcast or channel, who has made an application for registration to the Central Government on or before the date of commencement of this notification, for a period of six months from the date of such commencement, or till such registration has been granted or refused, whichever is earlier:

Provided further that channels uplinking from India, in accordance with permission for uplinking granted before 2nd December, 2005, shall be treated as "registered" television channels and can be carried or included in the cable service.

[F. No. 2302/1/2004-BC III]
P.K. TRIPATHI, Jt. Secy.

Footnote: The principal rules were published *vide* number GSR 729(E), dated the 29th September 1994 and amended *vide* number GSR 459(E), dated the 8th October, 1996 and GSR 710(E), dated the date of commencement of this notification, 18th September 2000.

* * * * * *

Ministry of Information and Broadcasting Notification
New Delhi, the 2nd August, 2006

G.S.R. 459(E). In exercise of the powers conferred by Sub-section (1) of Section 22 of the Cable Television Networks (Regulation) Act, 1995 (7 of 1995), the Central Government hereby makes the following rules further to amend the Cable Television Networks Rules. 1994, namely:

1. (1) These rules may be called Cable Television Networks (Amendment) Rules, 2006.
   (2) They shall come into force on the date of their publication in the Official Gazette,
2. In the Cable Television Networks Rules, 1994—
   (*i*) in Rule 6, in Sub-rule (1) after Clause (o) the following proviso shall be inserted, namely:
   "Provided that no film or film song or film promo or film trailer or music video or music albums or their promos, whether produced in India or abroad, shall be carried through cable service unless it has been certified by the Central Board of Film Certification (CBFC) as suitable for unrestricted public exhibition in India."
   (*ii*) in Rule 7, for Sub-rule (9) the following shall be substituted, namely;
   "(9) No advertisement which violates the Code for self-regulation in advertising, as adopted by the Advertising Standard Council of India (ASCD), Mumbai for public exhibition in India, from time to time, shall be carried in the cable service."

[F. No. 2302/1/2001-BC-II (Part))
N. BAIJENDRA KUMAR, Jt. Secy.

Note: The principal rules were published in Gazette of India, Part II, Section 3, Sub-section (*i*) *vide* number GSR, 729(E), dated the 29th September, 1994 and subsequently amended by GSR 459(E), dated the 8th October, 1996 and GSR 710(E), dated the 8th September 2000 and GSR 282(E), dated the 11th May, 2006.

* * * * * *

Ministry of Information and Broadcasting Notification
New Delhi, the 9th August, 2006

G.S.R. 469(E). In exercise of the powers conferred by sub-section (1) of Section 22 of the Cable Television Networks (Regulation) Act, 1995 (7 of 1995), the Central

Government hereby makes the following rules further to amend the Cable Television Network Rules, 1994, namely:

1. (1) These rules may be called the Cable Television Networks (Amendment) Rules, 2006.

   (2) They shall come into force on the date of their publication in the Official Gazette.

2. In the Cable Television Network Rules, 1994, in Rule 7, in Sub-rule (2), in Clause (*viii*), after Sub-clause (A), the following shall be inserted, namely:

"Provided that a product that uses a brand name or logo, which is also used for cigarettes, tobacco products, wine, alcohol, liquor or other intoxicants, may be advertised on cable service subject to the following conditions that—

(*i*) the story board or visual of the advertisement must depict only the product being advertised and not the prohibited products in any form or manner;

(*ii*) the advertisement must not make any direct or indirect reference to the prohibited products;

(*iii*) the advertisement must not contain any nuances or phrases promoting prohibited products;

(*iv*) the advertisement must not use particular colours and layout or presentations associated with prohibited products;

(*v*) the advertisement must not use situations typical for promotion of prohibited products when advertising the other products:

Provided further that all such advertisements shall be previewed and certified by the Central Board of Film Certification suitable for unrestricted public exhibition prior to telecast or transmission or retransmission";

[F. No. 804/3/2005-BC-III/BC-II]
N. BAIJENDRA KUMAR, Jt. Secy.

Note: The principal rules were published in the Gazette of India, Part II, Section 3, Sub-section (*i*) *vide* number G.S.R. 729(E), dated the 29th September, 1994 and subsequently amended by G.S.R. 459(E), dated the 8th October, 1996 and G.S.R. 282(E), dated 11th May, 2006.

* * * * * *

असाधारण
EXTRAORDINARY
भाग II—खण्ड 3—उपखण्ड (i)
Part II—Section 3—Sub-section (i)
प्राधिकार से प्रकाशित
Published by Authority

सं. 545] नई दिल्ली, शनिवार, नवम्बर 11, 2006/कार्तिक 20, 1928
No. 545] NEW DELHI, SATURDAY, NOVEMBER 11, 2006/KARTIKA 20, 1928

सूचना और प्रसारण मंत्रालय

अधिसूचना

नई दिल्ली, 11 नवम्बर, 2006

सा.का.नि. 697(अ).—केन्द्रीय सरकार, केबल टेलीविजन नेटवर्क (विनियमन) अधिनियम, 1995 (1955 का 7) की धारा 22 की उप-धारा (1) द्वारा प्रदत्त शक्तियों का प्रयोग करते हुए, केबल टेलीविजन नेटवर्क नियम, 1994 का और संशोधन करने के लिए निम्नलिखित नियम बनाती है, अर्थात्:

1. (1) इन नियमों का संक्षिप्त नाम केबल टेलीविज़न नेटवर्क (पाँचवां संशोधन) नियम, 2006 है ।
   (2) ये राजपत्र में इनके प्रकाशन की तारीख को प्रवृत्त होंगे ।
2. केबल टेलीविजन नेटवर्क नियम, 1994 के नियम 6 में उप-नियम (6) में, पहले परंतुक के स्थान पर निम्नलिखित परंतुक रखा जाएगा, अर्थात्—

"(परन्तु कोई केबल ऑपरेटर, जिसका रजिस्ट्रेशन के लिए आवेदन, केन्द्रीय सरकार को 11 मई, 2006 को या उससे पूर्व किया गया था और वह विचाराधीन है, इस अधिसूचना की तारीख से तीन मास की अवधि के लिए या ऐसा रजिस्ट्रीकरण मंजूर किए जाने या खारिज किए जाने तक, इनमें से जो भी पूर्वतर हो, किसी टेलीविजन प्रसारण या चैनल में अपनी केबल सेवा जारी रख सकेगा या शामिल कर सकेगा" ।

[फा. सं. 1601/71/2006—टीवी (आई)]

एन. बैजेन्द्र कुमार, संयुक्त सचिव

पाद टिप्पण: मूल नियम सं. सा.का.नि. 729(अ), तारीख 29 सितम्बर, 1994 द्वारा प्रकाशित किए गए थे और सं. सा.का.नि. 459(अ), तारीख 8 अक्तूबर, 1996, और सं. सा.का.नि. 710(अ), तारीख 8 सितम्बर, 2000, सा.का.नि. 282(अ), तारीख 11 मई, 2006. सा. का.नि. 452(अ), तारीख 31 जुलाई, 2006, सा.का.नि. 459(अ), तारीख 2 अगस्त, 2006 और सा.का.नि. 469(अ), तारीख 9 अगस्त, 2006 द्वारा संशोधित किए गए ।

Ministry of Information and Broadcasting Notification
New Delhi, the 11th November, 2006

G.S.R. 697(E).— In exercise of the powers conferred by Sub-section (1) of Section 22 of the Cable Television Networks (Regulation) Act, 1995 (7 of 1995), the Central Government hereby makes the following rules further to amend the Cable Television Networks Rules, 1994, namely:

1. (1) These rules may be called Cable Television Networks (Amendment) Rules, 2006.
   (2) They shall come into force on the date of their publication in the Official Gazette.
2. In the Cable Television Networks Rules, 1994, in Rule 6 in Sub-rule (6) for the first proviso the following proviso shall be substituted, namely:

   "Provided that a cable operator may continue to carry or include in his cable service any Television broadcast or channel, whose application for registration to the Central Government was made on or before 11th May, 2006 and is under consideration, for a period of three months from the date of this notification, or till such registration has been granted or refused, whichever is earlier:

[F. No. 1601/71/2006 —TV (I)]
N. Baijendra Kumak, Jt. Secy.

Footnote: The principal rules were published *vide* GSR 729(E), dated the 29th September, 1994 and amended *vide* GSR 459(E), dated the 8th October, 1996, GSR 710(E), dated the 18th September, 2000, GSR 282(E), dated the 11th May, 2006, GSR 452(E), dated the 31st July, 2006, GSR 459(E.), dated the 2nd August, 2006 and GSR 469(E), dated the 9th August, 2006.

* * * * * *

F. No. 2302/1/2004—BC-III (Part-1)
Ministry of Information and Broadcasting
Broadcasting Wing
....

Dated. 29.5.2006

Subject: Carrying illegal television channels in violation of the downlinking guidelines in Cable/DTH service.

The Undersigned is directed to inform you that as per the 'policy guidelines for downlinking of television channels' issued on 11.11.2005 by this Ministry all the television channels uplinked from abroad and downlinked into India have to register themselves before the expiry of 180 days from the date of this notification. The last date for such registration expired on 10.5.2006. The notification of the Cable Television Network (Amendment) Rules 2006 and the amendment to DTH guidelines was issued on 11.5.2006. As per this, a cable operator may continue to carry or include, in his cable service any television broadcast or channel, only those TV channels which had made an application for registration to the Central Government on or before the date of commencement of the notification, for a period of six months from the date of such commencement or till such registration has been granted or refused, whichever is earlier. The details of the 173 television channels permitted to uplink from India, the details of the 65 television channels uplinked from abroad and downlinked in India and notification issued by this Ministry on downlinking guidelines are posted on Ministry's web-site http/:mib.nic.in.

2. In the light of the above all MSOs/DTH Operators/cable Operators with head-ends are directed give the following information within seven (7) days of receipt of this letter.

- To intimate this Ministry the names of the channels that have been disconnected for telecasting, giving specific dates from which these have been disconnected.
- To intimate this Ministry the names of channels that are not permitted/ registered by the Ministry of I&B and which are still being carried in their networks and reasons for violation of the Cable Television Networks (Regulation) Act 1995 and the Rules framed there under, the notification of the Cable Television Networks (Amendment)

Rules 2006 vide F. No. 2302/1/2004 BC III, dated 11.5.2006 and DTH license agreement amendment order dated 11.5.2006.

3. Apart from the above, all MSOs/DTH Operators and COFI are directed to sensitize and activate all the Cable/DTH operators about the new regime and inform the action taken to this Ministry within seven days of receipt of this letter.

(Prawin Kumar)
Director
Tel. No: 2338 1246

To,

1. All MSO's
2. Smt. Roop Sharma, President, Cable Operators Federation of India (COFI) 13/97, New Rajori Apartments, Subash Nagar, New Delhi 1100027
3. Lt. Col. (Retd.) K.K. Sharma, Publisher & Chief Editor, Cable Quest, 13/97. New Rajori Apartments, Subash Nagar, New Delhi 1100027 (with a request to give a wide publicity in their magazine)
4. M/S ASC Enterprises (Agrani), J-27, South Extension, Part-I, New Delhi-110049. (Shri Rajiv Khattar, President-Projects, FC-19; Sector-16-A; Film City; NOIDA 201301.
5. DD-Direct Plus, Engineering-in-Chief, DG: Doordarshan, Doordarshan Bhavan Copernicus Marg, New Delhi-110001

TEXT OF THE DRAFT OF THE PROPOSED BROADCASTING SERVICES REGULATION BILL

To promote facilitate and develop in an orderly manner the carriage and content of Broadcasting,

To provide for regulation of broadcasting services in India for offering a variety of entertainment, news, views and information in a fair, objective and competitive manner and to provide for regulation of content for public viewing and matters connected therewith or incidental thereto.

To provide for the establishment of an independent authority to be known as the Broadcast Regulatory Authority of India for the purpose of regulating and facilitating development of broadcasting services in India

Whereas airwaves are public property and it is felt necessary to regulate the use of such airwaves in national and public interest, particularly with a view to ensuring proper dissemination of content and in the widest possible manner;

Whereas Government has issued guidelines from time to time, with the approval of the Union Cabinet, for regulating the Broadcasting Services and it is felt necessary to give a statutory effect to these guidelines with retrospective effect;

BE it enacted by Parliament in the Fifty "Eighth Year of the Republic of India as follows:

CHAPTER 1
PRELIMINARY

1. Short title, extent and commencement: (1) This Act may be called the Broadcasting Services Regulation Act, 2006.

(2) It extends to the whole of India.

(3) It shall come into force with immediate effect.

2. Definitions: In this Act, unless the context otherwise requires:

(*a*) "Authority" means the Broadcasting Regulatory Authority of India established under Section 12;

(*b*) "Authorized Officer" means, within his local limits of jurisdiction:

- (*i*) A District Magistrate, or
- (*ii*) A Sub-divisional Magistrate, or
- (*iii*) A Commissioner of Police,

And includes any other officer notified by the Central Government or State Government or the Authority, to be an authorized office for such local limits of jurisdiction as may be determined by that Government or Authority.

(*c*) "Broadcaster" means any person who provides a content broadcasting service and includes a broadcasting network service provider when he manages and operates his own television or radio channel service.

(*d*) "Broadcasting" means assembling and programming any form of communication content like signs, signals, writing, pictures, images and sounds, and either placing it in electronic form on electromagnetic waves on specified frequencies and transmitting it through space or cables to make it continuously available on the carrier waves, or continuously streaming it in digital data form on the computer networks, so as to be accessible to single or multiple users through receiving devices either directly or indirectly; and all its grammatical variations and cognate expressions;

(*e*) "Broadcasting Service" means assembling, programming and placing communication content in electronic form on the electromagnetic waves on specified frequencies and transmitting it continuously through broadcasting network or networks so as to enable all or any of the multiple users to access it by connecting their receiver devices to their respective broadcasting networks, and includes all the content broadcasting services and the broadcasting network services;

(*f*) "Broadcasting Network Service" means a service, which provides a network of infrastructure of cables or transmitting devices for carrying broadcasting content in electronic form on specified frequencies by means of guided or unguided electromagnetic waves to multiple users, and includes the management and operation of any of the following:

(*i*) Teleport/Hub/Earth Station
(*ii*) Direct-to-Home (DTH) Broadcasting Network
(*iii*) Multi-System Cable Television Network
(*iv*) Local Cable Television Network
(*v*) Satellite Radio Broadcasting Network
(*vi*) Such other Network Service as may be prescribed by the Central Government

(*g*) "Cable Operator" means any person who manages and operates, or is otherwise responsible for, a multi-system or a local cable television network.

(*h*) "Cable television channel service" means the assembly, programming and transmission by cables of any broadcast television content on a given set of frequencies to multiple subscribers.

(*i*) "Cable Television Network" means any system consisting of closed transmission paths and associated signal generation, control and distribution equipment, designed to receive and re-transmit television channels or programmes for reception by multiple subscribers;

(*j*) "Carrier" means the electromagnetic waves that can travel on air or cable and are capable of carrying communication content in electronic form on specified frequencies

(*k*) "Chairperson' means the Chairperson of the Authority appointed under Section 13;

(*l*) "Channel" means a set of frequencies used for transmission of a programme;

(*m*) "Competent Authority" means the Authority designated by the Government for the purpose of this Act;

(*n*) "Community radio service" means terrestrial radio broadcasting intended and restricted only to a specific community and within specified territory;

(*o*) "Content" means any sound, text, data, picture (still or moving), other audio-visual representation, signal or intelligence of any nature or any combination thereof which is capable of being created, processed, stored, retrieved or communicated electronically;

(*p*) "Content Broadcasting service" means the assembling, programming and placing content in electronic form and transmitting or re-transmitting the same on electromagnetic waves on specified frequencies, on a broadcasting network so as to make it available for access by multiple users by connecting their receiving devices to the network, and includes the management and operation of any of the following:

(*i*) Terrestrial television service;
(*ii*) Terrestrial radio service;
(*iii*) Satellite television service;
(*iv*) Satellite radio service;
(*v*) Cable television channel service;
(*vi*) Community radio service;
(*vii*) Such other content broadcasting services as may be prescribed by the Central Government.

(*q*) "Decoder" means an equipment for decoding an encrypted channel to facilitate its intelligible reception;

(*r*) "Direct-To-Home Broadcasting Service" means a service for multi-channel distribution of programmes direct to subscriber's premises without the help of a local delivery system by uplinking to a satellite system specified for the purpose by the Competent Authority;

(*s*) "Downlinking" with reference to satellite broadcast or DTH Broadcasting service means reception of programmes transmitted from a satellite to an earth station or a receiving device;

(*t*) "Encrypted" means treated electronically or otherwise for the purpose of preventing intelligible reception by unauthorized persons;

(*u*) "Frequency" means frequency of electromagnetic waves used for transmission of broadcasting service;

(*v*) "Foreign satellite broadcasting service" means a broadcasting service provided by using a satellite, up linked from a foreign country and receivable in India;

(*w*) "Free-to-air broadcasting service" means a non-encrypted broadcasting service made available for reception by receiving apparatus commonly available to the public without requiring payment of a subscription fee;

(*x*) "License" means a license issued for any of the broadcasting services by the relevant Licensing Authority prescribed by the Central Government under this Act;

(*y*) "Licensing Authority" means an officer of the Central Government or the Authority, so notified by the Central Government in respect of any of the broadcasting services and for such limits of jurisdiction as may be determined by the Government.

(*z*) "Licensed service" means a broadcasting service licensed by the Central Government or the Authority, as the case may be, under this Act;

(*aa*) "Local cable operator" means any person who manages and operates or is responsible for the management and operation of a cable television network to provide a cable television service to multiple subscribers in a particular area;

(*bb*) "Local Delivery service" means a service for multi-channel downlinking and distribution of television programmes by a land based transmission system using wired cable or wireless cable or a combination of both for simultaneous reception either by multiple subscribers directly or through one or more local cable operators

(*cc*) "Member" means a Whole-time Member or a Part-time Member, as the case may be, of the Authority referred to in section 13 and includes the Chairperson;

(*dd*) "Multi-System Cable Television Network" means a system for multi-channel downlinking and distribution of television programmes by a land based transmission system using wired cable or wireless cable or a combination of both for simultaneous reception either by multiple subscribers directly or through one or more local cable operators

(*ee*) "Multi-System Operator (MSO)" means any person who manages and operates a multi-system cable television network to provide a cable television service to multiple subscribers, which may or may not include other value added services including telecommunications and Internet.

(*ff*) "Network operator" means any person who provides a broadcasting network service.

(*gg*) "News and Current Affairs Channel" means a channel that broadcasts programmes containing reports and comments on recent events, ideas, individuals and institutions dealing with political, social, economic and such other subjects as are of general interest to the public at large, but does not include a channel that exclusively broadcasts scientific, cultural, educational or entertainment programmes including news relating thereto.

(*hh*) "Notification" means a notification published in the Official Gazette or posted on the official website of the Ministry of Information and Broadcasting or of the Authority, as the case may be, and the expression "notified" to be construed accordingly;

(*ii*) "Prescribed" means prescribed by rules notified under this Act;

(*jj*) "Private communication" means:

- (*a*) A communication between two or more persons that is of a private or domestic nature;
- (*b*) An internal communication of a business, government agency or other of a business, government agency or other organization for the purpose of the operation of the business, agency or organization; and
- (*c*) Communication in such other circumstances as may be prescribed.

(*kk*) "Programme" in relation to broadcasting service, means:

- (*i*) Any matter the purpose of which is related to entertain, educate or inform public or
- (*ii*) Any advertising or sponsorship matter, whether or not of a commercial kind;

But does not include any matter that is wholly related to or connected with any private communication.

(*ll*) "Public service broadcaster" means any entity whose primary objective is to provide broadcasting content to the public that is socially and culturally relevant and in public interest and welfare;

(*mm*) "Registered channel" means a broadcasting channel registered under this Act;

(*nn*) "Regulations" means regulations made by the Authority under this Act;

(*oo*) "Satellite television service" means a television broadcasting service provided by using a satellite, and received with or without the help of a local delivery system but does not include Direct-to-Home delivery service;

Explanation: Decision of the Authority whether a particular service falls in the category of a satellite broadcasting service or a Direct-to-Home delivery service shall be final.

(*pp*) "Satellite radio service" means a radio broadcasting service provided by using a satellite and directly receivable through receiver sets by multiple subscribers in India;

(*qq*) "Secretary" means the Secretary appointed under Sub-section (1) of Section 20;

(*rr*) "Service provider" means provider of a broadcasting service;

(*ss*) "Subscriber" of a service means a person who receives the service at a place indicated by him without further transmitting it to any other person;

(*tt*) "Subscription fee" means any form of consideration given by subscriber;

(*uu*) "Terrestrial television service" means a television broadcasting service provided over the air by using a land based transmitter and directly received through receiver sets by the public but does not include a local delivery service;

Explanation: Decision of the Authority whether a particular service falls in the category of a terrestrial television service or a local delivery service shall be final;

(*vv*) "Terrestrial radio service" means a radio broadcasting service for provided over the air by using a land-based transmitter and directly received through receiver sets by the public;

(*ww*) "Whole-time Member" means a Whole-time Member of the Authority appointed under Section 13;

(*xx*) "Wireless cable" means a land based wireless transmission system used for multi-point multi-channel distribution of programmes on frequencies designated for the purpose by the Competent Authority;

(*yy*) "Uplinking" with reference to satellite broadcast or Direct-to-Home service means uplinking of programme transmission from an earth station or a transmitting device to the satellite;

(zz) "Year" means the financial year.

CHAPTER 2
REGULATION OF BROADCASTING SERVICES

3. Broadcasting services not without license: (1) No person shall, after the commencement of this Act, provide any broadcasting service, or broadcast any programme or channel, without obtaining a license for such service or permission for such programme or registration of such channel, in accordance with the policy guidelines prescribed under this Act for regulating such broadcasting service, programme or channel.

Provided that the cable operators registered under the Cable Television Networks (Regulation) Act, 1995 may continue to provide cable services in accordance with the conditions laid down in Section 49 of this Act;

Provided further that the permissions issued, license agreements signed with private operators, and registration of channels done, by the Central Government, from time to time under respective guidelines listed under Sub-section (3) of this section, read with Indian Telegraph Act, 1885, prior to the commencement of this Act shall be deemed to be licenses issued under the provisions of this Act from the respective dates of issue of such permission or signing of such license agreement, or registration of such television channel, and shall be valid till the date of expiry of the original permission or license agreement or registration, as the case may be, or till the expiry of one year from the date of commencement of this Act, whichever is earlier, notwithstanding anything contained in this Act or any other law for the time being in force.

Provided further that the Central Government may, by notification, exempt a Public Service Broadcaster or such other category of broadcasters, as may be specified, from all or any of the provisions of this Act.

Provided further that the Government may, by notification, exempt such non-commercial establishments under common ownership from obtaining a license for a Local Delivery Service without using wireless cable, for the purpose of providing such service for the exclusive use of their members subject to such conditions and restrictions as may be specified.

(2) Notwithstanding anything contained in this Act or any other law for the time being in force, the guidelines issued by the Central Government, as specified in sub-section (3) below, and orders issued there under shall be deemed to have been issued as Rules under this Act and all actions taken by Central Government or any other person in pursuance of these guidelines, shall be deemed to have been taken under this Act.

(3) The following guidelines issued by the Central Government from time to time shall be deemed to have been issued as Rules under this Act:

(*i*) Uplinking Guidelines of 2000
(*ii*) FM Radio Policy for private agencies of 2000 (Phase 1)
(*iii*) DTH Policy Guidelines of 2001
(*iv*) SNG/DSNG Use Guidelines of 2002
(*v*) Community Radio Policy of 2002
(*vi*) Revision of Uplinking Policy Guidelines of March 2003
(*vii*) Revision of Uplinking Policy Guidelines of August 2003
(*viii*) FM Radio Policy Phase 2 of July 2005
(*ix*) Downlinking Guidelines of November 2005
(*x*) Consolidated Uplinking Guidelines of December 2005

4. Registration of channels and compliance with the content code: (1) Every service provider shall register his television or radio channel with the Authority in the manner prescribed.

(2) The Authority may refuse to register a channel, or cancel the registration of a channel, if it is of the considered opinion that the content of the channel is likely to threaten the security and integrity of the State or threaten peace and harmony or public order in the whole or a part of the country, or if the name or logo or symbol of the channel, either in part or full or abbreviated form, is:

(*a*) Obscene or vulgar;
(*b*) The same or similar to that of a terrorist or terrorist organization, either in full or in abbreviated form;
(*c*) The same or similar to that of any name or brand or symbol of a product, or a company making such a product, that is prohibited from being promoted or advertised, directly or indirectly, by any law for the time being in force;
(*d*) The same or similar to that of any other registered channel in India or any well known channels outside India, whether registered in India or not, except where valid permission is obtained from the owner of the original name or symbol or

logo, as the case may be, provided that any such permission shall not be treated as valid if the said owner does not have more than 26 per cent equity in the applicant company, or contributes or agrees to contribute from the original channel with the same or similar name or logo or symbol, as the case may be, more than 50 per cent of the content of the proposed channel of the applicant company.

Provided that no such order of refusal or cancellation of registration shall be issued without giving a reasonable opportunity to the applicant company or the service provider of being heard.

(3) No service provider shall provide any broadcasting content that is not in conformity with the broadcasting content certification and regulation rules, hereafter referred to as 'the Content Code', as may be prescribed by the Government under this Act.

Provided that till such time as the Content code is notified under this Act, all service providers shall adhere to the Programme Code and the Advertising Code prescribed under the Cable Television Network Rules, 1994.

5. Central Government to exercise certain powers in public interest: The Central Government may at any time, if it appears necessary or expedient to do so in public interest, in respect of any broadcasting service, which is considered prejudicial to friendly relations with a foreign country, public order, communal harmony or security of the State, direct the Licensing Authority to suspend or revoke its license or direct the service provider to stop broadcasting its service or transmit in its broadcasting service such announcements in such manner as may be considered necessary, and the service provider shall immediately comply with all or any such directions.

6. Mandatory sharing of certain sports broadcast signals: For the purpose of ensuring the widest availability of broadcast signals for viewing in India, no content rights owner or holder and no television or radio broadcasting service provider shall carry a live television broadcast on any cable or DTH network or radio commentary broadcast in India of such national or international sporting events, held in India or abroad, as may be notified by the Central Government to be of national importance, unless simultaneously, it shares the live broadcast signal, without its advertisements, with the public service broadcasters *i.e.* Doordarshan and All India Radio of Prasar Bharti, in such a manner as to enable them to retransmit the same on their respective terrestrial networks and DTH networks, on such terms and conditions as may be prescribed.

7. Compulsory transmission of public broadcasters' channels: (1) Every cable operator shall carry Lok Sabha and Rajya Sabha channels and at least two Doordarshan terrestrial channels and one regional language channel of a state in the prime band, in satellite mode on frequencies other than those carrying terrestrial frequencies.

(2) The channels referred to in sub-section (1) shall be retransmitted without any deletion or alteration of any programme transmitted on such channels.

(3) The Prasar Bharti (Broadcasting Corporation of India) established under Sub-section (1) of Section 3 of the Prasar Bharti (Broadcasting Corporation of India) Act, 1990 may, by notification in the Official Gazette, specify the additional number and name of every Doordarshan channel to be retransmitted by the cable operators in their cable service and the manner of reception and transmission of such channels.

8. Introduction of digital addressable systems (DASs) in broadcasting network services: (1) Where the Central Government is satisfied that it is necessary in public interest to do so, it may, by notification, make it obligatory for every broadcasting network service provider in the country to transmit or retransmit content of any or all channels provided by him, through a digital addressable system with effect from such date as may be specified in the notification.

(2) With a view to ensuring that the broadcasting network service providers comply with the obligation under Sub-section (1), the Central Government may, by notification, prescribe a transitional scheme for introduction of digital addressable systems (DASs) by service providers, with effect from such date as may be specified in the notification, and different dates may be specified for different types of service providers in different States, cities, towns or areas, which may, *inter alia,* provide for the following:

(*a*) Policy guidelines, transitional arrangements and the time frame within which the service providers in different areas shall complete the process of providing the DASs to all their viewers,

(*b*) Obligations of the broadcasters in terms of declaration of prices of their registered channels, commercial arrangements with their distributors and networks service providers etc.

(*c*) Obligations of the Multi-service Operators (MSOs) and Local Cable Operators (LCOs) who introduce DASs in terms of their supply, maintenance, quality of service standards, subscriber management system etc.

(*d*) Obligations of the MSOs and LCOs who continue for the time being with the existing non-addressable systems in terms of declaration of the available number, names and prices of channels, maintenance of subscriber registers and furnishing periodical information etc.

(*e*) Rights and obligations of the viewers in terms of getting quality of service, options to choose channels, making payments for the DASs and monthly subscriptions for the channels, proper upkeep and use of DASs etc.

(*f*) Powers and functions of the Authority in terms of regulation of, and adjudication on, the commercial arrangements among various service providers, prescribing quality of service standards, enforcement of license conditions and other obligations under the scheme on the service providers and the viewers etc.

(*g*) Such other terms and conditions of the scheme as are considered necessary and desirable for ensuring the successful transition from the existing technology to the digital addressable systems within the time frame prescribed under Sub-Section (1).

(3) Notwithstanding anything contained in Sub-sections (1) and (2) or any other law for the time being in force, the Central Government shall have the power, for reasons to be recorded in writing, to postpone or advance any specified date or dates, or by notification, modify, suspend or revoke a notification already issued or any other order or direction issued by it or the Authority

Provided that any order issued or action taken by the Central Government or the Authority or by any other person in pursuance of the earlier notification or order shall, unless specified otherwise, be deemed to be valid and continue to be in operation as if the earlier notification had never been modified, suspended or revoked, as the case may be.

9. Powers and functions of the Central Government: The Central Government shall have the authority to:

(*i*) Prescribe policy guidelines and procedures for the grant, refusal or revocation of licenses/registration for all types of broadcasting services;

(*ii*) Designate and notify such officers of the State Governments or the Authority as may be considered necessary, as the Licensing Authorities to grant, refuse or revoke licenses/registration in respect of such broadcasting services and for such limits of jurisdiction as may be prescribed;

(*iii*) Prescribe the terms and conditions of licenses/registration to service providers and procedures to ensure their compliance by the service providers;

(*iv*) Prescribe license fees and processing fees for grant of licenses/permissions/registration for different types of broadcasting services;

(*v*) Prescribe policy guidelines, including transitional arrangements, to facilitate the introduction of digital addressable systems in broadcasting services throughout the country in a time-bound manner;

(*vi*) Prescribe guidelines and norms to evaluate and certify broadcasting content and the terms and conditions of broadcasting different categories of content by the service-providers;

(*vii*) Prescribe policy guidelines and institutional arrangements for self-regulation of broadcasting content by the service providers in conformity with the prescribed norms;

(*viii*) Prescribe guidelines and institutional arrangements for complaint/grievance redressed against violations of the prescribed norms of broadcasting content code by service providers;

(*ix*) Prescribe policy guidelines to facilitate competition and promote efficiency in the operation of broadcasting services so as to facilitate growth in such services;

(*x*) Exercise, or authorize other existing institutions to exercise, any or all the powers and perform any or all the functions of the new institutions, pending their creation and operationalisation.

10. Restrictions on accumulation of interest: (1) The Central Government shall have the authority to prescribe such eligibility conditions and restrictions with regard to accumulation of interest in the print and broadcast segments of the media as may be considered necessary from time to time, to prevent monopolies across different segments of the media as well as within the broadcast segment, to ensure diversity of news and views.

(2) No content broadcasting service provider and its associated companies shall have more than 20 per cent share of paid up equity or have any other financing or commercial arrangement that may give it management control over the financial, management or editorial policies of any broadcasting network service provider.

(3) No broadcasting network service provider and its associated companies shall have more than 20 per cent share of paid up equity or have any other financing or commercial arrangement that may give it management control over the financial, management or editorial policies of any content broadcasting service provider.

(4) No content broadcasting service provider and its associated companies shall have more than the prescribed share of the total number of channels in a city or a state subject to the overall ceiling of 15 per cent for the whole country.

11. Public service broadcasting obligations: (1) Every broadcasting service provider shall discharge such public service broadcasting obligations as the Central Government may prescribe from time to time in accordance with the limits indicated below:

(*a*) The share of content produced in India shall not be less than 15 per cent of the total content of a channel broadcast during every week.

(*b*) The share of public service/social messaging through advertisements and such other promotional materials/messages shall not be less than 10 per cent of the total commercial time of a channel broadcast during every week.

(*c*) The share of public service/socially relevant programme content shall not be less than 10 per cent of the total programme content of a channel broadcast during every week.

(2) In the event of failure to comply with the public service obligation, every content-broadcasting service provider shall be liable to pay such amount as may be prescribed by the Central Government towards its public service obligation.

(3) The Central Government shall formulate detailed guidelines and institutional arrangement for evaluation of every television and radio broadcaster in respect of its public service broadcasting obligation.

CHAPTER 3
BROADCASTING REGULATORY AUTHORITY OF INDIA

12. Establishment and incorporation of the authority: (1) With effect from such date, as the Central Government may by notification appoint in this behalf, there shall be established for the purposes of this Act an Authority, to be known as the Broadcast Regulatory Authority of India.

(2) The Authority shall be a body corporate by the name aforesaid, having perpetual succession and a common seal with power to acquire, hold and dispose of property, both movable and immovable, and to contract, and shall by the said name sue and be sued.

(3) The Authority shall consist of one Chairperson and not more than six whole-time Members, to be appointed by the Central Government.

(4) The head office of the Authority shall be New Delhi.

13. Qualifications for appointment of chairperson and members: The Central Government shall, by notification, appoint a whole-time Chairperson and six whole-time members of the Authority at the rate of one each from amongst persons who have special knowledge of and professional experience in, the fields of

(*a*) Television, Radio, Cinema, Advertising, Audio-Visuals, Fine Arts etc.;

(*b*) Journalism, Mass Communication, Literature, Social Sciences etc.;

(*c*) Finance, Commerce, Audit, Accountancy etc.;

(*d*) Electronics, Telecommunication, Information Technology etc.;

(*e*) Consumer Affairs, Social Work/Service, Civil Society Organizations etc.;

(*f*) Law, Judiciary etc.;

(*g*) Public Administration, Management etc.

14. Term of office, conditions of service etc. of the chairman and other members: (1) Before appointing any person as the chairperson or a whole-time member, the

Central Government shall satisfy itself that the person does not have any such financial or other interest as is likely to affect prejudicially his functions as such member.

(2) The Chairperson and other whole-time members shall hold office for a term of five years from the date on which they enter upon their offices or till they attain the age of sixty-five years, whichever is earlier.

(3) The Chairperson or a member shall not be eligible for a second term but a member will be eligible for appointment as Chairperson of the Authority for the remaining part of his term.

(4) The Chairperson or a whole-time member shall not take up any commercial employment in the organizations that fall within the operational jurisdiction of the Authority, after demitting office within a period of one year without the prior permission of the Central Government.

(5) The salary and allowances payable to and other conditions of service of the Chairperson and other whole-time members shall be such as may be prescribed.

(6) A person having commercial employment or interest, direct or indirect, in any broadcasting services provider, advertising or programme producing agency shall not be eligible for appointment or continuation as Chairperson or a whole-time member.

15. Powers of the chairperson: The Chairperson shall have powers of general superintendence and direction in the conduct of the affairs of the Authority and he shall, in addition to presiding over the meetings of the Authority, exercise such powers of the Authority, and shall discharge such functions of the Authority, as may be prescribed.

16. Removal, suspension or resignation of chairperson and members: (1) The Central Government may remove from office or suspend the Chairperson or any member of the Authority who:

(*a*) Ceases to be a citizen of India; or
(*b*) Is adjudged an insolvent; or
(*c*) Is convicted or any offence involving moral turpitude; or
(*d*) Is, in the opinion of the Central Government, unfit to continue in office by reason of infirmity or body or mind; or
(*e*) Engages during his term of office in any paid employment outside the duties of his office;
(*f*) Acquires such financial or other interest as is likely to affect prejudicially his functions as a Chairperson or member;
(*g*) Abuses his position so as to render his continuance in office prejudicial to public interest.

(2) The Chairperson or any other member may resign his office by giving notice thereof in writing to the Central Government and on such resignation being accepted, the Chairperson or the member shall be deemed to have vacated his office.

17. Meetings of the authority or its committees: (1) The Authority may constitute committees of the Authority for specific purposes, and make regulations for the transaction of business at the meetings of the Authority as well as its committees.

(2) The Authority or its committee shall meet at such time and place and shall observe such procedure in regard to the transaction of business at its meetings as may be provided by regulations.

(3) The Chairperson shall preside at the meetings of the Authority or its committee, and if for any reason he is unable to attend any meeting, any other whole-time member elected by the members present at such meeting, shall preside at the meetings.

(4) A member shall be deemed to have vacated his office if he absents himself for three consecutive meetings of the Authority without the leave of the Chairperson.

(5) All questions which come up before any meeting of the Authority shall be decided by a majority of the votes of the members present and voting and, in the event of an equality of votes, the Chairperson, or in his absence, the person presiding, shall have and exercise a second or casting vote.

18. Vacancies not to invalidate proceedings: No act or proceedings of the Authority shall be invalid merely by reason of:

(*a*) Any vacancy in, or any defect in the constitution of, the Authority; or

(*b*) Any defect in the appointment of a person acting as a member; or

(*c*) Any irregularity in the procedure of the Authority not affecting the merits of the case.

19. Regional offices of the authority: The Authority may, with the prior approval of the Central Government set up Regional Offices at Delhi, Chennai, Kolkata and Mumbai, and such other regional offices at places to be notified by the Government, and to perform such functions and with such jurisdictions as may be prescribed. At each such Regional Offices there shall be one Regional Director to be appointed by the Central Government to discharge the functions delegated to him by the Authority.

20. Secretary and other officers and employees of the authority: (1) Secretary of the Authority shall be the Chief Executive Officer of the Authority. Subject to the provisions of Section 15 of the Act, the Secretary shall exercise such powers and discharge such functions of the Authority as may be delegated to him by the Authority.

(2) The Central Government shall make available to the Authority, a panel of not less than three officers of the rank of the Additional Secretary to the Government of India, and the Authority may select one of them and recommend his appointment as Secretary of the Authority to the Government.

(3) The Central Government shall make available a panel of not less than three officers of the rank of Joint Secretary to the Government of India for each of the five Regional Offices at Delhi, Chennai, Kolkota, Mumbai and Guwahati, and the Authority may select one from each panel and recommend his/her appointment to the Government. As and when more regional offices are opened, the Authority may seek officers of the rank of Joint Secretary or Director to the Government of India, as the case may be, for appointment as their Regional Directors.

(4) The Authority may appoint such officers and other employees, as it considers necessary for the efficient discharge of its functions under this Act in the manner as provided by the regulations.

(5) The salary and allowances payable to and other conditions of service of the officers and other employees of the Authority shall be such as may be determined by regulations.

21. Powers and functions of the authority: (1) Authority shall exercise the following powers and functions:

(*a*) Notify the terms and conditions of licenses for various categories of service providers, in accordance with the policy guidelines prescribed by the Government;

(*b*) Recommend to the Central Government, guidelines or norms or amendments of prescribed guidelines or norms, in the light of its experience in the discharge of its functions, as well as on such other issues as may be referred to it by the Government;

(*c*) Grant registration to TV and Radio channels as provided under Section 4 of the Bill;

(*d*) Lay-down the standards of quality of service to be provided by the service providers and conduct the periodical survey of such service provided by the service providers so as to protect interest of the consumers of broadcasting service;

(*e*) Notify detailed regulations to implement the policy guidelines prescribed by Government and take all necessary legal and administrative actions to ensure their compliance by the service providers;

(*f*) Formulate and determine conditions for fair, equitable and non discriminatory access to broadcasting services;

(*g*) Consider and publish its findings for wider public debate on issues of public importance relating to broadcasting services and their programme content;

(*h*) Facilitate competition and promote efficiency in the operation of broadcasting services so as to facilitate growth in such services;

(*i*) Advise the Central Government in the matters relating to the development of broadcasting technology and any other matter relatable to broadcasting industry in general;

(*j*) Evolve codes and practices in respect of such other services which are neither licensed nor registered under this Act as may be notified by the Central Government from time to time and lay down obligations on services providers for such codes and practices in a manner as may be prescribed;

(*k*) Ensure effective compliance of public service broadcasting obligations, and in the event of failure of a licensed service provider to meet such obligations, levy and collect such fees and in such manner as may be prescribed;

(*l*) Hear appeals against the orders and directions of the Licensing Authorities;

(*m*) Adjudicate on disputes between two or more Licensing Authorities or between a licensing authority and one or more service providers under jurisdiction of other licensing authorities, or between two or more service providers under jurisdiction of more than one licensing authority;

(*n*) Certify content in respect of such categories of programs or advertisements or promotional materials as require certification before broadcast, as may be prescribed in the Content Code;

(*o*) Adjudicate between licensing authorities or consumers or complainants and the service providers in respect of violations of the Content Code, and impose penalties in accordance with prescribed norms;

(*p*) Perform such other functions including such administrative and financial functions as may be entrusted to it by the Central Government or as may be necessary to carry out the provisions of this Act.

(2) The Authority may, for the discharge of its functions under Sub-section (1) of this section, issue such directions from time to time to the service providers, as it may consider necessary.

(3) The Authority may by general or special order, delegate to its Chairperson or a Member or Secretary or Regional officers or any other officer of the Authority or to any "Authorized Officer", subject to such conditions and limitations, if any, as may be specified therein, such of its powers and duties under this Act as it may deem fit.

22. Powers and functions of the Licensing Authorities: (1) Subject to such directions as the Central Government or the Authority may issue from time to time, the Licensing Authorities shall exercise all or any of the following powers and functions:

(*a*) Grant, refuse or revoke licenses/registration in respect of such broadcasting services and for such limits of jurisdiction as may be prescribed;

(*b*) Inspect, enquire or supervise, or direct an "authorized officer" to inspect, enquire or supervise all or any of the service providers to ensure compliance with the terms and conditions of their respective licenses;

(*c*) Ensure technical compatibility and effective interconnection between service providers;

(*d*) Arbitrate between service providers in respect of commercial arrangement mandated by the Central Government or the Authority for sharing their revenue derived from providing broadcasting services;

(*e*) Ensure effective compliance of such public service broadcasting obligations as may be prescribed for its licensees;

(*f*) Perform such other functions including such administrative and financial functions as may be entrusted to it by the Central Government or as may be necessary to carry out the provisions of this Act.

(*g*) Impose in accordance with prescribed norms, all or any of the penalties, individually or in combination, in case of breach of any terms and conditions of the license/permission/registration, after providing an opportunity to the concerned service provider of being heard.
Provided that the violations of the Content Code shall be punishable only by the Authority, and the licensing authority shall have the power to enforce compliance with such punishment by the service provider.

(*h*) Adjudicate between consumers and service providers licensed by it, in respect of complaints and disputes regarding the quality or standards of service and payments by the consumers.

23. Powers and functions of the 'Authorized Officers': Subject to such directions as may be given from time to time by the Central Government or the Authority, every authorized officer shall have the following powers:

(*i*) To inspect, search and seize equipment etc. under Section 24 of this Act.

(*ii*) To prosecute, on a written complaint by the concerned Licensing Authority, such licensed service providers or other persons as are found to have committed offences under the Act.

(*iii*) To co-ordinate with the Licensing Authorities to ensure that the terms and conditions of the licenses are not violated by any service provider;

(*iv*) To receive and enquire into complaints from the District Monitoring Committee or consumer groups or individual consumers regarding content or quality of service and report to the Licensing Authority for appropriate action.

(*v*) Any other powers and functions as may be delegated to him by the Authority as deemed necessary.

24. Seizure and confiscation of certain equipment: (1) If any authorized officer has reason to believe, or is directed by the Licensing Authority or the Authority or the Central Government, as the case may be, that the provisions of Sub-section (1) of Section 3, or Sub-section (1) of Section 4, or of Section 5 of this Act have been or are being contravened by any person, he may seize the equipment being used by such person for operating such unlicensed service or broadcasting such unregistered channel or programme or for failure to comply with the directions under Section 5 of the Act.

Provided that the authorized officer shall not retain such equipment for a period exceeding 30 days from the date of its seizure without the approval of the District Judge, within the local limits of whose jurisdiction such seizure has been made.

(2) The equipment so seized under Sub-section (1) above shall be liable to confiscation unless the person operating such service or channel complies with the provisions of the Act within a period of sixty days from the date of such seizure.

(3) The District Judge shall not pass any order adjudicating confiscation unless the person operating such service or channel has been given a reasonable opportunity in writing to make his representation against the proposed confiscation.

25. Finance, Accounts and Audit: (1) The proceeds of the license/registration/ permission fees in respect of broadcasting services shall be credited to the Consolidated Fund of India.

(2) The Central Government may for enabling the Authority to discharge its functions efficiently, after due appropriation made by Parliament by law in this behalf, pay to the Authority in each financial year such sums of money as the Government considers necessary by way of grants-in-aid.

(3) The Authority shall have its own fund and all the receipts of the Authority shall be credited to the fund and all payments by the Authority shall be made there from. All money belonging to the fund shall be deposited in one or more Scheduled Banks in such manner as the Authority may decide and Authority may spend such sums as it thinks fit for performing its function under this Act.

(4) The Authority shall prepare, in such form and at such time each year as may be prescribed, a budget in respect of the financial year next ensuing showing—

(*a*) The expenditure which is proposed to be met from the internal resource of the Authority; and

(*b*) The sums required from the Central Government to meet other expenses,

And copies thereof shall be forwarded to the Central Government.

(5) The Authority shall maintain proper accounts and other relevant records and prepare an annual statement of accounts in such form and in such manner as may be prescribed.

(6) The accounts of the Authority shall be audited by the Comptroller and Auditor General of India at such intervals as may be specified by him and any expenditure incurred in connection with such audit shall be payable by the Authority to the Comptroller and Auditor General.

Provided the matters relating to the adjudication by the Authority, manner and number of issue of licenses and quantum of license fee, levied by the Authority or the nature and quantum of penalties imposed by the Authority on any service provider, shall lie outside the purview of such Audit.

(7) The Comptroller and Auditor General of India and any person appointed by him in connection with the audit of the accounts of the Authority shall have the same rights and privileges and authority in connection with such audit as the Comptroller and Auditor General has in connection with the audit of Government accounts and, in particular, shall have the right to demand the production of books, accounts, connected vouchers and other documents and papers and to inspect any of the offices of the Authority.

(8) The accounts of the Authority as certified by the Comptroller and Auditor General of India or any other person appointed by him in this behalf together with the audit report thereon shall be forwarded annually to the Central Government and that Government shall cause the same to be laid before each House of Parliament.

(9) The Authority shall, after the end of each financial year, shall submit to the Central Government a report on their activities during the preceding financial year and containing such information relating to the proceedings and policy of the Authority, as the Government may prescribe from time to time.

(10) The Central Government shall cause such report to be laid before each House of Parliament.

26. Furnishing of returns, etc. to the Central Government: (1) The Authority shall furnish to the Central Government at such time and in such form and manner as may be prescribed or as the Central Government may direct, such returns and statements and such particulars in regard to any proposed or existing programme for the promotion and development of the broadcasting services, as the Central Government may, from time to time, require.

(2) The Authority shall prepare once every year in such form and at such time as may be prescribed, an annual summary of its activities during the previous year and copies of the report shall be forwarded to the Central Government.

(3) A copy of the report received under Sub-section (2) shall be laid, as soon as may be after it is received, before each House of Parliament.

27. Power of the Authority to make regulations: (1) The Authority may, by notification, make regulations not inconsistent with this Act and the rules made thereunder, for enabling it to perform its functions under this Act.

(2) Without prejudice to the generality of the foregoing power, such regulations may provide for all or any of the following matters, namely:

(*a*) The manner of appointment of officers and other employees of the Authority under Sub-section (4) of Section 20;

(*b*) The salary and allowances payable to and other conditions of service of the officers and other employees of the Authority under Sub-section (5) of Section 20;

(*c*) The terms and conditions, fees and procedure to be followed for granting licenses/registration under clause (*a*) of Sub-section (1) of Section 21;

(*d*) The times and places at which meetings of the Authority and its committees may be held and, the procedure to be followed in regard to the transaction of the business at such meetings under Sub-section (*l*) and Sub-section (2) of Section 17;

(*e*) The technical and other quality standards and the reasonable quality of reception under Clause (*d*) of Sub-section (1) of Section 21;

(*f*) The places and types and quantity of equipment to be provided, free of cost, by the licensee service provider for monitoring of content and the quality of technical standards of service, and the manner in which such monitoring may be carried out by the licensing authorities or authorized officers under Clause (*e*) of Sub-section (1) of Section 21.

(*g*) The delegation of powers and functions to the Chairman, members and other officers of the Authority under Sub-section (3) of Section 21;

(*h*) The documentary record and transmission schedule to be maintained by the licensees under Sub-section (1) of Section 40;

(*i*) The manner in which broadcasters shall establish and operate the system of self-certification of broadcasting content under Sub-section (vii) of Section 9;

(*j*) Any other matter in respect of which provision is, in the opinion of the Authority, necessary for the performance of its functions under this Act.

Provided that the regulations under Clauses (*a*), (*b*) and (*c*) shall be made with the prior approval of the Central Government.

CHAPTER 4
OFFENCES, PENALTIES AND APPEALS

28. Punishment for offences under this Act: (1) A person who in contravention of the provisions of this Act, provides, distributes or receives any broadcasting service which is not licensed under Sub-section (1) of Section 3 or broadcasts a channel which is not registered or a programme which is not permitted under Sub-section (1) of Section 4, or abets or assists transmission or distribution of such service or content, as the case may be, in any manner which may include collection of subscription for his principal, issuing of advertisements to such service, dealing in or distribution of decoders, shall be guilty of committing an offence of illegal broadcasting, and on conviction, shall be punishable with imprisonment which may extend up to three years, or with fine which may extend up to rupees twenty five Lakhs or both, and for subsequent offence and conviction such imprisonment may extend to five years or fine up to rupees fifty Lakhs, or with both.

Provided that unauthorized decoding or receiving of a programme that is not permitted or of a channel that is not registered or dealing in or distribution of equipment for the purpose shall also constitute an offence of illegal broadcasting and shall be dealt with accordingly.

(2) Whoever contravenes the provisions of Section 5 of this Act shall be punishable:

(*a*) For the first offence, with imprisonment for a term which may extend to two years or with fine which may extend to rupees ten lakhs or with both,

(*b*) For every subsequent offence, with imprisonment for a term which may extend to five years and with fine which may extend to rupees twenty-five lakhs.

29. Offences by companies: (1) Where an offence under this Act has been committed by a company, every person who, at the time the offence was committed, was in charge of, and was responsible to, the company for the conduct of the business of the company, as well as the company, shall be deemed to be guilty of the offence and shall be liable to be proceeded against and punished accordingly;

Provided that nothing contained in this sub-section shall render any such person liable for such punishment, if he proves that the offence was committed without his knowledge or that he had exercised all due diligence to prevent the commission of such offence.

(2) Notwithstanding anything contained in Sub-section (1), where an offence under this Act has been committed by a company and it is proved that it has been committed with the consent or connivance of, or is attributable to the negligence on the part of, any director, manager, secretary or other officer of the company, such director, manager, secretary or other officer shall also be deemed to be guilty of that offence and shall be liable to be proceeded against and punished accordingly.

Explanation: For the purpose of this section,

(*a*) "Company" means any body corporate and includes a firm or other association of individuals; and

(*b*) "Director" in relation to a firm, means a partner in the firm.

30. Cognizance of offences: (1) No court shall take cognizance of any offence punishable under this Act except upon a complaint made in writing by any authorized officer.

(2) No Court inferior to that of a Chief Metropolitan Magistrate or a Chief Judicial Magistrate of First Class shall try any offence punishable under this Act.

31. The Authority to prescribe penalties for violations of license conditions etc.: The Authority may prescribe the penalties to be imposed for violation of various terms and conditions of the license/permission/registration subject to the condition that such penalties shall not exceed a fine of rupees fifty lakhs, besides suspension or revocation of such license/permission/registration, subject further to the condition that no penalty shall be imposed unless and until a reasonable opportunity has been given to the service provider to explain its position.

32. The Licensing Authorities to impose penalties: (1) Subject to the provisions of Section 31 of this Act, every licensing authority shall have the power to impose any of the following penalties, individually or in combination, on its licensee service providers, in case of breach of any terms and conditions of the license or permission or registration, as the case may be, namely:

(*i*) Direct the licensee to broadcast a correction or an apology or not to repeat a programme; and/or

(*ii*) Impose a fine which may extend up to rupees twenty five lakhs;

(*iii*) Suspend the license for a specified period; or

(*iv*) Curtail the period of the license; or

(*v*) Revoke the license.

Provided that no such penalty shall be imposed without giving a reasonable opportunity to the concerned service provider of being heard in person or through a legal representative.

Provided that the violations of the Content Code shall be punishable only by the Authority, and the licensing authority shall have the power to enforce compliance with such punishment by the service provider.

(2) Pending disposal of the case, the Licensing Authority may, if it considers it expedient or desirable in public interest to do so, direct the concerned service provider to stop the repeat broadcast or broadcasts of a particular programme or portion thereof which is under investigation or enquiry, and the service provider shall immediately comply with such a direction.

Provided that no such interim direction shall be issued without giving a reasonable opportunity, as far as practical, to the concerned service provider of being heard in person or through a legal representative.

33. Appeals against the orders of the Licensing Authorities: An aggrieved person may prefer an appeal against an order or direction of any of the Licensing Authorities to the Authority within a period of thirty days of such an order or direction.

34. Appeals against the orders of the Authority: An aggrieved person may prefer an appeal against the order or direction of the Authority before the Film Certification Appellate Tribunal (FCAT) in respect of cases of violations of the Content Code, and before the Telecom Disputes Settlement and Appellate Tribunal (TDSAT) in respect of cases of all other violations of the terms and conditions of license.

35. Appeals before the Supreme Court: (1) Notwithstanding anything contained in the Code of Civil Procedure or in any other law, an appeal by either party to the dispute shall lie against any order, not being an interlocutory order, of the TDSAT or FCAT, as the case may be, to the Supreme Court on one or more of the grounds specified in Section 100 of that Code.

(2) No appeal shall lie against any decision or order made by the TDSAT or FCAT, as the case may be, with the consent of the parties.

(3) Every appeal under this section shall be preferred within a period of 90 days from the date of the decision or order appealed against,

Provided that the Supreme Court may entertain the appeal after expiry of the said period of 90 days if it is satisfied that the appellant was prevented by sufficient cause from preferring the appeal in time.

36. Transfer of pending cases to the Authority: (1) On the date to be notified by the Central Government, after the establishment of the Authority, all proceedings pending before the Telecom Regulatory Authority of India (TRAI) shall be deemed to be pending before the Authority and shall be disposed off in accordance with the provisions of this Act.

(2) On the date to be notified by the Central Government, after the establishment of the Authority, all proceedings pending before the Ministry of Information and Broadcasting, Government of India shall be deemed to be pending before the Authority and shall be disposed of in accordance with the provisions of this Act.

37. Civil Court not to have jurisdiction: No Civil Court shall have jurisdiction to entertain any suit or proceedings in respect of any matter which the Authority or the Licensing Authority, as the case may be, is empowered by or under this Act to determine and no injunction shall be granted by any civil court or other authority in respect of any action taken or to be taken in pursuance of any power conferred by and under this Act.

CHAPTER 5
MISCELLANEOUS

38. Power of the Central Government to issue directions: (1) The Central Government may, from time to time, issue to the Authority such directions as it may deem necessary in the interest of the sovereignty and integrity of India, the security of the State, friendly relations with foreign countries, public order, decency or morality.

(2) Without prejudice to the foregoing provisions, the Authority shall, in exercise of its powers or the performance of its functions, be bound by such directions on questions of policy as the Central Government may give in writing to it from time to time.

Provided that the Authority shall, as far as practicable, be given an opportunity to express its views before any such direction is given under this sub-section.

(3) The decision of the Central Government whether a question is one of policy or not shall be final.

39. The Authority to follow principles of natural justice: (1) The Authority shall not be bound by the procedure laid down by the Code of Civil Procedure, 1908, but shall be guided by the principles of natural justice and, subject to the other provisions of this Act and of any rules, the Authority shall have powers to regulate its own procedure including the fixing of places and times of its enquiry.

(2) The Authority shall have, for the purposes of discharging its functions under this Act, the same powers as are vested in a civil court under the Code of Civil Procedure, 1908, while trying a suit, in respect of the following matters, namely:

(*a*) Summoning and enforcing the attendance of any person and examining him on oath;

(*b*) Requiring the discovery and production of documents;

(*c*) Receiving evidence on affidavits;

(*d*) Issuing commissions for the examination of witnesses or documents;

(*e*) Requisitioning any public record or document or a copy of such record or document, from any office;

(*f*) Reviewing its decisions;

(*g*) Dismissing an application for default or deciding it, ex-party;

(*h*) Setting aside any order of dismissal of any application for default or any other passed by it, ex-party;

(*i*) Any other matter, which may be prescribed.

40. Service providers to maintain records: (1) Every service provider shall maintain such documentary records and transmission schedules as may be specified in the policy guidelines, notified under this Act and allow inspections of the facilities and such documentary records and transmission schedules by any person authorized by the Authority.

(2) The Authority may call for any information from the service provider, which is necessary for transparency and ascertaining the true ownership of the service provider.

(3) The Authority or any officer authorized by the Authority shall have power to inspect and obtain information wherever necessary, from programme producers, distributors and advertising agents.

(4) For effective enforcement of restrictions on holding of licenses, as provided under Section 10, the Authority or any officer authorized by the Authority for that purpose, shall have all the powers of an inspecting officer as provided under Section 209-A of the Companies Act, 1956.

(5) It shall be the duty of every service provider to carry out the directions of the Authority given under this section.

(6) If default is made by a service provider in complying with the provisions of Sub-section (5), the Authority may take such action as provided under Section 32(1) after providing him an opportunity of being heard.

41. Members and employees of the Authority to be public servants: The Chairman, every member, every officer or other employee of the Authority, shall be deemed to be a public servant within the meaning of Section 21 of the Indian Penal Code.

42. Protection of action taken in good faith: No suit or other legal proceeding shall lie against the Government, Authority, or any Member or Officer or other employee thereof for anything which is in, good faith done or intended to be done in pursuance of this Act or of any rules or regulations made there under.

43. Exemption from tax on wealth and income: Notwithstanding anything contained in the Wealth Tax Act, 1957, the Income Tax Act, 1961, or any other enactment for the time being in force relating to wealth, income, profit or gains, the Authority shall not be liable to pay wealth tax, income tax, or any other tax in respect of their wealth, income, profit or gains derived.

44. This Act to have overriding effect: (1) This Act shall have overriding effect over provisions of any other law for the time being in force and shall be given effect to, notwithstanding anything contained in any other law for the time being in force and notwithstanding any rights claimed under contract or created under any other law for the time being in force.

(2) Notwithstanding anything contained in Section 31 or Section 37 of the Indian Copyright Act, 1957, where one or more persons have made complaints in respect of a work which has been published or performed in public or which has already been broadcast or whose licensed reproductions have already been made available in public, licenses shall be granted to all such complainants under Sub-section (1) of Section 31 of the Indian Copyright Act 1957.

45. Power of the Central Government to make rules: (1) The Central Government may, by notification, makes rules for carrying out provisions of this Act.

(2) In particular and without prejudice to the generality of the foregoing power, such rules may provide for all or any of the following matters, namely:

(*a*) To determine other circumstances for communication under Sub-clause (*c*) of Clause (*ii*) of Section 2;

(*b*) To notify the sporting events and to lay down the procedure to be followed for enabling their being shared with Prasar Bharti under Section 6;

(*c*) The policy guidelines, designate licensing authorities, specify terms and conditions, and procedures for grant of the licenses/permissions/registration to the service provider under Clauses (*i*) to (*iv*) of Section 9;

(*d*) To lay down a time frame for change over to digital addressable networks for broadcasting content, and commercial and technical arrangements during the transition phase under Clause (*v*) of Section 9;

(*e*) The lay down the Content Code and procedures to be followed for content certification by the service providers, adjudication of complaints against content certification and appeals against imposition of penalties, under Clauses (*vi*) to (*viii*) of Section 9;

(*f*) The norms of public service broadcasting obligations, rates and procedures for levying and collection of fees, and setting up institutional arrangement and norms for managing and operating the public service broadcasting obligation fund under Clauses (*x*) and (*xi*) of Section 9;

(*g*) The eligibility conditions and restrictions to prevent accumulation of interest in licensed services and restrictions on controlling interest in print media and electronic media as well as within different segments of the electronic media under Section 10;

(*h*) The salaries and allowances payable and other conditions of service of the Chairperson and whole-time members under Sub-section (5) of Section 14;

(*i*) The places where the Regional Offices may be set up and the functions to be performed by such offices under Section 19;

(*j*) The form in which and the time at which in each year the Authority shall prepare a budget under Sub-section (4) of Section 25;

(*k*) The form and the manner in which the annual statement of accounts shall be prepared under Sub-section (5) of Section 25;

(*l*) The information relating to the proceedings and policy of the Authority to be contained in a report to be submitted by the Authority under Sub-section (9) of Section 25;

(*m*) Any other matter which is required to be or may be prescribed.

46. Rules and regulations to be laid before Parliament: Every rule and every regulation made under this Act shall be laid, as soon as may be after it is made, before each House of Parliament, while it is in session for a total period of thirty days which may be comprised in one session or in two or more successive sessions, and if, before the expiry of the session immediately following the session or the successive sessions aforesaid, both Houses agree in making any modification in, the rule or regulation, or both Houses agree that the rule or regulation should not be made, the rule or regulation shall thereafter have effect only in such modified form or be of no effect, as the case may be; so, however, that any such modification or annulment shall be without prejudice to the validity of anything previously done under that rule or regulation.

47. Application of certain laws: The provisions of this Act shall be in addition to the provisions of the Indian Telegraph Act, 1885 and Indian Wireless Telegraphy Act, 1933 and, in particular, nothing in this Act shall affect any jurisdiction, powers and functions required to be exercised or performed by the Telegraph Authority in relation to any area falling within the jurisdiction of such Authority.

48. Power to remove difficulties: (1) If any difficulty arises in giving effect to the provisions of this Act, the Central Government may, by other published in the Official Gazette, make such provisions, not inconsistent with the provisions of this Act, as it may deem necessary, for the removal of the difficulty.

Provided that no such order shall be made after the expiry of a period of three years from the commencement of this Act.

(2) Every order made under this section shall be laid, as soon as may be after it is made before each House of Parliament.

49. Repeal and saving: (1) The Cable Television Networks (Regulation) Act, 1995 is hereby repealed.

(2) Notwithstanding such repeal any cable operator registered under that Act as on the date of repeal, may continue to provide his services, provided he makes an application to the Authority for the grant of a license for any of the broadcasting network services within six months from the date of the commencement of this Act or where he has made such an application, till the disposal of such application, whichever is later.

(3) The Authority may on receipt of an application under Sub-section (2) grant a license for any of the broadcasting network services subject to fulfillment of such eligibility and other terms and conditions as may be prescribed.

(4) The cable operators operating under Sub-section (2) above shall continue to be regulated as if the Cable Television Networks (Regulation) Act, 1995 has not been repealed during the interregnum *i.e.* the period from the commencement of this Act and disposal of his application for the license or a period of six months, whichever is later.

(5) Notwithstanding such repeal, all cable operators registered under that Act as on the date of repeal, shall continue to comply with the provisions of the programme Code under Rule 6 and the Advertising Code under Rule 7 of the Cable Television Networks Rules, 1994 prescribed under that Act, till the said Codes are replaced by the new guidelines and norms (the Content Code) provided for under Sub-section (vi) of Section 9 of this Act.

* * * * * *

असाधारण
EXTRAORDINARY
भाग II—खण्ड 1
Part II—Section 1
प्राधिकार से प्रकाशित
PUBLISHED BY AUTHORITY

सं. 14] नई दिल्ली, शुक्रवार, फरवरी 2, 2007/माघ 13, 1928
No. 14] NEW DELHI, FRIDAY, FEBRUARY, 2, 2007/MAGHA 13, 1928

इस भाग में भिन्न पृष्ठ संख्या दी जाती है जिससे कि यह अलग संकलन के रूप में रखा जा सके ।
Separate paging is given to this Part in order that it may be filed as a separate compilation.

GUIDELINES BY LAW MINISTRY

New Delhi, the 2nd February, 2007/13 *Magha,* 1928 (*Saka*)

SPORTS BROADCASTING SIGNALS (MANDATORY SHARING WITH PRASAR BHARTI) ORDINANCE

No. 4 OF 2007

Promulgated by the President in the Fifty-eighth Year of the Republic of India.

An Ordinance to provide access to the largest number of listeners and viewers, on a Free-to-Air basis, of sporting events of national importance through mandatory sharing of sports broadcasting signals with Prasar Bharti and for matters connected therewith or incidental thereto.

Whereas Parliament is not in session and the President is satisfied that circumstances exist which render it necessary for him to take immediate action;

Now, therefore, in exercise of the powers conferred by Clause (1) of Article 123 of the Constitution, the President is pleased to promulgate the following Ordinance:

CHAPTER I
PRELIMINARY

1. (1) This Ordinance may be called the Sports Broadcasting Signals (Mandatory Sharing with Prasar Bharti) Ordinance, 2007.

(2) It extends to the whole of India.

(3) Save as otherwise provided, it shall be deemed to have come into force on the 11th day of November 2005.

Definitions.

2. (1) In this Ordinance, unless the context otherwise requiress—

(*a*) "Broadcaster" means any person who provides a content broadcasting service and includes a broadcasting network service provider when he manages and operates his own television or radio channel service;

(b) "Broadcasting" means assembling and programming any form of communication content, like signs, signals, writing, pictures, images and sounds, and either placing it in the electronic form on electromagnetic waves on specified frequencies and transmitting it through space or cables to make it continuously available on the carrier waves, or continuously streaming it in digital data form on the computer networks, so as to be accessible to single or multiple users through receiving devices either directly or indirectly; and all its grammatical variations and cognate expressions;

(c) "Broadcasting service" means assembling, programming and placing communication content in electronic form on the electromagnetic waves on specified frequencies and transmitting it continuously through broadcasting network or networks so as to enable all or any of the multiple users to access it by connecting their receiver devices to their respective broadcasting networks and includes the content broadcasting services and the broadcasting network services;

(*d*) "Broadcasting network service" means a service, which provides a network of infrastructure of cables or transmitting devices for carrying broadcasting content in electronic form on specified frequencies by means of guided or unguided electro-magnetic waves to multiple users, and includes the management and operation of any of the following:

(*i*) Teleport/Hub/Earth Station,

(*ii*) Direct-to-Home (DTH) Broadcasting Network,

(*iii*) Multi-system Cable Television Network,

(*iv*) Local Cable Television Network,

(*v*) Satellite Radio Broadcasting Network,

(*vi*) any other network service as may be prescribed by the Central Government;

(*e*) "Cable television channel service" means the assembly, programming and transmission by cables of any broadcasting television content on a given set of frequencies to multiple subscribers;

(*f*) "Cable television network" means any system consisting of closed transmission paths and associated signal generation, control and distribution equipment, designed to receive and re-transmit television channels or programmes for reception by multiple subscribers;

(*g*) "Community radio service" means terrestrial radio broadcasting intended and restricted only to a specific community and within specified territory;

(*h*) "content" means any sound, text, data, picture (still or moving), other audio-visual representation, signal or intelligence of any nature or any combination thereof which is capable of being created, processed, stored, retrieved or communicated electronically;

(*i*) "Content broadcasting service" means the assembling, programming and placing content in electronic form and transmitting or retransmitting the same on electromagnetic waves on specified frequencies, on a broadcasting network so as to make it available for access by multiple users by connecting their receiving devices to the network, and includes the management and operation of any of the following:

- (*i*) terrestrial television service,
- (*ii*) terrestrial radio service,
- (*iii*) satellite television service,
- (*iv*) satellite radio service,
- (*v*) cable television channel service,
- (*vi*) community radio service,
- (*vii*) any other content broadcasting services as may be prescribed by the Central Government.

(*j*) "Direct-to-Home (DTH) broadcasting service" means a service for multichannel distribution of programmes direct to a subscriber's premises without passing through an intermediary such as a cable operator by uplinking to a satellite system;

(*k*) "Guidelines" means the Guidelines issued under Section 5;

(*l*) "Multi-system cable television network" means a system for multi-channel downlinking and distribution of television programmes by a land-based transmission system using wired cable or wireless cable or a combination of both for simultaneous reception either by multiple subscribers directly or through one or more local cable operators;

(*m*) "Prasar Bharti" means the Corporation known as the Prasar Bharti (Broadcasting Corporation of India) established under Sub-section (1) of Section 3 of the Prasar Bharti (Broadcasting Corporation of India) Act, 1990;

(*n*) "Prescribed" means prescribed by rules made under this Ordinance;

(*o*) "Satellite television service" means a television broadcasting service provided by using a satellite, and received with or without the help of a local delivery system but does not include Direct-to-Home delivery service;

(*p*) "Satellite radio service" means a radio broadcasting service provided by using a satellite and directly receivable through receiver sets by multiple subscribers in India;

(*q*) "Service provider" means provider of a broadcasting service;

(*r*) "Specified" means specified under the Guidelines issued under Section 5;

(*s*) "Sporting events of national importance" means such national or international sporting events, held in India or abroad, as may be notified by the Central Government, in the Official Gazette to be of national importance;

(*t*) "Terrestrial television service" means a television broadcasting service provided over the air by using a land-based transmitter and directly received through receiver sets by the public;

(*u*) "Terrestrial radio service" means a radio broadcasting service provided over the air by using a land-based transmitter and directly received through receiver sets by the public.

(2) Words and expressions used and not defined in this Ordinance and defined in the Cable Television Networks (Regulation) Act, 1995, the Telecom Regulatory Authority of India Act, 1997, the Indian Telegraph Act, 1885, the Indian Wireless Telegraphy Act, 1933 shall have the meanings respectively assigned to them in those Acts.

CHAPTER II
MANDATORY SHARING OF SPORTS BROADCASTING SIGNALS WITH PRASAR BHARTI

3. (1) No content rights owner or holder and no television or radio broadcasting service provider shall carry a live television broadcast on any cable or Direct-to-Home network or radio commentary broadcast in India of sporting events of national importance, unless it simultaneously shares the live broadcasting signal, without its advertisements, with the Prasar Bharti to enable them to re-transmit the same on its terrestrial networks and Direct-to-Home networks in such manner and on such terms and conditions as may be specified.

(2) The terms and conditions under Sub-section (1) shall also provide that the advertisement revenue sharing between the content rights owner or holder and the Prasar Bharti shall be in the ratio of not less than 75:25 in case of television coverage and 50:50 in case of radio coverage.

(3) The Central Government may specify a percentage of the revenue received by the Prasar Bharti under Sub-section (2), which shall be utilised by the Prasar Bharti for broadcasting other sporting events.

4. The Central Government may specify penalties to be imposed, including suspension or revocation of license, permission or registration, for violation of various terms and conditions as may be specified under Section 3, subject to the condition that amount of a pecuniary penalty shall not exceed one crore rupees:

Provided that no penalty shall be imposed without giving a reasonable opportunity to the service provider:

Provided further that no act or omission on the part of any person after the 11th November 2005 and before the date of promulgation of the Sports Broadcasting Signals (Mandatory Sharing with Prasar Bharti) Ordinance, 2007 shall be subjected to penalties.

CHAPTER III
POWERS OF THE CENTRAL GOVERNMENT TO ISSUE GUIDELINES

5. The Central Government shall take all such measures, as it deems fit or expedient, by way of issuing Guidelines for mandatory sharing of broadcasting signals with Prasar Bharti relating to sporting events of national importance:

Provided that the Guidelines issued before the promulgation of the Sports Broadcasting Signals (Mandatory Sharing with Prasar Bharti) Ordinance, 2007 shall be deemed to have been issued validly under the provisions of this section.

CHAPTER IV
MISCELLANEOUS

6. (1) The provisions of the Guidelines issued by the Central Government for Downlinking of Television Channels on the 11th November 2005 and for Uplinking from India on the 2nd December 2005 for mandatory sharing of the sports broadcasting signals shall be deemed to be valid as if they have been issued under this Ordinance.

(2) Notwithstanding anything contained in any judgment, decree or order of any court, tribunal or other authority, any action taken by the Central Government or the Prasar Bharti in pursuance of the guidelines referred to in Sub-section (1) shall be deemed to be and to have always been for all purposes in accordance with the law, as if the Guidelines had been validly in force at all material times and notwithstanding anything as aforesaid and without prejudice to the generality of the foregoing provisions, no legal proceeding shall be maintained or continued in any court for the enforcement of any direction given by any court or any decree or order which would not have been so given had the Guidelines been validly in force at all material times.

7. The Central Government may, by notification in the Official Gazette, make rules for carrying out the provisions of this Ordinance.

8. Every rule and Guidelines made and issued, as the case may be, under this Ordinance shall be laid, as soon as may be after it is made or issued, before each House of Parliament, while it is in session for a total period of thirty days which may be comprised in one session or in two or more successive sessions, and if, before the expiry of the session immediately following the session or the successive sessions aforesaid, both Houses agree in making any modification in the rule or Guidelines, or both Houses agree that the rule or Guidelines should not be made, the rule or Guidelines shall thereafter have effect only in such modified form or be of no effect, as the case may be; so, however, that any such modification or annulment shall be without prejudice to the validity of anything previously done under that rule or Guidelines.

9. The relevant provisions under the Guidelines for Downlinking of Television Channels issued on the 11th November 2005 and the Guidelines for Uplinking from India issued on the 2nd December 2005 for mandatory sharing of sports broadcasting signals with Prasar Bharti. shall continue to remain in force till fresh Guidelines are issued under this Ordinance,

A.P.J. ABDUL KALAM,
President.

K.N. CHATURVEDI,
Secy. to the Govt, of India.

* * * * * *

GUIDELINES BY MINISTRY OF INFORMATION & BROADCASTING, PLAN COORDINATION CELL

Subject: Approved Annual Plan 2007-08—Regarding

The Annual Plan 2007-08 in respect of Ministry of I&B has been fixed at Rs. 475 Crores (Gross Budgetary Support) by the Planning Commission. The Sectoral break-up has been approved as under:

(Figures in Crores of Rupees)

S. No.	*Sector*	*GBS*	*IEBR*	*Total*
1.	Information sector	042.47	0.00	042.47
2.	Film Sector	041.98	0.00	041.98
3.	Broadcasting Sector	390.55	0.00	390.55
	Total:	475.00	0.00	475.00

2. The approved Media-Unit-Wise allocation of Annual Plan 2007-08 is indicated in Annexure-I and the schematic break-up is shown in Annexure-II. It may be noted that many new schemes have been introduced in Annual Plan 2007-08 for which only token provisions have been made. Mere inclusion of the schemes in the Annual Plan does not mean formal approval. Before incurring expenditure out of Plan budget, the following steps should be completed:

(*i*) In respect of the new schemes introduced in Annual Plan 2007-08, necessary "in-principle" approval of the Planning Commission should be obtained latest by 31.03.2007. The total requirement of funds for Eleventh Plan in respect of the new schemes should be assessed and indicated while seeking such "in principle" approval.

(*ii*) Necessary approval of SFC/EFC should be obtained at the earliest so that the implementation starts timely.

2.1. Relevant orders in this regard are contained under Rule 18 of the DFPRs, 1978 and other instructions in this regard.

3. All the Media Units/Organization should incur expenditure of an amount exceeding 2-3 per cent of their Budget for initiatives relating to furthering the use of Information Technology, including training, acquisition of hardware, software as well as development and maintenance of software. Media Units/Organizations are, therefore, requested to work out Action Plan for IT and forward the same to the concerned Administrative Divisions in the Ministry with a copy to Plan Coordination Cell latest by 15.3.2007. The progress in this regard will be monitored by the Planning Commission through the Half Yearly Performance Review reports. To facilitate monitoring of progress made in this regard, schematic break up of the outlays allocated for IT may be maintained/shown separately in the HPRs to be submitted.

4. As Heads of Departments/Media Units are aware, instructions have been repeatedly circulated to ensure phased and balanced Plan expenditure. All concerned are cautioned to ensure timely achievement of the physical and financial targets of Annual Plan 2007-08. Delay/failure on this account will be viewed seriously.

5. Heads of Department/Media Units are also aware of the instructions relating to Outcome Budget 2007-08 which should be finalized quickly and scrupulously monitored and implemented.

Encl.: Annexure I & II

Sd/-
(C Angrup Bodh)
Director (Fin. & PC)
Phone 23384484

LIST OF HEADS OF ALL MEDIA UNITS/ORGANISATIONS

Ministry of I&B's ID No. 4/73/2006-PC, dated 11/02/2007

Copy along with copies of Annexure—I&II forwarded to:

1. PS to MIB/PS to MSIB
2. Sr. PPS to Secretary (I&B)/PPS to AS/PPS to AS & FA
3. JS(P & A)/JS(B)/JS(F)/Economic Adviser.
4. All Directors/Deputy Secretaries
5. All Under Secretaries/Desk Officers/Section Officers, Administrative Sections.
6. Technical Director, NIC for putting on I & B's website (along with soft copy)

(C Angrup Bodh)
Director (Fin. and PC)

No. 603/1/2005-BC-III

GOVERNMENT OF INDIA

MINISTRY OF INFROMATION & BROADCASTING
'A' विंग शास्त्री भवन, नई दिल्ली-110001
'A' Wing Shastri Bhavan, New Delhi-110001

Dated: 18.04.2006

To

Shri N.P. Nawani
President
Indian Broadcasting Foundation (IBF)
B-3-4, 3rd Floor, Ansal Plaza, Khel Gaon Road,
New Delhi-49.

Sub: Sharing of Broadcasting rights of sports events with Prasar Bharti—meeting regarding.

Sir,

The undersigned is directed to enclose herewith a copy of the order No. 603/1/2005-BC-III dated 05.04.2006 regarding sharing of sports events between Prasar Bharti and sports channels and sports rights holder companies. This was decided after consultation with Ministry of Sports and Youth Affairs, Prasar Bharti and sports channels and sports rights holders companies as per Para 5.2 of the Policy guidelines for downlinking for television channels issued on 11.11.2005.

2. It is requested that the same may be disseminated to all the sports TV channels. This order has been posted on the Ministry's website www.mib.nic.in.

Yours faithfully,

(G.R. Raghavender)
Under Secretary (BC)
Tele: 2338 79 30

* * * * * *

No. 603/1/2005-BC-I

GOVERNMENT OF INDIA

MINISTRY OF INFROMATION & BROADCASTING
'A' विंग शास्त्री भवन, नई दिल्ली-110001
'A' Wing Shastri Bhavan, New Delhi-110001

Dated: 5th April 2006

ORDER

1. In pursuance of Para 5.2 of the policy guidelines for downlinking of television channels issued vide notice no. 13/2/2002-BP&L/BC-IV dated 11th November 2005 ***and after consultations with the Ministry of Sports & Youth Affairs, Prasar Bharti and the Sports Channels and Sports Rights Holders Companies,*** it is hereby ordered that live feeds without any advertisements of the sports channel/sports rights holder, of following sporting events of national importance held in India or abroad are required to be shared with Prasar Bharti with immediate effect by sports channels/sports management companies having television broadcasting rights for broadcast on their terrestrial and DTH networks:

A. International events:

- Summer Olympics
- Winter Olympics
- Commonwealth Games
- Asian Games
- Afro-Asian Games

B. (*i*) Tennis:

(*a*) *Davis Cup*—All matches featuring India and semi-final/final matches.
(*b*) *Grand Slam Tournaments*—finals of all tournaments *i.e.* Men's single, Women's single, mixed doubles, Men's double, Women's doubles. Further that if an Indian plays then all matches featuring him/her in quarter-final and above.
(*c*) *WTA Championships*—Same as for Grand Slam tournaments.

(*ii*) Hockey:

(*a*) *World Cup*—All matches featuring India and semi-finals and finals
(*b*) *Champions Trophy*—All matches featuring India and finals
(*c*) *Beighton Cup*—Semifinals and final
(*d*) *Indira Gandhi Gold Cup for Women*—Semifinals and finals

(*iii*) Football:

(*a*) *World Cup*—Semi-finals and finals.

(*b*) *European Cup*—Semi-finals and finals.
(*c*) *Asia Cup*—All matches featuring India and semi-finals & finals.
(*d*) *Subroto Cup*—Semi-finals and finals.
(*e*) *Santosh Trophy*—Semi-finals and finals.
(*f*) *Federation Cup*—Semi-finals and finals.
(*g*) *Durand Cup*—Semi-finals and finals.
(*h*) *National Women Football Championship*—semi finals and finals.
(*i*) Junior National Football Championship—semi finals and finals.

(*iv*) Chess:

(*a*) *World Championship*—Finals of the championship and all games featuring an Indian player in quarter finals and above.
(*b*) *Chess Olympiad*—Finals of the championship and all games featuring an Indian player in quarter finals and above.

(*v*) World Championships in Billiard & Snooker:

Finals of the championships and all games featuring an Indian player in quarter finals and above.

2. The events in the list shall be firm for five years from the date of issue of this order.
3. In case an event mentioned in the list is not telecast by Doordarshan (except for reasons beyond its control) the event would be considered of deletion in the next annual review, after giving an opportunity to Doordarshan to explain their position.
4. The Ministry shall annually review the implementation of this order and consider new proposals, if any.

(Seema Jere Bisht)
Director (BC)
Tele: 2338 1863

3

Towards Understanding the Audio Broadcast System, Sound Recording and Reproduction: Basic and Advanced Tools and Techniques

AUDIO

Audio may refer to:

- Sound that is capable of being heard:
  - Sound recording and reproduction,
  - Natural acoustic audio,
  - Audio frequencies.
- Audio content:
  - Audio book, a sound recording of a book
  - Audio content file format:
    - Windows Media Audio, Microsoft's proprietary digital audio format

Titles

- *Audio* (Blue Man Group album)

AUDIO FREQUENCY

An audio frequency (abbreviation: AF), or audible frequency is characterized as a periodic vibration whose frequency is audible to the average human. While the range of frequencies that any individual can hear is largely related to environmental factors, the generally accepted standard range of audible frequencies is 20 to 20,000 hertz. Frequencies below 20 Hz can usually be felt rather than heard, assuming the amplitude of the vibration is high enough. Frequencies above 20,000 Hz can sometimes be sensed by young people, but high frequencies are the first to be affected by hearing loss due to age and/or prolonged exposure to very loud noises.

Frequencies and Descriptions

Frequency (Hz)	*Octave*	*Description*
16 to 32	1st	The human threshold of feeling, and the lowest pedal notes of a pipe organ.
32 to 512	2nd to 5th	Rhythm frequencies, where the lower and upper bass notes lie.
512 to 2048	6th to 7th	Defines human speech intelligibility, gives a horn-like or tinny quality to sound.
2048 to 8192	8th to 9th	Gives presence to speech, where labial and fricative sounds lie.
8192 to 16384	10th	Brilliance, the sounds of bells and the ringing of cymbals. In speech, the sound of the letter "S" (8000-11000 Hz)

MIDI Note	*Frequency (Hz)*	*Description*
C-2	4.09	Lowest note for Gregg Bailey's 64' PVC sub-contrabass clarinet
C-1	8.18	Lowest organ note
C0	16.35	Lowest note for tuba, large pipe organs, Bösendorfer Imperial Grand Piano
C1	32.70	Lowest C on a standard 88-key piano.
C2	65.41	Lowest note for cello
C3	130.81	Lowest note for viola, mandola
C4	261.63	Middle C
C5	523.25	Lowest note for a piccolo.
C6	1046.50	Approximately the highest note reproducible by the average female human voice.
C7	2093	Highest note for a flute.
C8	4186	Highest note on a standard 88-key piano.
C9	8372	
C10	16744	Approximately the tone that a typical CRT television emits while running.

BASIC AUDIO

In most video programmes it's the audio portion that organizes and makes the visual intelligible. For some types of programmes the absence of sound would make the production completely useless even with the best visuals. Ideally, though, if attention is given to high values in both audio and video, each serves to compliment the other. The result is a programme that communicates powerfully and effectively.

In some ways, the general lack of good audio values in video might be attributed to the design of the video recorder. With most small, portable video units, a microphone is built into the camera, and sound synchronized to the action in the scene is automatically recorded along with the video. It's so easy that people tend to forget about the limitations in this setup and alternative techniques that are available.

Connections for composite video are pretty straightforward. If it says "video" then it's one volt peak to peak with an impedance of 75 ohms. Period. Audio connections are not so simple. To make connections from one piece of equipment to another with confidence, you need to know some basic audio terminology, and a little theory.

Technical Terminology

Unbalanced Audio Cable

Unbalanced lines are cables with only a single conductor and a grounded shield. They're used for "mic in" jacks rated at 600 ohms impedance and "line" or "auxiliary" in jacks rated at 10,000 ohms or higher. Unbalanced lines are subject to interference, especially in runs of twenty feet or longer. Unbalanced lines can usually be identified if they end in "RCA" jacks, mini-plugs or phone jacks.

Balanced Audio Cable

Balanced lines are those with two conductors and a grounded shield. The two conductors are used to carry signals which are identical except that one is inverted and is opposite in polarity from the other. Any interference picked up on the two conductors will have the same polarity on both. When the two signals are recombined in a transformer, the interference cancels itself out. This makes balanced lines the best choice for long cable runs. Balanced lines are generally used for 600 ohm "line" or 50-250 ohm microphone inputs. Generally, if the cable ends in a cannon (XL) connector it's balanced.

NOTE: Coupling a balanced line to an unbalanced line directly without using a transformer unbalances the entire length of the balanced line and defeats the purpose of using it.

Transformer

Impedance is a technical term that refers to the apparent resistance a circuit presents to an alternating current. This apparent resistance is measured in units called ohms. The maximum signal transmission between devices with the lowest distortion occurs when the input and output impedances are the same. Most audio devices fall into one of three categories; microphones generally have low impedance (50 to 250 ohms), balanced lines are rated at a nominal 600 ohms, and unbalanced lines (used in consumer stereo equipment) have high impedance (10,000 ohms and higher). Don't worry about an exact match. Simply connecting outputs to inputs in the same impedance range is sufficient.

Cables connecting high impedance devices are more susceptible to losses and interference as the length of cable increases. Cables connecting low impedance devices are less likely to have problems. Low impedance balanced cables can be run hundreds of feet with minimal problems.

Level—The sensitivity of audio inputs is another important variable. The standard line level is one volt peak-to-peak (.775 volts RMS) at 600 ohms. Microphone outputs and inputs vary. Specifications are given either in millivolts or in decibels. Using established convention, two typical microphone outputs are 1 millivolt (– 60 dB) and 100 millivolts (– 20 dB).

Signal to Noise Ratio is the difference in amplitude between unintelligible noise generated within the device and the maximum signal output of the device, again expressed in decibels. Most video recorders should be capable of an audio signal to noise ratio of forty to fifty dB. (Digital audio devices are capable of more than 100 dB.) You may have noticed that the range of output signal levels exceeds the signal to noise ratio of video recorders. If you put a mic level signal into a line level input, the signal is so low that it falls in the range of noise. You won't even hear it.

Equipment

Microphones

Microphones capture sound and transform it into electrical impulses that are sent to the video recorder. Although there are a number of different microphone designs, only two are used with most video equipment. From the user's point of view, the main difference is that condenser microphones need a power source (battery or external) and dynamic microphones don't.

Dynamic microphones are generally less expensive than condenser mics. Both are fine for general use. It's hard to find a quality microphone for less than a hundred dollars. Audio purists will spend hundreds of dollars on a microphone.

Microphones are also classified according to the shape of the area of sensitivity around the microphone.

Omnidirectional Pattern

An omnidirectional microphone picks up sound equally well from all directions. It's very flexible in that you can place an omni almost anywhere in most situations and pick up usable sound. Omnis are made for various purposes. One kind of omni is the microphone built into the camera. This microphone allows one person to handle both the audio and video. Another kind is called the lavalier, a small mic that clips to a lapel or other part of the wearer's clothing. It can be hidden and leaves the performer's hands free.

Cardioid Pattern

Directional microphones are designed to be more sensitive in some directions than others. One example of a directional microphone is the cardioid. Think of looking down over a microphone. A cardioid picks up the best sound in an area in front of the microphone. The shape of its coverage is like a heart. It's great for recording events on a stage where you don't want audience noise to be picked up. Bidirectional mics pick up sound on either side, but not in front or back.

Shotgun Pattern

Shotgun mics have a narrow range that can pull in sound from a distance in one direction.

Parabolic Dish Pattern

An omni can be used with a special parabolic dish to pick up sounds from great distances. You've seen them on the sideline at football games.

Boom

A boom is a long pole to which a microphone is attached. Usually there's a special rubber or foam shock absorber between the pole and the microphone so vibrations in the pole can't be picked up by the mic.

Windscreen

A windscreen is a small cover, usually of foam rubber, that fits over the top of the microphone. The wind screen is used outside and reduces (but doesn't eliminate) the sound of the wind. The windscreen doesn't cut down on the sensitivity of the mic very much. There's no need to remove it if you're working where it isn't needed.

Mixer

In some situations you'll find that certain sound sources will be louder than others. Some sources may be farther away from you than others and so they may not be picked up as clearly. Or, some sounds may be emitted in the presence of and overshadowed by other sounds. In these cases, the use of one omnidirectional mic won't let you record all the sounds you want to capture clearly. To resolve this problem you'll need more than one microphone. This is where you use a mixer, a device that takes the inputs of a number of microphones and combines them into one output for the recorder. The advantage of this technique is that a microphone can be placed in the optimum position to capture the sound of each source. In addition, the mixer enables you to adjust sound levels from each microphone. If, for example, you were recording a man explaining the skill involved in playing a tuba while the tuba was playing in the background, you might use a mixer to make sure that the speaker's words weren't drowned out.

On the front panel of the mixer are gain controls that adjust the sound level for each microphone. By turning some down and others up, you can get the right "mix" of sounds. After the sounds are mixed, the level of the combined sounds can be controlled by a master gain control so that the sound that goes on your videotape can be adjusted.

Transmitter Mics

Where you can't have microphone cables lying around, but you still need to mic specific sound sources, many people are using radio or transmitter mics. Actually, this involves a microphone plugged into a radio transmitter that sends the signal to a receiver, which is attached to the recorder. While it's a good idea, problems with interference, reflections, and obstacles can turn a good idea into a nightmare. The better systems operate in the VHF band, from 150 to 170 MHz.

Receivers for wireless microphones come in two basic types. Non diversity receivers have a single antenna and single receiver for each microphone. There is no protection against reflection or obstacles. Diversity receivers use multiple (2) antennas and may use one or two receivers for each microphone. The received signals are compared hundreds of times each second and the better signal is used. While diversity systems will help with reflections and obstacles, radio frequency interference will still cause problems.

The VU Meter

Audio recording systems have built-in limitations. When sounds are below a certain level, they're masked by noise. When sounds are too loud, the system can't handle the level and distortion results. If you're in charge of audio during a production, you want to make sure that the sound fed into the recorder falls in an acceptable range. In some instances, with some equipment, there is almost nothing you can do. With some mixers and some audio recorders equipped with VU meters, though, you can control the sound levels. A VU meter shows you a visual representation of the strength of the audio signal expressed in volume units. The maximum allowable sustained level is zero. Most VU meters range from –20 VU to +3 or +5 VU. Although digital recorders have considerably more range, any sound much below –20 VU will be masked by the inherent noise in an analog recording system. It is good practice to keep important audio between –10 VU and 0 VU.

Monitoring the sound using this meter is fairly easy. Set the audio level so that the loudest sound of any duration just hits 0 VU. Occasional peaks may go into the red. If you are recording to analog audio tape you can ignore these fluctuations when setting the levels. When recording digital audio you have a signal to noise ratio of up to 100 dB, but you should never exceed 0 dB, since there is no way to capture audio levels that exceed 100 per cent amplitude. Now you're all set and should leave the controls alone unless the sound levels change. For instance, suppose you're using a fixed position microphone and the speaker suddenly moves away from it after you set the levels. If the needle on the meter only moves a little at the lower end of the scale, you'll have to use the gain controls to boost the level of sound back into the acceptable range. If the speaker comes close to the microphone and starts to scream, and the needle on the meter goes consistently into the red, you'll have to reduce the sound level. Voice should be kept mostly between –7 and 0 VU.

Automatic Gain Control

Automatic Gain Control (AGC) is built into most consumer audio equipment to make the taping of sound easier. It boosts the sound signal automatically when the level gets too low and compresses the sound when it gets too loud. This feature allows one person to handle both video and audio without having to worry about monitoring the sound level. In many situations you'll get usable sound with AGC. Unfortunately, certain characteristics of AGC circuits cause problems in some situations.

Those problems are sensitivity to background (ambient) noise and the reaction time of the system. Most AGC circuits won't boost a sound until it reaches a certain threshold level. The circuit makes an arbitrary decision as to what is noise and what is signal. In a noisy environment (such as a room with a window air conditioner) the ambient sound will be boosted to an unacceptable level. AGC may boost the hum from an amplifier, turning it into a dull roar. Some mixers can emit a low level buzz that may also be boosted by AGC.

The other side of the coin is the problem of reaction time. If during a normal recording there's a sudden loud noise, the AGC circuit often will drive the recorded audio down below audible levels for three to four seconds.

If you can take control over your audio levels and operate manually, do it.

Production Tips

1. Scout the area where you want to tape before the actual recording. Try to visualize the kinds of recording situations that you'll encounter. If you're alone or short-handed, you might have to settle for the built-in microphone on the camera and hope for the best. If you have many sound sources and you can round up someone to handle the audio, use a mixer and multiple microphones where they're required. If you don't want the microphones to show in a scene, mount them on booms or hide them. Lavalier mics provide excellent pickup and can be hidden easily, but they restrict movement. Where movement is important, booms, sound parabolas, or transmitter mics might be appropriate.
2. Make sure all plugs and connectors on cables and equipment fit. Make sure the impedances and levels on all connected devices match. Do not assume that all microphones, mixers, and recorders are designed for compatible impedances or levels. Use adapters only where you are sure devices are compatible.
3. Try to visualize where the equipment and microphones will be placed and the dimensions of the area that will be used for taping. Use this information to estimate the amount of audio cable you will need. Again, it is better to take too much than too little.
4. Once on location, if you are using fixed microphones, set them at their positions. The optimum placement for a mic is six to twelve inches from and below the speaker's mouth. If it's too close you'll get too much bass response and not enough treble. If it's too far away, the level of the voice in relation to the noise in the surroundings may not be high enough. If the mic is directly in the speaker's wind stream, you may get popping and hissing when he pronounces certain consonants.
5. Lay out the cables and attach them either to a mixer or video recorder, then use gaffer's tape (or duct tape, if gaffer's tape is not available) to tape the cable to the ground every six to twelve feet. In high-traffic areas either cover the cable with a rubber mat or tape all along the cable so it's impossible to trip over. This will reduce the chances of someone hurting himself or damaging equipment.
6. Whenever possible, set sound levels using a VU meter.
7. Whenever possible, monitor the sound going to the recorder. Listen for high levels of background noise from the location, hum and other interference in the lines, and distortion, as well as a good sound mix. When a problem is discovered, it's generally better to correct it, even if it means delaying taping.
8. Watch for idiosyncrasies in the performers that might affect the sound. Tapping fingers or banging fists near table-mounted microphones are annoying. Some people are nervous on camera and rub their hands over hand-held mics or

microphone cables, causing a distracting scraping sound. People who tap or scratch their chests while wearing lavalier mics also can be a problem. Lavalier mics may click against buttons or jewelry if they're not carefully placed.

9. When using a sound mixer, use tape or a china marker (grease pencil) to label each control to indicate the source. You don't want to turn the wrong control at a critical moment.

If you are recording a live event it is important to be flexible and to be prepared. You probably will not have the only audio system on location. Musical groups are using sound reinforcement and so are most public speakers.

This raises an important question. What audio are you there to record? That answer may change with the nature of the event and your audience.

If, for example, you are recording a public speaker your interest is in getting the cleanest possible recording of the speaker. Any ambient sound is your enemy, particularly the public address system. You want your microphone as close to the speaker as you can get it. If there is only one speaker a lavalier microphone is the best solution. If there will be multiple speakers, a microphone on the podium is the best solution. If there are multiple speakers at multiple locations you will need an audio mixer and an audio operator to keep the active mike up and all of the others down.

If you are recording a musical performance there is more to consider. Four acoustic (unamplified) performances you could mic each instrument or group of instruments, mic the audience for applause and reactions, and manage it all with a mixing console. You might not be satisfied with the result if you don't get enough of the reverberation in the venue. You could place a couple of microphones above the front of the stage or performance area. The individual instruments will not be as clean, but your recording will be much closer to the experience in the audience. In well-designed concert halls you can actually get good results placing your microphones in the middle of the audience seating.

For electronic or amplified performances you will want to place your mics in the audience seating or at the front of the stage.

There are two problems you should consider in advance. First, what if the sound reinforcement is actually louder than the source when the two sounds reach your microphone? And what if the sound reinforcement is so loud that you literally cannot hear the sound in your headphones to judge the audio quality? If you anticipate this sort of problem, your best solution is to isolate your audio console and operator in an adjacent room or at least use a good headset designed to reduce unwanted ambient sound.

Equalization

Generally speaking, equalization is a tool which is used to correct deficiencies in sound. It involves changing the amplitude of narrow bands within the audio spectrum. It is (and this is important) a form of audio distortion. In other words, if something sounds all right to you, don't waste your time trying to improve it through equalization. To put it another way, any change you make in the audio system is by definition distortion.

The simplest equalizers are the bass, treble, and loudness controls on consumer receivers. Graphic equalizers slice the audio spectrum into a series of narrow bands, while parametric equalizers let you set the target frequency, the width of spectrum, and the amount of boost or attenuation you want. While graphic equalizers have a wide variety of uses, from matching sounds recorded with different microphones or under varying conditions, Parametric equalizers are better at isolating and reducing the impact of undesirable background sounds.

Sound is a more important part of most television programmes than the viewers ever realize. Unless you do an adequate job of treating the acoustical and aesthetic problems involved, the entire meaning of your programme can be distorted or obscured. As in any other area of television production, experience and common sense prove to be your most valuable tools.

SOUND RECORDING AND REPRODUCTION

Sound recording and reproduction is the electrical or mechanical inscription and recreation of sound waves, usually used for the voice or for music.

Technology

The two main classes of sound recording technology are analog recording and digital recording. Analog recording is achieved by a small microphone diaphragm that can detect changes in atmospheric pressure (acoustic sound waves) and record them as graphic sound waves on a medium. The first of these recordings were called sonograms and had no playback mechanism available. With an exclusively mechanical phonograph, the analog conversion is in the form of sonogram grooves carved by a stylus. Newer phonographs use electronics in the process. With magnetic tape, the analog conversion is first in the form of electrical current waves from the microphones conversion of diaphragm movement to electromagnetic fluctuation (flux) that modulate an electric signal, and second of magnetic particles drawn into sonogram-shaped clusters by flux from a tape head sensing the electrical current changes. Analog sound reproduction is the reverse process with a bigger loudspeaker diaphragm causing changes to atmospheric pressure to form acoustic sound waves.

Digital recording and reproduction uses the same analog technologies, with digitization of the sonographic data and signal, allowing it to be stored and transmitted on a wider variety of media. The digital binary numeric data is a representation of the periodic vector points in the raw analog acoustic data at a sample rate most often too frequent for the human ear to distinguish differences in quality. Digital recordings are not necessarily at a higher sample rate, but are often considered higher quality because of less interference from dust or electromagnetic interference in playback and less mechanical deterioration from corrosion or mishandling the storage medium.

Early Developments

The automatic reproduction of music can be traced back as far as the 9th century, when the Banū Musū brothers invented "the earliest known mechanical musical instrument", in this case a hydropowered organ which played interchangeable cylinders automatically. According to Charles B. Fowler, this "cylinder with raised pins on the surface remained the basic device to produce and reproduce music mechanically until the second half of the nineteenth century." The Banu Musa also invented an automatic flute player which appears to have been the first programmable machine.

In the 14th century, Flanders introduced a mechanical bell-ringer controlled by a rotating cylinder. Similar designs appeared in barrel organs (15th century), musical clocks (1598), barrel pianos (1805), and musical boxes (1815). All of these machines could play stored music, but they could not play arbitrary sounds, could not record a live performance, and were limited by the physical size of the medium. The first device that could record sound mechanically (but could not play it back) was the phonautograph, developed in 1857 by Edouard-Leon Scott. One of his paper recordings of *Au Clair de la Lune*, a French folk song, was digitally converted to sound in 2008. It is believed to be the oldest existing recording of a recognisable human voice. Since the above recording was recovered the same team have since recovered a recording of a 435 Hz tuning fork (at that time the French standard concert pitch for A'—now 440 Hz). The tuning fork is barely audible. This second recording has thus become the oldest known recording of a recognisable sound.

The player piano, first demonstrated in 1876, used a punched paper scroll that could store an arbitrarily long piece of music. This piano roll moved over a device known as the 'tracker bar', which first had 58 holes, was expanded to 65 and then was upgraded to 88 holes (generally, one for each piano key). When a perforation passed over the hole, the note sounded. Piano rolls were the first stored music medium that could be mass-produced, although the hardware to play them was much too expensive for personal use. Technology to record a live performance onto a piano roll was not developed until 1904. Piano rolls have been in continuous mass production since around 1898. A 1908 U.S. Supreme Court copyright case noted that, in 1902 alone, there were between 70,000 and 75,000 player pianos manufactured, and between 1,000,000 and 1,500,000 piano rolls produced. The use of piano rolls began to decline in the 1920s although one type is still being made today. The fairground organ, developed in 1892, used a similar system of accordion-folded punched cardboard books.

Phonograph Cylinder

The first practical sound recording and reproduction device was the mechanical phonograph cylinder, invented by Thomas Edison in 1877 and patented in 1878. The invention soon spread across the globe and over the next two decades the commercial recording, distribution and sale of sound recordings became a growing new international industry, with the most popular titles selling millions of units by the early 1900s. The development of mass-production techniques enabled cylinder recordings to become a major new consumer item in industrial countries and the cylinder was the main consumer format from the late 1880s until around 1910.

Disc Phonograph

The next major technical development was the invention of the gramophone disc, generally credited to Emile Berliner and commercially introduced in the United States in 1889.

Discs were easier to manufacture, transport and store, and they had the additional benefit of being louder (marginally) than cylinders, which by necessity, were single-sided. Sales of the Gramophone record overtook the cylinder ca. 1910, and by the end of World War I the disc had become the dominant commercial recording format. In various permutations, the audio disc format became the primary medium for consumer sound recordings until the end of the 20th century, and the double-sided 78 rpm shellac disc was the standard consumer music format from the early 1910s to the late 1950s.

Although there was no universally accepted speed, and various companies offered discs that played at several different speeds, the major recording companies eventually settled on a *de facto* industry standard of nominally 78 revolutions per minute, though the actual speed differed between America and the rest of the world. The specified speed was 78.26 rpm in America and 77.92 rpm throughout the rest of the world (this was related to the speed of a mains-driven synchronous motor). The nominal speed of the disc format gave rise to its common nickname, the "seventy-eight" (though not until other speeds had become available).

Discs were made of shellac or similar brittle plastic like materials, played with needles made from a variety of materials including mild steel, thorn and even sapphire. Discs had a distinctly limited playing life which was heavily dependent on how they were reproduced.

The earlier, purely acoustic methods of recording had limited sensitivity and frequency range. Mid-frequency range notes could be recorded but very low and very high frequencies could not. Instruments such as the violin transferred poorly to disc; however this was partially solved by retrofitting a conical horn to the sound box of the violin. The horn was no longer required once electrical recording was developed.

The vinyl microgroove record was introduced in the late 1940s, and the two main vinyl formats—the 7-inch single turning at 45 rpm and the 12-inch LP (long-playing) record turning at 33 1/3 rpm—had totally replaced the 78 rpm shellac (sometimes vinyl) disc by the end of the 1950s. Vinyl offered improved performance, both in stamping and in playback, and came to be generally played with polished diamond styli, and when played properly (precise tracking weight, etc.) offered longer life. Vinyl records were, over-optimistically, advertised as "unbreakable". They were not, but were much less brittle and breakable than shellac. Nearly all were tinted black, but some were coloured, as red, swirled, translucent, etc.

Electrical Recording

Sound recording began as a mechanical process and remained so until the early 1920s (with the exception of the 1899 Telegraphone) when a string of groundbreaking inventions in the field of electronics revolutionised sound recording and the young recording industry. These included sound transducers such as microphones and loudspeakers, and various electronic devices such as the mixing desk, designed for the amplification and modification of electrical sound signals.

After the Edison phonograph itself, arguably the most significant advances in sound recording were the electronic systems invented by two American scientists between 1900 and 1924.

In 1906 Lee De Forest invented the "Audion" triode vacuum-tube, electronic valve, which could greatly amplify weak electrical signals (one early use was to amplify long distance telephone in 1915), which became the basis of all subsequent electrical sound systems until the invention of the transistor. The valve was quickly followed by the invention of the Regenerative circuit, Super-Regenerative circuit and the Superheterodyne receiver circuit, all of which were invented and patented by the young electronics genius Edwin Armstrong between 1914 and 1922. Armstrong's inventions made higher fidelity electrical sound recording and reproduction a practical reality, facilitating the development of the electronic amplifier and many other devices; after 1925 these systems had become standard in the recording and radio industry.

While E.H. Armstrong published studies about the fundamental operation of the triode vacuum tube before World War I, scientists at Bell Telephone Laboratories achieved their own understanding about the triode and were utilizing the audion as a repeater in weak telephone circuits. By 1925 it was possible to place a long distance telephone call with these repeaters between New York and San Francisco in 20 minutes, both parties being clearly heard.

With this technical prowess, Joseph P. Maxfield and Henry C. Harrison from Bell Telephone Laboratories were skilled in using mechanical analogs of electrical circuits and applied these principles to sound recording and reproduction. They were ready to demonstrate their results by 1924 using the Wente condenser microphone and the vacuum tube amplifier to drive the "rubber line" wax recorder to cut a master audio disc.

Meanwhile, radio continued to develop. Armstrong's groundbreaking inventions (including FM radio) also made possible the broadcasting of long-range, high-quality radio transmissions of voice and music. The importance of Armstong's Superheterodyne circuit cannot be over-estimated—it is the central component of almost all analog amplification and both analog and digital radio-frequency transmitter and receiver devices to this day.

Beginning during World War I, experiments were undertaken in the United States and Great Britain to reproduce among other things, the sound of a Submarine (u-boat) for training purposes. The acoustical recordings of that time proved entirely unable to reproduce the sounds, and other methods were actively sought. Radio had developed independently to this point, and now Bell Laboriatories sought a marriage of the two disparate technologies, greater than the two separately. The first experiments were not very promising, but by 1920 greater sound fidelity was achieved using the electrical system than had ever been realized acoustically. One early recording made without fanfare or announcement was the dedication of the Tomb of the Unknown Soldier at Arlington Cemetery.

By early 1924 such dramatic progress had been made, that Bell Labs arranged a demonstration for the leading recording companies, Victor Talking Machine, and Columbia Phonograph Co's.

Columbia, always in financial straits, could not afford it, and Victor, essentially leaderless since the mental collapse of founder Eldridge Johnson, left the demonstration without comment. English Columbia, by then a separate company, got hold of a test pressing made by Pathe' from these sessions, and realized the immediate and urgent need to have the new system. Bell was only offering its method to United States Companies, and to circumvent this, Managing Director Louis Sterling of English Columbia, bought his once parent company, and signed up for electrical recording.

When Victor Talking Machine was apprised of the Columbia deal, they too quickly signed. Columbia made its first electrical recordings on February 25, 1925 with Victor following a few weeks later. The two then agreed privately to "be quiet" until November 1925, by which time enough electrical repertory would be available.

Other Recording Formats

This period also saw several other historic developments including the introduction of the first practical magnetic sound recording system, the magnetic wire recorder, which was based on the work of Danish inventor Valdemar Poulsen. Magnetic wire recorders were effective, but the sound quality was poor, so between the wars they were primarily used for voice recording and marketed as business dictating machines.

In the 1930s radio pioneer Guglielmo Marconi developed a system of magnetic sound recording using steel tape. This was the same material used to make razor blades, and not surprisingly the fearsome Marconi-Stille recorders were considered so dangerous that technicians had to operate them from another room for safety. Because of the high recording speeds required, they used enormous reels about one metre in diameter, and the thin tape frequently broke, sending jagged lengths of razor steel flying around the studio.

The K1 Magnetophon was the first practical tape recorder, developed by AEG in Germany in 1935.

The other major invention in sound recording in this period was the optical sound-on-film system, also generally credited to Lee De Forest. Although famous early "Talkies" like *The Jazz Singer* used a sound-on-disc system, the film industry eventually adopted the optical sound-on-film system and it revolutionised the movie industry in the 1930s, ushering in the era of 'talking pictures'. Optical sound-on-film, based on the photoelectric cell, became the standard film audio system throughout the world until it was superseded in the 1960s.

Magnetic Tape

Other important inventions of this period were magnetic tape and the tape-recorder (Telegraphone). Paper-based tape was first used but was soon superseded by polyester and acetate backing due to dust drop and hiss. Acetate was more brittle than polyester and snapped easily. This technology, the basis for almost all commercial recording from the 1950s to the 1980s, was invented by German audio engineers in the 1930s, who also discovered the technique of AC biasing, which dramatically improved the frequency response of tape recordings. Tape recording was perfected just after the war by American audio engineer John T. Mullin with the help of Crosby Enterprises (Bing Crosby), whose pioneering recorders were based on captured German recorders, and the Ampex company produced the first commercially available tape recorders in the late 1940s.

Magnetic tape brought about sweeping changes in both radio and the recording industry. Sound could be recorded, erased and re-recorded on the same tape many times, sounds could be duplicated from tape to tape with only minor loss of quality, and recordings could now be very precisely edited by physically cutting the tape and rejoining it.

Within a few years of the introduction of the first commercial tape recorder, the Ampex 200 model, launched in 1948, American musician-inventor Les Paul had invented the first multitrack tape recorder, bringing about another technical revolution in the recording industry. Tape made possible the first sound recordings totally created by electronic means, opening the way for the bold sonic experiments of the Musique Concrète school and avant garde composers like Karlheinz Stockhausen, which in turn led to the innovative pop music recordings of artists such as Frank Zappa, The Beatles and The Beach Boys.

Tape enabled the radio industry for the first time to pre-record many sections of programme content such as advertising, which formerly had to be presented live, and it also enabled the creation and duplication of complex, high-fidelity, long-duration recordings of entire programmes. It also, for the first time, allowed broadcasters, regulators and other interested parties to undertake comprehensive logging of radio broadcasts. Innovations like multitracking and tape echo enabled radio programmes and advertisements to be pre-produced to a level of complexity and sophistication that was previously unattainable and tape also led to significant changes to the pacing of programme content, thanks to the introduction of the endless-loop tape cartridge.

Stereo and Hi-Fi

Magnetic tape also enabled the development of the first practical commercial sound systems that could record and reproduce high-fidelity stereophonic sound. Experiments with stereo dated back to the 1880s and during the 1930s and 1940s there were many attempts to record in stereo using discs, but these were hampered by problems with synchronization.

The first major breakthrough in practical stereo sound was made by Bell Laboratories, who in 1937 demonstrated a practical system of two-channel stereo, using dual optical sound tracks on film. Major movie studios quickly developed three-track and four-track sound systems, and the first stereo sound recording in a commercial film was made by Judy Garland for the MGM movie *Listen, Darling* in 1938. The first commercially-released movie with a full surround soundtrack was Walt Disney's *Fantasia*, released in 1940. The sound for this production was originally recorded on a completely separate magnetic film, but because of the complex equipment required to present it, it was shown as a road show, but only in the United States. Regular releases of the film were on standard mono optical 35 mm stock until the film was transferred to multichannel 70 mm stock in the 1970s.

German audio engineers working on magnetic tape are reported to have developed stereo recording by 1943, but it was not until the introduction of the first commercial two-track tape recorders by Ampex in the late 1940s that stereo tape recording became commercially feasible. However, despite the availability of multitrack tape, stereo did not become the standard system for commercial music recording for some years and it remained a specialist market during the 1950s. This changed after the late 1957 introduction of the "Westrex stereo phonograph disc".

Decca Records in England came out with FFRR (Full Frequency Range Recording) in the 1940s which became internationally accepted and a worldwide standard for higher quality recordings on vinyl records. The Ernest Ansermet recording of Igor

Stravinsky's Petrushka was key in the development of full frequency range records and alterting the listening public to high fidelity in 1946.

Most pop singles were mixed into monophonic sound until the mid-1960s, it was common for major pop releases to be issued in both mono and stereo until the early 1970s. Many Sixties pop albums now available only in stereo were originally intended to be released only in mono, and the so-called "stereo" version of these albums were created by simply separating the two tracks of the master tape. In the mid Sixties, as stereo became more popular, many mono recordings (such as The Beach Boys' *Pet Sounds*) were remastered using the so-called "fake stereo" method, which spread the sound across the stereo field by directing higher-frequency sound into one channel and lower-frequency sounds into the other.

1950s and Beyond

Magnetic tape transformed the recording industry, and by the late-1950s the vast majority of commercial recordings were being mastered on tape. The electronics revolution that followed the invention of the transistor brought other radical changes, the most important of which was the introduction of the world's first "personal music device", the miniaturized transistor radio, which became a major consumer luxury item in the 1960s, transforming radio broadcasting from a static group experience into a mobile, personal listening activity.

The first multitrack recording made using magnetic tape was "How High the Moon" by Les Paul, on which Paul played eight overdubbed guitar tracks. In the 1960s Brian Wilson of The Beach Boys, Frank Zappa and The Beatles (with producer George Martin) were among the first popular artists to explore the possibilities of multitrack techniques and effects on their landmark albums *Pet Sounds, Freak Out!* and *Sgt. Pepper's Lonely Hearts Club Band.*

The next important innovation was small cartridge based tape systems of which the compact cassette, introduced by the Philips electronics company in 1964 is the best known. It eventually entirely replaced the competing formats, the larger 8-track tape (used primarily in cars) and the fairly similar 'Deutsche Cassette' developed by the German company Grundig. This latter system was not particularly common in Europe and practically unheard of in America. The compact cassette became a major consumer audio format and advances in microelectronics eventually allowed the development of the Sony Walkman, introduced in the 1970s, which was the first personal music player and gave a major boost to the mass distribution of music recordings. Cassettes became the first successful consumer recording/re-recording medium. The gramophone record was a pre-recorded playback only medium, and reel-to-reel tape was too difficult for most consumers and far less portable.

A key advance in audio fidelity came with the Dolby A noise reduction system, invented by Ray Dolby and introduced in 1966. A competing system dbx, invented by David Blackmer, found most success in professional audio. A simpler variant of Dolby's noise reduction system, known as Dolby B greatly improved the sound of cassette tape recordings by reducing the practical effect of the recorded hiss inherent in the narrow tape used. It, and variants, also eventually found wide application in the recording and film industries. Dolby B was crucial to the popularisation and commercial success of the compact cassette as a domestic recording and playback medium, and became a part of the booming "hi-fi" market of the 1970s and beyond. The compact cassette also benefited enormously from developments in the tape material itself as materials with wider frequency responses and lower inherent noise were developed, often based on cobalt and/or chrome oxides as the magnetic material instead of the more usual iron oxide.

The multitrack audio cartridge had been in wide use in the radio industry, from the late 1950s to the 1980s, but in the 1960s the pre-recorded 8-track cartridge was launched as a consumer audio format by Bill Lear of the Lear Jet aircraft company (and although its correct name was the 'Lear Jet Cartridge', it was seldom referred to as such). Aimed particularly at the automotive market, they were the first practical, affordable car hi-fi systems, and could produce superior sound quality to the compact cassette. However the smaller size and greater durability—augmented by the ability to create home-recorded music "compilations" since 8-track recorders were rare—saw the cassette become the dominant consumer format for portable audio devices in the 1970s and 1980s.

There had been experiments with multi-channel sound for many years—usually for special musical or cultural events—but the first commercial application of the concept came in the early 1970s with the introduction of Quadraphonic sound. This spin-off development from multitrack recording used four tracks (instead of the two used in stereo) and four speakers to create a 360-degree audio field around the listener. Following the release of the first consumer 4-channel hi-fi systems, a number of popular albums were released in one of the competing four-channel formats; among the best known are Mike Oldfield's *Tubular Bells* and Pink Floyd's *The Dark Side of the Moon*. Quadraphonic sound was not a commercial success, partly because of competing and somewhat incompatible four-channel sound systems (e.g., CBS, JVC, Dynaco and others all had systems) and generally poor quality, even when played as intended on the correct equipment, of the released music. It eventually faded out in the late 1970s, although this early venture paved the way for the eventual introduction of domestic Surround Sound systems in home theatre use, which have gained enormous popularity since the introduction of the DVD. This widespread adoption has occurred despite the confusion introduced by the multitude of available surround sound standards.

The replacement of the thermionic valve (vacuum tube) by the smaller, cooler and less power-hungry transistor also accelerated the sale of consumer high-fidelity "hi-fi" sound systems from the 1960s onward. In the 1950s most record players were monophonic and had relatively low sound quality; few consumers could afford high-quality stereophonic sound systems. In the 1960s, American manufacturers introduced a new generation of "modular" hi-fi components—separate turntables, pre-amplifiers, amplifiers, both combined as integrated amplifiers, tape recorders, and other ancillary equipment (like the graphic equaliser), which could be connected together to create a complete home sound system. These developments were rapidly taken up by Japanese electronics companies, which soon flooded the world market with relatively cheap, high-quality components. By the 1980s, corporations like Sony had become world leaders in the music recording and playback industry.

Digital Recording

The invention of digital sound recording and the compact disc in 1982 brought significant improvements in the durability of consumer recordings. The CD initiated another massive wave of change in the consumer music industry, with vinyl records effectively relegated to a small niche market by the mid-1990s. However, the introduction of digital systems was initially fiercely resisted by the record industry which feared wholesale piracy on a medium which was able to produce perfect copies of original released recordings. However, various protection system (principally SCMS) persuaded the industry to bow to the inevitable.

The most recent and revolutionary developments have been in digital recording, with the invention of purely electronic consumer recording formats such as the WAV digital music file and the compressed file type, the MP3. This generated a new type of portable solid-state computerised digital audio player, the MP3 player. Another invention, by Sony, was the minidisc player, using ATRAC compression on small, cheap, re-writeable discs. This was in vogue in the 1990s, and is still popular, especially in a newer, longer playing and higher fidelity version. New technologies such as Super Audio CD, DVD-A, Blu-ray Disc and HD DVD continue to set a very high rate of change in digital audio storage.

Fig. 3.1: A Digital Sound Recorder

This technology spreads across various associated fields, from hi-fi to professional audio, internet radio and podcasting.

Technological developments in recording and editing have transformed the record, movie and television industries in recent decades. Audio editing became practicable with the invention of magnetic tape recording, but the use of computers has made editing operations faster and easier to execute with software, and the use of hard-drives for storage has made recording cheaper. Today, the process of making a recording is separated into tracking, mixing and mastering. Multitrack recording makes it possible to capture signals from several microphones, or from different 'takes' to tape or disc, with maximized headroom and quality, allowing previously unavailable flexibility in the mixing and mastering stages for editing, level balancing, compressing and limiting, adding effects such as reverberation, equalisation, flanging, and much more.

In the 1920s, the early talkies featured the new sound-on-film technology which used photoelectric cells to record and reproduce sound signals that were optically recorded directly onto the movie film. The introduction of talking movies, spearheaded by *The Jazz Singer* in 1927 (though it used a sound on disk technique, not a photoelectric one), saw the rapid demise of live cinema musicians and orchestras. They were replaced with pre-recorded soundtracks, causing the loss of many jobs. The American Federation of Musicians took out ads in newspapers, protesting the replacement of real musicians with mechanical playing devices, especially in theatres.

Voice to Note

Voice-to-note refers to the capability of personal computers to be able to recognize notes that are sung, hummed, or whistled into a microphone. The pitch and duration of the notes are then calculated and converted into MIDI music files.

Legal Status

UK

Since 1934, sound recordings are treated differently from musical works under copyright law. *Copyright, Designs and Patents Act 1988* defines a sound recording to mean (*a*) *a recording of sounds, from which the sounds may be reproduced, or* (*b*) *a recording of the whole or any part of a literary, dramatic or musical work, from which sounds reproducing the work or part may be produced, regardless of the medium on which the recording is made or the method by which the sounds are reproduced or produced.* It thus covers vinyl records, tapes, compact discs, digital audiotapes, and MP3s which embody recordings.

MANUAL OF SOUND RECORDING

Types of Microphone:

- *Dynamic*: Most common/cheapest.
- *Condenser*: Most require Phantom Power. Known for producing more detail, especially in the upper frequencies.
- *Ribbon*: Was rare, becoming more common. Catching speed as being 'smooth' on guitars.

Electronics you should be Aware of Balanced Versus Unbalanced

Balanced audio connections use 3 wires for sending each channel: a plus phase, a negative phase, and a ground. The sending device sends its output over both the plus phase and the negative phase. But (and here's the clever bit) the signal is inverted on the negative phase. The receiving device then inverts the negative phase back (to match the positive phase) and adds it to the positive phase. Any noise picked up along a stretch of wire will be out of phase with itself (once the destination reverts the negative phase), and be cancelled out.

In short: Balanced is practically immune to noise (like "mains hum") and so you should use balanced connections as often as possible. It's absolutely vital to use balanced connections for long lengths of wire (lengths over a meter) and in situations where there's lots of electro-magnetic interference (EMI) like on a film set. (Those 20kW HMIs, for example!)

Grounding

Shielding

Phantom Power

Phantom power is used for condenser microphones that need power to run. It is also used to power direct boxes. Direct boxes turn unbalanced signal into balanced signal for reducing and preventing hum. You will most often see phantom power in 48v. You can get phantom power from a source such as many sound consoles, especially if you have a recording console. If you don't have it built into your console, you can buy a portable unit that takes up an outlet and has an xlr in and xlr out (with 48v power).

Mixing

As a quick rule of thumb for a TV mix, dialogue should average 3.5/4 ppm on a meter *i.e.* around –20 to 18 dB. You should record it like this and mix at these levels. Peak dialogue shouts etc. shouldn't really go above 6 ppm (– 10 dB). If you are recording or mixing for TV nothing should peak over 7 ppm (– 6 dB). And those peaks should last a minimal amount of time. Music is mixed at the dubbing mixer's discretion, so that it works with the programme and fits with the dialogue, but shouldn't peak above 6.5 ppm. A limiter would usually be placed across the output to ensure nothing goes above 7 ppm.

If you are mixing for DVD or Theatre release you would use the full digital scale. Dialogues should still average –20 to 18 dB however your fx peaks can go the full range to 0 dB but not over!

So you would have two mixes one for TV and one for DVD.

The BBC's audio delivery specification states:

> "Peak sound levels (when measured on a BS 5428 Peak Programme Meter) within the programme must not exceed PPM 6: that is, no greater than +8 dB with respect to the reference level of –18 dBFS."

In other words there should be no less than 10 dB of 'headroom' between the highest level you can record and your programme's highest peak.

You can find the full document at: http://www.bbc.co.uk/guidelines/delivering_quality/pdf/tv/tv_standards_london.doc

It is preferable to have sound with "hiss" rather than distortion. Distortion cannot be fixed, background noise can be somewhat fixed.

What to Record On?

The Video Camera

I've recorded onto camera quite a few times—the skinny is that you can get great audio from the cameras with XLR inputs and also:

The Canon XL1 has not got phantom power—you need an external mic power supply. The DVX-100a has small audio controls which are more difficult to manipulate, a little movement seems to make a big difference in level. One of the two DVX100a's I've used had a buzz only when the DV tape was installed. Very annoying, but the other one was quiet. The Sony PD170 has a good set of audio controls—especially the ch1/ch2 link function when using one microphone (two channels are better than one!)

The PD100 has needs a +48/XLR hot shoe attachment, otherwise it sounds fine.

It's wise to back up audio, and slate scenes without pausing, when using DV cameras—back up on DAT. On a recent 3 camera shoot, I had a total of 6 audio tracks, one into the DVx100a, one into a Canon Optura PI (fine little camera!), but with 1/8" connector and one into a Sony tcd-08 DAT—the DAT won as the best overall sound with the lowest noise and cleanest sound.

DAT

DAT-Heads concerns itself with Digital Audio Tape decks, with an emphasis on their use for the recording and distribution of live music.

MiniDisk

ATRAC 3 is a proprietary lossy perceptual audio codec developed by Sony and used for minidisc and other Sony products such as the PlayStation Portable. Uncompressed PCM offers higher quality, and therefore field recording with a portable DAT or harddisk recorder is almost always preferrable to a minidisc recorder. Personally, I'd trust a tape (DAT) more as I have accidentally recorded over material with the minidisk's chapter functions. It's easier to track down ABS (absolute time code) on a DAT, especially for sound logging purposes. DAT = Digital Audio Tape.

Hard Disk

Hard Disk recording has quickly become the industry standard (aside from analog tape.) Benefits include: Non-linear editing—no need to rewind or fast-forward to find different songs. Cost—You can buy a hard drive with well over a hundred gigs, for around a hundred bucks. 100 gigs can hold 300 hours of uncompressed single-channel audio, making it a very cheap way to record.

Wild Track

When on location you should always record a "wild track." This should be a few minutes of the ambient noise from your location (the sound of traffic in the distance, birds singing etc.). You should ask the assistant director to tell the entire crew to be quiet so you get an undisturbed track.

Why bother? In the edit it's very useful (and often absolutely required) to keep a wild track running in the background to smooth over the changes from cut to cut.

A Wild Track is an audio only recording of an actor's lines while the camera is NOT rolling. There are no sync marks or visible slates. These wild recordings are used to replace dialogue from a filmed take that may be un-usable for various reasons. Perhaps a plane flew over during the scene. The Wild Track Or Wild Line will be used in part or in whole to replace the on-camera dialogue. It is also used for Off-camera lines that need to be recorded on-mic. Many times wild Lines are used to replace compromised recordings made during a Wide master shot where the microphone could not be placed in the optimal position. Because the shot is wide, lip-sync of these lines is not as critical and sync errors are not as visible as for a close up.

"Room Tone" or "Presence" is a wild recording of just the ambient sound of a location (no one speaking). It is used in post production to cover unwanted sounds (like the director's verbal instruction during the take). To record Room tone you should place the same microphone in the same position as it was during the dialogue take. Record at the same level used for the actual take but have everyone remain still and quiet.

TAPE RECORDER

A tape recorder, tape deck, reel-to-reel tape deck, cassette deck or tape machine is an audio storage device that records and plays back sound using magnetic tape, either wound on a reel or in a cassette, for storage. It records a fluctuating signal by moving the tape across a tape head that polarizes the magnetic domains in the tape in proportion to the audio signal.

Fig. 3.2: Reel-to-Reel Tape Recorder

History

Early tape-recorders were created by replacing the steel wire of a wire recorder with a thin steel tape. The first of these modified wire recorders was the Blattnerphone, created in 1929 or 1930 by the Ludwig Blattner Picture Corporation. The first practical tape recorder was called K1 and demonstrated in Germany in 1935. Friedrich Matthias of IG Farben/BASF developed the recording tape, including the oxide, the binder, and the backing material. Development of magnetic tape recorders in the late 1940s and early 1950s is associated with the Brush Development Company and its licensee, Ampex; the equally important development of magnetic tape media itself was led by Minnesota Mining and Manufacturing Company (now known as 3M).

Description of Operation

Electrical

Electric current flowing in the coils of the tape head creates a fluctuating magnetic field. This causes the magnetic material on the tape, which is moving past and in contact with the head, to align in a manner proportional to the original signal. The signal can be reproduced by running the tape back across the tape head, where the reverse process occurs—the magnetic imprint on the tape induces a small current in the read head which approximates the original signal and is then amplified for playback. Many tape recorders are capable of recording and playing back at once by means of separate record and playback heads in line or combined in one unit.

Mechanical

Modern professional recorders usually use a three-motor scheme. One motor with a constant rotation speed provides traction for the capstan. This, usually combined with a rubber pinch roller, ensures that the tape speed does not fluctuate. Of the other two motors, one applies a very light torque to the supply reel, and the other a greater torque to the takeup reel, to maintain the tape's tension. During fast winding operation the pinch roller is disengaged and the reel motors provide the necessary power. The cheapest models use a single motor for all required functions, coupled to the capstan and reel spindles as needed with mechanical clutches and belts. There are also variants with two motors, in which one motor is used for rewinding only.

Later Developments

Since their first introduction, analog tape recorders have experienced a long series of progressive developments resulting in increased sound quality, convenience, and versatility.

Fig. 3.3: A Typical Portable Desktop Cassette Recorder from Radio Shack.

- Two-track and, later, multi-track heads permitted discrete recording and playback of individual sound sources, such as two stereophonic channels, or different microphones during live recording. The more versatile machines could be switched to record on some tracks while playing back others, permitting additional tracks to be "laid down" to match previously recorded material such as a rhythm track.
- Use of separate heads for recording vs. playback (three heads total, counting the erase head) enabled monitoring of the recorded signal a fraction of a second after recording. Mixing the playback signal back into the record input also created a primitive echo generator.
- Dynamic range compression during recording and expansion during playback expanded the available dynamic range and improved the signal-to-noise ratio. dbx and Dolby Laboratories introduced add-on products in this area, originally for studio use, and later in versions for the consumer market. In particular, "Dolby B" noise reduction became very common in all but the least expensive cassette tape recorders.
- Computer controlled analog tape recorders were introduced by Oscar Bonello in Argentina. The mechanical transport used three DC motors and introduced two new advances: automated microprocessor transport control and automatic adjustment of bias and frequency response. In 30 seconds the recorder adjusted its bias for minimum THD and best frequency response to match the brand and batch of magnetic tape used. The microprocessor control of transport allowed fast location of any point on the tape.

Limitations

The storage of an analogue signal on tape works well, but is not perfect. In particular, the granular nature of the magnetic material adds noise to the signal, which is usually heard as tape hiss. Also, the magnetic characteristics of tape are not linear. They exhibit a characteristic hysteresis curve, which causes unwanted distortion of the signal. Some of this distortion is overcome by using an inaudible high-frequency AC bias signal when recording, though the amount of bias needs careful adjustment for best results. Different tape material requires differing amounts of bias, which is why most recorders have a switch to select this (or, in a cassette recorder, switch automatically based on cutouts in the cassette shell). Additionally, systems such as Dolby B, Dolby C and Dolby HX-Pro have been devised to ameliorate some of the noise and distortion problems. Variations in tape speed cause flutter, which can be reduced by using dual capstans. Higher speeds used in professional recorders are prone to cause "head bumps," which are fluctuations in low-frequency response.

Variety of Tape-Recorders

There is a wide variety of tape-recorders in existence, from small hand-held devices to large multitrack machines. A machine with built-in speakers and audio power amplification to drive them is usually called a "tape recorder" or—if it has no record functionality—a "tape player," while one that requires external amplification for playback is usually called a "tape deck" (regardless of whether it can record).

Multitrack technology enabled the development of modern art music and one such artist, Brian Eno, described the tape recorder as "an automatic musical collage device".

Use of Tape-Recorders

An important use of tape-recorders is the recording of video. Video cassette recorders differ substantially from audio recorders due to the use of a rotating magnetic head that uses a helical scan over the tape medium. Helical scans increase the relative speed of the tape surface over the head.

While they are primarily used for sound recording, tape machines were also important for data storage before the advent of floppy disks and CDs, and are still used today, although primarily to provide an offline backup to hard disk drives.

Tapedeck Speeds

There are many different tape speeds which are in use in all sorts of tape recorders. Most often these speeds appear on tapedecks. But—while meaning the same speed—many tapedecks are either in centimeters per second (cm/s) or in inches per second (in/s).

To overcome this, here is an overview:

cm/s	*in/s*	*cm/s*	*in/s*
1.2	15/32	19	7 1/2
2.4	15/16	38	15
4.75	1 7/8	76	30
9.5	3 3/4		

DIGITAL AUDIO BROADCASTING

Until now, analogue radio signals such as AM or FM have been subject to numerous kinds of interference on their way from the transmitter to your radio. These problems are caused by mountains, high-rise buildings, local electrical interference and weather conditions.

Digital Audio Broadcasting (DAB), however, uses the most modern methods of radio transmission to produce a much more robust signal that can get around all these reception problems. DAB is broadcast on terrestrial networks, which means that it makes use of local transmitters in each community, much like AM and FM radio. Listeners are able to access these services using special new receivers. CD-like quality radio programmes can be received even in the car without any annoying interference and signal distortion. Aside from distortion-free reception and CD Quality sound, DAB offers further advantages as it has been designed for the multimedia age.

DAB can carry not only audio, but also text, pictures, data and even videos—all on radio! Listeners can hear their favorite music programmes and receive related video and text information all at the same time on suitably-equipped radios.

In Canada, DAB radio services utilizing the Eureka 147/DAB transmission standard have been implemented in Toronto, Montreal, Vancouver and Ottawa. Anyone with a DAB receiver capable of tuning "L-Band" spectrum from 1452-92 MHz can pick up these signals at no cost. At present, the programming services in these four cities consist of simulcasts of local CBC and private AM and FM radio stations, only in much higher quality.

The establishment of additional DAB stations across Canada awaits the conclusion of a federal government radio spectrum review that will determine where and when other L-Band radio frequencies for DAB services will be made available. This review is expected to commence in Fall 2008 and carry into 2009. In view of this, further DAB implementations by broadcasters are on hold, making suitable receivers hard to find in Canada. Although many such receivers are available in Europe and the UK, anyone buying such a device should ensure that it is capable of tuning to the L-Band frequency band mentioned previously.

NB: The DAB transmission system currently used in Canada is not technically compatible with the hybrid HD Radio IM digital radio technology being implemented by some US AM and FM radio stations. At present, no Canadian stations are transmitting digital signals using HD Radio TM; however, this may change should the US system be found capable of meeting part of Canada's future DAB needs. Likewise, digital receivers employed to access satellite pay radio services (*e.g.* Sirius and XM Radio) are not capable of receiving the free local DAB services offered by Canada's broadcasters.

Digital audio broadcasting (DAB), also known as digital radio and high-definition radio, is audio broadcasting in which analog audio is converted into a digital signal and transmitted on an assigned channel in the AM or (more usually) FM frequency range. DAB is said to offer compact disc (CD)—quality audio on the FM (frequency modulation) broadcast band and to offer FM-quality audio on the AM (amplitude modulation) broadcast band. The technology was first deployed in the United Kingdom in 1995, and has become common throughout Europe.

Digital audio broadcast signals are transmitted in-band, on-channel (IBOC). Several stations can be carried within the same frequency spectrum. Listeners must have a receiver equipped to handle DAB signals. At the transmitting site, the signal is compressed using MPEG algorithms and modulated using coded orthogonal frequency division multiplexing (COFDM). A digital signal offers several advantages over conventional analog transmission, including improved sound quality, reduced fading and multipath effects, enhanced immunity to weather, noise, and other interference, and expansion of the listener base by increasing the number of stations that can broadcast within a given frequency band.

A DAB receiver includes a small display that provides information about the audio content in much the same way that the menu screen provides an overview of programmes in digital television (DTV). Some DAB stations provide up-to-the-minute news, sports, and weather headlines or bulletins in a scrolled text format on the display. Using the DAB information, it may also be possible to see what song is coming up next.

4

Towards Understanding the Video Broadcast System: Basic and Additional Types

VIDEO

Video is the technology of electronically capturing, recording, processing, storing, transmitting, and reconstructing a sequence of still images representing scenes in motion.

History

Video technology was first developed for cathode ray tube television systems, but several new technologies for video display devices have since been invented. Standards for television sets and computer monitors have tended to evolve independently, but advances in computer performance and digital television broadcasting and recording are producing some convergence.

Computers can now display television and film-style video clips and streaming media, encouraged by increased processor speed, storage capacity, and broadband access to the Internet. General-purpose computing hardware can now be used to capture, store, edit, and transmit television and movie content, as opposed to older dedicated analog technologies.

Description of Video

The term *video* (from Latin: "I see") commonly refers to several storage formats for moving eye pictures: digital video formats, including DVD, QuickTime, and MPEG-4; and analog videotapes, including VHS and Betamax. Video can be recorded and transmitted in various physical media: in magnetic tape when recorded as PAL or NTSC electric signals by video cameras, or in MPEG-4 or DV digital media when recorded by digital cameras.

Quality of video essentially depends on the capturing method and storage used. Digital television (*DTV*) is a relatively recent format with higher quality than earlier television formats and has become a standard for television video.

3D-video, digital video in three dimensions, premiered at the end of 20th century. Six or eight cameras with realtime depth measurement are typically used to capture *3D-video* streams. The format of *3D-video* is fixed in MPEG-4 Part 16 Animation Framework eXtension (AFX).

In the UK, Australia, The Netherlands, Finland, Hungary and New Zealand, the term *video* is often used informally to refer to both Videocassette recorders and video cassettes; the meaning is normally clear from the context.

Characteristics of Video Streams

Number of Frames Per Second

Frame rate, the number of still pictures per unit of time of video, ranges from six or eight frames per second (*frame/s*) for old mechanical cameras to 120 or more frames per second for new professional cameras. PAL (Europe, Asia, Australia, etc.) and SECAM (France, Russia, parts of Africa etc.) standards specify 25 frame/s, while NTSC (USA, Canada, Japan, etc.) specifies 29.97 frame/s. Film is shot at the slower frame rate of 24 frame/s, which complicates slightly the process of transferring a cinematic motion picture to video. The minimum frame rate to achieve the illusion of a moving image is about fifteen frames per second.

Interlacing

Video can be interlaced or progressive. Interlacing was invented as a way to achieve good visual quality within the limitations of a narrow bandwidth. The *horizontal scan lines* of each interlaced frame are numbered consecutively and partitioned into two *fields*: the *odd field* (upper field) consisting of the odd-numbered lines and the *even field* (lower field) consisting of the even-numbered lines. NTSC, PAL and SECAM are interlaced formats. Abbreviated video resolution specifications often include an *i* to indicate interlacing. For example, PAL video format is often specified as *576i50,* where *576* indicates the vertical line resolution, *i* indicates interlacing, and *50* indicates 50 fields (half-frames) per second.

In *progressive scan* systems, each refresh period updates all of the scan lines. The result is a higher perceived resolution and a lack of various artifacts that can make parts of a stationary picture appear to be moving or flashing.

A procedure known as deinterlacing can be used for converting an interlaced stream, such as analog, DVD, or satellite, to be processed by progressive scan devices, such as TFT TV-sets, projectors, and plasma panels. Deinterlacing cannot, however, produce a video quality that is equivalent to true progressive scan source material.

Display Resolution

The size of a video image is measured in pixels for digital video, or horizontal scan lines and vertical lines of resolution for analog video. In the digital domain (*e.g.* DVD) standard-definition television (SDTV) is specified as *720/704/640×480i60* for NTSC and *768/720×576i50* for PAL or SECAM resolution. However in the analog domain, the number of visible scanlines remains constant (486 NTSC/576 PAL) while the horizontal measurement varies with the quality of the signal: approximately 320 pixels per scanline for VCR quality, 400 pixels for TV broadcasts, and 720 pixels for DVD sources. Aspect ratio is preserved because of non-square "pixels".

New high-definition televisions (HDTV) are capable of resolutions up to *1920×1080p60, i.e.* 1920 pixels per scan line by 1080 scan lines, progressive, at 60 frames per second.

Video resolution for 3D-video is measured in voxels (*volume picture element*, representing a value in three dimensional space). For example 512×512×512 voxels resolution, now used for simple 3D-video, can be displayed even on some PDAs.

Aspect Ratio

Aspect ratio describes the dimensions of video screens and video picture elements. All popular video formats are rectilinear, and so can be described by a ratio between width and height. The screen aspect ratio of a traditional television screen is 4:3, or about 1.33:1. High definition televisions use an aspect ratio of 16:9, or about 1.78:1. The aspect ratio of a full 35 mm film frame with soundtrack (also known as the Academy ratio) is 1.375:1.

Ratios where the height is taller than the width are uncommon in general everyday use, but do have application in computer systems where the screen may be better suited for a vertical layout. The most common tall aspect ratio of 3:4 is referred to as *portrait mode* and is created by physically rotating the display device 90 degrees from the normal position. Other tall aspect ratios such as 9:16 are technically possible but rarely used.

Pixels on computer monitors are usually square, but pixels used in digital video often have non-square aspect ratios, such as those used in the PAL and NTSC variants of the CCIR 601 digital video standard, and the corresponding anamorphic widescreen formats. Therefore, an NTSC DV image which is 720 pixels by 480 pixels is displayed with the aspect ratio of 4:3 (which is the traditional television standard) if the pixels are thin and displayed with the aspect ratio of 16:9 (which is the anamorphic widescreen format) if the pixels are fat.

Colour Space and Bits Per Pixel

Colour model name describes the video colour representation. *YIQ* was used in NTSC television. It corresponds closely to the *YUV* scheme used in NTSC and PAL television and the *YDbDr* scheme used by SECAM television.

The number of distinct colours that can be represented by a pixel depends on the number of *bits per pixel* (bpp). A common way to reduce the number of bits per pixel in digital video is by chroma subsampling (*e.g.* 4:4:4, 4:2:2, 4:2:0, 4:1:1).

Video Quality

Video quality can be measured with formal metrics like PSNR or with subjective video quality using expert observation.

The subjective video quality of a video processing system may be evaluated as follows:

- Choose the video sequences (the *SRC*) to use for testing.
- Choose the settings of the system to evaluate (the *HRC*).

- Choose a test method for how to present video sequences to experts and to collect their ratings.
- Invite a sufficient number of experts, preferably not fewer than 15.
- Carry out testing.
- Calculate the average marks for each *HRC* based on the experts' ratings.

Many subjective video quality methods are described in the ITU-T recommendation BT. 500. One of the standardized method is the *Double Stimulus Impairment Scale* (DSIS). In DSIS, each expert views an *unimpaired* reference video followed by an *impaired* version of the same video. The expert then rates the *impaired* video using a scale ranging from "impairments are imperceptible" to "impairments are very annoying".

Video Compression Method (Digital Only)

A wide variety of methods are used to compress video streams. Video data contains spatial and temporal redundancy, making uncompressed video streams extremely inefficient. Broadly speaking, spatial redundancy is reduced by registering differences between parts of a single frame; this task is known as *intraframe compression* and is closely related to image compression. Likewise, temporal redundancy can be reduced by registering differences between frames; this task is known as *interframe compression*, including motion compensation and other techniques. The most common modern standards are MPEG-2, used for DVD and satellite television, and MPEG-4, used for home video.

Bit Rate (Digital Only)

Bit rate is a measure of the rate of information content in a video stream. It is quantified using the bit per second (*bit/s* or *bps*) unit or *Megabits per second* (*Mbit/s*). A higher bit rate allows better video quality. For example VideoCD, with a bit rate of about 1 Mbit/s, is lower quality than DVD, with a bit rate of about 5 Mbit/s. HDTV has a still higher quality, with a bit rate of about 20 Mbit/s.

Variable bit rate (VBR) is a strategy to maximize the visual video quality and minimize the bit rate. On fast motion scenes, a variable bit rate uses more bits than it does on slow motion scenes of similar duration yet achieves a consistent visual quality. For real-time and non-buffered video streaming when the available bandwidth is fixed, *e.g.* in videoconferencing delivered on channels of fixed bandwidth, a constant bit rate (CBR) must be used.

Stereoscopic

Stereoscopic video can be created using several different methods:

- *Two channels*—A right channel for the right eye and a left channel for the left eye. Both channels may be viewed simultaneously by using light-polarizing filters 90 degrees off-axis from each other on two video projectors. These separately polarized channels are viewed wearing eyeglasses with matching polarization filters.

- One channel with two overlayed colour coded layers. This left and right layer technique is occasionally used for network broadcast, or recent "anaglyph" releases of 3D movies on DVD. Simple Red/Cyan plastic glasses provide the means to view the images discretely to form a stereoscopic view of the content.
- One channel with alternating left/right frames for each eye, using LCD shutter glasses which read the frame sync from the VGA Display Data Channel to alternately cover each eye, so the appropriate eye sees the correct frame. This method is most common in computer virtual reality applications such as in a a Cave Automatic Virtual Environment, but reduces the effective video framerate to one-half of normal (for example, from 120 Hz to 60 Hz).

New HD DVD and Blu-ray Discs will greatly improve the sharpness and detail of the two-colour 3D effect in colour coded stereo programmes. The first commercially available HD players were expected to debut at the 2006 NAB Show in Las Vegas in April.

Video Formats

There are different layers of video transmission and storage, each with its own set of formats to choose from.

For transmission, there is a physical connector and signal protocol ("video connection standard" below). A given physical link can carry certain "display standards" which specify a particular refresh rate, display resolution, and colour space. There are a number of analog and digital tape formats, though digital video files can also be stored on a computer file system which have their own formats. In addition to the physical format used by the storage or transmission medium, the stream of ones and zeros that is sent must be in a particular digital video "encoding", of which a number are available.

Video Connectors, Cables, and Signal Standards

Digital Television

New formats for digital television broadcasts use the MPEG-2 video codec and include:

- ATSC—USA, Canada, etc.; a DVB video standard
- Digital Video Broadcasting (DVB)—European
- Integrated Services Digital Broadcasting (ISDB)—Japanese; also a DVB video standard.

Analog Television

Analog television broadcast standards include:

- Field-sequential colour system—USA, Russia; obsolete
- Multiplexed Analogue Components (MAC)—Europe, obsolete
- Multiple sub-nyquist sampling Encoding (MUSE)—Japan, analog HDTV
- NTSC—USA, Canada, Japan, etc.
- PAL—Europe, Asia, Australia, etc.

   - PAL-M—PAL variation. Brazil
   - PALplus—PAL extension, Europe only

- RS-343 (military)
- SECAM—France, ex-USSR, Central Africa

An analog video format consists of more information than the visible content of the frame. Preceding and following the image are lines and pixels containing synchronization information or a time delay. This surrounding margin is known as a blanking interval or blanking region; the horizontal and vertical front porch and back porch are the building blocks of the blanking interval.

Many countries are planning a digital switchover to cease using these analog formats via terrestrial television broadcast. However, analog television sets expecting these older standards as input will be able to display standard definition digital signals if coupled with a converter box.

Computer Displays

See Computer display standard for a list of standards used for computer monitors and comparison with those used for television.

Recording Formats before Video Tape

- Kinescope

Analog Tape Formats

- 1" Type B video tape (Bosch)
- 1" Type C videotape (Ampex and Sony)
- 2" Quadruplex videotape (Ampex)
- Ampex
- Betacam
- Betacam SP
- Betamax (Sony)
- Philips videotape recorder EL3400 1" helical scan ca. 1963
- S-VHS (JVC)
- U-matic (Sony)
- VCR, VCR-LP, SVR
- VERA (BBC experimental format ca. 1958)
- VHS (JVC)
- VHS-C (JVC)
- Video 2000 (Philips)
- Video8
- Video Hi8

Digital Tape Formats

- Betacam IMX (Sony)
- D-VHS (JVC)
- D-Theater
- D1 (Sony)
- D2 (Sony)
- D3
- D5 HD
- Digital Betacam (Sony)
- Digital8 (Sony)
- DV
- HDV
- ProHD (JVC)
- MiniDV
- MicroMV

Optical Disc Storage Formats

- Blu-Ray Disc (Sony)
- DVD (was Super Density Disc, DVD Forum)
- Enhanced Versatile Disc (EVD, Chinese government-sponsored)
- HD DVD (NEC and Toshiba)
- HD-VMD
- Laserdisc (old, MCA and Philips)
- UMD (Sony)
- CBHD (Chinese government-sponsored)

Digital Encoding Formats

- CCIR 601 (ITU-T)
- H.261 (ITU-T)
- H.263 (ITU-T)
- H.264/MPEG-4 AVC (ITU-T + ISO)
- M-JPEG (ISO)
- MPEG-1 (ISO)
- MPEG-2 (ITU-T + ISO)
- MPEG-4 (ISO)
- Ogg-Theora
- VC-1 (SMPTE)

BASIC VIDEO

Nothing could be simpler than picking up your camcorder and shooting a little videotape out in the back yard. At least on the surface. It's useful to remember that television itself was only a laboratory curiosity in 1940. In the 1950's you could make black and white television images in a studio, but you couldn't record them on videotape until 1956 when Ampex introduced the first commercial videotape recorder at the modest cost of $ 75,000 per machine. In the 1960's colour television became common, and in the late 1970's videotape recorders found their way into businesses and schools. Cameras and recorders intended for individual use first hit the scene in the 1980's.

NTSC Video

Actually, there are three distinct analog television formats in use around the world today, with a number of variations. The American system (NTSC) was the first. The colour signal was designed to work with the pre-existing black and white standard. The same broadcast bandwidth that was designed for high-quality monochrome signals was made to accommodate the far more demanding colour signal. At the same time, colour transmissions had to be compatible with existing monochrome receivers. Compromise was the word for the day, and quality suffered as a result. The PAL system was designed for colour from the ground up, as was the SECAM system. PAL is used in England, Germany, and most countries having ties those two. The SECAM system is used in France, the Soviet Union, and countries associated with them.

There's no need to get into specific differences between standards. Since virtually all television in North America conforms to the NTSC standard, that's what we'll deal with. The television picture is generated by a complicated combination of signals. It's useful to look at these signals, collectively called composite video, from two different perspectives. First, we'll look at the mechanics of displaying, or writing, the television picture in terms of time. Then we'll see how the parts of the video waveform are combined to make a picture appear on the screen.

Writing on the Screen

In non-electronic visual media (photography and film), each complete picture is displayed or seen in its entirety instantly. The television image, like a wire photo, must be "written" onto the screen dot by dot and line by line. This done in the United States according to standards set by the NTSC (National Television Systems Committee). Like film, television consists of a series of pictures. While film pictures are presented at a rate of twenty-four frames per second, television pictures are displayed at a rate of thirty frames per second.

The Television Scan

The picture is actually created by a stream of electrons striking a phosphor screen on the face of a CRT (Cathode Ray Tube). When a phosphor dot is hit by this electron beam, it glows for a fraction of a second. To aim the electron beam, two control systems are used. The vertical circuits move the electron beam from the top of the screen to the bottom, while the horizontal circuits move the beam from left to right. This movement from top to bottom and left to right is called the trace. The return path (bottom to top and right to left) is called the retrace. The electron beam is turned off during the retrace. The NTSC picture consists of 525 horizontal lines displayed every thirtieth of a second. Instead of writing all 525 lines with each vertical trace, however, only every other line is written, odd numbered lines on one vertical trace and even numbered lines on the next. Each half of the picture is called a "field" and consists of 262 1/2 lines (half of 525). In order to write all 525 lines every thirtieth of a second, there must be two completed vertical traces for each picture. Thus, the field rate is sixty fields per second while the frame rate is half that, or thirty frames per second. A special series of signals, called equalizing pulses, is provided to make sure the two fields of video fit together, or interlace, properly.

Both PAL and SECAM signals have 625 horizontal lines, with a frame rate of 25 frames per second. Because of the slower frame rate both are able to display more picture detail than the NTSC system in the same bandwidth.

Composite Video

The portion of the waveform that causes the picture to be displayed on the screen in the right place at the correct rate is called "sync." The waveform that controls the brightness of the screen (by varying the strength of the electron beam) is called "video." Combined with the luminance signal is the signal that controls the hue and saturation of colour in the picture. The three signals combined are called "composite video."

Two Horizontal Fields

Composite video is distributed through television systems through cable at a level of one volt peak to peak with an impedance of 75 ohms. The scale used to measure the amplitude of the video signal is divided into IRE (Institute of Radio Engineers) units. The picture part of the signal (disregarding the chroma portion) should lie in the area above zero up to 100 IRE units. The sync portion of the signal should be a series of pulses going from zero IRE units down to – 40 IRE units.

The Vertical Interval, with Equalizing Pulses

Sync consists of horizontal pulses, vertical pulses, and equalizing pulses. The total amplitude of the signal, from the bottom tip of the sync pulses to the brightest part of the picture, is 140 IRE units. At a standard impedance of 75 ohms, the correct amplitude of the composite video signal is one volt, peak to peak, so one IRE unit is equal to 1/140 volt peak to peak. Picture sources are set up with "black" at about 7.5 to 10 IRE and maximum brightness for all but brief transient spikes just below 100 IRE units.

The Horizontal Interval, with Burst Flag

A third signal, neither sync nor video, is always present in colour pictures just after each horizontal sync pulse. This signal, called "burst," is a short sample of the colour subcarrier frequency and is used as a reference to control the colours displayed on the screen. The burst signal goes from + 20 to – 20 IRE units. Chroma is not considered in setting black level (pedestal) and level (gain). However, if the video signal including chroma goes below – 20 IRE, the picture will interfere with the sync signal, which controls how the picture is displayed.

Before the advent of colour television, the vertical and horizontal rates for NTSC television were actually 60 Hz and 15,750 Hz, respectively. In colour television the rates had to be altered slightly to 59.94 Hz and 15,734 Hz, respectively, to prevent interference with the colour sub-carrier, which has a frequency of 3.58 MHz.

Component Video

The colour NTSC signal is a clever interweaving of different elements. The colour portion in broadcast cameras is actually generated by three pickup tubes or chips. The colours are red, green, and blue. There are some pieces of equipment that actually use four independent signals; red, green, blue, and sync. Some combine sync with one of the colour signals. These systems are simply called "RGB systems."

It's also common to combine the three colour signals into two, called colour difference signals. If fact, the colour part of the broadcast television signal is a pair of colour difference sidebands. One of the most common "component" strategies comes from the way the signal is recorded on most VCR's. The colour and luminance parts of the signal are recorded separately in a scheme called "colour under." Every time the composite video signal is divided into luminance and chroma, and every time it's put back together into a composite signal, there is inevitable loss and distortion. Some systems can keep the luminance and chroma signals separate. The Sony Type V "RF Dub" edit mode is one example. "S Video" is another.

In the end, "component video" is not one standardized system, but rather any scheme that keeps parts of the total video signal separate in order to maintain higher quality. The problem is that these various formats are not directly compatible and the only universal NTSC standard for moving pictures from one machine to another is composite video.

Writing the Television Signal on Videotape

Almost all videotape recorders on the market today are "helical" recorders. All machines record from one to four audio signals on tape just as they would be on an audiotape recorder. Some are recorded by fixed heads in a linear fashion along the length of the tape, while others are recorded by the video heads.

The video signal contains enormous amounts of information. Just as the amount of detail in a photograph is dependant on the fineness of the grain structure of the film, the amount of information you can record on tape is dependant on the oxide structure on the tape. To record enough information for a full broadcast television signal using a fixed video head, the tape would have to be moving at over five hundred inches per second. Instead, two (or more) video heads are mounted on a drum rotating at 1800 rpm. Each head writes a diagonal stripe on the tape representing one field of video. A pair of heads, working together writes two stripes, representing one full frame of video. As the tape moves over the rotating video head drum, a series of diagonal stripes are written onto the tape.

Finding these stripes of video is the job of the last recorded signal, the control track. This signal is nothing more than a 60 Hz pulse recorded on the edge of the tape. Since the physical relationship between the diagonal video tracks and the individual control track pulses is fixed during recording, it's possible to use these pulses to find the video tracks on playback. The process of finding and reading the video tracks during playback is called "tracking." Failure to find the video tracks causes "snow" or noise in the video, or even complete picture loss.

Compromises

To record the full broadcast spectrum on tape, the original tape format was two inches wide and moved laterally at 15 inches per second. The Ampex videotape recorder had an effective head speed of 1500 inches of tape per second. Making the tape smaller and slowing it down required three key compromises.

The first was a reduction in signal-to-noise ratio. Even tapes recorded on one inch VTR's can be rerecorded up to five or six generations before there's noticeable noise in the picture. On the other hand, VHS tapes have noticeable noise in the first generation and objectionable noise by the third.

The second compromise was in resolution, or frequency response. The luminance bandwidth in broadcast television is 4.2 Megahertz, with a horizontal resolution of 336 lines. The luminance bandwidth of VHS tape is about 3 Megahertz, allowing a resolution of 230 to 240 horizontal lines.

The third compromise involves using the "colour under" technique to record a very low resolution version of the colour signal at a frequency below the luminance signal, on the assumption that a relatively sharper monochrome signal will mask the fuzzy colour signal. It works, to a point. In fact, first generation VHS or 8 mm tape looks reasonable. You can extend the resolution of a recorder if you're willing to accept more noise. Noise becomes objectionable at about three IRE units, or an overall signal to noise ratio of about 35 dB. You can fake resolution by using "image enhancement," which is a process that amplifies transitions between light and dark parts of the picture. Too much "enhancement" gives the overall picture a pasty look, especially in areas of fine detail.

While these tricks might make a first generation recording look somewhat better, as you copy a tape from one generation to the next the effects of all of your compromises and tricks are compounded. In the end, you can't beat the laws of physics. In the analog world, there are really only three ways to get better pictures on tape. The first is the traditional solution of moving the head over more tape by making the tape wider or by increasing the linear tape speed. The second is to improve the tape by reducing the size of the magnetic particles. This is the route taken by moving from metal oxide tapes to metal tapes. The third is to keep the luminance and chroma signals separate in some sort of "Y/C" scheme.

Digital Video

The first digital video format, D1, was introduced in 1986. Unfortunately there were no personal computers with enough storage, memory, or processor speed to use it.

Within four years Newtek had a viable add-on for the Amiga computer that could function as a video switcher, graphics generator, and 3D modeler. Still, there was no practical way to capture or store digital video. By the mid-1990's we were using video capture cards to convert the NTSC video signal to digital computer files and using nonlinear editing software. Digital video has no need for synchronizing signals, so only the picture content of the NTSC signal was digitized as a 640 × 480 pixel frame, the same as a VGA computer image, and maintaining the 1.33 aspect ratio.

By the year 2000 the DV (digital video) standard allowed direct digital recording on videotape. Unlike the NTSC standard, the digital video recording consists of 24 bit colour images, 720 pixels wide by 480 pixels high, that can be sent directly to disk as a computer file. DV is also referred to as SD, or Standard Definition, as opposed to HD, or High Definition. SD digital video does not have square pixels. To improve resolution over a standard 640 x 480 pixel VGA display, digital video pixels are nine tenths as wide as they are high, allowing for 720 horizontal pixels by 480 vertical pixels with the same 1.33 aspect ratio.

There is a second version of SD digital video which has pixels that are 1.2 times as wide as they are high. The same 720 × 480 picture in this format yields an aspect ratio of 1.78, or 16 × 9. It is not advisable to shoot in 16 × 9 SD unless you are sure that your software and hardware will recognize this format and play it back correctly at each stage of post production, including nonlinear editors, conversion programmes for MPEG2, Windows Media Files, Real Player, or Quicktime, DVD authoring software, and playback equipment. Compression schemes that look good with .9 to 1 pixels may not work as well with 1.2 to 1 pixels, especially where fast cameral movement is involved. Before shooting 16 × 9 SD, test every link in your production chain.

The 24 bit colour scheme allows for eight bits each to represent red, green, and blue. In effect, digital video is component video in digital form. Each eight bit colour can have 256 distinct steps from darkest to brightest. The total number of possible colours is 256 cubed, or 16,777,216. Any device or system that has "16 million colours" is 24 bit colour.

Unlike the original D1 digital standard, the DV standard is compressed to about one fifth the size of an uncompressed file. The data rate is about four megabytes per second. The way in which the data is compressed can vary from one manufacturer to the next. Even though audio/video files for Windows generally have the .avi extension (.mov for Apple), the ability to read (or decompress) these files resides in the hardware or software used for the original compression. The method of compression and subsequent decompression is called a codec. Literally dozens of codecs have been used by various capture card and video editing companies. Microsoft supplies most of the popular codecs, while others can be downloaded from sites on the internet. Still, always keep the original raw videotape if you can. As we move to digital broadcasting, we will be using a new collection of standards. While NTSC stands for the National Television Standards Committee, ATSC stands for Advanced Television Standards Committee. There are many different ATSC standards, all dealing with digital broadcasting. The three basic video formats are SD (1.33 aspect ratio with 720 × 480 non-square pixels and HD, either 720P or 1080i. 720P has 1280 × 720 pixels, while 1080i has 1080 × 1920 pixels. HD pixels are square. The aspect ratio is 1.78, or 16 × 9.

Video Sources

Although there are many sources of video, all fall into two categories: electronically generated sources and optical sources. Electronic sources include all of the standard test signals, character generators, computers, and background generators. Optically generated video is produced by television cameras, either directly or prerecorded on videotape.

The electronic test signals are used primarily to set up monitoring equipment and are rarely included in programme content. They include colour bars, gray scale, dots, crosshatch, and multiburst.

Colour Bars

While colour bars have several formats, all share a sequence of colours and gray scale values that are fixed and can be used as a standard reference in adjusting equipment. The colour sequence is always white, yellow, cyan, green, magenta, red, blue, and black, reading left to right. Each colour, going from left to right, has ten per cent less luminance than the preceding colour. Using this signal it's possible to set a monitor for the correct contrast and brightness, as well as for the correct colour saturation and hue, guaranteeing an optimum picture display. Colour bars are often used at the beginning of a programme to allow setup of tape processing equipment and playback receivers and monitors.

Gray Scale

Gray scale is either a five or a ten step scale plus black used to set up monitors for proper brightness and contrast range.

Dots and Crosshatch

Dots is a matrix of white dots on a black background. Crosshatch may be shown as a series of vertical or horizontal lines or as a combination of both. Dots and crosshatch are used to adjust the electron beams in colour monitors so that the red, green, and blue signals overlap properly. Neither signal has any burst or chroma content. Crosshatch can also be used to make sure graphics shown by cameras are straight.

Multiburst

Multiburst is a series of square waves with increasing frequency from left to right. It's used to check the overall frequency response of various pieces of video equipment and is used primarily as an engineering tool. The remaining electronically generated signals are used in the actual production of programmes.

Colour Black

The most basic is called "colour black." This signal has a luminance value of 7.5 IRE and no chroma in the picture. It does have sync and colour burst. It's the signal used every time the picture "fades to black."

Colour Background

The colour background generator provides a solid colour background in which the luminance, chroma, and hue can be adjusted. It's normally used as a background for text or graphics displayed on the screen. It's possible to adjust the background generator to create colour fields that exceed the technical specifications for video. This results in improper operation of home receivers and should be avoided if at all possible.

Character Generator

The character generator is used to write and display text on the screen. It's actually a microcomputer with the ability to store and display text in a video format compatible with NTSC colour signals. Some models provide for the ability to move text horizontally across the bottom of the screen or to roll text from bottom to top. Many character generators also may have the ability to store material on magnetic disks.

Computer

The computer is the tool of choice for artists working on television art and graphics. The ability to capture and digitize live or videotaped images, manipulate them, and store them for later use is essential to almost every television producer. Very few computers produce standard colour television signals out of the box. Most common desktop computers can be made to output NTSC-compatible graphics with the addition of a board here and a black box there. The quality of the output is generally proportional to the cost, but effective work can be done with equipment costing only a few thousand dollars. Artwork done for SD (Standard Definition) television should have an aspect ratio of 1.33. In graphics systems using square pixels the image should be 640 × 480 pixels. In systems using .9 × 1 pixels, the image should be 720 × 480 pixels.

Film Chain

The film chain, for broadcast purposes, is obsolete. A specialized camera is incorporated into the "film chain," a device used to show 35 mm slides and motion picture film. This camera is locked in a fixed location. Often it looks at a device called a "multiplexer," which sends one of three optical picture sources to the camera. A mirror is positioned by remote control to select the picture source. Slide projectors normally have two drums or carousels and can "dissolve" from one slide to the next. The film projectors have special shutter systems to adjust the normal film speed of 24 frames per second to the television frame rate of 30 frames per second.

Videotape

Video recorded on tape can be played back through a special computer called a "time base corrector." The signal from a videotape is not very stable compared to live sources, nor is it "locked" to the signal generator which drives all live sources. The time base corrector has the ability to take the picture from a videotape recorder, store it for a very short time, and send it on after adjusting the timing of the signal to conform to other video sources. Time base correctors usually have controls to adjust pedestal (black level), amplitude (gain), chroma amplitude, and chroma shift for colour correction, in addition to controls to shift horizontal and vertical timing and the width of the horizontal interval. Tapes played through a time base corrector do, however, have to conform to reasonable technical standards and must have proper sync signals. Many monochrome cameras are incompatible with time base correctors because they lack essential sync signals or process sync in a way that is incompatible with the NTSC colour system used in production studios for American television. The most common problems are lack of 2:1 interlace of video fields and lack of equalizing pulses.

Computer Disks

Both CD's and DVD's can be used as data disks with video content. Both can be used in live environments as video sources when connected to a computer with the proper video output. DVD players can be used to play back DVD's or (in some cases) CD's. It is hard to imagine a situation, however, in which it would not be better to introduce the content from a CD or DVD during editing, rather than during the recording of a live event.

Synchronization

Because of the complexity and the technical requirements of the video signal, pictures from different sources can't be combined without first making sure that all sources are synchronized. The biggest challenge in wiring a television control room or edit suite is to make sure that each signal reaching the special effects generator begins a new frame of video at the same time as every other incoming signal. To accomplish this, every colour television facility uses a signal generator which provides timing signals to all video equipment which must interact. In addition, all signals must arrive with the colour reference, or burst, at the same phase angle as all other signals.

Some cameras and recorders can't be locked to an external sync source. Those that can use either video or three discrete synchronizing signals. Those that use video have a "genloc" input which is used to lock an internal sync generator to the incoming signal. Those requiring discrete synchronizing signals use vertical drive, horizontal drive, subcarrier, and perhaps composite sync, produced by a special signal generator.

Timing and phase errors between sources are potential causes of bad pictures. If a picture problem is unique to a dissolve, wipe, or key situation, timing and colour phase are possible causes. There are a number of issues related to signal timing that keep television engineers busy. Just knowing that timing is important any time you connect or mix the outputs of two video devices should be enough to alert you to the cause of many otherwise mysterious problems.

Monitoring

Waveform Monitor

In judging pedestal and gain, and technical signal quality, a special oscilloscope called a waveform monitor is used. This monitor has a number of operating modes, but the most commonly used gives a display of two horizontal lines of picture, showing the combined effect of both the luminance and chroma portions of the picture. It's calibrated in IRE units, from – 40 IRE to 100, so precise measurement of the amplitude of both sync and picture is possible. It's also possible to isolate either the luminance portion or the chroma portion of the picture and to look at the horizontal sync portion alone, the vertical sync portion alone, or at two fields of video. Waveform monitors are valuable tools in evaluating the timing and technical quality of video sources and are therefore useful as trouble-shooting tools as well as production aids.

As you know, the amplitude of the video signal is set at one volt peak-to-peak into an impedance of 75 ohms. A glance at the waveform monitor can reveal one of the most common technical problems in television. Many devices allow you to "loop" an input through the device to another. Picture monitors generally allow you to do this. They also have a termination switch next to the looped input. Along the line from your picture source only one device should be terminated. A second termination will cut the signal amplitude in half. Lack of any termination will double the amplitude. If the sync portion of the composite signal on the waveform monitor is either much larger or much smaller than – 40 IRE, the problem is almost always improper termination.

Vectorscope

The vectorscope is used in analyzing the colour content of the video signal. It's set up like a polar graph, showing hue as a phase angle with reference to the "burst" signal, which should always be at zero degrees. Amplitude (distance from the center) of a colour indicates the saturation of the colour. One of the main functions of the vectorscope is the adjustment of colour phase of all colour video sources in the system. Using a standard reference signal, usually the colour subcarrier or colour black, each colour source is examined and the phase angle of its "burst" signal adjusted to zero degrees with reference to the standard signal. Only if all sources are "in phase" can they be used in special effects such as wipes and dissolves without objectionable colour shifts. The vectorscope is also useful in evaluating the accuracy of colour rendition of cameras and in setting up colour background fields.

Meters

Finally, videotape recorders and some other devices have video meters. These are not nearly as precise as the waveform monitor, but can be used to confirm the presence of a video signal and whether that signal is in a reasonable range. Although these meters may not have any calibration scale indicated, they do have a coloured section which conforms to a reasonable video level for most colour signals. The most obvious exception to this is colour black which gives a meter reading well below the "optimum" level. Video meters have only limited usefulness.

Switching

The heart of any video control room is the special effects generator, or video switcher. This is the device used to select pictures from the various video sources and to create the effects which are the "language" of television. While the average video switcher offers a bewildering number of possible effects, it's usually laid out in a logical and functional manner easily mastered if it's taken one step at a time.

The most common special effect is the "take." It's the instantaneous change from one picture source to another. The reason it's the most common is that it's almost always the most appropriate way to change picture content in the course of a programme. It may seem strange to use such an imposing piece of equipment as a video switcher for such a simple task, but it's crucial for any director to remember that all of the equipment around him serves only one central purpose: to transmit information to his audience cleanly and without confusion or distraction. The programme content must carry and maintain the interest of his audience. Any attempt to "dress up" a programme with unnecessary effects will simply distract or confuse the audience and will, therefore, be self-defeating. There is a video "language," just as there is a film language and just as there are spoken and written languages. In all of these it's the ability to communicate clearly that is the mark of the literate person.

The next commonly used effect is the dissolve. This is a gradual cross-fade from one picture to another during which one picture is superimposed on the other. The speed of the dissolve should be determined by the pace and mood of the programme material. The dissolve can be used to establish or enhance a lyrical mood. But it can also be used for major transitions in programme content that need to be softened; that is, where a take would be too jarring. Often a dissolve is used to indicate the passage of time or a change of location in dramatic programmes. In other contexts, it might be used in transition from a wide shot to a close-up to emphasize continuity.

The wipe has less ambiguous uses. When a complete wipe occurs, one picture is replaced by another as though it were pushing the other off of the screen. Most switchers offer a number of wipe patterns, including horizontal, vertical, various corners, circles, and perhaps some others of limited usefulness. The wipe is used in two ways. First, it's used to insert a portion of one picture into another, allowing the viewer to see two scenes at the same time. The wipe is sometimes used in the same way as the dissolve to indicate a change in time or location.

Keys and mattes are used to insert one picture into another. Luminance keys use the monochrome signal as a switching device. Any portion of the keyed signal reaching a specific video level replaces the video content of the background signal. The amount of luminance necessary to effect this replacement is adjusted to achieve the desired effect. A matte is similar to a key, except that a solid colour from the background generator is inserted into the background video in place of the video from the key source. Chroma keys work on the same principle, but use the colour saturation of a specific hue as the keying signal rather than the luminance level.

Luminance keys and mattes are used almost exclusively to superimpose text or graphics on the screen. A character generator, for example, uses a luminance key to put text over normal video. Chroma keys are used to insert more complicated video into the background. Because of the wide range of luminance values in video containing people or objects, a clean luminance key is often impossible. By carefully controlling the hues in a scene, though, it's often possible to generate a clean chroma key. The most common colour used in chroma keys is deep blue. The most common use of chroma keys is the insertion of video tape or computer graphics into newscasts.

VIDEO CLIP

Video clips are short clips of video, usually part of a longer piece. Video clips in digital format are often found on the internet where the massive influx of new video clips during 2006 was hailed as a new phenomenon having a profound impact on both the internet and other forms of media. Sources for video clips include news and sporting events, historical videos, music videos, television programmes, film trailers and vlogs. Webvideo in its current form distinguishes itself from what is mostly known as video on demand mainly in terms of technology, interface and cost for the user. The current hype in online video viewing only arose when sites were introduced that offered free hosting for the high-bandwidth content and the possibility to easily integrate these into personal Blogs or websites. This enabled online videos to crossover into the mainstream. The arrival of these sites also gave rise to more widespread use of the name webvideo. *Video on demand* however, is more closely associated with paid content of film studios, online video stores and cable providers. Video on demand also specifically references videos that start at a moment of the user's choice, as opposed to streaming, multicast and webcams in which the data is sent to the user live by a server.

The term is also more loosely used to mean any short video less than the length of a traditional television programme. With the proliferation of online news sites, whose appetite for content is becoming increasingly voracious, PR agencies are now making use of video clips as a new opportunity for clients to get their messages across.

On the Internet

With the spread of broadband Internet access, video clips have become very popular online. By mid 2006 there were tens of millions of video clips available online, with new websites springing up focusing entirely on offering free video clip to users and many established and corporate sites adding video clip content to their websites. With the spread of broadband Internet access, video clips have become very popular online. Whereas most of this content is non-exclusive and available on competing sites, some companies produce all their own videos and do not rely on the work of outside companies or amateurs.

While some video clips are taken from established media sources, community or individual-produced clips are becoming more common. Some individuals host their created works on vlogs, which are video blogs. The use of internet video is growing very fast. Between March and July of the year 2006 YouTube alone grew from 30 to 100 million views of videos per day. More recent developments includes the BBC's iPlayer, which was released for open beta testing in July 2007.

Distinctive Properties

As the developments in the area of internet video move very swiftly, it is difficult to define distinctive properties. There are however certain criteria, which seem to fit most web videos:

- Most commonly use FLV format (Flash Video), but also Windows Media Video, RealMedia, Quicktime or DivX;
- Usually freely available, which might help explain the current popularity;
- Most commonly uploaded by private persons, which explains the inferior technical quality when compared to paid content;
- Due to the lack of censorship there seems to be an abundance of free expressions, especially by youth;
- Commonly used on weblogs and other web 2.0 sites; and
- Commonly financed by advertising revenue at the hosting site. Although YouTube has announced plans to let creative users share in the advertising income, for now the only benefiting parties are the site owners.

Clip Culture

The widespread popularity of video clips, with the aid of new distribution channels, has evolved into clip culture. It is compared to "lean-back" experience of seeing traditional movies, refers to an internet activity of sharing and viewing a short video, mostly less than 15 minutes. The culture began as early as the development of broadband network, but it sees the boom since 2005 when websites for uploading clips are emerging on the market, including Shockinghumor, YouTube, Google Video, MSN Video and Yahoo! Video.

These video clips often show moments of significance, humour, oddity, or prodigy performance. Sources for video clips include news, movies, music video and amateur video shot. In addition to the clip recorded by high-quality camcorders, it is becoming common to produce clips with digital camera, webcam, and mobile phone.

Rise of Amateurs

Unlike traditional movies largely dominated by studios, clip movies were overwhelmingly supplied by amateurs. In May 2006, The Economist reported that 90 per cent of clips on YouTube came from amateurs, a few of whom are young comedians. It, in effect, also brought amateur talents.

In 2005, two Chinese students Huang Yixin and Wei Wei, now dubbed as "Back Dorm Boys" showed their talent in lip-synching in a song of the Backstreet Boys, with their self-conscious grimaces in a video uploaded to some clip websites, has instantly become renown. Not only did they appear on television shows, concerts, but were also granted a contract by a media company in Beijing for lip-syncing for cash.

An earlier celebrity was David Elsewhere, a talent at popping and liquiding. His performance to Kraftwerk's song Expo 2000 at the talent show Kollaboration in 2001 was widely spread on the internet leading later to his being hired to participate as a dancer in advertisements for Heineken, iPod and Pepsi.

Citizen Journalism

Citizen video reporting dates back as early as the development of camcorders, but all videos were screened by the local media outlets of the time, until its spread has been aided by free upload websites in which censorship is limited to make a vast amount of videos available to anyone who wants it. Scenes rarely broadcast on television, and many first-witnessed scenes have since become publicly available.

Fig. 4.1: The tsunami caused by the December 26, 2004 earthquake strikes Ao Nang, Thailand.

Notably, in December 2004, tourist videos on the Indian Ocean earthquake and tsunami offered worldwide audiences the first scenes of the disaster. In December 2003, videos in Hong Kong showing the bully in *De La Salle School* has outraged the public, raised a wide concern on school violence and led to the arrest of 11 students.

Vlog

In late 2005 to early 2006, a new form of blogging emerged called a vlog. It is a blog that takes video as the primary content, often accompanied by supporting text, image, and additional metadata to provide context. Su Li Walker, an analyst with the Yankee Group, said that like blogs, which have become an extension of traditional media, video blogs will be a supplement to traditional broadcasting.

Convergence with Traditional Media

The potential markets of video clips has caught the attention of traditional studios. In 2006, the producers of *Lucky Number Slevin,* a film with Morgan Freeman, Lucy Liu and Bruce Willis, made an 8-minute clip for YouTube. Celebrity in traditional media has proven to confer bigger popularity in clip culture.

Cyril Takayama, a Japanese-European magician, became famous by showing his theandric skills in Japanese TV magic show in 2004. His fame was achieved only in Japan and the international magicians' culture, until his video clips were later spread across the Internet.

HungryMan TV debuted in June of 2007 as a short-form web video channel developed by the advertising production studio, HungryMan. The website currently hosts seven web series and distributes videos on YouTube, Revver, MetaCafe, Veoh, and MySpaceTV.

Video Blog

A video blog, sometimes shortened to vlog is a blog that comprises video. Regular entries are typically presented in reverse chronological order and often combine embedded video or a video link with supporting text, images, and other metadata.

GETTING THE WORD OUT

Videotape

VHS videotape is still a viable distribution option preferred for audiences that are resistant to change.

CD

There are several ways to distribute video on CD's. They have been especially popular as a medium for motion pictures using the MPEG 1 standard. The quality of these "video CD's" is about the same as VHS. Some DVD authoring software can be used to make CD's that behave like DVD's. The total run time for these disks is about fifteen minutes. The special software needed to play back the CD content is included on the disk. These CD's are for computer CD/DVD drives only and are generally programmed to run the software automatically when the disk is inserted. While this is a viable way of distributing DVD-quality video to computer users, its usefulness diminishes as new computers are delivered with DVD drives as standard equipment.

It is also possible to make CD data disks that contain MPEG 2 or Windows Media Format files. Most computers now have the codecs needed to play MPEG 2 or WMF files. Again, at about four Mb/Sec a CD can hold about fifteen minutes of video. The increased compression of the WMF format allows more than sixty minutes on one CD. The WMF format fits the specifications for MPEG 4, the compression regimen designed to accommodate high definition television. Both Quicktime and Real Player also offer compressed video formats that can be included on data CD's. The appropriate players will have to be downloaded by your viewers.

Finally, there is software available for authoring data CD's, or CD-ROM's. These software packages allow the integration of files on the disk with files on the internet in addition to many of the navigation features common to DVD's.

DVD

One popular way to distribute video is the DVD. A DVD is an optical disk, actually a reflective film sandwiched between two protective acrylic layers, like a CD, but with some differences. The most important difference is that a typical DVD can hold up to

4.7 GB of data, including formatting information on a single layer disk and twice that on a dual layer disk. You have roughly four gigabytes of space available for project on a single layer disk.

There are two ways of using DVD technology to distribute video. The traditional method is to use DVD authoring software to create a DVD that can be played on a stand-alone DVD player, typically called a "set top" player. Set top players require a specific MPEG 2 format which makes it nearly impossible to reverse-engineer the video for editing. This DVD format is ideal for distribution. In small quantities you can make your own DVD's with relatively inexpensive software and hardware. Colour printers capable of printing directly on the DVD face are very affordable as well. It should be noted that from the beginning there have been problems with compatibility between DVD-R and DVD+R disks and some set top DVD players, especially models made before 2001.

For large quantities you'll want to use a commercial disk replicator. Replication is a two step process. First a glass master disk is made. Then the master disk is used to press or stamp a reflective disk, which is then sandwiched between two acrylic layers for protection. The minimum cost for replication is usually the same as the cost of making 800 to 1000 copies. In other words, whether you ask for one hundred, two hundred, or a thousand copies of your masterpiece, the total cost of replication (not including album cases or other packaging) will be about the same.

Most commercial disk replicators will now accept a DVD-R as a master, although the preferred medium for mastering DVD's is DLT, or digital linear tape. DLT was developed to backup or archive computer networks and servers. If you want digital copy protection for your DVD's you will have to submit your masters on DLT.

When dealing with a commercial replicator, be prepared to be able to prove you have the right to use all of the audio and video on your disk. Replicators do not like to be sued.

Making a DVD

A DVD can be as straightforward as a videotape. Pop it in the player and the programme runs from start to finish with no embellishments. Or it can have a complex system of menus allowing the viewer to select various programmes or go to specific points within programmes. Menus can allow viewers to select different audio channels or call up subtitles.

The first step in making a DVD is to assemble all of your finished media as digital files. There are only limited opportunities to edit materials in DVD authoring software. It is best if all of your materials are in final form before you go any further. Audio files should be in the .wav format. Your video files are probably either Quicktime or .avi files. They must be converted to MPEG 2. This option should be available in your video editing software. If you have optional audio tracks you can convert your video using your primary mix of audio tracks, then save your secondary mix of audio tracks separately as a .wav file. You can do this by turning the appropriate tracks on or off before exporting the file. In addition, you may have still images you want to use in your DVD, perhaps as menu backgrounds or buttons. Full frame stills should be 640 × 480 pixels for NTSC or 640 × 576 for PAL. Your DVD authoring programme will change these stills, which have square pixels, to 720 × 480 or 720 × 576 pixels where the width of each pixel is nine-tenths of the height. The difference is pixel aspect between digital stills and digital video affects all of your still images, whether full frame or smaller.

Your authoring software will allow you to import video, audio, and still image files. The categories may be straightforward or have more imaginative names, such as "Media," "Backgrounds," and "Buttons."

At this point it may or may not tell you if your project will fit on a DVD. You have about four gigabytes available. If your project is too large you can go back to your video editing software and change the MPEG 2 conversion settings to increase the compression and decrease the file size of each MPEG 2 file. While the DV files you generally work with in your editing software are compressed to about four Megabytes per second, MPEG 2 files are generally compressed to from 3.5 to 8 Megabits per second. At the lowest compression you have a little over an hour of video on a DVD. At the highest compression you can get about two hours on a disk. As you increase the compression of your video files you also increase the chance that you will lose detail in your video during quick movements. The loss of detail will take the form of pixilation. Your video will be reduced to a jumble of blocks until the rate of video change returns to a more normal rate. You should probably keep your data rate at four megabits per second or higher.

There is actually more to the MPEG 2 format than the data rate. While in the DV format compression is achieved frame by frame, MPEG 2 is divided into groups of pictures (GOP's) usually twelve to fifteen frames long. The first frame (*I*) of each GOP has all of the information necessary to reconstruct the frame. The remaining eleven to fourteen frames (P and B frames) contain only enough information to reconstruct the video by combining information from previous frames (P frames) or by combining information from both previous and following frames (B frames).

The best consumer authoring programmes will allow you to import your video and use it to create all of your menus and buttons in a very straightforward and intuitive way. Typically, once you've imported your video clips you can select one of several menu styles. If you have more than one video clip, you can assign each clip to a button on the menu. You may even be able to create intermediate menus and use the time line of your video you can select chapter points and drag those points to menu buttons. In some cases the video from the clip will form a still image in the button automatically. When you're done you usually have at least two options: burn one or more DVD's using the current project settings, or create a file that is an exact image of the contents of the DVD. When you burn your DVD's from the current project your programme will create a temporary file on your hard drive in which all of your materials are converted into the required DVD format. Your disks are burned from the temporary file, which is deleted as soon as the disks are done. When you elect to create an image file, the file is created on your hard drive but no disks are burned. You can use the image file to burn your disks later as you need them.

Professional software will allow you to do anything you'll see on a commercial DVD. Professional software is not, as a rule, either user-friendly or intuitive. It is more powerful and flexible.

The Internet

Using video on the internet creates a set of considerations and problems that should be part of the video planning process before any video is shot. The basic fact about the internet is that it was never designed to transmit video and audio at four megabytes per second or even four megabits per second. To send video over the internet more compression is necessary.

There are several compression schemes for internet video that rely on four ways of reducing picture information.

1. They generally reduce the frame size.
2. They reduce the frame rate.
3. They reduce the amount of information in each frame beyond the compression available in MPEG 2 by sacrificing picture quality when content in moving and maintaining higher resolution when images are relatively still.
4. They "buffer" the bit stream.

Reducing the frame size reduces the amount of picture detail available and should be an important consideration in shooting for the internet. Loss of detail can turn excellent images into mud. Just as commercial motion pictures are often shot not for the resolution available with 35 mm film, but with the more limited resolution of NTSC video in mind, you should shoot for resolutions much lower than standard video.

After decades of experimentation the film industry settled on a few frame rates. For silent consumer film either sixteen or eighteen frames per second was used. There was a noticeable flicker when films were projected at these rates. Commercial sound motion pictures are projected at twenty-four frames per second. The frame rate for NTSC television is thirty frames per second. Frame rates for streaming video are often below fifteen frames per second. The impact on motion is obvious. At fifteen frames per second, how many frames does it take to swing a baseball bat?

The third method of reducing the data rate, sacrificing detail during motion sequences, further "muddies" the picture. Motion and fine detail are mutually exclusive in the world of streaming video.

Buffering can be as simple as actually downloading the entire video at one rate in order to play it back on a computer at the designed normal rate. More commonly, playback is delayed until enough data has been downloaded to allow playback of a significant part of the video. When the playback catches up with the download (and runs out of data to play) the playback is paused until more data is downloaded. This process often causes awkward pauses during playback, but that's progress.

Streaming video should accommodate a range of users, from those with 56 Kbps dial-up modems to those with DSL and cable modems receiving in excess of one gigabit per second at the modem (but less than 54 Mbps over their wireless network). When you export video from your editing software you will have the option of two or three streaming formats. Pick the one you believe will offer your viewer the best picture quality, given the content of your video) with the least inconvenience and delay. Each of these will in turn allow you to choose either a single streaming rate or multiple rates dependent on the viewer's reception rate.

All that's left to be done is to move the finished streaming video file onto a web site for downloading.

Archiving Your Work

Most of the time most artists want their work to last at least as long as they live. Throughout recorded history we have been able to save some pieces of art or literature on cloth, paper, stone, or metal. Each of these has properties that cause the information to degrade, but all have one thing in common. It does not take any equipment beyond the human eye to recognize and read the information, although the eye may need a brain behind it trained in hieroglyphics or ancient Greek.

Times have changed. Your hardware may become obsolete or even incompatible with newer operating systems. Changes in the computer world have given an entirely new meaning to the word "legacy." Until recently the word referred to property inherited or traditions passed down from one generation to the next. In the computer world "legacy" has become an adjective referring to the data in any application that can no longer be used by readily available software or hardware. The 5¼ inch floppy disk is a legacy system in that no computers sold today can read those disks. The 3½ inch floppy disk is pretty close to legacy status itself. As you move from one operating system to the next or from one capture card to a different brand you risk rendering all of your .avi files unreadable. Keep the tape. And while you are at it, take very good care of your playback equipment, too.

So far we've gone through the following videotape formats: Two-inch quad, one inch helical of various formats up through type C, half-inch EIAJ reel to reel, U-Matic and U-Matic SP, Betamax, VHS, Betacam and Betacam SP, M2, S-VHS, 8 Millimeter, and Hi-8 analog formats; DV, Digital 8, DV Cam, DV Pro, Digital Betacam, a more. If your tape is stored properly at moderate temperature and humidity you are more likely to have trouble finding playback equipment than you are to have trouble with the videotape itself.

The best you can do is to make copies of your work in the highest quality digital format you believe has a user base large enough to keep it in use for a long period of time and that you can afford. While many are choosing to "archive" their work on DVD in MPEG 2, that medium is much more highly compressed than the DV format, which is in general use and slowing replacing both VHS and 8 mm as the recording format of choice, both by amateurs and many professionals. For works under fifteen minutes DV files can be stored as .avi or .mov files on DVD-R disks without further compression. A dual layer writable disk could hold up to thirty minutes. With the advent of high definition video there is no way to know how long the equipment to play back standard definition tapes will be generally available, while current DVD drives and both blue laser disk formats can play material on existing DVD-R disks. Properly stored DVD-R disks should last at least one hundred years, while rewritable disks can be expected to last at least twenty-five years. Considering the formats and equipment in common use twenty-five years ago, you should be prepared to re-record your work to new formats as it becomes advisable or necessary.

ADDITIONAL VIDEO

Titles and Artwork

Graphic material is very important in many types of programmes. Certainly almost any sort of show looks more polished and professional if it has, at least, opening titles, and credits for the major members of the production crew at the end. Other types of written and graphic material may also be needed.

There are four main ways to incorporate graphic information into a television programme:

1. The *Character Generator* is a computer that produces printed material digitally and converts it into a form which is directly usable as a video source.
2. Graphics can also be produced on *Live Cards,* usually cardboard sheets about 11 × 14 inches, which are shot by a camera.
3. *Slides* can be produced photographically in a variety of ways from the same sort of originals used for live cards and can then be projected into a special camera using a device called a film chain or projected onto a white surface and shot by a camera.
4. *Computers* are used to generate most of the graphics now used in television at all levels.

Character Generator

Character generators differ significantly in their versatility and ease of use, but mostly tend to look the same, consisting of a console with a typewriter-style keyboard and, usually, a dedicated video monitor. There are a number of special keys on the keyboard which control specific functions of the character generator, such as page advance, character size and type style, automatic centering, and perhaps other options. There is always a set of keys to position (up, down, left, right) a cursor which appears on the character generator's own monitor (but not in the signal sent to the switcher) and indicates exactly where on the screen the next letter will appear.

Most character generators allow for only a small number of characters on the screen at once; ten lines of thirty figures each is typical. Actually, this isn't a disadvantage. Small characters are difficult to see given the limited resolution and large viewing distances of TV sets in the home. This general principle applies to all graphics work for television: keep it simple, make all important elements large, and try to present complicated graphics in several pages, if needed, instead of all at once. The output of a character generator is usually inserted over other video by means of a key or matte.

As character generators become more sophisticated (and expensive), they may offer some of these additional features: Most units can store more than one "page" of graphics and allow you to recall them in order, or randomly, by pressing keys. The ability to roll (vertically) or crawl (horizontally) lettering across the screen is useful; rolling credits are common at the ends of programmes, and crawls are often used to make announcements during a programme at the bottom of the screen. Some machines offer a disk or tape cassette storage system which allows pages of characters to be stored for recall at any time, also extending the page-storage capability of the character generator enormously. Finally, more sophisticated character generators offer a wide variety of sizes and styles (and sometimes colours) of characters, variable italicization, outlines, shadows, and even the ability to create custom characters or logos for regeneration later. Less expensive machines may offer only one or two sizes of a single type font; the very cheapest don't even have lower-case letters.

The major disadvantage in the use of character generators for television graphics is that they are at their best only when presenting rather simple textual information. If you have in mind any kind of charts or graphs, or the use of some special type style, you'll have to use something else.

Live Cards

Before computer graphics we used live artwork cards in front of a camera to present graphics and photographs. Modestly stiff multiply cardboard in cards about 11 by 14 inches were the most common background material for live cards. This material is available at art supply houses in a variety of colours and textures.

Lettering on live cards can be done with dry transfer letters, again available at art and school supply stores. This material is provided in large sheets containing several complete alphabets of a particular type font. There are other lettering systems too, sometimes faster or cheaper but seldom as good-looking as well done dry transfer work.

In making up live cards, it's important to assure that everything you need will be seen on the television screen and that no extraneous material gets in. Always allow a 1-1/2 to 2 inch border on all sides of a live card to give some leeway in camera positioning and framing. This area should be completely clear of dirt, pencil marks and other distractions, as should, of course, the main picture area itself. Also, remember that the dimensions of the television screen are four units wide by three units high. A six by eight inch area in the center of an 11 by 14 card would be a very safe one in which to compose your graphics. Usually type no smaller than 24 point (1/3 inch high) would be used in a space of that size.

Slides

Any 35 mm still camera can be used to generate slides for use in television. In any photographic work for television, remember that the television system always crops the image slightly, so you'll see less on the TV screen than appears in the original slide or film. The 35 mm slide format also has a slightly different aspect ratio than the TV screen; the pictures are wider. Thus, anything at the extreme edges of the picture will not be reproduced.

Digital still cameras normally have a 1.33 aspect ratio and almost all have more than the 640 × 480 pixels used in SD television graphics.

It's wise to allow a border of about 20 per cent of the picture area on each side when framing in the still camera's viewfinder to allow for this image cutoff. This same precaution applies when shooting live-action photographs for use in television.

Some very expensive 35 mm cameras have interchangeable focusing screens and make available a screen marked with the appropriate television "safety" areas.

Here are the most important restrictions on the use of still photographs in television:

1. *Observe the safe action area.* As mentioned above, a border of about 20 per cent is needed. For a quick and conservative approach, turn a 35 mm camera on its side, as if shooting a vertical-format picture. The area seen from right to left in the viewfinder can be reasonably expected to be seen in the video image after you turn the camera back for the horizontally-framed shot.
2. *Shoot only in horizontal format.* Vertical slides appear on TV with severe cutoff at top and bottom and with a black border on each edge.
3. *Keep contrast low.* Pictures taken in bright sunlight without additional fill light, or indoors with a single flash unit, are often too high in contrast to reproduce properly on television (although they may look fine when projected on a screen). You should try to follow the same rules for lighting still photographs taken for television that you would in lighting for a video camera itself.

Film

It's not as easy to use film in television as it seems it ought to be. Two problems arise. First, film is usually shot without any regard for the television safe action and title areas. The outside 20 per cent or so of the film image is lost in the transfer process. Second, film is shot at 16, 18 or 24 frames per second. Broadcast film chains use special shutters in their projectors to repeat every fourth frame, bringing the frame rate up from twenty-four to the thirty frames per second required for television. Film shot at sixteen or eighteen frames per second can't be synchronized to television without special projection equipment.

Not so long ago virtually every television station had a film chain, both for news film and for theatrical films. Now they are rare indeed. To use film in a video production you will almost certainly have to convert it to video at a photo store of duplicator that has the necessary equipment. The transfer should be made to digital video, such as miniDV or DVCAM if possible.

Computers

Computers can be used to generate television graphics in live productions if their output signals are adapted to the NTSC standard. Most often computer graphics are integrated into programmes during editing using nonlinear editing programmes.

Computer screen outputs differ from standard NTSC video in several ways. First, most are "non-interlace." That is, there is no division of the picture into alternating odd-line and even-line fields. Second, the rate at which frames are displayed is usually much faster than the nominal thirty frames per second used in television. And third, many computer graphics displays leave a fairly large border, or "safe area," around the active graphics area. The television video area fills the entire screen. Although a variety of add-on products might allow recording of computer images on videotape, conversion to actual broadcast television standards requires a special video card. Even still images on computer take up a lot of space. Each true broadcast-quality image requires about one million bytes to display. To make transfer and storage of video images more practical, two basic compression techniques have been developed, with more on the way.

JPEG compression deals with discrete images, one at a time. Typical video frames can be compressed to one seventh of their original size with no discernable reduction in quality. It is usually possible in using JPEG compression to specify the degree of compression desired, so noticeable image degradation can be avoided.

MPEG compression works on the assumption that much of the image from one frame to the next in film or video remains the same. Except for key frames, no single MPEG frame is complete and each has meaning only with reference to the frame that preceded it.

5

Understanding Various Audiovisual Equipments: An Overview

AUDIOVISUAL

The term audio-visual (AV) may refer to works with both a sound and a visual component, the production or use of such works, or the equipment involved in presenting such works. Movies and television shows are examples of audiovisual presentations.

Business presentations are also usually audiovisual. In a typical presentation, the presenter provides the audio by speaking, and supplements it with a series of images projected onto a screen, either from a slide projector, or from a computer connected to a digital projector using software such as PowerPoint.

PROFESSIONAL AUDIOVISUAL INDUSTRY

The professional audiovisual industry is a multibillion-dollar industry, comprised of the manufacturers, dealers, systems integrators, consultants, programmers, presentation professionals and technology managers of audiovisual products and services.

Overview

The proliferation of audiovisual communications technologies, including sound, video, lighting, display and projection systems, is evident in every sector of society such as these:

- Business,
- Education,
- Government,
- The military,
- Healthcare,
- Retail environments, and
- Worship.

The application of audiovisual systems is found in:

- Collaborative conferencing presentation rooms,

- Auditoriums and lecture halls,
- Command and control centers, and
- Digital signage and more.

Concerts and corporate events are among the most obvious venues where audio-visual equipment is used in a staged environment. Providers of this type of service are known as rental and staging companies, although they may also be served by an in-house technology team (*e.g.*, in a hotel or conference center).

2006 is the fourth consecutive year that significant growth is projected for the industry. Revenue for surveyed North American companies is expected to grow by 40 per cent in 2006, and by 10.7 per cent for European audiovisual companies. The single biggest factor for this increase is the increased demand for networked audiovisual products due to the integration of audiovisual and IT technology. The two leading markets for AV equipment in North America and Europe continue to be business/IT and education.

AUDIOVISUAL EDUCATION

Audiovisual education or multimedia-based education (MBE) is instruction where particular attention is paid to the audio and visual presentation of the material with the goal of improving comprehension and retention.

After the use of training films and other visual aids during World War II, audiovisual technology gradually developed in sophistication and its use became more widespread in educational establishments such as schools, colleges, universities, museums and galleries, as well as at tourist destinations, such as the purpose-built circular cinema, Arromanches 360, at Arromanches-les-Bains, which shows a 360° film presentation of the Normandy landings.

Equipment Used for Audiovisual Presentations

- Dioramas,
- Magic lanterns,
- Planetarium,
- Film projectors,
- Slide projectors,
- Opaque projectors (episcopes and epidiascopes),
- Overhead projectors,
- Tape recorders,
- Television,
- Video,
- Camcorders,
- Video projectors,
- Interactive whiteboards, and
- Digital video clips.

DIORAMA

The word diorama can refer either to a nineteenth century mobile theatre device, or, in modern usage, a three-dimensional model, usually enclosed in a glass showcase for a museum.

Daguerre's Dirama

The Diorama was a popular entertainment in Paris, England, Scotland, and Ireland from 1822 to 1880. An alternative to the also popular "Panorama" (panoramic painting), the Diorama was a theatrical experience viewed by an audience in a highly specialized theatre. As many as 350 patrons would file in to view a landscape painting that would change its appearance both subtly and dramatically. Most would stand, though limited seating was provided. The show lasted 10 to 15 minutes, after which time the entire audience (on a massive turntable) would rotate to view a second painting. Later models of the Diorama theater even held a third painting.

The size of the proscenium was 24 feet (7.3 m) wide by 21 feet (6.4 m) high (7.3 m × 6.4 m). Each scene was hand-painted on linen, which was made transparent in selected areas. A series of these multi-layered, linen panels were arranged in a deep, truncated tunnel, then illuminated by redirected sunlight. Depending on the direction and intensity of the skillfully manipulated light, the scene would appear to change. The effect was so subtle and finely rendered that both critics and the public were astounded, believing they were looking at a natural scene.

The inventor and proprietor of the Diorama was Louis Jacques Mandé Daguerre (1787–1851), formerly a decorator, manufacturer of mirrors, painter of Panoramas, and masterly designer anc. painter of theatrical stage illusions. Daguerre would later co-invent the daguerreotype, the first widely used method of photography.

Daguerre opened a second Diorama in Regent's Park in London in 1823, a year after the debut of his Paris original. The show was a popular sensation, and spawned immediate imitations. English artists like Clarkson Stanfield and David Roberts produced ever-more elaborate dioramas through the 1830s; sound effects and even living performers were added. Some "typical diorama effects included moonlit nights, winter snow turning into a summer meadow, rainbows after a storm, illuminated fountains," waterfalls, thunder and lightning, and ringing bells.

Painters of the Romantic era like John Martin and Francis Danby were influenced to create large and highly dramatic pictures by the sensational dioramas and panoramas of their day. In one case, the connection between life and diorama art became intensely circular. On 1 February 1829, John Martin's brother Jonathan, known as "Mad Martin," set fire to the roof of York Minster. Clarkson Stanfield created a diorama re-enactment of the event, which premiered on 20 April of the same year; it employed a "safe fire" via chemical reaction as a special effect. On 27 May, the "safe" fire proved to be less safe than planned: it set a real fire in the painted cloths of the imitation fire, which burned down the theater and all of its dioramas.

Nonetheless, dioramas remained popular in England, Scotland, and Ireland through most of the nineteenth century, lasting until 1880.

A small scale version of the diorama called the Polyrama Panoptique could display images in the home. and was marketed from the 1820s. A diorama painted by Daguerre is currently housed in the church of the French town Bry-sur-Marne, where he lived and died.

The Modern Diorama

The current, popular understanding of the term "diorama" denotes a partially three-dimensional, full-size replica or scale model of a landscape typically showing historical events, nature scenes or cityscapes, for purposes of education or entertainment. Frank M. Chapman, a curator at the American Museum of Natural History during the late nineteenth and early twentieth centuries, helped popularize the style commonly seen today.

Modern museum dioramas may be seen in most major natural history museums. Typically, these displays use a tilted plane to represent what would otherwise be a level surface, a painted background of distant objects, and often employ false perspective, carefully modifying the scale of objects placed on the plane to reinforce the illusion through depth perception of viewing a larger space—representations of objects (of identical real-world size) placed further from the observer are smaller than those closer. Often the distant painted background or sky will be painted upon a continuous curved surface so that the viewer is not distracted by corners, seams, or edges. All of these techniques are means of presenting a realistic view of a large scene in a compact space. A photograph or single-eye view of such a diorama can be especially convincing since in this case there is no distraction by the binocular perception of depth.

Miniature dioramas, usually made in a shoe box, are used to represent scenes from historic events (*e.g.*, tin soldiers arranged in a display depicting a famous battle). A typical example of this type are the dioramas to be seen at the Norges Hjemmefrontmuseum (Norwegian Resistance Museum) in Oslo, Norway.

Room boxes and other doll housing can also be considered dioramas. So too, the landscapes built around model railways, although they often have to compromise scale accuracy for better operating characteristics.

One of the largest Dioramas ever created was a model of the entire state of California built for the Panama-Pacific International Exposition and that for a long time was installed in San Francisco's Ferry Building.

MAGIC LANTERN

The magic lantern or *Lanterna Magica* was the ancestor of the modern slide projector.

- 1558: Giovanni Battista della Porta describes projection with a lantern in his four volume, latin publication entitled *Magiae naturalis*, Naples 1558. The etymology of the sobriquet lanterna magica

Fig. 5.1: Magic Lantern

may harken back to this title. Sinophile Joseph Needham reports the device may have been first described in China.

- 1658: The description of projection with a lantern is included in the first English language edition of *Magiae naturalis* which is published with the English title: *Natural Magick by John Baptista Porta, A Neopolitane: In Twenty Books: J 1 Of the Causes of Wonderful Things 2 Of the Generation of Animals 3 Of the Production of new Plants 4 Of Increasing Household-Stuff 5 Of Changing Metals 6 Of Counterfeiting U Gold 7 Of the Wonders of Load-Stone 8 Of Strange Cures 9 Of Beautifying Women 10 Of Distillation 11 Of Perfuming 12 Of Artifical Fires 13 Of Tempering Steel 14 Of Cookery A 15 Of Fishing, Fowling and Hunting 16 Of Invisible Writing 17 Of Strange Glasses 18 Of Statick Experiments 19 Of Pneumatic Experiments 20 Of the Chaos Wherein are set forth N All the Riches and Delights Of the Natural Sciences.*
- 1671: A projecting lantern is described in *Ars Magna Lucis et Umbrae*, by the Jesuit Athanasius Kircher in 1671. He was describing an already existing device familiar to and employed by the Jesuits since the mid sixteenth century. With an oil lamp and a lens, images painted on glass plates could be projected on to a suitable screen.
- 17th-18th centuries: Physicists develop the use of optics and experiment with the system, improving it over the course of time. The impetus to develop the system was the use it found in phantasmagoria performances, especially those of Étienne-Gaspard Robert.
- 19th century: a thriving trade of itinerant projectionists travels around the United Kingdom with their magic lanterns and a large number of slides to put on shows in towns and villages. Some of the slides came with special effects, by means of extra sections that could slide or rotate across the main plate. One of the most famous of these, very popular with children, was The Rat Swallower, where a series of rats would be seen leaping into a sleeping man's mouth. During the Napoleonic wars, a series was produced of a British ship's encounter with a French navy ship, ending patriotically with the French ship sinking in flames, accompanied by the cheers of the audience.

The invention of photography enabled the inexpensive creation and reproduction of slides, and thereby greatly expanded the repertoire of available images. Slide shows would feature famous landmarks, foreign lands, and personages. Posed photographs were sold in series, telling uplifting stories and moral tales. Though there was a huge market for these lanterns and slides in the 19th century, they eventually fell out of favour after the invention of moving pictures, and the few surviving lanterns and slides are sought-after collector's items.

PLANETARIUM

A planetarium is a theatre built primarily for presenting educational and entertaining shows about astronomy and the night sky, or for training in celestial navigation. A dominant feature of most planetariums is the large dome-shaped projection screen onto which scenes of stars, planets and other celestial objects can be made to appear and move realistically to simulate the complex 'motions of the heavens'. The celestial scenes can be created using a wide variety of technologies, for example precision-engineered 'star balls' that combine optical and electro-mechanical technology, slide projector, video and fulldome projector systems, and lasers. Whatever technologies are used, the objective is normally to link them together to provide an accurate relative motion of the sky. Typical systems can be set to display the sky at any point in time, past or present, and often to show the night sky as it would appear from any point of latitude on Earth.

- The plural of *planetarium* can be either *planetariums* or *planetaria.*
- The term *planetarium* is sometimes used generically to describe other devices which illustrate the solar system, such as a computer simulation or an orrery.
- The term *planetarian* is used to describe a member of the professional staff of a planetarium.
- *Planetarium software* refers to a software application that renders a three dimensional image of the sky onto a two dimensional computer screen.

Planetariums have become well-nigh ubiquitous, with some privately owned. A rough estimate is that in the United States there is one planetarium per 100,000 population, ranging in size from the Hayden Planetarium's 20-meter dome seating 430 people, to three-meter inflatable portable domes where children sit on the floor. Such portable planetariums serve education programmes outside of the permanent installations of museums and science centers.

History

Timeline of planetariums for specific dates and events in the historical influences on and development of planetariums.

Early

Archimedes is attributed with possessing a primitive planetarium device that could predict the movements of the Sun and the Moon and the planets. The discovery of the Antikythera mechanism proved that such devices already existed during antiquity. Johannes Campanus (1220-96) described a planetarium in his *Theorica Planetarum,* and included instructions on how to build one. These devices would today usually be referred to as orreries (named for the Earl of Orrery, an Irish peer: an 18th century Earl of Orrery had one built). In fact, many planetariums today have what are called projection orreries, which project onto the dome a Sun with planets (usually limited to Mercury up to Saturn) going around it in something close to their correct relative periods.

The small size of typical 18th century orreries limited their impact, and towards the end of that century a number of educators attempted some larger scale simulations of the heavens. The efforts of Adam Walker (1730-1821) and his sons are noteworthy in their attempts to fuse theatrical illusions with educational aspirations. Walker's Eidouranion was the heart of his public lectures or theatrical presentations. Walker's son describes this "Elaborate Machine" as "twenty feet high, and twenty-seven in diameter: it stands vertically before the spectators, and its globes are so large, that they are distinctly seen in the most distant parts of the Theatre. Every Planet and Satellite seems suspended in space, without any support; performing their annual and diurnal revolutions without any apparent cause". Other lecturers promoted their own devices: R.E. Lloyd advertised his Dioastrodoxon, or Grand Transparent Orrery, and by 1825 William Kitchener was offering his Ouranologia, which was 42 feet (13 m) in diameter. These devices most probably sacrificed astronomical accuracy for crowd-pleasing spectacle and sensational and awe-provoking imagery.

The oldest, still working planetarium can be found in the Dutch town Franeker. It was built by Eise Eisinga (1744-1828) in the livingroom of his house. It took Eisinga seven years to build his planetarium, which was completed in 1781.

In 1905 Oskar von Miller (1855-1934) of the Deutsches Museum in Munich commissioned updated versions of a geared orrery and planetarium from M Sendtner, and later worked with Franz Meyer, chief engineer at the Carl Zeiss optical works in Jena, on the largest mechanical planetarium ever constructed, capable of displaying both heliocentric and geocentric motion. This was displayed at the Deutsches Museum in 1924, construction work having been interrupted by the war. The planets travelled along overhead rails, powered by electric motors: the orbit of Saturn was 11.25 m in diameter. 180 stars were projected onto the wall by electric bulbs.

While this was being constructed, von Miller was also working at the Zeiss factory with German astronomer Max Wolf, former director of the Baden Observatory in Heidelberg, on a new and novel design, inspired by Wallace W Atwood's work at the Chicago Academy of Sciences and by the ideas of Walther Bauersfeld at Zeiss. The result was a planetarium design which would generate all the necessary movements of the stars and planets inside the optical projector, and would be mounted centrally in a room, projecting images onto the white surface of a hemisphere. In August 1923, the first (Model I) Zeiss planetarium projected images of the night sky onto the white plaster lining of a 16 m hemispherical concrete dome, erected on the roof of the Zeiss works. The first official public showing was at the Deutsches Museum in Munich on October 21, 1923.

Before World War II nearly all planetariums were built by Zeiss, the only notable exceptions being one built by two brothers named Korkosz in Springfield, Massachusetts, and another for the Rosicrucian AMORC order in San Jose, California.

After WWII

When Germany was divided into East and West Germany after the war, the Zeiss firm was also split. Part remained in its traditional headquarters at Jena, in East Germany, and part migrated to West Germany. The designer of the first planetariums for Zeiss, Walther Bauersfeld, remained in Jena until his death in 1959.

The West German firm resumed making large planetariums in 1954, and the East German firm started making small planetariums a few years later. Meanwhile, the lack of planetarium manufacturers had led to several attempts at construction of unique models, such as one built by the California Academy of Sciences in Golden Gate Park, San Francisco, which operated 1952-2003. The Korkosz brothers built a large projector for the Boston Museum of Science, which was unique in being the first (and for a very long time only) planetarium to project the planet Uranus. Most planetariums ignore Uranus as being at best marginally visible to the naked eye.

A great boost to the popularity of the planetarium worldwide was provided by the Space Race of the 1950s and 60s when fears that the United States might miss out on the opportunities of the new frontier in space stimulated a massive programme to install over 1,200 planetariums in U.S. high schools.

Armand Spitz recognized that there was a viable market for small inexpensive planetariums. His first model, the Spitz A, was designed to project stars from a dodecahedron, thus reducing machining expenses in creating a globe. Planets were not mechanized, but could be shifted by hand. Several models followed with various upgraded capabilities, until the A3P, which projected well over a thousand stars, had motorized motions for latitude change, daily motion, and annual motion for Sun, Moon (including phases), and planets. This model was installed in hundreds of high schools, colleges, and even small museums from 1964 to the 1980s.

Japan entered the planetarium manufacturing business in the 1960s, with Goto and Minolta both successfully marketing a number of different models. Goto was particularly successful when the Japanese Ministry of Education put one of their smallest models, the E-3 or E-5 (the numbers refer to the metric diameter of the dome) in every elementary school in Japan.

Phillip Stern, as former lecturer at New York City's Hayden Planetarium, had the idea of creating a small planetarium which could be programmed. His Apollo model was introduced in 1967 with a plastic programme board, recorded lecture, and film strip. Unable to pay for this himself, Stern became the head of the planetarium division of Viewlex, a mid-size audiovisual firm on Long Island. About thirty canned programmes were created for various grade levels and the public, while operators could create their own or run the planetarium live. Purchasers of the Apollo were given their choice of two canned shows, and could purchase more. A few hundred were sold, but in the late 1970s Viewlex went bankrupt for reasons unrelated to the planetarium business.

During the 1970s, the OmniMax movie system (now known as IMAX Dome) was conceived to operate on planetarium screens. More recently, some planetariums have re-branded themselves as *dome theaters,* with broader offerings including wide-screen or "wraparound" films, fulldome video, and laser shows that combine music with laser-drawn patterns. StarLab in Massachusetts offered the first easily portable planetarium in 1977 which projected stars, constellation figures from many mythologies, celestial coordinate systems, and much else, from removable cylinders (Viewlex and others followed with their own portable versions).

When Germany reunified in 1989, the two Zeiss firms did likewise, and expanded their offerings to cover many different size domes.

Computerized Planetariums

In 1983, Evans and Sutherland installed the first planetarium projector displaying computer graphics—the Digistar I projector used a vector graphics system to display starfields as well as line art.

The newest generation of planetariums offer a fully digital projection system, using fulldome video technology. This gives the operator great flexibility in showing not only the modern night sky as visible from Earth, but any other image they wish (including the night sky as visible from points far distant in space and time).

A new generation of home planetariums was released in Japan by Takayuki Ohira in cooperation with Sega. Ohira is worldwide known as a mastermind for building portable planetariums used at exhibitions and events such as the Aichi World Expo in 2005. The Homestar Planetarium can be carried in a bag and is intended for home use, however by projecting 10,000 stars on the ceiling makes it semi-professional.

Planetarium Technology

Domes

Planetarium domes range in size from 3 to 30 m in diameter, accommodating from 1 to 500 people. They can be permanent or portable, depending on the application.

- Portable inflatable domes can be inflated in minutes. Such domes are often used for touring planetariums visiting, for example, schools and community centres.
- Temporary structures using Glass-reinforced plastic (GRP) segments bolted together and mounted on a frame are possible. As they may take some hours to construct, they are more suitable for applications such as exhibition stands, where a dome will stay up for a period of at least several days.
- Negative-pressure inflated domes are suitable in some semi-permanent situations. They use a fan to extract air from behind the dome surface, allowing atmospheric pressure to push it into the correct shape.
- Smaller permanent domes are frequently constructed from glass reinforced plastic. This is inexpensive but, as the projection surface reflects sound as well as light, the acoustics inside this type of dome can detract from its utility. Such a solid dome also presents issues connected with heating and ventilation in a large-audience planetarium, as air cannot pass through it.
- Older planetarium domes were built using traditional construction materials and surfaced with plaster. This method is relatively expensive and suffers the same acoustic and ventilation issues as GRP.
- Most modern domes are built from thin aluminium sections with ribs providing a supporting structure behind. The use of aluminium makes it easy to perforate the dome with thousands of tiny holes. This reduces the reflectivity of sound back to the audience (providing better acoustic characteristics), lets a sound system project through the dome from behind (offering sound that seems to come from appropriate directions related to a show), and allows air circulation through the projection surface for climate control.

The realism of the viewing experience in a planetarium depends significantly on the dynamic range of the image, *i.e.*, the contrast between dark and light. This can be a challenge in any domed projection environment, because a bright image projected on one side of the dome will tend to reflect light across to the opposite side, "lifting" the black level there and so making the whole image look less realistic. Since traditional planetarium shows consisted mainly of small points of light (*i.e.*, stars) on a black background, this was not a significant issue, but it became an issue as digital projection systems started to fill large portions of the dome with bright objects (*e.g.*, large images of the sun in context). For this reason, modern planetarium domes are often not painted white but rather a mid grey colour, reducing reflection to perhaps 35-50 per cent. This increases the perceived level of contrast.

A major challenge in dome construction is to make seams as invisible as possible. Painting a dome after installation is a major task and, if done properly, the seams can be made almost to disappear.

Traditionally, planetarium domes were mounted horizontally, matching the natural horizon of the real night sky. However, because that configuration requires highly inclined chairs for comfortable viewing "straight up", increasingly domes are being built tilted from the horizontal by between 5 and 30 degrees to provide greater comfort. Tilted domes tend to create a favoured 'sweet spot' for optimum viewing, centrally about a third of the way up the dome from the lowest point. Tilted domes generally have seating arranged 'stadium-style' in straight, tiered rows; horizontal domes usually have seats in circular rows, arranged in concentric (facing center) or epicentric (facing front) arrays.

Planetariums occasionally include controls such as buttons or joysticks in the armrests of seats to allow audience feedback that influences the show in real time.

Often around the edge of the dome (the 'cove') are:

- Silhouette models of geography or buildings like those in the area round the planetarium building.
- Lighting to simulate the effect of twilight or urban light pollution.
- In one planetarium the horizon decor included a small model of a UFO flying.

Traditionally, planetariums needed many incandescent lamps around the cove of the dome to help audience entry and exit, to simulate sunrise and sunset, and to provide working light for dome cleaning. More recently, solid-state LED lighting has become available that significantly decreases power consumption and reduces the maintenance requirement as lamps no longer have to be changed on a regular basis.

Traditional Electromechanical/Optical Projectors

Traditional planetarium projection apparatus uses a hollow ball with a light inside, and a pinhole for each star, hence the name "star ball". With some of the brightest stars (*e.g.*, Sirius, Canopus, Vega), the hole must be so big to let enough light through that there must be a small lens in the hole to focus the light to a sharp point on the dome. In late and modern planetarium star balls, the individual bright stars often have individual projectors, shaped like small hand-held torches, with focusing lenses for individual bright stars. Contact breakers prevent the projectors from projecting below the 'horizon'.

The star ball is usually mounted so it can rotate as a whole to simulate the Earth's daily rotation, and to change the simulated latitude on Earth. There is also usually a means of rotating to produce the effect of precession of the equinoxes. Often, one such ball is attached at its south ecliptic pole. In that case, the view cannot go so far south that any of the resulting blank area at the south is projected on the dome. Some star projectors have two balls at opposite ends of the projector like a dumbbell. In that case all stars can be shown and the view can go to either pole or anywhere between. But care must be taken that the projection fields of the two balls match where they meet or overlap.

Smaller planetarium projectors include a set of fixed stars, Sun, Moon, and planets, and various nebulae. Larger projectors also include comets and a far greater selection of stars. Additional projectors can be added to show twilight around the outside of the screen (complete with city or country scenes) as well as the Milky Way. Others add coordinate lines and constellations, photographic slides, laser displays, and other images.

Each planet is projected by a sharply focused spotlight that makes a spot of light on the dome. Planet projectors must have gearing to move their positioning and thereby simulate the planets' movements. These can be of these types:

- *Copernican*: The axis represents the Sun. The rotating piece that represents each planet carries a light that must be arranged and guided to swivel so it always faces towards the rotating piece that represents the Earth. This presents mechanical problems including:
  - The planet lights must be powered by wires, which have to bend about as the planets rotate, and repeatedly bending copper wire tends to cause metal fatigue.
  - When a planet is at opposition to the Earth, its light is liable to be blocked by the mechanism's central axle.
    (If the planet mechanism is set 180° rotated from reality, the lights are carried by the Earth and shines towards each planet, and the blocking risk happens at conjunction with Earth.)
- *Ptolemaic*: Here the central axis represents the Earth. Each planet light is on a mount which rotates only about the central axis, and is aimed by a guide which is steered by a deferent and an epicycle (or whatever the planetarium maker calls them). Here Ptolemy's number values must be revised to remove the daily rotation, which in a planetarium is catered for otherwise.
- *Computer-controlled*: Here all the planet lights are on mounts which rotate only about the central axis, and are aimed by a computer.

Despite offering a good viewer experience, traditional star ball projectors suffer several inherent limitations. From a practical point of view, the low light levels require several minutes for the audience to "dark adapt" its eyesight. "Star ball" projection is limited in education terms by its inability to move beyond an earth-bound view of the night sky. Finally, a challenge for most traditional projectors is that the various overlaid projection systems are incapable of proper occultation. This means that a planet image projected on top of a star field (for example) will still show the stars shining through the planet image, degrading the quality of the viewing experience. For related reasons, some planetariums show stars below the horizon projecting on the walls below the dome or on the floor, or (with a bright star or a planet) shining in the eyes of someone in the audience.

However, the new breed of Optical-Mechanical projectors using fiber-optic technology to display the stars, show a much more realistic view of the sky, and are far superior to any digital star projector.

Digital Projectors

An increasing number of planetariums are using digital technology to replace the entire system of interlinked projectors traditionally employed around a star ball to address some of their limitations. Digital planetarium manufacturers claim reduced maintenance costs and increased reliability from such systems compared with traditional "star balls" on the grounds that they employ few moving parts and do not generally require synchronisation of movement across the dome between several separate systems. Some planetariums mix both traditional opto-mechanical projection and digital technologies on the same dome.

In a fully digital planetarium, the dome image is generated by a computer and then projected onto the dome using a variety of technologies including cathode ray tube, LCD, DLP or laser projectors. Sometimes a single projector mounted near the centre of the dome is employed with a "fish eye lens" to spread the light over the whole dome surface, while in other configurations several projectors around the horizon of the dome are arranged to blend together seamlessly.

Digital projection systems all work by creating the image of the night sky as a large array of pixels. Generally speaking, the more pixels a system can display, the better the viewing experience. While the first generation of digital projectors were unable to generate enough pixels to match the image quality of the best traditional "star ball" projectors, high-end systems now offer a resolution that approaches the limit of human visual acuity, making their images subjectively indistinguishable from the very best "star balls" to most eyes.

However, these digital star projectors do not show "pin-point" stars like one would actually see in the real sky. The colours of the stars are also not correct. Although the digital projectors are good for "travelling" through space, their ability to show a realistic star field is decades away. And although the digital manufacturers may say that the costs of maintenance are reduced, in reality, the maintenance costs of the digital and video units are significantly more than those of their optical-mechanical counterparts.

LCD projectors have fundamental limits on their ability to project true black as well as light, which has tended to limit their use in planetariums. LCOS and modified LCOS projectors have improved on LCD contrast ratios while also eliminating the "screen door" effect of small gaps between LCD pixels. "Dark chip" DLP projectors improve on the standard DLP design and can offer relatively inexpensive solution with bright images, but the black level requires physical baffling of the projectors. As the technology matures and reduces in price, laser projection looks promising for dome projection as it offers bright images, large dynamic range and a very wide colour space.

Planetarium Show Content

Worldwide, most planetariums provide shows to the general public. Traditionally, shows for these audiences with themes such as "What's in the sky tonight?", or shows which pick up on topical issues such as a religious festival (often the Christmas star) linked to the night sky, have been popular. Pre-recorded and live presentation formats are possible. Live format are preferred by many venues (despite the increased expense) because a live expert presenter can answer on-the-spot questions raised by the audience.

Since the early 1990s, fully featured 3-D digital planetariums have added an extra degree of freedom to a presenter giving a show because they allow simulation of the view from any point in space, not only the earth-bound view which we are most familiar with. This new virtual reality capability to travel through the universe provides important educational benefits because it vividly conveys that space has depth, helping audiences to leave behind the ancient misconception that the stars are stuck on the inside of a giant celestial sphere and instead to understand the true layout of the solar system and beyond. For example, a planetarium can now 'fly' the audience towards one of the familiar constellations such as Orion, revealing that the stars which appear to make up a co-ordinated shape from our earth-bound viewpoint are at vastly different distances from Earth and so not connected, except in human imagination and mythology. For especially visual or spatially-aware people, this experience can be more educationally beneficial than other demonstrations.

Music is an important element to fill out the experience of a good planetarium show, often featuring forms of space-themed music, or music from the genres of space music, space rock, or classical music.

PROJECTOR

Projector may refer to:

- Video projector, a device that projects a video signal from computer, home theater system etc.
- Movie projector, a device that projects moving pictures from a filmstrip.
- Slide projector, a device that projects a still image with a transparent base.
- Overhead projector, a device that projects a transparent image.
- Opaque projector, a predecessor to the overhead projector.
- Magic lantern, a historic projection device.
- Camera obscura, the historic ancestor to projection devices.
- Enlarger, a device used to produce photographic prints from negatives.
- Ceiling projector, a device used to measure the height of clouds.
- *Projector* (album), an album by Dark Tranquility.
- A type of mortar (weapon).
- A version control system used in the Macintosh Programmer's Workshop.

FILM PROJECTOR

- Movie projector for projection of moving images from film.
- Slide projector for projection of still images from film.

MOVIE PROJECTOR

A movie projector is an opto-mechanical device for displaying moving pictures by projecting them on a projection screen. Most of the optical and mechanical elements, except for the illumination and sound devices, are present in movie cameras.

Fig. 5.2: 16 mm Movie Projector

Physiology

According to the theory of persistence of vision, the perceptual processes of the brain and the retina of the human eye retains an image for a brief moment of time. This theory is said to account for the illusion of motion which results when a series of film images is displayed in quick succession, rather than the perception of the individual frames in the series.

Persistence of vision should be compared with the related phenomena of beta movement and phi movement. A critical part of understanding these visual perception phenomena is that the eye *is not a camera, i.e.*, there is no "frame rate" or "scan rate" in the eye. Instead, the eye/brain system has a combination of motion detectors, detail detectors and pattern detectors, the outputs of all of which are combined to create the visual experience.

The frequency at which flicker becomes invisible is called the flicker fusion threshold, and is dependent on the level of illumination. Generally, the frame rate of 16 frames per second (frame/s) is regarded as the lowest frequency at which continuous motion is perceived by humans. (Interestingly this threshold varies across different species; a higher proportion of rod cells in the retina will create a higher threshold level.)

It is possible to view the black space between frames and the passing of the shutter by the following technique: Close your eyelids, then periodically rapidly blink open and closed. If done fast enough you will be able to randomly "trap" the image between frames, or during shutter motion. This will not work with television due to the persistence of the phosphors nor with LCD or DLP light projectors due to the continuity of image, although certain colour artifacts may appear with some digital projection technologies.

Since the birth of sound film, virtually all film projectors in commercial movie theaters project at a constant speed of 24 frame/s. This speed was chosen for financial and technical reasons—it was the slowest speed (and thus required the least film stock and was cheapest for producers) at which a satisfactory reproduction and amplification of sound could be conducted. There are some specialist formats (*e.g.* Showscan and Maxivision) which project at higher rates, often 48 frame/s.

Silent films usually were not projected at constant speeds but rather were varied throughout the show at the discretion of the projectionist, often with some notes provided by the distributor. Speeds ranged from about 18 frame/s on up—sometimes even faster than modern sound film speed (24 frame/s). Contrary to received opinion, 16 frame/s—though sometimes used as a camera shooting speed—was dangerously inadvisable for projection, due to the high risk of the nitrate-base prints catching fire in the projector. (A dramatic rendition of a nitrate print fire and its potentially devastating effects is famously found in *Nuovo Cinema Paradiso,* which revolves around the goings-on of a projectionist.)

Principles of Operation

Fig. 5.3: 35 mm Kinoton FP30ST Movie Projector, with Part Labeled.

Projection Elements

As in a slide projector there are essential optical elements:

Light Source

An incandescent lamp or an electric arc light produces light. The traditional carbon arc or modern light source produces sufficient heat to burn the film should the film remain stationary for more than a fraction of a second. Xenons were introduced in the 1950s and are now the more common source, being easier and safer to maintain for the most part.

Reflector and Condenser Lens

- A curved reflector redirects light that would otherwise be wasted toward the condensing lens.
- A positive curvature lens concentrates the reflected and direct light toward the film gate.

Douser (Dowser)

A metal blade which cuts off light before it can get to the film—usually this is part of the lamphouse, and may be manually or automatically operated. Some projectors have a second, electrically-controlled douser that is used for changeovers (sometimes called a "changeover douser" or "changeover shutter"). Some projectors have a third, mechanically-controlled douser that automatically closes when the projector slows down (called a "fire shutter" or "fire douser"), to protect the film if a failsafe causes the motor to shutdown. Dousers protect the film when the lamp is on but the film is not moving, preventing the film from melting from prolonged exposure to the direct heat of the lamp. It also prevents the lens from scarring or cracking from excessive heat.

Film Gate and Single Image

A single image of the series of images comprising the movie is positioned and held flat within an aperture called the gate. The gate also provides a slight amount of friction so that the film does not advance or retreat except when driven to advance the film to the next image.

Shutter

A commonly-held misconception is that film projection is simply a series of individual frames dragged very quickly past the projector's intense light source; this is not the case. If a roll of film were merely passed between the light source and the lens of the projector, all that would be visible on screen would be a continuous blurred series of images sliding from one edge to the other. It is the shutter that gives the illusion of one full frame being replaced exactly on top of another full frame. A rotating petal or gated cylindrical shutter interrupts the emitted light during the time the film is advanced to the next frame. The viewer does not see the transition, thus tricking the brain into believing a moving image is on screen. Modern shutters are designed with a flicker-rate of two times (48 Hz) or even sometimes three times (72 Hz) the frame rate of the film, so as to reduce the perception of screen flickering. Higher rate shutters are less light efficient, requiring more powerful light sources for the same light on screen.

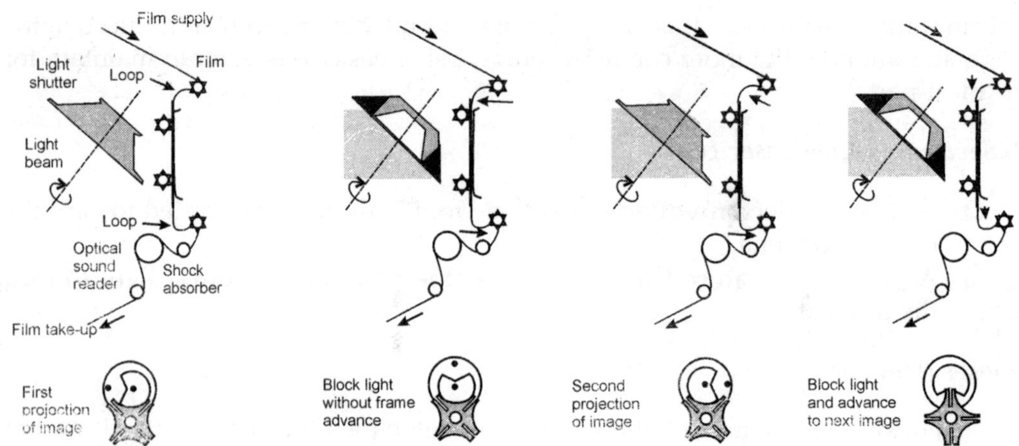

Fig. 5.4: Mechanical sequence when image is shown twice and then advanced. Outer sprockets rotate continuously while the frame advance sprockets are controlled by the mechanism shown.

Imaging Lens and Aperture Plate

A lens system with multiple optical elements directs the image of the film to a viewing screen. Different lenses are used for different aspect ratios. Each of these lenses comes with an aperture plate, a piece of metal with a precisely cut rectangular hole in the middle of equivalent aspect ratio. The aperture plate is placed just behind the gate, and masks off any light from hitting the image outside of the area intended to be shown (most modern films have extra image on the frame that is meant to be masked off in the projector).

Viewing Screen

In most cases this is a reflective surface which may be either aluminized (for high contrast in moderate ambient light) or a white surface with small glass beads (for high brilliance under dark conditions). In a commercial theater, the screen also has hundreds of small, evenly spaced holes in order to allow the passage of sound from the speakers and subwoofer which often are directly behind it.

Film Transport Elements

Film Supply and Takeup

Two Reel System

The two reel system is also known as a changeover system, after the switching mechanism that operates between the end of one reel and the beginning of the next. In a two reel system the feed reel has a slight drag to maintain tensioning in the film, while the takeup reel is driven with a constant tension by a mechanism that is allowed to slip.

The two reel system was almost universally used before the advent of the single reel system for movie theaters in order to be able to show feature-length films. Although one reel long-play systems tend to be more popular with the newer multiplexes, the two reel system is still in significant use to this day. The projector operator operates two projectors, threading one with the next reel while the other projector plays the current reel. As the outgoing reel approaches its end, the projectionist looks for cue marks, at the upper right corner of the picture. Usually these are dots or circles, although they can also be slashes. (Some older films have occasionally been known to have used squares or triangles, and even positioned the cues in the middle of the right edge of the picture.) The first cue appears twelve feet (3.7 m) or eight seconds at 24 frame/s before the end of the reel, and signals the projectionist to start the motor of the projector containing the incoming reel. After another ten and a half feet (3.2 m) or seven seconds at 24 frame/s, the changeover cue should appear, which signals the projectionist to actually make the changeover. When this second cue appears, the projectionist has one and a half feet (457 mm) or one second at 24 frame/s to make the changeover—if it doesn't occur within one second, the tail leader of the outgoing reel will be projected on the screen. On some projectors, the operator would be alerted to the change by a bell that operated when the feed reel rotation exceeded a certain speed (that reel rotates faster as the film is exhausted), or based on the diameter of the remaining film (Premier Changeover Indicator Pat. 411992), although many projectors do not have such an auditory system.

During the actual operation of a changeover, the two projectors use an interconnected electrical control connected to the changeover button so that as soon as the button is pressed, the changeover douser on the outgoing projector is closed in sync with the changeover douser on the incoming projector. If done properly, a changeover should be virtually unnoticeable to an audience. In older theaters, there may be manually operated, sliding covers in front of the projection booth's windows. A changeover with this system is often clearly visible as a wipe on the screen.

The size of the reels can vary based on the projectors, but generally films are divided and distributed in reels of up to 2000 feet (610 m, about 22 minutes at 24 frame/s). Some projectors can even accommodate up to 6000 feet (1,830 m), which minimizes the number of changeovers in a showing. Certain countries also divide their film reels up differently; Russian films, for example, often come on 1000 foot (305 m) reels, although it's likely that most projectionists working with changeovers would combine them into longer reels of at least 2000 feet (610 m), to minimize changeovers and also give sufficient time for threading and any possibly needed troubleshooting time.

Single Reel System

There are two largely used single reel systems (also known as long-play systems) today: the tower system (vertical feed and takeup) and the platter system (non-rewinding; horizontal feed and takeup).

The tower system largely resembles the two reel system, except in that the tower itself is generally a separate piece of equipment used with a slightly modified standard projector. The feed and takeup reels are held vertically on the axis, except behind the projector, on oversized spools with 12,000 foot (3,660 m) capacity or about 133 minutes at 24 frame/s. This large capacity alleviates the need for a changeover on an average-length feature; all of the reels are spliced together into one giant one. The tower is designed with four spools, two on each side, each with its own motor. This allows the whole spool to be immediately rewound after a showing; the extra two spools on the other side allow for a film to be shown while another is being rewound or even made up directly onto the tower. Each spool requires its own motor in order to set proper tensioning for the film, since it has to travel (relatively) much further between the projector film transport and the spools. As each spool gains or loses film, the tension must be periodically checked and adjusted so that the film can be transported on and off the spools without either sagging or snapping.

In a platter system the individual 20-minute reels of film are also spliced together as one large reel, but the film is then wound onto a horizontal rotating table called a platter. Three or more platters are stacked together to create a platter system. Most of the platters in a platter system will be occupied by film prints; whichever platter happens to be empty serves as the "take-up reel" to receive the film that is playing from another platter.

The way the film is fed from the platter to the projector is not unlike an eight-track audio cartridge. Film is unwound from the center of the platter through a mechanism called a payout unit which controls the speed of the platter's rotation so that it matches the speed of the film as it is fed to the projector. The film winds through a series of rollers from the platter stack to the projector, through the projector, through another series of rollers back to the platter stack, and then onto the platter serving as the take-up reel.

This system makes it possible to project a film multiple times without needing to rewind it. As the projectionist threads the projector for each showing, he transfers the payout unit from the empty platter to the full platter and the film then plays back onto the platter it came from. In the case of a double feature, each film plays from a full platter onto an empty platter, swapping positions on the platter stack throughout the day.

The advantage of a platter is that the film need not be rewound after each show, which can save labour. Rewinding risks rubbing the film against itself, which can cause scratching of the film and smearing of the emulsion which carries the pictures. The disadvantages of the platter system are that the film can acquire diagonal scratches on it if proper care is not taken while threading film from platter to projector, and the film has more opportunity to collect dust and dirt as long lengths of film are exposed to the air. A clean projection booth kept at the proper humidity is of great importance, as are cleaning devices that can remove dirt from the film print as it plays.

Automation and the Rise of the Multiplex

The single reel system can allow for the complete automation of the projection booth operations, given the proper auxiliary equipment. Since films are still transported in multiple reels they must be joined together when placed on the projector reel and taken apart when the film is to be returned to the distributor. It is the complete automation of projection that has enabled the modern "multiplex" cinema—a single site typically containing from 8 to 24 theaters with only a few projection and sound technicians, rather than a platoon of projectionists. The multiplex also offers a great amount of flexibility to a theater operator, enabling theaters to exhibit the same popular production in more than one auditorium with staggered starting times. It is also possible, with the proper equipment installed, to "interlock", *i.e.* thread a single length of film through multiple projectors. This is very useful when dealing with the mass crowds that an extremely popular film may generate in the first few days of showing, as it allows for a single print to serve more patrons.

Feed and Extraction Sprockets

Smooth wheels with triangular pins called sprockets engage perforations punched into one or both edges of the film stock. These serve to set the pace of film movement through the projector and any associated sound playback system.

Film Loop

As with motion picture cameras, the intermittent motion of the gate requires that there be loops above and below the gate in order to serve as a buffer between the constant speed enforced by the sprockets above and below the gate and the intermittent motion enforced at the gate. Some projectors also have a sensitive trip pin above the gate to guard against the upper loop becoming too big. If the loop hits the pin, it will close the dousers and stop the motor to prevent an excessively large loop from jamming the projector.

Film Gate Pressure Plate

A spring loaded pressure plate functions to align the film in a consistent image plane, both flat and perpendicular to the optical axis. It also provides sufficient drag to prevent film motion during the frame display, while still allowing free motion under control of the intermittent mechanism. The plate also has spring-loaded runners to help hold film while in place and advance it during motion.

Intermittent Mechanism

The intermittent mechanism can be constructed in different ways. For smaller gauge projectors (8 mm and 16 mm), a pawl mechanism engages the film's sprocket hole one side, or holes on each side. This pawl advances only when the film is to be moved to the next image. As the pawl retreats for the next cycle it is drawn back and does not engage the film. This is similar to the claw mechanism in a motion picture camera.

In 35 mm and 70 mm projectors, there usually is a special sprocket immediately underneath the pressure plate known as the intermittent sprocket. Unlike all the other sprockets in the projector, which run continuously, the intermittent sprocket operates in tandem with the shutter, and only moves while the shutter is blocking the lamp, so that the motion of the film cannot be seen. It also moves in a discrete amount at a time, equal to the number of perforations that make up a frame (4 for 35 mm, 5 for 70 mm). The intermittent movement in these projectors is usually provided by a Maltese Cross mechanism (also known as the Geneva Mechanism).

IMAX projectors use what is known as the rolling loop method, in which each frame is sucked into the gate by a vacuum, and positioned by registration pins in the perforations corresponding to that frame.

Types of Projectors

Projectors are classified by the size of the film used, *i.e.* the film format. Typical film sizes:

8 mm

Long used for home movies before the video camera, this uses double sprocketed 16 mm film, which is run through the camera twice. The 16 mm film is then split lengthwise into two 8 mm pieces that are spliced to make a single projectable film with sprockets on one side.

Super 8

Developed by Kodak, this film stock uses very small sprocket holes close to the edge that allow more of the film stock to be used for the images. This increases the quality of the image. The film is premade in the 8 mm width, not split during processing as is the earlier 8 mm. Magnetic stripes could be added to carry encoded sound to be added after film development.

9.5 mm

Film format introduced by Pathé Frères in 1922 as part of the Pathé Baby amateur film system. It was conceived initially as an inexpensive format to provide copies of commercially-made films to home users. The format uses a single, central perforation (sprocket hole) between each pair of frames, as opposed to 8 mm film which has perforations along one edge, and most other film formats which have perforations on each side of the image. It became very popular in Europe over the next few decades and is still used by a small number of enthusiasts today. Over 300,000 projectors were produced and sold mainly in France and England, and many commercial features were available in the format. In the sixties the last projectors of this format were being produced. They are now collectors' items.

16 mm

This was a popular format for audio-visual use in schools and as a high-end home entertainment system before the advent of broadcast television.

35 mm

The most common film size for theatrical productions during the 20th century. In fact, the common 35 mm camera, developed by Leica, was designed to use this film stock and was originally intended to be used for test shots by movie directors and cinematographers.

35 mm film is typically run vertically through the camera and projector. In the mid 1950's the VistaVision system presented wide screen movies in which the film moved horizontally, allowing much more film to be used for the image as this avoided the anamorphic reduction of the image to fit the frame width. As this required specific projectors it was largely unsuccessful as a presentation method while remaining attractive as filming, intermediate, and source for production printing and as an intermediate step in special effects to avoid film granularity, although the latter is now supplanted by digital methods.

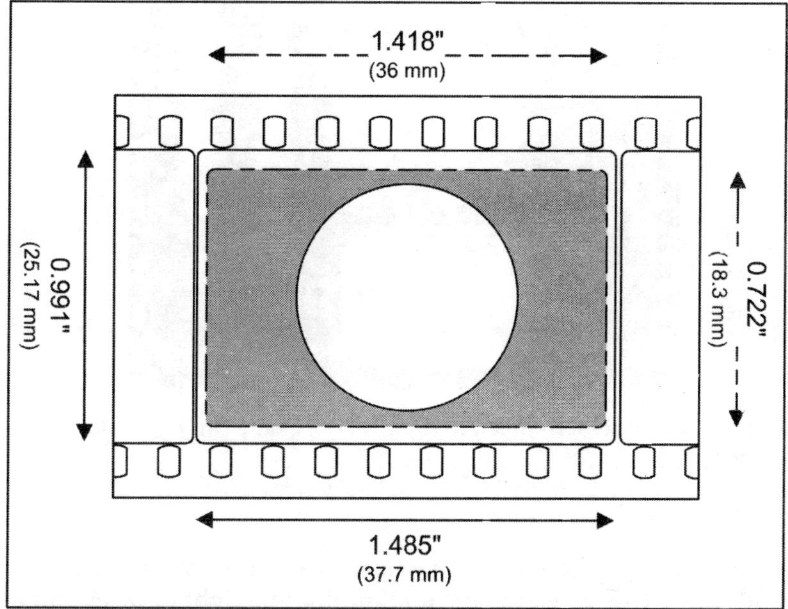

Fig. 5.5: A diagram of the VistaVision format.

70 mm

High end movie productions were often produced in this film gauge in the 1950s and 1960s and many very large screen theaters are still capable of projecting it in the 21st century. It is often referred to as 65/70, as the camera uses film 65 mm wide, but the projection prints are 70 mm wide. The extra five millimeters of film accommodated the soundtrack, usually a six track magnetic stripe. The most common theater installation would use dual gauge 35/70 mm projectors.

70 mm film is also used in both the flat and domed IMAX projection system. In IMAX the film is transported horizontally in the film gate, similar to VistaVision. Some productions intended for 35 mm anamorphic release were also released using 70 mm film stock. A 70 mm print made from a 35 mm negative is significantly better in appearance than an all 35 mm process, and allowed for a release with 6 track magnetic audio.

The advent of 35 mm prints with digital soundtracks in the 1990s largely supplanted the widespread release of the more expensive 70 mm prints.

Sound

Regardless of the sound format, any sound represented on the film image itself will not be the sound for the particular frame it occupies. All optical sound formats must be offset from the image because the image is projected with intermittent motion. If the sound head on the projector was adjacent to the gate, the sound would be a jerky start-stop-start-stop and so on. Therefore the sound head requires continuous motion and will be located a certain number of frames before or after the gate.

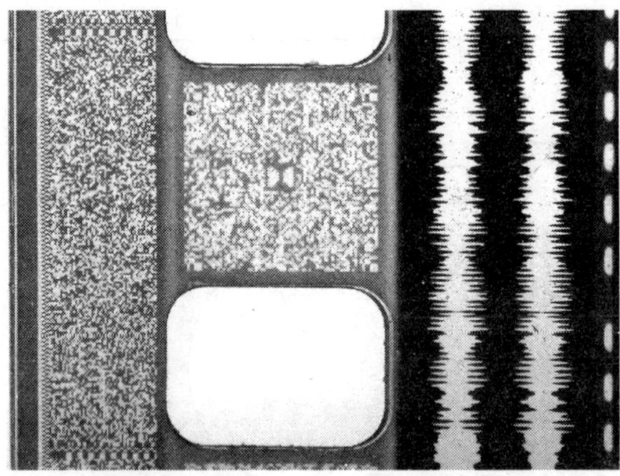

Fig. 5.6: 35 mm film audio tracks, from left to right: SDDS, Dolby Digital, analog optical, and DTS time code.

Optical

With 16 mm and the larger sizes it is practical to add a narrow channel of optically encoded sound track. This is read using an illuminating light or laser and a photocell or photodiode. In 16 mm, this is a single mono track, and the sound head is 26 frames after the gate. In 35 mm, this can be mono or stereo, the latter including several different Dolby noise reduction systems (including Dolby A and Dolby SR). The sound head is located twenty frames after the gate for 35 mm projectors. Originally optical sound was *variable density*, where the transparency/opacity level of the sound track was used to represent sound. This had disadvantages because the grain of the film caused a background hiss, and so was replaced with the now-universal standard *variable area*. In this system, a clear waveform on black background represents the sound, and the width of the waveform is equivalent to the amplitude. Variable area does have slightly less frequency response than variable density. In the 1970s and early 1980s, optical sound Super-8 mm copies were produced mainly for airline in-flight movies. This technology was soon made obsolete by video equipment.

Digital

Modern theatrical systems use optical representations of digitally encoded multi-channel sound. An advantage of digital systems is that the offset between the sound and picture heads can be varied and then set with the digital processors. Digital sound heads are usually above the gate. All digital sound systems currently in use have the ability to instantly and gracefully fall back to the optical sound system should the digital data be corrupt or the whole system fail.

Cinema Digital Sound (CDS)

Created by Kodak and ORC (Optical Radiation Corporation), Cinema Digital Sound was the first attempt to bring multi-channel digital sound to first-run theaters. CDS was available on both 35 mm and 70 mm films. Film prints equipped with CDS did not have the conventional analog optical or magnetic soundtracks to serve as a "back-up" in case the digital sound was unreadable. Another disadvantage of not having an analog back-up track is that CDS required extra film prints be made for the theaters equipped to play CDS. The three formats that followed, Dolby Digital, DTS and SDDS, can co-exist with each other and the analog optical soundtrack on a single version of the film print. This means that a film print carrying all three of these formats (and the analog optical format, usually Dolby SR) can be played in whichever format the theater is equipped to handle. CDS did not achieve wide spread use and ultimately failed. It premiered with the film *Dick Tracy* and was used with several other films, such as *Days of Thunder* and *Terminator 2: Judgement Day*.

Sony Dynamic Digital Sound (SDDS)

SDDS sound runs on the outside of 35 mm film, between the perforations and the edges, on both edges of the film. SDDS was the first digital system that could handle up to eight channels of sound. The additional two tracks are for an extra pair of screen channels (Left Center and Right Center) located between the 3 regular screen channels (Left, Center and Right). A pair of CCDs located in a unit above the projector read the two SDDS tracks. The information is decoded and decompressed before being passed along to the cinema sound processor. By default, SDDS units use an onboard Sony Cinema Sound Processor, and when the system is set up in this manner, the theatre's entire sound system can be equalized in the digital domain. In contrast, both DTS and Dolby Digital soundtracks must be passed through to standard analog cinema sound processors—which are also used for analog optical sound, so equalization of the sound remains in the analog domain. The audio data in an SDDS track is compressed in the 20-bit ATRAC2 compression scheme at a ratio of about 4.5:1. SDDS premiered with the film *Last Action Hero*. Sony ceased the sale of SDDS processors in 2001-2002.

Dolby Digital

Also known as Spectral Recording Digital or "SR•D." Sound is printed between the perforations and is 26 frames before the picture (the offset can be varied based on processing presets). Dolby Digital produces 6 discrete channels. In a variant called SR•D EX, the left and right surround channels can be dematrixed into left, right, and back surround, using Dolby Pro Logic. The audio data in a Dolby Digital track is compressed in the 16-bit AC-3 compression scheme at a ratio of about 12:1. The images between each perforation are read by a CCD located either above the projector or in the regular analog sound head below the film gate. The information is then decoded, decompressed, and converted to analog; this can happen either in a separate SR-D processor that feeds signals to the cinema sound processor, or SR-D decoding can be built-in to the cinema processor.

As of 2006, Dolby has discontinued sale of their external SR-D processor (the DA20), so, aside from the used market, purchasing a Dolby processor with integrated SR-D is the only way to purchase an SR-D decoder.

A consumer version of Dolby Digital is also used on most DVDs, often at higher data rates than the original film. Dolby Digital officially premiered with the film *Batman Returns*, but it was earlier tested at some screenings of *Star Trek: The Undiscovered Country*.

Digital Theater Systems (DTS)

DTS actually stores the sound information on separate CD-ROMs supplied with the film. The CDs are fed into a special modified computer which syncs up with the film through the use of DTS time code, decompresses the sound, and passes it through to a standard cinema processor. The time code is placed between the optical sound tracks and the actual picture, and is read by an optical LED ahead of the gate. The time code is actually the only sound system which is not offset within the film from the picture, but still needs to be physically set offset ahead of the gate in order to maintain continuous motion. Each disc can hold slightly over 90 minutes of sound, so longer films will require a second disc. Three types of DTS sound exist: DTS-ES (Extended Surround), an 8 channel digital system; DTS-6, a 6 track digital system, and a now obsolete 4 channel system. DTS-ES derives a back surround channel from the left surround and right surround channels using Dolby Pro Logic. The audio data in a DTS track is compressed in the 20-bit APTX-100 compression scheme at a ratio of about 4.5:1. Of the three digital formats currently in use, DTS is the only one that has been used with 70 mm presentations. DTS was premiered on *Jurassic Park*. A consumer version of DTS is available on some DVDs.

Magnetic Sound

70 mm, which had no optical sound, used the 5 millimeters gained between the 65 mm negative and the final release print to place three magnetic tracks on each side of the perforations, for a total of six tracks. Unlike all other non-double head magnetic sound, 70 mm magnetic heads are located before the gate. Until the introduction of digital sound, it was fairly common for 35 mm films to be blown up to 70 mm often just to take advantage of the greater number of sound tracks. 35 mm four-track magnetic sound was used from the 1950s through the mid 1970s for big-budget feature prints. It was of excellent quality, although somewhat prone to damage and erasure over time. As analog optical stereo gained popularity (it was also more durable and far less expensive to include on a film print), 35 mm four-track magnetic sound was increasingly only used for special road show screenings, and the development of digital sound systems made it completely obsolete.

35 mm and 16 mm each are sometimes run in sync with a separate reel of magnetic sound (known as double head projection because two reels are running on one projector in sync); the image goes through a gate while the magnetic reel passes over a sound head. Since the sound is on a separate reel, it does not need to be offset from the image. This system is usually used only for very low-budget or student productions, or for screening rough cuts of films before the creation of a final married print. Sync between the two reels is checked with SMPTE leader, also known as countdown leader. If the two reels are synced, there should be one frame of "beep" sound exactly on the "2" frame of the countdown—2 seconds or 48 frames before the picture start.

On certain stocks of Super 8 and 16 mm an iron-oxide sound recording strip was added for the direct synchronous recording of sound which could then be played by projectors with a magnetic sound head. It has since been discontinued by Kodak on both gauges.

Leaders

Academy leader is placed at the head of release prints containing information for the projectionist and featuring numbers which are black on a clear background, counting from 11 to 3 at 16 frame intervals (16 frames in 35 mm film = 1 ft). At – 12 feet there is a START frame.

SMPTE leader is placed at the head of release prints or video masters containing information for the projectionist or video playback tech. The numbers count down in seconds from 8 to 2 at 24 frame intervals ending at the first frame of the "2" followed by 47 frames of black.

Usually there's an audio POP that play 48 frames (2 seconds at 24 frame per second) before first frame of action (FFOA) that helps to sync audio and video during printing processes or postproduction.

Types of Lenses and Screens

Orthographic

Before the advent of certain wide screen technologies, lenses always reproduced the exact proportions of the film image onto the screen. Such lenses are relatively simple to design and manufacture. Prior to modern wide screen, the industry standard image ratio of width to height was 1.37:1.

35 mm VistaVision was a wide screen orthographic system. The wide image was obtained by running the film horizontally across the gate so that the width limitation of the film was transformed to a height limitation. See the VistaVision article for more information.

Anamorphic

The early 1950s saw the development of wide screen films using special lenses for filming and projection. The images on these films utilized a more squarish aspect ratio (1.18:1) in order to accommodate both magnetic and optical tracks. The wide image is compressed horizontally in half onto the film in the camera using additional cylindrical elements within the lens, with a corresponding lens used in the projector to expand the image to the wide screen. This technique is called anamorphic projection and various implementations have been marketed under several brand names, including CinemaScope, Panavision and Superscope, with Technirama implementing a slightly different anamorphic technique using vertical expansion to the film rather than horizontal compression. Large format anamorphic processes included Super (and Ultra) Panavision and VistaVision.

Fig. 5.7: Simulated wide screen image with 1.96 to 1 ratio as it would be seen in a camera viewfinder or on a theater screen.

Fig. 5.8: Simulated anamorphed image with 1.33 to 1 ratio (4:3) as it would appear on a frame of film.

Fish Eye with Dome

The IMAX dome projection method (called "OMNIMAX") uses 70 mm film oriented to maximize the image area and extreme wide angle lenses to obtain an almost hemispherical image. The field of view is tilted, as is the projection hemisphere, so one may view a portion of the ground in the foreground. Owing to the great area covered by the picture it is not as bright as seen with flat screen projection, but the immersive qualities are quite convincing. While there are not many theaters capable of displaying this format there are regular productions in the fields of nature, travel, science, and history, and productions may be viewed in most U.S. large urban regions. These dome theaters are mostly located in large and prosperous science and technology museums.

Wide and Deep Flat Screen

The IMAX flat screen system uses large format film, a wide and deep screen, and close and quite steep "stadium" seating. The effect is to fill the visual field to a greater degree than is possible with conventional wide screen systems. Like the IMAX dome, this is found in major urban areas, but unlike the dome system it is practical to reformat existing movie releases to this method. Also, the geometry of the theater and screen are more amenable to inclusion within a newly constructed but otherwise conventional multiple theater complex than is the dome style theater.

Multiple Cameras and Projectors

One wide screen development during the 1950s used non-anamorphic projection, but used three side by side synchronised projectors. Call Cinerama, the images were projected onto an extremely wide, curved screen. Some seams were said to be visible between the images but the almost complete filling of the visual field made up for this. This showed some commercial success as a limited location (only in major cities) exhibition of the technology in *This is Cinerama,* but the only memorable story-telling film of two made for this technology was *How the West Was Won,* widely seen only in its Cinemascope re release.

While neither a technical nor a commercial success, the business model survives as implemented by the documentary production, limited release locations, and long running exhibitions of IMAX dome movies.

Three-Dimensional

For techniques used to display pictures with a three-dimensional appearance, see the 3-D film article for some movie history and the stereoscopy article for technical information.

SLIDE PROJECTOR

A slide projector is an opto-mechanical device to view photographic slides. It has four main elements: a fan-cooled electric light bulb or other light source, a reflector and "condensing" lens to direct the light to the slide, a holder for the slide and a focusing lens. A flat piece of heat absorbing glass is often placed in the light path between the condensing lens and the slide, to avoid damaging the latter. This glass transmits visible wavelengths but absorbs infrared. Light passes through the transparent slide and lens, and the resulting image is enlarged and projected onto a perpendicular flat screen so the audience can view its reflection. Alternatively the image may be projected onto a translucent "rear projection" screen, often used for continuous automatic display for close viewing. This form of projection also avoids the audience's interrupting the light stream or bumping into the projector.

Slide projectors were common in the 1950s and 1960s as a form of entertainment; family members and friends would gather to view slideshows.

In-home photographic slides and slide projectors have largely been replaced by low cost paper prints, digital cameras, DVD media, video display monitors and digital projectors.

As of October 2004, Kodak no longer manufactures slide projectors. It is also increasingly difficult in some countries to locate photo processors who will process slide film.

Types of Slide Projector

- Carousel slide projectors (includes tray-style projectors),
- Dual slide projectors,
- Large format slide projectors,
- Overhead projectors,
- Single slide projectors (manual/form),
- Viewer slide projectors,
- Slide Cube projectors, and
- Stereo slide projectors (projects two slides simultaneously with different polarizations; slides appear as three-dimensional with polarizing glasses).

VIDEO PROJECTOR

A video projector takes a video signal and projects the corresponding image on a projection screen using a lens system. All video projectors use a very bright light to project the image, and most modern ones can correct any curves, blurriness, and other inconsistencies through manual settings. Video projectors are widely used for conference room presentations, classroom training, and home theatre applications.

Overview

A video projector, also known as a Digital Projector, may be built into a cabinet with a rear-projection screen (rear-projection TV, or RPTV) to form a single unified display device, now popular for "home theater" applications.

Common display resolutions for a portable projector include SVGA (800 × 600 pixels), XGA (1024 × 768 pixels), 720p (1280 × 720 pixels), and 1080p (1920 × 1080 pixels).

The cost of a device is not only determined by its resolution, but also by its light output, acoustic noise output, contrast, and other characteristics. While most modern projectors provide sufficient light for a small screen at night or under controlled lighting such as in a basement with no windows, a projector with a higher light output (measured in lumens, abbreviated "lm") is required for a larger screen or a room with a higher amount of ambient light. A rating of 1500 to 2500 ANSI lumens or lower is suitable for smaller screens with controlled lighting or low ambient light. Between

2500 and 4000 lm is suitable for medium-sized screens with some ambient light or dimmed light. Over 4000 lm is appropriate for very large screens in a large room with no lighting control (for example, a conference room). Projected image size is important; because the total amount of light does not change, as size increases, brightness decreases. Image sizes are typically measured in linear terms, diagonally, obscuring the fact that larger images require much more light (proportional to the image area, not just the length of a side). Increasing the diagonal measure of the image by 25 per cent reduces the image brightness by 35 per cent; an increase of 41 per cent reduces brightness by *half*.

Projection Technologies

- CRT projector using cathode ray tubes. This typically involves a blue, a green, and a red tube. Minimal maintenance is required (unlike projectors that use expensive lamps which must be periodically replaced after they burn out). This is the oldest system and falling out of favour largely because of the bulky cabinet. However, it does provide the largest screen size for a given cost. This also covers three tube home models, which, while bulky, can be moved.
- LCD projector using LCD light gates. This is the simplest system, making it one of the most common and affordable for home theaters and business use. Its most common problem is a visible "screen door" or pixelation effect, although recent advances have minimized this.
- DLP projector using Texas Instruments' DLP technology. This uses one, two, or three microfabricated light valves called digital micromirror devices (DMDs). The single-and double-DMD versions use rotating colour wheels in time with the mirror refreshes to modulate colour. The most common problem with the single- or two-DMD varieties is a visible "rainbow" which some people perceive when moving their eyes. More recent projectors with higher speed (2x or 4x) and otherwise optimised colour wheels have lessened this artifact. Systems with 3 DMDs never have this problem, as they display each primary colour simultaneously.
- LCOS projector using Liquid crystal on silicon.
- D-ILA JVC's Direct-drive Image Light Amplifier based on LCOS technology.
- LED Use an array of Light Emitting Diodes as the light source, negating the need for lamp replacement.

Obsolete Technologies

- Eidophor oil-film projectors
- Talaria oil-film projectors
- ILA (Light Image Amplifier) light valves
- Schmidt-CRT, developed by Kloss Video

DIY Video Projectors

With a growing DIY-community and an increasing interest in low cost devices, some hobbyists have endeavored to build their own projectors from kits, sourced components, or from scratch. Through the internet, the community is now able to obtain plans to construct DIY-video projectors and there is a growing trend toward building them for domestic requirements and classroom use. The DIY-projectors are now being used both in developed countries and in developing countries in the interest of providing education as well as for entertainment purposes.

OVERHEAD PROJECTOR

An overhead projector (OHP) is a variant of slide projector that is used to display images to an audience.

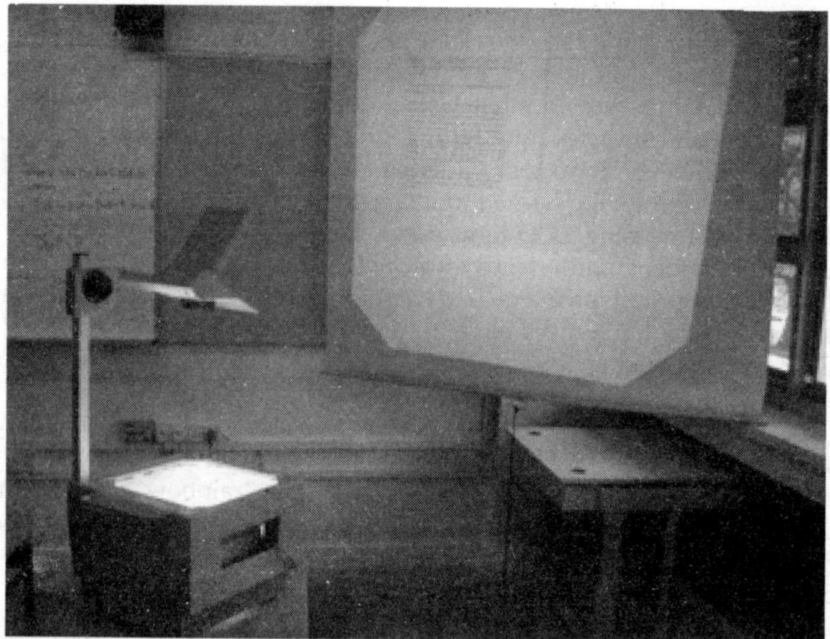

Fig. 5.9: Overhead projector in operation, during a classroom lesson.

Mechanism

An overhead projector typically consists of a large box containing a very bright lamp and a fan to cool it off, on top of which is a large fresnel lens that collimates the light. Above the box, typically on a long arm, is a mirror and lens that focusses and redirects the light forward instead of up.

Transparencies are placed on top of the lens for display. The light from the lamp travels through the transparency and into the mirror where it is shone forward onto a screen for display. The mirror allows both the presenter and the audience to see the image at the same time, the presenter looking down at the transparency as if writing, the audience looking forward at the screen. The height of the mirror can be adjusted, to both focus the image and to make the image larger or smaller depending on how close the projector is to the screen.

Focal-Length Adjustment

Better-quality overhead projectors offer an adjustment wheel or screw on the body of the projector, to move the lamp towards or away from the fresnel lens. When the mirror above the lens is moved too high or too low, it moves out of the best focal distance for an evenly white image, resulting in a projected image with either blue or brown colour fringing around the outside edge of the screen. Turning the adjustment wheel moves the lamp to correct the focal distance and restores the all-white projected image.

Illumination

The lamp technology of an overhead projector is typically very simple compared to a modern LCD or DLP video projector. Most overheads use an extremely high-power halogen lamp that may consume up to 750 watts yet produces a fairly dim, yellowed image. A high-flow blower is required to keep the bulb from melting itself due to the heat output. Further, the intense heat usually causes the halogen lamp to fail quickly, often lasting less than 100 hours before failing and requiring replacement. A modern LCD or DLP uses an arc lamp which has a higher luminous efficacy and lasts for thousands of hours. A negative to LCD/DLP technology is the warm up time required for arc lamps, but it is the instant turn-on of halogen lamps that may be the biggest factor in their rapid rate of failure.

Older overhead projectors used a tubular quartz lamp body containing the filament only, which mounted above a bowl-shaped polished reflector. However because the lamp was suspended above and outside the reflector, a large amount of light was cast to the sides inside the projector body that was wasted and required a very large lamp for sufficient screen illumination. More recent projectors use an integrated lamp and conical reflector assembly that allows the lamp to be located deep within the reflector so that more light is focused towards the fresnel lens, allowing for a lower-power lamp.

The most recent innovation for overhead projectors with integrated lamps/ reflectors is the quick-swap dual-lamp control, allowing two lamps to be installed in the projector in movable sockets. If during a presentation one lamp were to fail, the presenter can merely move a lever to slide the spare into position and continue with the presentation, without needing to open the projection unit or waiting for the failed bulb to cool before replacing it.

History

The first overhead projector was used for police identification work. It used a cellophane roll over a 9-inch stage allowing facial characteristics to be rolled across the stage. The U.S. Army in 1945 was the first to use it in quantity for training as World War II wound down. It began to be widely used in schools and businesses in the late 1950s and early 1960s.

A major manufacturer of overhead projectors in this early period was the company 3M. As the demand for projectors grew, Buhl Industries was founded in 1953, and became the leading US contributor for several optical refinements for the overhead projector and its projection lens. In 1957 the United States' first Federal Aid to Education programme stimulated overhead sales which remained high up to the late 1990s and into the 21st Century.

Use in Education

The overhead projector facilitates an easy low-cost interactive environment for educators. Teaching materials can be pre-printed on plastic sheets, upon which the educator can directly write using a non-permanent, washable colour marking pen. This saves time, since the transparency can be pre-printed and used repetitively, rather than having materials written manually before each class.

The overhead is typically placed at a comfortable writing height for the educator and allows the educator to face the class, facilitating better communication between the students and teacher. The enlarging features of the projector allow the educator to write in a comfortable small script in a natural writing position rather than writing in an overly large script on a blackboard and having to constantly hold his arm out in midair to write on the blackboard.

When the transparency sheet is full of written or drawn material, it can simply be replaced with a new, fresh sheet with more pre-printed material, again saving class time vs a blackboard that would need to be erased and teaching materials rewritten by the educator. Following the class period, the transparencies are easily restored to their original unused state by washing off with soap and water.

LCD Overhead Displays

In the early 1980s-90s, overhead projectors were often used as part of a classroom computer display/projection system. A liquid-crystal panel mounted in a plastic frame was placed on top of the overheard projector and connected to the video output of the computer, often splitting off the normal monitor output. A cooling fan in the frame of the LCD panel would blow cooling air across the LCD to prevent overheating that would fog the image.

The first of these LCD panels were monochrome-only, and could display NTSC video output such as from an Apple II computer or VCR. In the late 1980s colour models became available, capable of "thousands" of colours (16-bit colour), for the colour Macintosh and VGA PCs. The displays were never particularly fast to refresh or update, resulting in the smearing of fast-moving images, but it was acceptable when nothing else was available.

Decline in Use

Overhead projectors were once a common fixture in most classrooms and business conference rooms, but today are slowly being replaced by Document Cameras, large computer monitors, dedicated computer projection systems and interactive whiteboards. Such systems allow to make animated, interactive presentations with movement and video, typically using software like Microsoft PowerPoint.

The primary reason for this gradual replacement is the deeply ingrained use of computing technology in modern society and the inability of overheads to easily support the features that modern users demand. While an overhead can display static images fairly well, it performs poorly at displaying moving images. The LCD video display panels that were once used have fallen out of favour due to the limited resolution available and relatively dim, fuzzy image produced by the overhead.

The standards of users have also increased, so that a dim, fuzzy overhead projection that is too bright in the center and too dim around the edges is no longer acceptable. The optical focus, linearity, brightness and clarity of an overhead generally cannot match that of a video projector primarily due to the plastic fresnel lens, which can only approximate what would normally be an extremely large and heavy glass lens.

Video projectors utilize extremely small picture generation mechanisms, allowing for precision optics that far exceed the plastic fresnel lens' optical performance. They also include additional optics that eliminate the *hotspot* in the center of the screen directly above the light source, so that the brightness is uniform everywhere on the projection screen.

Critics feel that there are some downsides as these technologies are more prone to failure and have a much steeper learning curve for the user than a standard overhead projector. While a computer projection system eliminates the need to create hard copy transparencies (which can be quite expensive, particularly if made in colour) of the slide show presentation, many presenters make both in case the computer hardware fails. Furthermore, the overhead projector allows a more direct interaction through live writing on the transparency.

Pop Culture References

- In the film Apollo 13 Gene Kranz attempts to use an overhead projector to draw up a plan for rescuing the stranded astronauts, only to have the bulb fail a few seconds after turning on the projector.
- *The Art of the Overhead*: An art and media festival dedicated to this almost outdated technology was arranged for the first time in Copenhagen, October 2005. The project spawned a row of overhead installations and performances, like the song "Farewell to the Overhead". The festival is an ongoing project.
- *Farewell to Overhead*: In 2005 the group Monochrom created a melancholic electro pop song about the "dead medium" overhead projector and adolescence/socialisation.

OPAQUE PROJECTOR

The opaque projector, *epidioscope, epidiascope* or *episcope* is a device which displays opaque materials by shining a bright lamp onto the object from above. A system of mirrors, prisms and/or imaging lenses is used to focus an image of the material onto a viewing screen. Because they must project the reflected light, opaque projectors require brighter bulbs and larger lenses than overhead projectors. Care must be taken that the materials are not damaged by the heat generated by the light source. Opaque projectors are not as common as the modern "overhead."

Opaque projectors are typically used to project images of book pages, drawings, mineral specimens, leaves, etc. They have been produced and marketed as artists' enlargement tools to allow images to be transferred to surfaces such as prepared canvas, or for lectures and discourses

History

The opaque projector is a predecessor to the overhead projector. The light source in early opaque projectors was often limelight. Incandescent light bulbs and halogen lamps are most commonly used today. In the early and middle parts of the 20th century, low-cost opaque projectors were produced and marketed as toys for children.

In educational settings, the specific role of the opaque projector has been superseded by the *presenter*, a lighted table with a fixed video camera above it. The image from the camera is displayed using a separate projector. The desktop presenter unit is sometimes called an opaque projector.

Types

At the beginning of the 20th century, projection was split into two classes: *"If the light traverses the object, the projection is said to be diascopic, if by reflected light, episcopic."*

Two main classes of opaque projectors thus existed:

1. the episcope, which solely projected images of opaque objects
2. the epidiascope, which was capable of projecting images of both opaque and transparent images.

CAMERA OBSCURA

The camera obscura (Lat. *dark chamber*) was an optical device used in drawing, and one of the ancestral threads leading to the invention of photography. In English, today's photographic devices are still known as "cameras."

The principle of the camera obscura can be demonstrated with a rudimentary type, just a box (which may be room-sized, or even hangar sized) with a hole in one side. Light from only one part of a scene will pass through the hole and strike a specific part of the back wall. The projection is made on paper on which an artist can then copy the image. The advantage of this technique is that the perspective is accurate, thus greatly increasing the realism of the image.

With this simple do-it-yourself apparatus, the image is always upside-down. By using mirrors, as in the 18th century overhead version (illustrated in the Discovery and Origins section below), it is also possible to project a right-side-up image. Another more portable type, is a box with an angled mirror projecting onto tracing paper placed on the glass top, the image upright as viewed from the back.

As a pinhole is made smaller, the image gets sharper, but the light-sensitivity decreases. With too small a pinhole the sharpness again becomes worse due to diffraction. Practical camerae obscurae use a lens rather than a pinhole because it allows a larger aperture, giving a usable brightness while maintaining focus.

Discovery and Origins

The first mention and discovery of the principles behind the pinhole camera, a precursor to the camera obscura, belong to Mozi (470 BC to 390 BC), a Chinese philosopher and founder of Mohism. The Mohist tradition is also highly unusual in Chinese thought in that it devoted time to developing principles of logic. Further down the line, Aristotle (384 to 322 BC) understood the optical principle of the pinhole camera. He viewed the crescent shape of a partially eclipsed sun projected on the ground through the holes in a sieve, and the gaps between leaves of a plane tree.

The first camera obscura was later built by an Arab scientist named Abu Ali Al-Hasan Ibn al-Haitham, born in Basra (965-1039 AD), known in the West as *Alhacen* or *Alhazen*, who carried out practical experiments on optics in his *Book of Optics*. Most of his professional career took place in Cairo, where he was summoned for his first engineering task of regulating the flow of the Nile river. In his various experiments, Ibn Al-Haitham used the term "*Al-Bayt al-Muthlim*, translated in English as dark room. In the experiment he undertook, in order to establish that light travels in time and with speed, he says: "If *the hole was covered with a curtain and the curtain was taken off, the light traveling from the hole to the opposite wall will consume time.*" He reiterated the same experience when he established that light travels in straight lines. The most revealing experiment which indeed introduced the camera obscura was in his studies of the half-moon shape of the sun's image during eclipses which he observed on the wall opposite a small hole made in the window shutters. In his famous essay "On the form of the Eclipse" (*Maqalah-fi-Surat-al-Kosuf*) he commented on his observation "The *image of the sun at the time of the eclipse, unless it is total, demonstrates that when its light passes through a narrow, round hole and is cast on a plane opposite to the hole it takes on the form of a moon-sickle*".

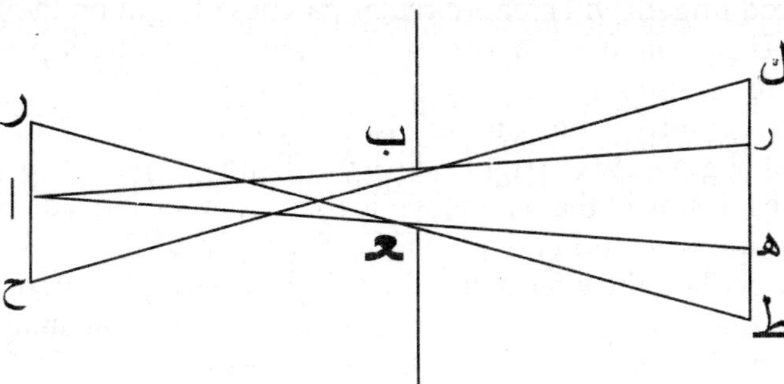

Fig. 5.10: Alhacen's observations of light's behaviour through a pinhole with a second hole the image is doubled.

In his experiment of the sun light he extended his observation of the penetration of light through the pinhole to conclude that when the sunlight reaches and penetrates the hole it makes a conic shape at the points meeting at the pinhole, forming later another conic shape reverse to the first one on the opposite wall in the dark room.

This happens when sunlight diverges from point "1" until it reaches an aperture and is projected through it onto a screen at the luminous spot. Since the distance between the aperture and the screen is insignificant in comparison to the distance between the aperture and the sun, the divergence of sunlight after going through the aperture should be insignificant. In other words, should be about equal to. However, it is observed to be much greater when the paths of the rays which form the extremities of are retraced in the reverse direction, it is found that they meet at a point outside the aperture and then diverge again toward the sun as illustrated in figure 5.10. This was indeed the first accurate description of the Camera Obscura phenomenon.

In camera terms, the light converges into the room through the hole transmitting with it the object(s) facing it. The object will appear in full colour but upside down on the projecting screen/wall opposite the hole inside the dark room. The explanation is that light travels in a straight line and when some of the rays reflected from a bright subject pass through the small hole in thin material they do not scatter but cross and reform as an upside down image on a flat white surface held parallel to the hole. Ibn Al-Haitham established that the smaller the hole is, the clearer the picture is.

History

Although both the pinhole camera and camera obscura are credited to Ibn al-Haytham (Alhazen, 965-1039), for providing the first clear description and correct analysis of the device and for first describing how an image is formed in the eye using the camera obscura as an analogy, primitive forms of a camera obscura were known to earlier scholars since the time of Mozi and Aristotle. When Ibn al-Haytham began experimenting with the camera obscura phenomenon, he himself stated (in the Latin translation), with respect to the camera obscura phenomenon, *Et nos non inventimus ita*, "we did not invent this".

In the 4th century BC, Aristotle noted that "sunlight traveling through small openings between the leaves of a tree, the holes of a sieve, the openings wickerwork, and even interlaced fingers will create circular patches of light on the ground." In the 4th century AD, Theon of Alexandria observed how "candlelight passing through a pinhole will create an illuminated spot on a screen that is directly in line with the aperture and the center of the candle." In the 9th century, Al-Kindi (Alkindus) demonstrated that "light from the right side of the flame will pass through the aperture and end up on the left side of the screen, while light from the left side of the flame will pass through the aperture and end up on the right side of the screen." While these earlier scholars described the effects of a single light passing through a pinhole, none of them suggested that what is being projected onto the screen is an image of everything on the other side of the aperture. Ibn al-Haytham's *Book of Optics* (1021) was the first to demonstrate this with his lamp experiment where several different light sources are arranged across a large area, and he was thus the first scientist to successfully project an entire image from outdoors onto a screen indoors with the camera obscura.

Several decades after Ibn al-Haytham's death, the Song Dynasty Chinese scientist Shen Kuo (1031–95) experimented with camera obscura, and was the first to apply geometrical and quantitative attributes to it in his book of 1088 AD, the *Dream Pool Essays*. However, Shen Kuo alluded to the fact that the *Miscellaneous Morsels from*

Youyang written in about 840 AD by Duan Chengshi (d. 863) during the Tang Dynasty (618–907) mentioned inverting the image of a Chinese pagoda tower beside a seashore. In fact, Shen makes no assertion that he was the first to experiment with such a device. Shen wrote of Cheng's book: "[*Miscellaneous Morsels from Youyang*] said that the image of the pagoda is inverted because it is beside the sea, and that the sea has that effect. This is nonsense. It is a normal principle that the image is inverted after passing through the small hole."

Its potential as a drawing aid may have been familiar to artists by as early as the 15th century; Leonardo da Vinci (1452-1519 AD) described camera obscura in *Codex Atlanticus*. Johann Zahn's *Oculus Artificialis Teledioptricus Sive Telescopium* was published in 1685. This work contains many descriptions and diagrams, illustrations and sketches of both the camera obscura and of the magic lantern.

The Dutch Masters, such as Johannes Vermeer, who were hired as painters in the 17th century, were known for their magnificent attention to detail. It has been widely speculated that they made use of such a camera, but the extent of their use by artists at this period remains a matter of considerable controversy, recently revived by the Hockney-Falco thesis.

Early models were large; comprising either a whole darkened room or a tent (as employed by Johannes Kepler). By the 18th century, following developments by Robert Boyle and Robert Hooke, more easily portable models became available. These were extensively used by amateur artists while on their travels, but they were also employed by professionals, including Paul Sandby, Canaletto and Joshua Reynolds, whose camera (disguised as a book) is now in the Science Museum (London). Such cameras were later adapted by Louis Daguerre and William Fox Talbot for creating the first photographs.

Tourist Attractions

Some camera obscura have been built as tourist attractions, often taking the form of a large chamber within a high building that can be darkened so that a 'live' panorama of the world outside is projected onto a horizontal surface through a rotating lens. Although few now survive, examples can be found at the following locations:

- Turin in Italy—at the Cinema Museum inside the Mole Antonelliana by Antonelli
- Edinburgh in Scotland—See the Camera obseuza sile
- Grahamstown in South Africa
- Johannesburg in South Africa
- Pretoria in South America NOTTTT
- Cape Town in South Africa
- the Observatory in Bristol
- Portslade village and Eastbourne Pier in England
- Kentwell Hall, Long Melford, Suffolk, England
- Aberystwyth and Portmeirion in Wales
- Kirriemuir, Dumfries and Edinburgh in Scotland
- Douglas, Isle of Man

- Dumfries Museum and Camera Obscura, Scotland
- Trondheim, Norway
- Lisbon and Tavira in Portugal
- Santa Monica, California at Pacific Palisades Park
- Los Angeles at the Griffith Observatory
- San Francisco, California's Camera Obscura
- North Carolina's "Cloud Chamber for the Trees and Sky"
- Havana in Cuba
- Eger in Hungary
- Cádiz in Spain in the Torre Tavira
- Great Orme at Llandudno in North Wales
- Royal Observatory, Greenwich, London
- Perdika, Aegina Island, Greece.
- Marburg, Universitie of Physik, Germany
- The Science Museum of Minnesota, St. Paul
- Greenport on Long Island, New York

There is also a portable example which Willett and Patteson tour around England and the world.

CEILING PROJECTOR

The ceiling projector or cloud searchlight is used to measure the height of the base of clouds (called the ceiling) above the ground. It is used in conjunction with an alidade, usually positioned 1000 ft (304.8 m) away and wherever possible set at the same level.

The projector is normally set at 90°, although 71° 31' may be used, in relation to the terrain. The projector consists of a 430 W incandescent bulb set in a weatherproof housing. Inside the housing are two mirrors; the first, above the bulb, reflects the light downwards to the second mirror, that then reflects the light upwards to the cloud. Both mirrors are focused to produce a high intensity beam of light that renders a visible spot on the base of the cloud.

The alidade is mounted on a post at a height of 5 ft (1.524 m) from the ground. It consists of an arm with a pointer and open sight at one end and a rubber eyepiece at the other. The arm is mounted onto a curved scale that is marked both in meters and the coded cloud height (feet). The observer looks through the eyepiece and sets the sight onto the spot projected on the cloud and reads the height from the attached scale.

When the cloud is thin the beam of light may penetrate into the cloud. The observer should read the scale where the light first enters the cloud and not at the top. However, a remark may be made as to how far into the cloud the light was able to penetrate as this may be useful. In the case of fog or blizzard conditions the observer should read the scale where the beam disappears.

ENLARGER

An enlarger is a specialised transparency projector used to produce photographic prints from film or glass negatives using the gelatin-silver process, or transparencies.

All enlargers consist of a light source—normally an incandescent light bulb, a holder for the negative or transparency and a specialised lens for projection. The light passes through a film holder, which holds a photographic negative or transparency, having been previously exposed in a camera and developed.

Prints made with an enlarger are called *enlargements*. Typically, enlargers are used in a darkroom, an enclosed space from which extraneous light may be excluded; some commercial enlargers have an integral dark box so that they can be used in a light-filled room.

Fig. 5.11: Photographic Enlarger.

Types of Enlarger

1. A *condenser* enlarger consists of a light source, a condensing lens, a holder for the negative and a projecting lens. The condenser provides even illumination to the negative beneath it.
2. A *diffuser* enlarger's light source is diffused by translucent glass or plastic, providing even illumination for the film.
3. Condenser enlargers produce higher contrast than diffusers because light is scattered from its path by the negative's image silver; this is called the Callier Effect. The condenser's increased contrast emphasises any negative defects, such as dirt and scratches, and image grain.
4. Diffuser enlargers produce an image of the same contrast as a contact print from the negative.
5. Dedicated colour enlargers contain an adjustable filter mechanism between the light source and the negative, enabling the user to control the amount of cyan, magenta and yellow light reaching the negative. Other models have a

drawer where cut filters can be inserted into the light path. These enlargers can also be used with variable-contrast monochrome papers.

6. Digital enlargers project an image from an LCD screen at the film plane, to produce a photographic enlargement from a digital file.

Enlarger Physical Arrangements

Most modern enlargers are vertically mounted with the head pointing downward and adjusted up or down to change the size of the image projected onto the enlarger's base, or a work table if the unit is mounted to the wall.

Horizontal enlargers are comprised of a trestle, with the head mounted on crossbars between two or more posts for extra stability. Horizontal enlarger structures are used when high quality, large format enlargements are required such as when photographs are taken from aircraft for mapping and taxation purposes.

The parts of the enlarger includes baseboard, enlarger head, elevation knob, filter holder, negative carrier, glass plate, focus knob, girder scale, timer, bellows, and housing lift.

Principles of Operation

The image from the negative or transparency is projected through a lens fitted with an adjustable iris aperture, onto to a flat surface bearing the sensitized photographic paper. By adjusting the ratio of distance from film to lens to the distance from lens to paper, various degrees of enlargement may be obtained, with the physical enlargement ratio limited only by the structure of the enlarger and the size of the paper. As the image size is changed it is also necessary to change the focus of the lens. Some enlargers, such as Leica's "Autofocus" enlargers, perform this automatically.

An easel is used to hold the paper perfectly flat. Some easels are designed with adjustable overlapping flat steel "blades" to crop the image on the paper to the desired size while keeping an unexposed white border about the image. Paper is sometimes placed directly on the table or enlarger base, and held down flat with metal strips.

The enlargement is made by first focusing the image with the lamp on, the lens at maximum aperture and the easel empty, usually with the aid of a focus finder. The lamp is turned off, or in some cases, shuttered by a light-tight mechanism.

The image is focused by changing the distance between the lens and the film, achieved by adjusting the length of a light-tight bellows with a geared rack and pinion mechanism.

The lens is set to its working aperture. Enlarging lenses have an optimum range of apertures which yield a sharp image from corner to corner, often around f8. The lens is normally set to this aperture and any colour filtration dialed in, if making a colour print or one on variable-contrast black and white paper.

The enlarger's lamp or shutter mechanism is controlled either by an electronic timer, or by the operator—who marks time with a clock, metronome or simply by counting seconds—shuttering or turning off the lamp when the exposure is complete. The exposed paper can be processed immediately or placed in a light-tight container for later processing.

Digitally-controlled commercial enlargers typically adjust exposure in steps known as printer points; twelve printer points makes a factor of two change in exposure.

Paper Processing

After exposure, photographic paper is developed, fixed, washed and dried using the gelatin-silver process.

Automated Print Machines

Automated photo print machines comprise the same basic elements and integrate each of the steps outlined above in a single complex machine under operator and computer control. Rather than project directly from the film negative to the print paper, a digital image may first be captured from the negative. This allows the operator or computer to quickly determine adjustments to brightness, contrast, clipping, and other characteristics. The image is then rendered by passing light through negative and a built-in computer controlled enlarger optically projects this image to the paper for final exposure. As a byproduct of the process a compact disk recording may be made of the digital images, although a subsequent print made from these may be quite inferior to an image made from the negative due to digitization noise and lack of dynamic range which are characteristics of the digitizing process. For better images, the negatives may be reprinted using the same automated machine under operator selection of the print to be made. For better quality images the negatives should be reprinted using manually operated equipment as would be found in a specialty photographic store or laboratory. Highest quality images are obtained using several preliminary test images to determine the correct exposure and filter adjustments to obtain an appropriate effect.

Advantages

- The image may be printed to a size different than the negative or transparency. Without an enlarger, only a contact print would be possible, and large images would require large size negatives and hence very large cameras.
- Local contrast and density of various parts of the print can be easily controlled. Changing the amount of light exposing the paper in various areas will change the image density in those areas. A mask with a hole can be used to add extra light to an area "burning", which will have the effect of darkening the regions with additional exposure, while the use of a small wand to reduce the total exposure to a region is called "dodging" and has the effect of lightening the regions with reduced exposure. The tool is kept moving to avoid producing a sharp edge at the region boundary. Using these techniques it is possible to make significant changes to the mood or emphasis of a photographic print. Similar methods are available with contact printing, but it is more difficult to see the image as it is being manipulated.
- It is also possible to make composite photographs by overlaying the print with a hand-cut mask, performing an exposure, and then using the inverse of that mask to perform another exposure with a different negative. This is much

more difficult to do well using photographic methods than it is now by using the methods of modern digital image manipulation.

Image Enlargement Limits

The practical amount of enlargement (irrespective of the enlarger structure) will depend upon the grain size of the negative, the sharpness (accuracy) of both the camera and projector lenses, blur in the image due to subject motion and camera shake during the exposure, and the intended viewing distance of the final product.

For example, a 5 by 7 inch print intended for viewing in a scrapbook at 18 inches may be unsuitable for enlargement as an 8 by 10 inch print to be hung on a hallway wall to be viewed at the same distance, but usable at a larger 5 by 7 feet (twelve times larger) on a billboard to be viewed no closer than eighteen feet (twelve times more distant).

Manufacturers

Because of the change to digital, many manufacturers no longer make enlargers for the professional photographer. Durst, who made high quality enlargers, stopped producing them in 2005, but still supports already sold models. Manufacturers old and new include:

- Leitz
- Durst
- Dunco
- Meopta
- Beseler
- Omega
- Kaiser Fototechnik
- De Vere

INTERACTIVE WHITEBOARD

An interactive whiteboard is a large interactive display that connects to a computer and projector. A projector projects the computer's desktop onto the board's surface, where users control the computer using a pen, finger or other device. The board is typically mounted to a wall or on a floor stand.

They are used in a variety of settings such as in classrooms at all levels of education, in corporate board rooms and work groups, in training rooms for professional sports coaching, broadcasting studios and more.

The interactive-whiteboard industry is expected to reach sales of $1 billion worldwide by 2008; one of every seven classrooms in the world will feature an interactive whiteboard by 2011 according to market research by Futuresource Consulting.

Uses for interactive whiteboards include:

- Operating any softw are that is loaded onto the connected PC, including Internet browsers or proprietary software.
- Using software to capture notes written on a whiteboard or whiteboard-like surface.
- Controlling the PC (click and drag), mark-up (annotating a programme or presentation) and translating cursive writing to text (not all whiteboards).
- In some instances the Interactive Whiteboard may be provided with an integrated Audience Response System so presenters can carry out polls and quizzes and capture the feedback on the Interactive Whiteboard.

Operation

The interactive whiteboard is connected to a computer through a wired medium (USB, a serial port cable) or with a wireless connection (Bluetooth).

Usually, the device driver software is loaded onto the attached computer where it enables the Interactive Whiteboard to act as a Human Input Device (HID). The interactive whiteboard usually becomes active once connected and the driver is running.

Classroom Uses

Interactive whiteboards are used in many schools as replacements for traditional whiteboards or flipcharts or video/media systems such as a DVD player and TV combination. Users can also connect to a school network digital video distribution system using an Interactive Whiteboard. Interactive whiteboards can also interact with online shared annotation and drawing environments in the form of interactive vector based graphical websites.

The software supplied with the Interactive Whiteboard will usually allows the teacher to keep their notes and annotations as an electronic file for later distribution either on paper or through a number of electronic formats.

In addition, some interactive whiteboards allow teachers to record their instruction as digital video files and post the material for review by students at a later time. This can be a very effective instructional strategy for students who benefit from repetition, who need to see the material presented again, for students who are absent from school, for struggling learners, and for review for examinations. Brief instructional blocks can be recorded for review by students—they will see the exact presentation that occurred in the classroom with the teacher's audio input. This can help transform learning and instruction.

Many companies and projects now focus on creating supplemental instructional materials specifically designed for interactive whiteboards.

Integration with a Learner Response System

Some manufacturers are providing classroom response systems that are integrated with their interactive whiteboard products. These take the form of handheld 'clickers' operating via Infrared or Radio. Simple clickers offer basic multiple choice and polling options, while more sophisticated clickers offer text and numeric responses and will export an analysis of the student performance for subsequent review.

With classroom response and interactive whiteboard systems combined, teachers can present material and receive feedback from students in order to direct instruction more effectively as well as carry out formal assessments. For example, the interactive whiteboard allows students to solve puzzles and math problems and then demonstrate their knowledge through a test.

Research into Impact of Interactive Whiteboards on Education Standards

A substantial body of evidence is now emerging that looks at the impact of the Interactive Whiteboard technology on teaching and learning practices and student performance on standardized tests.

The DfES Primary Schools Whiteboard Expansion Project

Evidence of impacts on attainment when Interactive Whiteboards is appearing. The BECTA (UK) commissioned study into the impact of Interactive Whiteboards over a two year period showing very significant learning gains, particularly with second cohorts of students, where they benefited from the teacher's experience with the device.

The DfES Primary Schools Whiteboard Expansion project (PSWE) provided substantial funding to 21 Local Authorities in 2003-04 to support the acquisition and use of interactive whiteboards in UK primary schools.

The implementation and impacts of the project were evaluated by a team at Manchester Metropolitan University, led by Professor Bridget Somekh.

This major study into the impact of interactive technologies on student performance standards, involved 20 Local Authorities and 7272 learners in 97 schools. Variables considered in this detailed research included; length of exposure to interactive whiteboard technology, the age of pupils (down to individual birthdays), gender, special needs, entitlement to free schools meals and other socio-economic groupings. To date it is the largest and longest study conducted into the impact of Interactive Whiteboards.

Key Findings

The research showed that interactive whiteboard technology led to consistent gains across all key stages and subjects with increasingly significant impact on the second cohorts, indicating that embedding of the technology into the classroom and teacher experience with the technology are key factors.

Gains were measured in 'months progress' against standard measures of attainment over the two year study period.

In infant classes, ages 5-7:

- In Key Stage 1 Maths, high attaining girls made gains of 4.75 months over the two years, enabling them to catch up with high attaining boys.

- In Key Stage 1 Science, there was improved progress for girls of all attainment levels and for average and high attaining boys.
- In Key Stage 1 English, average and high attending pupils all benefited from increased exposure to interactive whiteboards.

There was also clear evidence of similar impacts in Key stage two ages 7-11:

- In Key Stage 2 Maths, average and high attaining boys and girls who had been taught extensively with the Interactive Whiteboard made the equivalent of an extra 2.5 to 5 months progress over the course of the two years.
- In Key Stage 2 Science, all pupils, except high attaining girls made greater progress with more exposure to the IWB, with low attaining boys making as much as 7.5 months additional progress.
- In Key Stage 2 writing, boys with low attainment made 2.5 months of additional progress.

There was no adverse impact observed at any level.

The study also indicated how interactive whiteboards have very positive impacts on the attention, attitude and motivation of all pupils and produces a co-operative, 'community of learning' ethos in the class. It also shows how Interactive Whiteboards help with teaching abstract and difficult concepts and complex ideas—visual tools help pupils concentrate for longer and understand more fully.

Becta summarizes the research as follows:

- *"This study clearly shows the benefits that can be gained from effective use of an interactive whiteboard. We know that technology has the capability of bringing lessons to life and making that much more enjoyable for the learner.*
- *Not only do the lessons become more fun, the study clearly shows the very real benefits in terms of learner attainment and engaging pupils in lessons."*

Impact on English Language Learner (ELL) Students

Lighting the Flame of Learning for English Language Learners Through the use of Interactive Whiteboard Technology by The Corporation for Public School Education K16 (2006) highlights the rising need to address students challenged by learning in their non-native language, identifying the Interactive Whiteboard as a powerful, multi-modal tool for supporting the effective social learning environment necessary for ELL students:

- *The active classroom's capacity to present a range of multimedia resources efficiently is also argued to help students learn. This is not only because there is more information available, there is also a wider variety of information so that ideas and concepts become more tangible and students find the concepts easier to assimilate (Levy, 2002). Moreover, teachers report that they can more easily accommodate a wider range of student learning styles using IWBs, when needed for particular students' needs (Bell, 2002; Billard, 2002).*

- *Walker-Tileston (2004) argues that children learn best through their dominant senses, seeing, hearing and touching. Active classrooms can appeal to all three senses simultaneously through a variety of visual representations, sounds and the capacity to touch and interact with the board.*

Digital Learning Classroom Project Findings

Impacts of Interactive Whiteboards on Pedagogy

Glover and Miller from Keele University highlight the following advantages of Interactive Whiteboard technology in teaching and learning contexts:

- *Theoretically, the interactive whiteboard is more than a computer, a projector, or a screen–its sum is greater than its parts, and when all the technology is turned off the board surface can be used as a conventional dry-wipe whiteboard should it be required. It can enable the teacher to use high-quality material previously prepared by a teacher or group of teachers using software packages, and to use multimedia material, including electronic microscopes, video-clips, board work, data tables, sketches, CD-ROM, or Internet images; and it facilitates simulation activities incorporating pupil input and reasoned discussion, and immediate recording of the contents of the board at any stage in the development of an argument*
- *Where teachers have access to an interactive whiteboard in their classroom, and can base their teaching around it, their reactions are unfailingly positive. The boards are seen as technology that empowers them, affords them creativity and enables them to provide learning experiences that meet the needs of all of their students. Those schools that have boards in all their classrooms have seen the greatest effects: those that have limited resources that have to be shared, or where they are restricted to ICT suites, have seen the least impact on the ways in which teachers teach and students learn. Despite that, there have been changes in teaching and learning within those specific areas.*

As with most educational technology, impact on improved pedagogy is a professional development issue:

- *If learners are to use the affordances offered by IWBs and become interactive autonomous learners then classroom organisation and the role of students needs to move away from a model based on curriculum content and didactic teaching. The problem is not with the technology, but rather the ways in which we choose to use it.*

A research review by the British Educational Communications and Technology Agency reported the following benefits for students:

- Increased enjoyment and motivation,
- Greater opportunities for participation and collaboration,
- Improved personal and social skills,
- Less need for note-taking,

- Ability to cope with more complex concepts,
- Accommodation for different learning styles, and
- Increased self-confidence.

Pedagogical Impacts of Using a Responder Technology with an Interactive Whiteboard

A number of Interactive Whiteboards designed for the education sector may be supplied with an integrated Audience Response System that allows the teacher to ask questions and elicit feedback from the audience. This data can be used either used to personalize instruction through dynamic assessment or, in the case of more sophisticated responder devices which allow the students to contribute their own ideas, involve the students in generating the content itself.

Henrico County Schools engaged in a study to determine *if the combination of the Interactive Whiteboard and the responder devices had a positive impact on the teaching/learning process*. The study was designed to determine if:

- The use of the interactive whiteboards with responder technology would increase student engagement in their learning.
- The use of the interactive whiteboards with responder software would allow for more frequent monitoring of student learning and allow for quick adjustments to the teaching process based on this monitoring.
- The use of interactive whiteboards with responder technology would be used as an information/communication tool and would raise the level of technology use/integration as a 21st century skill.
- The use of the interactive boards with responders would enhance student acquisition of content, concepts and skills taught using this technology.

The report concluded that:

- Students were more engaged in classes with teachers using Interactive Whiteboards and Responders when compared to their match classes. There was a doubling of students observed in higher level activities as defined by more student centered activity as compared with their match classes.
- Teachers in classrooms with Interactive Whiteboards and Responders asked students questions more frequently than their match classroom. They were also seen to monitor the learning of all students in the classroom more frequently than their match teacher.
- Teachers with the Interactive Whiteboards and Responders were observed to ask significantly more questions at the higher end of Bloom's Taxonomy—Application, Analysis, Synthesis and Application.
- Teachers with Interactive Whiteboards and Responders incorporated 21st century skills in the area of communication, problem solving, and collaboration more often than their match teachers.
- Students in classrooms with Interactive Whiteboards and Responders had a significantly higher pass rate on the Standards of Learning tests than their match class.

Criticisms

A report from London's Institute of Education on Interactive Whiteboards said: *"Although the newness of the technology was initially welcomed by pupils any boost in motivation seems short-lived. Statistical analysis showed no impact on pupil performance in the first year in which departments were fully equipped."*

The report highlighted the following issues:

- *Sometimes teachers focused more on the new technology than on what pupils should be learning.*
- *The focus on interactivity as a technical process can lead to some relatively mundane activities being over-valued. Such an emphasis on interactivity was particularly prevalent in classes with lower-ability students.*
- *In lower-ability groups it could actually slow the pace of whole class learning as individual pupils took turns at the board.*

Only around 1 in 15 of the teachers studied had received any form of training or professional development in the use of the technology which is considered by commentators as a key factor in the deployment of anything intended to impact teaching and learning.

Academic Literature Reviews and Research

There are a number of literature reviews, findings and papers on the use of interactive whiteboards in the classroom:

- DCSF and Becta (2007) Evaluation of the DCSF Primary Schools Whiteboard Expansion Project.
- Painter, D. Whiting, E. and Wolters, B. (2005) The Use of an Interactive Whiteboard in promoting interactive teaching and learning.
- Beauchamp, G. and Parkinson, J. (2005) Beyond the wow factor: developing interactivity with the interactive whiteboard. School Science Review (86) 316: 97-103.
- Glover, D., Miller D., Averis D. and Door V. (2005) The interactive whiteboard: a literature survey. Technology, Pedagogy and Education (14) 2: 155-170.
- Moss, G., Jewitt C., Levaĉic' R., Armstrong V., Cardini A. and Castle F., Allen B., Jenkins A. and Hancock M. with High S. (2007) The Interactive Whiteboards, Pedagogy and Pupil Performance Evaluation: An Evaluation of the Schools Whiteboard Expansion (SWE) Project: London Challenge http://www.dfes.gov.uk/research/data/uploadfiles/RR816.pdf
- Smith, H. J., Higgins S., Wall K., and Miller J. (2005) Interactive whiteboards: boon or bandwagon? A critical review of the literature, Journal of Computer Assisted Learning, 21(2), pp. 91-101.

Interactive Whiteboard Technologies

Interactive whiteboards may use one of several types of sensing technology to track interaction on the screen surface: resistive, electromagnetic, infrared optical, laser, ultra-sonic, and camera-based (optical).

- *Optical and Infrared*—When pressed to the whiteboard surface, the finger or marker sees the infrared light. Software then manipulates the information to triangulate the location of the marker or stylus. This technology allows whiteboards to be made of any material; with this system no dry-erase marker or stylus is needed. In 2007, Carnegie Mellon University PhD student Johnny Chung Lee demonstrated a low-cost method of this type of whiteboard, using the infrared camera inside a Wii Remote video game controller. Lee provides tutorial videos, and the software required to run the system for free on his website.
- *Resistive*—Resistive touchscreens are composed of two flexible sheets coated with a resistive material and separated by an air gap or microdots. When contact is made to the surface of the touchscreen, the two sheets are pressed together, registering the precise location of the touch. This technology allows one to use a finger, a stylus, or any other pointing device on the surface of the board. By their nature they do not support the full function of a mouse and interface effects such as hover/popups require additional interactions or software helper functions. Resistive touchscreens typically have a resolution of 4096 × 4096 DPI providing accurate touch control.
- *Electromagnetic*—These digital boards feature an array of wires embedded behind the board surface interacts with a coil in the stylus tip to determine the (X, Y) coordinate of the stylus. Styli are either active (require a battery or wire back to the whiteboard) or passive (alter electrical signals produced by the board, but contain no power source). In other words, there are magnetic sensors in the board that react and send a message back to the computer when they are activated by a magnetic pen. These types of board usually support the full range of mouse functions, mouseover, hover effects and right click and are directly related to Graphics Tablets used by professional digital artists and designers. They may accommodate pressure sensing and multiple users touching and pointing on the surface. Electromagnetic touchscreens typically have a resolution of 30,000 × 30,000 DPI.
- *Capacitive*—Just like the electromagnetic type, the capacitive type works with an array of wires behind the board. In this case however the wires interact with fingers touching the screen. The interaction between the different wires (laminated in a patented X- and Y-axis manner) and the tip of the finger is measured and calculated to a (x, y) coordinate.
- *Laser*—An infrared laser is located in each upper corner of the whiteboard. The laser beam sweeps across the whiteboard surface—much like a lighthouse sweeps light across the ocean—by using a rotating mirror. Reflectors on the stylus or marker reflect the laser beam back to the source and the (X, Y) position can be triangulated. This technology may be combined with a hard (usually

ceramic on steel) surface, which has long life and erases cleanly. Markers and styli are passive, but must have reflective tape to work.

- *Ultrasonic and Infrared*—When pressed to the whiteboard surface, the marker or stylus sends out both an ultrasonic sound and an infrared light. Two ultrasonic microphones receive the sound and measure the difference in the sound's arrival time, and triangulate the location of the marker or stylus. This technology allows whiteboards to be made of any material, but requires a suitably adapted active dry-erase marker or stylus.
- *Ultrasonic only*—These devices have two ultrasonic transmitters in two corners and two receivers in the other two corners. The ultrasonic waves are transmitted by the whiteboard surface. Some little marks in the whiteboard borders create reflecting waves for each ultrasonic transmiter at different and recognizable distances. Touching with a pen or even the finger in the whiteboard causes these point waves to be suppressed, and the receivers communicate the fact to the controller.
- *Frustrated Internal Reflection*—Infrared light bounces within a flexible and transparent surface. When the surface is deformed through a finger press the internal reflection is disrupted and the light escapes the surface where it is then sensed by cameras. Image processing software turns the light spots observed by the cameras into mouse or pointer movements.
- *Using digital pens (e.g. Anoto)*—The embedded IR-cameras of the pen can track a tiny dot-pattern which can be printed on a large piece of paper (or on a special rear-projection foil). This technology allows a highly accurate tracking with approximately 600 dpi. Moreover, the tracking results are independent from the shape and from the size.

Potential Issues

Interactive whiteboards have some issues similar to regular whiteboards. Permanent markers, for example, can create problems on some interactive whiteboard surfaces. Punctures, dents and other damage to surfaces are a risk with membrane based devices but do not typically occur in the normal course of classroom use.

Front and Rear Projection

Interactive whiteboards are generally available in two forms: front projection and rear projection.

- Front-projection interactive whiteboards have a video projector in front of the whiteboard. The only disadvantage to these boards is that the presenter must stand in front of the screen and their body will cast a shadow. Presenters quickly learn to compensate for the shadow by slightly extending their arm with or without a stylus.
- Rear-projection interactive whiteboards locate the projector or emmisive display behind the whiteboard sensing surface so that no shadows occur. Rear-projection boards are also advantageous because the presenter does not have

to look into the projector light while speaking to the audience. The disadvantages of these systems are that they are generally more expensive than front-projection boards, are often very large, and cannot be mounted flush on a wall; however, in-wall installations are possible.

Some manufacturers also provide an option to raise and lower the display to accommodate users of different heights.

Short-Throw Projection Systems and Interactive Whiteboards

Some manufacturers offer short-throw projection systems in which a projector with a special wide angle lens is mounted much closer to the interactive whiteboard surface and projects down at an angle of around 45°. These vastly reduce the shadow effects of traditional front-projection systems and eliminate any chance for a user to see the projector beam. The risk of projector theft, which is problematic for some school districts, is reduced by integrating the projector with the interactive whiteboard.

At least one manufacturer has provided a unified system where the whiteboards, short throw projection system and audio system are all combined into a single unit which can also move up and down and enable young children and those in wheelchairs to access all areas of the board. Reduced installation costs make these very cost effective.

Calibration

In most cases, the touch surface must be initially calibrated with the display image. This process involves displaying a sequence of dots or crosses on the touch surface and having the user select these dots either with a stylus or their finger. This process is called alignment, calibration, or orientation. Fixed installations with projectors and boards bolted to roof and wall greatly reduce or eliminate the need to calibrate.

A few interactive whiteboards can automatically detect projected images during a different type of calibration. The technology was developed by Mitsubishi Electric Research Laboratories, Inc and is disclosed in patent 7,001,023. The computer projects a Gray Code sequence of white and black bars on the touch surface and light sensitive sensors behind the touch surface detect the light passing through the touch surface. This sequence allows the computer to align the touch surface with the display; however, it has the disadvantage of having "dead spots" in the resistive touch surface where the light sensors are present. The "dead spots" do not allow touches in that area to be presented to the computer.

Associated Equipment

A variety of accessories is available for interactive whiteboards:

- *Projector*—Allows a computer display to be projected onto the whiteboard. 'Short Throw' projectors are available from some manufacturers that mount directly above the board minimizing shadow effects.

- *Track*—Allows the whiteboard to be placed over a traditional whiteboard or tackboard to provide additional wall space at the front of the room. Some tracks provide power and data to the whiteboard as well.
- *Mobile stand*—Allows the interactive whiteboard to be moved between rooms. Many are height adjustable as well.
- *Printer*—Allows copies of the whiteboard notes to be made.
- *Slate or tablet*—Allows students control of the whiteboard away from the front of the room.
- *Personal Response System*—Allows students to answer test questions posted on the whiteboard or take part in polls and surveys.
- *Wireless unit*—Allows the interactive whiteboard to operate without wires to the computer, *e.g.* Bluetooth.
- *Remote control*—Allows the presenter to control the board from different parts of the room and eliminates on-screen toolbars.

6

Television and Television Systems: Types, Components and Standards

TELEVISION

Television is a widely used telecommunication medium for sending (broadcasting) and receiving moving images, either monochromatic ("black and white") or colour, usually accompanied by sound. "Television" may also refer specifically to a television set, television programming or television transmission. The word is derived from mixed Latin and Greek roots, meaning "far sight": Greek *tele* = far, and Latin *visio*, sight (from *video, vis-* to see, or to view in the first person).

Commercially available since the late 1930s, the television set has become a common communications receiver in homes, businesses and institutions, particularly as a source of entertainment and news. Since the 1970s, recordings on video cassettes, and later, digital media such as DVDs, have resulted in the television frequently being used for viewing recorded as well as broadcast material.

A standard television set comprises multiple internal electronic circuits, including those for tuning and decoding broadcast signals. A display device which lacks these internal circuits is therefore properly called a monitor, rather than a television. A television set may be designed to handle other than traditional broadcast or recorded signals and formats, such as closed-circuit television (CCTV), digital television (DTV) and high-definition television (HDTV).

History

In its early stages of development, television included only those devices employing a combination of optical, mechanical and electronic technologies to capture, transmit and display a visual image. By the late 1920s, however, those employing only optical and electronic technologies were being explored. All modern television systems rely on the latter, however the knowledge gained from the work on mechanical-dependent systems was crucial in the development of fully electronic television.

In 1884 Paul Gottlieb Nipkow, a 20-year old university student in Germany patented the first electromechanical television system which employed a scanning disk, a spinning disk with a series of holes spiraling toward the center, for "rasterization", the process of converting a visual image into a stream of electrical pulses. The holes were spaced at equal angular intervals such that in a single rotation the disk would allow light to pass through each hole and onto a light-sensitive selenium sensor which produced the electrical pulses. As an image was focused on the rotating disk, each hole captured a horizontal "slice" of the whole image.

Nipkow's design would not be practical until advances in amplifier tube technology became available in 1907. Even then the device was only useful for transmitting still halftone images—those represented by equally spaced dots of varying size—over telegraph or telephone lines. Later designs would use a rotating mirror-drum scanner to capture the image and a cathode ray tube (CRT) as a display device, but moving images were still not possible, due to the poor sensitivity of the selenium sensors.

Scottish inventor John Logie Baird demonstrated the transmission of moving silhouette images in London in 1925, and of moving, monochromatic images in 1926. Baird's scanning disk produced an image of 30 lines resolution, barely enough to discern a human face, from a double spiral of lenses.

By 1927, Russian inventor Léon Theremin developed a mirror drum-based television system which used interlacing to achieve an image resolution of 100 lines.

Also in 1927, Herbert E. Ives of Bell Labs transmitted moving images from a 50-aperture disk producing 16 frames per minute over a cable from Washington, DC to New York City, and via radio from Whippany, New Jersey. Ives used viewing screens as large as 24 by 30 inches (60 by 75 centimeter). His subjects included Secretary of Commerce Herbert Hoover.

In 1928, Philo Farnsworth made the world's first working television system with electronic scanning of both the pickup and display devices, which he first demonstrated to news media on 1928, televising a motion picture film.

Geographical Usage

Timeline of the introduction of television in countries.

Content Programming

Getting TV programming shown to the public can happen in many different ways. After production the next step is to market and deliver the product to whatever markets are open to using it. This typically happens on two levels:

1. *Original Run* or *First Run*—A producer creates a programme of one or multiple episodes and shows it on a station or network which has either paid for the production itself or to which a license has been granted by the producers to do the same.
2. *Syndication*—This is the terminology rather broadly used to describe secondary programming usages (beyond original run). It includes secondary runs in the country of first issue, but also international usage which may or may not be managed by the originating producer. In many cases other companies, TV stations or individuals are engaged to do the syndication work, in other words to sell the product into the markets they are allowed to sell into by contract from the copyright holders, in most cases the producers.

First run programming is increasing on subscription services outside the U.S., but few domestically produced programmes are syndicated on domestic FTA elsewhere. This practice is increasing however, generally on digital-only FTA channels, or with subscriber-only first run material appearing on FTA.

Unlike the U.S., repeat FTA screenings of a FTA network programme almost only occur on that network. Also, Affiliates rarely buy or produce non-network programming that is not centred around local events.

Funding

Around the globe, broadcast television is financed by either government, advertising, licensing (a form of tax), subscription or any combination of these. To protect revenues, subscription TV channels are usually encrypted to ensure that only subscription payers receive the decryption codes to see the signal. Non-encrypted channels are known as Free-to-Air or FTA.

Advertising

Advertising attempts to influence people's behaviour and beliefs and television is therefore a powerful and attractive medium for advertisers to use. TV stations sell air time to advertisers in order to fund their programming.

United States

Since inception in the U.S. in 1940, TV commercials have become one of the most effective, persuasive, and popular method of selling products of many sorts, especially consumer goods. U.S. advertising rates are determined primarily by Nielsen Ratings. The time of the day and popularity of the channel determine how much a television commercial can cost. For example, the highly popular American Idol can cost approximately $ 750,000 for a thirty second block of commercial time; while the same amount of time for the World Cup and the Super Bowl can cost several million dollars.

In recent years, the paid programme or infomercial has become common, usually in lengths of 30 minutes or one hour. Some drug companies and other businesses have even created "news" items for broadcast, known in the industry as video news releases, paying programme directors to use them.

Some TV programmes also weave advertisements into their shows, a practice begun in film and known as product placement. For example, a character could be drinking a certain kind of soda, going to a particular chain restaurant, or driving a certain make of car. (This is sometimes very subtle, where shows have vehicles provided by manufacturers for low cost, rather than wrangling them.) Sometimes a specific brand or trade mark, or music from a certain artist or group, is used. (This excludes guest appearances by artists, who perform on the show.)

United Kingdom

The TV regulator oversees TV advertising in the United Kingdom. Its restrictions have applied since the early days of commercially funded TV. Despite this, an early TV mogul, Lew Grade, likened the broadcasting licence as a being a "licence to print money". Restrictions mean that the big three national commercial TV channels, ITV, Channel 4, and Five can show an average of only seven minutes of advertising per hour (eight minutes in the peak period). Other broadcasters must average no more than nine minutes (twelve in the peak). This means that many imported TV shows from the US have unnatural breaks where the UK company has edited out the breaks intended for US advertising. Advertisements must not be inserted in the course of any broadcast of a news or current affairs programme of less than half an hour scheduled duration, or in a documentary of less than half an hour scheduled duration, or in a programme for children of less than half an hour scheduled duration. Nor may advertisements be carried in a programme designed and broadcast for reception in schools or in any religious service or other devotional program, or during a formal Royal ceremony or occasion. There also must be clear demarcations in time between the programs and the advertisements.

The BBC, being strictly non-commercial is not allowed to show advertisements on television in the UK, although it has many advertising-funded channels abroad. The majority of its budget comes from TV licencing (see below) and the sale of content to other broadcasters.

Taxation or TV License

Television services in some countries may be funded by a television licence, a form of taxation which means advertising plays a lesser role or no role at all. For example, some channels may carry no advertising at all and some very little.

- United Kingdom (BBC)
- Australia (ABC)
- Sweden (SVT)
- Norway (NRK)

The BBC carries no advertising on its UK channels and is funded by an annual licence paid by all households owning a television. This licence fee is set by government, but the BBC is not answerable to or controlled by government and is therefore genuinely independent.

The two main BBC TV channels are watched by almost 90 per cent of the population each week and overall have 27 per cent share of total viewing. This in spite of the fact that 85 per cent of homes are multichannel, with 42 per cent of these having access to 200 Free-to-Air channels via satellite and another 43 per cent having access to 30 or more channels via Freeview. The licence that funds the seven advertising-free BBC TV channels costs less than £136 a year (about US$270) irrespective of the number of TV sets owned. When the same sporting event has been presented on both BBC and commercial channels, the BBC always attracts the lion's share of the audience, indicating viewers prefer to watch TV uninterrupted by advertising.

The Australian Broadcasting Corporation (ABC) carries no advertising (except for the ABC shop) as it is banned under law ABC Act 1983. The ABC receives its funding from the Australian Government every three years. In the 2006/07 Federal Budget the ABC received Au$822.67 million this covers most of the ABC funding commitments and as with the BBC also funds radio channels, transmitters and the ABC websites. The ABC also receives funds from its many ABC Shops in Australia.

Subscription

Some TV channels are partly funded from subscriptions and therefore the signals are encrypted before broadcast to ensure that only paying subscribers have access to the decryption codes. Most subscription services are also funded by advertising.

Television Genres

Television genres include a broad range of programming types that entertain, inform, and educate viewers. The most expensive entertainment genres to produce are usually drama and dramatic miniseries. However, other genres, such as historical Western genres, may also have high production costs.

Popular entertainment genres include action-oriented shows such as police, crime, detective dramas, horror or thriller shows. As well, there are also other variants of the drama genre, such as medical dramas and daytime soap operas. Science fiction shows can fall into either the drama or action category, depending on whether they emphasize philosophical questions or high adventure. Comedy is a popular genre which includes situation comedy (sitcom) and animated shows for the adult demographic such as *South Park.*

The least expensive forms of entertainment programming are game shows, talk shows, variety shows, and reality TV. Game shows show contestants answering questions and solving puzzles to win prizes. Talk shows feature interviews with film, television and music celebrities and public figures. Variety shows feature a range of musical performers and other entertainers such as comedians and magicians introduced by a host or Master of Ceremonies. There is some crossover between some talk shows and variety shows, because leading talk shows often feature performances by bands, singers, comedians, and other performers in between the interview segments. *Reality TV* shows "regular" people (*i.e.,* not actors) who are facing unusual challenges or experiences, ranging from arrest by police officers (*COPS*) to weight loss (*The Biggest Loser*). A variant version of reality shows depicts celebrities doing mundane activities such as going about their everyday life (*The Osbournes*) or doing manual labour (*Simple Life*).

Social Aspects

Television has played a pivotal role in the socialization of the 20th and 21st centuries. There are many social aspects of television that can be addressed, including:

- Positive effects,
- Negative effects,
- Gender and television,
- Politics and television,
- Socializing children,
- Technology trends,

- ❑ Suitability for audience,
- ❑ Alleged dangers,
- ❑ Propaganda delivery, and
- ❑ Educational advantages.

Environmental Aspects

With high lead content in CRTs, and the rapid diffusion of new, flat-panel display technologies, some of which (LCDs) use lamps containing mercury, there is growing concern about electronic waste from discarded televisions. Related occupational health concerns exist, as well, for disassemblers removing copper wiring and other materials from CRTs. Further environmental concerns related to television design and use relate to the devices' increasing electrical energy requirements.

In Numismatics

Television has had such an impact in today's life, that it has been the main motif for numerous collectors' coins and medals. One of the most recent ones is the Austrian 50 years of Television commemorative coin minted in March 9, 2005. The obverse of the coin shows a "test pattern", while the reverse shows several milestones in the history of television.

Fig. 6.1: The 50 years of Television commemorative coin.

TERRESTRIAL TELEVISION

Terrestrial television is a term which refers to modes of television broadcasting which do not involve satellite transmission. The term is uncommon in the United States, and more common in Europe.

Terrestrial television broadcasting dates back to the very beginnings of television as a medium itself with the first long-distance public television broadcast from Washington, D.C., on April 7, 1927. Aside from transmission by high-flying planes moving in a loop using a system developed by Westinghouse called Stratovision, there was virtually no other method of television delivery until the 1950s with the beginnings of cable television, or *community antenna television* (CATV). The first non-terrestrial method of delivering television signals that in no way depended on a signal originating from a traditional terrestrial source began with the use of communications satellites during the 1960s and 1970s.

Europe

In Europe, a planning conference ("ST61") held under the auspices of the International Telecommunications Union in Stockholm in 1961 allocated frequencies the Bands IV and V for the first time for broadcast television use. It also superseded the 1951 Plan (also made in Stockholm) which had first allocated Band II frequencies for FM radio and Band III frequencies for television.

Following the ST61 conference, UHF frequencies were first used in the UK in 1964 with the introduction of BBC2. In UK, VHF channels were kept on the old 405-line system, while UHF was used solely for 625-line broadcasts (which later used PAL colour). Television broadcasting in the 405-line system continued after the introduction of four analogue programmes in the UHF bands until the last 405-line transmitters were switched off on January 6, 1985. VHF Band III is still used in other countries around Europe for PAL broadcasts, though many have plans to phase it out.

The success of terrestrial analogue television across Europe varies from country to country. Although each country has rights to a certain number of frequencies by virtue of the ST61 plan, not all of them have been bought into service.

North America

In the United States and most of the rest of North America as well, terrestrial television underwent a revolutionary transformation with the eventual acceptance of the NTSC standard for colour television broadcasts in 1953. Later, Europe and the rest of the world either chose between the later PAL and SECAM colour television standards, or adopted NTSC. Japan also uses a version of NTSC.

In addition to the threat from Cable Television, analog terrestrial television is now also subject to competition from satellite television and distribution of video and film content over the Internet. The technology of digital terrestrial television has been developed as a response to these challenges. The rise of digital terrestrial television, especially HDTV, may mark an end to the decline of broadcast television reception via traditional receiving antennas, which can receive over-the-air HDTV signals.

In North America, terrestrial broadcast television operates on TV channels 2 through 6 (VHF-low band, known as band I in Europe), 7 through 13 (VHF-high band, known as band III elsewhere), and 14 through 69 (UHF television band, elsewhere bands IV and V). Channel numbers represent actual frequencies used to broadcast the television signal. Additionally, television translators and boosters can be used to rebroadcast a terrestrial TV signal using an otherwise unused channel to cover areas with marginal reception. A chart showing the North American television bandplan can be found here.

Digital Television

By the mid 1990s, the interest in digital television across Europe was such the CEPT convened the "Chester '97" conference to agree means by which digital television could be inserted into the ST61 frequency plan.

The introduction of digital television in the late 1990s and early years of the 21st century led the ITU to call a Regional Radiocommunication Conference to abrogate the ST61 plan and to put a new plan for digital broadcasting only in its place.

In December 2005 the EU has decided to cease all analogue television transmissions by the year 2012 and switch all terrestrial television broadcasting to digital (all EU countries have agreed on using DVB-T). The Netherlands completed the transition in December 2006, and some EU member states have decided to complete this switchover as early as 2008 (Sweden) and 2009 (Denmark), while the UK began the switch over in late 2007 it will not be a nationwide switch over until mid-2012. Two member states (not specified in the announcement) have expressed concerns that they might not be able to proceed to the switchover by 2012 due to technical limitations, the rest of the EU member states are expected to stop analogue television transmissions by 2012.

Many countries are developing and evaluating digital terrestrial television systems.

In North America a specification laid out by the ATSC has become the standard for digital terrestrial television. In the United States the FCC has set a final deadline for the switchoff of analog service for February 17, 2009. All television receivers must now include a digital tuner. In Canada, the Canadian Radio-television and Telecommunications Commission (CRTC), has set August 31, 2011 as the date that over-the-air analog transmission service will cease in most parts of the country except in Northern Canada.

DIGITAL TELEVISION

Digital television (DTV) is the sending and receiving of moving images and sound by discrete (digital) signals, in contrast to the analog signals used by analog TV. Introduced in the late 1990s, this technology appealed to the television broadcasting business and consumer electronics industries because it offers new financial opportunities.

Digital television is more flexible and efficient than analog television. When properly used by broadcasters, digital television can allow higher-quality images, sound, and more programming choices than analog does. However, a digital signal does not necessarily carry a higher-quality image or sound than an analog signal.

After February 17, 2009, *full-power* television stations in the USA will broadcast in digital only.

While the majority of the viewed TV broadcast stations are full-power stations, about 1800 in number, there are three other categories of TV stations that exist: "low-power" stations, "Class A" stations, and "TV translator" stations. There is presently *no deadline* for these stations, about 7100 in number, to convert to digital broadcasting.

Technical Information

Formats and Bandwidth

With digital television, two formats—HDTV and SDTV—of TV programmes are broadcast.

High-definition television (HDTV), which is usually used over DTV, uses one of two formats: 1280 × 720 pixels in progressive scan mode (abbreviated *720p*) or 1920 × 1080 pixels in interlace mode (*1080i*). Each of these utilizes a 16:9 aspect ratio.

(Some televisions are capable of receiving an HD resolution of 1920 × 1080 at a 60 Hz progressive scan frame rate—known as 1080p60—but this format is not standard and no broadcaster is able to transmit these signals over the air at acceptable quality yet.)

Standard definition TV (SDTV), by comparison, may use one of several different formats taking the form of various aspect ratios depending on the technology used in the country of broadcast. For 4:3 aspect-ratio broadcasts, the 640 × 480 format is used in countries, while 720 × 576 (rescaled to 768 × 576) is used in PAL countries. For 16:9 broadcasts, the 704 × 480 (rescaled to 848 × 480) format is used in NTSC countries, while 720 × 576 (rescaled to 1024 × 576) is used in PAL countries. However, broadcasters may choose to reduce these resolutions to save bandwidth (*e.g.*, many DVB-T channels in the United Kingdom use a horizontal resolution of 544 or 704 pixels per line). The perceived quality of such programming is surprisingly acceptable because of interlacing—the effective vertical resolution is halved to 288 lines.

Each DTV channel is permitted to be broadcast at a data rate up to 19 megabits per second, or 2.375 megabytes per second. However, the broadcaster does not need to use this entire bandwidth for just one broadcast channel. Instead the broadcast can be subdivided across several video subchannels of varying quality and compression rates, including non-video datacasting services that allow one-way high-bandwidth streaming of data to computers.

A broadcaster may opt to use a standard-definition digital signal instead of an HDTV signal, because current convention allows the bandwidth of a DTV channel (or "multiplex") to be subdivided into multiple subchannels (similar to what most FM stations offer with HD Radio), providing multiple feeds of entirely different programming on the same channel. This ability to provide either a single HDTV feed or multiple lower-resolution feeds are often referred to as distributing one's "bit budget" or multicasting. This can sometimes be arranged automatically, using a statistical multiplexer (or "stat-mux"). With some implementations, image resolution may be less directly limited by bandwidth; for example in DVB-T, broadcasters can choose from several different modulation schemes, giving them the option to reduce the transmission bitrate and make reception easier for more distant or mobile viewers.

Reception

There are a number of different ways to receive digital television. One of the oldest means of receiving DTV (and TV in general) is using an antenna (known as an *aerial* in some countries). This way is known as Digital Terrestrial Television (DTT). With DTT, viewers are limited to whatever channels the antenna picks up. Signal quality will also vary.

Other ways have been devised to receive digital television. Among the most familiar to people are digital cable and digital satellite. In some countries where transmissions of TV signals are normally achieved by microwaves, digital MMDS is used. Other standards, such as DMB and DVB-H, have been devised to allow handheld devices such as mobile phones to receive TV signals. Another way is IPTV, that is receiving TV via Internet Protocol, relying on DSL or optical cable line. Finally, an alternative way is to receive digital TV signals via the open Internet. For example, there is a lot of P2P Internet Television software that can be used to watch TV on your computer.

Some signals carry encryption and specify use conditions (such as "may not be recorded" or "may not be viewed on displays larger than 1 m in diagonal measure") backed up with the force of law under the WIPO Copyright Treaty and national legislation implementing it, such as the U.S. Digital Millennium Copyright Act. Access to encrypted channels can be controlled by a removable smart card, for example via the Common Interface (DVB-CI) standard for Europe and via Point Of Deployment (POD) for IS or named differently CableCard.

Protection Parameters for Terrestrial DTV Broadcasting

In order for digital television to be broadcast, it must initially interoperate with analog television. When analog television ceases to exist, digital television signals must not interfere with each other. Propagation research carried out by several important digital television regulators has derived a table of acceptable parameters for tolerable interference margins. This table below provides all the important acceptable interference margins.

System Parameters (protection ratios)	*Canada*	*USA*	*EBU ITU-mode M3*	*Japan & Brazil*
C/N for AWGN Channel	+19.5 dB (16.5 dB)	+15.19 dB	+19.3 dB	+19.2 dB
Co-Channel DTV into Analog TV	+33.8 dB	+34.44 dB	+34 ~ 37 dB	+38 dB
Co-Channel Analog TV into DTV	+7.2 dB	+1.81 dB	+4 dB	+4 dB
Co-Channel DTV into DTV	+19.5 dB (16.5 dB)	+15.27 dB	+19 dB	+19 dB
Lower Adjacent Channel DTV into Analog TV	–16 dB	–17.43 dB	–5 ~ –11 dB	–6 dB
Upper Adjacent Channel DTV into Analog TV	–12 dB	–11.95 dB	–1 ~ –10db	–5 dB
Lower Adjacent Channel Analog TV into DTV	–48 dB	–47.33 dB	–34 ~ –37 dB	–35 dB
Upper Adjacent Channel Analog TV into DTV	–49 dB	–48.71 dB	– 38 ~ –36 dB	–37 dB
Lower Adjacent Channel DTV into DTV	–27 dB	–28 dB	–30 dB	–28 dB
Upper Adjacent Channel DTV into DTV	–27 dB	–26 dB	–30 dB	–29 dB

Interaction

Interaction happens between the TV watcher and the DTV system. It can be understood in different ways, depending on which part of the DTV system is concerned. It can also be an interaction with the STB only (to tune to another TV channel or to browse the EPG).

Modern DTV systems are able to provide interaction between the end-user and the broadcaster through the use of a return path. With the exceptions of coaxial and fiber optic cable, which can be bidirectional, a dialup modem, Internet connection, or other method is typically used for the return path with unidirectional networks such as satellite or antenna broadcast.

In addition to not needing a separate return path, cable also has the advantage of a communication channel localized to a neighbourhood rather than a city (terrestrial) or an even larger area (satellite). This provides enough customizable bandwidth to allow true video on demand.

Advantages to Conversion

DTV has several advantages over analog TV, the most significant being that digital channels take up less bandwidth (and the bandwidth needs are continuously variable, at a corresponding cost in image quality depending on the level of compression). This means that digital broadcasters can provide more digital channels in the same space, provide high-definition television service, or provide other non-television services such as multimedia or interactivity. DTV also permits special services such as multiplexing (more than one programme on the same channel), electronic programme guides and additional languages, spoken or subtitled. The sale of non-television services may provide an additional revenue source. In many cases, viewers perceive DTV to have superior picture quality, improved audio quality, and easier reception than analog.

Disadvantages to Conversion

Impact on Existing Analog Technology

The analog switch-off ruling, which so far has met with little opposition from consumers or manufacturers, would render all non-digital televisions obsolete on the switch-off date unless connected to an external off-the-air tuner, analog or digital cable, or a satellite system. An external converter box can be added to non-digital televisions to lengthen their useful lifespan. Several of these devices have already been shown and, while few were initially available, they are becoming more available by the day. In the United States, a government-sponsored coupon is available to offset the cost of an external converter box. Once connected to the converter unit, operation of non-digital units is achievable and, in most cases, rich in new features (in comparison to previous analog reception operation). At present, analog switchoff is scheduled for February 17, 2009 in the United States and August 31, 2011 in Canada.

Some existing analog equipment will be less functional with the use of a converter box. For example, television remote controls will no longer be effective at changing channels, because that function will instead be handled by the converter box. Similarly, video recorders for analog signals (including both tape-based VCRs and hard-drive-based DVRs) will not be able to select channels, limiting their ability to automatically record programmes via a timer or based on downloaded programme information. ATSC-capable VCRs are likely to be far less common than their NTSC counterparts, with most current offerings being VCR/DVD combo units. Also, older handheld televisions, which rely primarily on over-the-air signals and battery operation, will be rendered impractical since the proposed converter boxes are not portable nor powered with batteries.

Portable radios that are able to listen to television audio on VHF channels 2-13 would also lose this ability, while television stations which formerly broadcast on

Channel 6 (with analog FM audio on 87.75 MHz) would no longer be heard on standard FM broadcast band radios. These stations would lose the ability for commuters to listen to their broadcasts.

If any new TVs contained only an ATSC tuner, this could prevent older devices such as VCRs and video game consoles with only an analog RF output from connecting to the TV. Connection would require an analog to digital converter box, which is the opposite of what is currently being sold. Such a box would also likely introduce additional delay into the video signal. Fortunately, analog inputs suitable for connection to VCRs have remained available on all current digital-capable TV's.

Compression Artifacts and Allocated Bandwidth

DTV images have some picture defects that are not present on analog television or motion picture cinema, because of present-day limitations of bandwidth and compression algorithms such as MPEG-2.

When a compressed digital image is compared with the original programme source, some hard-to-compress image sequences may have digital distortion or degradation. For example:

- Quantization noise,
- Incorrect colour,
- Blockiness, and
- A blurred, shimmering haze.

Broadcasters attempt to balance their needs to show high quality pictures and to generate revenue by using a fixed bandwidth allocation for more services.

Buffering and Preload Delay

Unlike analog televisions, digital televisions have a significant delay when changing channels, making "channel surfing" more difficult.

Different devices need different amounts of preload time to begin showing the broadcast stream, resulting in an undesirable and annoying audio echo effect when two televisions in adjacent rooms of a house are tuned to the same channel.

Effects of Poor Reception

Changes in signal reception from factors such as degrading antenna connections or worsening weather conditions may gradually reduce the quality of analog TV. The nature of digital TV results in a perfect picture initially, until the receiving equipment starts picking up noise or losing signal. Some equipment will show a picture even with significant damage, while other devices may go directly from perfect to no picture at all (and thus not show even a slightly damaged picture). This latter effect is known as the *digital cliff* or cliff effect.

For remote locations, distant analog channels that were previously acceptable in a snowy and degraded state may be anything from perfect to completely unavailable. The use of higher frequencies will add to these problems, especially in cases where a clear line-of-sight from the receiving antenna to the transmitter is not available. Many intermittent signal fading conditions, such as the rapid-fade effect caused by reflections of UHF television signals from passing aircraft, will not produce intermittently-snowy video, but potential intermittent loss of the entire signal.

Multi-path interference is a much more significant problem for DTV than for analog TV and affects reception, particularly when using simple antennas such as rabbit ears. This is perceived as "ghosting" in the analog domain, but this same problem manifests itself in a much more insidious way with DTV. Unlike the problems of the preceding paragraph, multi path can in fact be worse for DTV under high signal conditions. It is perceived by the viewer as a spotty loss of audio or picture freezing and pixelation as people move about in the vicnity of the antenna and is often worse in wet weather due to increased reflection re-polarization of the DTV signal arriving from multiple paths. In extreme cases—the signal is lost completely. The cure is to employ a directional antenna outdoors, aligned with the transmitting location.

Limitations

The greatest DTV detail level currently available is 1080i, which is a 1920x1080 interlaced widescreen format. Interlacing is done to reduce the image bandwidth to one-half of full-frame quality, which gives better frame update speed for quick-changing scenes such as sports, but at the same time reduces the overall image quality and introduces image flickering and "crawling scanlines" because of the alternating field refresh.

Full-frame progressive-scan 1920x1080 (1080p) requires up to twice the data bandwidth currently available in the DTV channel specification. High frame-rate 1080p may become an option in the near future, as a result of recent technology advances such as H.264/MPEG-4 AVC video coding, allowing more detail to be sent via the same channel bandwidth allocations that are used now.

The limitations of interlacing can be partially overcome through the use of advanced image processors in the consumer display device, such as the use of Faroudja DCDi and using internal frame buffers to eliminate scanline crawling.

Conversion

As of late 2007, six countries had completed the process of turning off analog terrestrial broadcasting. Many other countries had plans to do so or were in the process of a staged conversion. IEEE in Jamaica also decided to switch over the same time as the US.

NATIONAL TELEVISION SYSTEM COMMITTEE (NTSC)

National Television System Committee (NTSC) is the analog television system used in the United States, Canada, Japan, Mexico, the Philippines, South Korea, Taiwan, and some other countries. NTSC is also the name of the U.S. standardization body that adopted it. The first black-and-white NTSC standard for broadcast was developed in 1941 and had no provision for colour transmissions. The standard called for 525 lines of picture information in each frame, and 30 interlaced frames per second; the frame rate was later slightly adjusted for the colour standard. Civilian development of commercial television was halted with the entry of the United States into the war. In 1953 a second standard was issued, which allowed colour broadcasting to be compatible with the existing stock of black-and-white receivers, while maintaining the broadcast channel bandwidth already in use. This was an important commercial advantage over incompatible colour systems that had also been proposed. NTSC was the first widely adopted broadcast colour system. After over a half-century of use, the vast majority of over-the-air NTSC transmissions will be replaced with ATSC by February 17, 2009 in the United States, and August 31, 2011 in Canada. Various digital television systems have replaced the vacuum-tube era standard.

Television encoding systems by nation, countries using the NTSC system are shown in green.

History

The National Television System Committee was established in 1940 by the United States Federal Communications Commission (FCC) to resolve the conflicts that arose between companies over the introduction of a nationwide analog television system in the United States. In March 1941, the committee issued a technical standard for black-and-white television that built upon a 1936 recommendation made by the Radio Manufacturers Association (RMA). Technical advancements of the vestigial sideband technique allowed for the opportunity to increase the image resolution broadcast to consumer televisions. The NTSC compromised between RCA's desire to keep a 441-scan line standard (which was already being used by RCA's NBC TV network) and Philco's desire to increase the number of scan lines to between 605 and 800: A 525-line transmission standard was selected. Other technical standards in the final recommendation were a frame rate (image rate) of 30 frames per second consisting of two interlaced fields per frame (2:1 interlacing) at 262.5 lines per field or 60 fields per second, along with an aspect ratio of 4:3, and frequency modulation (FM) for the sound signal (which was quite new at the time).

In January 1950 the Committee was reconstituted to standardize colour television. In December 1953, it unanimously approved what is now called simply the NTSC colour television standard (later defined as RS-170a). The updated standard retained full backwards compatibility ("compatible colour") with older black-and-white television sets. Colour information was added to the black-and-white image by adding a colour subcarrier of 4.5 × 455/572 MHz (approximately 3.58 MHz) to the video signal. In order to minimize interference between the chrominance signal and FM sound carrier, the addition of the colour subcarrier also required a slight reduction of the frame rate from 30 frames per second to 30/1.001 (very close to 29.97) frames per second, and changing the line frequency from 15,750 Hz to 15,734.26 Hz.

The FCC had briefly approved a different colour television standard, starting in October 1950, which was developed by CBS. However, this standard was incompatible with black-and-white broadcasts. It used a rotating colour wheel (a technique re-used in the first DLP projectors developed in the late 1980s), reduced the number of scan lines from 525 to 405, and increased the field rate from 60 to 144 (but had an effective frame rate of only 24 frames a second). Legal action by rival RCA kept commercial use of the system off the air until June 1951, and regular broadcasts only lasted a few months before manufacture of all colour television sets was banned by the Office of Defense Mobilization (ODM) in October, ostensibly due to the Korean War. CBS rescinded its system in March 1953, and the FCC replaced it on December 17, 1953 with the NTSC colour standard, which was cooperatively developed by several companies (including RCA and Philco). The first publicly announced network TV broadcast of a programme using the NTSC "compatible colour" system was an episode of NBC's *Kukla, Fran and Ollie* on August 30, 1953, although it was viewable in colour only at the network's headquarters. The first nationwide view of NTSC colour came on the following January 1 with the coast-to-coast broadcast of the Tournament of Roses Parade, viewable on prototype colour receivers at special presentations across the country.

The first colour NTSC television camera was the RCA TK-40, used for experimental broadcasts in 1953; an improved version, the TK-40A, introduced in March 1954, was the first commercially available colour TV camera. It was replaced later that year by an improved version, the TK-41, which became the standard camera used throughout much of the 1960s. The NTSC standard has been adopted by other countries, including most of the Americas and Japan. With the advent of digital television, analog broadcasts are being phased out. NTSC broadcasts are mandated by the FCC to end in the United States on February 17, 2009.

Technical Details

Lines and Refresh Rate

NTSC colour encoding is used with the *M* format, which consists of 30/100.1 per cent (or approximately 29.97) interlaced frames of video per second. Each frame consists of a total of 525 scanlines, of which 486 make up the visible raster. The remainder (the vertical blanking interval) are used for synchronization and vertical retrace, and can contain other data such as closed captioning and vertical interval timecode. In the complete raster (ignoring half-lines), the even-numbered or 'lower" scanlines (lines 21 to 263 in the video signal) are drawn in the first field, and the odd-numbered or "upper" (signal lines 283 to 525) are drawn in the second field, to yield a flicker-free image at the field refresh frequency of approximately 59.94 Hertz (actually 60 Hz/ 100.1%). For comparison, PAL uses 625 lines (576 visible), and so has a higher vertical resolution, but a lower temporal resolution of 25 frames or 50 fields per second.

The NTSC field refresh frequency was originally exactly 60 Hz in the black-and-white system, chosen because it matched the nominal 60 Hz frequency of alternating current power used in the United States. Matching the field refresh rate to the power source avoided wave interference which produces rolling bars on the screen. Synchronization of the refresh rate to the power incidentally helped kinescope cameras record early live television broadcasts, as it was very simple to synchronize a film camera to capture one frame of video on each film frame by using the alternating current frequency as a shutter trigger.

The figure of 525 lines was chosen as a consequence of the limitations of the vacuum-tube-based technologies of the day. In early TV systems, a master voltage-controlled oscillator was run at twice the horizontal line frequency, and this frequency was divided down by the number of lines used (in this case 525) to give the field frequency (60 Hz in this case). This frequency was then compared with the 60 Hz power-line frequency and any discrepancy corrected by adjusting the frequency of the master oscillator.

The only practical method of frequency division available at the time was the use of multivibrators, which could only divide by small numbers. For interlaced scanning an odd number of lines per frame was required in order to make the vertical retrace distance identical for the odd and even fields; an extra odd line means that the same distance is covered in retracing from the final odd line to the first even line as from the final even line to the first odd line, so simplifying the retrace circuitry. This meant that a chain of multivibrators was needed, each of which had to divide by a small, odd number. (Note that an odd number is never integrally divisible by any even number). The closest practical sequence to 500 was 3 × 5 × 5 × 7 = 525. Similarly, 625-line PAL and SECAM uses 5 × 5 × 5 × 5. The British 405-line system used 3 × 3 × 3 × 3 × 5, the French 819-line system used 3 × 3 × 7 × 13. Although other values were theoretically possible, all of them involved division by unacceptably large numbers, which produced reliability problems. Modern systems derive all their frequencies from the colour subcarrier frequency.

In the colour system the refresh frequency was shifted slightly downward to 59.94 Hz to eliminate stationary dot patterns in the colour carrier, as explained below in "Colour encoding".

Colour Encoding

There are three main standards in use around the world, PAL (Phase Alternating Line), NTSC (National Television System Committee) and SECAM (Séquentiel Couleur à Mémoire—Sequential Colour with Memory).

The system used in North America is NTSC. Western Europe, Australia, and Eastern South America use PAL. Eastern Europe used SECAM, but switched to PAL after the change of the political regimes there. France still uses SECAM. Generally, a device (such as a television) can only read or display video encoded to a standard which the device is designed to support; otherwise, the source must be converted (such as when European programmes are broadcast in North America or vice versa).

This table illustrates the differences:

	NTSC M	*PAL B, G, H*	*PAL I*	*PAL N*	*PAL M*	*SECAM B, G, H*	*SECAM D, K, K', L*
Lines/Fields	525/60	625/50	625/50	625/50	525/60	625/50	625/50
Horizontal Frequency	15.734 kHz	15.625 kHz	15.625 kHz	15.625 kHz	15.750 kHz	15.625 kHz	15.625 kHz
Vertical Frequency	60 Hz	50 Hz	50 Hz	50 Hz	60 Hz	50 Hz	50 Hz
Colour Subcarrier Frequency	3.579545 MHz	4.43361875 MHz	4.43361875 MHz	3.582056 MHz	3.575611 MHz		
Video Bandwidth	4.2 MHz	5.0 MHz	5.5 MHz	4.2 MHz	4.2 MHz	5.0 MHz	6.0 MHz
Sound Carrier	4.5 MHz	5.5 MHz	5.9996 MHz	4.5 MHz	4.5 MHz	5.5 MHz	6.5 MHz

For backward compatibility with black-and-white television, NTSC uses a luminance-chrominance encoding system invented in 1938 by Georges Valensi. Luminance (derived mathematically from the composite colour signal) takes the place of the original monochrome signal. Chrominance carries colour information. This allows black-and-white receivers to display NTSC signals simply by ignoring the chrominance.

The original chromaticities of the NTSC colour primaries were R = [0.67, 0.33], G = [0.21, 0.71], B = [0.14, 0.08], yielding a far larger gamut than most of today's monitors. Over the decades, however, desire for a brighter picture prompted TV manufacturers to deviate from that specification, sacrificing saturation for increased brightness. This deviation from the standard, which happened both at the receiver and broadcaster stage, was the source of considerable colour variation in the 1960s As a result, in 1968 the SMPTE recommended a new set of phosphor primaries for studio use, which in 1979 became part of SMPTE 170M, the engineering standard describing the American broadcasting system. Although the old 1953 NTSC specifications are still part of the United States Code of Federal Regulations, all modern broadcast equipment follows the SMPTE 170M standard instead and thus encodes a signal for the SMPTE "C" set of phosphor primaries.

In NTSC, chrominance is encoded using two 3.579545 MHz signals which are 90 degrees out of phase, known as I (in-phase) and Q (quadrature) QAM. Mathematically, the combination of two sine waves 90 degrees out of phase with each other, with varying respective amplitudes, can be viewed as a single sine wave with varying phase relative to a reference, and varying amplitude. In essence, the phase represents the instantaneous colour hue captured by a TV camera and the amplitude represents the colour saturation.

For a TV or a display to recover hue information from the I/Q phase as just described, it must know the reference for it (*i.e.* what phase is zero). It also needs a reference against which to compare the amplitude to make saturation sense out of it. So the NTSC signal includes a short sample of this reference signal, known as the colour burst, located on the 'back porch' of each horizontal line (the time between the end of the horizontal synchronization pulse and of the blanking pulse on each line). The colour burst consists of a minimum of eight cycles of the unmodulated (fixed phase and amplitude) colour subcarrier. By comparing the reference signal derived from colour burst to the chrominance signal's amplitude and phase at a particular point in the scan, the device determines what chrominance to assign to the pixel then being displayed. Combining that with the amplitude of the luminance signal, the receiver calculates exactly what colour to make the pixel.

When a transmitter broadcasts an NTSC signal, it amplitude-modulates a radio-frequency carrier with the NTSC signal just described, while it frequency-modulates a carrier 4.5 MHz higher with the audio signal. If non-linear distortion happens to the broadcast signal, the 3.58 MHz colour carrier may beat with the sound carrier to produce a dot pattern on the screen. To make the resulting pattern less noticeable, designers adjusted the original 60 Hz field rate down by a factor of 1.001 (0.1%), to approximately 59.94 fields per second.

The 59.94 rate is derived from the following calculations. Designers chose to make the chrominance subcarrier frequency an n + 0.5 multiple of the line frequency to minimize interference between the luminance signal and the chrominance signal. They then chose to make the audio subcarrier frequency an integer multiple of the line frequency to minimize interference between the audio signal and the chrominance signal. The original black-and-white standard, with its 15750 Hz line frequency and 4.5 MHz audio subcarrier, does not meet these requirements, so designers had either to raise the audio subcarrier frequency or lower the line frequency. Raising the audio subcarrier frequency would prevent existing receivers from properly tuning in the audio signal. Lowering the line frequency is comparatively innocuous, because the horizontal and vertical synchronization information in the NTSC signal allows a receiver to tolerate a substantial amount of slop in the line frequency. So that is the route the colour standard took. In the black-and-white standard, the ratio of audio subcarrier frequency to line frequency is 4.5 MHz/15,750 = 285.71. In the colour standard, this becomes rounded to the integer 286, which means the colour standard's line rate is 4.5 MHz/286 ~ 15,734 lines per second. Dividing by 262.5 lines per field, this gives approximately 59.94 fields per second.

Transmission Modulation Scheme

An NTSC television channel as transmitted occupies a total bandwidth of 6 MHz. A guard band, which does not carry any signals, occupies the lowest 250 kHz of the channel to avoid interference between the video signal of one channel and the audio signals of the next channel down. The actual video signal, which is amplitude-modulated, is transmitted between 500 kHz and 5.45 MHz above the lower bound of the channel. The video carrier is 1.25 MHz above the lower bound of the channel. Like most AM signals, the video carrier generates two sidebands, one above the carrier and one below. The sidebands are each 4.2 MHz wide. The entire upper sideband is transmitted, but only 750 kHz of the lower sideband, known as a vestigial sideband, is transmitted. The colour subcarrier, as noted above, is 3.579545 MHz above the video carrier, and is quadrature-amplitude-modulated with suppressed carrier. The highest 25 kHz of each channel contains the audio signal, which is frequency-modulated, making it compatible with the audio signals broadcast by FM radio stations in the 88–108 MHz band. The main audio carrier is 4.5 MHz above the video carrier. Sometimes a channel may contain an MTS signal, which is simply more than one audio signal. This is normally the case when stereo audio and/or second audio programme signals are used.

- One odd thing about NTSC is the *Cvbs* (Composite vertical blanking signal) is something called "setup". This is a voltage offset between the "black" and "blanking" levels. *Cvbs is unique to NTSC.*
- Cvbs has one defect: it makes NTSC more easily separated from its primary sync signals, but Cvbs has a smaller dynamic range when compared with PAL or SECAM.

Framerate Conversion

There is a large difference in framerate between film, which runs at 24.0 frames per second, and the NTSC standard, which runs at approximately 29.97 frames per second.

Unlike the two other video formats, PAL and SECAM, this difference cannot be overcome by a simple speed-up.

A complex process called "3:2 pulldown" is used. One film frame is transmitted for three video fields (1.5 video frame times), and the next frame is transmitted for two video fields (1 video frame time). Two 24 frame/s film frames are therefore transmitted in five 60 Hz video fields, for an average of 2.5 video fields per film frame. The average frame rate is thus 60/2.5 = 24 frame/s, so the average film speed is exactly what it should be. There are drawbacks, however. Still-framing on playback can display a video frame with fields from two different film frames, so any motion between the frames will appear as a rapid back-and-forth flicker. There can also be noticeable jitter/ "stutter" during slow camera pans.

To avoid 3:2 pulldown, film shot specifically for NTSC television is often taken at 30 frame/s.

For viewing native PAL or SECAM material (such as European television series and some European movies) on NTSC equipment, a standards conversion has to take place. There are basically two ways to accomplish this.

- The framerate can be slowed from 25 to 23.976 frames per second (a slowdown of about 4%) to subsequently apply 3:2 pulldown.
- Interpolation of the contents of adjacent frames in order to produce new intermediate frames; this introduces artifacts, and even the most modestly trained of eyes can quickly spot video which has been converted between formats.

Modulation for Analog Satellite Transmission

Because satellite power is severely limited, analog video transmission through satellites differs from terrestrial TV transmission. AM is a linear modulation method, so a given demodulated signal-to-noise ratio (SNR) requires an equally high received RF SNR. The SNR of studio quality video is over 50 dB, so AM would require prohibitively high powers and/or large antennas.

Wideband FM is used instead to trade RF bandwidth for reduced power. Increasing the channel bandwidth from 6 to 36 MHz allows a RF SNR of only 10 dB or less. The wider noise bandwidth reduces this 40 dB power saving by 36 MHz/6 MHz = 8 dB for a substantial net reduction of 32 dB.

Sound is on a FM subcarrier as in terrestrial transmission, but frequencies above 4.5 MHz are used to reduce aural/visual interference. 6.8, 5.8 and 6.2 MHz are commonly used. Stereo can be multiplex or discrete, and unrelated audio and data signals may be placed on additional subcarriers.

A triangular 60 Hz energy dispersal waveform is added to the composite baseband signal (video plus audio and data subcarriers) before modulation. This limits the satellite downlink power spectral density in case the video signal is lost. Otherwise the satellite might transmit all of its power on a single frequency, interfering with terrestrial microwave links in the same frequency band.

In half transponder mode, the frequency deviation of the composite baseband signal is reduced to 18 MHz to allow another signal in the other half of the 36 MHz transponder. This reduces the FM benefit somewhat, and the recovered SNRs are further reduced because the combined signal power must be "backed off" to avoid intermodulation distortion in the satellite transponder. A single FM signal is constant amplitude, so it can saturate a transponder without distortion.

Use with Progressive Sources

When NTSC is used to transmit content which was originally composed of 29.97 progressive full frames per second, the even field of the frame is transmitted first. This is opposite from PAL, and opposite from what might be expected ('Even first' means the frame starts being drawn on the second line). Systems which recover progressive frames or transcode video should ensure that this 'Field Order' is obeyed, otherwise the recovered frame will consist of a field from one frame and a field from an adjacent frame, resulting in 'comb' interlacing artifacts.

Comparative Quality

Video professionals and television engineers jokingly referred to NTSC as "Never The Same Colour" or "Never Twice the Same Colour". Reception problems can degrade an NTSC picture by changing the phase of the colour signal, so the colour balance of the picture will be altered unless a compensation is made in the receiver. This necessitates the inclusion of a tint control on NTSC sets, which is not necessary on PAL or SECAM systems.

However, the mismatch between NTSC's 30 frames per second and film's 24 frames is well overcome by an ingenious process which capitalizes on the *field* rate of the interlaced NTSC signal, thus avoiding the film playback speedup used for PAL and SECAM at 25 frames per second (which causes the accompanying audio to increase in pitch slightly).

There is no question the NTSC system reflects the technology of its originating era, but its compatibility and flexibility has been the key to its longevity over seven decades. The coming of digital television and high-definition television may end the need for analog television systems.

Variants

NTSC-M

Unlike PAL, with its many varied underlying broadcast television systems in use throughout the world, NTSC colour encoding is invariably used with broadcast system *M*, giving NTSC-M.

NTSC-J

Only Japan's variant "NTSC-J" is slightly different: in Japan, black level and blanking level of the signal are identical (at 0 IRE), as they are in PAL, while in American NTSC, black level is slightly higher (7.5 IRE) than blanking level. Since the difference is quite small, a slight turn of the brightness knob is all that is required to enjoy the "other" variant of NTSC on any set as it is supposed to be; most watchers might not even notice the difference in the first place.

PAL-M

The Brazilian PAL-M system uses the same broadcast bandwidth, frame rate, and number of lines as NTSC, but using PAL colour encoding. It is therefore partially NTSC-compatible. NTSC-M tv sets can receive terrestrial PAL-M broadcasts, NTSC VCRs can play videotapes recorded in PAL-M and vice versa, but only in black and white due to the fact that the colour information cannot be decoded. Conversely, DVD players sold for the PAL-M market are identical to NTSC DVD players, as the frame rates match and the difference in analogue colour encoding becomes irrelevant in digital formats.

NTSC-N

This is used in Paraguay and Bolivia (though Paraguay has recently switched to NTSC-M from PAL-N). This is very similar to PAL-M (used in Brazil). It is also closely related to PAL-Nc (used in Argentina) and PAL-N (used in Uruguay).

The similarities of NTSC-M and NTSC-N can be seen on the broadcast television systems#ITU identification scheme table, which is reproduced here:

World Television System

System	*Lines*	*Frame rate*	*Channel b/w*	*Visual b/w*	*Sound offset*	*Vestigial sideband*	*Vision mod.*	*Sound mod.*	*Notes*
M	525	29.97	6	4.2	+4.5	0.75	Neg.	FM	Most of the Americas and Caribbean, Philippines, South Korea, Taiwan (all NTSC-M) and Brazil (PAL-M).
N	625	25	6	4.2	+4.5	0.75	Neg.	FM	Argentina, Paraguay, Uruguay (all PAL-N). Greater number of lines results in higher quality.

As it is shown, aside from the number of lines and frames per second, the systems are identical. NTSC-N/PAL-N/PAL-Nc are compatible with sources such as game consoles, VHS/Betamax VCRs, and DVD players. However, they are not compatible with baseband broadcasts (which are received over an antenna), though some newer sets come with baseband NTSC 3.58 support (NTSC 3.58 being the frequency for colour modulation in NTSC: 3.58 MHz).

NTSC 4.43

In what can be considered an opposite of PAL-60, NTSC 4.43 is a pseudo colour system which transmits NTSC encoding (525/29.97) in a colour subcarrier of 4.43 MHz instead of 3.58 MHz. The resulting output is only viewable by TVs which support the resulting pseudo-system (usually multi-standard TVs). Using a native NTSC TV to decode the signal yields no colour, while using a PAL TV to decode the system yields erratic colours (observed to be lacking red and flickering randomly). The format is apparently limited to few early laserdisc players and some game consoles sold in markets where the PAL system is used.

The NTSC 4.43 system, while not a broadcast format, appears most often as a playback function of PAL cassette format VCRs, beginning with the Sony 3/4" U-Matic format and then following onto Betamax and VHS format machines. As Hollywood has the claim of providing the most cassette software (movies and television series) for VCRs for the world's viewers, and as not *all* cassette releases were made available in PAL formats, a means of playing NTSC format cassettes was highly desired.

Multi-standard video monitors were already in use in Europe to accommodate broadcast and professional needs regarding PAL, SECAM, and NTSC video formats from sources dedicated to just one of those formats. The heterodyne colour-under process of U-Matic, Betamax and VHS lent itself to minor modification of VCR players to accommodate NTSC format cassettes. The colour-under format of VHS uses a 629 kHz subcarrier while U-Matic and Betamax use a 688 kHz subcarrier to carry an *amplitude modulated* chroma signal for both NTSC and PAL formats. Since the VCR was ready to play the colour portion of the NTSC recording using PAL colour mode, the PAL scanner and capstan speeds had to be adjusted upwards from PAL's slower 50 Hz field rate to match NTSC's 59.94 Hz field rate, and faster linear tape speed.

Although easier to do than explain, the changes to the PAL VCR are very minor thanks to the existing VCR recording formats. The output of the VCR when playing an NTSC cassette in NTSC 4.43 mode is 525 lines/29.97 frames per second with PAL compatible heterodyned colour. The multi-standard receiver is already set to support the NTSC H&V frequencies; it just needs to do so while receiving PAL colour.

The existence of those multi-standard receivers was probably part of the need for region coding of DVDs. As the colour signals are component on disc for all display formats almost no changes would be required for PAL DVD players to play NTSC (525/29.97) discs as long as the display was frame-rate compatible.

NTSC-Film

NTSC with a frame rate of 23.976 frame/s is described in the NTSC-film standard.

Canada/US Video Game Region

Sometimes *NTSC-US* or *NTSC-U/C* is used to describe the video gaming region of North America, as regional lockout usually restricts games released within a region to that region.

Vertical Interval Reference

The standard NTSC video image contains some lines (lines 1–21 of each field) which are not visible; all are beyond the edge of the viewable image, but only lines 1–9 are used for the vertical-sync and equalizing pulses. The remaining lines were deliberately blanked in the original NTSC specification to provide time for the electron beam in CRT-based screens to return to the top of the display.

VIR (or Vertical interval reference), widely adopted in the 1980s, attempts to correct some of the colour problems with NTSC video by adding studio-inserted reference data for luminance and chrominance levels on line 19. Suitably-equipped television sets could then employ these data in order to adjust the display to a closer match of the original studio image. The actual VIR signal contains three sections, the first having 70 per cent luminance and the same chrominance as the colour burst signal, and the other two having 50 per cent and 7.5 per cent luminance respectively.

A less-used successor to VIR, GCR, also added ghost (multipath interference) removal capabilities.

The remaining vertical blanking interval lines are typically used for datacasting or ancillary data such as video editing timestamps (vertical interval timecodes or SMPTE timecodes on lines 12–14), test data on lines 17–18, a network source code on line 20 and closed captioning, XDS, and V-chip data on line 21. Early teletext applications also used vertical blanking interval lines 14–18 and 20, but teletext over NTSC was never widely adopted by viewers.

Many stations transmit TV Guide On Screen (TVGOS) data for an electronic programme guide on VBI lines. The primary station in a market will broadcast 4 lines of data, and backup stations will broadcast 1 line. In most markets the PBS station is the primary host. TVGOS data can occupy any line from 10-25, but in practice its limited to 11-18, 20 and line 22. Line 22 is only used for 2 broadcast, DirecTV and CFPL-TV.

Countries and Territories Using NTSC

North America

- Canada, NTSC broadcast to be abandoned by August 2011, simulcast in ATSC
- Mexico, NTSC broadcast to be abandoned by 2022, simulcast in ATSC
- United States, NTSC broadcast to be abandoned in February 2009, simulcast in ATSC

Central America and the Caribbean

- Antigua and Barbuda
- Bahamas
- Belize
- British Virgin Islands
- Costa Rica
- Dominica
- El Salvador
- Grenada
- Honduras
- Leeward Islands
- Netherlands Antilles
- Panama
- Saint Kitts and Nevis
- Saint Vincent and the Grenadines
- U.S. Virgin Islands
- Aruba
- Barbados
- Bermuda
- Cayman Islands
- Cuba
- Dominican Republic
- Guatemala
- Haiti
- Jamaica
- Montserrat
- Nicaragua
- Puerto Rico (U.S.)
- Saint Lucia
- Trinidad and Tobago

South America

- Bolivia
- Colombia
- Chile
- Ecuador

- ❑ Guyana
- ❑ Peru
- ❑ Venezuela
- ❑ Paraguay (*until 2006 Paraguay used PAL*)
- ❑ Suriname

Asia

- ❑ Japan
- ❑ Philippines
- ❑ South Korea
- ❑ Republic of China (Taiwan)
- ❑ Union of Myanmar (Burma)
- ❑ North Korea (*Propaganda station aimed at South Korea; domestic broadcasts use PAL*)
- ❑ Cambodia (*Historic; Cambodia now uses PAL*)
- ❑ Vietnam (*Historic; all of Vietnam now uses PAL*)
- ❑ Thailand (*Historic; Thailand now uses PAL*)

Pacific

US Territories

- ❑ American Samoa
- ❑ Guam
- ❑ Northern Mariana Islands
- ❑ Midway Atoll (a US military base)

Other Pacific Island Nations

- ❑ Marshall Islands (in Compact of Free Association with US; US aid funded NTSC adoption).
- ❑ Micronesia (in Compact of Free Association with US).
- ❑ Palau (in Compact of Free Association with US; adopted NTSC before independence).
- ❑ Samoa (closely tied to American Samoa; US aid funded NTSC adoption).
- ❑ Tonga (US aid funded NTSC adoption).

Historic (Used NTSC Experimentally Before Adopting PAL)

- ❑ Fiji (*Historic; used before 1989, Fiji has used PAL since 1990*)

Indian Ocean

- ❑ Diego Garcia

Middle East

- ❑ South Yemen (*Historic; all of Yemen now uses PAL*)

Europe

- ❑ *United Kingdom (Experimented with a 405-line variant of NTSC in the 1950s and 1960s; dropped in favour of PAL)*

PHASE ALTERNATING LINE (PAL)

PAL, short for *Phase Alternating Line,* is a colour-encoding system used in broadcast television systems in large parts of the world. Other common analogue television systems are SECAM and NTSC. This page discusses the colour encoding system *only*. See Broadcast television systems and analogue television for discussion of frame rates, image resolution and audio modulation. For discussion of the 625-line 25 frame/s television standard.

History of the PAL Standard

In the 1950s, when the Western European countries were planning to establish colour television, they were faced with the problem that the already existing American NTSC standard would not fit the 50 Hz AC frequency of the European power grids. In addition to that NTSC demonstrated several weaknesses, including colour tone shifting under poor transmission conditions. For these reasons the development of the SECAM and PAL standards began. The goal was to provide a colour TV standard with a picture frequency of 50 fields per second (50 hertz), and sporting a better colour picture than NTSC.

PAL was developed by Walter Bruch at Telefunken in Germany. The format was first unveiled in 1963, with the first broadcasts beginning in the United Kingdom and Germany in 1967.

Telefunken was later bought by the French electronics manufacturer Thomson. Thomson also bought the *Compagnie Générale de Télévision* where Henri de France developed SECAM, historically the first European colour television standard. Thomson nowadays also co-owns the RCA brand for consumer electronics products, which created the NTSC colour TV standard before Thomson became involved.

The term PAL is often used informally to refer to a 625-line/50 Hz (576i, principally European) television system, and to differentiate from a 525-line/60 Hz (480i, principally North American/Central American/Japanese) NTSC system. Accordingly, DVDs are labelled as either PAL or NTSC (referring informally to the line count and frame rate) even though technically the European discs do not have PAL composite colour. This usage may lead readers to believe that PAL defines image resolution, even though it does not. The PAL colour system can be used in conjunction with any resolution and frame rate, and various such combinations exist. NTSC, by contrast does define the video line and frame format.

Technical Details

The basics of PAL and the NTSC system are very similar; a quadrature amplitude modulated subcarrier carrying the chrominance information is added to the luminance video signal to form a composite video baseband signal. The frequency of this subcarrier is approximately 4.43 MHz for PAL, compared to approximately 3.58 MHz for NTSC. The SECAM system, on the other hand, uses a frequency modulation scheme on its colour subcarrier.

The name "Phase Alternating Line" describes the way that the phase of part of the colour information on the video signal is reversed with each line, which automatically corrects phase errors in the transmission of the signal by cancelling them out. Lines where the colour phase is reversed compared to NTSC are often called PAL or phase-alternation lines, which justifies one of the expansions of the acronym, while the other lines are called NTSC lines. Early PAL receivers relied on the imperfections of the human eye to do that cancelling; however this resulted in a comblike effect on larger phase errors. Thus, most receivers now use a chrominance delay line, which stores the received colour information on each line of display; an average of the colour information from the previous line and the current line is then used to drive the picture tube. The effect is that phase errors result in saturation changes, which are less objectionable than the equivalent hue changes of NTSC. A minor drawback is that the vertical colour resolution is poorer than the NTSC system's, but since the human eye also has a colour resolution that is much lower than its brightness resolution, this effect is not visible. In any case, NTSC, PAL and SECAM all have chrominance bandwidth (horizontal colour detail) reduced greatly compared to the luminance signal.

For a 1:1 pixel aspect (square pixels) on a 50 Hz interlaced PAL signal the pixel rate should be 14.75.

The 4.43361875 MHz frequency of the colour carrier is a result of 283.75 colour clock cycles per line plus a 25 Hz offset to avoid interferences. Since the line frequency is 15625 Hz, the colour carrier frequency calculates as follows: 4.43361875 MHz = 283.75 × 15625 Hz + 25 Hz.

- CVBS is an initialism, but it does not stand for "composite video baseband signal", CVBS actually stands for (C)hroma, (V)ideo, (B)urst, and (S)ync; which are the four basic components of a composite video signal. That's why it's called "composite".

PAL vs. NTSC

NTSC receivers have a tint control to perform colour correction manually. If this is not adjusted correctly, the colours may be faulty. The PAL standard automatically removes hue errors by utilizing phase alternation of the colour signal, so a tint control is unnecessary. Chrominance phase errors in the PAL system are cancelled out using a 1H delay line resulting in lower saturation, which is much less noticeable to the eye than NTSC hue errors.

However, the alternation of colour information—Hanover bars—can lead to picture grain on pictures with extreme phase errors even in PAL systems, if decoder circuits are misaligned or use the simplified decoders of early designs (to overcome royalty restrictions). Usually such extreme phase shifts do not occur; this effect will usually be observed when the transmission path is poor, typically in built up areas or where the terrain is unfavourable. The effect is more noticeable on UHF signals than VHF as VHF signals tend to be more robust.

A PAL decoder can be seen as a pair of NTSC decoders:

- PAL can be decoded with two NTSC decoders.
- By switching between the two NTSC decoders every other line it is possible to decode PAL without a phase delay line or two phase-locked loop (PLL) circuits.
- This works because one decoder receives a colour subcarrier with negated phase in relation to the other decoder. It then negates the phase of that sub carrier when decoding. This leads to smaller phase errors being cancelled out. However a delay line PAL decoder gives superior performance. Some Japanese TVs originally used the dual NTSC method to avoid paying royalty to Telefunken.
- PAL and NTSC have slightly divergent colour spaces, but the colour decoder differences here are ignored.
- PAL supports SMPTE 498.3 while NTSC is compliant with EBU Recommendation 14.
- The issue of frame rates and colour subcarriers is ignored in this technical explanation. These technical details play no direct role (except as subsystems and physical parameters) to the decoding of the signal.

PAL vs. SECAM

SECAM is an earlier attempt at compatible colour television which also tries to resolve the NTSC hue problem. It does so by applying a different method to colour transmission, namely alternate transmission of the U and V vectors and frequency modulation, while PAL attempts to improve on the NTSC method.

SECAM transmissions are more robust over longer distances than NTSC or PAL. However, owing to their FM nature, the colour signal remains present, although at reduced amplitude, even in monochrome portions of the image, thus being subject to stronger cross colour. Like PAL, a SECAM receiver needs a delay line.

Broadcast Systems PAL has been Used with PAL B/G/D/K/I

The majority of countries using PAL have television standards with 625 lines and 25 frames, differences concern the audio carrier frequency and channel bandwidths. Standards B/G are used in most of Western Europe, standard I in the UK, Ireland, Hong Kong and Macau, standards D/K in most of Eastern Europe and Standard D in mainland China.

7 MHz channels are used in VHF (B, D) and 8 MHz channels in UHF (G, K, I), although Australia used 7 MHz channels in UHF and Ireland uses 8 MHz channels in VHF.

PAL-M Standard (Brazil)

In Brazil, PAL is used in conjunction with the 525 line, 29.97 frame/s system *M*, using (very nearly) the NTSC colour subcarrier frequency. Exact colour subcarrier frequency of PAL-M is 3.575611 MHz:

- Almost all other countries using system M use NTSC.

The PAL colour system (either baseband or with any RF system, with the normal 4.43 MHz subcarrier unlike PAL-M) can also be applied to an NTSC-like 525-line (480i) picture to form what is often known as "PAL-60" (sometimes "PAL-60/525" or "Pseudo PAL"). PAL-M (a broadcast standard) however should not be confused with "PAL-60".

PAL-Nc

In Argentina, the PAL-Nc (combination N) variant is used. It employs the 625 line/50 field per second waveform of PAL-B/G, D/K, H, I but with a chrominance subcarrier frequency of 3.582 MHz. VHS tapes recorded from a PAL-Nc or a PAL-B/G, D/K, H, I broadcast are indistinguishable because the downconverted subcarrier on the tape is the same.

PAL-N

In Paraguay and Uruguay, PAL is used with the standard 625 line/50 fields per second system, but again with (very nearly) the NTSC subcarrier frequency.

- PAL-N should not be viewed as wildly incompatible versions of the PAL system, only the choice of colour subcarrier is different.
- A VHS recorded off TV (or released) in Europe will play in colour on any PAL-N VCR and PAL-N TV in Argentina, Paraguay, and Uruguay. Likewise, any tape recorded in Argentina or Uruguay off a PAL-N TV broadcast, can be sent to anyone in European countries that use PAL (and Australia/New Zealand, etc.) and it will display in colour. This has been very convenient for video collectors in the past.

People in Uruguay, Argentina and Paraguay usually own TV sets that also display NTSC-M, in addition to PAL-N of course. Direct TV broadcasts in NTSC-M for North, Central and South America so this is very convenient too. Most DVD players sold in Argentina, Uruguay and Paraguay also play PAL discs. However this is usually output in the European variant (colour subcarrier frequency 4.433618 MHz), so people who own a TV set that only works in PAL-N (plus NTSC-M in most cases) will have to watch those PAL DVD imports in black and white, as the colour subcarrier frequency in the TV set is the PAL-N variation, 3.582056 MHz. Some DVD players (usually lesser known brands) include an internal transcoder and the signal can be output in NTSC-M, with some video quality loss because of the systems conversion from a 625/50 PAL DVD disc to the output in NTSC-M 525/60. A few DVD players sold in Argentina and Uruguay allow to output the signal in NTSC-M, PAL, or PAL-N. In that case, a PAL disc (imported from Europe) can be played back on a PAL-N TV. Because there is no fields/lines conversion, quality is excellent.

Extended features of the PAL specification such as teletext are implemented quite differently in PAL-N. PAL-N supports a modified 608 closed captioning format that is designed to ease compatibility with NTSC originated content carried on line 18, and a modified teletext format that can occur several lines.

PAL L

The PAL L (Phase Alternating Line with L-sound system) standard uses the System "PAL" video standard, which is the same as PAL B/G/H (625 lines, 50 Hz field rate, 15.625 kHz line rate) except that it uses 6 MHz video bandwidth rather than 5.5 MHz, lifting the audio subcarrier to 6.5 MHz. When System L is used with SECAM, the audio carrier is amplitude modulated, but when used with PAL, the more usual FM sound system is usually used. The sound offset in B and G is +5.5 whereas in L its +6.5. In layman's language, PAL-L is PAL-BG with positive and AM sound modulation. An 8 MHz channel spacing is used with PAL L.

PAL L is used on some hotel internal distribution systems, as well as other public display and plant television systems. It is not used by any national TV networks. One example of a TV with PAL-L support is Thomson 24WK25. This signal has been defined by Sandipan Bhattacharjee, India.

System A

The BBC tested their pre-war 405 line monochrome system with all three colour standards including PAL, before the decision was made to abandon 405 and transmit colour on 625/System I only.

All PAL Systems Interoperable Except PAL-M (525/60)

The PAL colour system is usually used with a video format that has 625 lines per frame (576 visible lines, the rest being used for other information such as sync data and captioning) and a refresh rate of 50 interlaced fields per second (*i.e.* 25 full frames per second), such as systems B, G, H, I, and N.

- Some countries in Eastern Europe which formerly used SECAM with systems D and K have switched to PAL while leaving other aspects of their video system the same.
- However, some European countries have changed completely from SECAM-D/K to PAL-B/G.

On RF (*i.e.* through a Modulator or TV Aerial) the difference between I, D/H and B/G is audio. These use different audio subcarriers, so with mismatch on Modulator Settings or an imported TV there will be perfectly normal Colour Video, but possibly no audio. Some TVs and VHS tuners have multiple filters in parallel or switched for the 6 MHz, 5.5 MHz, 6.5 MHz or 4.5 MHz sound carriers. Nicam is an additional 6.5 MHz offset carrier carrying stereo digitally, on 6.0 MHz PAL I systems. Germany particularly uses two separate FM sound carriers on PAL B/G. (Stereo FM Radio uses a mono signal with a DSBSC L-R audio centred on 38 kHz with a 19 kHz pilot to aid decoding. Hence the German Zweiton and Nicam both give better performance than FM Radio).

Multisystem PAL Support and "PAL 60"

Recently manufactured PAL television receivers can typically decode all of these systems except, in some cases, PAL-M and PAL-N. Many of them can also receive

Eastern European and Middle Eastern SECAM, though rarely French broadcast SECAM (because France uses the unique positive video modulation), unless they are made for the French market. They will correctly display plain CVBS or S-video SECAM signals. Many can also accept baseband NTSC-M, such as from a VCR or game console, though not usually broadcast NTSC. Many sets also support NTSC with a 4.43 MHz subcarrier.

Many newer Video Cassette recorders and DVD players sold in Europe can play back NTSC tapes/discs. When operating in this mode most of them do not output a true (625/25) PAL signal but rather a hybrid of PAL and NTSC known as "PAL 60" (or "pseudo PAL") with "60" standing for 60 Hz, instead of 50 Hz. Some video game consoles also output a signal in this mode. Most newer television sets can display such a signal correctly but some will only do so (if at all) in black and white and/or with flickering/foldover at the bottom of the picture, or picture rolling (it can be noted, however, that many analogue-era TV sets can receive the picture by means of adjusting the V-Hold and V-Height knobs—assuming they have them). Very few TV tuner cards or video capture cards will support this mode (a small number can, although software/driver modification is usually required and the manufacturers' specs are usually unclear). A "PAL 60" signal is similar to an NTSC (525/30) signal but with a PAL chrominance subcarrier at 4.43 MHz (instead of 3.58) and with the PAL-specific phase alternation of the red colour difference signal between the lines.

Countries and Territories Using PAL

Over 120 countries and territories use or once used the terrestrial PAL system. Many of these are currently converting terrestrial PAL to DVB-T (PAL still often used by cable TV or in conjunction with a digital standard, such as DVB-C).

PAL B, G, D, K or I

- Afghanistan
- Albania DVB-T introduction started in 2005
- Australia DVB-T introduction started in 2001 (PAL to be abandoned for DVB-T by 2012)
- Austria DVB-T introduction started in 2006
- Bahrain
- Bangladesh
- Belgium
- Bosnia and Herzegovina
- Brunei
- Bulgaria (migrated from SECAM 1994-1996) (set to migrate to DVB-T in 2012, although such broadcasts are currently only available in Sofia)
- China, Mainland (PAL-D, digital broadcast using DMB-T/H):
  - Hong Kong (PAL-I, DMB-T/H introduced since Dec 31, 2007, PAL-I broadcast planned to be abandoned in 2012).
  - Macau (PAL-I).
- Croatia (PAL to be abandoned for DVB-T by 01.01.2011)
- Cyprus

- Czech Republic (migrated from SECAM 1992-94) (DVB-T introduction started in 2006, PAL to be abandoned for DVB-T by 2012)
- Denmark (including Faroe Islands and Greenland) (PAL broadcast to be abandoned by 31 October 2009; DVB-T since 31 March 2006)
- East Timor (Timor-Leste)
- Estonia (migrated from SECAM 1995-99; PAL to be abandoned for DVB-T at latest in 2012)
- Germany (PAL broadcast to be abandoned; DVB-T introduction started in 2003)
- Gibraltar
- Greece (migrated from SECAM in ca. 1992)
- Hungary (migrated from SECAM 1995-96; PAL broadcast to be abandoned by 31 December 2011; is converting to DVB-T)
- Iceland
- India
- Indonesia (PAL broadcast to be abandoned by 2016; is converting to DVB-T since 2007)
- Iran
- Iraq
- Ireland (VHF and UHF)
- Israel
- Italy (PAL broadcast to be abandoned by 2012; is converting to DVB-T)
- Jordan
- Kuwait
- Latvia (migrated from SECAM 1997-99)
- Lebanon
- Liechtenstein
- Lithuania (migrated from SECAM 1997-99)
- Republic of Macedonia
- Malaysia (Preliminary DVB-T Trials ended, further trials planned. Set top box and Digital TV not yet available on sale, but USB DVB-T receivers for viewing on a computer are widely available now. Plans to abandon PAL broadcast by 2015)
- Maldives
- Malta
- Montenegro
- Myanmar
- Nepal
- New Zealand
- Norway PAL broadcast to be abandoned by 2008–09, simulcast in DVB-T
- Poland (migrated from SECAM 1993-95; PAL broadcast to be abandoned by 2015; is converting to DVB-T)
- Portugal, including Madeira and Azores
- Romania (PAL broadcast to be abandoned by 2010-11; is converting to DVB-T since early 2007)
- Serbia

- Slovenia (PAL broadcast to be abandoned by 2012; is converting to DVB-T)
- Slovakia (migrated from SECAM 1993-96 PAL to be abandoned by 2012, is converting to DVB-T)
- Spain (including Canary Islands) PAL broadcast to be fully abandoned by 2010, simulcast in DVB-T
- Turkey
- Ukraine
- United Kingdom (UHF only), PAL broadcast to be abandoned by 2012, simulcast in DVB-T
- Vatican City
- North Korea
- Oman
- Pakistan
- Palestine (Gaza and West Bank)
- Qatar
- Saudi Arabia (which also uses SECAM)
- Singapore
- Sri Lanka
- Syria
- Thailand
- United Arab Emirates
- Vietnam
- Yemen
- Botswana
- Cameroon
- Cape Verde
- Egypt
- Eritrea
- Ethiopia
- Gambia
- Ghana
- Guinea
- Guinea-Bissau
- Kenya
- Liberia
- Malawi
- Mozambique
- Morocco
- Nigeria
- Seychelles
- Sierra Leone
- Somalia
- Sudan
- Swaziland
- Tanzania
- Tunisia
- Uganda
- Zambia
- Zanzibar
- Zimbabwe
- Angola
- Ascension Island, PAL broadcast to be abandoned by 2012, simulcast in DVB-T
- Lesotho
- Namibia
- South Africa PAL broadcast to be abandoned by 2011; is converting to DVB-T
- Tristan da Cunha
- Christmas Island (see Australia)
- Cook Islands (see New Zealand)
- Easter Island
- Fiji
- Norfolk Island (see Australia)
- Papua New Guinea
- Samoa, Samoa is converting to NTSC and probably ATSC
- Solomon Islands
- Tonga, Tonga is converting to NTSC and probably ATSC
- Vanuatu

- Falkland Islands (UHF only)

PAL-M

- Brazil (simulcast in ISDB-T, compressed using H.264/MPEG-4 AVC, started in December 2007 until 2016)
- Laos (also uses SECAM)

PAL-N and PAL-Nc

- Argentina
- Paraguay
- Uruguay (will use DVB but no date decided yet)

Countries and Territories that Once Used PAL

- Andorra (switched to DVB-T completed September 25, 2007).
- Finland (switched to DVB-T completed September 1, 2007).
- Luxembourg (switched to DVB-T completed September 1, 2006).
- Netherlands (switched to DVB-T completed December 11, 2006).
- Sweden (switch to DVB-T completed October 15, 2007).
- Switzerland (switch to DVB-T completed November 26, 2007).

SECAM

SECAM, also written SÉCAM (*Séquentiel couleur à mémoire,* French for "Sequential Colour with Memory"), is an analog colour television system first used in France. A team led by Henri de France working at Compagnie Française de Télévision (later bought by Thomson) invented SECAM. It is, historically, the first European colour television standard.

Technical Details

Just as the other colour standards adopted for broadcast usage over the world, SECAM is a *compatible* standard, which means that monochrome television receivers predating its introduction are still able to show the programmes, although only in black and white. Because of this compatibility requirement, colour standards add a second signal to the basic monochrome signal, and this signal carries the colour information, called chrominance or C in short, while the black and white information is called the luminance (Y in short). Old TV receivers only see the luminance, while colour receivers process both signals.

Additionally, for compatibility, it is required to use no more bandwidth than the monochrome signal alone; the colour signal has to be somehow inserted into the monochrome signal, without disturbing it. This insertion is possible because the spectrum of the monochrome TV signal is not continuous, hence empty space exists which can be utilized. This lack of continuity results from the discrete nature of the signal, which is divided into frames and lines. Analogue colour systems differ by the way in which empty space is used. In all cases, the colour signal is inserted at the end of the spectrum of the monochrome signal.

In order to be able to separate the colour signal from the monochrome one in the receiver, a fixed frequency subcarrier has to be used, this subcarrier being modulated by the colour signal.

The colour space is three dimensional by the nature of the human vision, so after subtracting the luminance, which is carried by the base signal, the colour subcarrier still has to carry a two dimensional signal. Typically the red (R) and the blue (B) information are carried because their signal difference with luminance (R-Y and B-Y) is stronger than that of green (G-Y).

SECAM differs from the other colour systems by the way the R-Y and B-Y signals are carried.

First, SECAM uses frequency modulation to encode chrominance information on the sub carrier.

Second, instead of transmitting the red and blue information together, it only sends one of them at a time, and uses the information about the other colour from the preceding line. It uses a delay line, an analog memory device, for storing one line of colour information. This justifies the "Sequential, With Memory" name.

Because SECAM transmits only one colour at a time, it is free of the colour artifacts present in NTSC and PAL resulting from the combined transmission of both signals.

This means that the vertical colour resolution is halved relative to NTSC. It is however not halved compared to PAL. Although PAL does not eliminate half of vertical colour information during encoding, it combines colour information from adjacent lines at the decoding stage, in order to compensate for "colour subcarrier phase errors" occurring during the transmission of the Amplitude-Modulated colour subcarrier. This is normally done using a delay line borrowed from SECAM (the result is called *PAL DL* or PAL Delay-Line, sometimes interpreted as DeLuxe), but can be accomplished "visually" in cheap TV sets (*PAL standard*). Because the FM modulation of SECAM's colour sub carrier is insensitive to phase (or amplitude) errors, phase errors do not cause loss of colour saturation in SECAM, although they do in PAL. In NTSC, such errors cause colour shifts.

The colour difference signals in SECAM are actually calculated in the YDbDr colour space, which is a scaled version of the YUV colour space. This encoding is better suited to the transmission of only one signal at a time.

FM modulation of the colour information allows SECAM to be free of the dot crawl problem commonly encountered with the other analog standards and first widely noticed with Laserdiscs. Dot crawl can be removed from PAL and NTSC-encoded signals using a comb filter. Such filters are usually only included in high-end displays. Dot crawl patterns (*animated checkerboard*) are easily visible along vertical lines in DVD menus displayed even by expensive (*e.g.* plasma) displays if these displays are connected to a signal source (DVD player) using a composite PAL or NTSC connection rather than, for example, RGB.

The idea of reducing the vertical colour resolution comes from Henri de France, who observed that colour information is approximately identical for two successive lines. Because the colour information was designed to be a cheap, backwards compatible addition to the monochrome signal, the colour signal has a lower bandwidth than the luminance signal, and hence lower horizontal resolution. Fortunately, the human visual system is similar in design: it perceives changes in luminance at a higher resolution than changes in chrominance, so this asymmetry has minimal visual impact. It was therefore also logical to reduce the vertical colour resolution.

DVD and other digital television formats have continued to exploit this visual artifact, sub sampling colour both horizontally and vertically. Hence, paradoxically, VHS NTSC videos and especially NTSC Laserdiscs can have a greater vertical colour resolution than DVD.

A similar paradox applies to the vertical resolution in television in general: reducing the bandwidth of the video signal will preserve the vertical resolution, even if the image loses sharpness and is smudged in the horizontal direction. Hence, video could be sharper vertically than horizontally. However, because of the interlacing, vertical resolution is effectively not as great as the number of scan lines. Additionally, transmitting an image with too much vertical detail will cause annoying flicker on television screens, as small details will only appear on a single line, and hence be refreshed at half the frequency. Computer-generated text and inserts have to be carefully low-pass filtered to prevent this.

History

Work on SECAM began in 1956. The technology was ready by the end of the fifties, but this was too soon for a wide introduction. Initially, a version of SECAM for the French 819-line television standard was devised and tested, but not introduced. Following a pan-European agreement to introduce colour TV only in 625 lines, France had to start the conversion by switching over to a 625-line television standard, which happened at the beginning of the 1960s with the introduction of a second network.

The first proposed system was called *SECAM I* in 1961, followed by other studies to improve compatibility and image quality.

These improvements were called *SECAM II* and *SECAM III* with the later being presented at the 1965 CCIR General Assembly in Vienna.

Further improvements were *SECAM III A* followed by *SECAM III B*, the adopted system for general usage in 1967.

Soviet technicians were involved in the development of the standard, and even created their own incompatible variant called *NIR* or *SECAM IV*, which was not deployed. The team was working in Moscow's Telecentrum under Professor Chmakov's direction. The *NIR* designation comes from the name of the *Nautchno-Issledovatelskiy Institut Radio* NIIR research institute involved in the studies. Two standards were developed: *Non-linear NIR* in which a process analogous to gamma correction is used and *Linear NIR* or *SECAM IV* that omits this process.

SECAM was inaugurated in France on October 1, 1967, on *la deuxième chaîne* (the second channel), now called France 2. A group of four suited men—a presenter and 3 contributors to the system's development, including De France—was shown standing in a studio. Following a count from 10, the originally black and white image switched to colour; the presenter then declared *"Et voici la couleur !"* (*fr:* And here is colour!)

The first colour television sets cost 5000 Francs. Colour TV was not very popular initially; only about 1500 people watched the inaugural programme in colour. A year later, only 200,000 sets had been sold of an expected million. This pattern was similar to the earlier slow build-up of colour television popularity in the USA.

SECAM was later adopted by former French and Belgian colonies, Greece, the Soviet Union and Eastern bloc countries (except Romania), and Middle Eastern countries. However, with the fall of communism, and following a period when multi-standard TV sets became a commodity, many Eastern European countries decided to switch to PAL.

Development

Some have argued that the primary motivation for the development of SECAM in France was to protect French television equipment manufacturers. However, incompatibility had started with the earlier decision to unusually adopt positive video modulation for French broadcast signals. The earlier British System A was the only other system to use positive video modulation. In addition, SECAM development predates PAL. NTSC was considered undesirable in Europe because of its tint problem requiring an additional control, which SECAM and PAL solved. The joke was that "SECAM" stood for «*System Essentially Contrary to the American Method*» versus NTSC «*Never Twice the Same Colour*» whilst «*Peace At Last*» could only be obtained through the PAL system. (But another version of the joke expands PAL as «*People Are Lavender*»). Nonetheless, SECAM was partly developed for reasons of national pride. Henri de France's personal charisma and ambition may have been a contributing factor. PAL was developed by Telefunken, a German company, and in the post-war De Gaulle era there would have been much political resistance to dropping a French-developed system and adopting a German-developed one instead.

Unlike some other manufacturers, the company where SECAM was invented, Thomson, still sells TV sets worldwide under different brands; this may be due in part to the legacy of SECAM. Thomson bought the company that developed PAL, Telefunken, and today even co-owns the RCA brand—RCA being the creator of NTSC. Thomson also co-authored the ATSC standard which is used for American high-definition TV.

Why SECAM Elsewhere?

The adoption of SECAM in Eastern Europe has been attributed to Cold War political machinations. According to this explanation, Western TV was popular in the East, authorities were well aware of this and adopted SECAM rather than the PAL encoding used in West Germany. This did not hinder mutual reception in black and white, because the underlying TV standards remained essentially the same in both parts of Germany. However, East Germans responded by buying PAL decoders for their SECAM sets. Eventually, the government in East Berlin stopped paying attention to so-called "Republikflucht via Fernsehen", or "defection via television". Later East German produced TV sets even included a dual standard PAL/SECAM decoder. In any case the majority of TV sets in East Germany were monochrome (black and white) until well into the 1980s.

However, PAL and SECAM are just standards for the colour subcarrier, used in conjunction with older standards for the base monochrome signals. The names for these monochrome standards are letters, such as M, B/G, D/K, and L.

These signals are much more important to compatibility than the colour sub-carriers are. They differ by AM or FM sound modulation, signal polarisation, relative frequencies within the channel, bandwidth, etc. For example, a PAL D/K TV set will be able to receive a SECAM D/K signal (although in black and white), while it will not be able to decode the sound of a PAL B/G signal. So even before SECAM came to Eastern European countries, most viewers could not have received Western programmes—and colour TV sets were not exactly widespread in the Communist bloc anyway, so the monochrome — only reception did not pose a significant problem.

SECAM Varieties

L, B/G, D/K, H (Broadcast)

There are five varieties of SECAM:

1. *French SECAM (SECAM-L)*: French SECAM (SECAM-L) is used only in France, Luxembourg (only RTL9 on CH 21 from Dudelange) and Tele Monte-Carlo Transmitters in the south of France.
2. *SECAM-B/G*: SECAM-B/G is used in the Middle East, former East Germany and Greece.
3. *SECAM D/K*: SECAM D/K is used in the Commonwealth of Independent States and Eastern Europe (this is simply SECAM used with the D and K monochrome TV transmission standards).
4. *SECAM-H*: Around 1983-84 a new colour identification standard ("Line SECAM or SECAM-H") has been introduced in order to make more space available inside the signal for adding teletext information (originally according to the Antiope standard). Identification bursts have been made per-line (like in PAL) rather than per-picture. Very old SECAM TV sets might not be able to display colour for today's broadcasts. Although any sets manufactured after the mid-1970s should be able to receive either variant.
5. *SECAM-K*: France also introduced the SECAM standard to its dependencies. However, the SECAM standard used in France's overseas possessions (as well as African countries that were once ruled by France) was slightly different from the SECAM used in Metropolitan France. The SECAM standard used in Metropolitan France used the SECAM-L and a variant of the channel information for VHF channels 2-10. French overseas possessions and many French-speaking African countries use the SECAM-K standard and a mutually incompatible variant of the channel information for VHF channels 4-9 (not channels 2-10).

MESECAM (Home Recording)

Reference is sometimes made to MESECAM as an alternative form of broadcast SECAM used in the Middle East. This is incorrect, MESECAM is meaningful only in terms of video recording. When a colour signal is recorded onto VHS or Betamax video tape, the luminance signal is recorded in its original form (albeit with some reduction of bandwidth) but the chrominance signal of about 4.4 MHz is too sensitive to small changes in frequency caused by inevitable small variations in tape speed to be recorded directly. Instead, it is first down converted to the lower frequency of 630 kHz, and the complex nature of the PAL subcarrier means that the down conversion must be done via a superhet mixer to ensure that information is not lost.

The SECAM subcarrier, being a simple FM signal, does not need such complex processing. The VHS specification requires that it be simply divided by 4 on recording to give a subcarrier of approximately 1.1 MHz, and multiplied by 4 again on playback. A true dual-standard PAL and SECAM video recorder therefore requires two colour processing circuits, adding to complexity and expense. Since some countries in the Middle East use PAL and others use SECAM, the region has adopted a shortcut, and uses the PAL mixer-down converter approach for both PAL and SECAM. This works well and simplifies VCR design.

The resultant signal on tape is not, of course, compatible with a true standard SECAM recording, and so is referred to as MESECAM. This is the only time the term MESECAM is meaningful. It is interesting to note that it is often possible to record SECAM video on an unmodified PAL VCR, thus creating MESECAM tapes, which can be played back in colour through another PAL VCR into a SECAM TV. Basic PAL VCRs work better for this, ones that are more sophisticated detect the SECAM signal as "not-PAL" and refuse to record it in colour.

Problems with the Standard

Unlike PAL or NTSC, analog SECAM television cannot easily be edited in its native analog form. Because it uses frequency modulation, SECAM is not linear with respect to the input image (this is also what protects it against signal distortion), so electrically mixing two (synchronized) SECAM signals does not yield a valid SECAM signal, unlike with analog PAL or NTSC. For this reason, to mix two SECAM signals, they must be demodulated, the demodulated signals mixed, and are remodulated again. Hence, post-production is often done in PAL, or in component formats, with the result encoded or transcoded into SECAM at the point of transmission. Reducing the costs of running television stations is one reason for some countries' recent switchovers to PAL.

TVs currently sold in SECAM countries support both SECAM and PAL, and more recently baseband NTSC as well (though not usually broadcast NTSC, that is, they cannot accept a broadcast signal from an antenna). Although the older analog camcorders (VHS, VHS-C) were produced in SECAM versions, none of the 8 mm or Hi-band models (S-VHS, S-VHS-C, and Hi-8) recorded it directly. Camcorders and VCRs of these standards sold in SECAM countries are internally PAL. They use an internal SECAM to PAL converter for recording of broadcast TV transmitted in SECAM. The result could be converted back to SECAM in some models; most people buying such expensive equipment would have a multistandard TV set and as such would not need a conversion. Digital camcorders or DVD players (with the exception of some early models) do not accept or output a SECAM analog signal. However, this is of dwindling importance: since 1980 most European domestic video equipment uses French-originated SCART connectors, allowing the transmission of RGB signals between devices. This eliminates the legacy of PAL, SECAM, and NTSC colour sub-carrier standards.

In general, modern professional equipment is now all-digital, and uses component-based digital interconnects such as CCIR 601 to eliminate the need for any analog processing prior to the final modulation of the analog signal for broadcast. However, large installed bases of analog professional equipment still exist, particularly in third world countries.

Countries and Territories that Use SECAM

This is a list of nations that currently authorize the use of the SECAM standard for television broadcasting. Nations that have moved to PAL or DVB-T are listed separately.

Africa

- ❑ Benin
- ❑ Burundi
- ❑ Chad
- ❑ Congo-Kinshasa
- ❑ Djibouti
- ❑ Egypt (Simulcast in PAL-B/G)
- ❑ Libya (Simulcast in PAL-B/G)
- ❑ Mali
- ❑ Mauritius
- ❑ Niger
- ❑ Réunion (see France)
- ❑ Togo
- ❑ Burkina Faso
- ❑ Central African Republic
- ❑ Congo-Brazzaville
- ❑ Côte d'Ivoire
- ❑ Equatorial Guinea
- ❑ Gabon
- ❑ Madagascar
- ❑ Mauritania
- ❑ Morocco
- ❑ Rwanda
- ❑ Senegal
- ❑ Tunisia

Asia

- ❑ Afghanistan (Simulcast in PAL-B)
- ❑ Cambodia (Kampuchea) (Simulcast in PAL-B/G)
- ❑ Iran (Simulcast in PAL-B/G)
- ❑ North Korea (Simulcast in PAL-D/K)
- ❑ Saudi Arabia (Simulcast in PAL-B)
- ❑ Syria (Simulcast in PAL-G)
- ❑ Vietnam (Simulcast in NTSC-M)

Pacific Islands

- ❑ French Polynesia (incl. Tahiti)

- New Caledonia
- Wallis and Futuna

Europe

- Andorra (Simulcast in PAL).
- France (SECAM broadcast to be abandoned by 2011, simulcast in IPTV/ADSL and DVB-T).
- Luxembourg (Simulcast in PAL-B/G).
- Monaco (Simulcast in PAL-G).

Former USSR

Due to some slight differences in the type of SECAM adopted by the former USSR, the former USSR states that adopted SECAM are listed separately.

- Armenia
- Azerbaijan
- Belarus
- Georgia
- Kazakhstan
- Kyrgyzstan
- Moldova
- Russia
- Tajikistan
- Turkmenistan
- Uzbekistan

Americas

- French Guiana
- Guadeloupe
- Saint-Pierre and Miquelon
- Martinique

Migration from SECAM to PAL

Some former SECAM countries are in the process of migrating to PAL or have already finished doing so.

Europe

- Bulgaria (migrated 1994-96)
- Czech Republic (migrated 1992-94)
- Estonia (migrated 1995-99)
- East Germany (switchover on December 14, 1990 because of German reunification)
- Greece (migrated in ca. 1992)
- Hungary (migrated 1995-96)
- Latvia (migrated 1997-99)
- Lithuania (migrated 1997-99)
- Poland (migrated 1993-95)
- Slovakia (migrated 1993-96)
- Ukraine

Asia

- Iraq
- Mongolia

The Czech Republic, Slovakia, Hungary and the Baltic countries also changed their underlying sound carrier standard from D/K to B/G which is used in most of Western Europe, to facilitate use of imported broadcast equipment. This required viewers to purchase multistandard receivers though. The other countries mentioned kept their existing standards (B/G in the cases of East Germany and Greece, D/K for the rest).

FIELD-SEQUENTIAL COLOUR SYSTEM

A field-sequential colour system is a colour television system in which the primary colour information is transmitted in successive images, and which relies on the human vision system to fuse the successive images into a colour picture. One field-sequential system was developed by Dr. Peter Goldmark for CBS, which was its sole user in commercial broadcasting. It was first demonstrated to the press on September 4, 1940, and first shown to the general public on January 12, 1950. The Federal Communications Commission adopted it on October 11, 1950 as the standard for colour television in the United States, but it was later withdrawn.

Operation

The CBS field-sequential system was an example of a mechanical television system because it relied in part on a disc of colour filters rotating at 1440 rpm inside the camera and the receiver, capturing and displaying red, green, and blue television images in sequence. The field rate was increased from 60 to 144 fields per second to overcome the flicker from the separate colour images, resulting in 24 complete colour frames per second (each of the three colours was scanned twice, double interlacing being standard for all electronic television: 2 scans × 3 colours × 24 frames per second = 144 fields per second). If the 144-field colour signal were transmitted with the same detail as a 60-field monochrome signal, 2.4 times the bandwidth would be required. Therefore, to keep the signal within the standard 6 MHz bandwidth of a channel, the image's vertical resolution was reduced from 525 lines to 405. Because of these variances from the NTSC standards for television broadcasting, field-sequential colour broadcasts could not be seen on existing black and white receivers without an adapter (to see them in monochrome), or adapter-converter (to see them in colour).

Commercial Failure

CBS purchased its own television manufacturer in April 1951 when no other company would produce colour sets using the system. Production of CBS-Columbia colour receivers began in September, and were first offered for retail sale in October.

Field-sequential colour broadcasts were suspended by CBS on October 21, 1951, ostensibly by request of the National Production Authority, which in November 1951 prohibited the manufacture of colour sets for the general public during the Korean War. Only 200 colour sets had been manufactured for commercial sale, and only 100 of those had shipped, when CBS suspended its colour broadcasts. CBS announced in March 1953 that it had abandoned any further plans for its colour system. RCA was the leading company in the television field, with a larger technical staff, more development funds, and more political success in getting the NTSC compatible colour television system. RCA developed the hardware for NTSC which superseded the field-sequential system as the U.S. standard in December 1953.

Baird Predecessor

Television pioneer John Logie Baird demonstrated the earliest version of field-sequential colour television on July 3, 1928, using a mechanical television system before the use of cathode ray tubes, and producing a vertical colour image about 4 inches (10 cm) high. It was described in the journal *Nature*:

- The process consisted of first exploring the object, the image of which is to be transmitted, with a spot of red light, next with a spot of green light, and finally with a spot of blue light. At the receiving station a similar process is employed, red, blue and green images being presented in rapid success to the eye. The apparatus used at the transmitter consists of a disc perforated with three successive spiral curves of holes. The holes in the first spiral are covered with red filters, in the second with green filters and in the third with blue. Light is projected through these holes and an image of the moving holes is projected onto the object. The disc revolves at 10 revolutions per second and so thirty complete images are transmitted every second—ten blue, ten red, and ten green.
- At the receiving station a similar disc revolves synchronously with the transmitting disc, and behind this disc, in line with the eye of the observer, are two glow discharge lamps. One of these lamps is a neon tube and the other a tube containing mercury vapour and helium. By means of a commutator the mercury vapour and helium tube is placed in circuit for two-thirds of a revolution and the neon tube for the remaining third. The red light from the neon is accentuated by placing red filters over the view holes for the red image. Similarly, the view holes corresponding to the green and blue images are covered by suitable filters. The blue and green lights both come from the mercury helium tube, which emits rays rich in both colours.

Baird demonstrated a modified version on July 27, 1939 that used a cathode ray tube in the receiver.

Later Use

For the first nine months of NTSC colour in 1953–54, CBS continued to use its field-sequential colour television cameras, with the field rate and signal adapted for NTSC standards, until RCA delivered its first production model of an NTSC colour camera in time for the 1954–55 season.

Russia was the only other country to experiment with a field-sequential colour system. It manufactured a small number of colour receivers in 1954 that used a mechanical colour disc.

The field sequential system was used in specialized applications long after it had replaced for broadcast television. A notable example was the Apollo lunar landing cameras which transmitted colour television images from the Moon during missions from 1969 to 1972.

MULTIPLEXED ANALOGUE COMPONENTS

Multiplexed Analogue Components (MAC) was a satellite television transmission standard, originally proposed for use on a Europe-wide terrestrial HDTV system, although it was never used terrestrially.

MAC FAQ

MAC transmits luminance and chrominance data separately in time rather than separately in frequency (as other analog television formats do, such as composite video).

Audio and Scrambling (selective access):

- Audio, in a format similar to NICAM was transmitted digitally rather than as an FM sub-carrier.
- The MAC standard included a standard scrambling system, EuroCrypt, a precursor to the standard DVB-CSA encryption system.

History

It was originally developed by the Independent Broadcasting Authority (IBA) (dates unknown) in the UK for delivering high quality pictures via direct broadcast satellites that would be independent of European countries' choice of terrestrial colour coding standard.

Variants

A number of broadcasting variants of the MAC standard exist.

- A-MAC Designed as a test-bed for the MAC concept. A-MAC was never deployed by any broadcaster. S-MAC is design descendant A-MAC.
- B-MAC used in South Africa by Multichoice, Australia by Optus and also used in parts of Asia until 2005 when digital compression finally replaced B-MAC.
- C-MAC has a wide-screen backwardly compatible variant called E-MAC.
- D-MAC (used by British Satellite Broadcasting) but not used on cable systems.

This is a satellite only MAC format. Also used by NRK. This because D-MAC has 4 audio channels (D2-MAC just has 2 audio channels). Then it was possible to transmit 3 radio channels and 1 TV channel at one D-MAC channel.

- D2-MAC used until July 2006 in Scandinavia and until the mid-1990s for German and French satellite television. Some cable systems may still be using D2-MAC in Europe and Asia.
- HD-MAC, an early high-definition television standard allowing for 2048×1152 resolution.

Studio (Non Broadcast) MAC Variants

S-MAC (*Studio MAC*): Used mostly in North America.

- Processing NTSC component signals yields better results (a higher quality image) than manipulating NTSC directly—thus the need to create S-MAC.
- It is not possible to mix standard MAC signals in the studio environment because the (R-Y) and (B-Y) components are carried on alternate lines.
- S-MAC's SECAM like approach to bandwidth reduction is technical annoyance, but most studio users are not affected by it.
- In S-MAC the luminance is compressed by 2:1 and the two chrominance signals by 4:1 so that all three may occupy the same line.
- S-MAC's vision bandwidth is 11 MHz, only ~2.8x that of NTSC's vision bandwidth of 4.2 MHz.
- S-MAC can be carried on a single circuit and converted losslessly to and from C-MAC at any stage.
- S-MAC is well suited for SNG applications (AKA: news gathering trucks).

MAC System Innovations

Mathematical

- A-MAC proved the mathematical principle that separating vision from colour for TV transmission was technologically viable.

Broadcast Engineering

- The MAC audio subsystem is very similar to NICAM, so much so that identical chip-sets are used.
- D-MAC satellite broadcasts provided the first broadcast sourced wide-screen television in Europe, and HD-MAC provided the first HDTV broadcasts, in 1992.

Technical Challenges

Although the MAC technique is capable of superior video quality (similar to the improvement of component video over composite in a DVD player), its major drawback was that this quality was only ever realized when the video signals being transmitted remained in component form from source to transmitter. If at any stage the video had to be handled in composite form, the necessary encoding/decoding processes would severely degrade the picture quality.

- Terrestrial TV broadcasters were never able to take full advantage of MAC image quality due to multiple interactions between their composite and component signal paths.
- *Direct to Home* and TVRO broadcasters were able to take advantage of MAC's improved image quality because their studios and routing facilities were far less complex.
- The success of NICAM audio for terrestrial television can be traced to the success of MAC technology. The MAC audio subsystem is nearly identical in design and function to NICAM.

Technological Obsolescence

Since the vast majority of TV stations and similar installations were only wired for composite video, the fitting of a MAC transmitter at the end of the chain had the effect of degrading the transmitted image quality, rather than improving it.

For this and other technical reasons, MAC systems never really caught on with broadcasters. MAC transmission technology was made obsolete by the radically new digital systems (like DVB-T and ATSC) in the late 1990s.

Although MAC transmission systems are still used, the technology is obsolete. It is expected that MAC will cease to be used for TV transmission by 2012.

MULTIPLE SUB-NYQUIST SAMPLING ENCODING SYSTEM

Multiple Sub-nyquist Sampling Encoding System (MUSE), also known as *Hi-Vision* for marketing purposes was an early Japanese analog television standard. Japan had the earliest working HDTV system, with design efforts going back to 1979. The country began broadcasting analog HDTV signals in the late 1980s using an interlaced resolution of 1035 or 1080 active lines (1035i) or 1125 total lines.

History

The Japanese system, developed by NHK *Science and Technical Research Laboratories* (STRL) in the 1980s, employed filtering tricks to reduce the original source signal to decrease bandwidth utilization. MUSE was marketed as "Hi-Vision" by NHK.

- Japanese broadcast engineers immediately rejected conventional vestigial sideband broadcasting for well-founded technical reasons.
- It was decided early on that MUSE would be a satellite broadcast format as Japan economically supports satellite broadcasting.

Modulation Research

- The idea of FM modulation of a conventionally constructed composite (Y+C, like NTSC and PAL) signal was first tested.

- MUSE initially had a signal structure similar to NTSC. Early MUSE had with the Y at the lower frequencies and the C at higher frequencies just like NTSC. This worked moderately well and was adopted for initial satellite trials in the 1980s.
- Separate transmission of Y and C components was then explored. The MUSE format that is transmitted today uses separated component signalling. The improvement in picture quality was so great that the original test systems were recalled.
- One more power saving tweak was made: Lack of visual response to low frequency noise allows significant reduction in transponder power if the higher video frequencies are emphasized prior to modulation at the transmitter and de-emphasized at the receiver.

Technical Specifications

- Aspect Ratio: 16:9
- Scanlines (active/total): 1,125/1,250
- Pixels per line (active/total): 1,920/2,200
- Interlaced ratio: 2:1
- Refresh rate: 59.94 (as with NTSC).
- Sampling frequency for broadcast: 16.2 MHz
- Vector motion compensation: horizontal ± 16 samples (32.4 MHz clock)/frame, a vertical line ± 3/Field
- Audio: 48 KHz 16 bit (2ch) 32 KHz 12 bit (4ch: 3.1)

DPCM Audio compression format: DPCM quasi-instantaneous companding

MUSE is a 1125 line system (1035 visible), and is not pulse and sync compatible with the digital 1080 line system used by modern HDTV. Originally, it was a 1125 line, interlaced, 60 Hz, system with a 5/3 ((1.66:1) aspect ratio and an optimal viewing distance of roughly 3.3 H.

For terrestrial MUSE transmission a bandwidth limited FM modulation system was devised. A satellite transmission system uses uncompressed FM modulation.

The pre-compression bandwidth for Y is 20 MHz, and the pre-compression bandwidth for chrominance is a 7 MHz carrier.

The Japanese initially explored the idea of FM modulation of a conventionally constructed composite signal. This would create a signal similar in structure to the Y/C NTSC signal—with the Y at the lower frequencies and the C above. Approximately 3 kW of power would be required, in order to get 40 dB of signal to noise ratio for a composite FM signal in the 22 GHz band. This was incompatible with satellite broadcast techniques and bandwidth.

To overcome this limitation, it was decided to use a separate transmission of Y and C. This reduces the effective frequency range and lowers the required power. Approximately 570 W (360 for Y and 210 for C) would be needed in order to get a 40 dB of signal to noise ratio for a separate Y/C FM signal in the 22 GHz satellite band. This was feasible.

There is one more power saving that appears from the character of the human eye. The lack of visual response to low frequency noise allows significant reduction in transponder power if the higher video frequencies are emphasized prior to modulation at the transmitter and then de-emphasized at the receiver. This method was adopted, with crossover frequencies for the emphasis/de-emphasis at 5.2 MHz for Y and 1.6 MHz for C. With this in place, the power requirements drop to 260 W of power (190 for Y and 69 for C).

Sampling Systems and Ratios

The subsampling in a video system is usually expressed as a three part ratio. The three terms of the ratio are: the number of brightness ("luminance" "luma" or Y) samples, followed by the number of samples of the two colour ("chroma") components: U/Cb then V/Cr, for each complete sample area. For quality comparison, only the ratio between those values is important, so 4:4:4 could easily be called 1:1:1; however, traditionally the value for brightness is always 4, with the rest of the values scaled accordingly.

Sometimes, four part relations are written, like 4:2:2:4. In these cases, the fourth number means the sampling frequency ratio of a key channel. In virtually all cases, that number will be 4, since high quality is very desirable in keying applications.

The sampling principles above apply to both digital and analog television.

MUSE implements a varible sampling system of ~4:2:1 … ~4:0.5:0.25 depending on the amount of motion on the screen.

Exotic Digital Audio Broadcasting Subsystem

MUSE had a discrete 2- or 4-channel digital audio system called "DANCE", which stood for *D*igital *A*udio *N*ear-instantaneous *C*ompression and *E*xpansion. It used differential audio transmission (DPCM) that was not psychoacoustics-based like MPEG-1 Layer II. It used 1350 kbp/s and was not nearly as 'mysterious' or 'complex' as some people have claimed. Like the PAL NICAM stereo system, it used near-instantaneous companding (as opposed to Syllabic-companding like the dbx system uses) and non-linear 13-bit digital encoding at a 32 kHz sample rate. It could also operate in a 48 kHz 16-bit mode. The DANCE system was well documented in numerous NHK technical papers and in a NHK-published book issued in the USA called *Hi-Vision Technology*.

The DANCE audio codec was superseded by Dolby AC-3 (a.k.a Dolby Digital), DTS Coherent Acoustics (a.k.a DTS Zeta 6x20 or ARTEC), MPEG-1 Layer III and many other audio coders. The methods of this codec are described in the IEEE paper:

Real World Performance Issues

In the typical setup, three picture elements on a line were actually derived from three separate scans. Stationary images were transmitted at full resolution. However, as MUSE lowers the horizontal and vertical resolution of material that varies greatly from frame to frame, moving images were blurred in a manner similar to using 16 mm movie film for HDTV projection. In fact, whole-camera pans would result in a loss of 50 per cent of horizontal resolution.

MUSE's "1125 lines" are an analog measurement, which includes non-video "scan lines" during which a CRT's electron beam returns to the top of the screen to begin scanning the next field. Only 1035 lines have picture information. Digital signals count only the lines (rows of pixels) that have actual detail, so NTSC's 525 lines become 480i, PAL's 625 lines become 576i, and muse would be 1035i. To convert the bandwidth of Hi-Vision MUSE into 'conventional' lines-of-horizontal resolution (as is used in the NTSC world), multiply 29.9 lines per MHz of bandwidth. (NTSC and PAL/SECAM are 79.9 lines per MHz)—this calculation of 29.9 lines works for all current HD systems including Blu-ray and HD-DVD. So, for MUSE, during a still picture, the lines of resolution would be: 598-lines of luminance resolution per-picture-height. The chroma resolution is: 209-lines. This 'seems' the same as Standard Def but remember, HD has a wider aspect ratio and more vertical scanning lines. The horizontal luminance measurement approximately matches the vertical resolution of a 1080 interlaced image when the Kell Factor and Interlace Factor are taken into account. Shadows and multipath still plague this analog frequency modulated transmission mode.

Considering the technological limitations of the time, MUSE was a very cleverly-designed system. One thing most people don't seem to realize however is that MUSE, except for the actual transmission over the air, was a 100 per cent digital system—All encoding/decoding was done in the digital domain. ONLY the actual transmission was analog and used Pulse Amplitude Modulation. So, it's rather unfair to call MUSE "analog", when it really was a digital compression system. Japan has since switched to a digital HDTV system based on ISDB, but the original MUSE-based BS Satellite channel 9 (NHK BS Hi-vision) was broadcast until September 30, 2007.

Muse Laserdiscs

There were a few MUSE laserdisc players available in Japan (Panasonic LX-HD10/20 and Sony HIL-C2EX). These could play Hi-Vision as well as standard NTSC discs.

Sega Saturn

The Japanese Sega Saturn could output a Hi-Vision signal (352×480p or 704×480p) with special cables.

EIA STANDARDS

Here is a list of Electronic Industries Alliance (EIA) Standards:

- EIA-232 RS-232 electrical characteristics single-ended voltage digital interface circuit.
- EIA/ECA-310 Cabinets, racks (including 19-inch racks), panels and associated equipment standard.
- EIA-343 Formerly RS-343. Signal standard for non-broadcast high resolution monochrome video.

- EIA-343A Formerly RS-343 A. Video signal standard for high resolution monochrome CCTV. Based on EIA-343.
- TIA-422 RS-422 electrical characteristics of the balanced voltage digital interface circuit
- EIA-485 RS-485 multi-point electrical characteristics of the balanced voltage digital interface circuit
- EIA-535 defines capacitor dielectric classes: class 1, class 2
- TIA-568-B cable wiring standard for twisted pair cabling
- TIA-574 D-subminiature 9 pin connector
- EIA-608 standard for closed captioning for NTSC TV broadcasts in the United States and Canada
- EIA-708 is the standard for closed captioning for ATSC digital television streams in the United States and Canada.
- TIA-968-A unkeyed RJ45 connector to ethernet

Note: the above list of standards is not only incomplete, but also out of date. For example, the standard on capacitor dielectric classes is as of November 2002:

- EIA-198-1-F Ceramic Dielectric Capacitors: Classes I, II, III, and IV.

7

Towards Better Understanding of Modulation: Principles, Types and Techniques

MODULATION

In A device that performs modulation is known as a modulator and a device that performs the inverse operation of modulation is known as a demodulator (sometimes *detector* or *demod*). A device that can do both operations is a modem (short for "Modulator-Demodulator").

Aim

The aim of digital modulation is to transfer a digital bit stream over an analog bandpass channel, for example over the public switched telephone network (where a filter limits the frequency range to between 300 and 3400 Hz) or a limited radio frequency band.

The aim of analog modulation is to transfer an analog lowpass signal, for example an audio signal or TV signal, over an analog bandpass channel, for example a limited radio frequency band or a cable TV network channel.

Analog and digital modulation facilitate frequency division multiplexing (FDM), where several low pass information signals are transferred simultaneously over the same shared physical medium, using separate bandpass channels.

The aim of digital baseband modulation methods, also known as line coding, is to transfer a digital bit stream over a lowpass channel, typically a non-filtered copper wire such as a serial bus or a wired local area network.

The aim of pulse modulation methods is to transfer a narrowband analog signal, for example a phone call over a wideband lowpass channel or, in some of the schemes, as a bit stream over another digital transmission system.

Analog Modulation Methods

In analog modulation, the modulation is applied continuously in response to the analog information signal.

Common analog modulation techniques are:

- Amplitude modulation (AM) (here the amplitude of the modulated signal is varied):
  - Double-sideband modulation (DSB),

- Double-sideband modulation with unsuppressed carrier (DSB-WC) (used on the AM radio broadcasting band),
- Double-sideband suppressed-carrier transmission (DSB-SC),
- Double-sideband reduced carrier transmission (DSB-RC).

◆ Single-sideband modulation (SSB, or SSB-AM):

- SSB with carrier (SSB-WC),
- SSB suppressed carrier modulation (SSB-SC).

◆ Vestigial sideband modulation (VSB, or VSB-AM).
◆ Quadrature amplitude modulation (QAM).

❑ Angle modulation:

◆ Frequency modulation (FM) (here the frequency of the modulated signal is varied).
◆ Phase modulation (PM) (here the phase shift of the modulated signal is varied).

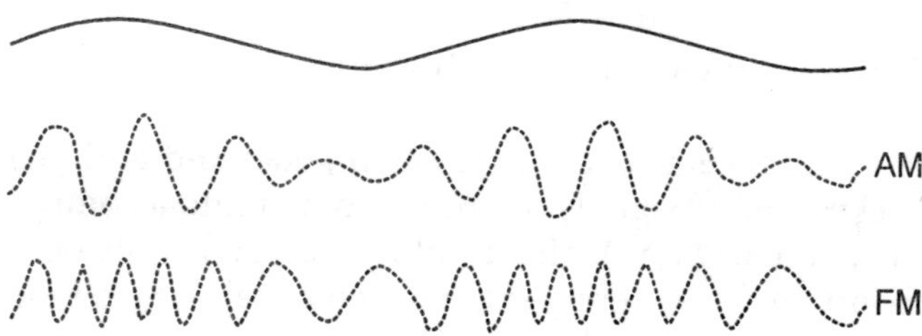

Fig. 7.1: A low-frequency message signal (top) may be carried by an AM or FM radio wave.

Digital Modulation Methods

In digital modulation, an analog carrier signal is modulated by a digital bit stream. Digital modulation methods can be considered as digital-to-analog conversion, and the corresponding demodulation or detection as analog-to-digital conversion. The changes in the carrier signal are chosen from a finite number of M alternative symbols (the *modulation alphabet*).

Fundamental Digital Modulation Methods

These are the most fundamental digital modulation techniques:

❑ In the case of PSK, a finite number of phases are used.
❑ In the case of FSK, a finite number of frequencies are used.
❑ In the case of ASK, a finite number of amplitudes are used.
❑ In the case of QAM, a finite number of at least two phases, and at least two amplitudes are used.

In QAM, an inphase signal (the I signal, for example a cosine waveform) and a quadrature phase signal (the Q signal, for example a sine wave) are amplitude modulated with a finite number of amplitudes, and summed. It can be seen as a two-channel system, each channel using ASK. The resulting signal is equivalent to a combination of PSK and ASK.

In all of the above methods, each of these phases, frequencies or amplitudes are assigned a unique pattern of binary bits. Usually, each phase, frequency or amplitude encodes an equal number of bits. This number of bits comprises the *symbol* that is represented by the particular phase.

If the alphabet consists of $M = 2^N$ alternative symbols, each symbol represents a message consisting of N bits. If the symbol rate (also known as the baud rate) is f_S symbols/second (or baud), the data rate is Nf_S bit/second.

For example, with an alphabet consisting of 16 alternative symbols, each symbol represents 4 bits. Thus, the data rate is four times the baud rate.

In the case of PSK, ASK or QAM, where the carrier frequency of the modulated signal is constant, the modulation alphabet is often conveniently represented on a constellation diagram, showing the amplitude of the I signal at the x-axis, and the amplitude of the Q signal at the y-axis, for each symbol.

Modulator and Detector Principles of Operation

PSK and ASK, and sometimes also FSK, are often generated and detected using the principle of QAM. The I and Q signals can be combined into a complex-valued signal $I + jQ$ (where j is the imaginary unit). The resulting so called equivalent lowpass signal or equivalent baseband signal is a representation of the real-valued modulated physical signal (the so called passband signal or RF signal).

These are the general steps used by the modulator to transmit data:

1. Group the incoming data bits into codewords, one for each symbol that will be transmitted.
2. Map the codewords to attributes, for example amplitudes of the I and Q signals (the equivalent low pass signal), or frequency or phase values.
3. Adapt pulse shaping or some other filtering to limit the bandwidth and form the spectrum of the equivalent low pass signal, typically using digital signal processing.
4. Perform digital-to-analog conversion (DAC) of the I and Q signals (since today all of the above is normally achieved using digital signal processing, DSP).
5. Generate a high-frequency sine wave carrier waveform, and perhaps also a cosine quadrature component. Carry out the modulation, for example by multiplying the sine and cosine wave form with the I and Q signals, resulting in that the equivalent low pass signal is frequency shifted into a modulated passband signal or RF signal. Sometimes this is achieved using DSP technology, for example direct digital synthesis using a waveform table, instead of analog signal processing. In that case the above DAC step should be done after this step.
6. Amplification and analog bandpass filtering to avoid harmonic distortion and periodic spectrum.

At the receiver side, the demodulator typically performs:

1. Bandpass filtering.
2. Automatic gain control, AGC (to compensate for attenuation, for example fading).
3. Frequency shifting of the RF signal to the equivalent baseband I and Q signals, or to an intermediate frequency (IF) signal, by multiplying the RF signal with a local oscillator sinewave and cosine wave frequency (see the superheterodyne receiver principle).
4. Sampling and analog-to-digital conversion (ADC) (Sometimes before or instead of the above point, for example by means of undersampling).
5. Equalization filtering, for example a matched filter, compensation for multipath propagation, time spreading, phase distortion and frequency selective fading, to avoid intersymbol interference and symbol distortion.
6. Detection of the amplitudes of the I and Q signals, or the frequency or phase of the IF signal.
7. Quantization of the amplitudes, frequencies or phases to the nearest allowed symbol values.
8. Mapping of the quantized amplitudes, frequencies or phases to codewords (bit groups).
9. Parallel-to-serial conversion of the codewords into a bit stream.
10. Pass the resultant bit stream on for further processing such as removal of any error-correcting codes.

As is common to all digital communication systems, the design of both the modulator and demodulator must be done simultaneously. Digital modulation schemes are possible because the transmitter-receiver pair have prior knowledge of how data is encoded and represented in the communications system. In all digital communication systems, both the modulator at the transmitter and the demodulator at the receiver are structured so that they perform inverse operations.

Non-coherent modulation methods do not require a receiver reference clock signal that is phase synchronized with the sender carrier wave. In this case, modulation symbols (rather than bits, characters, or data packets) are asynchronously transferred. The opposite is coherent modulation.

List of Common Digital Modulation Techniques

The most common digital modulation techniques are:

- Phase-shift keying (PSK):
  - Binary PSK (BPSK), using M=2 symbols
  - Quadrature (QPSK), using M=4 symbols
  - 8 PSK, using M=8 symbols
  - 16 PSK, usign M=16 symbols
  - Differential PSK (DPSK)

- Differential QPSK (DQPSK)
- Offset QPSK (OQPSK)
- π/4–QPSK

- Frequency-shift keying (FSK):
  - Audio frequency-shift keying (AFSK)
  - Multi-frequency shift keying (M-ary FSK or MFSK)
  - Dual-tone multi-frequency (DTMF)
  - Continuous-phase frequency-shift keying (CPFSK)
- Amplitude-shift keying (ASK)
- On-off keying (OOK), the most common ASK form
  - M-ary vestigial sideband modulation, for example 8 VSB
- Quadrature amplitude modulation (QAM)—a combination of PSK and ASK:
  - Polar modulation like QAM a combination of PSK and ASK.
- Continuous phase modulation (CPM) methods:
  - Minimum-shift keying (MSK)
  - Gaussian minimum-shift keying (GMSK)
- Orthogonal frequency division multiplexing (OFDM) modulation:
  - Discrete multitone (DMT)—including adaptive modulation and bit-loading.
- Wavelet modulation.
- Trellis coded modulation (TCM), also known as trellis modulation.

MSK and GMSK are particular cases of continuous phase modulation. Indeed, MSK is a particular case of the sub-family of CPM known as continuous-phase frequency-shift keying (CPFSK) which is defined by a rectangular frequency pulse (*i.e.* a linearly increasing phase pulse) of one symbol-time duration (total response signaling).

OFDM is based on the idea of frequency division multiplexing (FDM), but is utilized as a digital modulation scheme. The bit stream is split into several parallel data streams, each transferred over its own sub-carrier using some conventional digital modulation scheme. The modulated sub-carriers are summed to form an OFDM signal. OFDM is considered as a modulation technique rather than a multiplex technique, since it transfers one bit stream over one communication channel using one sequence of so-called OFDM symbols. OFDM can be extended to multi-user channel access method in the Orthogonal Frequency Division Multiple Access (OFDMA) and MC-OFDM schemes, allowing several users to share the same physical medium by giving different sub-carriers or spreading codes to different users.

Of the two kinds of RF power amplifier, switching amplifiers (Class C amplifiers) cost less and use less battery power than linear amplifiers of the same output power.

However, they only work with relatively constant-amplitude-modulation signals such as angle modulation (FSK or PSK) and CDMA, but not with QAM and OFDM. Nevertheless, even though switching amplifiers are completely unsuitable for normal QAM constellations, often the QAM modulation principle are used to drive switching amplifiers with these FM and other waveforms, and sometimes QAM demodulators are used to receive the signals put out by these switching amplifiers.

Digital Baseband Modulation or Line Coding

The term digital baseband modulation is synonymous to line codes, which are methods to transfer a digital bit stream over an analog lowpass channel using a pulse train, *i.e.* a discrete number of signal levels, by directly modulating the voltage or current on a cable. Common examples are unipolar, non-return-to-zero (NRZ), Manchester and alternate mark inversion (AMI) coding.

Pulse Modulation Methods

Pulse modulation schemes aim at transferring a narrowband analog signal over an analog lowpass channel as a two-level quantized signal, by modulating a pulse train. Some pulse modulation schemes also allow the narrowband analog signal to be transferred as a digital signal (*i.e.* as a quantized discrete-time signal) with a fixed bit rate, which can be transferred over an underlying digital transmission system, for example some line code. They are not modulation schemes in the conventional sense since they are not channel coding schemes, but should be considered as source coding schemes, and in some cases analog-to-digital conversion techniques.

- Pulse-code modulation (PCM) (Analog-over-digital).
- Pulse-width modulation (PWM) (Analog-over-analog).
- Pulse-amplitude modulation (PAM) (Analog-over-analog).
- Pulse-position modulation (PPM) (Analog-over-analog).
- Pulse-density modulation (PDM) (Analog-over-digital).
- Sigma-delta modulation (ΣΔ) (Analog-over-digital).
- Continuously variable slope delta modulation (CVSDM), also called Adaptive-delta modulation (ADM) (Analog-over-digital).
- Direct-sequence spread spectrum (DSSS) is based on pulse-amplitude modulation.

Miscellaneous Modulation Techniques

- The use of on-off keying to transmit Morse code at radio frequencies is known as continuous wave (CW) operation.
- Adaptive modulation.
- Space modulation A method whereby signals are modulated within airspace, such as that used in Instrument landing systems.

AMPLITUDE MODULATION

Amplitude modulation (AM) is a technique used in electronic communication, most commonly for transmitting information via a radio carrier wave. AM works by varying the strength of the transmitted signal in relation to the information being sent. For example, changes in the signal strength can be used to reflect the sounds to be reproduced by a speaker, or to specify the light intensity of television pixels. (Contrast this with frequency modulation, also commonly used for sound transmissions, in which the frequency is varied; and phase modulation, often used in remote controls, in which the phase is varied).

In the mid-1870s, a form of amplitude modulation—initially called "undulatory currents"—was the first method to successfully produce quality audio over telephone lines. Beginning with Reginald Fessenden's audio demonstrations in 1906, it was also the original method used for audio radio transmissions, and remains in use today by many forms of communication—"AM" is often used to refer to the mediumwave broadcast band.

Forms of Amplitude Modulation

As originally developed for the electric telephone, amplitude modulation was used to add audio information to the low-powered direct current flowing from a telephone transmitter to a receiver. As a simplified explanation, at the transmitting end, a telephone microphone was used to vary the strength of the transmitted current, according to the frequency and loudness of the sounds received. Then, at the receiving end of the telephone line, the transmitted electrical current affected an electromagnet, which strengthened and weakened in response to the strength of the current. In turn, the electromagnet produced vibrations in the receiver diaphragm, thus closely reproducing the frequency and loudness of the sounds originally heard at the transmitter.

In contrast to the telephone, in radio communication what is modulated is a continuous wave radio signal (carrier wave) produced by a radio transmitter. In its basic form, amplitude modulation produces a signal with power concentrated at the carrier frequency and in two adjacent sidebands. Each sideband is equal in bandwidth to that of the modulating signal and is a mirror image of the other. Amplitude modulation that results in two sidebands and a carrier is often called *double sideband amplitude modulation* (DSB-AM). Amplitude modulation is inefficient in terms of power usage and much of it is wasted. At least two-thirds of the power is concentrated in the carrier signal, which carries no useful information (beyond the fact that a signal is present); the remaining power is split between two identical sidebands, though only one of these is needed since they contain identical information.

To increase transmitter efficiency, the carrier can be removed (suppressed) from the AM signal. This produces a reduced-carrier transmission or *double-sideband suppressed-carrier* (DSBSC) signal. A suppressed-carrier amplitude modulation scheme is three times more power-efficient than traditional DSB-AM. If the carrier is only partially suppressed, a *double-sideband reduced-carrier* (DSBRC) signal results. DSBSC and DSBRC signals need their carrier to be regenerated (by a beat frequency oscillator, for instance) to be demodulated using conventional techniques.

Even greater efficiency is achieved—at the expense of increased transmitter and receiver complexity—by completely suppressing both the carrier and one of the sidebands. This is single-sideband modulation, widely used in amateur radio due to its efficient use of both power and bandwidth.

A simple form of AM often used for digital communications is *on-off keying*, a type of *amplitude-shift keying* by which binary data is represented as the presence or absence of a carrier wave. This is commonly used at radio frequencies to transmit Morse code, referred to as continuous wave (CW) operation.

In 1982, the International Telecommunications Union (ITU) designated the various types of amplitude modulation as follows:

Designation	*Description*
A3E	Double-sideband full-carrier—the basic AM modulation scheme
R3E	Single-sideband reduced-carrier
H3E	Single-sideband full-carrier
J3E	Single-sideband suppressed-carrier
B8E	Independent-sideband emission
C3F	Vestigial-sideband
Lincompex	Linked compressor and expander

Example: A carrier wave is modelled as a simple sine wave, such as:

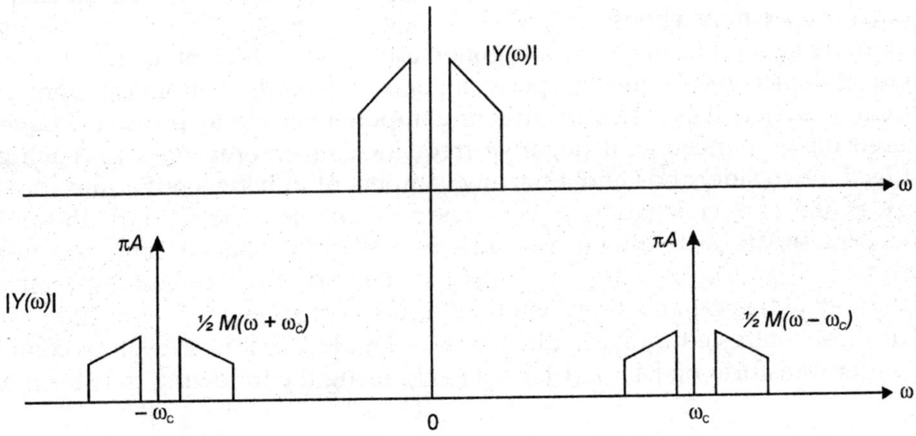

Fig 7.2: The (2-sided) spectrum of an AM signal.

$$c(t) = C\sin(\omega_c t + \phi_c),$$

where the radio frequency (in Hz) is given by: $\omega_c/(2\pi)$.

For generality, C and ϕ_c are arbitrary constants that represent the carrier amplitude and initial phase. For simplicity, we set their respective values to 1 and 0.

Let $m(t)$ represent an arbitrary waveform that is the message to be transmitted. And let the constant M represent its largest magnitude. For instance:

$$m(t) = M\cos(\omega_m t + \phi).$$

Thus, the message might be just a simple audio tone of frequency $\omega_m/(2\pi)$. It is generally assumed that $\omega_m \ll \omega_c$ and that min $[m(t)] = -M$. Then amplitude modulation is created by forming the product:

$$y(t) = [A + m(t)]\, c(t),$$
$$= [A + M\cos(\omega_m t + \phi)] \,.\, \sin(\omega_c t)$$

A represents another constant we may choose. The values $A = 1$, and $M = 0.5$, produce a $y(t)$ depicted by the graph labelled "50 per cent Modulation" in Figure 7.4.

For this simple example, $y(t)$ can be trigonometrically manipulated into the following equivalent form:

$$y(t) = A\sin(\omega_c t) + \frac{M}{2}\left[\sin((\omega_c + \omega_m)t + \phi) + \sin((\omega_c - \omega_m)t - \phi)\right].$$

Therefore, the modulated signal has three components, a carrier wave and two sinusoidal waves (known as sidebands) whose frequencies are slightly above and below ω_c.

Also notice that the choice A = 0 eliminates the carrier component, but leaves the sidebands. That is the DSBSC transmission mode. To generate double-sideband full carrier (A3E), we must choose: $A \geq M$.

For more general forms of $m(t)$, trigonometry is not sufficient. But if the top trace of Figure 2 depicts the frequency spectrum, of $m(t)$, then the bottom trace depicts the modulated carrier. It has two groups of components: one at positive frequencies (centered on $+\omega_c$) and one at negative frequencies (centered on $-\omega_c$). Each group contains the two sidebands and a narrow component in between that represents the energy at the carrier frequency. We need only be concerned with the positive frequencies. The negative ones are a mathematical artifact that contains no additional information. Therefore, we see that an AM signal's spectrum consists basically of its original (2-sided) spectrum shifted up to the carrier frequency.

For those interested in the mathematics of Figure 7.2, it is a result of computing the Fourier transform of: $[A + m(t)]$. c sin ($\omega_c t$), using the following transform pairs:

$$m(t) \overset{F}{\Longleftrightarrow} M(\omega)$$
$$\sin(\omega_c t) \overset{F}{\Longleftrightarrow} i\pi\,[\delta(\omega + \omega_c) - \delta(\omega - \omega_c)]$$
$$A\sin(\omega_c t) \overset{F}{\Longleftrightarrow} i\pi A\,[\delta(\omega + \omega_c) - \delta(\omega - \omega_c)]$$
$$m(t)\sin(\omega_c t) \overset{F}{\Longleftrightarrow} \frac{1}{2\pi}\{M(\omega)\} * \{i\pi[\delta(\omega + \omega_c) - \delta(\omega - \omega_c)]\}$$
$$= \frac{i}{2}\left[M(\omega + \omega_c) - M(\omega - \omega_c)\right]$$

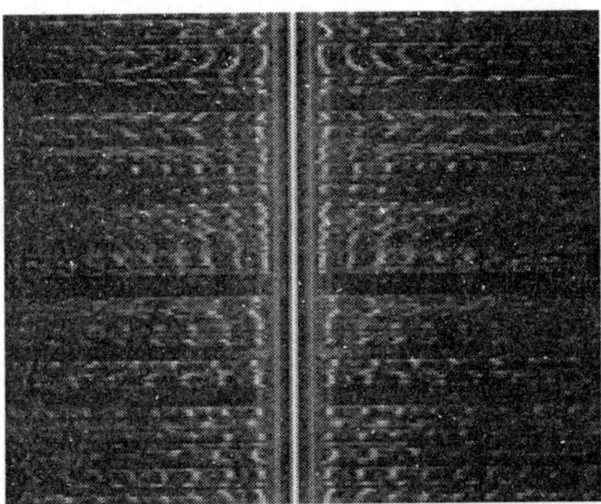

Fig. 7.3: The spectrogram of an AM broadcast shows its two sidebands (green) separated by the carrier signal (red).

In terms of the positive frequencies, the transmission bandwidth of AM is twice the signal's original (baseband) bandwidth—since both the positive and negative sidebands are shifted up to the carrier frequency. Thus, double-sideband AM (DSB-AM) is spectrally inefficient, meaning that fewer radio stations can be accommodated in a given broadcast band. The various suppression methods in Forms of AM, can be readily understood in terms of the diagram in Figure 7.2. With the carrier suppressed there would be no energy at the center of a group. And with a sideband suppressed, the "group" would have the same bandwidth as the positive frequencies of $M(\omega)$. The transmitter power efficiency of DSB-AM is relatively poor (about 33%). The benefit of this system is that receivers are cheaper to produce. The forms of AM with suppressed carriers are found to be 100 per cent power efficient, since no power is wasted on the carrier signal which conveys no information.

Modulation Index

As with other modulation indices, in AM, this quantity, also called *modulation depth,* indicates by how much the modulated variable varies around its 'original' level. For AM, it relates to the variations in the carrier amplitude and is defined as:

$$h = \frac{\text{Peak value of } m(t)}{A} = \frac{M}{A}, \text{ where } M \text{ and } A \text{ were introduced above.}$$

So if $h = 0.5$, the carrier amplitude varies by 50 per cent above and below its unmodulated level, and for $h = 1.0$ it varies by 100 per cent. To avoid distorsion in the A3E transmission mode, modulation depth greater than 100 per cent must be avoided. Practical transmitter systems will usually incorporate some kind of limiter circuit, such as a VOGAD, to ensure this.

Variations of modulated signal with percentage modulation are shown below. In each image, the maximum amplitude is higher than in the previous image. Note that the scale changes from one image to the next.

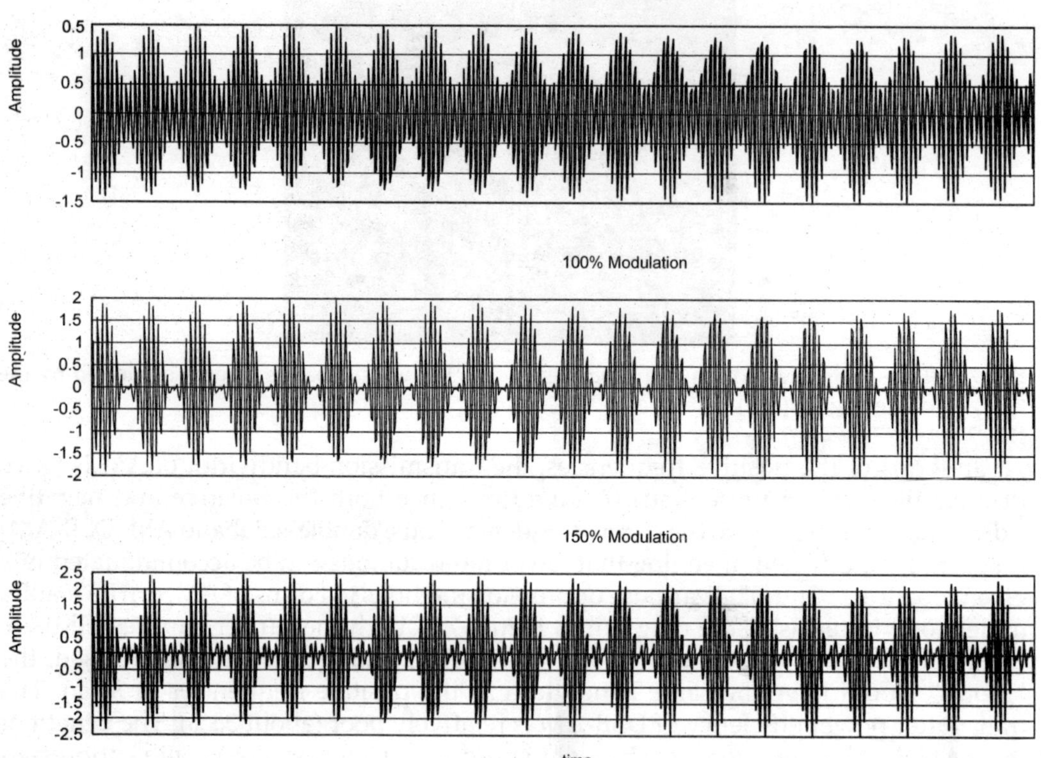

Fig 7.4: Modulation depth.

Amplitude Modulator Designs

Circuits

A wide range of different circuits have been used for AM, but one of the simplest circuits uses anode or collector modulation applied via a transformer. While it is perfectly possible to create good designs using solid-state electronics, valved (vacuum tube) circuits are shown here. In general, valves are able to more easily yield RF powers, in excess of what can be easily achieved using solid-state transistors. Most high-power broadcast stations still use valves.

Modulation circuit designs can be broadly divided into low and high level.

Low Level

Here a small audio stage is used to modulate a low power stage, the output of this stage is then amplified using a linear RF amplifier.

Advantages

The advantage of using a linear RF amplifier is that the smaller early stages can be modulated, which only requires a small audio amplifier to drive the modulator.

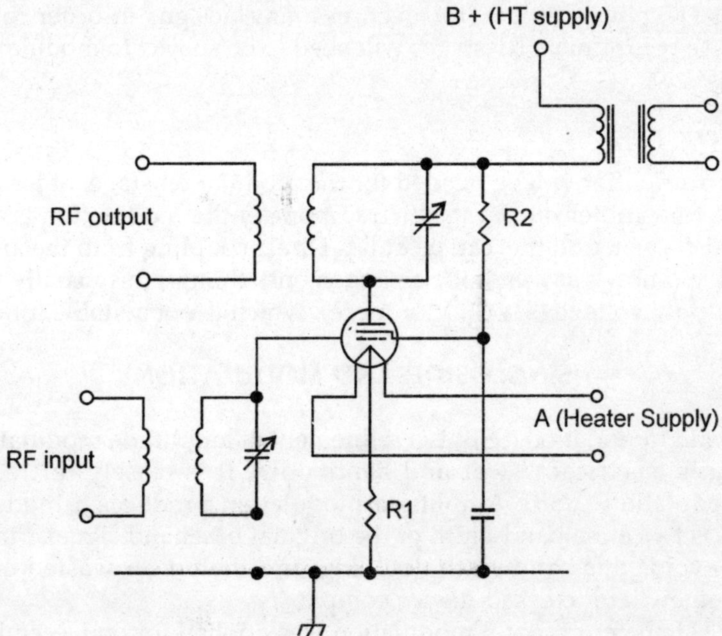

Fig. 7.5: Anode modulation using a transformer. The tetrode is supplied with an anode supply (and screen grid supply) which is modulated via the transformer. The resistor R1 sets the grid bias, both the input and outputs are tuned LC circuits which are tapped into by inductive coupling

Disadvantages

The great disadvantage of this system is that the amplifier chain is less efficient, because it has to be linear to preserve the modulation. Hence Class C amplifiers cannot be employed.

An approach which marries the advantages of low-level modulation with the efficiency of a Class C power amplifier chain is to arrange a feedback system to compensate for the substantial distortion of the AM envelope. A simple detector at the transmitter output (which can be little more than a loosely coupled diode) recovers the audio signal, and this is used as negative feedback to the audio modulator stage. The overall chain then acts as a linear amplifier as far as the actual modulation is concerned, though the RF amplifier itself still retains the Class C efficiency. This approach is widely used in practical medium power transmitters, such as AM radiotelephones.

High Level

Advantages

One advantage of using class C amplifiers in a broadcast AM transmitter is that only the final stage needs to be modulated, and that all the earlier stages can be driven at a constant level. These class C stages will be able to generate the drive for the final stage for a smaller DC power input. However, in many designs in order to obtain better quality AM the penultimate RF stages will need to be subject to modulation as well as the final stage.

Disadvantages

A large audio amplifier will be needed for the modulation stage, at least equal to the power of the transmitter output itself. Traditionally the modulation is applied using an audio transformer, and this can be bulky. Direct coupling from the audio amplifier is also possible (known as a cascode arrangement), though this usually requires quite a high DC supply voltage (say 30 V or more), which is not suitable for mobile units.

SINGLE-SIDEBAND MODULATION

Single-sideband modulation (SSB) is a refinement of amplitude modulation that more efficiently uses electrical power and bandwidth. It is closely related to vestigial sideband modulation (VSB). Amplitude modulation produces a modulated output signal that has twice the bandwidth of the original baseband signal. Single-sideband modulation avoids this bandwidth doubling, and the power wasted on a carrier, at the cost of somewhat increased device complexity.

The first U.S. patent for SSB modulation was applied for on December 1, 1915 by John Renshaw Carson. Patent 1,449,382, titled "Method and Means for Signaling with High Frequency Waves" was awarded to Carson on March 27, 1923 and assigned to AT&T.

The U.S. Navy experimented with SSB over its radio circuits prior to World War I. SSB first entered commercial service in January 7, 1927 on the longwave transatlantic public radiotelephone circuit between New York and London. The high power SSB transmitters were located at Rocky Point, New York and Rugby, England. The receivers were in very quiet locations in Houlton, Maine and Cupar Scotland.

SSB was also used over long-distance telephone lines, as part of a technique known as frequency-division multiplexing. (FDM) was pioneered by telephone companies in the 1930s. This enabled many voice channels to be sent down a single physical circuit. The use of SSB meant that the channels could be spaced (usually) just 4,000 Hz apart, while offering a speech bandwidth of nominally 300-3,400 Hz.

Amateur radio operators began to seriously experiment with SSB after World War II. It has become a de facto standard for long-distance voice radio transmissions since then.

Signal Generation

Bandpass Filtering

Consider an amplitude-modulated signal, which will have two frequency-shifted copies of the modulating signal (the lower one is frequency-inverted) on either side of the remaining carrier wave. These are known as sidebands.

One method of producing an SSB signal is to remove one of the sidebands via filtering, leaving only either the *upper sideband* (USB) or less commonly the *lower sideband* (LSB). Most often, the carrier is reduced or removed entirely (suppressed), being referred to in full as *single sideband suppressed carrier* (SSBSC). Assuming both sidebands are symmetric, no information is lost in the process. Since the final RF amplification is now concentrated in a single sideband, the effective power output is greater than in normal AM (the carrier and redundant sideband account for well over half of the power output of an AM transmitter). Though SSB uses substantially less bandwidth and power, it cannot be demodulated by a simple envelope detector like standard AM.

Hartley Modulator

An alternate method of generation known as a *Hartley modulator*, named after R.V.L. Hartley, uses phasing to suppress the unwanted sideband. To generate an SSB signal with this method, two versions of the original signal are generated, mutually 90° out of phase. Each one of these signals is then mixed with carrier waves that are also 90° out of phase with each other. By either adding or subtracting the resulting signals, a lower or upper sideband signal results. A benefit of this approach is to allow an analytical expression for SSB signals, which can be used to understand effects such as synchronous detection of SSB.

Shifting the baseband signal 90° out of phase cannot be done simply by delaying it, as it contains a large range of frequencies. In analog circuits, a phasing network is used. The method was popular in the days of vacuum-tube radios, but later gained a bad reputation due to poorly adjusted commercial implementations. Modulation using this method is again gaining popularity in the homebrew and DSP fields. This method, utilizing the Hilbert transform to phase shift the baseband audio, can be done at low cost with digital circuitry.

Weaver Modulator

Another variation, the *Weaver modulator*, uses only lowpass filters and quadrature mixers, and is a favored method in digital implementations.

In Weaver's method, the band of interest is first translated to be centered at zero, conceptually by modulating a complex exponential exp (jwt) with frequency in the middle of the voiceband, but implemented by a quadrature pair of sine and cosine modulators at that frequency (*e.g.* 2 kHz). This complex signal or pair of real signals is then lowpass filtered to remove the undesired sideband that is not centered at zero. Then, the single-sideband complex signal centered at zero is upconverted to a real signal, by another pair of quadrature mixers, to the desired center frequency.

Mathematical Highlights

Let $s(t)$ be the baseband waveform to be transmitted. Its Fourier transform, $S(f)$, is Hermitian symmetrical about the $f = 0$ axis, because $s(t)$ is real-valued. Double sideband modulation of $s(t)$ to a radio transmission frequency, F_c, moves the axis of symmetry to $f = \pm F$ and the two sides of each axis are called sidebands.

Let $\widehat{s}(t)$ represent the Hilbert transform of $s(t)$. Then

$$s\hat{a} = s(t) + j \, . \, \widehat{s}(t)$$

is a useful mathematical concept, called an analytic signal. The Fourier transform of $s_a(t)$ equals 2. $S(f)$, for $f > 0$, but it has no negative-frequency components. So it can be modulated to a radio frequency and produce just a *single* sideband.

The analytic representation of cos $(2\pi F_c t)$ is:

$$\cos(2\pi F_c t) + j.\sin(2\pi F_c . t) = e^{j2\pi F_c . t} \quad \text{(the equality is Euler's formula)}$$

whose Fourier transform is $\delta(f - F_c)$.

When $s_a(t)$ is modulated (*i.e.* multiplied) by $e^{j2\pi F_c . t}$, all frequency components are shifted by $+F_c$, so there are still no negative-frequency components. Therefore, the complex product is an *analytic representation* of the single sideband signal:

$$s_a(t)e^{j2\pi F_c . t} = s_{ssb}(t) + j.\hat{s}_{ssb}(t)$$

where $s_{ssb}(t)$ is the real-valued, single sideband waveform. Therefore,

$$\begin{aligned} s_{ssb}(t) &= Re\{s_s(t).e^{i2\pi F_c . t}\} \\ &= \text{Re}\{[s(t) + j.\hat{s}(t)][\cos(2\pi F_c.t) + j.\sin(2\pi F_c.t)]\} \\ &= s(t).\cos(2\pi F_c.t) - s(t).\sin(2\pi F_c.t) \end{aligned}$$

And the "out-of-phase carrier waves" mentioned earlier are evident.

Lower Sideband

$s_a(t)$ represents the baseband signal's upper sideband, $s_+(t)$. It is also possible, and useful, to convey the baseband information using its lower sideband, $s\_(t)$, which is a mirror image about $f = 0$ Hz. By a general property of the Fourier transform, that symmetry means it is the complex conjugate of $s_+(t)$:

$$s\_(t) = s_+^*(t) = s_a^*(t) = s(t) - j.\hat{s}(t)$$

Note that:

$$s_+(t) + s\_(t) = 2s(t)$$

The gain of 2 is a result of defining the analytic signal (one sideband) to have the same total energy as $s(t)$ (both sidebands).

As before, the signal is modulated by $e^{j2\pi F_c . t}$. The typical F_c is large enough that the translated lower sideband (LSB) has no negative-frequency components. Then the result is another analytic signal, whose real part is the actual transmission.

$$s_{lsb}(t) = Re\left\{s_a^*(t).e^{j2\pi F_c t}\right\}$$

$$= s(t)\cos(2\pi F_c.t) + \hat{s}(t)\sin(2\pi F_c.t)$$

Note that the sum of the two sideband signals is:

$$2s(t) \cos (2\pi F_c . t)$$

which is the classic model of suppressed-carrier double sideband AM.

SSB and VSB can also be regarded mathematically as special cases of analog quadrature amplitude modulation.

Demodulation

The front end of an SSB receiver is similar to that of an AM or FM receiver, consisting of a superheterodyne RF front end that produces a frequency-shifted version of the radio frequency (RF) signal within a standard intermediate frequency (IF) band.

To recover the original signal from the IF SSB signal, the single sideband must be frequency-shifted down to its original range of baseband frequencies, by using a product detector which mixes it with the output of a beat frequency oscillator (BFO). In other words, it is just another stage of heterodyning.

For this to work, the BFO frequency must be accurately adjusted. If the BFO is mis-adjusted, the output signal will be frequency-shifted, making speech sound strange and "Donald Duck"-like, or unintelligible. Some receivers use a carrier recovery system, which attempts to automatically lock on to the exact frequency.

As an example, consider an IF SSB signal centered at frequency F_{if} = 45000 Hz. The baseband frequency it needs to be shifted to is F_b = 2000 Hz. The BFO output waveform is cos $(2\pi.F_{bfo}.t)$. When the signal is multiplied by (a.k.a. 'heterodyned with') the BFO waveform, it shifts the signal to $(F_{if} + F_{bfo})$ and to $\left|F_{if} - F_{bfo}\right|$, which is known as the *beat frequency* or *image frequency*. The objective is to choose an F_{bfo} that results in $\left|F_{if} - F_{bfo}\right| = F_b$ 2000 Hz. (The unwanted components at $\left(F_{if} + F_{bfo}\right)$ can be removed by a lowpass filter (such as the human ear).

Note that there are two choices for F_{bfo}: 43000 Hz and 47000 Hz, a.k.a. *low-side* and *high-side* injection. With high-side injection, the spectral components that were distributed around 45000 Hz will be distributed around 2000 Hz in the reverse order, also known as an *inverted spectrum*. That is in fact desirable when the IF spectrum is also inverted, because the BFO inversion restores the proper relationships. One reason for that is when the IF spectrum is the output of an inverting stage in the receiver. Another reason is when the SSB signal is actually a lower sideband, instead of an upper sideband. But if both reasons are true, then the IF spectrum in not inverted, and the non-inverting BFO (43000 Hz) should be used.

If F_{bfo} is off by a small amount, then the beat frequency is not exactly F_b, which can lead to the speech distortion mentioned earlier.

Suppressed Carrier SSB

Suppressed carrier SSB modulation is used by ATSC. DSL modems implement suppressed carrier SSB modulation as well.

Vestigial Sideband (VSB)

A vestigial sideband (in radio communication) is a sideband that has been only partly cut off or suppressed. Television broadcasts (in NTSC, PAL, or SECAM analog video format) use this method if the video is transmitted in AM, due to the large bandwidth used. It may also be used in digital transmission, such as the ATSC standardized 8-VSB. The Milgo 4400/48 modem (circa 1967) used vestigial sideband and phase-shift keying to provide 4800 bit/s transmission over a 1600 Hz channel.

The video baseband signal used in TV in countries that use NTSC or ATSC has a bandwidth of 6 MHz. To conserve bandwidth, SSB would be desirable, but the video signal has significant low frequency content (average brightness) and has rectangular synchronising pulses. The compromise is vestigial sideband modulation. In vestigial sideband the full upper sideband of bandwidth W2 = 4 MHz is transmitted, but only W1 = 1.25 MHz of the lower sideband is transmitted, along with a carrier. This effectively makes the system AM at low modulation frequencies and SSB at high modulation frequencies. The absence of the lower sideband components at high frequencies must be compensated for, and this is done by the RF and IF filters.

FREQUENCY MODULATION

In telecommunications, frequency modulation (FM) conveys information over a carrier wave by varying its frequency (contrast this with amplitude modulation, in which the amplitude of the carrier is varied while its frequency remains constant). In analog applications, the instantaneous frequency of the carrier is directly proportional to the instantaneous value of the input signal. Digital data can be sent by shifting the carrier's frequency among a set of discrete values, a technique known as frequency-shift keying.

Theory

Suppose the baseband data signal (the message) to be transmitted is: $x_m(t)$ and is restricted in amplitude to be $|x_m(t)| \leq 1$, and the sinusoidal carrier is

$$x_c(t) = A_c \cos(2\pi f_c t)$$

where f_c is the carrier's base frequency and A_c is the carrier's amplitude. The modulator combines the carrier with the baseband data signal to get the transmitted signal,

$$y(t) = A_c \cos\left(2\pi \int_0^t f(\tau) d\tau\right)$$

$$= A_c \cos\left(2\pi \int_0^t \left[f_c + f\Delta x_m(\tau)\right] d\tau\right)$$

$$= A_c \cos\left(2\pi f_c t + 2\pi f\Delta \int_0^t x_m(\tau) d\tau\right)$$

In this equation, $f(\tau)$ is the *instantaneous frequency* of the oscillator and $f\Delta$ is the *frequency deviation*, which represents the maximum shift away from f_c in one direction, assuming $x_m(t)$ is limited to the range ±1.

Although it may seem that this limits the frequencies in use to $f_c \pm f_\Delta$, this neglects the distinction between *instantaneous frequency* and *spectral frequency*. The frequency spectrum of an actual FM signal has components extending out to infinite frequency, although they become negligibly small beyond a point.

The harmonic distribution of a sine wave carrier modulated by a sine wave signal can be represented with Bessel functions—this provides a basis for a mathematical understanding of frequency modulation in the frequency domain.

Modulation Index

As with other modulation indices, this quantity indicates by how much the modulated variable varies around its unmodulated level. It relates to the variations in the frequency of the carrier signal:

$$h = \frac{\Delta f}{f_m} = \frac{f\Delta |x_m(t)|}{f_m}$$

where f_m is the highest modulating frequency of $x_m(t)$. If $h \ll 1$, the modulation is called *narrowband FM*, and its bandwidth is approximately $2f_m$. If $h \gg 1$, the modulation is called *wideband FM* and its bandwidth is approximately $2f_\Delta$. While wideband FM uses more bandwidth, it can improve signal-to-noise ratio significantly.

With a tone-modulated FM wave, if the modulation frequency is held constant and the modulation index is increased, the (non-negligible) bandwidth of the FM signal increases, but the spacing between spectra stays the same; some spectral components decrease in strength as others increase. If the frequency deviation is held constant and the modulation frequency increased, the spacing between spectra increases.

Carson's Rule

A rule of thumb, *Carson's rule* states that nearly all (~98%) of the power of a frequency-modulated signal lies within a bandwidth B_T of

$$B_T = 2(f\Delta + f_m)$$

where f_Δ is the peak deviation of the instantaneous frequency $f(t)$ from the center carrier frequency f_c (assuming x_m is in the range ±1).

Noise Quieting

The noise power decreases as the signal power increases, therefore the SNR goes up significantly.

Wideband Noise Reduction

Since B_T increases with the deviation ratio and the SNR is proportional to the deviation ratio, we can reduce signal power and keep the SNR constant as long as we increase the bandwidth.

Bessel Functions

The carrier and sideband amplitudes are illustrated for different modulation indices of FM signals. Based on the Bessel functions.

Modulation Index	*Carrier*	*1*	*2*	*3*	*4*	*5*	*6*	*7*	*8*	*9*	*10*	*11*	*12*	*13*	*14*	*15*	*16*
0.00	1.00																
0.25	0.98	0.12															
0.5	0.94	0.24	0.03														
1.0	0.77	0.44	0.11	0.02													
1.5	0.51	0.56	0.23	0.06	0.01												
2.0	0.22	0.58	0.35	0.13	0.03												
2.41	0	0.52	0.43	0.20	0.06	0.02											
2.5	–.05	0.50	0.45	0.22	0.07	0.02	0.01										
3.0	–.26	0.34	0.49	0.31	0.13	0.04	0.01										
4.0	–.40	–.07	0.36	0.43	0.28	0.13	0.05	0.02									
5.0	–.18	–.33	0.05	0.36	0.39	0.26	0.13	0.05	0.02								
5.53	0	–.34	–.13	0.25	0.40	0.32	0.19	0.09	0.03	0.01							
6.0	0.15	–.28	–.24	0.11	0.36	0.36	0.25	0.13	0.06	0.02							
7.0	0.30	0.00	–.30	–.17	0.16	0.35	0.34	0.23	0.13	0.06	0.02						
8.0	0.17	0.23	–.11	–.29	–.10	0.19	0.34	0.32	0.22	0.13	0.06	0.03					
8.65	0	0.27	0.06	–.24	–.23	0.03	0.26	0.34	0.28	0.18	0.10	0.05	0.02				
9.0	–.09	0.25	0.14	–.18	–.27	–.06	0.20	0.33	0.31	0.21	0.12	0.06	0.03	0.01			
10.0	–.25	0.04	0.25	0.06	–.22	–.23	–.01	0.22	0.32	0.29	0.21	0.12	0.06	0.03	0.01		
12.0	0.05	–.22	–.08	0.20	0.18	–.07	–.24	–.17	0.05	0.23	0.30	0.27	0.20	0.12	0.07	0.03	0.01

Implementation

FM signals can be generated using either direct or indirect frequency modulation.

- ❑ Direct FM modulation can be achieved by directly feeding the message into the input of a VCO.
- ❑ For indirect FM modulation, the message signal is integrated to generate a phase modulated signal. This is used to modulate a crystal controlled oscillator, and the result is passed through a frequency multiplier to give an FM signal.

A common method for recovering the information signal is through a Foster-Seeley discriminator.

Applications in Broadcasting

FM is commonly used at VHF radio frequencies for high-fidelity broadcasts of music and speech (see FM broadcasting). Normal (analog) TV sound is also broadcast using FM. A narrow band form is used for voice communications in commercial and amateur radio settings. The type of FM used in broadcast is generally called wide-FM, or W-FM. In two-way radio, narrowband narrow-fm (N-FM) is used to conserve bandwidth. In addition, it is used to send signals into space.

Applications in Hardware

FM is also used at intermediate frequencies by most analog VCR systems, including VHS, to record the luminance (black and white) portion of the video signal. FM is the only feasible method of recording video to and retrieving video from magnetic tape without extreme distortion, as video signals have a very large range of frequency components—from a few hertz to several megahertz, too wide for equalizers to work with due to electronic noise below – 60 dB. FM also keeps the tape at saturation level, and therefore acts as a form of noise reduction, and a simple limiter can mask variations in the playback output, and the FM capture effect removes print-through and pre-echo. A continuous pilot-tone, if added to the signal—as was done on V2000 and many Hi-band formats—can keep mechanical jitter under control and assist timebase correction.

Applications in Sound

FM is also used at audio frequencies to synthesize sound. This technique, known as FM synthesis, was popularized by early digital synthesizers and became a standard feature for several generations of personal computer sound cards.

Applications in Radio

Edwin Armstrong presented his paper: "A Method of Reducing Disturbances in Radio Signaling by a System of Frequency Modulation", which first described FM radio, before the New York section of the Institute of Radio Engineers on November 6, 1935. The paper was published in 1936.

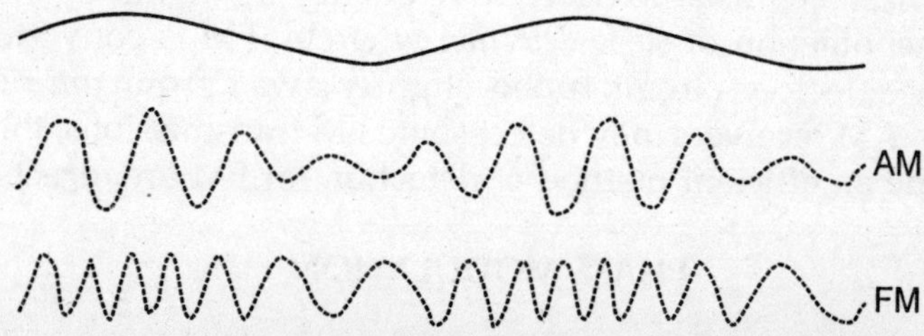

Fig. 7.6: An audio signal (top) may be carried by an AM or FM radio wave.

As the name implies, wideband FM (W-FM) requires a wider signal bandwidth than amplitude modulation by an equivalent modulating signal, but this also makes the signal more robust against noise and interference. Frequency modulation is also more robust against simple signal amplitude fading phenomena. As a result, FM was chosen as the modulation standard for high frequency, high fidelity radio transmission: hence the term "FM radio" (although for many years the BBC called it "VHF radio", because commercial FM broadcasting uses a well-known part of the VHF band; in certain countries, expressions referencing the more familiar wavelength notion are still used in place of the more abstract modulation technique name).

FM receivers employ a special detector for FM signals and exhibit a phenomenon called *capture effect*, where the tuner is able to clearly receive the stronger of two stations being broadcast on the same frequency. Problematically however, frequency drift or lack of selectivity may cause one station or signal to be suddenly overtaken by another on an adjacent channel. Frequency drift typically constituted a problem on very old or inexpensive receivers, while inadequate selectivity may plague any tuner.

An FM signal can also be used to carry a stereo signal: see FM stereo. However, this is done by using multiplexing and demultiplexing before and after the FM process, and is not part of FM proper. The rest of this article ignores the stereo multiplexing and demultiplexing process used in "stereo FM", and concentrates on the FM modulation and demodulation process, which is identical in stereo and mono processes.

A high-efficiency radio-frequency switching amplifier can be used to transmit FM signals (and other constant-amplitude signals). For a given signal strength (measured at the receiver antenna), switching amplifiers use less battery power and typically cost less than a linear amplifier. This gives FM another advantage over other modulation schemes that require linear amplifiers, such as AM and QAM.

Miscellaneous

- Note that frequency modulation can be regarded as a special case of phase modulation where the carrier phase modulation is the time integral of the FM modulating signal.
- *Frequency-shift keying* is the frequency modulation using only a discrete number of frequencies. Morse code can be implemented this way, most early telephone-line modems, and radioteletype applications.
- When used in supervisory signaling in telephony, the term frequency-change signaling has been used to describe frequency modulation.
- By the phenomenon of *slope detection* whereby FM is converted to AM in a frequency-selective circuit tuned slightly away from the nominal signal frequency, AM receivers may detect some FM transmissions, though this does not provide an efficient method of detection for FM broadcasts.

PHASE MODULATION

Phase modulation (PM) is a form of modulation that represents information as variations in the instantaneous phase of a carrier wave.

Unlike its more popular counterpart, frequency modulation (FM), PM is not very widely used. This is because it tends to require more complex receiving hardware and there can be ambiguity problems in determining whether, for example, the signal has changed phase by +180° or –180°.

Theory

Suppose that the signal to be sent (called the modulating or message signal) is $m(t)$.

The carrier onto which the signal is to be modulated is

$$c(t) = A_c \sin(\omega_c t + \phi_c).$$

Then the modulated signal is

$$y(t) = A_c \sin(\omega_c t + m(t) + \phi_c),$$

This shows how $m(t)$ modulates the phase. Clearly, it can also be viewed as a change of the frequency of the carrier signal. PM can thus be considered a special case of FM in which the carrier frequency modulation is given by the time derivative of the phase modulation.

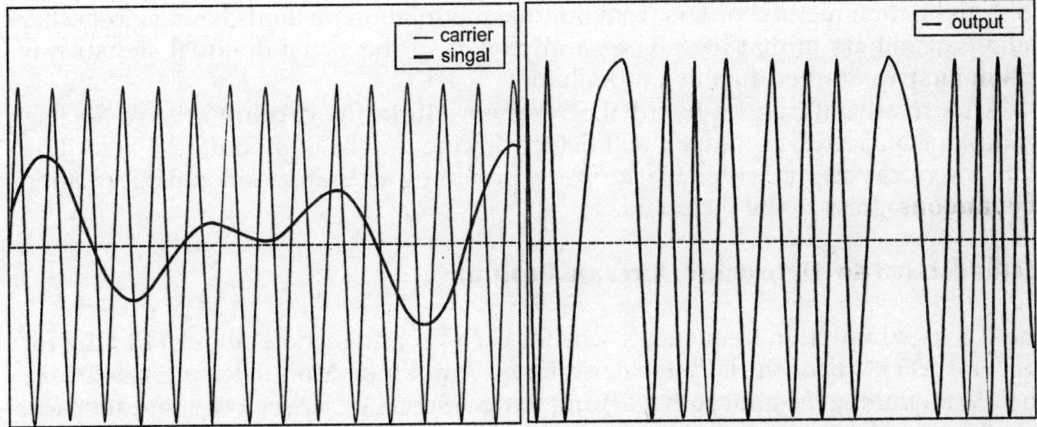

Fig. 7.7: An example of phase modulation. The top diagram shows the modulating signal superimposed on the carrier wave. The bottom diagram shows the resulting phase-modulated signal.

The spectral behaviour of phase modulation is difficult to derive, but the mathematics reveals that there are two regions of particular interest:

- For small amplitude signals, PM is similar to amplitude modulation (AM) and exhibits its unfortunate doubling of baseband bandwidth and poor efficiency.
- For a single large sinusoidal signal, PM is similar to FM, and its bandwidth is approximately.

$$2(h+1)\,f_M$$

where $f_M = \omega_m/2\pi$ and h is the modulation index defined below. This is also known as Carson's Rule for PM.

Modulation Index

As with other modulation indices, this quantity indicates by how much the modulated variable varies around its unmodulated level. It relates to the variations in the phase of the carrier signal:

$$h = \Delta\theta$$

where $\Delta\theta$ is the peak phase deviation. Compare to the modulation index for frequency modulation.

SPACE MODULATION

Space modulation is a radio Amplitude Modulation technique used in Instrument Landing Systems that incorporates the use of multiple antennas fed with various radio frequency powers and phases to create different depths of modulation within airspace. This modulation method differs from internal modulation methods inside most other radio transmitters in that the phases and powers of the two individual signals mix within airspace, rather than in a modulator.

An aircraft with an on-board ILS receiver within the capture area of an ILS, (glideslope and localiser range), will detect varying depths of modulation according to the aircraft's position within that airspace, providing accurate positional information about the progress to the threshold.

Method Used to Determine Aircraft Position

The ILS uses two radio frequencies, one for each ground station (about 110 Mhz for LLZ and 330 Mhz for the GP), to transmit two Amplitude Modulated signals (90 Hz and 150 Hz), along the glidepath (GP) and the localiser (LLZ) trajectories into airspace. it is this signal projected up from the runway that an aircraft using an instrument approach, uses to land.

The modulation depth of each 90 Hz and 150 Hz signal changes according to the deviation of the aircraft from the correct position for the aircraft to touchdown on the threshold. The difference between the two signal modulation depths is zero when the aircraft is on the correct approach—*i.e.* No difference (zero DDM), produces no deviation from the middle indication of the instrument's needle within the cockpit of the aircraft.

FREQUENCY-SHIFT KEYING

Frequency-shift keying (FSK) is a frequency modulation scheme in which digital information is transmitted through discrete frequency changes of a carrier wave. The simplest FSK is *binary FSK* (BFSK). BFSK literally implies using a couple of discrete frequencies to transmit binary (0s and 1s) information. With this scheme, the "1" is called the mark frequency and the "0" is called the space frequency. The time domain of an FSK modulated carrier is illustrated in the figures to the right.

Other Forms of FSK

Minimum-Shift Keying

Minimum frequency-shift keying or minimum-shift keying (MSK) is a particularly spectrally efficient form of coherent FSK. In MSK the difference between the higher and lower frequency is identical to half the bit rate. Consequently, the waveforms used to represent a 0 and a 1 bit differ by exactly half a carrier period. This is the smallest FSK modulation index that can be chosen such that the waveforms for 0 and 1 are orthogonal. A variant of MSK called GMSK is used in the GSM mobile phone standard.

FSK is commonly used in Caller ID and remote metering applications: see FSK standards for use in Caller ID and remote metering for more details.

Audio FSK

Audio frequency-shift keying (AFSK) is a modulation technique by which digital data is represented by changes in the frequency (pitch) of an audio tone, yielding an encoded signal suitable for transmission via radio or telephone. Normally, the transmitted audio alternates between two tones: one, the "mark", represents a binary one; the other, the "space", represents a binary zero.

AFSK differs from regular frequency-shift keying in performing the modulation at baseband frequencies. In radio applications, the AFSK-modulated signal normally is being used to modulate an RF carrier (using a conventional technique, such as AM or FM) for transmission.

AFSK is not always being used for high-speed data communications, since it is far less efficient in both power and bandwidth than most other modulation modes. In addition to its simplicity, however, AFSK has the advantage that encoded signals will pass through AC-coupled links, including most equipment originally designed to carry music or speech.

Applications

Most early telephone-line modems used audio frequency-shift keying to send and receive data, up to rates of about 300 bits per second. The common Bell 103 modem used this technique, for example. Even today, North American caller ID uses 1200 baud AFSK in the form of the Bell 202 standard. Some early microcomputers used a specific form of AFSK modulation, the Kansas City standard, to store data on audio cassettes. AFSK is still widely used in amateur radio, as it allows data transmission through unmodified voiceband equipment. Radio control gear uses FSK, but calls it FM and PPM instead.

AFSK is also used in the United States' Emergency Alert System to transmit warning information. It is used at higher bitrates for Weathercopy used on Weatheradio by NOAA in the U.S., and more extensively by Environment Canada.

The CHU shortwave radio station in Ottawa, Canada broadcasts an exclusive digital time signal encoded using AFSK modulation.

ON-OFF KEYING

On-off Keying (OOK) is a type of modulation that represents digital data as the presence or absence of a carrier wave. In its simplest form, the presence of a carrier for a specific duration represents a binary one, while its absence for the same duration represents a binary zero. Some more sophisticated schemes vary these durations to convey additional information. On-off keying is most commonly used to transmit Morse code over radio frequencies (referred to as continuous wave operation), although in principle any digital encoding scheme may be used. OOK has been used in the ISM bands to transfer data between computers, for example.

OOK is not very spectrally efficient due to the abrupt changes in amplitude of the carrier wave. At low to medium signalling speeds, this can be mitigated by adjusting the rise and fall rates of the carrier's amplitude. At high speeds, more efficient modulation modes (such as frequency-shift keying) are normally used instead.

In addition to RF carrier waves, OOK is also used in optical communication systems (*e.g.* IrDA). In aviation, some possibly unmanned airports have equipment that let pilots key their VHF radio a number of times in order to request an Automatic Terminal Information Service broadcast, or turn on runway lights.

AMPLITUDE-SHIFT KEYING

Amplitude-shift keying (ASK) is a form of modulation that represents digital data as variations in the amplitude of a carrier wave.

The amplitude of an analog carrier signal varies in accordance with the bit stream (modulating signal), keeping frequency and phase constant. The level of amplitude can be used to represent binary logic 0s and 1s. We can think of a carrier signal as an ON or OFF switch. In the modulated signal, logic 0 is represented by the absence of a carrier, thus giving OFF/ON keying operation and hence the name given.

Like AM, ASK is also linear and sensitive to atmospheric noise, distortions, propagation conditions on different routes in PSTN, etc. Both ASK modulation and demodulation processes are relatively inexpensive. The ASK technique is also commonly used to transmit digital data over optical fiber. For LED transmitters, binary 1 is represented by a short pulse of light and binary 0 by the absence of light. Laser transmitters normally have a fixed "bias" current that causes the device to emit a low light level. This low level represents binary 0, while a higher-amplitude lightwave represents binary 1.

Encoding

The simplest and most common form of ASK operates as a switch, using the presence of a carrier wave to indicate a binary one and its absence to indicate a binary zero. This type of modulation is called *on-off keying*, and is used at radio frequencies to transmit Morse code (referred to as continuous wave operation).

More sophisticated encoding schemes have been developed which represent data in groups using additional amplitude levels. For instance, a four-level encoding scheme can represent two bits with each shift in amplitude; an eight-level scheme can represent three bits; and so on. These forms of amplitude-shift keying require a high signal-to-noise ratio for their recovery, as by their nature much of the signal is transmitted at reduced power.

Here is a diagram showing the ideal model for a transmission system using an ASK modulation:

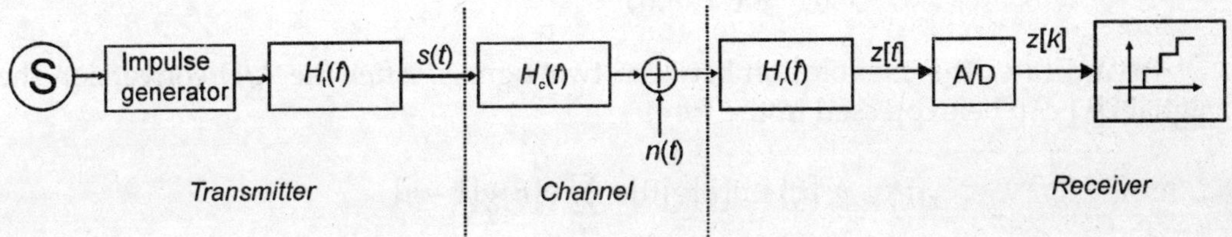

Fig. 7.8:

It can be divided into three blocks. The first one represents the transmitter, the second one is a linear model of the effects of the channel, the third one shows the structure of the receiver. The following notation is used:

- $h_t(t)$ is the carrier signal for the transmission,
- $h_c(t)$ is the impulse response of the channel,
- $n(t)$ is the noise introduced by the channel,
- $h_r(t)$ is the filter at the receiver,
- L is the number of levels that are used for transmission, and
- T_s is the time between the generation of two symbols.

Different symbols are represented with different voltages. If the maximum allowed value for the voltage is A, then all the possible values are in the range $[-A, A]$ and they are given by:

$$v_i = \frac{2A}{L-1} i - A; \ \mathrm{i} = 0,1, \ldots, \mathrm{L}-1$$

the difference between one voltage and the other is:

$$\Delta = \frac{2A}{L-1}$$

Considering the picture, the symbols $v[n]$ are generated randomly by the source S, then the *impulse generator* creates impulses with an area of $v[n]$. These impulses are sent to the filter h_t to be sent through the channel. In other words, for each symbol a different carrier wave is sent with the relative amplitude.

Out of the transmitter, the signal $s(t)$ can be expressed in the form:

$$s(t) = \sum_{n=-\infty}^{\infty} v[n] \, . \, h_t\left(t - nT_s\right)$$

In the receiver, after the filtering through $h_r(t)$ the signal is:

$$z(t) = n_r(t) + \sum_{n=-\infty}^{\infty} v[n] \, . \, g\left(t - nT_s\right)$$

where we use the notation:

$$n_r(t) = n(t) * h_r(t)$$
$$g(t) = h_t(t) * h_c(t) * h_r(t)$$

where indicates the convolution between two signals. After the A/D conversion the signal $z[k]$ can be expressed in the form:

$$z[k] = n_r[k] + v[k]g[0] + \sum_{n \neq k} v[n]g[k-n]$$

In this relationship, the second term represents the symbol to be extracted. The others are unwanted: the first one is the effect of noise, the second one is due to the intersymbol interference.

If the filters are chosen so that $g(t)$ will satisfy the Nyquist ISI criterion, then there will be no intersymbol interference and the value of the sum will be zero, so:

$$z[k] = n_r[k] + v[k]g[0]$$

the transmission will be affected only by noise.

Probability of Error

The probability density function to make an error after a certain symbol has been sent can be modelled by a Gaussian function; the mean value will be the relative sent value, and its variance will be given by:

$$\sigma_N = \int_{-\infty}^{+\infty} \Phi_N(f) . \left|H_r(f)\right|^2 df$$

where $F_N(f)$ is the spectral density of the noise within the band and $H_r(f)$ is the continuous Fourier transform of the impulse response of the filter $h_r(f)$.

The possibility to make an error is given by:

$$P_c = P_{c/H_0} . P_{H_0} + P_{c/H_1} . P_{H_1} + \ldots + P_{c/H_{L-1}} . P_{H_{L-1}}$$

where $P_{c/H0}$ is the conditional probability of making an error after a symbol v_i has been sent and P_{H0} is the probability of sending a symbol v_0.

If the probability of sending any symbol is the same, then:

$$P_{H_i} = \frac{1}{L}$$

If we represent all the probability density functions on the same plot against the possible value of the voltage to be transmitted, we get a picture like this (the particular case of $L = 4$ is shown):

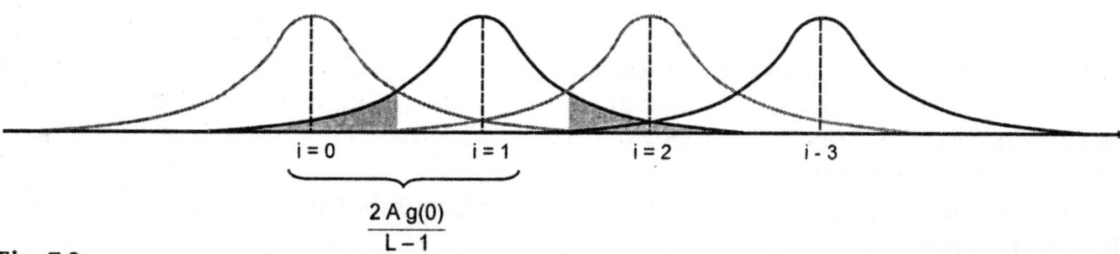

Fig. 7.9:

The possibility of making an error after a single symbol has been sent is the area of the Gaussian function falling under the other ones. It is shown in cyan just for one of them. If we call P^+ the area under one side of the Gaussian, the sum of all the areas will be: $2LP^+ - 2P^+$. The total probability of making an error can be expressed in the form:

$$P_c = 2\left(1-\frac{1}{L}\right)P^+$$

We have now to calculate the value of P^+. In order to do that, we can move the origin of the reference wherever we want: the area below the function will not change. We are in a situation like the one shown in the following picture:

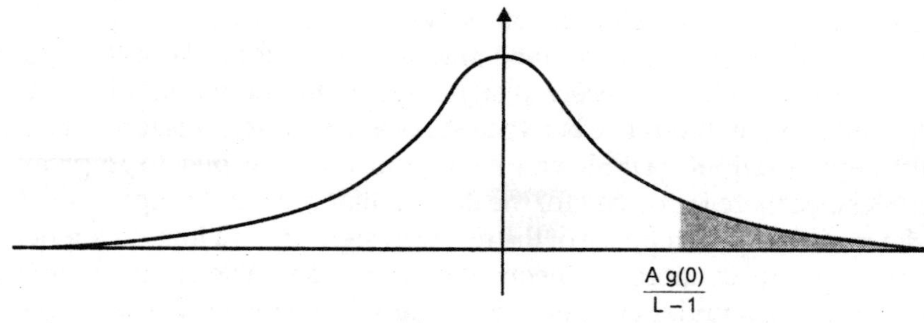

Fig. 7.10:

It does not matter which Gaussian function we are considering, the area we want to calculate will be the same. The value we are looking for will be given by the following integral:

$$P^+ = \int_{\frac{Ag(0)}{L-1}}^{\infty} \frac{1}{\sqrt{2\pi}\sigma_N} e^{-\frac{x^2}{2\sigma_N^2}} dx = \frac{1}{2}\,\text{erfc}\left(\frac{Ag(0)}{\sqrt{2}(L-1)\sigma_N}\right)$$

where erfc() is the complementary error function. Putting all these results together, the probability to make an error is:

$$P_c = \left(1 - \frac{1}{L}\right) \text{erfc}\left(\frac{Ag(0)}{\sqrt{2}(L-1)\sigma_N}\right)$$

from this formula we can easily understand that the probability to make an error decreases if the maximum amplitude of the transmitted signal or the amplification of the system becomes greater; on the other hand, it increases if the number of levels or the power of noise becomes greater.

This relationship is valid when there is no intersymbol interference, *i.e.* $g(t)$ is a Nyquist function.

PHASE-SHIFT KEYING

Phase-shift keying (PSK) is a digital modulation scheme that conveys data by changing, or modulating, the phase of a reference signal (the carrier wave).

Any digital modulation scheme uses a finite number of distinct signals to represent digital data. PSK uses a finite number of phases, each assigned a unique pattern of binary bits. Usually, each phase encodes an equal number of bits. Each pattern of bits forms the symbol that is represented by the particular phase. The demodulator, which is designed specifically for the symbol-set used by the modulator, determines the phase of the received signal and maps it back to the symbol it represents, thus recovering the original data. This requires the receiver to be able to compare the phase of the received signal to a reference signal—such a system is termed coherent (and referred to as CPSK).

Alternatively, instead of using the bit patterns to *set* the phase of the wave, it can instead be used to *change* it by a specified amount. The demodulator then determines the *changes* in the phase of the received signal rather than the phase itself. Since this scheme depends on the difference between successive phases, it is termed differential phase-shift keying (DPSK). DPSK can be significantly simpler to implement than ordinary PSK since there is no need for the demodulator to have a copy of the reference signal to determine the exact phase of the received signal (it is a non-coherent scheme). In exchange, it produces more erroneous demodulations. The exact requirements of the particular scenario under consideration determine which scheme is used.

Introduction

There are three major classes of digital modulation techniques used for transmission of digitally represented data:

- Amplitude-shift keying (ASK).
- Frequency-shift keying (FSK).
- Phase-shift keying (PSK).

All convey data by changing some aspect of a base signal, the carrier wave (usually a sinusoid), in response to a data signal. In the case of PSK, the phase is changed to represent the data signal. There are two fundamental ways of utilizing the phase of a signal in this way:

- By viewing the phase itself as conveying the information, in which case the demodulator must have a reference signal to compare the received signal's phase against; or
- By viewing the *change* in the phase as conveying information—*differential* schemes, some of which do not need a reference carrier (to a certain extent).

A convenient way to represent PSK schemes is on a constellation diagram. This shows the points in the Argand plane where, in this context, the real and imaginary axes are termed the in-phase and quadrature axes respectively due to their 90° separation. Such a representation on perpendicular axes lends itself to straightforward implementation. The amplitude of each point along the in-phase axis is used to modulate a cosine (or sine) wave and the amplitude along the quadrature axis to modulate a sine (or cosine) wave.

In PSK, the constellation points chosen are usually positioned with uniform angular spacing around a circle. This gives maximum phase-separation between adjacent points and thus the best immunity to corruption. They are positioned on a circle so that they can all be transmitted with the same energy. In this way, the moduli of the complex numbers they represent will be the same and thus so will the amplitudes needed for the cosine and sine waves. Two common examples are "binary phase-shift keying" (BPSK) which uses two phases, and "quadrature phase-shift keying" (QPSK) which uses four phases, although any number of phases may be used. Since the data to be conveyed are usually binary, the PSK scheme is usually designed with the number of constellation points being a power of 2.

Definitions

For determining error-rates mathematically, some definitions will be needed:

- E_b = Energy-per-bit.
- E_s = Energy-per-symbol = kE_b with k bits per symbol.
- T_b = Bit duration.
- T_s = Symbol duration.
- $N_0/2$ = Noise power spectral density (W/Hz).
- P_b = Probability of bit-error.
- P_s = Probability of symbol-error.

$Q(x)$ will give the probability that a single sample taken from a random process with zero-mean and unit-variance Gaussian probability density function will be greater or equal to x. It is a scaled form of the complementary Gaussian error function:

$$Q(x) = \frac{1}{\sqrt{2\pi}}\int_x^\infty e^{-t^2/2}dt = \frac{1}{2}\,\mathrm{erfc}\left(\frac{x}{\sqrt{2}}\right),\ x \geq 0.$$

The error-rates quoted here are those in additive white Gaussian noise (AWGN). These error rates are lower than those computed in fading channels, hence, are a good theoretical benchmark to compare with.

Applications

Owing to PSK's simplicity, particularly when compared with its competitor quadrature amplitude modulation, it is widely used in existing technologies.

The wireless LAN standard, IEEE 802.11b-1999, uses a variety of different PSKs depending on the data-rate required. At the basic-rate of 1 Mbit/s, it uses DBPSK. To provide the extended-rate of 2 Mbit/s, DQPSK is used. In reaching 5.5 Mbit/s and the full-rate of 11 Mbit/s, QPSK is employed, but has to be coupled with complementary code keying. The higher-speed wireless LAN standard, IEEE 802.11g-2003 has eight data rates: 6, 9, 12, 18, 24, 36, 48 and 54 Mbit/s. The 6 and 9 Mbit/s modes use OFDM modulation where each sub-carrier is BPSK modulated. The 12 and 18 Mbit/s modes use OFDM with QPSK. The fastest four modes use OFDM with forms of quadrature amplitude modulation.

Because of its simplicity BPSK is appropriate for low-cost passive transmitters, and is used in RFID standards such as ISO 14443 which has been adopted for biometric passports, credit cards such as American Express's ExpressPay, and many other applications.

Bluetooth 2 will use π/4-DQPSK at its lower rate (2 Mbit/s) and 8-DPSK at its higher rate (3 Mbit/s) when the link between the two devices is sufficiently robust. Bluetooth 1 modulates with Gaussian minimum-shift keying, a binary scheme, so either modulation choice in version 2 will yield a higher data-rate. A similar technology, IEEE 802.15.4 (the wireless standard used by ZigBee) also relies on PSK. IEEE 802.15.4 allows the use of two frequency bands: 868–915 MHz using BPSK and at 2.4 GHz using OQPSK.

Notably absent from these various schemes is 8-PSK. This is because its error-rate performance is close to that of 16-QAM—it is only about 0.5 dB better—but its data rate is only three-quarters that of 16-QAM. Thus 8-PSK is often omitted from standards and, as seen above, schemes tend to 'jump' from QPSK to 16-QAM (8-QAM is possible but difficult to implement).

Binary Phase-Shift Keying (BPSK)

BPSK (also sometimes called PRK, Phase Reversal Keying) is the simplest form of PSK. It uses two phases which are separated by 180° and so can also be termed 2-PSK. It does not particularly matter exactly where the constellation points are positioned, and in this figure they are shown on the real axis, at 0° and 180°. This modulation is the most robust of all the PSKs since it takes serious distortion to make the demodulator reach an incorrect decision. It is, however, only able to modulate at 1 bit/symbol (as seen in the figure) and so is unsuitable for high data-rate applications when bandwidth is limited.

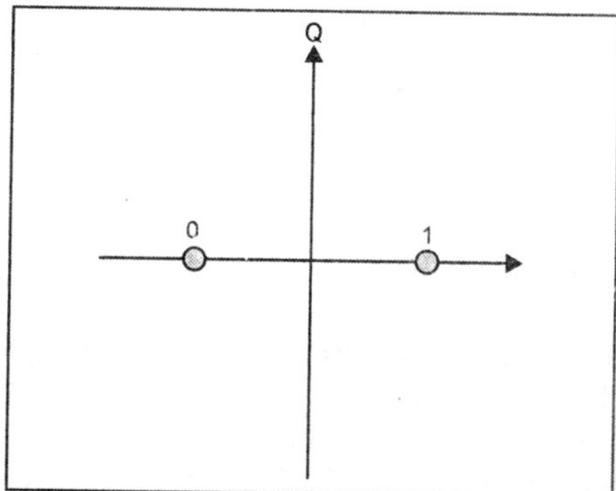

Fig. 7.11: Constellation diagram for BPSK.

The bit error rate (BER) of BPSK in AWGN can be calculated as:

$$P_b = Q\left(\sqrt{\frac{2E_b}{N_0}}\right) \text{ or } P_b = \frac{1}{2}\,\text{erfc}\left(\sqrt{\frac{E_b}{N_0}}\right)$$

Since there is only one bit per symbol, this is also the symbol error rate.

In the presence of an arbitrary phase-shift introduced by the communications channel, the demodulator is unable to tell which constellation point is which. As a result, the data is often differentially encoded prior to modulation.

Implementation

Binary data is often conveyed with the following signals:

$$s_0(t) = \sqrt{\frac{2E_b}{T_b}}\cos(2\pi f_c t + \pi) = -\sqrt{\frac{2E_b}{T_b}}\cos(2\pi f_c t) \text{ for binary "0"}$$

$$s_1(t) = \sqrt{\frac{2E_b}{T_b}}\cos(2\pi f_c t) \text{ for binary "1"}$$

where f_c is the frequency of the carrier-wave.

Hence, the signal-space can be represented by the single basis function

$$\phi(t) = \sqrt{\frac{2}{T_b}}\cos(2\pi f_c t)$$

where 1 is represented by $\sqrt{E_b}\phi(t)$ and 0 is represented by $-\sqrt{E_b}\phi(t)$. This assignment is, of course, arbitrary.

The use of this basis function is shown at the end of the next section in a signal timing diagram. The topmost signal shows PSK modulating a cosine wave, and is the signal that the BPSK modulator would produce. The bit-stream that causes this output is shown above the signal (the other parts of this figure are relevant only to QPSK).

Quadrature Phase-Shift Keying (QPSK)

Sometimes known as quaternary or quadriphase PSK, 4-PSK, or 4-QAM, QPSK uses four points on the constellation diagram, equispaced around a circle. With four phases, QPSK can encode two bits per symbol, shown in the diagram with Gray coding to minimize the BER—twice the rate of BPSK. Analysis shows that this may be used either to double the data rate compared to a BPSK system while maintaining the bandwidth of the signal or to maintain the data-rate of BPSK but halve the bandwidth needed.

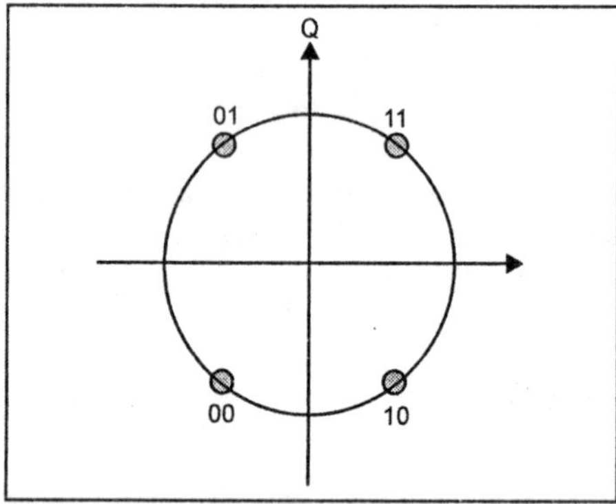

Fig. 7.12: Constellation diagram for QPSK with Gray coding. Each adjacent symbol only differs by one bit.

Although QPSK can be viewed as a quaternary modulation, it is easier to see it as two independently modulated quadrature carriers. With this interpretation, the even (or odd) bits are used to modulate the in-phase component of the carrier, while the odd (or even) bits are used to modulate the quadrature-phase component of the carrier. BPSK is used on both carriers and they can be independently demodulated.

As a result, the probability of bit-error for QPSK is the same as for BPSK:

$$P_b = Q\left(\sqrt{\frac{2E_b}{N_0}}\right).$$

However, in order to achieve the same bit-error probability as BPSK, QPSK uses twice the power (since two bits are transmitted simultaneously).

The symbol error rate is given by:

$$P_s = (1 - P_b)^2$$

$$= 2Q\left(\sqrt{\frac{2E_s}{N_0}}\right) - Q^2\left(\sqrt{\frac{E_s}{N_0}}\right).$$

If the signal-to-noise ratio is high (as is necessary for practical QPSK systems) the probability of symbol error may be approximated:

$$P_s \approx 2Q\left(\sqrt{\frac{E_s}{N_0}}\right)$$

As with BPSK, there are phase ambiguity problems at the receiver and differentially encoded QPSK is more normally used in practice.

Implementation

The implementation of QPSK is more general than that of BPSK and also indicates the implementation of higher-order PSK. Writing the symbols in the constellation diagram in terms of the sine and cosine waves used to transmit them:

$$s_i(t) = \sqrt{\frac{2E_s}{T}}\cos\left(2\pi f_c t + (2i-1)\frac{\pi}{4}\right), \quad i = 1, 2, 3, 4.$$

This yields the four phases $\pi/4$, $3\pi/4$, $5\pi/4$ and $7\pi/4$ as needed.
This results in a two-dimensional signal space with unit basis functions:

$$\phi_1(t) = \sqrt{\frac{2}{T_s}}\cos(2\pi f_c t)$$

$$\phi_2(t) = \sqrt{\frac{2}{T_s}}\sin(2\pi f_c t)$$

The first basis function is used as the in-phase component of the signal and the second as the quadrature component of the signal.

Hence, the signal constellation consists of the signal-space 4 points

$$\left(\pm\sqrt{E_s/2}, \pm\sqrt{E_s/2}\right)$$

The factors of 1/2 indicate that the total power is split equally between the two carriers.

Comparing these basis functions with that for BPSK shows clearly how QPSK can be viewed as two independent BPSK signals. Note that the signal-space points for BPSK do not need to split the symbol (bit) energy over the two carriers in the scheme shown in the BPSK constellation diagram.

QPSK systems can be implemented in a number of ways. An illustration of the major components of the transmitter and receiver structure are shown below.

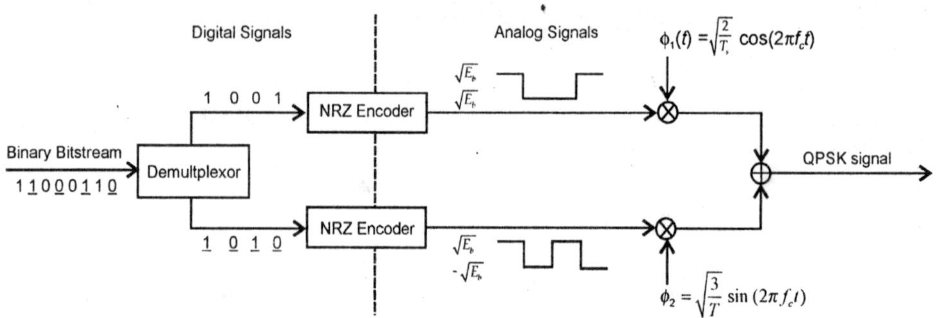

Fig. 7.13: Conceptual transmitter structure for QPSK. The binary data stream is split into the in-phase and quadrature-phase components. These are then separately modulated onto two orthogonal basis functions. In this implementation, two sinusoids are used. Afterwards, the two signals are superimposed, and the resulting signal is the QPSK signal. Note the use of polar non-return-to-zero encoding. These encoders can be placed before for binary data source, but have been placed after to illustrate the conceptual difference between digital and analog signals involved with digital modulation.

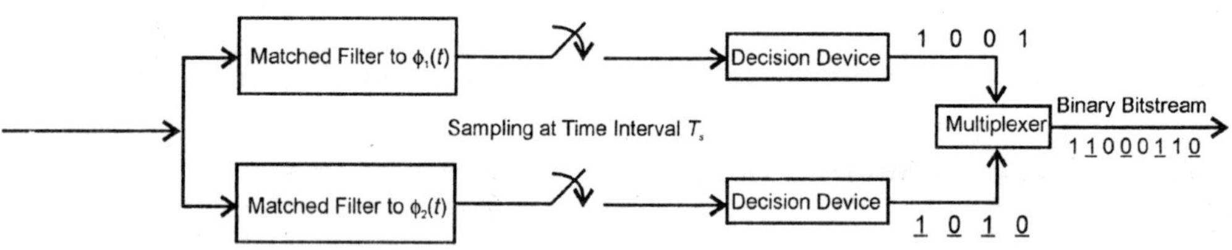

Fig. 7.14: Receiver structure for QPSK. The matched filters can be replaced with correlators. Each detection device uses a reference threshold value to determine whether a 1 or 0 is detected.

QPSK Signal in the Time Domain

The modulated signal is shown below for a short segment of a random binary data-stream. The two carrier waves are a cosine wave and a sine wave, as indicated by the signal-space analysis above. Here, the odd-numbered bits have been assigned to the in-phase component and the even-numbered bits to the quadrature component (taking the first bit as number 1). The total signal—the sum of the two components—is shown at the bottom. Jumps in phase can be seen as the PSK changes the phase on each component at the start of each bit-period. The topmost waveform alone matches the description given for BPSK above.

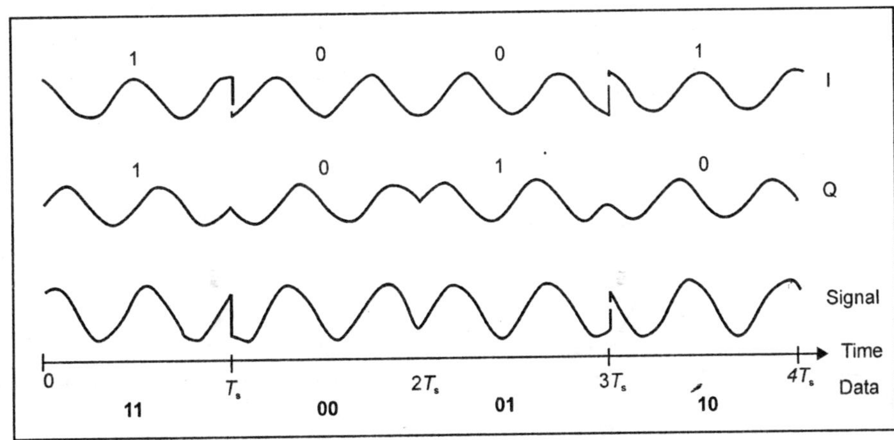

Fig. 7.15: Timing diagram for QPSK. The binary data stream is shown (below) beneath the time axis. The two signal components with their bit assignments are shown the top and the total, combined signal at the bottom. Note the abrupt changes in phase at some of the bit-period boundaries.

The binary data that is conveyed by this waveform is: **1** 1 **0** 0 **0** 1 **1** 0.

- The odd bits, highlighted here, contribute to the in-phase component: **1** 1 **0** 0 **0** 1 **1** 0
- The even bits, highlighted here, contribute to the quadrature-phase component: 1 **1** 0 **0** 0 **1** 1 **0**

Offset QPSK (OQPSK)

Offset quadrature phase-shift keying (*OQPSK*) is a variant of phase-shift keying modulation using 4 different values of the phase to transmit. It is sometimes called *Staggered quadrature phase-shift keying* (*SQPSK*).

Taking four values of the phase (two bits) at a time to construct a QPSK symbol can allow the phase of the signal to jump by as much as 180° at a time. When the signal is low-pass filtered (as is typical in a transmitter), these phase-shifts result in large amplitude fluctuations, an undesirable quality in communication systems. By offsetting the timing of the odd and even bits by one bit-period, or half a symbol-period, the in-phase and quadrature components will never change at the same time. In the constellation diagram shown on the right, it can be seen that this will limit the phase-shift to no more than 90° at a time. This yields much lower amplitude fluctuations than non-offset QPSK and is sometimes preferred in practice.

The picture on the right shows the difference in the behaviour of the phase between ordinary QPSK and OQPSK. It can be seen that in the first plot the phase can change by 180° at once, while in OQPSK the changes are never greater than 90°.

The modulated signal is shown below for a short segment of a random binary data-stream. Note the half symbol-period offset between the two component waves. The sudden phase-shifts occur about twice as often as for QPSK (since the signals no longer change together), but they are less severe. In other words, the magnitude of jumps is smaller in OQPSK when compared to QPSK.

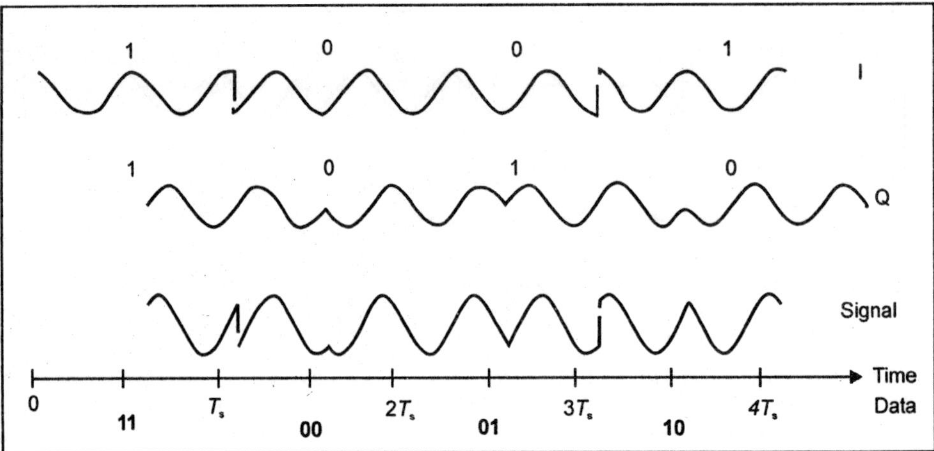

Fig. 7.16: Timing diagram for offset-QPSK. The binary data stream is shown beneath the time axis. The two signal components with their bit assignments are shown the top and the total, combined signal at the bottom. Note the half-period offset between the two signal components.

π/4–QPSK

This final variant of QPSK uses two identical constellations which are rotated by 45° (π/z4 radians, hence the name) with respect to one another. Usually, either the even or odd data bits are used to select points from one of the constellations and the other bits select points from the other constellation. This also reduces the phase-shifts from a maximum of 180°, but only to a maximum of 135° and so the amplitude fluctuations of π/4–QPSK are between OQPSK and non-offset QPSK.

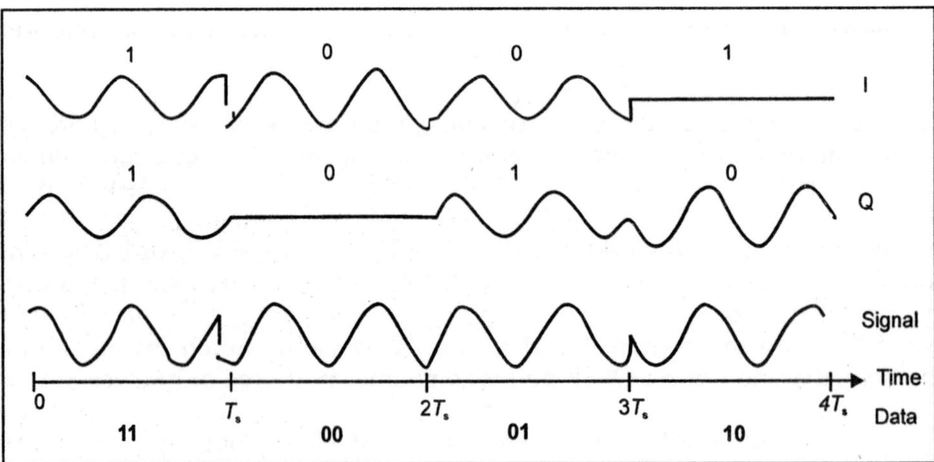

Fig. 7.17: Timing diagram for π/4-QPSK. The binary data stream is shown beneath the time axis. The two signal components with their bit assignments are shown the top and the total, combined signal at the bottom. Note that successive symbols are taken alternately from the two constellations, starting with the 'blue' one.

One property this modulation scheme possesses is that if the modulated signal is represented in the complex domain, it does not have any paths through the origin. In other words, the signal does not pass through the origin. This lowers the dynamical range of fluctuations in the signal which is desirable when engineering communications signals.

On the other hand, π/4–QPSK lends itself to easy demodulation and has been adopted for use in, for example, TDMA cellular telephone systems.

The modulated signal is shown below for a short segment of a random binary data-stream. The construction is the same as above for ordinary QPSK. Successive symbols are taken from the two constellations shown in the diagram. Thus, the first symbol (1 1) is taken from the 'blue' constellation and the second symbol (0 0) is taken from the 'green' constellation. Note that magnitudes of the two component waves change as they switch between constellations, but the total signal's magnitude remains constant. The phase-shifts are between those of the two previous timing-diagrams.

SOQPSK

The license-free *shaped-offset QPSK* (SOQPSK) is interoperable with Feher-patented QPSK (FQPSK), in the sense that an integrate-and-dump offset QPSK detector produces the same output no matter which kind of transmitter is used.

These modulations carefully shape the I and Q waveforms such that they change very smoothly, and the signal stays constant-amplitude even during signal transitions. (Rather than traveling instantly from one symbol to another, or even linearly, it travels smoothly around the constant-amplitude circle from one symbol to the next).

The standard description of SOQPSK-TG involves ternary symbols.

Higher-Order PSK

Any number of phases may be used to construct a PSK constellation but 8-PSK is usually the highest order PSK constellation deployed. With more than 8 phases, the error-rate becomes too high and there are better, though more complex, modulations available such as quadrature amplitude modulation (QAM). Although any number of phases may be used, the fact that the constellation must usually deal with binary data means that the number of symbols is usually a power of 2—this allows an equal number of bits-per-symbol.

For the general *M*-PSK there is no simple expression for the symbol-error probability if $M > 4$. Unfortunately, it can only be obtained from:

$$P_s = 1 - \int_{-\frac{\pi}{M}}^{\frac{\pi}{M}} p\Theta_r(\Theta_r)\, d\Theta_r$$

where

$$P_{\Theta r}(\Theta r) = \frac{1}{2\pi} e^{-2\gamma_s \sin^2 \Theta_r} \int_0^{\infty} V e^{-\left(V - \sqrt{4\gamma_s} \cos\Theta_r\right)^2/2}$$

$$V = \sqrt{r_1^2 + r_2^2},$$

$$\Theta_r = \tan^{-1}(r_2/r_1),$$

$$\gamma_s = \frac{E_s}{N_0} \text{ and}$$

$P_s \sim N\left(\sqrt{E_s}, N_0/2\right)$ and $r_2 \sim N\left(0, N_0/2\right)$ are jointly-Gaussian random variables.

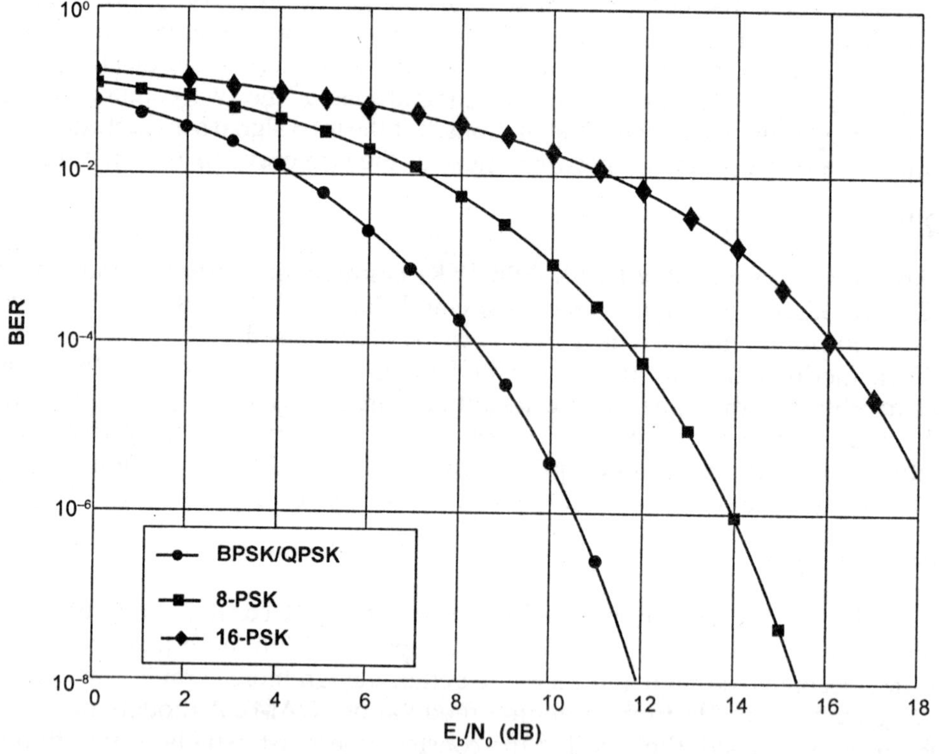

Fig. 7.18: Bit-error rate curves for BPSK, QPSK, 8-PSK and 16-PSK.

This may be approximated for high M and high E_b/N_0 by:

$$P_s \approx 2Q\left(\sqrt{2\gamma_s}\sin\frac{\pi}{M}\right).$$

The bit-error probability for M-PSK can only be determined exactly once the bit-mapping is known. However, when Gray coding is used, the most probable error from one symbol to the next produces only a single bit-error and

$$P_b \approx \frac{1}{k}P_s.$$

The graph on the left compares the bit-error rates of BPSK, QPSK (which are the same, as noted above), 8-PSK and 16-PSK. It is seen that higher-order modulations exhibit higher error-rates; in exchange however they deliver a higher raw data-rate.

Bounds on the error rates of various digital modulation schemes can be computed with application of the union bound to the signal constellation.

Differential Encoding

As mentioned for BPSK and QPSK there is an ambiguity of phase if the constellation is rotated by some effect in the communications channel the signal passes through. This problem can be overcome by using the data to *change* rather than *set* the phase.

For example, in differentially-encoded BPSK a binary '1' may be transmitted by adding 180° to the current phase and a binary '0' by adding 0° to the current phase. In differentially-encoded QPSK, the phase-shifts are 0°, 90°, 180°, –90° corresponding to data '00', '01', '11', '10'. This kind of encoding may be demodulated in the same way as for non-differential PSK but the phase ambiguities can be ignored. Thus, each received symbol is demodulated to one of the M points in the constellation and a comparator then computes the difference in phase between this received signal and the preceding one. The difference encodes the data as described above.

The modulated signal is shown below for both DBPSK and DQPSK as described above. It is assumed that the *signal starts with zero phase,* and so there is a phase shift in both signals at $t = 0$.

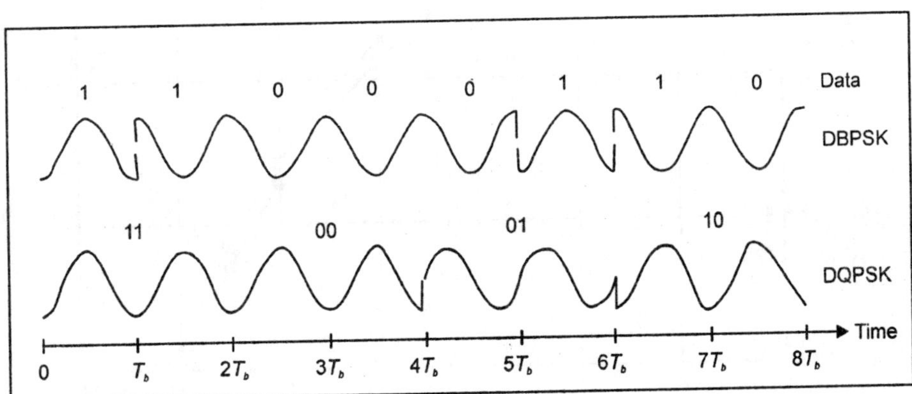

Fig. 7.19: Timing diagram for DBPSK and DQPSK. The binary data stream is above the DBPSK signal. The individual bits of the DBPSK signal are grouped into pairs for the DQPSK signal, which only changes every $T_s = 2T_b$.

Analysis shows that differential encoding approximately doubles the error rate compared to ordinary M-PSK but this may be overcome by only a small increase in E_b/N_0. Furthermore, this analysis (and the graphical results below) are based on a system in which the only corruption is additive white Gaussian noise. However, there will also be a physical channel between the transmitter and receiver in the communication system. This channel will, in general, introduce an unknown phase-shift to the PSK signal; in these cases the differential schemes can yield a *better* error-rate than the ordinary schemes which rely on precise phase information.

Example: Differentially-Encoded BPSK

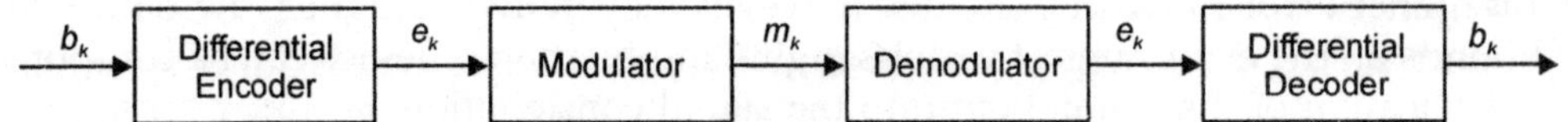

Fig. 7.20: Differential encoding/decoding system diagram.

At the *k*th time-slot call the bit to be modulated b_k, the differentially-encoded bit e_k and the resulting modulated signal $m_k(t)$. Assume that the constellation diagram positions the symbols at ±1 (which is BPSK). The differential encoder produces:

$$e_k = e_{k-1} \oplus b_k$$

where + indicates binary or modulo-2 addition.

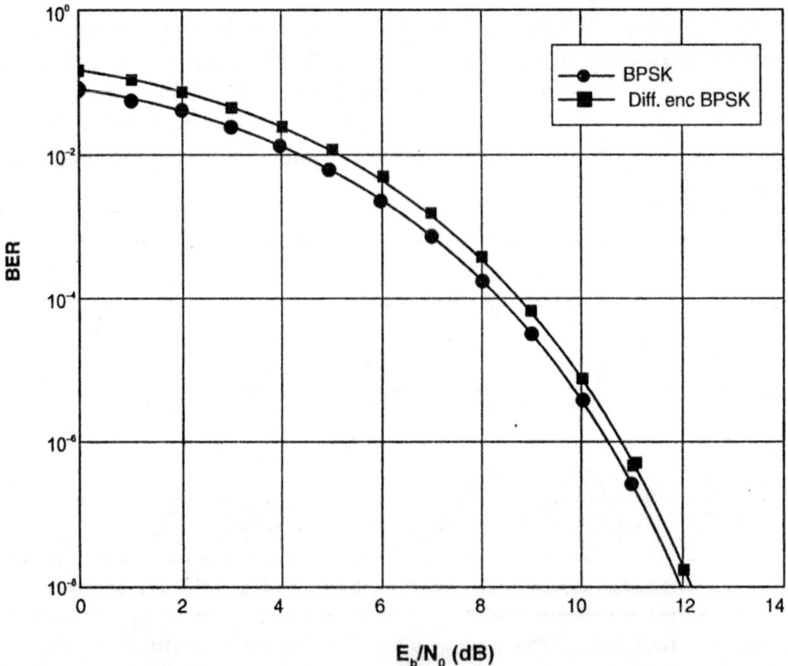

Fig. 7.21: BER comparison between BPSK and differentially-encoded BPSK with gray-coding operating in white noise.

So e_k only changes state (from binary '0' to binary '1' or from binary '1' to binary '0') if b_k is a binary '1'. Otherwise it remains in its previous state. This is the description of differentially-encoded BPSK given above.

The received signal is demodulated to yield $e_k = \pm 1$ and then the differential decoder reverses the encoding procedure and produces:

$b_k = e_k \oplus e_{k-1}$ since binary subtraction is the same as binary addition.

Therefore, $b_k = 1$ if e_k and e_{k-1} differ and $b_k = 0$ if they are the same. Hence, if both e_k and e_{k-1} are *inverted*, b_k will still be decoded correctly. Thus, the 180° phase ambiguity does not matter.

Differential schemes for other PSK modulations may be devised along similar lines. The waveforms for DPSK are the same as for differentially-encoded PSK given above since the only change between the two schemes is at the receiver.

The BER curve for this example is compared to ordinary BPSK on the right. As mentioned above, whilst the error-rate is approximately doubled, the increase needed in E_b/N_0 to overcome this is small. The performance degradation is a result of noncoherent transmission—in this case it refers to the fact that tracking of the phase is completely ignored.

Differential Phase-Shift Keying (DPSK)

For a signal that has been differentially encoded, there is an obvious alternative method of demodulation. Instead of demodulating as usual and ignoring carrier-phase ambiguity, the phase between two successive received symbols is compared and used to determine what the data must have been. When differential encoding is used in this manner, the scheme is known as differential phase-shift keying (DPSK). Note that this is subtly different to just differentially-encoded PSK since, upon reception, the received symbols are *not* decoded one-by-one to constellation points but are instead compared directly to one another.

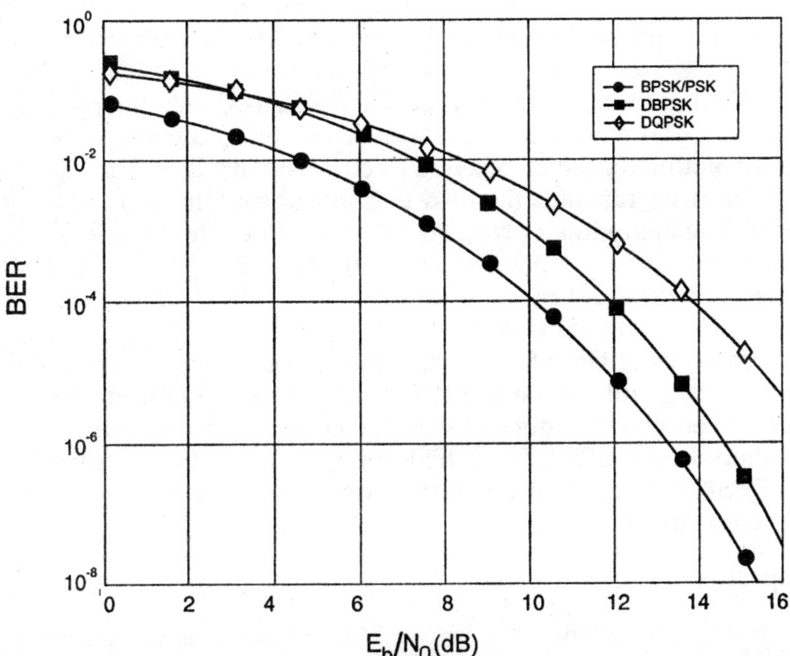

Fig. 7.22: BER comparison between DBPSK, DQPSK and their non-differential forms using gray-coding and operating in white noise.

Call the received symbol in the kth timeslot r_k and let it have phase φ_k. Assume without loss of generality that the phase of the carrier wave is zero. Denote the AWGN term as n_k. Then

$$r_k = \sqrt{E_s e^{j\phi_k}} + n_k.$$

The decision variable for the k–1th symbol and the kth symbol is the phase difference between r_k and r_{k-1}. That is, if r_k is projected onto r_{k-1}, the decision is taken on the phase of the resultant complex number:

$$r_k r^*_{k-1} = E_s e^{j(\theta_k - \theta_{k-1})} + \sqrt{E_s} e^{j\theta_k} n^*_{k-1} + \sqrt{E_s} e^{-j\theta_{k-1}} n_k + n_k n_{k-1}$$

where superscript * denotes complex conjugation. In the absence of noise, the phase of this is $\theta_k - \theta_{k-1}$, the phase-shift between the two received signals which can be used to determine the data transmitted.

The probability of error for DPSK is difficult to calculate in general, but, in the case of DBPSK it is:

$$P_b = \frac{1}{2} e^{-E_b/N_0},$$

which, when numerically evaluated, is only slightly worse than ordinary BPSK, particularly at higher E_b/N_0 values.

Using DPSK avoids the need for possibly complex carrier-recovery schemes to provide an accurate phase estimate and can be an attractive alternative to ordinary PSK.

In optical communications, the data can be modulated onto the phase of a laser in a differential way. The modulation is a laser which emits a continuous wave, and a Mach-Zehnder modulator which receives electrical binary data. For the case of BPSK for example, the laser transmits the field unchanged for binary '1', and with reverse polarity for '0'. The demodulator consists of a delay line interferometer which delays one bit, so two bits can be compared at one time. In further processing, a photo diode is used to transform the optical field into an electric current, so the information is changed back into its original state.

The bit-error rates of DBPSK and DQPSK are compared to their non-differential counterparts in the graph to the right. The loss for using DBPSK is small enough compared to the complexity reduction that it is often used in communications systems that would otherwise use BPSK. For DQPSK though, the loss in performance compared to ordinary QPSK is larger and the system designer must balance this against the reduction in complexity.

Channel Capacity

Like all M-ary modulation schemes with M = 2^*b* symbols, when given exclusive access to a fixed bandwidth, the channel capacity of any phase shift keying modulation scheme rises to a maximum of *b* bits/s as the SNR increases.

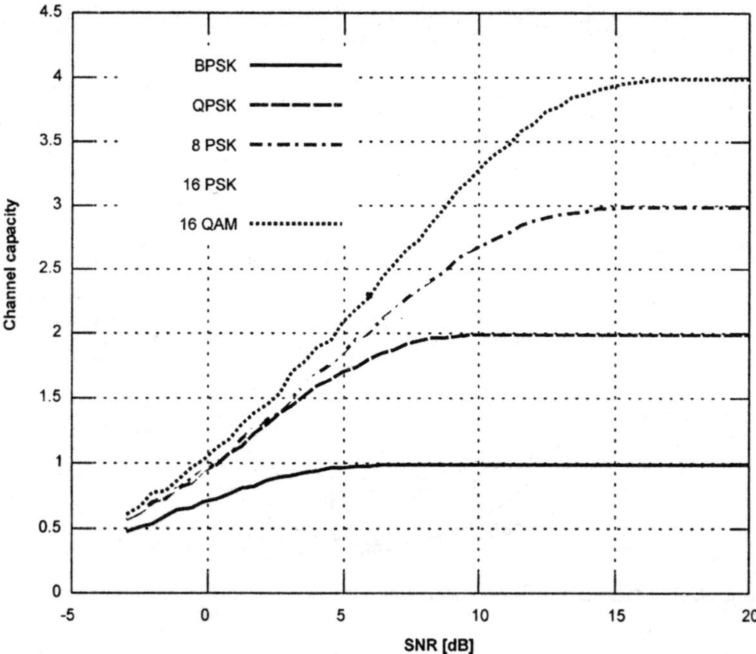

Fig. 7.23: Given a fixed bandwidth, channel capacity vs. SNR for some common modulation schemes.

QUADRATURE AMPLITUDE MODULATION

Quadrature amplitude modulation (QAM) (Pronounced kwa:m) is a modulation scheme which conveys data by changing (*modulating*) the amplitude of two carrier waves. These two waves, usually sinusoids, are out of phase with each other by 90° and are thus called quadrature carriers—hence the name of the scheme.

Overview

Like all modulation schemes, QAM conveys data by changing some aspect of a carrier signal, or the carrier wave (usually a sinusoid), in response to a data signal. In the case of QAM, the amplitude of two waves, 90 degrees out-of-phase with each other (in quadrature) are changed (*modulated* or *keyed*) to represent the data signal.

Phase modulation (analog PM) and phase-shift keying (digital PSK) can be regarded as a special case of QAM, where the magnitude of the modulating signal is a constant, with only the phase varying. This can also be extended to frequency modulation (FM) and frequency-shift keying (FSK), for these can be regarded a special case of phase modulation.

Analog QAM

When transmitting two signals by modulating them with QAM, the transmitted signal will be of the form:

$$s(t) = I(t) \cos (2\pi f_0 t) + Q(t) \sin (2\pi f_0 t),$$

where $I(t)$ and $Q(t)$ are the modulating signals and f_0 is the carrier frequency.

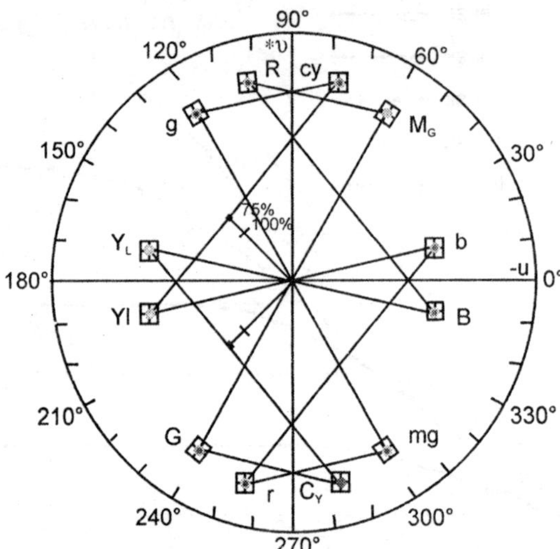

Fig. 7.24: Analog QAM: measured PAL colour bar signal on a vector analyser screen.

At the receiver, these two modulating signals can be demodulated using a coherent demodulator. Such a receiver multiplies the received signal separately with both a cosine and sine signal to produce the received estimates of $I(t)$ and $Q(t)$ respectively. Because of the orthogonality property of the carrier signals, it is possible to detect the modulating signals independently.

In the ideal case $I(t)$ is demodulated by multiplying the transmitted signal with a cosine signal:

$$\begin{aligned} r_i(t) &= s(t)\cos(2\pi f_0 t) \\ &= I(t)\cos(2\pi f_0 t)\cos(2\pi f_0 t) + Q(t)\sin(2\pi f_0 t)\cos(2\pi f_0 t) \end{aligned}$$

Using standard trigonometric identities, we can write it as:

$$\begin{aligned} r_i(t) &= \frac{1}{2}I(t)\left[1+\cos(4\pi f_0 t)\right]+\frac{1}{2}Q(t)\sin(2\pi f_0 t) \\ &= \frac{1}{2}I(t)+\frac{1}{2}\left[I(t)\cos(4\pi f_0 t)+Q(t)\sin(4\pi f_0 t)\right] \end{aligned}$$

Low-pass filtering $r_i(t)$ removes the high frequency terms (containing $4\pi f_0 t$), leaving only the $I(t)$ term. This filtered signal is unaffected by $Q(t)$, showing that the in-phase component can be received independently of the quadrature component. Similarly, we may multiply $s(t)$ by a sine wave and then low-pass filter to extract $Q(t)$.

It should be noted that here we assumed that the phase of the received signal is known at the receiver. If the demodulating phase is even a little off, it results in crosstalk between the modulated signals. This issue of carrier synchronization at the receiver must be handled somehow in QAM systems. The coherent demodulator needs to be exactly in phase with the received signal, or otherwise the modulated signals cannot be independently received. For example analog television systems transmit a burst of the transmitting colour subcarrier after each horizontal synchronization pulse for reference.

Analog QAM is used in NTSC and PAL television systems, where the I- and Q-signals carry the components of chroma (colour) information. "Compatible QAM" or C-QUAM is used in AM stereo radio to carry the stereo difference information.

Fourier Analysis of QAM

In the frequency domain, QAM has a similar spectral pattern to DSB-SC modulation. Using the properties of the Fourier transform, we find that:

$$S(f) = \frac{1}{2}\left[M_I(f - f_0) + M_I(f + f_0)\right] + \frac{1}{2j}\left[M_Q(f - f_0) - M_Q(f + f_0)\right]$$

where $S(f)$, $M_I(f)$ and $M_Q(f)$ are the Fourier transforms (frequency-domain representations) of $s(t)$, $I(t)$ and $Q(t)$, respectively.

Quantized QAM

As with many digital modulation schemes, the constellation diagram is a useful representation. In QAM, the constellation points are usually arranged in a square grid with equal vertical and horizontal spacing, although other configurations are possible (*e.g.* Cross-QAM). Since in digital telecommunications the data is usually binary, the number of points in the grid is usually a power of 2 (2, 4, 8 ...). Since QAM is usually square, some of these are rare—the most common forms are 16-QAM, 64-QAM, 128-QAM and 256-QAM. By moving to a higher-order constellation, it is possible to transmit more bits per symbol. However, if the mean energy of the constellation is to remain the same (by way of making a fair comparison), the points must be closer together and are thus more susceptible to noise and other corruption; this results in a higher bit error rate and so higher-order QAM can deliver more data less reliably than lower-order QAM, for constant mean constellation energy.

If data-rates beyond those offered by 8-PSK are required, it is more usual to move to QAM since it achieves a greater distance between adjacent points in the I-Q plane by distributing the points more evenly. The complicating factor is that the points are no longer all the same amplitude and so the demodulator must now correctly detect both phase and amplitude, rather than just phase.

64-QAM and 256-QAM are often used in digital cable television and cable modem applications. In the US, 64-QAM and 256-QAM are the mandated modulation schemes for digital cable (see QAM tuner) as standardised by the SCTE in the standard ANSI/SCTE 07 2000. Note that many marketing people will refer to these as QAM-64 and QAM-256. In the UK, 16-QAM and 64-QAM are currently used for digital terrestrial television (Freeview and Top Up TV).

Ideal Structure

Transmitter

The following picture shows the ideal structure of a QAM transmitter, with a carrier frequency f_0 and H_t the frequency response of the transmitter's filter:

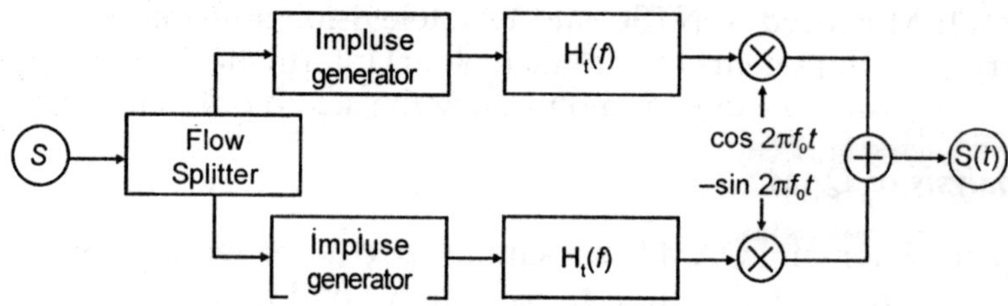

Fig. 7.25:

First the flow of bits to be transmitted is split into two equal parts: this process generates two independent signals to be transmitted. They are encoded separately just like they were in an amplitude-shift keying (ASK) modulator. Then one channel (the one "in phase") is multiplied by a cosine, while the other channel (in "quadrature") is multiplied by a sine. This way there is a phase of 90° between them. They are simply added one to the other and sent through the real channel.

The sent signal can be expressed in the form:

$$s(t) = \sum_{n=-\infty}^{\infty}\left[v_i[n].h_t(t-nT_s)\cos(2\pi f_0 t) - v_s[n].h_t(t-nT_s)\sin(2\pi f_0 t)\right],$$

where $v_c[n]$ and $v_s[n]$ are the voltages applied in response to the nth symbol to the cosine and sine waves respectively.

Receiver

The receiver simply performs the inverse process of the transmitter. Its ideal structure is shown in the picture below with H_r the receive filter's frequency response:

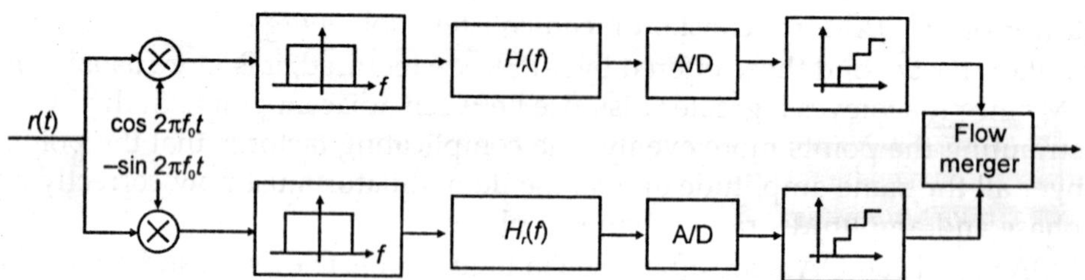

Fig. 7.26:

Multiplying by a cosine (or a sine) and by a low-pass filter it is possible to extract the component in phase (or in quadrature). Then there is only an ASK demodulator and the two flows of data are merged back.

In practice, there is an unknown phase delay between the transmitter and receiver that must be compensated by *synchronization* of the receivers local oscillator, *i.e.* the sine and cosine functions in the above figure. In mobile applications, there will often be an offset in the relative *frequency* as well, due to the possible presence of a Doppler shift proportional to the relative velocity of the transmitter and receiver. Both the phase and frequency variations introduced by the channel must be compensated by properly tuning the sine and cosine components, which requires a *phase reference,* and is typically accomplished using a Phase-Locked Loop (PLL).

In any application, the low-pass filter will be within $h_r(t)$: here it was shown just to be clearer.

Quantized QAM Performance

The following definitions are needed in determining error rates:

- M = Number of symbols in modulation constellation,
- E_b = Energy-per-bit,
- E_s = Energy-per-symbol = kE_b with k bits per symbol,
- N_0 = Noise power spectral density (W/Hz),
- P_b = Probability of bit-error,
- P_{bc} = Probability of bit-error per carrier,
- P_s = Probability of symbol-error, and
- P_{sc} = Probability of symbol-error per carrier.

$Q(x)$ is related to the complementary Gaussian error function by:

$Q(x) = \frac{1}{2}\operatorname{erfc}\left(\frac{x}{\sqrt{2}}\right)$, which is the probability that x will be under the tail of the Gaussian PDF towards positive infinity.

The error-rates quoted here are those in additive white Gaussian noise (AWGN).

Where coordinates for constellation points are given in this article, note that they represent a *non-normalised* constellation. That is, if a particular mean average energy were required (*e.g.* unit average energy), the constellation would need to be linearly scaled.

Rectangular QAM

Rectangular QAM constellations are, in general, sub-optimal in the sense that they do not maximally space the constellation points for a given energy. However, they have the considerable advantage that they may be easily transmitted as two pulse amplitude modulation (PAM) signals on quadrature carriers, and can be easily demodulated. The non-square constellations, dealt with below, achieve marginally better bit-error rate (BER) but are harder to modulate and demodulate.

The first rectangular QAM constellation usually encountered is 16-QAM, the constellation diagram for which is shown here. A Gray coded bit-assignment is also given. The reason that 16-QAM is usually the first is that a brief consideration reveals that 2-QAM and 4-QAM are in fact binary phase-shift keying (BPSK) and quadrature phase-shift keying (QPSK), respectively. Also, the error-rate performance of 8-QAM is close to that of 16-QAM (only about 0.5 dB better), but its data rate is only three-quarters that of 16-QAM.

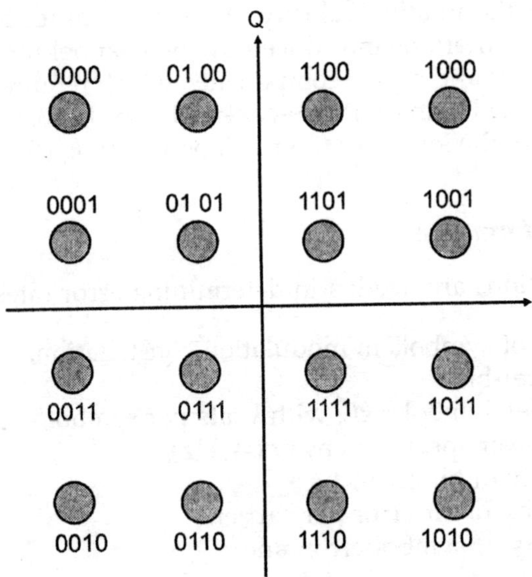

Fig. 7.27: Constellation diagram for rectangular 16-QAM.

Expressions for the symbol error-rate of rectangular QAM are not hard to derive but yield rather unpleasant expressions. For an even number of bits per symbol, k, exact expressions are available. They are most easily expressed in a *per carrier* sense:

$$P_{sc} = 2\left(1-\frac{1}{\sqrt{M}}\right)Q\left(\sqrt{\frac{3}{M-1}\frac{E_s}{N_0}}\right),$$

So

$$P_s = 1-(1-P_{sc})^2.$$

The bit-error rate will depend on the exact assignment of bits to symbols, but for a Gray-coded assignment with equal bits per carrier:

$$P_{bc} = \frac{2}{k}\left(1-\frac{1}{\sqrt{M}}\right)Q\left(\sqrt{\frac{3k}{M-1}\frac{E_b}{N_0}}\right),$$

So

$$P_s = 1-(1-P_{bc})^2.$$

Odd-k QAM

For odd k, such as 8-QAM ($k = 3$) it is harder to obtain symbol-error rates, but a tight upper bound is:

$$P_s \leq 4Q\left(\sqrt{\frac{3kE_b}{(M-1)N_0}}\right)$$

Two rectangular 8-QAM constellations are shown below without bit assignments. These both have the same minimum distance between symbol points, and thus the same symbol-error rate (to a first approximation).

The exact bit-error rate, P_b will depend on the bit-assignment.

Note that neither of these constellations are used in practice, as the non-rectangular version of 8-QAM is optimal.

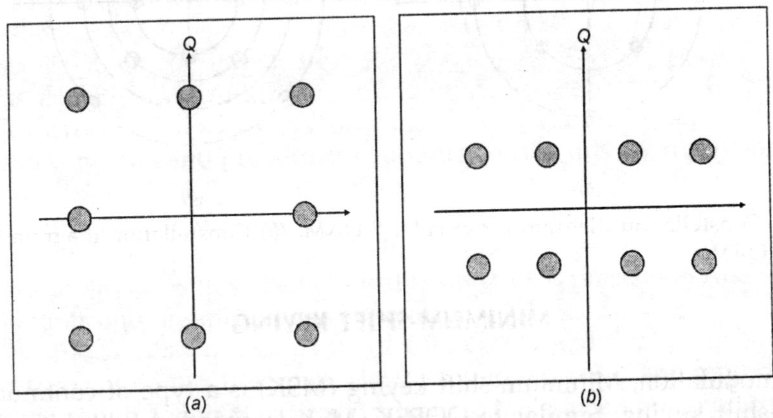

Fig. 7.28: (*a*) Constellation diagram for rectangular 8-QAM. (*b*) Alternative constellation diagram for rectangular 8-QAM.

Non-Rectangular QAM

It is the nature of QAM that most orders of constellations can be constructed in many different ways and it is neither possible nor instructive to cover them all here. This article instead presents two, lower-order constellations.

Two diagrams of circular QAM constellation are shown, for 8-QAM and 16-QAM. The circular 8-QAM constellation is known to be the optimal 8-QAM constellation in the sense of requiring the least mean power for a given minimum Euclidean distance. The 16-QAM constellation is suboptimal although the optimal one may be constructed along the same lines as the 8-QAM constellation. The circular constellation highlights the relationship between QAM and PSK. Other orders of constellation may be constructed along similar (or very different) lines. It is consequently hard to establish expressions for the error-rates of non-rectangular QAM since it necessarily depends on the constellation. Nevertheless, an obvious upper bound to the rate is related to the minimum Euclidean distance of the constellation (the shortest straight-line distance between two points):

$$P_s < (M-1)Q\left(\sqrt{d_{min}^2 / 2N_0}\right).$$

Again, the bit-error rate will depend on the assignment of bits to symbols.

Although, in general, there is a non-rectangular constellation that is optimal for a particular M, they are not often used since the rectangular QAMs are much easier to modulate and demodulate.

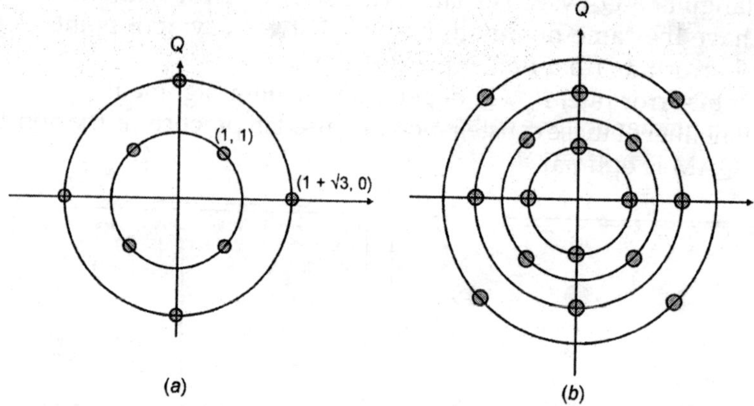

Fig. 7.29: (*a*) Constellation diagram for circular 8-QAM. (*b*) Constellation diagram for circular 16-QAM.

MINIMUM-SHIFT KEYING

In digital modulation, Minimum-shift keying (MSK) is a type of continuous phase frequency-shift keying. Similar to OQPSK, MSK is encoded with bits alternating between quarternary components, with the Q component delayed by half the symbol period. However, instead of square pulses as OQPSK uses, MSK encodes each bit as a half sinusoid. This results in a constant-modulus signal, which reduces problems caused by non-linear distortion.

MSK, a proven and widely used technique, should not be confused with the completely unworkable Very minimum-shift keying (VMSK).

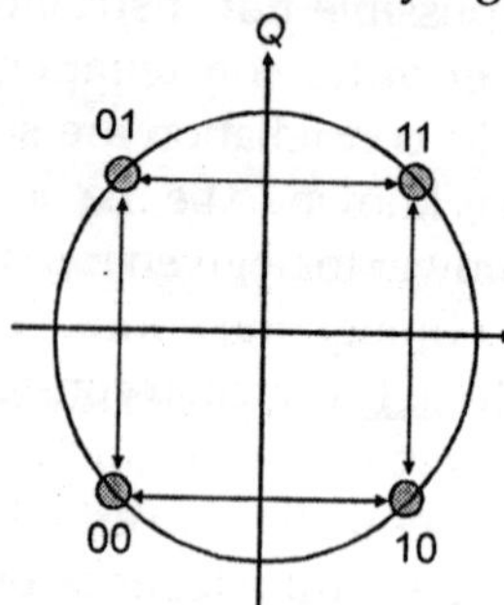

Fig. 7.30: Mapping changes in continuous phase.

Mathematical Representation

The resulting signal is represented by the formula:

$$s(t) = a_I(t)\cos\left(\frac{\pi t}{2T}\right)\cos(2\pi f_c t) - a_Q(t)\sin\left(\frac{\pi t}{2T}\right)\sin(2\pi f_c t)$$

where $a_I(t)$ and $a_Q(t)$ encode the even and odd information respectively with a sequence of square pulses as of duration $2T$. Using the trigonometric identity, this can be rewritten in a form where the phase and frequency modulation is more obvious,

$$s(t) = \cos\left[2\pi f_c t + b_k(t)\frac{\pi t}{2T} + \phi_k\right]$$

where $b_k(t)$ is +1 when $a_I(t) = a_Q(t)$ and –1 if they are of opposite signs, and φ_k is 0 if $a_I(t)$ is 1, and π otherwise. Therefore, the signal is modulated in frequency and phase, and the phase continuously and linearly changes.

Gaussian Minimum-Shift Keying

In digital communication, *Gaussian minimum shift keying* or GMSK is a continuous-phase frequency-shift keying modulation scheme. It is similar to standard *minimum-shift keying* (MSK); however the digital data stream is first shaped with a Gaussian filter before being applied to a frequency modulator. This has the advantage of reducing sideband power, which in turn reduces out-of-band interference between signal carriers in adjacent frequency channels. However, the Gaussian filter increases the modulation memory in the system and causes intersymbol interference, making it more difficult to discriminate between different transmitted data values and requiring more complex channel equalization algorithms such as an adaptive equalizer at the receiver.

Applications

GMSK is most notably used in the Global System for Mobile Communications (GSM).

Spectral Efficiency

GMSK has high spectral efficiency, but it needs a higher power level than QPSK, for instance, in order to transmit the same amount of data reliably.

CONTINUOUS PHASE MODULATION

Continuous phase modulation (CPM) is a method for modulation of data commonly used in wireless modems. In contrast to other coherent digital phase modulation techniques where the carrier phase abruptly resets to zero at the start of every symbol (*e.g.* M-PSK), with CPM the carrier phase is modulated in a continuous manner. For instance, with QPSK the carrier instantaneously jumps from a sine to a cosine (*i.e.* a 90 degree phase shift) whenever one of the two message bits of the current symbol differs from the two message bits of the previous symbol. This discontinuity requires a relatively large percentage of the power to occur outside of the intended band (*e.g.*, high fractional out-of-band power), leading to poor spectral efficiency. Furthermore, CPM is typically implemented as a constant-envelope waveform, *i.e.* the transmitted carrier power is constant. Therefore, CPM is attractive because the phase continuity yields high spectral efficiency, and the constant-envelope yields excellent power efficiency. The primary drawback is the high implementation complexity required for an optimal receiver.

Phase Memory

Each symbol is modulated by gradually changing the phase of the carrier from the starting value to the final value, over the symbol duration. The modulation and demodulation of CPM is complicated by the fact that the initial phase of each symbol is determined by the cumulative total phase of all previous transmitted symbols, which is known as the *phase memory*. Therefore, the optimal receiver cannot make decisions on any isolated symbol without taking the entire sequence of transmitted symbols into account. This requires a Maximum Likelihood Sequence Estimator (MLSE), which is efficiently implemented using the Viterbi algorithm.

Phase Trajectory

Minimum-shift keying (MSK) is another name for CPM with an excess bandwidth of 1/2 and a linear *phase trajectory*. Although this linear phase trajectory is continuous, it is not *smooth* since the derivative of the phase is not continuous. The spectral efficiency of CPM can be further improved by using a smooth phase trajectory. This is typically accomplished by filtering the phase trajectory prior to modulation, commonly using a Raised Cosine or a Gaussian filter. The raised cosine filter has a strictly finite duration, and can yield a *full-response* CPM waveform that prevents Intersymbol Interference (ISI).

Partial Response CPM

Partial-response signaling, such as duo-binary signaling, is a form of intentional ISI where a certain number of adjacent symbols interfere with each symbol in a controlled manner. A MLSE must be used to optimally demodulate any signal in the presence of ISI. Whenever the amount of ISI is known, such as with any partial-response signaling scheme, MLSE can be used to determine the exact symbol sequence (in the absence of noise). Since the optimal demodulation of full-response CPM already requires MLSE detection, using partial-response signaling requires little additional complexity, but can afford a comparatively smoother phase trajectory, and thus, even greater spectral efficiency. One extremely popular form of partial-response CPM is GMSK, which is used by GSM in most of the world's 2nd generation cell phones. It is also used in 802.11 FHSS, Bluetooth, and many other proprietary wireless modems.

Continuous-Phase Frequency-Shift Keying

Continuous-phase frequency-shift keying (CPFSK) is a commonly-used variation of frequency-shift keying (FSK), which is itself a special case of analog frequency modulation. FSK is a method of modulating digital data onto a sinusoidal carrier wave, encoding the information present in the data to variations in the carrier's instantaneous frequency between one of two frequencies (referred to as the space frequency and mark frequency). In general, a standard FSK signal does not have continuous phase, as the modulated waveform switches instantaneously between two sinusoids with different frequencies.

As the name suggests, the phase of a CPFSK is in fact continuous; this attribute is desirable for signals that are to be transmitted over a bandlimited channel, as discontinuities in a signal introduce wideband frequency components. In addition, some classes of amplifiers exhibit nonlinear behaviour when driven with nearly-discontinuous signals; this could have undesired effects on the shape of the transmitted signal.

Theory

If a finitely-valued digital signal to be transmitted (the message) is $m(t)$, then the corresponding CPFSK signal is:

$$s(t) = A_c \cos\left(2\pi f_c t + D_f \int_{-\infty}^{t} m(\alpha)d\alpha\right)$$

where A_c represents the amplitude of the CPFSK signal, f_c is the base carrier frequency, and D_f is a parameter that controls the frequency deviation of the modulated signal. The integral located inside of the cosine's argument is what gives the CPFSK signal its continuous phase; an integral over any finitely-valued function (which $m(t)$ is assumed to be) will not contain any discontinuities. If the message signal is assumed to be causal, then the limits on the integral change to a lower bound of zero and a higher bound of t. Note that this does not mean that $m(t)$ must be continuous; in fact, most ideal digital data waveforms contain discontinuities. However, even a discontinuous message signal will generate a proper CPFSK signal.

PULSE-POSITION MODULATION

Pulse-position modulation is a form of signal modulation in which M message bits are encoded by transmitting a single pulse in one of 2^M possible time-shifts. This is repeated every T seconds, such that the transmitted bit rate is M/T bits per second. It is primarily useful for optical communications systems, where there tends to be little or no multipath interference.

Synchronization

One of the key difficulties of implementing this technique is that the receiver must be properly synchronized to align the local clock with the beginning of each symbol.

Therefore, it is often implemented differentially as *Differential Pulse-position modulation,* where by each pulse position is encoded relative to the previous pulse, such that the receiver must only measure the difference in the arrival time of successive pulses. It is possible to limit the propagation of errors to adjacent symbols, so that an error in measuring the differential delay of one pulse will affect only two symbols, instead of effecting all successive measurements.

Sensitivity to Multipath Interference

Aside from the issues regarding receiver synchronization, the key disadvantage of PPM is that it is inherently sensitive to multipath interference that arises in channels with frequency-selective fading, whereby the receiver's signal contains one or more echoes of each transmitted pulse. Since the information is encoded in the time of arrival (either differentially, or relative to a common clock), the presence of one or more echoes can make it extremely difficult, if not impossible, to accurately determine the correct pulse position corresponding to the transmitted pulse.

Non-Coherent Detection

One of the principal advantages of Pulse Position Modulation is that it is an M-ary modulation technique that can be implemented non-coherently, such that the receiver does not need to use a Phase-locked loop (PLL) to track the phase of the carrier. This makes it a suitable candidate for optical communications systems, where coherent phase modulation and detection are difficult and extremely expensive. The only other common M-ary non-coherent modulation technique is M-ary Frequency Shift Keying, which is the frequency-domain dual to PPM.

PPM vs. M-FSK

PPM and M-FSK systems with the same bandwidth, average power, and transmission rate of M/T bits per second have identical performance in an AWGN (Additive White Gaussian Noise) channel. However, their performance differs greatly when comparing frequency-selective and frequency-flat fading channels. Whereas frequency-selective fading produces echoes that are highly disruptive for any of the M time-shifts used to encode PPM data, it selectively disrupts only some of the M possible frequency-shifts used to encode data for M-FSK. Conversely, frequency-flat fading is more disruptive for M-FSK than PPM, as all M of the possible frequency-shifts are impaired by fading, while the short duration of the PPM pulse means that only a few of the M time-shifts are heavily impaired by fading.

Optical communications systems (even wireless ones) tend to have weak multipath distortions, and PPM is a viable modulation scheme in many such applications.

Applications for RF Communications

Narrowband RF (Radio Frequency) channels with low power and long wavelengths (*i.e.*, low frequency) are affected primarily by flat fading, and PPM is better suited than M-FSK to be used in these scenarios. One common application with these channel characteristics is the radio control of model aircraft, boats and cars. PPM is employed in these systems, with the position of each pulse representing the angular position of an analogue control on the transmitter, or possible states of a binary switch. The number of pulses per frame gives the number of controllable channels available. The advantage of using PPM for this type of application is that the electronics required to decode the signal are extremely simple, which leads to small, light-weight receiver/decoder units. (Model aircraft require parts that are as lightweight as possible). Servos made for model radio control include some of the electronics required to convert the pulse to the motor position—the receiver is merely required to demultiplex the separate channels and feed the pulses to each servo.

More sophisticated R/C systems are now often based on pulse-code modulation, which is more complex but offers greater flexibility and reliability.

Pulse position modulation is also used for communication to the ISO 15693 contactless Smart card as well as the HF implementation of the EPC Class 1 protocol for RFID tags.

TRELLIS MODULATION

In telecommunication, trellis modulation (also known as trellis coded modulation, or simply TCM) is a modulation scheme which allows highly efficient transmission of information over band-limited channels such as telephone lines. Trellis modulation was invented by Gottfried Ungerboeck in 1982.

In the late 1980s, modems operating over plain old telephone service ("POTS") typically achieved 9.6 kbit/s by employing 4 bits per symbol QAM modulation at 2400 baud (symbols/second). This bit rate ceiling existed despite the best efforts of many researchers, and some engineers predicted that without a major upgrade of the public phone infrastructure, the maximum achievable rate for a POTS modem might be 14 kbit/s for two-way communication (3429 baud × 4 bits/symbol using QAM). However, 14 kbit/s is only 40 per cent of the theoretical maximum bit rate predicted by Shannon's Theorem for POTS lines (approximately 35 kbit/s).

A New Modulation Method

The name "trellis" was coined because a state diagram of the technique, when drawn on paper closely resembles the trellis lattice used in rose gardens. The scheme is basically a convolutional code of rates $(r, r + 1)$. Ungerboeck's unique contribution is to apply the parity check on a per symbol basis instead of the older technique of applying it to the bit stream then modulating the bits. The key idea he termed Mapping by Set Partitions. This idea was to group the symbols in a tree like fashion then separate them into two limbs of equal size. At each limb of the tree, the symbols were further apart. Although in multi-dimensions, it is hard to visualize, a simple one dimension example illustrates the basic procedure. Suppose the symbols are located at [1, 2, 3, 4,...]. Then take all odd symbols and place them in one group, and the even symbols in the second group. This is not quite accurate because Ungerboeck was looking at the two dimensional problem, but the principle is the same, take every other one for each group and repeat the procedure for each tree limb. He next described a method of assigning the encoded bit stream onto the symbols in a very systematic procedure. Once this procedure was fully described, his next step was to programme the algorithms into a computer and let the computer search for the best codes. The results were astonishing. Even the most simple code (4 state) produced error rates nearly 1000 times lower than an equivalent uncoded system. For two years Ungerboeck kept these results private and only conveyed them to close colleagues. Finally, in 1982, Ungerboeck published a paper describing the principles of trellis modulation.

A flurry of research activity ensued, and by 1990 the International Telecommunication Union had published modem standards for the first trellis-modulated modem at 14.4 kbit/s (2400 baud and 6 bits per symbol). Over the next several years further advances in encoding, plus a corresponding symbol rate increase from 2400 to 3429 baud, allowed modems to achieve rates up to 34.3 kbit/s (limited by maximum power regulations to 33.8k). Today, the most common trellis-modulated V.34 modems use a 4-dimensional set partition which is achieved by treating two 2-dimensional symbols as a single lattice. This set uses 8, 16, or 32 state convolutional codes to squeeze the equivalent of 6 to 10 bits into each symbol sent by the modem (example: 2400 baud * 8 bits/symbol = 19,200 bits per second).

Once manufacturers introduced modems with trellis modulation, transmission rates increased to the point where interactive transfer of multimedia over the telephone became feasible (a 200 kilobyte image and a 5 megabyte song could be downloaded in less than 1 minute and 30 minutes, respectively). Sharing a floppy disk via a BBS could be done in just a few minutes, instead of an hour. Thus Ungerboeck's invention played a key role in the Information Age.

ORTHOGONAL FREQUENCY-DIVISION MULTIPLEXING

Orthogonal frequency-division multiplexing (OFDM)—essentially identical to Coded OFDM (COFDM) and Discrete multi-tone modulation (DMT)—is a frequency-division multiplexing (FDM) scheme utilized as a digital multi-carrier modulation method. A large number of closely-spaced orthogonal *sub-carriers* are used to carry data. The data are divided into several parallel data streams or channels, one for each sub-carrier. Each sub-carrier is modulated with a conventional modulation scheme (such as quadrature amplitude modulation or phase shift keying) at a low symbol rate, maintaining total data rates similar to conventional *single-carrier* modulation schemes in the same bandwidth.

OFDM has developed into a popular scheme for wideband digital communication, whether wireless or over copper wires, used in applications such as digital television and audio broadcasting, wireless networking and broadband internet access.

The primary advantage of OFDM over single-carrier schemes is its ability to cope with severe channel conditions—for example, attenuation of high frequencies in a long copper wire, narrowband interference and frequency-selective fading due to multipath—without complex equalization filters. Channel equalization is simplified because OFDM may be viewed as using many slowly-modulated narrowband signals rather than one rapidly-modulated wideband signal. The low symbol rate makes the use of a guard interval between symbols affordable, making it possible to handle time-spreading and eliminate intersymbol interference (ISI). This mechanism also facilitates the design of single-frequency networks, where several adjacent transmitters send the same signal simultaneously at the same frequency, as the signals from multiple distant transmitters may be combined constructively, rather than interfering as would typically occur in a traditional single-carrier system.

Example of Applications

The following list is a summary of existing OFDM based standards and products. For further details, see the Usage section in the end of the Table 7.1.

Cable

- ADSL and VDSL broadband access via POTS copper wiring.
- Power line communication (PLC).
- Multimedia over Coax Alliance (MoCA) home networking.

Wireless

- The wireless LAN radio interfaces IEEE 802.11a, g, n and HIPERLAN/2.
- The digital radio systems DAB/EUREKA 147, DAB+, Digital Radio Mondiale, HD Radio, T-DMB and ISDB-TSB.
- The terrestrial digital TV system DVB-T.
- The terrestrial mobile TV systems DVB-H, T-DMB, ISDB-T and MediaFLO forward link.
- The cellular communication systems Flash-OFDM.
- The mobile broadband 3GPP Long Term Evolution air interface named High Speed OFDM Packet Access (HSOPA).
- The Wireless MAN/Fixed broadband wireless access (BWA) standard IEEE 802.16 (or WiMAX).
- The Mobile Broadband Wireless Access (MBWA) standards IEEE 802.20, IEEE 802.16e (Mobile WiMAX) and WiBro.
- The wireless Personal Area Network (PAN) Ultra wideband (UWB) IEEE 802.15.3a implementation suggested by WiMedia Alliance.

Key Features

The advantages and disadvantages listed below are further discussed in the Characteristics and principles of operation section.

Summary of Advantages

- Can easily adapt to severe channel conditions without complex equalization,
- Robust against narrow-band co-channel interference,
- Robust against Intersymbol interference (ISI) and fading caused by multipath propagation,
- High spectral efficiency,
- Efficient implementation using FFT,
- Low sensitivity to time synchronization errors,
- Tuned sub-channel receiver filters are not required (unlike conventional FDM), and
- Facilitates Single Frequency Networks, *i.e.* transmitter macrodiversity.

Table 7.1: Key features of some common OFDM based systems.

Standard name	*DAB Eureka 147*	*DVB-T*	*DVB-H*	*DMB-T/H*	*IEEE 802.11a*
Ratified year	1995	1997	2004	2006	1999
Frequency range of today's equipment (MHz)	174-240 1452-1492	470-862 174-230	470-862	470-862	4915-5825
Channel spacing B (MHz)	1.712	8, 7, 6,	8, 7, 6 & 5	8	20
Number of subcarriers N	192, 384, 768 or 1536	2K mode: 1705 8K mode: 6817	1705, 3409, 6817	1 (single-carrier) 3780 (multi-carrier)	52
Subcarrier modulation scheme	DQPSK	QPSK, 16 QAM or 64 QAM	QPSK, 16 QAM or 64 QAM	4 QAM, 4 QAM-NR, 16 QAM, 32 QAM and 64 QAM.	BPSK, QPSK, 16 QAM or 64 QAM
Useful symbol length T_U (µs)		2K mode: 224 8K mode: 896	224, 448, 896	500 (multi-carrier)	3.2
Additional guard interval T_G (Fraction of T_U)		1/4, 1/8, 1/16, 1/32	1/4, 1/8, 1/16, 1/32	¼, 1/6, 1/9	1/4
Subcarrier spacing $\Delta f = 1/(T_U)$? B/N (Hz)		2K mode: 4464 8K mode: 1116	4464, 2232, 1116	8 M (single-carrier) 2000 (multi-carrier)	312.5K
Net bit rate R (Mbit/s)	0.576-1.152	4.98-31.67 (typically 24)	3.7-23.8	4.81-32.49	6-54
Link spectral efficiency R/B (bit/s/Hz)	0.34-0.67	0.62-4.0	0.62-4.0	0.60-4.1	0.30-2.7
Inner FEC	Conv coding with code rates 1/4, 3/8 or 1/2	Conv coding with code rates 1/2, 2/3, 3/4, 5/6 or 7/8	Conv coding with code rates 1/2, 2/3, 3/4, 5/6 or 7/8	LDPC with code rates 0.4, 0.6 or 0.8	Conv coding with code rates 1/2, 2/3 or 3/4
Outer FEC (if any)	None	RS(204, 188, t = 8)	RS(204, 188, t=8) + MPE-FEC	BCH code (762, 752)	
Maximum traveling speed (km/h)	200-600	53-185 depends on transmission frequency			
Time interleaving depth (ms)	385	0.6-3.5	0.6-3.5	200-500	
Adaptive transmission (if any)	None	None			
Multiple access method (if any)	None	None			
Typical source coding	192 kbit/s MPEG2 Audio layer 2	2-18 Mbit/s Standard-HDTV H.264 or MPEG2		Not defined (MPEG-2 or H.264 w/MP2)	

Summary of Disadvantages

- Sensitive to Doppler shift.
- Sensitive to frequency synchronization problems.
- High peak-to-average-power ratio (PAPR), requiring linear transmitter circuitry, which suffers from poor power efficiency.

Characteristics and Principles of Operation

Orthogonality

In OFDM, the sub-carrier frequencies are chosen so that the sub-carriers are orthogonal to each other, meaning that cross-talk between the sub-channels is eliminated and inter-carrier guard bands are not required. This greatly simplifies the design of both the transmitter and the receiver; unlike conventional FDM, a separate filter for each sub-channel is not required.

The orthogonality requires that the sub-carrier spacing is $\Delta f = k/(T_U)$ Hertz, where T_U seconds is the useful symbol duration (the receiver side window size), and k is a positive integer, typically equal to 1. Therefore, with N sub-carriers, the total passband bandwidth will be $B \approx N \cdot \Delta f$ (Hz).

The orthogonality also allows high spectral efficiency, with a total symbol rate near the Nyquist rate. Almost the whole available frequency band can be utilized. OFDM generally has a nearly 'white' spectrum, giving it benign electromagnetic interference properties with respect to other co-channel users.

OFDM requires very accurate frequency synchronization between the receiver and the transmitter; with frequency deviation the sub-carriers will no longer be orthogonal, causing *inter-carrier interference* (ICI), *i.e.* cross-talk between the sub-carriers. Frequency offsets are typically caused by mismatched transmitter and receiver oscillators, or by Doppler shift due to movement. While Doppler shift alone may be compensated for by the receiver, the situation is worsened when combined with multipath, as reflections will appear at various frequency offsets, which is much harder to correct. This effect typically worsens as speed increases, and is an important factor limiting the use of OFDM in high-speed vehicles. Several techniques for ICI suppression are suggested, but they may increase the receiver complexity.

Implementation using the FFT Algorithm

The orthogonality allows for efficient modulator and demodulator implementation using the FFT algorithm on the receiver side, and inverse FFT on the sender side. Although the principles and some of the benefits have been known since the 1960s, OFDM is popular for wideband communications today by way of low-cost digital signal processing components that can efficiently calculate the FFT.

Guard Interval for Elimination of Inter-Symbol Interference

One key principle of OFDM is that since low symbol rate modulation schemes (*i.e.* where the symbols are relatively long compared to the channel time characteristics) suffer less from intersymbol interference caused by multipath, it is advantageous to transmit a number of low-rate streams in parallel instead of a single high-rate stream. Since the duration of each symbol is long, it is feasible to insert a guard interval between the OFDM symbols, thus eliminating the intersymbol interference.

The guard interval also eliminates the need for a pulse-shaping filter, and it reduces the sensitivity to time synchronization problems.

> *A simple example*: If one sends a million symbols per second using conventional single-carrier modulation over a wireless channel, then the duration of each symbol would be one microsecond or less. This imposes severe constraints on synchronization and necessitates the removal of multipath interference. If the same million symbols per second are spread among one thousand sub-channels, the duration of each symbol can be longer by a factor of thousand, *i.e.* one millisecond, for orthogonality with approximately the same bandwidth. Assume that a guard interval of 1/8 of the symbol length is inserted between each symbol. Intersymbol interference can be avoided if the multipath time-spreading (the time between the reception of the first and the last echo) is shorter than the guard interval, *i.e.* 125 microseconds. This corresponds to a maximum difference of 37.5 kilometers between the lengths of the paths.

The cyclic prefix, which is transmitted during the guard interval, consists of the end of the OFDM symbol copied into the guard interval, and the guard interval is transmitted followed by the OFDM symbol. The reason that the guard interval consists of a copy of the end of the OFDM symbol is so that the receiver will integrate over an integer number of sinusoid cycles for each of the multipaths when it performs OFDM demodulation with the FFT.

Simplified Equalization

The effects of frequency-selective channel conditions, for example fading caused by multipath propagation, can be considered as constant (flat) over an OFDM sub-channel if the sub-channel is sufficiently narrow-banded, *i.e.* if the number of sub-channels is sufficiently large. This makes equalization far simpler at the receiver in OFDM in comparison to conventional single-carrier modulation. The equalizer only has to multiply each detected sub-carrier (each Fourier coefficient) by a constant complex number, or a rarely changed value.

> *Our example*: The OFDM equalization in the above numerical example would require $N = 1000$ complex multiplications per OFDM symbol, *i.e.* one million multiplications per second, at the receiver. The FFT algorithm requires $N\log_2 N = 10000$ complex-valued multiplications per OFDM symbol, *i.e. 10 million multiplications per second*, at both the receiver and transmitter side. This should be compared with the corresponding one million symbols/second single-carrier modulation case mentioned in the example, where the equalization of 125 microseconds time-spreading using a FIR filter would require 125 multiplications per symbol, *i.e. 125 million multiplications per second.*

Some of the sub-carriers in some of the OFDM symbols may carry pilot signals for measurement of the channel conditions, *i.e.* the equalizer gain and phase shift for each sub-carrier. Pilot signals and training symbols may also be used for time synchronization (to avoid inter-symbol interference, ISI) and frequency synchronization (to avoid inter-carrier interference, ICI, caused by Doppler shift).

If differential modulation such as DPSK or DQPSK is applied to each sub-carrier, equalization can be completely omitted, since these non-coherent schemes are insensitive to slowly changing amplitude and phase distortion.

Channel Coding and Interleaving

OFDM is invariably used in conjunction with channel coding (forward error correction), and almost always uses frequency and/or time interleaving. Frequency (subcarrier) interleaving increases resistance to frequency-selective channel conditions such as fading. For example, when a part of the channel bandwidth is faded, frequency interleaving ensures that the bit errors that would result from those subcarriers in the faded part of the bandwidth are spread out in the bit-stream rather than being concentrated. Similarly, time interleaving ensures that bits that are originally close together in the bit-stream are transmitted far apart in time, thus mitigating against severe fading as would happen when travelling at high speed. However, time interleaving is of little benefit in slowly fading channels, such as for stationary reception, and frequency interleaving offers little to no benefit for narrowband channels that suffer from flat-fading (where the whole channel bandwidth is faded at the same time).

The reason why interleaving is used on OFDM is to attempt to spread the errors out in the bit-stream that is presented to the error correction decoder, because when such decoders are presented with a high concentration of errors the decoder is unable to correct all the bit errors, and a burst of uncorrected errors occurs.

A common type of error correction coding used with OFDM-based systems is convolutional coding, which is often concatenated with Reed-Solomon coding. Convolutional coding is used as the inner code and Reed-Solomon coding is used for the outer code—usually with additional interleaving (on top of the time and frequency interleaving mentioned above) in between the two layers of coding. The reason why this combination of error correction coding is used is that the Viterbi decoder used for convolutional decoding produces short errors bursts when there is a high concentration of errors, and Reed-Solomon codes are inherently well-suited to correcting bursts of errors.

Newer systems, however, usually now adopt the near-optimal types of error correction coding that use the turbo decoding principle, where the decoder iterates towards the desired solution. Examples of such error correction coding types include turbo codes and LDPC codes. These codes only perform close to the Shannon limit for the Additive White Gaussian Noise (AWGN) channel, however, and some systems that have adopted these codes have concatenated them with either Reed-Solomon (for example on the MediaFLO system) or BCH codes (on the DVB-S2 system) to improve performance further over the wireless channel.

Adaptive Transmission

The resilience to severe channel conditions can be further enhanced if information about the channel is sent over a return-channel. Based on this feedback information, adaptive modulation, channel coding and power allocation may be applied across all sub-carriers, or individually to each sub-carrier. In the latter case, if a particular range of frequencies suffers from interference or attenuation, the carriers within that range can be disabled or made to run slower by applying more robust modulation or error coding to those sub-carriers.

The term discrete multitone modulation (DMT) denotes OFDM based communication systems that adapt the transmission to the channel conditions individually for each sub-carrier, by means of so called *bit-loading*. Examples are ADSL and VDSL.

The upstream and downstream speeds can be varied by allocating either more or fewer carriers for each purpose. Some forms of Rate-adaptive DSL use this feature in real time, so that the bitrate is adopted to the co-channel interference and bandwidth is allocated to whichever subscriber that needs it most.

OFDM Extended with Multiple Access

OFDM in its primary form is considered as a digital modulation technique, and not a multi-user channel access technique, since it is utilized for transferring one bit stream over one communication channel using one sequence of OFDM symbols. However, OFDM can be combined with multiple access using time, frequency or coding separation of the users.

In Orthogonal Frequency Division Multiple Access (OFDMA), frequency-division multiple access is achieved by assigning different OFDM sub-channels to different users. OFDMA supports differentiated quality-of-service by assigning different number of sub-carriers to different users in a similar fashion as in CDMA, and thus complex packet scheduling or media access control schemes can be avoided. OFDMA is used in the IEEE 802.16 Wireless MAN standard, commonly referred to as WiMAX.

In Multi-carrier code division multiple access (MC-CDMA), also known as OFDM-CDMA, OFDM is combined with CDMA spread spectrum communication for coding separation of the users. Co-channel interference can be mitigated against, meaning that manual fixed channel allocation (FCA) frequency planning is simplified, or complex dynamic channel allocation (DCA) schemes are avoided.

Space Diversity

In OFDM based wide area broadcasting, receivers can benefit from receiving signals from several spatially-dispersed transmitters simultaneously, since transmitters will only destructively interfere with each other on a limited number of sub-carriers, whereas in general they will actually reinforce coverage over a wide area. This is very beneficial in many countries, as it permits the operation of national single-frequency networks (SFNs), where many transmitters send the same signal simultaneously over the same channel frequency. SFNs utilise the available spectrum more effectively than conventional multi-frequency broadcast networks (MFN), where programme content is replicated on different carrier frequencies. SFNs also result in a diversity gain in receivers situated midway between the transmitters. The coverage area is increased and the outage probability decreased in comparison to an MFN, due to increased received signal strength averaged over all sub-carriers.

Although the guard interval only contains redundant data, which means that it reduces the capacity, some OFDM-based systems, such as some of the broadcasting systems, deliberately use a long guard interval in order to allow the transmitters to be spaced farther apart in an SFN, and longer guard intervals allow larger SFN cell-sizes. A rule of thumb for the maximum distance between transmitters in an SFN is equal to the distance a signal travels during the guard interval—for instance, a guard interval of 200 microseconds would allow transmitters to be spaced 60 km apart.

Single-frequency networks is a form of transmitter macrodiversity. The concept can be further utilized in Dynamic single-frequency networks (DSFN), where the SFN grouping is changed from timeslot to timeslot.

OFDM may be combined with other forms of space diversity, for example antenna arrays and MIMO channels. This is done in the IEEE802.11n Wireless LAN standard.

Linear Transmitter Power Amplifier

An OFDM signal exhibits a high peak-to-average power ratio (PAPR) because the independent phases of the sub-carriers mean that they will often combine constructively. Handling this high PAPR requires:

- ❑ A high-resolution digital-to-analog converter (DAC) in the transmitter,
- ❑ A high-resolution analog-to-digital converter (ADC) in the receiver, and
- ❑ A linear signal chain.

Any non-linearity in the signal chain will cause intermodulation distortion that:

- ❑ Raises the noise floor,
- ❑ May cause inter-carrier interference, and
- ❑ Generates out-of-band spurious radiation.

The linearity requirement is demanding, especially for transmitter RF output circuitry where amplifiers are often designed to be non-linear in order to minimise power consumption. In practical OFDM systems a small amount of peak clipping is allowed to limit the PAPR in a judicious tradeoff against the above consequences. However, the transmitter output filter which is required to reduce out-of-band spurs to legal levels has the effect of restoring peak levels that were clipped, so clipping is not an effective way to reduce PAPR.

Although the spectral efficiency of OFDM is attractive for both terrestrial and space communications, the high PAPR requirements have so far limited OFDM applications to terrestrial systems.

Idealized System Model

This section describes a simple idealized OFDM system model suitable for a time-invariant AWGN channel.

Transmitter

An OFDM carrier signal is the sum of a number of orthogonal sub-carriers, with baseband data on each sub-carrier being independently modulated commonly using some type of quadrature amplitude modulation (QAM) or phase-shift keying (PSK). This composite baseband signal is typically used to modulate a main RF carrier.

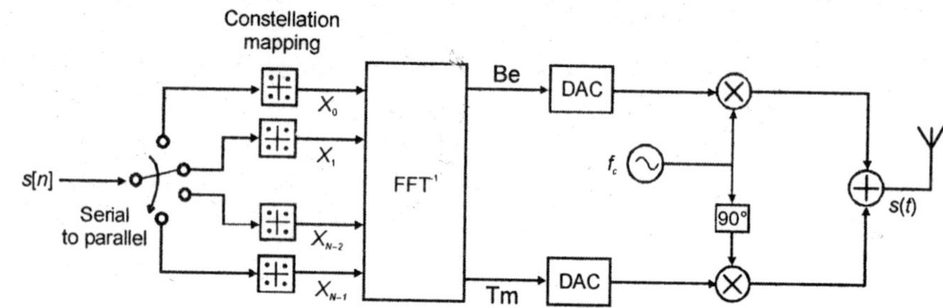

Fig. 7.31:

$s[n]$ is a serial stream of binary digits. By inverse multiplexing, these are first demultiplexed into N parallel streams, and each one mapped to a (possibly complex) symbol stream using some modulation constellation (QAM, PSK, etc.). Note that the constellations may be different, so some streams may carry a higher bit-rate than others.

An inverse is computed on each set of symbols, giving a set of complex time-domain samples. These samples are then quadrature-mixed to passband in the standard way. The real and imaginary components are first converted to the analogue domain using digital-to-analogue converters (DACs); the analogue signals are then used to modulate cosine and sine waves at the carrier frequency, f, respectively. These signals are then summed to give the transmission signal, $s(t)$.

Receiver

The receiver picks up the signal $r(t)$, which is then quadrature-mixed down to baseband using cosine and sine waves at the carrier frequency. This also creates signals centered on $2f$ so low-pass filters are used to reject these. The baseband signals are then sampled and digitised using analogue-to-digital converters (ADCs), and a forward FFT is used to convert back to the frequency domain.

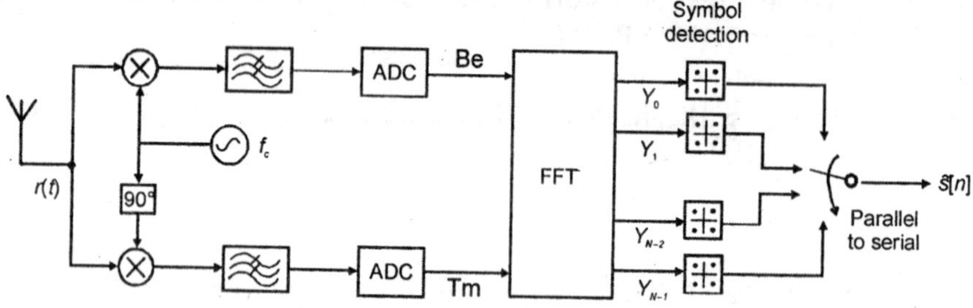

Fig. 7.32:

This returns N parallel streams, each of which is converted to a binary stream using an appropriate symbol detector. These streams are then re-combined into a serial stream, $\hat{s}(n)$, which is an estimate of the original binary stream at the transmitter.

Mathematical Description

If N sub-carriers are used, and each sub-carrier is modulated using M alternative symbols, the OFDM symbol alphabet consists of M^N combined symbols.

The low-pass equivalent OFDM signal is expressed as:

$$v(t) = \sum_{k=0}^{N-1} X_k e^{j2\pi kt/T}, \qquad 0 \le t < T,$$

where $\{X_k\}$ are the data symbols, N is the number of sub-carriers, and T is the OFDM symbol time. The sub-carrier spacing of $1/T$ makes them orthogonal over each symbol period; this property is expressed as:

$$\frac{1}{T}\int_0^T \left(e^{j2\pi k_1 t/T}\right)^* \left(e^{j2\pi k_2 t/T}\right) dt$$

$$= \frac{1}{T}\int_0^T e^{j2\pi (k_2-k_1)t/T} dt = \delta_{k_1 k_2}$$

where $(.)^*$ denotes the complex conjugate operator and δ is the Kronecker delta.

To avoid intersymbol interference in multipath fading channels, a guard interval of length T_g is inserted prior to the OFDM block. During this interval, a *cyclic prefix* is transmitted such that the signal in the interval $-T_g \le t < 0$ equals the signal in the interval $(T - T_g) \le t < T$. The OFDM signal with cyclic prefix is thus:

$$v(t) = \sum_{k=0}^{N-1} X_k e^{j2\pi kt/T}, \qquad -T_g \le t < T$$

The low-pass signal above can be either real or complex-valued. Real-valued low-pass equivalent signals are typically transmitted at baseband—wireline applications such as DSL use this approach. For wireless applications, the low-pass signal is typically complex-valued; in which case, the transmitted signal is up-converted to a carrier frequency f_c. In general, the transmitted signal can be represented as:

$$s(t) = \frac{1}{2}\Re\left\{v(t)e^{j2\pi f_c t}\right\}$$

$$= \sum_{k=0}^{N-1} |X_k| \cos\left(2\pi\left[f_c + k/T\right]t + \arg\left[X_k\right]\right)$$

Usage

OFDM System Comparison Table

Key features of some common OFDM based systems are presented in the Table 7.1.

ADSL

OFDM is used in ADSL connections that follow the G.DMT (ITU G.992.1) standard, in which existing copper wires are used to achieve high-speed data connections.

Long copper wires suffer from attenuation at high frequencies. The fact that OFDM can cope with this frequency selective attenuation and with narrow-band interference are the main reasons it is frequently used in applications such as ADSL modems. However, DSL cannot be used on every copper pair; interference may become significant if more than 25 per cent of phone lines coming into a central office are used for DSL.

For experimental amateur radio applications, users have even hooked up commercial off-the-shelf ADSL equipment to radio transceivers which simply shift the bands used to the radio frequencies the user has licensed.

Powerline Technology

OFDM is used by powerline devices to extend Ethernet connections to other rooms in a home through its power wiring. Adaptive modulation is particularly important with such a noisy channel as electrical wiring.

Wireless Local Area Networks (LAN) and Metropolitan Area Networks (MAN)

OFDM is also now being used in some wireless LAN and MAN applications, including IEEE 802.11a/g (and the defunct European alternative HIPERLAN/2) and WiMAX.

IEEE 802.11a, operating in the 5 GHz band, specifies airside data rates ranging from 6 to 54 Mbit/s. Four different modulation schemes are used: BPSK, QPSK, 16-QAM, and 64-QAM, along with a number of convolutional encoding schemes. This allows the system to adapt to the optimum data rate vs. error rate for the current conditions.

Clearwire, a wireless Internet Service Provider who provides access to metropolitan areas across the United States, utilizes OFDM in both their current 2.5 GHz network and the planned expansion of their WiMax network.

Wireless Personal Area Networks (PAN)

OFDM is also now being used in the WiMedia/Ecma-368 standard foı high-speed wireless personal area networks in the 3.1-10.6 GHz ultrawideband spectrum.

Terrestrial Digital Radio and Television Broadcasting

Much of Europe and Asia has adopted OFDM for terrestrial broadcasting of digital television (DVB-T, DVB-H and T-DMB) and radio (EUREKA 147 DAB, Digital Radio Mondiale, HD Radio and T-DMB).

DVB-T

By Directive of the European Commission, all television services transmitted to viewers in the European Community must use a transmission system that has been standardized by a recognized European standardization body, and such a standard has been developed and codified by the DVB Project, *Digital Video Broadcasting (DVB); Framing structure, channel coding and modulation for digital terrestrial television*. Customarily referred to as DVB-T, the standard calls for the exclusive use of COFDM for modulation. DVB-T is now widely used in Europe and elsewhere for terrestrial digital TV.

SDARS

The ground segments of the SDARS systems used by XM Satellite Radio and Sirius Satellite Radio are transmitted using COFDM.

COFDM vs. VSB

The question of the relative technical merits of COFDM versus 8VSB has been a subject of some controversy, especially between Europe and USA. The United States has rejected several proposals to adopt COFDM for its digital television services, and has instead opted for 8VSB (vestigial sideband modulation) operation.

One of the major benefits provided by COFDM is that it renders radio broadcasts relatively immune to multipath distortion and signal fading due to atmospheric conditions or passing aircraft. Proponents of COFDM argue that it resists multipath far better than 8VSB. Early 8VSB DTV (digital television) receivers often had difficulty receiving a signal in urban environments.

However, newer 8VSB receivers are far better at dealing with multipath, hence the difference in performance may diminish with advances in demodulator design. Moreover, 8VSB modulation requires less power to transmit a signal the same distance, i.e., the received carrier-to-noise threshold is lower for the same bit error rate. In less-populated areas, 8VSB may have an advantage because of this. In urban areas, however, COFDM is believed to offer better reception than 8VSB.

In practice, it may be impossible to settle this debate without empirical history. One difficulty in fully assessing the two systems' relative performance in multipath environments is that the spatial distribution of multipath cannot be modeled well. Due to the chaotic nature of multipath, the process is non-stationary, both temporally and spatially, in the stochastic sense. Thus, the probability distribution of impaired receiving locations is not tractable.

Digital Radio

COFDM is also used for other radio standards, for digital audio broadcasting (DAB), the standard for digital audio broadcasting at VHF frequencies, and also for Digital Radio Mondiale (DRM), the standard for digital broadcasting at shortwave and mediumwave frequencies (below 30 MHz).

The USA again uses an alternate standard, a proprietary system developed by iBiquity dubbed "HD Radio". However, it uses COFDM as the underlying broadcast technology to add digital audio to AM (medium wave) and FM broadcasts.

Both Digital Radio Mondiale and HD Radio are classified as in-band on-channel systems, unlike Eureka 147 (DAB: Digital audio broadcasting) which uses separate VHF or UHF frequency bands instead.

BST-OFDM Used in ISDB

The BST-OFDM (Band Segmented Transmission Orthogonal Frequency Division Multiplexing) system proposed for Japan—in the ISDB-T, ISDB-TSB and ISDB-C broadcasting systems—improves upon COFDM by exploiting the fact that some OFDM carriers may be modulated differently from others within the same multiplex. Some forms of COFDM already offer this kind of hierarchical modulation, though BST-OFDM is intended to make it more flexible. The 6 MHz television channel may therefore be "segmented", with different segments being modulated differently and used for different services.

It is possible, for example, to send an audio service on a segment that includes a segment comprised of a number of carriers, a data service on another segment and a television service on yet another segment—all within the same 6 MHz television channel. Furthermore, these may be modulated with different parameters so that, for example, the audio and data services could be optimized for mobile reception, while the television service is optimized for stationary reception in a high-multipath environment.

Ultra-Wideband

UWB (ultra-wideband) wireless personal area network technology may also utilise OFDM, such as in Multiband OFDM (MB-OFDM). This UWB specification is advocated by the WiMedia Alliance (formerly by both the Multiband OFDM Alliance {MBOA} and the WiMedia Alliance, but the two have now merged), and is one of the competing UWB radio interfaces.

Flash-OFDM

Flash-OFDM (Fast Low-latency Access with Seamless Handoff Orthogonal Frequency Division Multiplexing), which is also referred to as F-OFDM, is a system that is based on OFDM and specifies also higher protocol layers. It has been developed and is marketed by Flarion. Flash-OFDM has generated interest as a packet-switched cellular bearer, on which area it would compete with GSM and 3G networks. As an example, old 450 MHz frequency bands that were used by NMT-450 and C-Net C450 (both 1G analog networks, now mostly decommissioned) in Europe are already being licensed to Flash-OFDM operators.

A Flash-OFDM service delivers wireless broadband right where it is needed. It is a digital mobile network, which offer ADSL telecommunications connections for private and business use. Flash-OFDM is the only broadband solution that you can take with you wherever you go.

In Finland the license holder Digita has begun deployment of its nationwide "@450" wireless network, operational in parts of the country since April 2007 and planned coverage of all of Finland in 2009.

T-Mobile Slovakia already offers Flash-OFDM connection to its subscribers in Slovakia. The maximum download speed is 5.3 Mbit/s, whereas upload speed is limited to 1.8 Mbit/s. Slovakia is nearly full covered by Flash-OFDM.

T-Mobile Germany uses Flash-OFDM to backhaul Wi-Fi HotSpots on the Deutsche Bahn's ICE high speed trains. This deployment showcases shows the excellent mobility support of Flash-OFDM as the ICE trains reach speeds up to 300 km/h.

American wireless carrier Sprint Nextel had stated plans for field testing Flash-OFDM (along with other wireless broadband network technologies) for their 4G offering, which will be deployed using the licenses they own nationwide in the 2.5 GHz frequency range. Sprint subsequently has decided to deploy the mobile version of WiMAX, which is based on SOFDMA, scalable orthogonal frequency division multiple access technology.

Citizens Telephone Cooperative launched a Flash-OFDM service to subscribers in parts of Virginia in March, 2006. The maximum speed available is 1.5 Mbit/s.

Digiweb Ltd. launched a mobile broadband network using FLASH-OFDM technology at 872 MHz in July 2007 in Ireland and also will be launching in Norway. Voice handsets are not yet available at the time of writing (November 2007). The deployment is live in a small area north of Dublin only.

Butler Networks is currently trialing FLASH-OFDM technology in Denmark at 872 MHz as well.

In The Netherlands, KPN-telecom will start a pilot around July 2007.

History

- 1957: Kineplex, multi-carrier HF modem (R.R. Mosier & R.G. Clabaugh)
- 1966: Chang, Bell Labs: OFDM paper and US patent 3488445
- 1971: Weinstein and Ebert proposed use of FFT and guard interval
- 1985: Cimini described use of OFDM for mobile communications
- 1985: Telebit Trailblazer Modem introduced incorporating a 512 carrier Packet Ensemble Protocol
- 1987: Alard and Lasalle: COFDM for digital broadcasting
- September 1988: TH-CSF LER, first experimental Digital TV link in OFDM, Paris area
- 1989: OFDM international patent application PCT/FR 89/00546, filed in the name of THOMSON-CSF, Fouche, de Couasnon, Travert, Monnier and all.http://www.wipo.int/pctdb/en/wo.jsp?WO=1990/04893
- October 1990: TH-CSF LER, first OFDM equipment field test, 34 Mbit/s in an 8 MHz channel, experiments in Paris area
- December 1990: TH-CSF LER, first OFDM test bed comparison with VSB in Princeton USA
- September 1992: TH-CSF LER, second generation equipment field test, 70 Mbit/s in an 8 MHz channel, twin polarisations. Wuppertal, Germany
- October 1992: TH-CSF LER, second generation field test and test bed with BBC, near London, UK
- 1993: TH-CSF show in Montreux SW, 4 TV channel and one HDTV channel in a single 8 MHz channel
- 1993: Morris: Experimental 150 Mbit/s OFDM wireless LAN
- 1994: US patent 5282222, *Method and apparatus for multiple access between transceivers in wireless communications using OFDM spread spectrum*

- 1995: ETSI Digital Audio Broadcasting standard EUreka: first OFDM based standard
- 1997: ETSI DVB-T standard
- 1998: Magic WAND project demonstrates OFDM modems for wireless LAN
- 1999: IEEE 802.11a wireless LAN standard (Wi-Fi)
- 2000: Proprietary fixed wireless access (V-OFDM, Flash-OFDM, etc.)
- 2002: IEEE 802.11g standard for wireless LAN
- 2004: IEEE 802.16-2004 standard for wireless MAN (WiMAX)
- 2004: ETSI DVB-H standard
- 2004: Candidate for IEEE 802.15.3a standard for wireless PAN (MB-OFDM)
- 2004: Candidate for IEEE 802.11n standard for next generation wireless LAN
- 2005: OFDMA is candidate for the 3GPP Long Term Evolution (LTE) air interface E-UTRA downlink.
- 2007: The first complete LTE air interface implementation was demonstrated, including OFDM-MIMO, SC-FDMA and multi-user MIMO uplink.

FREQUENCY-HOPPING SPREAD SPECTRUM

Frequency-hopping spread spectrum (FHSS) is a method of transmitting radio signals by rapidly switching a carrier among many frequency channels, using a pseudorandom sequence known to both transmitter and receiver.

A spread-spectrum transmission offers three main advantages over a fixed-frequency transmission:

1. Spread-spectrum signals are highly resistant to narrowband interference. The process of re-collecting a spread signal spreads out the interfering signal, causing it to recede into the background.
2. Spread-spectrum signals are difficult to intercept. An FHSS signal simply appears as an increase in the background noise to a narrowband receiver. An eavesdropper would only be able to intercept the transmission if they knew the pseudorandom sequence.
3. Spread-spectrum transmissions can share a frequency band with many types of conventional transmissions with minimal interference. The spread-spectrum signals add minimal noise to the narrow-frequency communications, and vice versa. As a result, bandwidth can be utilized more efficiently.

Basic Algorithm

Typically, the initiation of an FHSS communication is as follows:

1. The initiating party sends a request via a predefined frequency or control channel.
2. The receiving party sends a number, known as a seed.
3. The initiating party uses the number as a variable in a predefined algorithm, which calculates the sequence of frequencies that must be used. Most often the period of the frequency change is predefined, as to allow a single base station to serve multiple connections.

4. The initiating party sends a synchronization signal via the first frequency in the calculated sequence, thus acknowledging to the receiving party it has correctly calculated the sequence.
5. The communication begins, and both the receiving and the sending party change their frequencies along the calculated order, starting at the same point in time.

In some uses, most often military, a predefined frequency-hopping sequence is negotiated, and after completing the first step the procedure is continued from number 5.

Military Use

Spread-spectrum signals are highly resistant to deliberate jamming, unless the adversary has knowledge of the spreading characteristics. Military radios use cryptographic techniques to generate the channel sequence under the control of a secret Transmission Security Key (TRANSEC) that the sender and receiver share.

By itself, frequency hopping provides only limited protection against eavesdropping and jamming. To get around this weakness most modern military frequency hopping radios often employ separate encryption devices such as the KY-57. U.S. military radios that use frequency hopping include HAVE QUICK and SINCGARS.

Technical Considerations

The overall bandwidth required for frequency hopping is much wider than that required to transmit the same information using only one carrier frequency. However, because transmission occurs only on a small portion of this bandwidth at any given time, the effective interference bandwidth is really the same. Whilst providing no extra protection against wideband thermal noise, the frequency-hopping approach does reduce the degradation caused by narrowband interferers.

One of the challenges of frequency-hopping systems is to synchronize the transmitter and receiver. One approach is to have a guarantee that the transmitter will use all the channels in a fixed period of time. The receiver can then find the transmitter by picking a random channel and listening for valid data on that channel. The transmitter's data is identified by a special sequence of data that is unlikely to occur over the segment of data for this channel and the segment can have a checksum for integrity and further identification. The transmitter and receiver can use fixed tables of channel sequences so that once synchronized they can maintain communication by following the table. On each channel segment, the transmitter can send its current location in the table.

In the US, FCC part 15 on unlicensed system in the 900 MHz and 2.4 GHz bands permits more power than non-spread spectrum systems. Both frequency hopping and direct sequence systems can transmit at 1 Watt. The limit is increased from 1 milliwatt to 1 watt or a thousand times increase. The Federal Communications Commission (FCC) prescribes a minimum number of channels and a maximum dwell time for each channel.

In a real multipoint radio system, space allows multiple transmissions on the same frequency to be possible using multiple radios in a geographic area. This creates the possibility of system data rates that are higher than the Shannon limit for a single channel. Spread spectrum systems do not violate the Shannon limit. Spread spectrum systems rely on excess signal to noise ratios for sharing of spectrum. This property is also seen in MIMO and DSSS systems. Beam steering and directional antennas also facilitate increased system performance by providing isolation between remote radios.

Multiple Inventors of Frequency Hopping Concepts

Perhaps the earliest mention of frequency hopping in the open literature is in radio pioneer Johannes Zenneck's book *Wireless Telegraphy* (German, 1908, English translation McGraw Hill, 1915), although Zenneck himself states that Telefunken had already tried it.

A Polish army officer, Leonard Danielewicz, came up with his own version of the idea in 1929. Several other patents were taken out in the 1930s, including one by Willem Broertjes [(Germany 1929, U.S. Patent No. 1,869,659 (issued Aug. 2, 1932)].

During World War II, the US Army Signal Corp was inventing a communication system called SIGSALY, which incorporated spread spectrum in a single frequency context. However, SIGSALY was top secret communications system so its existence did not become known until the 1980s.

The most celebrated invention of frequency hopping was that of actress Hedy Lamarr and composer George Antheil, who in 1942 received patent number 2,292,387 for their "Secret Communications System."

This early version of frequency hopping used a piano-roll to change between 88 frequencies, and was intended to make radio-guided torpedoes harder for enemies to detect or to jam. The patent was rediscovered in the 1950s during patent searches when private companies independently developed Code Division Multiple Access, a civilian form of spread-spectrum.

Variations

Adaptive Frequency-hopping spread spectrum (AFH) (as used in Bluetooth) improves resistance to radio frequency interference by avoiding using crowded frequencies in the hopping sequence. This sort of adaptive transmission is easier to implement with FHSS than with DSSS. The key idea behind AFH is to hop only over the "good" frequencies, by avoiding the frequency channels that are experiencing radio frequency interference from a certain transmitter. Therefore, AFH should be complemented by a mechanism for detecting good/bad channels.

However, if the radio frequency interference is itself dynamic, then the strategy of "bad channel removal", applied in AFH might not work well. For example, if there are several colocated frequency-hopping networks (as Bluetooth Piconet), then they are mutually interfering and the strategy of AFH fails to avoid this interference.

In this case, there is a need to use strategies for dynamic adaptation of the frequency hopping pattern. Such a situation can often happen in the scenarios that use Unlicensed spectrum.

In addition, dynamic radio frequency interference is expected to occur in the scenarios related to Cognitive radio, where the networks and the devices should exhibit frequency-agile operation. Chirp modulation can be seen as a form of frequency-hopping that simply scans through the available frequencies in consecutive order.

DIRECT-SEQUENCE SPREAD SPECTRUM

In telecommunications, direct-sequence spread spectrum (DSSS) is a modulation technique. As with other spread spectrum technologies, the transmitted signal takes up more bandwidth than the information signal that is being modulated. The name 'spread spectrum' comes from the fact that the carrier signals occur over the full bandwidth (spectrum) of a device's transmitting frequency.

Features

1. It phase-modulates a sine wave pseudorandomly with a continuous string of pseudonoise (PN) code symbols called "chips", each of which has a much shorter duration than an information bit. That is, each information bit is modulated by a sequence of much faster chips. Therefore, the chip rate is much higher than the information signal bit rate.
2. It uses a signal structure in which the sequence of chips produced by the transmitter is known *a priori* by the receiver. The receiver can then use the same *PN sequence* to counteract the effect of the PN sequence on the received signal in order to reconstruct the information signal.

Transmission Method

Direct-sequence spread-spectrum transmissions multiply the data being transmitted by a "noise" signal. This noise signal is a pseudorandom sequence of 1 and – 1 values, at a frequency much higher than that of the original signal, thereby spreading the energy of the original signal into a much wider band.

The resulting signal resembles white noise, like an audio recording of "static". However, this noise-like signal can be used to exactly reconstruct the original data at the receiving end, by multiplying it by the same pseudorandom sequence (because $1 \times 1 = 1$, and $-1 \times -1 = 1$). This process, known as "despreading", mathematically constitutes a correlation of the transmitted PN sequence with the PN sequence that the receiver believes the transmitter is using.

For de-spreading to work correctly, the transmit and receive sequences must be synchronized. This requires the receiver to synchronize its sequence with the transmitter's sequence via some sort of timing search process. However, this apparent drawback can be a significant benefit: if the sequences of multiple transmitters are synchronized with each other, the relative synchronizations the receiver must make between them can be used to determine relative timing, which, in turn, can be used to calculate the receiver's position if the transmitters' positions are known. This is the basis for many satellite navigation systems.

The resulting effect of enhancing signal to noise ratio on the channel is called *process gain*. This effect can be made larger by employing a longer PN sequence and more chips per bit, but physical devices used to generate the PN sequence impose practical limits on attainable processing gain.

If an undesired transmitter transmits on the same channel but with a different PN sequence (or no sequence at all), the de-spreading process results in no processing gain for that signal. This effect is the basis for the code division multiple access (CDMA) property of DSSS, which allows multiple transmitters to share the same channel within the limits of the cross-correlation properties of their PN sequences.

As this description suggests, a plot of the transmitted waveform has a roughly bell-shaped envelope centered on the carrier frequency, just like a normal AM transmission, except that the added noise causes the distribution to be much wider than that of an AM transmission.

In contrast, frequency-hopping spread spectrum pseudo-randomly re-tunes the carrier, instead of adding pseudo-random noise to the data, which results in a uniform frequency distribution whose width is determined by the output range of the pseudo-random number generator.

Benefits

- Resistance to intended or unintended jamming.
- Sharing of a single channel among multiple users.
- Reduced signal/background-noise level hampers interception (stealth).
- Determination of relative timing between transmitter and receiver.

Uses

- The United States GPS and European Galileo satellite navigation systems.
- CDMA cellular phones.
- Cordless phones operating in the 900 MHZ, 2.4 GHZ and 5.8 GHz bands.
- 802.11 and 802.11b Wi-Fi standards (The faster modes in 802.11g use OFDM, not spread spectrum, although it can fall back to the slower 802.11b modes).
- ZigBee/802.15.4.
- Automatic meter reading.

8

Television Programme Production, Organization and Studies: An Overview

TELEVISION PROGRAMME

A television programme (US), television programme (UK) or simply television show is a segment of programming in television broadcasting. It may be a one-off broadcast or, more usually, part of a periodically returning television series. A television series that is intended to be broadcast a finite number of episodes is usually called a miniseries or serial (although the latter term also has other meanings). Americans call a short run lasting less than a year a *season*; People of the United Kingdom and the Republic of Ireland generally call this a *series*. This season or series usually consists of 6–26 installments. U.S. industry practice tends to favour longer seasons than those of some other countries.

A single instance of a programme is called an episode, although this is sometimes also called a "show" or "programme." A one-off broadcast may be called a "special". A television movie ("made-for-TV" movie) is a film that is initially broadcast on television rather than being released in theaters or direct-to-video, although many successful television movies are later released on video.

Today, advertisements play a role in most television programming, such that each hour of programming can contain up to 15 minutes of advertisements in some countries. By contrast, being publicly funded, the BBC in the United Kingdom does not run advertisements, except to trail (promote) its own output. Its promotions appear between and near the end of shows but not in the middle of them, much like the Public Broadcasting Service (PBS) in the United States and the Australian Broadcasting Corporation (ABC) in Australia. With rise of internet video clips, there is serious debate about where the future of television programmes is going.

Programme Content

The content of television programmes may be factual, as in documentaries, news, and reality television, or fictional as in comedy and drama. It may be topical as in the case of news and some made-for-television movies or historical as in the case of such documentaries or fictional series. It may be primarily instructional as in the case of educational programming, or entertaining as is the case in situation comedy, reality TV, or game shows, or for income as advertisements.

A drama programme usually features a set of actors in a somewhat familiar setting. The programme follows their lives and their adventures. Many shows, especially before the 1980s, maintained a status quo where the main characters and the premise changed little. If some change happened to the characters lives during the episode, it was usually undone by the end. (Because of this, the episodes could usually be watched in any order.) Since the 1980s, there are many series that feature progressive change to the plot, the characters, or both.

Common TV programme periods include regular broadcasts (like TV news), TV series (usually seasonal and ongoing with a duration of only a few episodes to many seasons), or TV miniseries which is an extended film, usually with a small pre-determined number of episodes and a set plot and timeline. Miniseries usually range from about 3 to 10 hours in length, though critics often complain when programmes hit the short end of that range and are still marketed as "minis." In the UK, the term "miniseries" is only usually used in references to imported programmes, and such short-run series are usually called "serials".

Older American television shows began with a Pilot title sequence, showed opening credits at the bottom of the screen during the beginning of the show, and included closing credits at the end of the show. However, beginning in the 1990s some shows began with a "cold open," followed by a title sequence and a commercial break. Many serialistic shows begin with a "Previously on..." (such as 24) introduction before the teaser. And, to save time, some shows omit the title sequence altogether, folding the names normally featured there into the opening credits. The title sequence has not been completely eliminated, however, as many major television series still use them in 2007.

While television series appearing on TV networks are usually commissioned by the networks themselves, their producers earn greater revenue when the programme is sold into syndication. With the rise of the DVD home video format, box sets containing entire seasons or the complete run of a programme have become a significant revenue source as well.

Genres

- Category: Television series by genre

Scripted Entertainment

- Dramatic television series (including dramedy, police procedural, serial drama, science-fiction, or soap operas) or Television comedy (typically situation comedy or sketch comedy)
- Animated television series
- Miniseries and TV Movies
- Award show

Unscripted Entertainment

- Talk shows
- Reality television
- Game shows

Informational

- News programmes
- Documentary
- Television news magazine, dealing with current affairs
- TV infomercials, which are advertising paid spots

Development

A person decides to create a new television *series*. The show's creator develops the show's elements, consisting of the concept, the characters, the crew, and various actors (in some cases, "big-name" actors). They will then offer ("pitch") it to the various television networks in an attempt to find one that is interested in the series and order a prototype first episode of the series, known as a *pilot*.

To create the pilot, the structure and team of the whole series needs to be put together. If the network likes the pilot, they will "pick up" the show for their next *season* (UK: *series*). Sometimes they'll save it for "midseason" or request re-writes and further review (known in the industry as "Development hell"). And other times they'll *pass* entirely, leaving the show's creator forced to "shop it around"' to other networks. Many shows never make it past the pilot stage. If the show is picked up, a "run" of episodes is ordered. Usually only 13 episodes are ordered at first, although a series will typically last for at least 22 episodes (the last nine episodes sometimes being known as the "back nine", borrowing a term from golf).

The show hires a "stable" of writers, who usually work in parallel: the first writer works on the first episode, the second on the second episode, and so forth. When all of the writers have been used, the assignment of episodes continues starting with the first writer again. On other shows, however, the writers work as a team. Sometimes they will develop story ideas individually, and pitch them to the show's creator, who then folds them together into a script and rewrites them.

A UK/US Comparison

In contrast to the US model illustrated above, the UK procedure is operated on a sometimes similar, but much smaller scale.

The method of "team writing" is employed on some longer dramatic series (usually running up to a maximum of around thirteen episodes). The idea for such a show may be generated "in-house" by one of the networks; it could originate from an independent production company; it will sometimes be a product of both. For example, the BBC's long-running soap opera *EastEnders* is wholly a BBC production, whereas its popular drama *Life on Mars* was developed by Kudos in association with the network.

However, there are still a significant number of programs (usually sitcoms) that are built around just one or two writers and a small, close-knit production team. These are "pitched" in the traditional way, but since the creator(s) will handle all the writing requirements, there will be a run of six or seven instalments per series once approval has been given. Many of the most popular British comedies have been made this way, including *Monty Python's Flying Circus* (albeit with an exclusive team of six writer-performers), *Fawlty Towers, Blackadder* and *The Office.*

Production

The executive producer, often the show's creator, is in charge of running the show. They pick crew and cast (subject to approval by the network), approve and often write series plots, and sometimes write and direct major episodes. A whole host of other producers of various names work under him or her, to make sure the show is always running smoothly.

As with films or other media production, production of an individual episode can be divided into three parts: pre-production, principal photography, and post-production.

Pre-production begins when a script is approved for production. A director is chosen to plan what the episode will actually look like in the end. Pre-production tasks include storyboarding, construction of sets, props, and costumes, casting guest stars, budgeting, acquiring resources like lighting, special effects, stunts, etc. Once the show is planned, it must then be scheduled; scenes are often filmed out of sequence, guest actors or even regulars may only be available at certain times, sometimes the principal photography of different episodes must be done at the same time, complicating the schedule (*i.e.* a guest star might shoot scenes from two episodes on the same afternoon). Complex scenes are translated from storyboard to animatics to further clarify the action. Scripts are adjusted to meet altering requirements.

Some shows have a small stable of directors, but also usually rely on outside directors. Given the time constraints of broadcasting, a single show might have two or three episodes in pre-production, one or two episodes in principal photography, and a few more in various stages of post-production. The task of directing is complex enough that a single director can usually not work on more than one show at a time, hence the need for multiple directors.

Principal photography is the actual filming of the episode. Director, actors and crew will gather at soundstages or on location to film a scene. A scene is further divided into shots, which should be planned during preproduction; depending on scheduling, a scene may be shot not in the chronological order of the story. Conversations may be filmed twice from different angles, often using stand-ins, so one actor might perform all their lines in one set of shots, and then the other side of the conversation will be filmed from the opposite perspective. In order to complete a production on time, a second unit may be filming a different scene on another set or location at the same time, using a different set of actors, an assistant director, and a second unit crew. A director of photography takes care of making the show look good, doing things with lighting and so on.

Once principal photography is complete, producers coordinate post-production tasks. Visual and digital effects are added to the film; this is often outsourced to companies specializing in these areas. Often music is performed with the conductor using the film as a time reference (other musical elements may be previously recorded). An editor cuts the various pieces of film together, adds the musical score and effects, determines scene transitions, and assembles the completed show.

Distribution

The show is then turned over to the network, which sends it out to its affiliates, which broadcast it in the specified timeslot. If the Nielsen Ratings are good, the show is kept alive as long as possible. If not, the show is usually cancelled. The show's creators are then left to shop around remaining episodes, and the possibility of future episodes, to other networks. On especially successful series, the producers sometimes call a halt to a series on their own like *The Cosby Show* and end it with a concluding episode which sometimes is a big production called a series finale.

If the show is popular or lucrative, and a number of episodes (usually 100 episodes or more) are made, it goes into syndication where broadcast rights are then resold.

Seasons/Series

The terminology used to define a set of episodes produced by a television series varies from country to country. In North America and Australia, the term used to describe a regular run of episodes is a television season or simply, season. For example, a season of a television series might consist of 22-24 episodes broadcast regularly between September and April with a hiatus during the holidays. Alternatively, it may comprise 22-24 consecutive episodes between September and December or January and May. The latter is often referred to as a "non-stop season", which are usually used for serial television series (*e.g.*, *24* and *Lost*). Another example might be a series that airs only 6-13 episodes broadcast during the summer.

In the United Kingdom, on the ABC in Australia and in other countries, these sets of episodes are now referred to as series (the term is used separately from "television series" which refers to a complete production), although in the UK historically "season" was used on certain series, and remains in use in reference to them (*e.g. Doctor Who*, *Blake's 7*, etc.). In the United States, most regular television series have 22 episodes per year. In general, dramas usually last 44 minutes (an hour with advertisements), while comedies last 22 (30 with advertisements). However, with the rise of cable networks, especially pay ones, series and episode lengths have been changing. Cable networks usually feature series lasting around thirteen episodes (*e.g. The Sopranos* from HBO, with 12- to 13-episode seasons). Many British series have significantly shorter yearly runs, such as *The Office* and *Extras*, which feature 6 episodes per series. Recently, American non-cable networks have also begun to experiment with shorter seasons for some programs, particularly reality shows such as *Survivor*.

This is a reduction from the 1950s, in which many American shows (*e.g.*, *The Twilight Zone*) had between 29 to 39 episodes per season. Actual storytelling time within a commercial television hour has also gradually reduced over the years, from 50 minutes out of every 60 in the early days down to the current 44 (and, on some networks, less) in the 2000s.

The Japanese have sometimes subdivided television series and dramas into *küru*, possibly from the French term "cours" or German "kur" for "course", which is a 3-month period usually of 13 episodes. Each *kûru* generally has its own opening and ending image sequence and song, recordings of which are often sold.

INTRODUCTION TO TV PRODUCTION: AN OVERVIEW

There are essentially two ways of doing television. Programmes are shot either in a specially designed television studio using several cameras which are fed into a control room and assembled in "real time," or they are shot using a single camera on location and assembled later in an editing room or on a computer. Obviously, almost all non-professional video is shot using a single camera. That makes it what the pros call "electronic field production," or EFP.

In electronic field production, the director is like a composer of music, creating and assembling images and impressions, fitting them together carefully, weighing the quality and importance of each as he goes. He works much as a film director would, in a linear fashion from one shot to the next, one scene to the next. He is dealing with only one picture and one situation at a time. Since the programme will be edited later, he can shoot out of sequence, repeat shots, and record extra shots to be included later. Electronic field production allows for a richness of scene and artistic creativity born sometimes out of necessity and sometimes out of opportunities suggested by the location itself.

Professionals spend most of their time planning, scripting, and organizing their productions. The amount of time spent actually recording the programme is surprisingly short compared to the time spent preparing for it. Each programme goes through several important stages, from development of the concept through planning and scripting, then on to set design or location scouting, acquisition of performers and rehearsal. Along the way, the producer schedules his equipment, finds a competent crew, and brings all of the necessary elements together for actual production of the program.

Television is an amalgam of many diverse disciplines. Professional productions often depend on the skill and cooperation of many people, as well as the ability of the producer and director to bring these people together in a cooperative effort. On the other hand, with digital technology, it is also possible to be a "one man band," performing all of the various functions yourself, and produce a "broadcast quality" programme. While this book will deal with many of the techniques of production, it doesn't pretend to tell you how to do anything. After all, rules are made to be broken. Or ignored. Still, picking the mind of a professional television producer will help you get better results every time you pick up a camera.

I'm going to assume you're serious and want to learn more than you'd need to know just to make home movies of your vacation, your little brother's birthday party, or your trip to Disneyland. The instruction manual that came with your camcorder should cover these needs.

Although most who use these modules study in class situations, many people go through these modules on an individual basis—i.e., they work for government agencies, TV production facilities, or they just need a personal understanding of the concepts.

Completing this course could mean an exciting career in broadcast television, Internet webcasting, institutional videography, satellite programming, mobile video, and other areas—including advertising and public relations aspects of any of these. And video production now includes feature films—the kind you see at your local theater. I have trained thousands of people in television production and have worked professionally in the field for many years—and I guarantee that, by the end of this course, you'll have a good understanding of the production process.

Although the modules emphasize studio and field production for broadcast television, what's presented will be applicable to a wide variety of audio- and video-based media. It's all pretty much the same once you know the basics. Of course, it's desirable to have audio and video equipment to work with—either personal equipment or equipment provided in a school or lab setting. Some equipment may not be available to you. That's okay; it's important to understand the equipment and techniques that are part of larger production facilities. For one thing, you may suddenly be confronted with an internship or job opportunity where this knowledge is essential. Camerapersons, writers, directors, producers, and even on-camera talent find that having a solid understanding of the tools and techniques of the entire process makes a major difference in the success of productions—not to mention their careers. In television production, as in most of today's high-tech areas, *knowledge is power*.

Enough of the sales pitch. Let's get down to business.

A Bird's Eye View of the Production Process

Let's take a whirlwind tour of the production process. But unlike a whirlwind tour of Europe (if it's Tuesday, this must be Barcelona), we'll come back to these people and places later. For now, let's take a quick look at the production process from the standpoint of the key people.

We'll start by thinking big—big productions, that is—because many of these things can be scaled down, combined, or eliminated in smaller productions.

Who Does What and Why

This list is long, but have you noticed the lengthy credit lists for major films and TV programs? The person generally in charge of launching entire production is the producer. He or she comes up with the programme concept, lays out the budget for the production, and makes the major decisions. This person is the team leader, the one who works with the writers, hires the director, decides on the key talent, and guides the general direction of the production. In smaller productions, the producer may also take charge of the more mundane activities. And in small productions, the *director* may handle the producer's responsibilities. In this case, the combined job title becomes (want to guess?), producer-director.

Some productions may also have an associate producer who sets up schedules for the talent and crew and who generally assists the producer. On a major production, one of the producer's first jobs is to hire a writer to write the script (the document that tells everyone what to do and say). The script is like a written plan or blueprint for the production.

The producer will next consider the key talent for the production. In general, the talent includes actors, reporters, hosts, guests, and off-camera narrators—anyone whose voice is heard or who appears on camera. Sometimes *talent* is broken down into three sub-categories: actors (who portray other people in dramatic productions), performers (who appear on camera in nondramatic roles), and announcers (who generally don't appear on camera). In a large production, the producer will hire a director. The director is in charge of working out *preproduction* (before the production) details, coordinating the activities of the production staff and on-camera talent, working out camera and talent positions on the set, selecting the camera shots during production, and supervising *postproduction* work.

In other words, once the producer sets things in motion, the director is in charge of taking the script from the beginning to the very end of the production process. Assisting a director in the control room is typically a technical director who operates the *video switcher*. (A rather elaborate version is shown on the right.) The technical director, or TD, is also responsible for coordinating the technical aspects of the production. One or more production assistants (PAs) may be hired to help the producer and director. Among other things, PAs keep notes on ongoing production needs and changes. The lighting director (LD) designs the lighting plan, arranges for the lighting equipment, and sets up and checks the lighting. As we'll see, lighting is a key element in the overall look of a production. Some productions have a set designer who, along with the producer and director, designs the set and supervises its construction, painting, and installation. The makeup person, with the help of, for example, cosmetics and hair spray, sees that the talent look their best/or worst, if that's what the script calls for. Makeup is just one of the areas where a link will take you to advanced information. (We'll discuss the meaning of the coloured squares below). It should be emphasized that specific responsibilities of production personnel will vary widely, depending on the production facility. In Europe, and in particular at the BBC (British Broadcasting System) in London, these distinctions are made. Before you move on to Part Two of this module, let me call your attention to some things:

- First, you'll notice the *Site Search/Key Terms* link at the end of each module. This link is useful in finding terms and phrases anywhere on the site.
- Links will also take you to about 100 associated files intended to add to the basic information presented in these modules.
- For further readings on any topic, click on the link at the bottom of each module for a bibliography of additional readings (the hardcopy type).
- For important background information on the television medium, check out the series of modules.
- After you visit any of these links, you can either close the window that pops up or click on the back arrow at the top of your browser to get back to the module you were reading.

These modules are available on independent Internet servers in the United States and Brazil. In case you get lost in cyberspace at some point, you might want to make a note of the following independent sites in the U.S. where these materials can be found:

- http://www.CyberCollege.com/tvp_ind.htm
- http://www.CyberCollege.org/tvp_ind.htm
- http://www.InternetCampus.com/tvp_ind.htm
- http://www.InternetCampus.org/tvp_ind.htm

If you find that one site bogs down—we've all known the Internet to do that on occasion—try another site. All these sites carry the same TV Production and Mass Media modules.

The "Quick Quiz" button at the end of each chapter takes you to a very short interactive matching game that acts as a review of some of the major concepts in the chapter (and checks to see if you really were awake while you were reading it!).

Green, Yellow, Blue, and Red Readings

And now to explain those little colored squares before most links.

- A green square in front of a link indicates information that's *important to what's being discussed*. We cover this information in the interactive tests and puzzles.
- A yellow square indicates helpful *background reading*. This material is not included on the interactive tests, but instructors may include the readings on their own tests.
- A blue square indicates *technical information* designed for advanced classes and professionals; again, this material may or may not be required by an instructor (if you are in a classroom setting).
- A red square indicates *external links* with related information not included on the interactive tests—but your instructor, of course, has the option of asking that you read this information. Please note that the links to these external sources should in no way be considered endorsements, and no compensation is received by Cyber College or the Internet Campus for including these links. Unlike the links which go to information on this site, we have no control over the content of these external links.

NOTE: If you find that some of the interactive features on this site don't work, you are probably using an old browser or you have JavaScript disabled. Note that the wavy underline here indicates the mouse over option of more information.

TELEVISION PRODUCTION TIPS

- *Shooting Video For Editing*—There's a trick to shooting video out of sequence and editing it together later.
- *Just 4 shots*—The magic of television. There are only four different shots in television and once you learn them and their uses, you'll know-how to do the magic too.

- *Basic storyboarding*—It takes a lot of planning to develop a video production that makes sense. It's been said that 90 per cent of the work on a good video production is done before you take the camera out of the box.
- *Continuity is essential*—If a person is signing their name with their right hand and you cut to a close-up of their left hand doing the writing, that's a continuity problem.
- *Using Cutaways*—A cutaway is a shot that allows you to cover up an edit. They are very useful when editing interviews.
- *Simple lighting techniques*—Using inexpensive lighting instruments, you can add snap to your video.

ORGANIZATION OF MATERIALS

The materials needed to produce a television programme fall into two broad categories. The first consists of the material itself, including the script, on-camera talent, sets, and props. The second consists of the videotape, equipment, and crew which will be involved in production. It's the job of the producer to see to it that both come together at the time of production. Even if you're just shooting home movies, you can appreciate the difficulty in getting the "cast" and your equipment together and ready all at the same time. In the world of professional film and video the problems are the same, only bigger.

Planning and Pre-Production

The first step in planning a production is usually called a "treatment." This is nothing more than a brief description of the way the material is to be organized and the programmatic goals of the production. For example:

> This programme is designed to present the services provided by Moving Pictures, including programme production, tape duplication, and computer graphics and animation.

This might be followed by an outline showing sequences in the order in which they will appear in the final programme and detailing the objectives for each sequence.

I. Open with variety of location shots.
II. Brief description of range of services.
III. POC explains advantages of television over other media.
IV. Examples of too small—too large—too far away—too dangerous concepts.
V. Examples of narrations in different languages.
VI. Computer animation and graphics examples
VIII. Closing statement

The next step is a shot sheet, or storyboard. While a shot sheet describes each shot in writing, a storyboard does the same thing using pictures.

RIGHTS AND RESPONSIBILITIES

Television, more than any other medium, by nature can invade the privacy and trample on the rights of the people it uses. The television producer makes himself responsible to the people shown on camera and to the creators of materials he might use. He must also guarantee that he will use his medium responsibly and fairly. The ability to make and distribute television programmes depends largely on the continuing trust these people have for the producer and his crew.

Rights can be divided broadly into those involving people who actually appear on camera and those involving the acquisition and use of the creative works of others. The two sometimes overlap when musical or dramatic performances are involved. Both need to be given careful attention.

People on Camera

In certain kinds of programmes everyone who appears on camera does so by choice. This doesn't necessarily give the producer the free and clear right to use recordings made under these circumstances in any way he pleases. First, those appearing should be informed of the intended use of the recording and its potential distribution. Understanding the producer's intentions, they should then give the producer permission to carry out those intentions by signing a "release form" stating the intent of the producer and any compensation to be received by the performer.

In other programmes, people may be videotaped without permission. This may be done if the following conditions are met:

1. The taping is done in a public place.
2. No attempt is made to hide the fact that a recording is being made.

In any case, a person appearing on camera is in the hands of the producer, who has certain responsibilities toward him:

1. To respect any verbal promises or understandings made at the time the recording was make.
2. To refrain from using or editing the material in a way that alters the meaning of any statements made by the person appearing.
3. To refrain from editing the material in such a way as to misrepresent the circumstances of the recording in a way detrimental to the person appearing.
4. To refrain from distributing the material beyond the distribution agreed to and stated in the release form.

A talent release can be anything from the simple form below to a contract running hundreds of pages. It all depends on the complexity of the issues and the need to guard against unforeseen circumstances. This sample is a simple expression of good faith by both parties.

Sample release form:

General Release

In consideration of the payment to me of the sum of $____________, receipt whereof is hereby acknowledged, I hereby agree as follows:

1. I give and grant for a period of ____________ years (hereinafter referred to as the "Term") to MOVING PICTURES, its successors and assigns, the right to use, publish, and copyright my name, picture, portrait and likeness in a television programme produced by MOVING PICTURES ________________ ______________ and in all media and types of advertising and promotion of the above programme.
2. I agree that all videotape of me used and taken by MOVING PICTURES is owned by them and that they may copyright material containing same. If I should receive any copy thereof, I shall not authorize its use by anyone else.
3. I agree that no material need be submitted to me for any further approval and that MOVING PICTURES shall be without liability to me resulting from the publication of my likeness.
4. I warrant and represent that this license does not in any way conflict with any existing commitment on my part.
5. Nothing herein will constitute any obligation of MOVING PICTURES to make any use of any of the rights set forth herein.

________________________ ____________

(Signature) (Date)

____

(Printed Full Name)

____

____

(Address)

If releaser is not yet 21 years old, complete the following form:

I, the undersigned, hereby warrant that I am______________________________*of ______________________, a minor, and have full authority to authorize the above release which I have read and approved. I hereby release and agree to indemnify MOVING PICTURES and their successors and assigns, from and against any and all liability arising out of the exercise of the rights granted by the above release.

______________________________ __________

(Signature of Parent or Guardian) (Date)

*Insert the word "parent" or "guardian," as appropriate.

In addition, it's important to respect the wishes of people who appear on camera. It's possible, for example, that a person recorded during a traumatic event might later decide to ask that he not be used in your programme. Unless you can make a good case for the importance of that person's appearance, it would be wise to accede to his wishes. It's also a common courtesy to allow people appearing in your programmes to preview material before it's shown in public. While this does not suggest that they have any right to edit or control your product, they may be able to make suggestions for changes that would improve the accuracy or impact of a programme.

You also have an obligation to be fair in your treatment of issues. The composition of every shot, as well as its duration, is an editorial judgment. The process of selecting and rejecting sequences for inclusion, too, implies editorial judgments. If you have a bias or an axe to grind, get it out front both in dealing with those who appear in your programme and in presenting it to your audience. No one is free of all bias, but in the communications media you have a special responsibility to the public to deal honestly and fairly with facts and with issues, as well as with people.

Copyright

Copyright is the great two-edged sword everyone in the media must face sooner or later. In copyright, as in most areas of law, the more you know the more confusing it can become. Far from being legal advice, what follows is intended to let you know when to start asking the hard questions and not to lull you into a false sense of security.

Copyright is designed to foster the creation and publication of ideas by allowing the author to sell his ideas on the open market. It's thought that only if the creative process can provide economic rewards to creative people can the maximum flow of ideas be promoted. Thus, to deprive an author of his right to earn money by selling his product, whether a photograph, book, song, or videotape, harms us all by discouraging him from publishing his work.

Any use of a copyrighted work without the copyright holder's permission is an infringement of his rights. In certain cases, however, such use can be defended using the principles of "fair use." This basically means that the use will not cause financial injury to the author and that the need of the public to have use of the material can be demonstrated to be more important than the author's right to protect his creative work. Except in broadcast news and educational situations there is little point in considering "fair use" further.

The proliferation of home recorders (both video and audio) has created a right to record materials for personal, private use. You do not have the right to "distribute, duplicate, or perform (present to an audience)" your home recordings except under very limited fair use guidelines. There are limited exceptions for educational use, but whether you make a profit violating someone else's copyright is irrelevant. The mere fact that you're not making any money does not give you permission to break the law.

A perfect (and common) technical violation of copyright takes place when you videotape your child's performance in a school concert or play. As long as the recording is for personal use only this kind of taping is permissible. If the recording will be used by the participants as part of their training it's okay. Again, any public performance, distribution, or duplication of your private copy (outside your immediate family) creates a real copyright violation.

The number one copyright rule is not to step on someone else's toes. It must be assumed that anything printed or published or shown is protected by copyright. This isn't literally true, but it's better to assume a work is protected until you can prove otherwise than to infringe on someone's copyright. Virtually everything in print is copyrighted. Most music, whether in sheet form or recorded is also protected. Broadcast radio and television stations pay a licensing fee to ASCAP and BMI for the right to use music on the air. Since you don't have a license to use copyrighted music, you'll have to resort to one of three alternatives: write and perform your own, buy limited rights for a specific recording or song, or buy a record library which you can use without restriction.

Dramatic works are a problem in that there are two considerations beyond merely purchasing rights. Not only will the licensing agent make sure your "performance" of a work won't conflict with any theatrical production in the same region of the country, but the agent may feel that a videotape recording of a work might, by virtue of its amateurish performance, actually harm the reputation of the work and deny permission on that ground alone. This is also true of short stories and novels, where the author has a legitimate right to impose conditions on adaptations of his work. Regardless of the type of work involved, the best way to find out who has the rights and how to acquire them is to write to the publisher of the work.

On the brighter side, as a creator of television programmes, you are also protected from copyright infringement. In order to obtain protection, you should place a copyright notice prominently on your work. On a script or book it should appear on or near the title page. On a film or videotape the notice may appear at the beginning or end, as long as a viewer is likely to see it. Although an explicit copyright notice is no longer required by law, if you publish or distribute a work without a copyright notice you may give the impression you do not intend to protect your rights and are implicitly placing the work in the public domain.

Technically, you're required to register your copyright with the Register of Copyrights, Library of Congress, Washington, D.C. 20559, by sending in an application along with two copies of your work. In practice this is rarely done. You can file your copyright at any time. Usually actual applications are made only if the copyright holder intends to sue someone for infringement. Obviously, the copyright has to be registered before such a suit can be brought.

In summary, a reasonable respect for the rights of people you deal with in the production of television programmes is perhaps the most important single responsibility you have as a television producer. Respect for the rights of others will pave the way for your own work and the work of those who follow you. On the other hand, a disregard for the rights of others will make people reluctant to work with you, on or off camera, and close doors for everyone who depends on the good will of the public.

Taking it to the Next Level

If you intend to distribute your work commercially or have large quantities made by a commercial replicator you will want to take special care in documenting your rights.

Many replicators are members of the International Recording Media Association. As one of the conditions of membership, these companies will require you to fill out a form supplied by the association and to provide documentation of the rights and permissions related to your project. If you are using pre-recorded music you must be able to produce proof that you have the right to use the music. This could take the form of a copy of your original contract with the music distributor, such as a "buy out" license or a letter from the distributor verifying your rights. If your audio is licensed separately you will need proof of audio/video synchronization licensing. For CD's containing special software to make them play back like DVD's you will need distribution licensing documentation for the software. You should be able to affirm that you have all of the releases necessary for your talent and permission to use any other copyrighted materials. Needless to say, it is much easier to keep track of all of your paperwork as you go along than it is to assemble it after the fact.

TV PRODUCTION SHOTS

There are four types of shots used in video production. All TV shows are just combinations of these four shots put in order to make sequences.

	Long shot (LS) A long shot allows your audience to see everything. It shows the big picture.
	Medium shot (MS) This shot gets rid of any distractions in the picture and starts the process of zeroing in on the action.
	Close-up (CU) This shot cuts out extraneous visual material. Faces should fill up most of the screen.
	Extreme close-up (ECU) Use this shot to focus attention on what's important. It enlarges small objects to show details.

STORYBOARDING

When you draw pictures of what you are going to see it forces you think visually. Storyboards will also help you identify the shots you will need to construct a sequence. Listing the audio will help you decide what microphones, sound effects, music, or narration you'll need.

	Storyboard Titles: The Entrance Shot 1: Long shot. Show the front of the building For continuity, man enters the frame and goes into building from right to left. Audio: Natural sounds
	Shot 2: Long shot. Interior of the building as man enters. For continuity, make sure man enters from right and exits to the left. Audio: Natural sound
	Shot 3: Medium shot. Man approaches front desk and signs in. For continuity, use right to left movement. Audio: Typing in the background.
	Shot 4: Extreme Close-up. Shot of hands signing paper. For continuity, Have hand in same position as in MS of man approaching front desk. Make sure nothing but paper shows in this shot. Audio: Typing in the background
	Shot 5: Close-up. Receptionist turns to the camera and says good morning. For continuity, use a high camera angle so it looks like the man is looking at her while standing. Audio: Receptionist says a cheery "Good morning." Typing stops.
	Shot 6: Medium shot. Man finishes signing in and moves out of the frame. For continuity, this shot needs to be a continuation of the first medium shot. Audio: Man Mumbles "Good morning."

STORYBOARD ARTWORK PROJECT

In this project, you create educational materials for schools. If you like to draw human figures or if you have Poser or DAZ Studio, you can join.

Fig. 8.1: The Storyboard Artwork Project.

The artwork that you will create in this project turns Tux Paint into a storyboarding program. The artwork is a human figure viewed from many angles. Once you have drawn the artwork, you mask the figures so they can be used as "stamps" in Tux Paint for kids to create storyboards for motion pictures.

These special stamps allow Tux Paint to work like a simple version of Storyboard Quick and Storyboard Artist.

Hopefully, this project teaches you everything you need to know to create storyboarding stamps for Tux Paint. If you need more information, please contact the coordinator for this project. The coordinator for this project is Robert Elliott.

Fig. 8.2:

We need you to create illustrations of people from multiple angles.

Fig. 8.3:

We need both photo realistic images and hand drawings.

The Lessons in the Project

Fig. 8.4:

The Lessons

Here are four lessons to help you get started creating stamps for Tux Paint:

1. The artwork needed for storyboarding
2. How to create stamps for Tux Paint
3. 2D—How to create artwork for storyboarding in Tux Paint using 2D software
4. 3D—How to create artwork for storyboarding in Tux Paint using 3D software

Optional

There are also optional lessons for creating props and background scenery.

(*a*) How to create blank storyboard frames for Tux Paint (optional) (*b*) How to create background scenery and props for Tux Paint Storyboards (optional)

Tux Paint

Tux Paint is a fun drawing programme for kids. It allows kids to add pictures called "Stamps" to their artwork.

Storyboard Quick and Storyboard Artist also uses stamps to draw storyboards but unlike Tux Paint, these programs are not free.

These special stamps are pictures of people in various poses. Storyboard Quick uses hand drawn pictures of people while Storyboard Artist uses pictures from Poser.

Anyone who likes to draw figures or is learning to use Poser or DAZ Studio can participate. All they have to do is create poses of people in various positions. I will show you how!

2D Human Figures

Hand Drawn Artwork

We need artists who can draw human figures from many different angles. If you are interested, you can practice by drawing the same figure from 3 or more angles. This can be stick figures, realistic artwork, or cartoon art. We need them all.

- ❑ ArtRage Free
- ❑ ArtRage 2
- ❑ Painter
- ❑ Photoshop, etc.

3D Human Figures

3D Art Programmes

We need artist who can render 3D human figures from many angles. If you are interested in learning to use 3D programmes, you can practice by drawing the same figure from 5 or more angles.

- ❑ DAZ Studio
- ❑ Poser

Blank Storyboard Frames

Storyboard Work Sheet for Tux Paint

Once the artwork is created and masked, we need a storyboard worksheet in Tux Paint ready for children to be painting on. These sheets can be done with:

- ❑ Adobe Photoshop
- ❑ Adobe Illustrator
- ❑ Freehand

USING CUTAWAYS IN INTERVIEWS

Cutaways are shots the videographer gets that can be used to cover up edits. They are very helpful when editing an interview. The cutaway is usually something related to the location or what the person on camera is saying. The video "cuts away" from the person talking so the editor can cut out unnecessary audio.

	This is the unedited interview. The man gives a good sound bite, but with a little bit of irrelevant material in the middle.
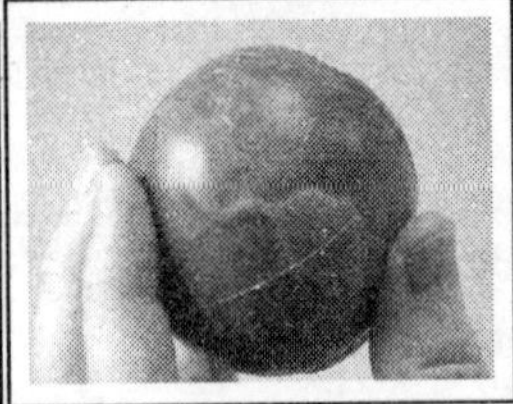	The edited interview. We have taken out the irrelevant material and placed a cutaway of a globe over the audio to hide the edit point.

This brings up the issue of ethical editing. In the examples below you can see how an editor can make someone say something they didn't intend. This is why so many people argue they were quoted out of context or were simply misquoted. When editing, care must be taken so you don't change the intended meaning.

	The unedited comment. You'd think it wouldn't be easy to change the intent of the speaker.
	By rearranging what the speaker says, the meaning is totally changed. Of course, it's easy to spot this edit because the speaker jumps around in the frame.
	Editors use cutaways to cover up the edit. In this example the meaning has been totally changed and a cutaway has been used to cover the edit.

CASE STUDY: DEGREE IN ASSOCIATE OF APPLIED SCIENCE IN TELEVISION PRODUCTION

You might be surprised by the range of careers in television production and by the variety of employers in this field. Broadcast television stations, industrial video firms, cable companies and satellite operations head the list. Helping you prepare for an entry-level position as a production specialist at employers such as these, is the aim of the Associate of Applied Science Degree programme in Television Production.

You'll have an opportunity to learn all the positions behind the camera, and you can experience substantial hands-on training in a multi-camera studio and on location with this television production programme. Concepts of both linear and non-linear editors are also taught. The curriculum includes an internship or practicum project. The television production programme's General Education component can contribute to the shaping of a well-informed broadcast professional, and can help you develop the problem-solving and human relations skills sought by today's employers.

Career Opportunities for Television Production Graduates

- Camera operator
- Floor director
- Graphics operator
- Producer
- Production assistant
- Video editor.

The Television Production programme is available at the Mendota Heights campus.

"It doesn't feel like school. It feels like you are really producing news or commercials."

—*Bandon Rickert*
Graduate, Television Production

Associate of Applied Science Degree

18 months—6 quarters—90 quarter credits

RTV 101	Lec: 3	Lab: 0	Cred: 3	FV

Audio Techniques

This course is an introduction to the tools and processes involved in audio production, including basic training in the operation of sound recording and playback systems.

Pre Req.: Departmental approval for nondegree-seeking students.

RTV 109	Lec: 2	Lab: 3	Cred: 3	FV

Writing for Electronic Media

This course covers writing techniques for radio, television and other electronic media. Emphasis is placed on broadcast news writing, TV and radio commercial writing and short form story telling. It is recommended that students enrolling in RTV 109 be familiar with basic computer functions and word processing software.

Pre Req.: ENG 100 and basic computer skills.

RTV 111	Lec: 2	Lab: 3	Cred: 3	FV

Radio Studio Techniques I

This course includes an introduction to the broadcasting studio utilizing the audio control console and recording devices.

Pre Req.: RTV 101, RTV 109, RTV 121, departmental approval for nondegree-seeking.

RTV 112	Lec: 2	Lab: 3	Cred: 3	FV

Radio Studio Techniques II

This course covers commercial production, news formatting and programme assembly techniques.

Pre Req.: RTV 111, departmental approval for nondegree-seeking students.

RTV 121	Lec: 3	Lab: 0	Cred: 3	FV

Introduction to Broadcasting

This course covers the history of broadcasting, federal communications policies and basic operational practices.

Pre Req.: ENG 100.

RTV 211	Lec: 2	Lab: 3	Cred: 3	FV

Radio Studio Techniques III

This course further studies advanced techniques of commercial production, news formatting and programme assembly techniques.

Pre Req.: RTV 111, RTV 112, departmental approval required for nondegree-seeking students.

RTV 231	Lec: 0	Lab: 12	Cred: 3	FV

SCWE in Broadcasting I

This course includes supervised production experience at a television or radio location. This course cannot be audited. This course may only be taken twice. A grade of C or better is required to advance to RTV 232.

Pre Req.: RTV 101, RTV 103, RTV 105, RTV 109, RTV 111, RTV 121, RTV 222, departmental approval for nondegree-seeking students.

RTV 232	Lec: 0	Lab: 12	Cred: 3	FV

SCWE in Broadcasting II

This course includes supervised production experience at a television or radio production location. This course cannot be audited. This course may only be taken twice. This course may not be taken concurrently with RTV 231. A grade of C or higher must be earned to receive credit for the course.

Pre Req.: RTV 231 with a minimum grade of C, departmental approval for nondegree-seeking students.

TELEVISION STUDIES

Television studies is an academic discipline that deals with critical approaches to television. Usually, it is distinguished from mass-communication research, which tends to approach the topic from an empirical perspective. Defining the field is problematic; some institutions and syllabuses do not distinguish it from media studies or classify it as a subfield of popular culture studies.

Television studies is roughly equivalent to the longer-standing discipline of film studies in that it is often concerned with textual analysis. For example, analyses of so-called "quality television," such as *Cathy Come Home* and *Twin Peaks,* have attracted the interests of researchers for their cinematic qualities. However, television studies can also incorporate the study of television viewing and how audiences make meaning from texts, which is commonly known as audience studies or reception theory.

History

Charlotte Brunsdon argues that television studies is an "aspirationally disciplinary name given to the academic study of television." Since it is a relatively new discipline, Brunsdon notes that "...many of the key television scholars are employed in departments of sociology, politics, communication arts, speech, theatre, media and film studies." She argues that television studies developed during the 1970s and 1980s

"...from three major bodies of commentary on television: journalism, literary/dramatic criticism and the social sciences." Critical methods for television have been "...extrapolated from traditional literary and dramatic criticism."

As a result, television studies is marked by a great deal of "disciplinary hybridity." Perhaps because television scholars are approaching the subject from so many different disciplinary and theoretical perspectives, there are many debates about how television should be understood and conceptualized from a political and methodological point of view. Another impact of the disciplinary hybridity is the diversity in the types of studies carried out. Early television studies included histories of television, biographies of television producers, archival research by historians, and sociological studies of the role the television set played in 1950s homes.

In television studies, television and other mass media forms are "...conceptualised within frameworks" such as "...ownership; national and international regulation of media production and distribution; professional ideologies; public opinion; [and] media audiences." As the field of television studies was being developed, it was influenced by the medium's longstanding issue of invoking "distrust, fear and contempt", as a purported cause of social ills. As well, television scholars had to prove that television was different from other "mass media", often by pointing to how television differed from radio and cinema.

In the 1970s and 1980s, television studied developed three strands of commentary: a journalistic approach which reviews recent television programmes; a literary/ dramatic criticism approach which examines the television screenwriter in the same way that literary and dramatic criticism examine novels and plays; and the social sciences, which examined the "production, circulation and function of television in contemporary society."

The social science stream examined the social function and effects of television and analyzed the role that television plays in the social order and the public sphere. Some television scholars applied Marxist frameworks or the "critical sociology of the Frankfurt School". Since the 1970s, feminist television scholars have focused "... on programmes for women and those which have key female protagonists", such as Julie *Cagney and Lacey* and the "...now substantial literature on soap opera." Television studies in the 1990s includes "work on the definition and interpretation of the television text and the new media ethnographies of viewing" and histories of "production studies"—how television shows are developed, financed, and produced.

Television Scholars

Scholars who principally work in television studies include:

- Robert C. Allen
- Ien Ang
- Charlotte Brunsdon
- Jane Feuer
- John Fiske
- Christine Geraghty
- John Hartley

- Henry Jenkins
- David Lusted
- Toby Miller
- Jason Mittell
- David Morley
- Horace Newcomb
- Neil Postman
- Lynn Spigel
- Raymond Williams

List of Television-Studies Journals

The following journals are either devoted to television studies or, at the least, frequently include TV-studies essays.

English Language

- *Camera Obscura*—Feminist media theory.
- *Cinema Journal*—Published by the Society for Cinema and Media Studies.
- *Critical Studies in Television: Scholarly Studies for Small Screen Fictions*—Peer-reviewed journal devoted to a study of television.
- *Flow*—An online journal of television and media studies published biweekly by the Department of Radio-TV-Film at the University of Texas at Austin.
- *Journal of Film and Video*—Published by the University Film and Video Association.
- JUMP CUT—Review of contemporary media.
- *Screen*—Influential film and TV journal of the 1970s and 1980s.
- *Television and New Media*—One of the few television-specific journals.
- *The Velvet Light Trap*—Long-running film and media journal.

Television Studies

Television studies is the relatively recent, aspirationally disciplinary name given to the academic study of television. Modeled by analogy with longer established fields of study, the name suggests that there is an object, "television", which, in courses named, for example, "Introduction to Television Studies", is the self-evident object of study using accepted methodologies. This may be increasingly the case, but it is important to grasp that most of the formative academic research on television was inaugurated in other fields and contexts. The "television" of television studies is a relatively new phenomenon, just as many of the key television scholars are employed in departments of sociology, politics, communication arts, speech, theatre, media and film studies. If it is now possible, in 1996, to speak of a field of study, "television studies" in the Anglophone academy, in a way in which it was not in 1970, the distinctive characteristics of this field of study include its disciplinary hybridity and continuing debate about how to conceptualize the object of study "television." These debates, which are and have been both political and methodological, are further complicated in an international frame by the historical peculiarities of national broadcasting systems. Thus, for example, the television studies that developed in Britain or Scandinavia, while often addressing U.S. television programmes, did so within the taken-for-granted dominance of public service models. In contrast, the U.S. system is distinguished by the normality of advertising spots and breaks. In the first instance then, television studies signifies the contested, often nationally inflected, academic address to television as primary object of study—rather than, for example, television as part of international media economies or television as site of drama in performance.

There have been two prerequisites for development of television studies in the "West"—and it is primarily a western phenomenon, which is not to imply that there is not, for example, a substantial literature on Indian television (cf. Krishnan and Dighe, 1990). The first was that television as such be regarded as worthy of study. This apparently obvious point is significant in relation to a medium which has historically attracted distrust, fear and contempt. These responses, which often involve the invocation of television as both origin and symptom of social ills, have, as many scholars have pointed out, homologies with responses to earlier popular genres and forms such as the novel and the cinema. The second prerequisite was that television be granted, conceptually, some autonomy and specificity as a medium. Thus television had to be regarded as more than simply a transmitter of world, civic or artistic events and as distinguishable from other of the "mass media". Indeed, much of the literature of television studies could be characterised as attempting to formulate accounts of the specificity of television, often using comparison with, on the one hand, radio (broadcast, liveness, civic address) and on the other, cinema (moving pictures, fantasy), with particular attention, as discussed below, to debate about the nature of the television text and the television audience. Increasingly significant also are the emergent histories of television whether it be the autobiographical accounts of insiders, such as Grace Wyndham Goldie's history of her years at the BBC, *Facing the Nation*, or the painstaking archival research of historians such as William Boddy with his history of the quiz scandals in 1950s U.S. television or Lynn Spigel with her pioneering study of the way in which television was "installed"' in the U.S. living room in the 1950s, *Make Room for TV.*

Television studies emerges in the 1970s and 1980s from three major bodies of commentary on television: journalism, literary/dramatic criticism and the social sciences. The first, and most familiar, was daily and weekly journalism. This has generally taken the form of guides to viewing and reviews of recent programmes. Television reviewing has, historically, been strongly personally voiced, with this authorial voice rendering continuity to the diverse topics and programmes addressed. Some of this writing has offered formulations of great insight in its address to television form—for example the work of James Thurber, Raymond Williams, Philip Purser or Nancy Banks-Smith—which is only now being recognised as one of the origins of the discipline of television studies. The second body of commentary is also organised through ideas of authorship, but here it is the writer or dramatist who forms the legitimation for the attention to television. Critical method here is extrapolated from traditional literary and dramatic criticism, and the television attracts serious critical attention as an "home theatre". Indicative texts here would be the early collection edited by Howard Thomas, *Armchair Theatre* (1959) or the later, more academic volume edited by George Brandt, British *Television Drama* (1981). Until the 1980s, the address of this type of work was almost exclusively to "high culture": plays and occasionally series by known playwrights, often featuring theatrical actors. Only with an understanding of this context is it possible to see how exceptional Raymond William's defence of television soap opera is in Drama In Performance (1968), or Horace Newcomb's validation of popular genres in *TV: The Most Popular Art* (1974).

Both of these bodies of commentary are mainly concerned to address what was shown on the screen, and thus conceive of television mainly as a text within the arts humanities academic traditions. Other early attention to television draws, in different ways, on the social sciences to address the production, circulation and function of television in contemporary society. Here, research has tended not to address the television text as such, but instead to conceptualise television either through notions of its social *function and effects*, or within a governing question of *cui bono?* (whose good is served?). Thus television, along with other of the mass media, is conceptualised within frameworks principally concerned with the maintenance of social order; the reproduction of the status quo, the relationship between the state, media ownership and citizenship, the constitution of the public sphere. With these concerns, privileged areas of inquiry have tended to be non-textual: patterns of international cross-media ownership; national and international regulation of media production and distribution; professional ideologies; public opinion; media audiences. Methodologies here have been greatly contested, particularly in the extent to which Marxist frameworks, or those associated with the critical sociology of the Frankfurt School have been employed. These debates have been given further impetus in recent years by research undertaken under the loose definition of cultural studies. The privileged texts, if attention has been directed at texts, have been news and current affairs, and particularly special events such as elections, industrial disputes and wars. It is this body of work which is least represented in "television studies", which, as an emergent discipline, tends towards the textualisation of its Object of study. The British journal Media, Culture and Society provides an exemplary instance of media research—in which television plays some part—in the traditions of critical sociology and political economy.

Much innovatory work in television studies has been focused on the definition of the television text. Indeed, this debate could be seen as one of the constituting frameworks of the field. The common-sense view points to the individual programme as a unit, and this view has firm grounding in the way television is produced. Television is, for the most part, made as programmes or runs of programmes: series, serials and miniseries. However, this is not necessarily how television is watched, despite the considerable currency of the view that it is somehow better for the viewer to choose to watch particular programmes rather that just having the television on. Indeed, BBC television in the 1950s featured "interludes" between programmes, most famously, "The Potter's Wheel", a short film showing a pair of hands making a clay pot on a wheel, to ensure that viewers did not just drift from one programme to another. It is precisely this possible "drifting" through an evening's viewing that has come to seem, to many commentators, one of the unique features of television watching, and hence something that must be attended to in any account of the television text.

The inaugural formulation is Raymond William's argument, in his 1974 book, *Television: Technology and Cultural Form*, that "the defining feature of broadcasting" is "planned flow". Williams developed these ideas through reflecting on four years of reviewing television for the weekly periodical *The Listener,* when he suggests that the separating of the television text into recognisable generic programme units, which makes the reviewer's job much easier, somehow misses "the central television experience: the fact of flow" (1974). Williams's own discussion of flow draws on analysis of both British and U.S. television and he is careful to insist on the national variation of broadcasting systems and types and management of flow, but his attempt to describe what is specific to the watching of television has been internationally generative, particularly in combination with some of the more recent empirical studies of how people do (or don't) watch television.

If Williams's idea of flow has been principally understood to focus attention on television viewing as involving more viewing and less choosing than a critical focus on individual programmes would suggest, other critics have picked up the micro-narratives of which so much television is composed. Thus John Ellis approached the television text using a model ultimately derived from film studies, although he is precisely concerned, in his book *Visible Fictions,* to differentiate cinema and television. Ellis suggests that the key unit of the television text is the "segment", which he defines as "small, sequential unities of images and sounds whose maximum duration seems to be about five minutes" (1982). Broadcast television, Ellis argues, is composed of different types of combination of segment: sometimes sequential, as in drama series, sometimes cumulative, as in news broadcasts and commercials. As with Williams's "flow", the radical element in Ellis's "segment" is the way in which it transgresses common sense boundaries like "programme" or "documentary" and "fiction" to bring to the analyst's attention common and defining features of broadcast television as a medium.

However, it has also been argued that the television text cannot be conceptualised without attention to the structure of national broadcasting institutions and the financing of programme production. In this context, Nick Browne has argued that the U.S. television system is best approached through a notion of the "super-text". Browne is concerned to address the specificities of the U.S. commercial television system in contrast to the public service models—particularly the British one—which have been so generative a context for formative and influential thinking on television such as that of Raymond Williams and Stuart Hall. Browne defines the "super-text" as, initially, a television programme and all introductory and interstitial material in that programme's place in a schedule. He is thus insisting on an "impure" idea of the text, arguing that the programme as broadcast at a particular time in the working week, interrupted by ads and announcements, condenses the political economy of television. Advertising, in Browne's schema, is the central mediating institution in U.S. television, linking programme schedules to the wider world of production and consumption.

The final concept to be considered in the discussion about the television text is Newcomb and Hirsch's idea of the "viewing strip" (1987). This concept suggests a mediation between broadcast provision and individual choice, attempting to grasp the way in which each individual negotiates his or her way through the "flow" on offer, putting together a sequence of viewing of their own selection. Thus different individuals might produce very different "texts"—viewing strips—from the same nights viewing. Implicit within the notion of the viewing strip—although not a prerequisite—is the remote control device, allowing channel change and channel surfing. And it is this tool of audience agency which points us to the second substantial area of innovatory scholarship in television studies, the address to the audience.

The hybrid disciplinary origins of television studies are particularly evident in the approach to the television audience. Here, particularly in the 1980s, we find the convergence of potentially antagonistic paradigms. Very simply, on the one hand, research traditions in the social sciences focus on the empirical investigation of the already existing audience. Research design here tends to seek representative samples of particular populations and/or viewers of a particular type of programming (adolescent boys and violence; women and soap opera). Research on the television audience has historically been dominated, particularly in the U.S., by large-scale quantitative surveys, often designed using a model of the "effects" of the media, of which television is not necessarily a differentiated element. Within the social sciences, this "effects" model has been challenged by what is known as the "uses and gratifications" model. In James Halloran's famous formulation, "we should ask not what the media does to people, but what people do to the media." (Halloran, 1970). Herta Herzog's 1944 research on the listeners to radio daytime serials was an inaugural project within this "uses and gratifications" tradition, which has recently produced the international project on the international decoding of the U.S. prime time serial, Dallas (Liebes and Katz, 1990).

This social science history of empirical audience investigation has been confronted, on the other hand by ideas of a textually-constituted "reader" with their origins in literary and film studies. This is a very different conceptualisation of the audience, drawing on literary, semiotic and psychoanalytic theory to suggest—in different and disputed ways—that the text constructs a "subject position" from which it is intelligible. In this body of work, the context of consumption and the social origins of audience members are irrelevant to the making of meaning which originates in the text. However—and it is thus that we seen the potential convergence with social science "uses and gratifications" models—literary theorists such as Umberto Eco (1979) have posed the extent to which the reader should be seen as active in meaning-making. It is, in this context, difficult to separate the development of television studies, as such, from that of cultural studies, for it is within cultural studies that we begin to find the most sophisticated theorisations and empirical investigations of the complex, contextual interplay of text and "reader" in the making of meaning.

The inaugural formulations on television in the field of cultural studies are those of Stuart Hall in essays such as "Encoding and Decoding in Television Discourse" (1974) (Hall, 1997) and David Morley's audience research (1980). However this television specific work cannot theoretically be completely separated from other cultural studies work conducted at Birmingham University in the 1970s such as the work of Dick Hebdige and Angela McRobbie which stressed the often oppositional agency of individuals in response to contemporary culture. British cultural studies has proved a successful export, the theoretical paradigms there employed meeting and sometimes clashing with those used, internationally, in more generalised academic re-orientation towards the study of popular culture and entertainment in the 1970s and 1980s. Examples of influential scholars working within or closely related to cultural studies paradigms would by Ien Ang and John Fiske. Ang's work on the television audience ranges from a study of *Dallas* fans in the Netherlands to the interrogation of existing ideas of audience in a postmodern, global context. John Fiske's work has been particularly successful in introducing British cultural studies to a U.S. audience, and his 1987 book, *Television Culture* was one of the first books about television to take seriously the feminist agenda that has been so important to the recent development of the field. For if television studies is understood as a barely established institutional space, carved out by scholars of television from, on the one hand, mass communications and traditional Marxist political economy, and on the other, cinema, drama and literary studies, the significance of feminist research to the establishment of this connotationally feminized field cannot be underestimated, even if it is not always recognised. E. Ann Kaplan's collection, *Regarding Television*, with papers from a 1981 conference gives some indication of early formulations here.

The interest of new social movements in issues of representation, which has been generative for film and literary studies as well as for television studies, has produced sustained interventions by a range of scholars, approaching mainly "texts" with questions about the representation of particular social groups and the interpretation of programmes such as, for example, *thirty something, Cagney and Lacey, The Cosby Show* or various soap operas. Feminist scholars have, since the mid-1970s, tended to focus particularly on programmes for women and those which have key female protagonists. Key work here would include Julie D'Acci's study of *Cagney and Lacey* and the now substantial literature on soap opera (Seiter *et al.*, 1989). Research by Sut Jhally and Justin Lewis has addressed the complex meanings about class and "race" produced by viewers of *The Cosby Show*, but most audience research in this "representational" paradigm has been with white audiences. Jacqueline Bobo and Ellen Seiter argue that this is partly a consequence of the "whiteness" of the academy which makes research about viewing in the domestic environment potentially a further extension of surveillance for those ethnicized by the dominant culture.

Television studies in the 1990s, then, is characterised by work in four main areas. The most formative for the emergent discipline have been the work on the definition and interpretation of the television text and the new media ethnographies of viewing which emphasize both the contexts and the social relations of viewing. However, there is a considerable history of "production studies" which trace the complex interplay of factors involved in getting programmes on screen. Examples here might include Tom Burn's study of the professional culture of the BBC (1977), Philip Schlesinger's study of "The News" (1978) or the study of MTM co-edited by Jane Feuer, Paul Kerr and Tise Vahimagi (1984). Increasingly significant also is the fourth area, that of television history. Not only does the historical endeavour frequently necessitate working with vanished sources—such as the programmes—but it has also involved the use of material of contested evidentiary status. For example, advertisements in women's magazines as opposed to producer statements. This history of television is a rapidly expanding field, creating a retrospective history for the discipline, but also documenting the period of nationally regulated terrestrial broadcasting—the "television" of "television studies"—which is now coming to an end.

9

Radio, Radio Programming and Radio Production: An Overview

RADIO

Radio is the transmission of signals, by modulation of electromagnetic waves with frequencies below those of visible light. Electromagnetic radiation travels by means of oscillating electromagnetic fields that pass through the air and the vacuum of space. It does not require a medium of transport. Information is carried by systematically changing (modulating) some property of the radiated waves, such as their amplitude or their frequency. When radio waves pass an electrical conductor, the oscillating fields induce an alternating current in the conductor. This can be detected and transformed into sound or other signals that carry information.

Although Nikola Tesla first demonstrated the feasibility of wireless communications in 1893, Guglielmo Marconi, an Italian inventor, was the first to develop workable radio communication. He sent and received his first radio signal in Italy in 1895. The word 'radio' is used to describe this phenomenon, and radio transmissions are classed as radio frequency emissions.

Etymology

Originally, radio or radioteleography was called 'wireless telegraphy', which was shortened to 'wireless'. The prefix *radio-* in the sense of wireless transmission was first recorded in the word *radioconductor*, coined by the French physicist Edouard Branly in 1897 and based on the verb *to radiate* (in Latin "radius" means "spoke of a wheel, beam of light, ray"). 'Radio' as a noun is said to have been coined by advertising expert Waldo Warren (White 1944). The word appears in a 1907 article by Lee de Forest, was adopted by the United States Navy in 1912 and became common by the time of the first commercial broadcasts in the United States in the 1920s. (The noun 'broadcasting' itself came from an agricultural term, meaning 'scattering seeds'.) The term was then adopted by other languages in Europe and Asia, although British Commonwealth countries retained the term 'wireless' until the mid-20th century. In Japanese, the term 'wireless' is the basis for the term 'radio wave' although the term for the device that listens to radio waves is literally 'device for receiving sounds'.

In recent years the term 'wireless' has gained renewed popularity through the rapid growth of short range networking, *e.g.*, WLAN ('Wireless Local Area Network'),

WiFi and Bluetooth as well as mobile telephony, *e.g.*, GSM and UMTS. Today, the term 'radio' often refers to the actual transceiver device or chip, whereas 'wireless' refers to the system and/or method used for radio communication. Hence one talks about radio transceivers and Radio Frequency Identification (RFID), but about wireless devices and wireless sensor networks.

Invention

Although invention was long attributed to Guglielmo Marconi, the identity of the original inventor of radio, at the time called wireless telegraphy, is contentious. Development from a laboratory demonstration to commercial utility spanned several decades and required the efforts of many practitioners. The controversy over who invented the radio, with the benefit of hindsight, can be broken down as follows:

- In 1887, David E. Hughes transmitted Morse code by radio at and below the Super low frequency range (via a clockwork transmitter).
- In 1888, Heinrich Hertz produced and measured the Ultra High Frequency range (via a sparkgap transmitter).
- In 1891, Nikola Tesla began wireless research. He developed means to reliably produce radio frequencies, publicly demonstrated the principles of radio, and transmitted long-distance signals.
- Between 1893 and 1894, Roberto Landell de Moura, a Brazilian priest and scientist, conducted experiments. He did not publicise his achievement until 1900 but later obtained Brazilian patent.
- In 1894 in Kolkata (Calcutta), Sir Jagdish Chandra Bose (J.C. Bose) invented the mercury coherer, together with the telephone receiver.
- Alexander Stepanovich Popov, in 1894, built his first radio receiver, which contained a coherer but actually coherer was first demonstrated by J.C. Bose. Popov demonstrated the coherer, further refined as a lightning detector, to the Russian Physical and Chemical Society on May 7, 1895.
- In 1894, Guglielmo Marconi read about Hertz's and Tesla's work on wireless telegraphy, and began his own experiments.
- In December of 1901 Guglielmo Marconi used J.C. Bose's inventions to receive the radio signal in his first transatlantic radio communication over a distance of 2000 miles from Poldhu, UK, to St. Johns, Newfoundland. Marconi was celebrated worldwide for this achievement. Soon after the patent was given to Marconi. He even received the Nobel Prize.
- In early 1900s Reginald Fessenden and Lee de Forest invented amplitude-modulated (AM) radio allowing an audio signal to be sent over the air.
- In 1935 Edwin H. Armstrong invented frequency-modulated (FM) radio, so that an audio signal can avoid "static," that is, interference from electrical equipment and atmospherics.
- In 1943, the U.S. Supreme Court acknowledged that Marconi's work wasn't original, and the patent ownership is given back to Nikola Tesla. However, Tesla died shortly before the decision was announced.

History

Tesla demonstrating wireless transmissions during his high frequency and potential lecture of 1891. After continued research, Tesla gave the fundamentals of radio in 1893. In 1893, in St. Louis, Missouri, Nikola Tesla made devices for his experiments with electricity. Addressing the *Franklin Institute* in Philadelphia and the *National Electric Light Association*, he described and demonstrated in detail the principles of his wireless work. The descriptions contained all the elements that were later incorporated into radio systems before the development of the vacuum tube. He initially experimented with magnetic receivers, unlike the coherers (detecting devices consisting of tubes filled with iron filings which had been invented by Temistocle Calzecchi-Onesti at Fermo in Italy in 1884) used by Guglielmo Marconi and other early experimenters.

In 1894 Alexander Stepanovich Popov built his first radio receiver, which contained a coherer. Further refined as a lightning detector, it was presented to the Russian Physical and Chemical Society on May 7, 1895.

The first public demonstration of wireless telegraphy took place in the lecture theatre of the Oxford University Museum of Natural History on August 14, 1894, carried out by Professor Oliver Lodge and Alexander Muirhead. During the demonstration a radio signal was sent from the neighbouring Clarendon laboratory building, and received by apparatus in the lecture theatre.

In 1896, Marconi was awarded the British patent 12039, *Improvements in transmitting electrical impulses and signals and in apparatus therefore*, for radio. In 1897 he established the world's first radio station on the Isle of Wight, England. Marconi opened the world's first "wireless" factory in Hall Street, Chelmsford, England in 1898, employing around 50 people.

The next great invention was the vacuum tube detector, invented by Westinghouse engineers. On Christmas Eve, 1906, Reginald Fessenden used a synchronous rotary-spark transmitter for the first radio programme broadcast, from Brant Rock, Massachusetts. Ships at sea heard a broadcast that included Fessenden playing *O Holy Night* on the violin and reading a passage from the Bible. The first radio news programme was broadcast August 31, 1920 by station 8 MK in Detroit, Michigan. The first college radio station began broadcasting on October 14, 1920, from Union College, Schenectady, New York under the personal call letters of Wendell King, an African-American student at the school. That month 2ADD, later renamed WRUC in 1940, aired what is believed to be the first public entertainment broadcast in the United States, a series of Thursday night concerts initially heard within a 100 mile radius and later for a 1,000 mile radius. In November 1920, it aired the first broadcast of a sporting event. At 9 pm on August 27, 1920, Sociedad Radio Argentina aired a live performance of Richard Wagner's Parsifal opera from the Coliseo Theater in downtown Buenos Aires, only about twenty homes in the city had a receiver to tune in. Meanwhile, Regular entertainment broadcasts commenced in 1922 from the Marconi Research Centre at Writtle, near Chelmsford, England.

One of the first developments in the early 20th century (1900-59) was that aircraft used commercial AM radio stations for navigation. This continued until the early 1960s when VOR systems finally became widespread (though AM stations are still marked on U.S. aviation charts). In the early 1930s, single sideband and frequency modulation were invented by amateur radio operators. By the end of the decade, they were established commercial modes. Radio was used to transmit pictures visible as television as early as the 1920s. Commercial television transmissions started in North America and Europe in the 1940s. In 1954, Regency introduced a pocket transistor radio, the TR-1, powered by a "standard 22.5 V Battery".

In 1960, Sony introduced its first transistorized radio, small enough to fit in a vest pocket, and able to be powered by a small battery. It was durable, because there were no tubes to burn out. Over the next 20 years, transistors replaced tubes almost completely except for very high-power uses. By 1963 colour television was being regularly transmitted commercially, and the first (radio) communication satellite, TELSTAR, was launched. In the late 1960s, the U.S. long-distance telephone network began to convert to a digital network, employing digital radios for many of its links. In the 1970s, LORAN became the premier radio navigation system. Soon, the U.S. Navy experimented with satellite navigation, culminating in the invention and launch of the GPS constellation in 1987. In the early 1990s, amateur radio experimenters began to use personal computers with audio cards to process radio signals. In 1994, the U.S. Army and DARPA launched an aggressive, successful project to construct a software radio that could become a different radio on the fly by changing software. Digital transmissions began to be applied to broadcasting in the late 1990s.

Uses of Radio

Early uses were maritime, for sending telegraphic messages using Morse code between ships and land. The earliest users included the Japanese Navy scouting the Russian fleet during the Battle of Tsushima in 1905. One of the most memorable uses of marine telegraphy was during the sinking of the RMS *Titanic* in 1912, including communications between operators on the sinking ship and nearby vessels, and communications to shore stations listing the survivors. The first radio couldn't transmit sound or speech and was called the "wireless telegraph"

Radio was used to pass on orders and communications between armies and navies on both sides in World War I; Germany used radio communications for diplomatic messages once its submarine cables were cut by the British. The United States passed on President Woodrow Wilson's Fourteen Points to Germany via radio during the war. Broadcasting began from San Jose in 1909, and became feasible in the 1920s, with the widespread introduction of radio receivers, particularly in Europe and the United States. Besides broadcasting, point-to-point broadcasting, including telephone messages and relays of radio programmes, became widespread in the 1920s and 1930s. Another use of radio in the pre-war years was the development of detecting and locating aircraft and ships by the use of radar (*RA*dio *D*etection *A*nd *R*anging).

Today, radio takes many forms, including wireless networks and mobile communications of all types, as well as radio broadcasting. Before the advent of television, commercial radio broadcasts included not only news and music, but dramas, comedies, variety shows, and many other forms of entertainment. Radio was unique among methods of dramatic presentation in that it used only sound.

Audio

AM broadcast radio sends music and voice in the Medium Frequency (MF—0.300 MHz to 3 MHz) radio spectrum. AM radio uses amplitude modulation, in which the amplitude of the transmitted signal is made proportional to the sound amplitude captured (transduced) by the microphone while the transmitted frequency remains unchanged. Transmissions are affected by static and interference because lightning and other sources of radio that are transmitting at the same frequency add their amplitudes to the original transmitted amplitude. The most wattage an AM radio station in the United States is allowed to use is 50,000 watts and the majority of stations that emit signals this powerful were grandfathered in; these include WGN (AM), WJR, and CKLW. In 1986 KTNN received the last granted 50,000 watt license.

FM broadcast radio sends music and voice with higher fidelity than AM radio. In frequency modulation, amplitude variation at the microphone causes the transmitter frequency to fluctuate. Because the audio signal modulates the frequency and not the amplitude, an FM signal is not subject to static and interference in the same way as AM signals. FM is transmitted in the Very High Frequency (VHF—30 MHz to 300 MHz) radio spectrum. VHF radio waves act more like light, traveling in straight lines, hence the reception range is generally limited to about 50-100 miles. During unusual upper atmospheric conditions, FM signals are occasionally reflected back towards the Earth by the ionosphere, resulting in Long distance FM reception. FM receivers are subject to the capture effect, which causes the radio to only receive the strongest signal when multiple signals appear on the same frequency. FM receivers are relatively immune to lightning and spark interference.

High power is useful in penetrating buildings, diffracting around hills, and refracting for some distance beyond the horizon. Consequently, 100,000 watt FM stations can regularly be heard up to 100 miles (160 km) away, and farther (*e.g.*, 150 miles, 240 km) if there are no competing signals.

A few old "grandfathered" stations do not conform to these power rules. WBCT-FM (93.7) in Grand Rapid, Michigan, runs 320,000 watts ERP, and can increase to 500,000 watts ERP by the terms of its original license. This huge power level does not usually help to increase range as much as one might expect, because VHF frequencies travel in nearly straight lines over the horizon and off into space. Nevertheless, when there were fewer FM stations competing, this station could be heard near Bloomington, Illinois, almost 300 miles (500 km) distant.

FM Sub-carrier services are secondary signals transmitted "piggyback" along with the main programme. Special receivers are required to utilize these services. Analog channels may contain alternative programming, such as reading services for the blind, background music or stereo sound signals. In some extremely crowded metropolitan areas, the sub-channel programme might be an alternate foreign language radio programme for various ethnic groups. Sub-carriers can also transmit digital data, such as station identification, the current song's name, web addresses, or stock quotes. In some countries, FM radios automatically re-tune themselves to the same channel in a different district by using sub-bands.

Aviation voice radios use VHF AM. AM is used so that multiple stations on the same channel can be received. (Use of FM would result in stronger stations blocking out reception of weaker stations due to FM's capture effect). Aircraft fly high enough that their transmitters can be received hundreds of miles (or kilometres) away, even though they are using VHF.

Marine voice radios can use AM in the shortwave High Frequency (HF—3 MHz to 30 MHz) radio spectrum for very long ranges or narrowband FM in the VHF spectrum for much shorter ranges. Government, police, fire and commercial voice services use narrowband FM on special frequencies. Fidelity is sacrificed to use a smaller range of radio frequencies, usually five kHz of deviation, rather than the 75 kHz used by FM broadcasts and 25 kHz used by TV sound.

Civil and military HF (high frequency) voice services use shortwave radio to contact ships at sea, aircraft and isolated settlements. Most use single sideband voice (SSB), which uses less bandwidth than AM. On an AM radio SSB sounds like ducks quacking. Viewed as a graph of frequency versus power, an AM signal shows power where the frequencies of the voice add and subtract with the main radio frequency. SSB cuts the bandwidth in half by suppressing the carrier and (usually) lower sideband. This also makes the transmitter about three times more powerful, because it doesn't need to transmit the unused carrier and sideband.

TETRA, Terrestrial Trunked Radio is a digital cell phone system for military, police and ambulances. Commercial services such as XM, WorldSpace and Sirius offer encrypted digital Satellite radio.

Telephony

Mobile phones transmit to a local cell site (transmitter/receiver) that ultimately connects to the public switched telephone network (PSTN) through an optic fiber or microwave radio and other network elements. When the mobile phone nears the edge of the cell site's radio coverage area, the central computer switches the phone to a new cell. Cell phones originally used FM, but now most use various digital modulation schemes. Recent developments in Sweden (such as DROPme) allow for the instant downloading of digitial material from a radio broadcast (such as a song) to a mobile phone.

Satellite phones use satellites rather than cell towers to communicate. They come in two types: INMARSAT and Iridium. Both types provide worldwide coverage. INMARSAT uses geosynchronous satellites, with aimed high-gain antennas on the vehicles. Iridium uses 66 Low Earth Orbit satellites as the cells.

Video

Television sends the picture as AM and the sound as FM, with the sound carrier a fixed frequency (4.5 MHz in the NTSC system) away from the video carrier. Analog television also uses a vestigial sideband on the video carrier to reduce the bandwidth required.

Digital television uses 8VSB modulation in North America (under the ATSC digital television standard), and COFDM modulation elsewhere in the world (using the DVB-T standard). A Reed-Solomon error correction code adds redundant correction codes and allows reliable reception during moderate data loss. Although many current and future codecs can be sent in the MPEG-2 transport stream container format, as of 2006 most systems use a standard-definition format almost identical to DVD: MPEG-2 video in Anamorphic widescreen and MPEG layer 2 (*MP2*) audio. High-definition television is possible simply by using a higher-resolution picture, but H.264/AVC is being considered as a replacement video codec in some regions for its improved compression. With the compression and improved modulation involved, a single "channel" can contain a high-definition programme and several standard-definition programmes.

Navigation

All satellite navigation systems use satellites with precision clocks. The satellite transmits its position, and the time of the transmission. The receiver listens to four satellites, and can figure its position as being on a line that is tangent to a spherical shell around each satellite, determined by the time-of-flight of the radio signals from the satellite. A computer in the receiver does the math.

Radio direction-finding is the oldest form of radio navigation. Before 1960 navigators used movable loop antennas to locate commercial AM stations near cities. In some cases they used marine radiolocation beacons, which share a range of frequencies just above AM radio with amateur radio operators. Loran systems also used time-of-flight radio signals, but from radio stations on the ground. VOR (Very High Frequency Omnidirectional Range), systems (used by aircraft), have an antenna array that transmits two signals simultaneously. A directional signal rotates like a lighthouse at a fixed rate. When the directional signal is facing north, an omnidirectional signal pulses. By measuring the difference in phase of these two signals, an aircraft can determine its bearing or radial from the station, thus establishing a line of position. An aircraft can get readings from two VORs and locate its position at the intersection of the two radials, known as a "fix." When the VOR station is collocated with DME (Distance Measuring Equipment), the aircraft can determine its bearing and range from the station, thus providing a fix from only one ground station. Such stations are called VOR/DMEs. The military operates a similar system of navaids, called TACANs, which are often built into VOR stations. Such stations are called VORTACs. Because TACANs include distance measuring equipment, VOR/DME and VORTAC stations are identical in navigation potential to civil aircraft.

Radar

Radar (Radio Detection and Ranging) detects objects at a distance by bouncing radio waves off them. The delay caused by the echo measures the distance. The direction of the beam determines the direction of the reflection. The polarization and frequency of the return can sense the type of surface. Navigational radars scan a wide area two to four times per minute. They use very short waves that reflect from earth and stone. They are common on commercial ships and long-distance commercial aircraft

General purpose radars generally use navigational radar frequencies, but modulate and polarize the pulse so the receiver can determine the type of surface of the reflector. The best general-purpose radars distinguish the rain of heavy storms, as well as land and vehicles. Some can superimpose sonar data and map data from GPS position.

Search radars scan a wide area with pulses of short radio waves. They usually scan the area two to four times a minute. Sometimes search radars use the doppler effect to separate moving vehicles from clutter. Targeting radars use the same principle as search radar but scan a much smaller area far more often, usually several times a second or more. Weather radars resemble search radars, but use radio waves with circular polarization and a wavelength to reflect from water droplets. Some weather radar use the doppler to measure wind speeds.

Data (Digital Radio)

Most new radio systems are digital, The oldest form of digital broadcast was spark gap telegraphy, used by pioneers such as Marconi. By pressing the key, the operator could send messages in Morse code by energizing a rotating commutating spark gap. The rotating commutator produced a tone in the receiver, where a simple spark gap would produce a hiss, indistinguishable from static. Spark gap transmitters are now illegal, because their transmissions span several hundred megahertz. This is very wasteful of both radio frequencies and power.

The next advance was continuous wave telegraphy, or CW (Continuous Wave), in which a pure radio frequency, produced by a vacuum tube electronic oscillator was switched on and off by a key. A receiver with a local oscillator would "heterodyne" with the pure radio frequency, creating a whistle-like audio tone. CW uses less than 100 Hz of bandwidth. CW is still used, these days primarily by amateur radio operators (hams). Strictly, on-off keying of a carrier should be known as "Interrupted Continuous Wave" or ICW or on-off keying (OOK).

Radio teletypes usually operate on short-wave (HF) and are much loved by the military because they create written information without a skilled operator. They send a bit as one of two tones. Groups of five or seven bits become a character printed by a teletype. From about 1925 to 1975, radio teletype was how most commercial messages were sent to less developed countries. These are still used by the military and weather services.

Aircraft use a 1200 Baud radioteletype service over VHF to send their ID, altitude and position, and get gate and connecting-flight data. Microwave dishes on satellites, telephone exchanges and TV stations usually use quadrature amplitude modulation (QAM). QAM sends data by changing both the phase and the amplitude of the radio signal. Engineers like QAM because it packs the most bits into a radio signal when given an exclusive (non-shared) fixed narrowband frequency range. Usually the bits are sent in "frames" that repeat. A special bit pattern is used to locate the beginning of a frame.

Communication systems that limit themselves to a fixed narrowband frequency range are vulnerable to jamming. A variety of jamming-resistant spread spectrum techniques were initially developed for military use, most famously for Global Positioning System satellite transmissions. Commercial use of spread spectrum begin in the 1980s. Bluetooth, most cell phones, and the 802.11b version of Wi-Fi each use various forms of spread spectrum.

Systems that need reliability, or that share their frequency with other services, may use "coded orthogonal frequency-division multiplexing" or COFDM. COFDM breaks a digital signal into as many as several hundred slower subchannels. The digital signal is often sent as QAM on the subchannels. Modern COFDM systems use a small computer to make and decode the signal with digital signal processing, which is more flexible and far less expensive than older systems that implemented separate electronic channels. COFDM resists fading and ghosting because the narrow-channel QAM signals can be sent slowly. An adaptive system, or one that sends error-correction codes can also resist interference, because most interference can affect only a few of the QAM channels. COFDM is used for WiFi, some cell phones, Digital Radio Mondiale, Eureka 147, and many other local area network, digital TV and radio standards.

Heating

Radio-frequency energy generated for heating of objects is generally not intended to radiate outside of the generating equipment, to prevent interference with other radio signals. Microwave ovens use intense radio waves to heat food. (Note: It is a common misconception that the radio waves are tuned to the resonant frequency of water molecules. The microwave frequencies used are actually about a factor of ten below the resonant frequency.) Diathermy equipment is used in surgery for sealing of blood vessels. Induction furnaces are used for melting metal for casting.

Amateur Radio Service

Amateur radio is a hobby in which enthusiasts purchase or build their own equipment and use radio for their own enjoyment. They may also provide an emergency and public-service radio service. This has been of great use, saving lives in many instances. Radio amateurs are licensed to use frequencies in a large number of narrow bands throughout the radio spectrum. They use all forms of encoding, including obsolete and experimental ones. Several forms of radio were pioneered by radio amateurs and later became commercially important including FM, single-sideband (SSB), AM, digital packet radio and satellite repeaters. Some amateur frequencies may be disrupted by power-line internet service.

Unlicensed Radio Services

Personal radio services such as Citizens' Band Radio, Family Radio Service, Multi-Use Radio Service and others exist in North America to provide simple (usually) short range communication for individuals and small groups, without the overhead of licensing. Similar services exist in other parts of the world. These radio services involve the use of handheld units. The commonest form of unlicensed radio is known as Free or Pirate radio, the main differences being that a Free radio station does not advertise or make any money, while the Pirate station could not exist without adverts, payolas, etc.

Radio Control (RC)

Radio remote controls use radio waves to transmit control data to a remote object as in some early forms of guided missile, some early TV remotes and a range of model boats, cars and airplanes. Large industrial remote-controlled equipment such as cranes and switching locomotives now usually use digital radio techniques to ensure safety and reliability.

In Madison Square Garden, at the Electrical Exhibition of 1898, Nikola Tesla successfully demonstrated a radio-controlled boat. He was awarded U.S. patent No. 613,809 for a "Method of and Apparatus for Controlling Mechanism of Moving Vessels or Vehicles."

The Electromagnetic Spectrum

Radio waves are a form of electromagnetic radiation, created whenever a charged object (in normal radio transmission, an electron) accelerates with a frequency that lies in the radio frequency (RF) portion of the electromagnetic spectrum. In radio, this acceleration is caused by an alternating current in an antenna. Radio frequencies occupy the range from a few tens of hertz to three hundred gigahertz, although commercially important uses of radio use only a small part of this spectrum. Other types of electromagnetic radiation, with frequencies above the RF range, are microwave, infrared, visible light, ultraviolet, X-rays and gamma rays. Since the energy of an individual photon of radio frequency is too low to remove an electron from an atom, radio waves are classified as non-ionizing radiation.

Other

Energy autarkic radio technology consists of a small radio transmitter powered by environmental energy (push of a button, temperature differences, light, vibrations, etc.). A number of schemes have been proposed for Wireless energy transfer. Various plans included transmitting power using microwaves, and the technique has been demonstrated. These schemes include, for example, solar power stations in orbit beaming energy down to terrestrial users.

ALL INDIA RADIO

All India Radio (abbreviated as AIR), officially known as Akashvani (Devanagari: आकाशवाणी), is the radio broadcaster of India and a division of Prasar Bharti (Broadcasting Corporation of India), an autonomous corporation of the Ministry of Information and Broadcasting, Government of India. It is the sister service of Prasar Bharti's Doordarshan, the national television broadcaster.

All India Radio is one of the largest radio networks in the world. The headquarters is at the Akashwani Bhavan, New Delhi. Akashwani Bhavan houses the drama section, the FM section and the National service. The Doordarshan Kendra (Delhi) is also located on the 6th floor of Akashvani Bhavan.

History

Experimentation with radio in India began in 1915. Broadcasting began in India with the formation of a private radio service in Madras in 1924. In the same year, the British colonial government granted a license to a private company, the Indian Broadcasting Company, to open Radio stations in Bombay and Calcutta. The company went bankrupt in 1930 but the colonial government took over the two transmitters and the Department of Labour and Industries started operating them as the Indian State Broadcasting Corporation. In 1936, the Corporation was renamed All India Radio (AIR) and placed under the Department of Communications. When India became independent in 1947, AIR was made a separate Department under the Ministry of Information and Broadcasting. AIR was officially renamed to *Akashwani* in 1957. This name was given by Late Pandit Narendra Sharma a noted lyricist and renowned Hindi poet. however all English usage refers to it as All India Radio.

In the era of government control, All India Radio was known for taking an overwhelmingly government line. Indira Gandhi famously stated in 1975 that All India Radio is "a Government organ, it is going to remain a Government organ..."

Despite the growth of private radio channels since the 1990s, All India Radio (AIR) remains a popular media resource, being accessible even in the remotest parts of the country.

Coverage

The All India Radio website claims that the station reaches 99.37 per cent of India's populace of over one billion. AIR maintains approximately 225 broadcasting centres around the country including one in the capital of every state, a total of 384 channels and transmits in 24 different languages and dialects. In spite of recent penetration by other media such as Cable TV, AIR remains the most common means of gaining access to information and entertainment, as the radio receivers are relatively cheap and affordable. AIR today has a network of 229 broadcasting centres with 148 medium frequency (MW), 54 high frequency (SW) and 168 FM transmitters. The coverage is 91.79 per cent of the area, serving 99.14 per cent of the people in the largest democracy of the world. AIR covers 24 languages and 146 dialects in home services. In Externel services, it covers 27 languages; 17 national and 10 foreign languages

AIR in Popular Culture

Broadcasting House is an old building next to Akashwani Bhavan. The News Service Division of All India Radio under the Director General (New) functions from this building. Built during the British rule, it is a very popular location and easily recognised building in New Delhi.

Several scenes of *Dil Se*, a popular Bollywood film starring Shahrukh Khan, were shot in and around this building; in the film Khan plays a reporter for All India Radio. All India Radio also featured prominently in the film *Rang De Basanti.*

Services

AIR has many different services each catering to different regions/languages across India. One of the most famous services of the AIR is the *Vividh Bharti Seva* (roughly translating to "Multi-Indian service"). This service is the most commercial of all and is is popular in Mumbai and other cities of India. This service offers a wide range of programmes including news, film music, comedy shows, etc. The Vividh Bharti service operates on different MW band frequencies for each city as shown below.

Some programmes broadcast on the Vividh Bharti:

- *Hawa-mahal*—Skit based on some novels/plays.
- *Santogen ki mehfil*—Jokes and humour.

The following is a partial list of AIR services:

North Regional Service

- Agra 1530 kHz
- Allahabad 1026 kHz
- Delhi 'Indraprastha' 819 kHz
- Delhi 'Rajdhani' 666 kHz
- Delhi 'D' 1017 kHz
- Jaipur 'A' 1476 kHz
- Jalandhar 'A' 873 kHz
- Jammu 'A' 990 kHz
- Jodhpur 'A' 531 kHz
- Lucknow 'A' 747 kHz
- Srinagar 'A' 1116 kHz
- Varanasi 'A' 1242 kHz

East Regional Service

- Bhagalpur 1458 kHz
- Cuttack 'A' 972 kHz
- Darbhanga 1296 kHz
- Jamshedpur 1584 kHz
- Kolkata 'A' 657 kHz
- Kolkata 'B' 1008 kHz
- Kolkata 'C' 1323 kHz
- Patna 'A' 621 kHz
- Ranchi 'A' 549 kHz
- AIR FM Kolkata has two stations 107FM Rainbow and 100.2 FM Gold.

These stations broadcast live programmes in Bangla, English and Hindi.

North-East Regional Service

- Agartala 1269 kHz
- Guwahati 'A' 729 kHz
- Shillong 864 kHz

West Regional Service

- Ahmedabad 'A' 846 kHz
- Aurangabad 1521 kHz
- Bhopal 'A' 1593 kHz
- Gwalior 1386 kHz
- Indore 'A' 648 kHz
- Jalgaon 963 kHz
- Mumbai 'A' 1044 kHz
- Mumbai 'B' 558 kHz
- Nagpur 'A' 585 kHz
- Panaji 'A' 1287 kHz
- Pune 'A' 792 kHz
- Rajkot 'A' 810 kHz
- Ratnagiri 1143 kHz
- Sholapur 1602 kHz
- Sangli 1251 kHz

South Regional Service

- ❑ Adilabad 1485 kHz
- ❑ Chennai 'A' 720 kHz
- ❑ Hyderabad 'A' 738 kHz
- ❑ Kozhikode 'A' 684 kHz
- ❑ Ootakamund 1602 kHz
- ❑ Port Blair 684 kHz
- ❑ Tiruchirapalli 'A' 936 kHz
- ❑ Visakhapatnam 927 kHz
- ❑ Bangalore 'A' 612 kHz
- ❑ Gulbarga 1107 kHz
- ❑ Hyderabad 'B' 1377 kHz
- ❑ Madurai 1269 kHz
- ❑ Pondicherry 1215 kHz
- ❑ Thiruvananthapuram 'A' 1161 kHz
- ❑ Vijayawada 'A' 837 kHz

Vividh Bharti Service

- ❑ Chennai 'C' 783 kHz
- ❑ Delhi 'C' 1368 kHz
- ❑ Jalandhar 'C' 1350 kHz
- ❑ Kolkata 'C' 1323 kHz
- ❑ Mumbai 'C' 1188 kHz
- ❑ Vijayawada 'B' 1503 kHz
- ❑ Varanasi FM' 100.6 MHz
- ❑ Cuttack 'B' 1314 kHz
- ❑ Hyderabad 'C 102.8 MHz
- ❑ Kanpur 1449 kHz
- ❑ Lucknow 'C' 1278 kHz
- ❑ Panaji 'B' 1539 kHz
- ❑ Varanasi 'B' 1602 kHz

External Services

The External Services Division of All India Radio broadcasts in 27 languages to countries outside of India, primarily by high powered Short wave broadcasts although Medium wave is also used to reach neighbouring countries. In addition to broadcasts targeted at specific countries by language there is a General Overseas Service which broadcasts in English with 8-1/4 hours of programming each day and is aimed at a general international audience.

Yuv-vani*: The Voice of Youth*

The *Yuv-vani* service of AIR provides an enriching and novel radio-experience by encouraging youth participation and experimenting with varied script ideas. It is broadcast at 1017 kHz which corresponds to 294.9 meter. Its Broadcast begins every evening at 7 pm. With shows like "Mehfil", "In the groove" and "The Roving Microphone" which have been around for more than three decades, Yuv-vani still holds a firm ground of its own.

Some of the big names on the Indian media scene began their journey with Yuv-vani. Comments Praful Thakkar, a well known documentary maker—"Yuv-vani came as a breath of fresh air in our reckless college days. It was a great learning experience for me and it made me realize that radio is not all about goofy quotes and PJs."

Some of the other names that have been associated with Yuv-vani in the past include Celebrity game show host Roshan Abbas, VJ Gaurav Kapoor, DJ Kaushal Khanna and DJ Pratham among others.

News-On-Phone Service

All India Radio, after launching the news-on-phone service on 25 February 1998 from New Delhi, is running the service from Chennai, Mumbai, Hyderabad, Patna and Bangalore also. The service is accessible through STD, ISD and local telephone calls. The service is going to be started from 9 more cities—Ahmedabad, Guwahati, Imphal, Jaipur, Kolkata, Lucknow, Raipur, Simla and Thiruvanthapuram shortly.

English and Hindi hourly news bulletins can be heard live on http://www.newsonair.com/. The news in MP3 format can be directly played from the site. In the file name the hourly time of news is mentioned. Text of the English and Hindi bulletins can be read from http://www.newsonair.com/BulletinsInd.html.

AIR news bulletins are available in 9 regional languages (Tamil, Kannada, Gujarati, Bengali, Marathi, North East, Punjabi, Telugu, Urdu) from http://www.newsonair.com/index_regional.htm.

PIRATE RADIO

The term Pirate Radio usually refers to illegal or unregulated radio transmissions. The term is most commonly used to describe illegal broadcasting for entertainment or political purposes, but is also sometimes used for illegal two-way radio operation. Rules and regulations vary largely from country to country. In countries such as the USA and many countries in Europe, many types of radio licenses exist, and often the term pirate radio generally describes the unlicensed broadcasting of FM radio, AM radio, or shortwave signals over a significant coverage area that could be picked up by listeners.

Sometimes radio stations are deemed legal where the signal is transmitted, but illegal and considered "pirate stations" where the signals are received—especially when the signals cross a country's border. In other cases, a broadcast may be considered "pirate" due to the nature of its content, its transmission format (especially a failure to transmit a station identification according to regulations), or the transmit power (wattage) of the station, even if the broadcast is not technically illegal (such as a webcast or a ham radio broadcast). Therefore pirate radio can sometimes mean different things to different people. Pirate radio stations are sometimes called bootleg stations (a term especially associated with two-way radio), clandestine stations or Free Radio stations.

Pirate Radio History and Examples

Denmark had the first known radio station in the world to broadcast commercial radio from a vessel in international waters without permission from the authorities in the country that it broadcast to (Denmark in this case). The station was named Radio Mercur and began transmission on August 2nd, 1958. In the Danish newspapers it was soon called a "pirate radio".

In the 1960s in the UK, the term referred to not only a perceived theft of the state-run airwaves by the unlicensed broadcasters but also the risk-taking nature of offshore radio stations that actually operated on anchored ships or marine platforms.

A good example of this kind of activity was Radio Luxembourg located in the Grand Duchy of Luxembourg. The English language evening broadcasts from Radio Luxembourg were intentionally beamed toward the British Isles by Luxembourg licensed transmitters, while the intended audience in the United Kingdom originally listened to their radio sets by permission of a Wireless License issued by the British General Post Office (GPO). However, under terms of that Wireless License, it was an offense under the Wireless Telegraphy Act to listen to *unauthorized* broadcasts, which possibly included those transmitted by Radio Luxembourg. Therefore as far as the British authorities were concerned, Radio Luxembourg was a "pirate radio station" and British listeners to the station were breaking the law (although as the term 'unauthorised' was never properly defined it was somewhat of a legal grey area). This did not stop British newspapers from printing programme schedules for the station, or a British weekly magazine aimed at teenage girls, "Fab 28" from promoting the deejays and their lifestyle (Radio Luxembourg's wavelength was 208 metres).

Radio Luxembourg was later joined by two other well known pirate stations received in the UK in violation of UK licensing, Radio Caroline and Radio London, both of which broadcast from vessels anchored outside of territorial limits and were therefore legitimate but unauthorised in much the same way as Luxembourg. Indeed, all three stations even had registered offices based in mainland UK.

Where actual sea faring vessels are not involved, the term *pirate radio* is a political term of convenience as the word "pirate" suggests an illegal venture, regardless of the broadcast's actual legal status. The radio station XERF located at Ciudad Acuña, Coahuila, Mexico, just across the Rio Grande from Del Rio, Texas, USA, is an example.

While Mexico issued radio station XERF with a license to broadcast, the power of its 250,000 watts transmitter was far greater than the maximum of 50,000 watts authorized for commercial use by the government of the United States of America. Consequently, XERF and many other radio stations in Mexico, which sold their broadcasting time to sponsors of English-language commercial and religious programmes, were labeled as "border blasters", but not "pirate radio stations", even though the content of many of their programs were in violation of US law. Predecessors to XERF, for instance, had originally broadcast in Kansas, advocating "goat-gland surgery" for improved masculinity, but moved to Mexico to evade US laws about advertising medical treatments, particularly unproven ones.

In 1924, New York City station WHN was accused of being an "outlaw" station by AT&T (then American Telephone and Telegraph Company) for violating trade licenses which permitted only AT&T stations to sell airtime on their transmitters. As a result of the AT&T interpretation a landmark case was heard in court, which even prompted comments from Secretary of Commerce Herbert Hoover when he took a public stand in the station's defense. Although AT&T won its case, the furor created was such that those restrictive provisions of the transmitter license were never enforced.

Free Radio

Another variation on the term *pirate radio* came about during the "Summer of Love" in San Francisco during the hippie days when many things were named "free". Examples include "free store", "free love" and even "free radio", which usually referred to clandestine and unlicensed land-based transmissions. These were also tagged as being pirate radio transmissions.

The term *free radio* crossed the Atlantic Ocean, where it was adopted by the Free Radio Association of listeners who defended the rights of the offshore "pirate radio stations" broadcasting from ships and marine structures off the coastline of the United Kingdom. However, the term *free radio* also has another meaning, because it differentiates between that form of licensed broadcasting supported by the sale of commercial airtime which anyone can hear free of charge, from that form of licensed commercial broadcasting (especially television) that listeners and especially viewers have to subscribe to and which is usually known as Pay TV.

Félix Guattari points out:

"Technological development, and in particular the miniaturization of transmitters and the fact that they can be put together by amateurs, 'encounters' a collective aspiration for some new means of expression."

In Europe, in addition to adopting the term free radio, supportive listeners of what had been called pirate radio adopted the term offshore radio, which was usually the term used by the owners of the marine broadcasting stations.

Freebooter was yet another variation of the term *pirate radio* and it was sometimes used by the business press in the USA when describing marine broadcasting in Europe.

While *pirate radio* began as a defamatory term in Britain, it later became accepted as having a secondary meaning to describe adventurous forms of licensed broadcasting that had roots in true offshore unlicensed broadcasting. To this end the British licensing authorities have allowed both independent stations and to date even one local BBC station to use this name, while the government retained use of the term *pirate radio* to describe any stations on land or at sea, which are broadcasting without a license and contrary to law.

Pirate Radio by Geographical Area

Since this subject covers both national territories, international waters and international airspace, the only effective way to treat this subject is on a country by country, international waters and international airspace basis. Because the laws vary, the interpretation of the term *pirate radio* also varies considerably.

Questions have been raised about various types of broadcasting conducted by national governments against the interests of other national governments, which have in turn created jamming stations transmitting noises on the same frequency so as to destroy the receivability of the incoming signal.

While the USA transmitted its programmes towards the USSR, which attempted to jam them, in 1970 the government of the United Kingdom decided to employ a jamming transmitter to drown out the incoming transmissions from the commercial station Radio North Sea International, which was based aboard the Motor Vessel (MV) *Mebo II* anchored off Southeast England in the North Sea.

Other examples of this type of unusual broadcasting include the Coast Guard Cutter *USCGC Courier,* which both originated and relayed broadcasts of the Voice of America from an anchorage at the island of Rhodes, Greece to Soviet bloc countries. Balloons have been flown above Key West, Florida to support the TV transmissions of

TV Martí, which are directed at Cuba. Military broadcasting aircraft have been flown over Vietnam, Iraq and many other nations by the United States Air Force. The European Union financially supported a radio station broadcasting news and information into the former Yugoslavia from a ship anchored in international waters.

New Media Pirate Radio

Pirate radio has long been synonymous with AM (LW, MW and SW) and FM (VHF) unlicensed broadcasting and "border blasting" in most parts of the world. With the advent of the internet, many conventional AM/FM radio stations have also taken to simulcasting via the web. These range from public broadcasters, licensed commercial radio, and in some countries, the 3rd tier of low power license exempt radio stations.

Despite pirate radio being known for over the air transmission, a new type of pirate radio stations now operate online. The distinguishing feature is that these online pirates will usually not pay music copyright fees, like most of their AM/FM pirate cousins. These online pirate radio stations will usually attract a small and loyal audience and may go unnoticed by the authorities, unlike AM/FM pirates who can easily be heard and traced on a conventional radio.

A recent case of online pirate radio was seen in the UK. Hitz Radio (UK) and not to be confused with HitzRadio.com (USA) managed to attract large amounts of mainstream media publicity in early 2007. This publicity resulted from Ryan Dunlop, the owner of the station, nominating Hitz Radio for various business awards. After this publicity, many people with radio industry knowledge began to probe the station, which had claimed "millions of fans" and tens of thousands of listeners online. These claims, along with others, were part of the portfolio put forward for the business awards. When industry insiders checked these claims, it resulted in the UK music copyright agencies PPL and MCPS-PRS Alliance chasing back fees owed by Ryan Dunlop and Hitz Radio. That in turn resulted in the audience claims to be false, based upon the amount of back dated fees owed for copyright.

Piracy in Amateur and Two-Way Radio

Illegal use of licensed radio spectrum (also known as bootlegging in CB circles) is fairly common and takes several forms:

- *Unlicensed operation*—Particularly associated with amateur radio and licensed personal communication services such as GMRS, this refers to use of radio equipment on a section of spectrum for which the equipment is designed but on which the user is not licensed to operate (most such operators are informally known as "bubble pack pirates" from the sealed plastic retail packaging common to such walkie-talkies). While piracy on the US GMRS band, for example, is widespread (some estimates have the number of total GMRS users outstripping the number of licensed users by several orders of magnitude), such use is generally disciplined only in cases where the pirate's activity interferes with a licensee. (A notable case is that of United States amateur operator and political activist Jack Gerritsen (operating under the revoked call sign KG61RO), who was successfully prosecuted by the FCC for unlicensed operation and malicious interference.) A subcategory of this is freebanding, the use of allocations nearby a legal allocation (most typically the 27MHz Citizen's Band) on modified or purpose-built gear.

- *Inadvertent interference*—Common when personal communications gear is brought into countries where it is not certified to operate. Such interference results from clashing frequency allocations, and occasionally requires wholesale reallocation of an existing band due to an insurmountable interference problem; for example, the 2004 approval in Canada of the unlicensed use of the United States General Mobile Radio Service frequencies due to interference from users of FRS/GMRS radios from the United States, where Industry Canada had to transfer a number of licensed users on the GMRS frequencies to unoccupied channels to accommodate the expanded service.
- *Deliberate or malicious interference*—Refers to the use of two-way radio to harass or jam other users of a channel. Such behaviour is widely prosecuted, especially when it interferes with mission-critical services such as aviation radio or marine VHF radio.
- *Illegal equipment*—This refers to the use of illegally modified equipment or equipment not certified for a particular band. Such equipment includes illegal linear amplifiers for CB radio, antenna or circuit modifications on walkie-talkies, the use of "export" radios for freebanding, or the use of amateur radios on unlicensed bands that amateur gear is not certified for. The use of marine VHF radio gear for inland mobile radio operations is common in some countries, with enforcement difficult since marine VHF is generally the province of maritime authorities.

List of Known Pirate Radio Stations

- Radio Mercur, Denmark
- Radio Caroline, United Kingdom
- Radio London, United Kingdom
- Radio Luxembourg
- 94.5 FM The Doja, Athens, Ohio, United States
- 96.9 FM The Darklife Radio Show, United States

In Popular Culture

- Christian Slater's character in tshe movie *Pump Up the Volume* (1990) runs a pirate radio station from his basement.
- In the best selling novel *Harry Potter and the Deathly Hallows*, rebels use a pirate radio station to inspire the population.
- In the Teenage Mutant Ninja Turtles Season 5 (1991) episode "Pirate Radio", Pirate Radio is something everyone listens to and Krang uses it to hypnotize people into walking through an inter-dimension portal into Krang's Chasm.

- In an episode of Sealab 2021, captain Murphy runs a pirate radio station using the emergency transmission equipment, until it is shut down by the FCC.

RADIO COMMERCIAL

A radio commercial (often called an advert in the United Kingdom, or a spot to people in the business) is a form of advertising in which goods, services, organizations, ideas, etc. are promoted via the medium of radio. Many commercials are produced by an outside ad agency or radio production company and, airtime is purchased from a station or network in exchange for sponsorship of its programming.

Radio commercials are sold in 10, 20, 30, 40, 50, 60 or 120 second increments. While a : 60 radio commercial is twice as long as a : 30 radio commercial, it is rarely sold at twice the price. While practices vary, most radio stations only charge 20-30 per cent more for the longer spot.

While many commercials are professionally produced, radio is not out of reach for the small retail business owner. Most local radio stations have the ability to produce radio commercials in house using their own announcers. Often local radio stations will write and even produce the radio commercials for local retail advertisers at no additional cost when the merchant purchases a schedule of "spots" on the station.

Radio commercials can be delivered to a network of radio stations directly from the recording studio on a DAT cassette or transmitted via satellite or ISDN.

The first radio commercial is credited to WEAF, New York on August 28, 1922 for the Queensboro real estate corporation. The ten-minute live commercial was voiced by H.M. Blackwell, a representative of Queensboro.

RADIO PROPAGATION

Radio propagation is a term used to explain how radio waves behave when they are transmitted, or are propagated from one point on the Earth to another.

In free space, all electromagnetic waves (radio, light, X-rays, etc.) obey the inverse-square law which states that the power density of an electromagnetic wave is proportional to the inverse of the square of "*r*" (where "*r*" is the distance [radius] from the source). Doubling the distance from a transmitter means that the power density of the radiated wave at that new location is reduced to one-quarter of its previous value.

The far-field magnitudes of the electric and magnetic field components of electromagnetic radiation are equal, and their field strengths are inversely proportional to distance. The power density per surface unit is proportional to the product of the two field strengths, which are expressed in linear units. Thus, doubling the propagation path distance from the transmitter reduces their received field strengths by one-half.

Electromagnetic wave propagation is also affected by several other factors determined by its path from point to point. This path can be a direct line of sight path or an over-the-horizon path aided by refraction in the ionosphere.

Lower frequencies (between 30 and 3,000 kHz) have the property of following the curvature of the earth via groundwave propagation in the majority of occurrences.

The interaction of radio waves with the ionized regions of the atmosphere makes radio propagation more complex to predict and analyze than in free space. Ionospheric radio propagation has a strong connection to space weather.

Since radio propagation is somewhat unpredictable, such services as emergency locator transmitters, in-flight communication with ocean-crossing aircraft, and some television broadcasting have been moved to satellite transmitters. A satellite link, though expensive, can offer highly predictable and stable line of sight coverage of a given area.

A sudden ionospheric disturbance is often the result of large solar flares directed at Earth. These solar flares can disrupt HF radio propagation and affect GPS accuracy.

Radio waves at different frequencies propagate in different ways.

Antenna

The beginning and end of a communication circuit is the antenna. The antenna can provide gain and directivity on both transmit and receive. The take-off angle of the antenna is based on the type of antenna, the height of the antenna above ground, and the terrain below and in front of the antenna. The take-off angle will determine the angle of incidence on the ionosphere, which will affect where the signal will be refracted by the ionosphere.

Radio Frequencies and Their Primary Mode of Propagation

Band		Frequency	Wavelength	Propagation via
VLF	Very Low Frequency	3-30 kHz	100-10 km	Guided between the earth and the ionosphere.
LF	Low Frequency	30-300 kHz	10-1 km	Guided between the earth and the D layer of the ionosphere. Surface waves.
MF	Medium Frequency	300-3000 kHz	1000-100 m	Surface waves. E, F layer ionospheric refraction at night, when D layer absorption weakens.
HF	High Frequency (Short Wave)	3-30 MHz	100-10 m	E layer ionospheric refraction. F1, F2 layer ionospheric refraction.
VHF	Very High Frequency	30-300 MHz	10-1 m	Infrequent E ionospheric refraction. Extremely rare F1, F2 layer ionospheric refraction during high sunspot activity up to 80 MHz. Generally direct wave. Sometimes tropospheric ducting.
UHF	Ultra High Frequency	300-3000 MHz	100-10 cm	Direct wave. Sometimes tropospheric ducting.
SHF	Super High Frequency	3-30 GHz	10-1 cm	Direct wave.
EHF	Extremely High Frequency	30-300 GHz	10-1 mm	Direct wave limited by absorption.

Radio Spectrum

ELF	SLF	ULF	VLF	LF	MF	HF	VHF	UHF	SHF	EHF
3 Hz	30 Hz	300 Hz	3 kHz	30 kHz	300 kHz	3 MHz	30 MHz	300 MHz	3 GHz	30 GHz
30 Hz	300 Hz	3 kHz	30 kHz	300 kHz	3 MHz	30 MHz	300 MHz	3 GHz	30 GHz	300 GHz

The above table listed as radio spectrum is incorrect in its identification of frequency bands for ULF, ELF and AF (audio frequency) ULF = 3 to 30 Hz, ELF = 30 to 300 Hz, Audio Frequency = 300 to 3000 Hz, VLF = 3000 to 30000 Hz, LF = 30 kHz to 300 kHz, MF = 300 kHz to 3 MHz, HF = 3 to 30 MHz, VLF = 30 to 300 MHz, UHF = 300 to 3000 MHz, SHF = 3 to 30 GHz EHF = 30 to 300 HGz

Modes

Surface Modes

The mode is commonly called the "Ground wave". This can cause confusion since the Direct mode is also sometimes called the "Ground wave".

In this mode the radio wave propagates by interacting with the semi-conductive surface of the earth. The wave "clings" to the surface and thus follows the curvature of the earth. Vertical polarization is used to alleviate short circuiting the electric field through the conductivity of the ground. Since the ground is not a perfect electrical conductor, ground waves are attenuated [need reference to properties and effects of attenuation] rapidly as they follow the earth's surface. Attenuation is proportional to the frequency making this mode mainly useful for LF and VLF frequencies.

Today LF and VLF are mostly used for time signals, and for military communications, especially with ships and submarines. Early commercial and professional radio services relied exclusively on long wave, low frequencies and ground-wave propagation. To prevent interference with these services, amateur and experimental transmitters were restricted to the higher (HF) frequencies, felt to be useless since their ground-wave range was limited. Upon discovery of the other propagation modes possible at medium wave and short wave frequencies, the advantages of HF for commercial and military purposes became apparent. Amateur experimentation was then confined only to authorized frequency segments in the range.

Direct Modes (Line-of-Sight)

Line-of-sight is the direct propagation of radio waves between antennas that are visible to each other. This is probably the most common of the radio propagation modes at VHF and higher frequencies. Because radio signals can travel through many non-metallic objects, radio can be picked up through walls. This is still line-of-sight propagation. Examples would include propagation between a satellite and a ground antenna or reception of television signals from a local TV transmitter.

Ground plane reflection effects are an important factor in VHF line of sight propagation. The interference between the direct beam line-of-sight and the ground reflected beam often leads to an effective inverse-fourth-power law for ground-plane limited radiation.

Ionospheric Modes (Sky-Wave)

Skywave propagation, also referred to as skip, is any of the modes that rely on refraction of radio waves in the ionosphere, which is made up of one or more ionized layers in the upper atmosphere. F2-layer is the most important ionospheric layer for HF propagation, though F1, E, and D-layers also play some role. These layers are directly affected by the sun on a daily cycle, the seasons and the 11-year sumspot cycle determines the utility of these modes. During solar maxima, the whole HF range up to 30 MHz can be used and F2 propagation up to 50 MHz are observed frequently depending upon daily solar flux values. During solar minima, propagation of higher frequencies is generally worse.

Forecasting of skywave modes is of considerable interest to amateur radio operators and commercial marine and aircraft communications, and also to shortwave broadcasters.

Meteor Scattering

Meteor scattering relies on reflecting radio waves off the intensely ionized columns of air generated by meteors. While this mode is very short duration, often only from a fraction of second to couple of seconds per event, digital Meteor burst communications allows remote stations to communicate to a station that may be hundreds of miles up to over 1,000 miles (1,600 km) away, without the expense required for a satellite link. This mode is most generally useful on VHF frequencies between 30 and 250 MHz.

Auroral Reflection

Intense columns of Auroral ionization at 100 km altitudes within the auroral oval reflect radio waves, perhaps most notably on HF and VHF. The reflection is angle-sensitive—incident ray vs. magnetic field line of the column must be very close to right-angle. Random motions of electrons spiraling around the field lines create a Doppler-spread that broadens the spectra of the emission to more or less noise-like—depending on how high radio frequency is used. The radio-aurora is observed mostly at high latitudes and rarely extend down to middle latitudes. The occurrences of radio-auroras depends on solar activity (flares, coronal holes, CMEs) and annually the events are more numerous during solar cycle maximas. Radio aurora includes the so-called afternoon radio aurora which produces stronger but more distorted signals and after the Harang-minima, the late-night radio aurora (sub-storming phase) returns with variable signal strength and lesser doppler spread. The propagation range for this predominantly back-scatter mode extends up to about 2000 km in east-west plane, but strongest signals are observed most frequently from north at nearby sites on same latitudes.

Rarely, a strong radio-aurora is followed by Auroral-E, which resembles both propagation types in some ways.

Sporadic-E Propagation

Sporadic E (Es) propagation can be observed on HF and VHF bands. It must not be confused with ordinary HF E-layer propagation. Sporadic-E at mid-latitudes occurs mostly during summer season, from May to August in the northern hemisphere and from November to February in the southern hemisphere. There is no single cause for this mysterious propagation mode. The reflection takes place in a thin sheet of ionisation around 90 km height. The ionisation patches drift westwards at speeds of few hundred km per hour. There is a weak periodicity noted during the season and typically Es is observed on 1 to 3 successive days and remains absent for a few days to reoccur again. Es do not occur during small hours, the events usually begin at dawn, there is a peak in the afternoon and a second peak in the evening. Es propagation is usually gone by local midnight.

Maximum observed frequency (MOF) for Es is found to be lurking around 30 MHz on most days during the summer season, but sometimes MOF may shoot up to 100 MHz or even more in ten minutes to decline slowly during the next few hours. The peak-phase includes oscillation of MOF with periodicity of approximately 5...10 minutes, possibly related to gravity waves. The propagation range for Es single-hop is typically 1000...2000 km, but with multi-hop, double range is observed. The signals are very strong but also with slow deep fading.

Thomas F. Giella, a noted retired Meteorologist, Space Plasma Physicist and Amateur Radio Operator, KN4LF cites the following from his professional research.

Just as the E layer is the main refraction medium for medium frequency (300-3000 kc) signal propagation within approximately 5000 km/3100 mi, so is a Sporadic-E (Es) cloud. Sporadic-E (Es) clouds occur at approximately 100 km/60 miles in altitude and generally move from ESE to WNW. Like Stratosphere level warming and Troposphere level temperature and moisture discontinuities, Sporadic-E (Es) clouds can depending on the circumstances absorb, block or refract medium, high and very high frequency RF signals in an unpredictable manner.

The main source for "high latitude" Sporadic E (Es) clouds is geomagnetic storming induced radio aurora activity.

The main source for "mid-latitude" Sporadic-E (Es) clouds is wind shear produced by internal buoyancy/gravity waves (IBGW's), that create travelling ionosphere disturbances (TID's), most of which are produced by severe thunderstorm cell complexes with overshooting tops that penetrate into the Stratosphere. Another tie in between Sporadic-E (Es) and a severe thunderstorm is the Elve.

The main sources for "low latitude" Sporadic-E (Es) clouds is wind shear produced by internal buoyancy/gravity waves (IBGW's), that create travelling ionosphere disturbances, most of which are produced by severe thunderstorm cell complexes tied to tropical cyclones. High electron content in the Equatorial Ring Current also plays a role.

The forecasting of Sporadic-E (Es) clouds has long been considered to be impossible. However it is possible to identify certain troposphere level meteorological conditions that can lead to the formation of Sporadic E (Es) clouds. One is as mentioned above the severe thunderstorm cell complex.

Sporadic-E (Es) clouds have been observed to initially occur within approximately

150 km/90 mi to the right of a severe thunderstorm cell complex in the northern hemisphere, with the opposite being observed in the southern hemisphere. To complicate matters is the fact that Sporadic-E (Es) clouds that initially form to the right of a severe thunderstorm complex in the northern hemisphere, then move from ESE-WNW and end up to the left of the severe thunderstorm complex in the northern hemisphere. So one has to look for Sporadic-E (Es) clouds on either side of a severe thunderstorm cell complex. Things get even more complicated when two severe thunderstorm cell complexes exist approximately 1000-2000 miles apart.

Not all thunderstorm cell complexes reach severe levels and not all severe thunderstorm cell complexes produce Sporadic-E (Es). This is where knowledge in tropospheric physics and weather analyses/forecasting is necessary.

Some of the key elements in identifying which severe thunderstorm cell complexes have the potential to produce Sporadic-E (Es) via wind shear, from internal buoyancy/ gravity waves, that produce traveling ionosphere disturbances include:

1. Negative tilted mid and upper level long wave troughs.
2. Approximate 150 knot/170 mph jet stream jet maxes that produce divergence and therefore create a sucking vacuum effect above thunderstorm cells, that assist thunderstorm cells in reaching and penetrating the Tropopause into the Stratosphere.
3. 500 mb temperatures of –20 deg. C or colder, which produce numerous positive and negative lightning bolts and inter-related Sprites and Elves.
4. Approximate 150-175 knot/172-200 mph updrafts within thunderstorm cells complexes that create overshooting tops that penetrate the Tropopause into the Stratosphere, launching upwardly propagating internal buoyancy/gravity waves, which create traveling ionosphere disturbances and then wind shear.

Tropospheric Modes

Tropospheric Scattering

At VHF and higher frequencies, small variation (turbulence) in the density of the atmosphere at a height of around 6 miles (10 km) can scatter some of the normally line-of-sight beam of radio frequency energy back toward the ground, allowing over-the-horizon communication between stations as far as 500 miles (800 km) apart.

Tropospheric Ducting and Enhancement or Refraction via Inversion Layer

Sudden changes in the atmosphere's vertical moisture content and temperature profiles can on random occasions make microwave and UHF and VHF signals propagate hundreds of kilometers up to about 2,000 kilometers (1,300 mi)—and for ducting mode even farther—beyond the normal radio-horizon. The inversion layer is mostly observed over high pressure regions, but there are several tropospheric weather conditions which create these randomly occurring propagation modes. Inversion layer's altitude for non-ducting is typically found between 100 meters (300 ft) to about 1 kilometer (3,000 ft) and for ducting about 500 meters (1,600 ft) to 3 kilometers (2 mi), and the duration of the events are typically from several hours up to several days. Higher frequencies experience the most dramatic increase of signal strengths, while on low-VHF and HF the effect is negligible. Propagation path attenuation may be below free-space loss. Some of the lesser inversion types related to warm ground and cooler air moisture content occur regularly at certain times of the year and time of day.

Rain Scattering

Rain scattering is purely a microwave propagation mode and is best observed around 10 GHz, but extends down to few GHz—the limit being the size of the scattering particle size vs. wavelength. This mode scatters signals mostly forwards and backwards when using horizontal polarization and side-scattering with vertical polarization. Forward-scattering typically yields propagation ranges of 800 km. Scattering from snowflakes and ice pellets also occurs, but scattering from ice without watery surface is less effective. The most common application for this phenomenon is microwave rain radar, but rain scatter propagation can be a nuisance causing unwanted signals to intermittently propagate where they are not anticipated or desired. Similar reflections may also occur from insects though at lower altitudes and shorter range. Rain also causes attenuation of point-to-point and satellite microwave links. Attenuation values up to 30 dB have been observed on 30 GHz during heavy tropical rain.

Aeroplane Scattering

Aeroplane scattering (or most often reflection) is observed on VHF through microwaves and besides back-scattering, yields momentary propagation up to 500 km even in a mountain-type terrain. The most common back-scatter application is air-traffic radar and bistatic forward-scatter guided-missile and aeroplane detecting trip-wire radar and the US space radar.

Lightning Scattering

Lightning scattering has sometimes been observed on VHF and UHF over distance of about 500 km. The hot lightning channel scatters radiowaves for a fraction of a second. The RF noise burst from the lightning makes the initial part of the open channel unusable and the ionisation disappears soon because of combination at low latitude high atmospheric pressure. This mode has no practical use.

Other Effects

Diffraction

Knife-Edge diffraction is the propagation mode where radio waves are bent around sharp edges. For example, this mode is used to send radio signals over a mountain range when a line-of-sight path is not available. However, the angle cannot be too sharp or the signal will not diffract. The diffraction mode requires increased signal strength, so higher power or better antennas will be needed than for an equivalent line-of-sight path.

Diffraction depends on the relationship between the wavelength and the size of the obstacle. In other words, the size of the obstacle in wavelengths. Lower frequencies diffract around large smooth obstacles such as hills more easily. For example, in many cases where VHF (or higher frequency) communication is not possible due to shadowing by a hill, one finds that it is still possible to communicate using the upper part of the HF band where the surface wave is of little use.

Diffraction phenomena by small obstacles are also important at high frequencies. Signals for urban cellular telephony tend to be dominated by ground-plane effects as they travel over the rooftops of the urban environment. They then diffract over roof edges into the street, where multipath propagation, absorption and diffraction phenomena dominate.

Absorption

Low-frequency radio waves travel easily through brick and stone and VLF even penetrates sea-water. As the frequency rises, absorption effects become more important. At microwave or higher frequencies, absorption by molecular resonance in the atmosphere (mostly water, H_2O and oxygen, O_2) is a major factor in radio propagation. For example, in the 58-60 GHz band, there is a major absorption peak which makes this band useless for long-distance use. This phenomenon was first discovered during radar research during World War II. Beyond around 400 GHz, the Earth's atmosphere blocks some segments of spectra while still passes some—this is true up to UV light, which is blocked by ozone, but visible light and some of the NIR is transmitted.

Heavy rain and snow also affect microwave reception.

RADIO PROGRAMMING

Radio programming is the content that is broadcast by radio stations. In the early radio age, content typically included a balance of comedy, drama, news, music and sports reporting. U.S. radio programmes included the most famous talent of the day. Radio soap operas began in the U.S. in 1930 with *Painted Dreams*. Despite radio's majority use being spoken entertainment, the *Grand Ole Opry*, as of 2006 being the longest-running radio programme, has been focused on broadcasting country music since it began in 1925.

In the late 1940s and early 1950s, television eroded the popularity of radio comedy, drama and variety shows. By the late 1950s, radio broadcasting took on much the form it has today—strongly focused on music, news and sports, though drama can still be heard, especially on the BBC.

In Britain during the 1950s, radio broadcasting was dominated entirely by the BBC. Rock and pop music fans, dissatisfied with the BBC's output, often listened to Radio Luxembourg. During the post-1964 period, western Europe offshore radio (such as Radio Caroline broadcasting from ships at anchor or abandoned forts) helped to supply the demand for the pop and rock music. The BBC launched their own pop music station, BBC Radio 1 in 1967.

In South Asia, Radio Ceylon (the oldest radio station in the region) was the King of the Airwaves from the 1950s and 1960s. Broadcasting in Ceylon was launched by British Engineer, Edward Harper in 1925. Radio Ceylon became a public corporation in 1967 and was known as the Sri Lanka Broadcasting Corporation when the island turned into a republic in 1972.

There has been a recent resurgence of interest in what is now called old-time radio with surviving shows being traded and collected in reel-to-reel, cassette, CD and MP3 formats.

PRODUCING RADIO PROGRAMMES

Most Popular

- ❑ 30 People Who Shaped Sound
- ❑ Videos From AES 2007
- ❑ Tracking Paul McCartney's Memory
- ❑ Read-Watch-Listen-Play!
- ❑ SONAR 7 Videos

Classics

- ❑ Alicia Keys Opens Recording Studio
- ❑ Making Tool's *10,000 Days*
- ❑ Behind the Scenes at Pink Martini's 2006 tour
- ❑ Meet Daft Punk
- ❑ Phil Collins' "In the Air Tonight" Advertisement

RHLA Ramps Up November 8-10

Participating artists and producers include 9th Wonder, Aloe Blacc, Carmen Rizzo and Freq Nasty. Click here for complete details about RHLA and to register.

Apple Logic Pro 8 Classes at Remix Hotel L.A.

Apple Computer will host daily classes and demos on its flagship DAW, Logic Pro 8. For dates, times and locations, go to remixmag.com/remixhotel.

Looking for new revenue possibilities for your studio? Producing radio programmes can provide income that doesn't come with clients who have fist fights during recording sessions or want the monitors turned up to 11. In fact, in the best cases, the client comes in, records the voice tracks and splits, leaving you the flexibility to put the show together as it suits you.

Radio programme production might seem as simple as sequencing recorded elements-sort of like sequencing music tracks on a CD. Unlike CD sequencing, however, producing a music radio programme often combines widely divergent audio elements that challenge a producer's ability to make the show hang together. Jazz musicologist Jim Murphy's "Journey Into Jazz," a one-hour weekly programme that covers 50 years of music, provided just that sort of challenge.

When you have recordings from Sinatra, Tito Puente, the Four Freshmen, The Rippingtons, The Hi-Los, Max Roach, MJQ, Oscar Peterson, Spyro Gyra and Sonny Rollins, you've got a very listenable but very wide hour of music.

The show, with 13 weeks of programming already in the can, was produced on an Orban Audicy workstation, with the music loaded in a cut at a time. Under direction not to "mess with the music" (which I interpreted as no EQ or compression), I found the loudest passage of each cut and set record levels accordingly. Against my gut instincts, all of the voice and music elements of the first two shows were mixed without processing.

After listening to the mixed programmes, Murphy was not happy. The first problem was that the intros to some of the pieces started at rather low levels, which became more apparent when sequenced with the voice tracks. I explained that raising the level would be changing the dynamic properties of the music, and that's what he said he did not want. He cleared things up by saying he wanted the audio to sound like it did on the radio.

That changed everything and made my gut feel better. Almost everything on the radio is EQ'd, compressed and limited. Part of running a "tight board" (radio lingo for no dead air and consistent levels) is raising the level of soft intros and backing them off as the song builds. After that, you let the station's compressor, limiter and clipper do the work. If the song fades at the end, it's not unusual to increase its level until the subjectively "best" musical moment for either a segue to the next tune or the back announce. That part of the recipe was working.

The other part is the appropriate use of compression and limiting on both the voice and music. I know some people think music should not be messed with—it is a complete art form and the degree of compression and limiting is part of the art form. I also know that in the 17 years I spent working at radio stations, every single one compressed, limited and clipped at the transmitter. (So, no flame mail!) In the '60s and early '70s, stations were using the CBS Audimax and Volumax. They were crude by today's standards, but they increased the average modulation level. In AM (amplitude-modulated) signals, a good portion of the signal strength and coverage area is produced by the modulation in the side bands. The harder you bang it, the bigger it gets. Bigger coverage area means more listeners.

In the late '70s, Bob Orban's multiband Optimod 8000 revolutionized the sound of FM radio by reducing the amount of artifacts produced by massive amounts of gain reduction. Multibanding was part of the solution; using a small amount of delay to prepare the gain reduction circuits for what was about to hit them was another. Other manufacturers contributed boxes with their own "secret sauce," resulting in some truly hideous audio when too many radio stations tried to turn it up to 11.

The point is, you never know if the programming you're producing is going to end up being aired on a station where management has decided that louder is better. If you give them the full, unadulterated stuff, with no ...er...preprocessing, it will sound a lot worse on the air than if you do some of the gain reduction work with relatively transparent gear beforehand. That way, their equipment doesn't have to work as hard, which generally means fewer artifacts and better sound.

Preprocessing also falls right into line when loading said audio into a workstation. The more bits you use, the better the sound, but digital "overs" suck. Striking the right balance of compressor and limiter settings took some time because the production styles and mix techniques within 50 years of jazz vary wildly. In the end, I found that an Aphex Compellor followed by a Studio Dominator set at light but fast settings contributed a consistency. The Compellor is a very transparent device, and the tri-band stereo limiting of the Studio Dominator kept the lid on without pumping.

Compression ran at a fairly constant 2 to 4 dB. The Studio Dominator was set to catch the occasional peaks, most of which required 1 to 3 dB of gain reduction. A few of the selections, some with bongo accents and drum and vibe solos, had extremely high peaks, requiring the Dominator release times to be set faster to avoid pumping. From there, the input level to the Compellor/Dominator stage was varied as needed to account for level differences on the LPs and CDs. In most cases, the newer tunes were produced with more overall compression than some of the earlier ones. The more gain reduction I heard in the original recording, the less I used.

After testing several mics on Murphy's voice, I settled on a Gefell UM 70 through a GML mic preamp with no EQ. The voice tracks were recorded through the Compellor/ Studio Dominator chain using the same settings as for the music tracks. The Audicy was used to cut the center out of Murphy's breaths, leaving enough to imply natural breathing.

A good turntable, stylus, cartridge and preamp all make a difference. You can't "get by" with bad stuff. I used a Stanton 981 HZ-Mk II-S cartridge with a II D98S stylus in a Technics SL-D1 direct drive turntable and a Stanton Model 210 phone preamp. Murphy's LP collection is in very good condition, requiring only that a standard, moistened Dishwasher be used to remove the usual dust buildup. Some of the older, more frequently played discs had developed some crackles and pops. The Audicy got rid of the pops with no problem, but the budget wasn't there for more extensive noise removal.

The show was mixed to a Panasonic SV-3900 DAT in quarter-hour segments. It's very easy to let the level of a sequenced show creep away from you. The tendency is to make each segment just a little louder than the last. I used the –6 dB peak hold indicator on the DAT meters as a guide, with rare excursions to –4 dB and –2 dB.

After making high-speed DAT backup copies of each programme with a Tascam DA-302 dual-well DAT, the DATs were sent off for CD replication. The house with the best price is not always the best deal. Of the first ten shows sent out, 1 to 7 came back in mono, and 8 and 9 came back in stereo with the channels reversed, but that's another story.

RADIO PRODUCTION

Students interested in radio use a radio production facility encompassing five studios. All studios contain state-of-the-art radio production equipment.

Our Facilities

- 24 channel Teac mixing console,
- 10 channel on-air board,
- Digital audio cassette recorders,
- Digital Minidisk recorders and players,
- The latest digital signal processing equipment,
- Digital computerized editing suites, and
- Adobe audition sound editing software.

Radio Station WIUS

- Radio station WIUS is a licensed operation that broadcasts live in the Macomb area.
- The station is completely run by WIU students and plays a variety of formats including urban contemporary and alternative rock.
- WIUS is an excellent opportunity for broadcast majors and other students interested in radio to get professional air time.
- Listen Live to WIUS-FM.

Advanced Radio Production

- If you are looking for more challenging radio production work, the advanced radio production classes have what you are looking for.
- Students complete more intricate technical and dramatic projects using state-of-the-art digital equipment.
- You will learn to master the "big board" with all the latest in signal processors, digital players and recorders, and multi-track recording.

Certificate: Industrial Technology

Credit Requirements: 24 Semester Credit Hours

This certificate is designed for students who wish to pursue a career in Radio Production primarily as board operators and production assistants but also in some cases as on-the-air talent.

Admission into the programme requires proof of high school graduation (or GED) and qualifying scores on SAT, ACT, or the TTC placement test.

Recommended Sequence of Courses
First Semester—Fall

RTV 101	Audio Techniques	3
RTV 109	Writing for Electronic Media	3
RTV 111	Radio Studio Techniques I	3
		Total 9

Second Semester—Spring

RTV 112	Radio Studio Techniques II	3
RTV 121	Introduction to Broadcasting	3
RTV 231	SCWE in Broadcasting I	3
		Total 9

Third Semester—Summer

RTV 211	Radio Studio Techniques III	3
RTV 232	SCWE in Broadcasting II	3
		Total 6

RADIO SOFTWARE

Almost all radio stations today use some form of broadcast automation. Although some only use small scripts in audio players, a more robust solution is using a full Radio Automation Suite. There are many commercial and free radio automation packages available.

Free and Open-Source Developments

- Soma Suite
- Campcaster
- Rivendell
- IKRA

Commercial Products

- Raduga
- Pulsar Multimídia
- Backbone Networks

RADIO FORMAT

A radio format or programming format describes the overall content broadcast on a radio station. Radio formats are frequently employed as a marketing tool, and constantly evolve. Music radio; All-news radio; Sports radio; Talk radio and Weather radio describe the operation of different genres of radio format and each format can often be sub-divided into many speciality formats.

RADIO DOCUMENTARY

A radio documentary or feature is a radio documentary programme devoted to covering a particular topic in some depth, usually with a mixture of commentary and sound pictures. Some radio features, especially those including specially composed music or other pieces of audio art, resemble radio drama in many ways, though non-fictional in subject matter, while others consist principally of more straightforward, journalistic-type reporting—but at much greater length than found in an ordinary news report.

> "At its best, radio combines the power and immediacy of great documentary films with the intimacy and poetry of a *New Yorker*-style magazine piece."
>
> —*Columbia Graduate School of Journalism*

"Staring red-eyed at the mirror in front of me, having spent another day and half of the night with my computer, I ask myself fundamental questions: Why radio? Why documentary? Answer: No other medium can provide me with more freedom of creation and investigation. It meets my urgent interest in reality and the desire for a 'musical' expression. The material (*der Werkstoff*) is sound. And sound always surrounds us. And: I'm not so much interested in the description of stable situations, but in processes. Our medium is not space, but time; our stories are not glued to the ground, but have motion, life ... That's why!"

—*Helmut Kopetzky*, German author

Notable Radio Documentary and Feature Makers

- American RadioWorks
- John Biewen
- Kyla Brettle
- Ira Glass
- Berit Hedemann (Prix Europa Yleisradio 1997 and 1998)
- David Isay
- Bill Lichtenstein
- Ewan MacColl
- Charles Parker
- Joe Richman
- Steve Rowland

CASE STUDY: ASSOCIATE OF APPLIED SCIENCE DEGREE

For over 60 years, Brown has been educating successful radio broadcasters and producers. In fact, 17 of our grads have found their way into the Minnesota Radio Broadcasting Hall of Fame. But broadcasting's best days lie ahead. Streaming audio, podcasts, and satellite radio are just a few of the emerging technologies that will demand skilled broadcasters and producers for years to come.

The Associate of Applied Science degree in Radio Broadcasting is designed to help you develop an on-air presence and the technical skills needed for positions in this growing industry. Business aspects of broadcasting are illuminated, including station management and sales. The programme also explores the relationship between broadcasting and the Internet, and includes an internship or practicum project.

Career Opportunities for Radio Broadcasting Graduates

- Audio production director,
- Newscaster,
- On-air talent,
- Producer,
- Radio newscaster,
- Media sales account executive, and
- Sports play-by-play announcer and reporter.

Listen Live to The VBC The Voice of Brown College available at the Mendota Heights campus.

The instructors guide and mentor you throughout the programme.

—Siobhan Kierans,
Graduate, School of Broadcasting

10

Camera: Types, Materials and Processes

CAMERA

A camera is a device used to capture images, either as still photographs or as sequences of moving images (movies or videos). The term comes from the *camera obscura* (Latin for "dark chamber"), an early mechanism of projecting images where an entire room functioned as a real-time imaging system; the modern camera evolved from the camera obscura.

Cameras may work with the light of the visible spectrum or with other portions of the electromagnetic spectrum. A camera generally consists of an enclosed hollow with an opening (aperture) at one end for light to enter, and a recording or viewing surface for capturing the light at the other end. A majority of cameras have a lens positioned in front of the camera's opening to gather the incoming light and focus all or part of the image on the recording surface. The diameter of the aperture is often controlled by a diaphragm mechanism, but some cameras have a fixed-size aperture.

History

The forerunner to the camera was the camera obscura. The camera obscura is an instrument consisting of a darkened chamber or box, into which light is admitted through a convex lens, forming an image of external objects on a surface of paper or glass, etc., placed at the focus of the lens. The camera obscura was first invented by the Iraqi scientist Ibn al-Haytham (Alhazen) as described in his *Book of Optics* (1015-1021). Irish scientist Robert Boyle and his assistant Robert Hooke later developed a portable camera obscura in the 1660s.

The first camera that was small and portable enough to be practical for photography was built by Johann Zahn in 1685, though it would be almost 150 years before technology caught up to the point where this was practical. Early photographic cameras were essentially similar to Zahn's model, though usually with the addition of sliding boxes for focusing. Before each exposure, a sensitized plate would be inserted in front of the viewing screen to record the image. Jacques Daguerre's popular daguerreotype process utilized copper plates, while the calotype process invented by William Fox Talbot recorded images on paper.

The first permanent photograph was made in 1826 by Joseph Nicéphore Niépce using a sliding wooden box camera made by Charles and Vincent Chevalier in Paris. Niépce built on a discovery by Johann Heinrich Schultz (1724): a silver and chalk mixture darkens under exposure to light. However, while this was the birth of photography, the camera itself can be traced back much further. Before the invention of photography, there was no way to preserve the images produced by these cameras apart from manually tracing them.

The development of the collodion wet plate process by Frederick Scott Archer in 1850 cut exposure times dramatically, but required photographers to prepare and develop their glass plates on the spot, usually in a mobile darkroom. Despite their complexity, the wet-plate ambrotype and tintype processes were in widespread use in the latter half of the 19th century. Wet plate cameras were little different from previous designs, though there were some models, such as the sophisticated Dubroni of 1864, where the sensitizing and developing of the plates could be carried out inside the camera itself rather than in a separate darkroom. Other cameras were fitted with multiple lenses for making cartes de visite. It was during the wet plate era that the use of bellows for focusing became widespread.

The first colour photograph was made by James Clerk Maxwell, with the help of Thomas Sutton, in 1861.

Mechanics

Image Capture

Traditional cameras capture light onto photographic film or photographic plate. Video and digital cameras use electronics, usually a charge coupled device (CCD) or sometimes a CMOS sensor to capture images which can be transferred or stored in tape or computer memory inside the camera for later playback or processing.

Cameras that capture many images in sequence are known as movie cameras or as ciné cameras in Europe; those designed for single images are still cameras. However these categories overlap, as still cameras are often used to capture moving images in special effects work and modern digital cameras are often able to trivially switch between still and motion recording modes. A video camera is a category of movie camera that captures images electronically (either using analogue or digital technology).

Focus

Due to the optical properties of photographic lenses, only objects within a limited range of distances from the camera will be reproduced clearly. The process of adjusting this range is known as changing the camera's focus. There are various ways of focusing a camera accurately. The simplest cameras have fixed focus and use a small aperture and wide-angle lens to ensure that everything within a certain range of distance from the lens, usually around 3 metres (10 ft) to infinity, is in reasonable focus. Fixed focus cameras are usually inexpensive types, such as single-use cameras. The camera can also have a limited focusing range or scale-focus that is indicated on the camera body.

The user will guess or calculate the distance to the subject and adjust the focus accordingly. On some cameras this is indicated by symbols (head-and-shoulders; two people standing upright; one tree; mountains).

Rangefinder cameras allow the distance to objects to be measured by means of a coupled parallax unit on top of the camera, allowing the focus to be set with accuracy. Single-lens reflex cameras allow the photographer to determine the focus and composition visually using the objective lens and a moving mirror to project the image onto a ground glass or plastic micro-prism screen. Twin-lens reflex cameras use an objective lens and a focusing lens unit (usually identical to the objective lens) in a parallel body for composition and focusing. View cameras use a ground glass screen which is removed and replaced by either a photographic plate or a reusable holder containing sheet film before exposure. Modern cameras often offer autofocus systems to focus the camera automatically by a variety of methods.

Exposure Control

The size of the aperture and the brightness of the scene controls the amount of light that enters the camera during a period of time, and the shutter controls the length of time that the light hits the recording surface. Equivalent exposures can be made with a larger aperture and a faster shutter speed or a corresponding smaller aperture and with the shutter speed slowed down.

The Camera

We're well on our way to the world of fully automatic "point and shoot" television cameras. Smart cameras are great most of the time and they certainly cut down on the common mistakes most people (even pros) make from time to time. When automatic operation doesn't work, though, the results can be pretty bad. Knowing what the conditions were that fooled your "smart" camera will help you to know when to turn these features off and do it the old-fashioned way. But before you do, you need to know what cameras do and how they work.

The television camera changes light into an electronic signal that can be stored (using video tape, optical disks, or computer memory, transmitted, and displayed on a television receiver or monitor. Television cameras are probably easier to operate well than film or still cameras because you can watch and control the camera output as you record. There are few electronic controls, and the manual controls on the lens will be familiar to anyone who has used a good still or motion picture camera. Since video cameras can, as a rule, produce sharper, clearer pictures than the recording media they were designed to work with, the quality of your camera is seldom an excuse for fuzzy pictures. Understanding how to use the camera correctly will help you avoid poor results.

Lens Controls

The modern television lens has three controls: iris, focus, and zoom. On a fully automatic camera you may not have to adjust the focus or iris except under unusual conditions, but you should know what's going on so you can use manual settings with confidence.

Iris

The ring closest to the camera body controls the amount of light passing through the lens to the light-sensitive surface of the pickup tube or chip. It is called the iris, aperture, or f-stop control and is marked off in f-numbers. The lowest f-stop lets in the most light, and the highest f-stop lets in the least. Some lenses even have a "C" setting after the highest f-stop which means the lens is completely closed, letting no light through at all.

More light——————Less light
1 1.4 2 2.8 4 5.6 8 11 16 22 32
STANDARD F-NUMBERS

Each standard f-stop lets half as much light through the lens as the f-stop below it.

If the camera gets too little light, the image will look fuzzy and drab, even though it may be in focus. The camera image may lag behind quick changes in the picture and the picture will be grayish, with little contrast.

Too much light will produce too much contrast. Details in both the very bright and the very dark parts of the picture will be lost. Bright spots may grow "halos" or "bloom." So-called "point sources" of light may cause light vertical stripes on CCD cameras.

The correct setting is between these extremes, generally about one f-stop higher than the f-stop at which the bright parts of the picture lose details and grow halos, or "bloom." To find this point, begin with the lens in the closed or highest f-stop position and open it slowly until you start losing details in the brightest parts of the picture. Then reduce the amount of light coming through by going down to the next highest f-stop.

Indoors it's often necessary to add light to get a good picture. Outdoors on bright sunny days it may be necessary to reduce the light reaching the pickup tube even more than the lens will allow. This is done by adding a neutral density filter between the lens and lens hood. A two power (2X) filter has the same effect as using the next highest f-stop, while a four power (4X) filter gives the effect of going up two f-stops.

Zoom

The center ring on most lenses is the zoom control. Most cameras use a rocker switch beside the lens. This allows you to change the focal length of the lens through a range from wide angle (short focal length) to telephoto (long focal length). It's common for inexpensive zoom lenses to have a range of about six to one. That is, the longest focal length is about six times the shortest. Zoom lenses for television cameras with two-thirds inch pickup tubes or chips range from about 12 mm to 75 mm, with a normal focal length of about 33 mm.

A wide angle setting makes the subject smaller as the angle of view is increased. Distances from the camera are exaggerated, with objects nearer the camera appearing abnormally large. This is especially true of people who are too close to a wide angle lens. Straight lines near the edges of the picture are often bent with an effect known as barrel distortion.

A telephoto setting makes the subject larger as the angle of view is reduced. Distances from the camera are compressed. More than one feature film director has used this effect to make an action (like running toward the camera) seem to take much longer than it should.

The normal lens settings offer the most natural perspective to the viewer. It's possible to change the focal length of a zoom lens during a shot by "zooming" in or out. Inexperienced camera operators often over-use this capability. The main value of the lens is in controlling the field of view of the camera when it's inconvenient or impossible to change the distance from the subject to the camera.

Focus

The focus control is the ring farthest from the camera body, on the front of the lens. Distance settings are marked in meters and in feet. While a non-zoom (fixed focal length) lens is focused simply by turning the ring until the image is sharp, the zoom lens must be zoomed in to the smallest angle of view and the largest image size to adjust focus. The lens should then be zoomed out to the widest angle of view and the smallest image size to make sure the image stays in focus through the entire zoom range. If the image stays sharp, the lens will remain focused at any focal length as long as the distance from the subject does not change.

Depth of field is the range of distances in front of the lens in which objects appear to be in acceptable focus. It's longer for short (wide angle) lenses than for long (telephoto) lenses, and it increases as you use higher f-stops. It is often wise to use a higher f-stop when lighting conditions permit, if you expect the distance between the camera and the subject to change often while you're taping, since you'll have less trouble keeping the subject sharply focused with greater depth of field.

While all cameras with zoom lenses must control iris, focal length, and focus, the functions of the three rings described here may be automated or provided by remote control. Most lenses also have a "macro" setting on the zoom ring. This changes the characteristics of the lens to let you focus on objects right up to the front of the lens.

Electronic Controls

Some or all of the following controls may be automatic or preset and thus not adjustable by the user.

Pedestal

Also called the "set-up" control, sets the level of the darkest parts of the picture. On portable cameras it's generally automatic or totally absent.

Gain

Also called "level," this control sets the level of the brightest parts of the picture. It can be used to reduce the level when too much light is striking the pickup tube, but it will not make the picture brighter without making it grainy or snowy if the pickup tube or chip isn't getting enough light. Automatic gain controls can be extremely sensitive to even small bright parts of the picture, driving medium and darker parts into black. They may also bring dark parts up into the medium range if there's not enough light for a good picture.

White Balance

If you use outdoor film with normal indoor lighting (no flash) everything comes out orange. The color temperature of sunlight is very different from an incandescent light bulb. Most consumer cameras now sense the overall colour temperature and adjust color electronically. In older or professional cameras it may be necessary with each change in location or lighting to "tell" the camera how to interpret colour. This is done by showing the camera a white card, which represents the total absence of color. Controls on the camera are then used to minimize the colour output of the camera.

Viewfinder

There are often controls to adjust a camera viewfinder. To state the obvious, these controls have absolutely nothing to do with the actual output of the camera. It's helpful to adjust the viewfinder under controlled conditions so it shows a faithful representation of actual camera output. Otherwise, if you want viewfinders to tell you the truth, they should never be adjusted just to make a "pretty" picture.

DIGITAL SINGLE-LENS REFLEX CAMERA

A digital single-lens reflex camera (digital SLR or DSLR) is a digital camera that uses an automatic mirror system and pentaprism or pentamirror to direct light from the lens through the viewfinder eyepiece.

The basic operation of a DSLR is as follows: for viewing purposes, the mirror reflects the light coming through the attached lens upwards at an approximately 90 degree angle. It is then reflected by the pentaprism to the photographer's eye. During exposure (when the photograph is taken), the mirror swings upward, and a shutter opens, allowing the lens to project light onto the image sensor.

Brief Difference Between a DSLR and a Digicam

This design scheme is a major difference compared to an ordinary digital camera (digicam), which typically exposes the sensor constantly to the light projected by the lens, allowing the camera's screen to be used as an electronic viewfinder.

In contrast, the mirror arrangement in a DSLR usually precludes the ability to view the scene on the LCD screen before the photograph is taken. However, many newer DSLR models feature live preview, allowing LCD display to be used as a viewfinder in the same way as a normal digicam, although with certain limitations and with the optical viewfinder disabled.

In most other respects, a DSLR is similar in principle and operation to a standard (non-SLR) digital camera.

DSLR Design Principles

A camera based on the single-lens reflex (SLR) principle uses a mirror to show the image that will be captured in a viewfinder. The cross-section (side-view) of the optical components of an SLR shows how the light passes through the lens assembly (1), is reflected into the pentaprism by the reflex mirror (which must be at an exact 45 degree angle) (2) and is projected on the matte focusing screen (5). Via a condensing lens (6) and internal reflections in the roof pentaprism (7) the image is projected, either focused or unfocused through the eyepiece (8) to the photographer's eye. Focusing is usually automatic, activated by pressing half-way on the shutter release or a dedicated AF button, as is mainly the case with an autofocusing film SLR; or manual, where the photographer manually focuses the lens by turning a lens ring on the lens barrel. When an image is photographed, the mirror moves upwards in the direction of the arrow, the focal-plane shutter (3) opens, and the image is projected and captured on the sensor (4), after which actions, the shutter closes, the mirror returns to a critical 45 degree angle, and the diaphragm reopens and the built in drive mechanism retensions the shutter for the next exposure.

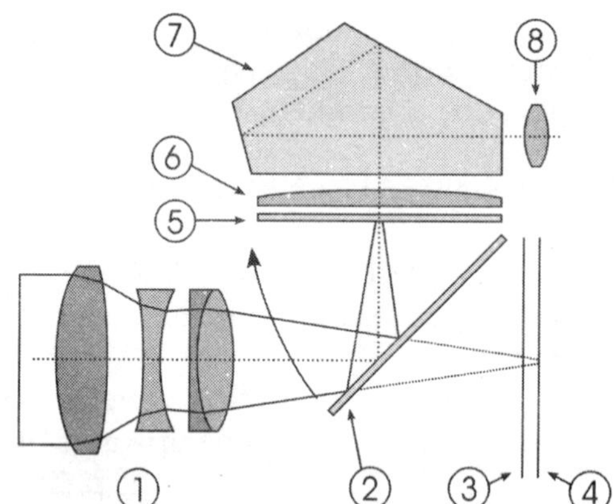

Fig. 10.1: Cross-section view of SLR system.

1. 4-element lens,
2. Reflex mirror,
3. Focal-plane shutter,
4. Sensor,
5. Matte focusing screen,
6. Condenser lens,
7. Pentaprism, and
8. Eyepiece.

Fast Phase-Detection Autofocus

The diagram shown here is an over-simplification in that it omits the sensors used to activate the drive for the autofocus system.

DSLRs typically use a phase detection autofocus system. This method of focus is very fast, and results in less focus "searching", but requires the insertion of a special sensor into the optical path, so it is usually only used in SLR designs. Digicams that use the main sensor to create a live preview on the LCD or electronic viewfinder need to use the slower contrast method of autofocus.

DSLR Optical Viewfinder vs. Digicam LCD Display

Depending on the viewing position of the reflex mirror (down or up), the light from the scene can only reach either the viewfinder or the sensor. Therefore, most DSLRs do not currently provide "live preview" (allowing focusing, framing, and depth-of-field preview using the display), a facility that is always available on digicams.

The advantages of an optical viewfinder are that it alleviates eye-strain sometimes caused by electronic view finders (EVF), and that it constantly shows (except during the split second of time for the sensor to be exposed) the exact image that will be exposed because its light is routed directly from the lens itself. Compared to ordinary digital cameras with their LCD displays and/or electronic viewfinders the advantage is that there is no time lag in the image; it is always correct as it is being "updated" at the speed of light. This is important for action and/or sports photography, or any other situation where the subject or the camera is moving too quickly. Furthermore, the "resolution" of the viewed image is much better than that provided by an LCD display or an electronic viewfinder, which can be important if manual focusing is desired for precise focusing, as would be the case in photomacrography or photomicrography (commonly referred to as "macro-photography" and "micro-photography").

Compared to some low cost cameras that provide an optical viewfinder that uses a small auxiliary lens, the DSLR design has the advantage of being parallax-free; that is, it never provides an off-axis view.

A disadvantage of the DSLR optical viewfinder system is that it prevents the possibility of using the LCD display for viewing and composing the picture before taking it. Some people prefer to compose pictures on the display—for them this has become the natural way to use a camera. LCD displays and electronic viewfinders may also provide a brighter display in low light situations, as the picture can be electronically amplified; conversely, LCD displays can be difficult to see in very bright sunlight.

DSLRs with Live Preview

A fairly recent development in DSLRs is the emergence of live preview options, which make it possible to use either the optical viewfinder or the LCD display when composing the picture (but not both). This can be an advantage because some people simply prefer to use the display and because in some situations it is not convenient or possible to hold the camera up to one's face to look through the viewfinder. Underwater photography, where the camera is enclosed in a plastic waterproof case, is an example of a situation where composing on the display is preferred.

Olympus introduced the first DSLR with live preview—albeit an atypical design with a fixed lens—the Olympus E-10, in the summer of 2000. Since then other manufacturers have launched DSLR models with live preview, and it is likely that other new DSLRs will eventually have this feature.

As of early 2008, the Canon EOS-1D Mark III, Canon EOS-1Ds Mark III, Canon EOS 40D, Canon EOS Rebel XSI, Nikon D3, Nikon D300, Olympus E-330, Olympus E-410, Olympus E-510, Olympus E-3, Panasonic Lumix DMC-L1, Panasonic Lumix DMC-L10, Leica Digilux 3, Pentax K20D, and Canon EOS 450D all provide continuous live preview as an option. Additionally, the Fujifilm FinePix S5 Pro offers 30 seconds of live preview.

Some live preview systems make use of the primary sensor to provide the image on the LCD display (which is the way all non-DSLR digicams work), and some systems use a secondary sensor. Possible advantages of using a secondary sensor for live preview is to avoid additional noise that might result from the primary sensor heating up from continuous use, and allowing faster auto-focus.

A new feature via a separate software package introduced from Breeze Systems in October, 2007, features live view from a distance. The software package is named "DSLR Remote Pro v1. 5" and enables support for the Canon EOS 40D and 1D Mark III.

DSLR Lenses

The ability to exchange lenses, to select the best lens for the current photographic need, and to allow the attachment of specialized lenses, is a key to the popularity of DSLR cameras.

Lens Mounts and Lens Manufacturers

Interchangeable lenses for SLRs and DSLRs are built to operate correctly with a specific lens mount. A photographer will often use lenses made by the same manufacturer as the camera body (for example, Canon lenses on a Canon body). There are also many independent lens manufacturers, such as Sigma, Tamron, Tokina, and Vivitar, to name a few, that make lenses for a variety of different lens mounts. There are also lens adapters that allow a lens for one lens mount to be used on a camera body with a different lens mount, but with reduced functionality.

Many lenses are mountable, "diaphragm-and-meter-compatible," on modern DSLRs and on older film SLRs that use the same lens mount.

DSLR Design Considerations

Pentaprism vs. Penta-Mirror

Some DSLRs use a pentamirror instead of the traditional pentaprism. The pentamirror design is composed mostly of plastic and is lighter and cheaper to produce.

Sensor Size and Image Quality

Image sensors used in DSLRs come in a range of sizes. The very largest are the ones used in "medium format" cameras, typically via a "digital back" which can be used as an alternative to a film back. Because of the manufacturing costs of these large sensors the price of these cameras is typically over $20,000 as of December 2007.

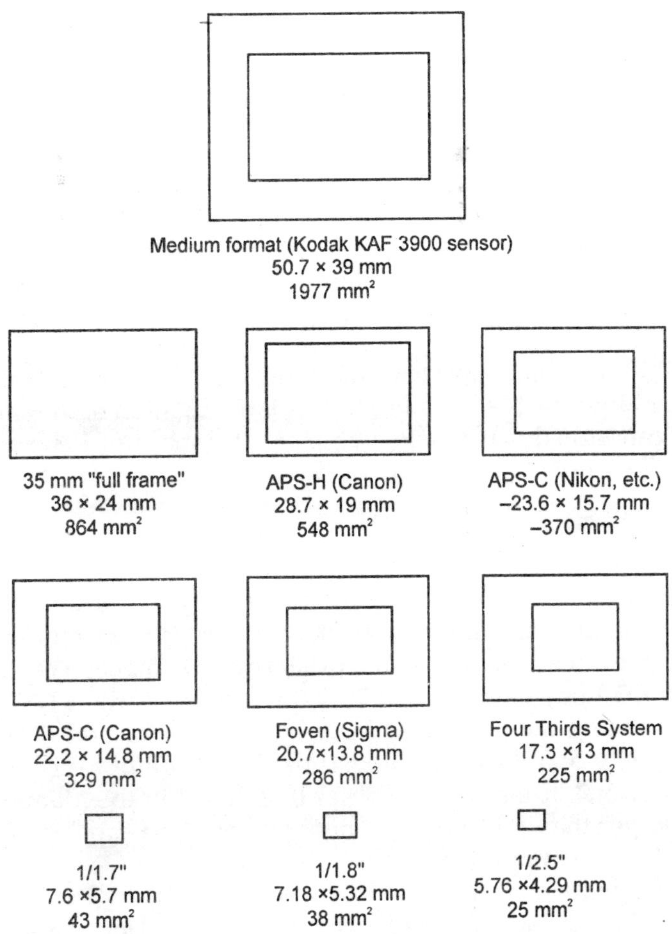

Fig. 10.2: Drawing showing the relative size of sensors used in current DSLRs.

Neglecting medium format DSLRs, the largest sensors are referred to as "full-frame", and are the same size as 35 mm film (135 film); these sensors are used in quite expensive DSLRs such as the Canon EOS-1Ds Mark III, the Canon EOS 5D, and the Nikon D3. Most modern DSLRs use a smaller sensor commonly referred to as APS-C sized, that is, approximately 22 mm × 15 mm, a little smaller than the size of an APS-C film frame, or about 40 per cent of the area of a full-frame sensor. Other sensor sizes found in DSLRs include the Four Thirds System sensor at 26 per cent of full frame, APS-H sensors (used, for example, in the Canon EOS-1D Mark III) at around 61 per cent of full frame, and the Foveon X3 sensor at 33 per cent of full frame.

All of the sensors used in current DSLRs are much larger than the sensors found in digicam-style cameras, most of which use sensors known as 1/2.5", whose area is only 3 per cent of a full frame sensor. Even high-end digicams such as the Canon

PowerShot G9 or the Nikon CoolPix P5000 use sensors that are approximately 5 and 4 per cent of the area of a full frame sensor, respectively.

There is a connection between sensor size and image quality; in general, a larger sensor provides lower noise, higher sensitivity, and increased latitude and dynamic range. There is also a connection between sensor size and depth of field, with the larger sensor resulting in shallower depth of field.

Depth-of-Field Control

The larger size of the sensors (and therefore lens focal lengths) of DSLRs compared to digicams makes it much easier to limit the depth of field, for example to emphasize a face by blurring the background. This reduced depth of field can be a disadvantage when the photographer prefers to take pictures where as much of the scene as possible is sharply rendered.

Note that DSLR's typically have lens apertures smaller than the typical digicam's aperture setting ability, which is usually f/8. This is a limitation of the small sensor. In contrast, a DSLR can 'stop down' to f/16, f/22 or smaller aperture, depending upon the lens mounted on the camera and its f/stop range.

Angle of View

The angle of view of a lens depends upon its focal length and the camera's image sensor size; a sensor smaller than 35 mm film format (36 × 24 mm frame) gives a narrower angle of view for a lens of a given focal length than does a camera equipped with a full-frame (35 mm) sensor. As of 2007, only a few current DSLRs have full-frame sensors, including the Canon EOS-1Ds Mark II, the Canon EOS 5D, and the Nikon D3. The scarcity of full-frame DSLRs is partly a result of the cost of such large sensors. Medium format size sensors, such as those used in the Mamiya ZD among others, are even larger than full-frame (35 mm) sensors, and capable of even greater image quality, but are even more expensive.

The impact of sensor size on field of view is referred to as the "crop factor" or "focal length multiplier", which is a factor by which a lens focal length can be multiplied to give the full-frame-equivalent focal length for a lens. Roughly APS-sized sensors have a crop factor of 1.5 to 1.7, so a lens with a focal length of 50 mm will give a field of view equal to that of a 75 mm to 85 mm lens on a full-frame camera. This crop factor makes achieving long telephoto images on an APS-sensor camera easier than on a full-frame camera, though wide-angle views suffer by the same amount. Shallow depth-of-field images also tend to be more limited, since the wider the lens you use the more depth of field you get, so the smaller the sensor the more depth of field with the same f-number and field of view.

Mode Dial

Digital SLR cameras, along with most other digital cameras, generally have a mode dial to access standard camera settings or automatic scene-mode settings. Sometimes called a "PASM" dial, they typically provide as minimum Programme, Aperture-priority, Shutter-priority, and full Manual modes. Scene modes vary and are inherently less customizable. They often include full-auto, landscape, portrait, action, macro, and night modes, among others. Professional DSLRs seldom contain automatic scene modes because professionals understand their equipment and can quickly adjust the settings to take the image that they want.

Medium Format Digital

Many medium format roll-film SLRs can accept a digital camera back to turn the camera into a DSLR with very high image resolution and quality (typically 22–39 megapixels as of January 2007). However, the combination is very expensive and bulky, and more suited to still life than to action photography.

As of 2007 integrated medium formats like the Hasselblad H System and Leaf AFi have started to appear.

Unusual Features—Infrared and Ultraviolet Photography

On July 13, 2007, FujiFilm announced the FinePix IS Pro, which uses Nikon F-mount lenses. This camera, in addition to having live preview, has the ability to record in the infrared and ultraviolet spectra of light.

History

At Photokina in 1986, Nikon revealed a prototype analog electronic still SLR camera, the Nikon SVC, a precursor to the digital SLR. The prototype body shared many features with the N8008.

In 1991, Kodak released the first commercially available digital SLR, the Kodak DCS-100. It consisted of a modified Nikon F3 SLR body, modified drive unit, and an external storage unit connected via cable. The 1.3 megapixel camera cost approximately US$ 30,000. This was followed by the Kodak DCS-200 with integrated storage.

Over the next decade, DSLRs have been released by various companies such as Canon, Nikon, Kodak, Pentax, Olympus, Panasonic, Samsung, Konica Minolta, which was acquired by SONY, Fujifilm, and Sigma with higher resolution and lower prices.

In 1999, Nikon announced the Nikon D1, the first DSLR to truly compete, and begin to replace, film cameras in the professional photojournalism and sports photography fields. This camera was able to use current autofocus Nikkor lenses available at that time for the Nikon film series cameras, and was also able to utilize the older Nikon and similar, independent mount lenses designed for those cameras. A combination of price, speed, and image quality was the beginning of the end of 35 mm film for these markets.

In January 2000, Fujifilm announced the FinePix S1 Pro, the first DSLR marketed to non-professionals.

In 2003, Canon introduced the 6.3 megapixel EOS 300D SLR camera (known in the United States as the Digital Rebel) with an MSRP of US$999. Its popularity encouraged other manufacturers to produce affordable digital SLR cameras, lowering entry costs and allowing more amateur photographers to purchase DSLR's.

Since 2003, the number of megapixels in imaging sensors have increased steadily, with most companies focusing on build quality, high ISO performance, speed, the elimination of digital 'noise' produced by the imaging sensor, and price reductions to lure new customers.

Present Day

Canon, Fujifilm, Nikon, Olympus, Panasonic, Pentax, Samsung, Sigma, and Sony currently produce DSLR cameras. Hasselblad and Mamiya also produce expensive, professional medium-format DSLRs.

- Canon's EOS digital line includes the 400D, 40D, 5D and the 1D Mark III. Canon's latest cameras, the 40D and the 1Ds Mark III were introduced on August 20, 2007. All current Canon DSLRs use CMOS sensors.
- Nikon also has a broad line of DSLRs currently including the D40, D40x, D80, D200, D2Hs, and D2Xs. Nikon announced two new cameras on August 23, 2007, the D300 and the D3. The latter is the company's first full-frame digital SLR.
- Fujifilm currently sells the Fujifilm FinePix S5 Pro DSLR camera body, compatible only with the Nikon F-mount lens system. This camera is based upon the magnesium-alloy body of the Nikon D200, but utilizes Fuji's sensor (Fujifilm SuperCCD SR Pro) technology and Fuji's menu system. Another DSLR from Fuji is the Fujifilm FinePix IS Pro, which has the unique ability to capture light in the infrared and ultraviolet spectrums.
- Olympus, Panasonic, and Leica make DSLR cameras that conform to the Four Thirds System of bodies and lenses designed specifically for digital photography. Current Olympus models are the E-410, E-510, and E-3, while the Lumix DMC-L10 is the latest Panasonic model. Innovative features of these models include live preview in addition to the optical viewfinder, and supersonic dust reduction. The Olympus E-3 and E-510 feature in-body image stabilization while Panasonic and Leica feature in-lens stabilization.
- Pentax (in collaboration with Samsung) currently offers the Pentax K100D Super and K10D. The Samsung GX-10 is a clone of the K10D. Innovative features include in-body image stabilization, dust reduction system, use of standard AA batteries in the K100D Super, weather-proof sealing on the K10D (a feature otherwise found only in semi-pro models such as the Nikon D200), and adoption of Adobe's DNG standard raw image format. Also, these cameras are based on the Pentax K mount lens system, so they can accept all K-mount lenses made since 1975 (though the automatic light metering functionality of some early lenses does not work).
- Sony, which acquired Konica Minolta's DSLR line in 2006, produces the Sony α line of DSLRs with in-body image stabilization.
- Sigma produces an innovative DSLR with the multi-layered Foveon X3 sensor to deliver excellent color and detail.
- Hasselblad and Mamiya produce medium format-sized DSLRs which produce the highest quality digital images. Their high-resolution sensors (over 39

megapixels in some cases) are able to capture much more detail than the 35 mm full-frame and smaller sensors found in other cameras.

DSLRs Compared to other Digital Cameras

Fixed-Lens Cameras

Non-SLR digital cameras generally fall into two types: compact digicams, and SLR-like bridge digital cameras (also known as advanced *digital cameras*) which offer larger zoom ranges, better optics, and more manual controls. Both types have permanently fixed lenses. While the only *defining* feature of an SLR is its reflex viewfinder system, extant digital SLR models generally offer the following advantages over fixed-lens cameras of the same generation:

- Choice of interchangeable (and often higher-quality) lenses.
- Image sensors of much larger size and often higher quality, offering lower noise, which is useful in low light, and greater dynamic range.
- Optical viewfinders which tend to be more comfortable and efficient, especially for action photography and in low-light conditions.
- DSLRs often offer faster and more responsive performance, with less shutter lag, faster autofocus systems, and faster frame rates.
- The larger focal length for the same field of view allows creative use of depth of field effects.
- Ability to attach additional accessories including hot shoe-mounted flash units, battery grips for additional power and hand positions, external light meters, and remote controls.

There are also certain drawbacks to current DSLR designs, compared to fixed-lens cameras:

- Generally greater size and weight.
- Generally greater cost.
- Lack of a video mode. No DSLRs produced so far can record full-motion video, while this has become a standard feature of compact digital cameras.
- Many DSLR models lack live preview on their LCD screens, a universal feature among compact digital cameras.
- Noisier operation, due to the SLR mirror mechanism.
- Potential contamination of the sensor by dust particles, when the lens is changed (though recent dust reduction systems alleviate this).
- Small digicams generally can focus on closer objects than typical DSLR lenses.

SLR-like Cameras—"Bridge Cameras"

The "SLR-like" or "advanced" digicams (*e.g.* the Olympus SP series, Nikon Coolpix models such as the 5700, 8400, 8700 and 8800 to name a few; the Sony Cyber-shot DSC V, DSC H, DSC F and DSC R series, the Panasonic FZ series, the Canon PowerShot A, G, some S and Pro models, Minolta DiMAGE 7/7i/7hi, A1, A2, A200, and some Fujifilm

FinePix models such as the S7000 and S9000) offer a non-optical electronic through-the-lens (TTL) view through the focusing lens, via the eye-level electronic viewfinder (EVF) as well as the rear LCD screen.

The difference in views compared to a DSLR is that the EVF shows a digitally-created TTL image, whereas the viewfinder in a DSLR shows an actual optical TTL image via the reflex viewing system. An EVF image has lag-time (i.e., it reacts more slowly to view changes and has a lower resolution than an optical viewfinder) but achieves parallax-free viewing using less bulk and mechanical complexity than a DSLR with its reflex viewing system.

One limitation of a bridge digital camera is its fixed, non-interchangeable lens. Some of these lenses are limited to approximately a 7:1 zoom ratio range, as is the range of the Fujifilm FinePix S9100; to about a 12:1 focal-length range with the Canon PowerShot S5-IS. An advantage, however, is that the fixed zoom lens eliminates the risk of dust accumulating on the imaging sensor from the changing of an interchangeable lens.

Several of the high-end bridge cameras such as the current Canon PowerShot S5-IS have a movable LCD screen (other examples: the now-discontinued Canon PowerShot Pro1 and Konica Minolta A200), which can be used instead of the regular viewfinder to provide waist-level or low-angle viewing, overhead viewing, and viewing for a self-timer group shot or portrait. The LCD screen also enables the photographer to review the stored images in a convenient way.

Digicams (Compact 'Point-and-Shoot' Digital Cameras)

Digicams, some commonly referred to as 'point-and-shoot' cameras because of their ease of use, can usually be operated at arm's length using only the LCD display screen at the rear of the camera. Some models also have simple optical viewfinders like traditional compact 35 mm film cameras. Like the SLR-like bridge cameras, digicams lack the ability to accept interchangeable lenses, with the exception of certain digital rangefinder cameras such as the Leica M8 and the Epson RD-1, which use the Leica M-mount lens system.

Most digicams are manufactured with a zoom lens that covers the most commonly used fields of view, with "super-zoom" models becoming more popular. Digicam lenses can be adapted to telephoto or wide-angle as the above-mentioned 'bridge-cameras'.

Digicams were once significantly slower in image capture (time measured from pressing the shutter release to the writing of the digital image to the storage medium) than DSLR cameras, but this situation is changing with the introduction of faster capture memory cards and faster in-camera processing chips. Currently, however, these cameras present a significant disadvantage for action, wildlife, sports and other photography requiring a high burst rate (frames per second).

Non-SLR Interchangeable Lens Digital Cameras

The ability to switch lenses is shared by certain rangefinder cameras, both film and digital in operation. Two such digital rangefinders are the Epson R-D1 (possibly discontinued) and the Leica M8; both use sensors smaller than the full format of 35 mm rangefinder cameras.

TWIN-LENS REFLEX CAMERA

A twin-lens reflex camera (TLR) is a type of camera with two objective lenses of the same focal length. One of the lenses is the photographic objective (the lens that takes the picture), while the other is used for the waist-level viewfinder system. In addition to the objective, the viewfinder consists of a 45-degree mirror (the reason for the word *reflex* in the name), a matte focusing screen at the top of the camera, and a pop-up hood surrounding it. The two objectives are connected, so that the focus shown on the focusing screen will be exactly the same as on the film. However, many inexpensive TLRs are fixed-focus models.

Higher-end TLRs may have a pop-up magnifying glass to assist the user in focusing the camera. In addition, many have a "sports finder" consisting of a square hole punched in the back of the pop-up hood, and a knock-out in the front. Photographers can sight through these instead of using the matte screen. This is especially useful in tracking moving subjects such as animals or race cars, since the image on the matte screen is reversed left-to-right.

Mamiya's C-Series, introduced in the 60s, the C-3, C-2, C-33, C-22 and the Mamiya C330 and Mamiya C220 are the only conventional TLR cameras to feature truly interchangeable lenses.

Rollei Rolleiflex model TLRs have an additional feature for the "sports finder" that allows precise focusing. When the hinged front hood knock-out is moved to the sports finder position a secondary mirror swings down over the view screen to reflect the image to a secondary magnifier on the back of the hood, just below the direct view cutout. This permits precise focusing while using the sports finder feature. The magnified central image is reversed both top to bottom and left to right.

TLRs are different from single-lens reflex cameras (SLR) in several respects. First, unlike virtually all SLRs, TLRs provide a continuous image on the finder screen. The view does not black out during exposure. Additionally, models with leaf shutters rather than focal-plane shutters can synchronize with flash at higher speeds than can SLRs. However, because the photographer views through one lens but takes the photograph through another, parallax error makes the photograph different from the view on the screen. This difference is negligible when the subject is far away, but is critical for nearby subjects. For accuracy in tabletop photography, in which the subject might be within a foot (30 cm) of the camera, devices are available that move the camera upwards so that the taking lens goes to the exact position that the viewing lens occupied.

A primary advantage of the TLR is its simplicity as compared to the more common single-lens reflex cameras. The SLR must employ some method of blocking light from reaching the film during focusing, either with a focal plane shutter (most common) or with the reflex mirror itself. Both methods add significant noise to the camera's operation. Most TLRs use a leaf shutter in the lens. The only mechanical noise during exposure is from the shutter leaves opening and closing.

The TLR is especially useful for action portrait photography (*e.g.*, martial arts portraits) as the action of the shutter can be very responsive to the photographer compared to the time required to move the mirror of an SLR. Owing availability of medium format cameras and the ease of image composition it is also preferred by many portrait studios for static poses.

The typical TLR is medium format, using 120 roll film with square 6 × 6 cm images. Presently, the Chinese Seagull Camera and the German Rollei are in production, but in the past, many manufacturers made them. Models with the Mamiya, Minolta and Yashica brands are common on the used-camera market, and many other companies made TLRs that are now classics. The Mamiya C series TLRs had interchangeable lenses, allowing focal lengths from 55 mm (wide angle) to 250 mm (telephoto) to be used.

There were smaller TLR models, using 127 roll film with square 4×4 cm images, most famous the "Baby" Rolleiflex and the Yashica 44. The TLR style was also popular in the 1950s for inexpensive fixed focus cameras such as the Kodak Duaflex and Argus 75.

The smallest TLR camera is the Swiss made Tessina, using performated 35 mm film forming images of 14×21 mm.

PHOTOGRAPHIC FILM

Photographic film is a sheet of plastic (polyester, nitrocellulose or cellulose acetate) coated with an emulsion containing light-sensitive silver halide salts (bonded by gelatin) with variable crystal sizes that determine the sensitivity, contrast and resolution of the film. When the emulsion is sufficiently exposed to light (or other forms of electromagnetic radiation such as X-rays), it forms a latent (invisible) image. Chemical processes can then be applied to the film to create a visible image, in a process called film developing.

In black-and-white photographic film there is usually one layer of silver salts. When the exposed grains are developed, the silver salts are converted to metallic silver, which block light and appear as the black part of the film *negative*.

Colour film uses at least three layers. Dyes, which adsorb to the surface of the silver salts, make the crystals sensitive to different colours. Typically the blue-sensitive layer is on top, followed by the green and red layers. During development, the exposed silver salts are converted to metallic silver, just as with black and white film. But in a colour film, the by-products of the development reaction simultaneously combine with chemicals known as colour couplers that are included either in the film itself or in the developer solution to form coloured dyes. Because the by-products are created in direct proportion to the amount of exposure and development, the dye clouds formed are also in proportion to the exposure and development. Following development, the silver is converted back to silver salts in the *bleach step*. It is removed from the film in the *fix step*. This leaves behind only the formed colour dyes, which combine to make up the colored visible image.

Newer colour films, like Kodacolour II, have as many as 12 emulsion layers, with upwards of 20 different chemicals in each layer.

Because photographic film is widespread in the production of motion pictures, or movies, these are also known as *films*.

Film Basics

There are two primary types of photographic film:

- *Print film,* when developed, turns into a negative with the colours (or black and white values, in black and white film) inverted. This type of film must be "printed"—either projected through a lens or placed in contact—to photographic paper in order to be viewed as intended. Print films are available in both black-and-white and colour.
- *Color reversal film* after development is called a transparency and can be viewed directly using a loupe or projector. Reversal film mounted with plastic or cardboard for projection is often called a slide. It is also often marketed as "slide" film. This type of film is often used to produce digital scans or colour separations for mass-market printing. Photographic prints can be produced from reversal film, but the process is expensive and not as simple as that for print film. Black and white reversal film exists, but is uncommon—one of the reasons reversal films are popular among professional photographers is the fact that they are generally superior to print films with regards to colour reproduction. (Conventional black and white negative stock can be reversal-processed, to give "black and white slides", and kits are available to enable this to be done by home-processors. As indicated by Grant Haist's published book *Modern Photographic Processing,* B&W transparencies can be produced from most all B&W films.)

In order to produce a usable image, the film needs to be exposed properly. The amount of exposure variation that a given film can tolerate while still producing an acceptable level of quality is called its exposure latitude. Colour print film generally has greater exposure latitude than other types of film. Additionally, because print film must be printed to be viewed, after-the-fact corrections for imperfect exposure are possible during the printing process.

The concentration of dyes or silver salts remaining on the film after development is referred to as optical density, or simply density; the optical density is proportional to the logarithm of the optical transmission coefficient of the developed film. A dark image on the negative is of higher density than a more transparent image.

Most films are affected by the physics of silver grain activation (which sets a minimum amount of light required to expose a single grain) and by the statistics of random grain activation by photons. The film requires a minimum amount of light before it begins to expose, and then responds by progressive darkening over a wide dynamic range of exposure until all of the grains are exposed and the film achieves (after development) its maximum optical density.

Over the active dynamic range of most films, the density of the developed film is proportional to the logarithm of the total amount of light to which the film was exposed, so the transmission coefficient of the developed film is proportional to a power of the reciprocal of the brightness of the original exposure. This is due to the statistics of grain activation: as the film becomes progressively more exposed, each incident photon is less likely to impact a still-unexposed grain, yielding the logarithmic behaviour. A simple, idealized statistical model yields the equation density = 1—(1-k) ^ light, where "light" is proportional to the number of photons hitting a unit area of film, "k" is the probability of a single photon striking a grain (based on the size of the grains and how closely spaced they are), and density is the proportion of grains that where hit by at least one photon.

If parts of the image are exposed heavily enough to approach the maximum density possible for a print film, then they will begin losing the ability to show tonal variations in the final print. Usually those areas will be deemed to be overexposed and will appear as featureless white on the print. Some subject matter is tolerant of very heavy exposure; brilliant light sources like a bright lightbulb, or the sun, included in the image generally appear best as a featureless white on the print.

Likewise, if part of an image receives less than the beginning threshold level of exposure, which depends upon the film's sensitivity to light—or speed—the film there will have no appreciable image density, and will appear on the print as a featureless black. Some photographers use their knowledge of these limits to determine the optimum exposure for a photograph; for one example, see the Zone system. Most automatic cameras instead try to achieve a particular average density.

Film Speed

Film speed describes a film's threshold sensitivity to light. The international standard for rating film speed is the ISO scale which combines both the ASA speed and the DIN speed in the format ASA/DIN. Using ISO convention film with an ASA speed of 400 would be labeled 400/27°. A fourth naming standard is GOST, developed by the Russian standards authority. See the film speed article for a table of conversions between ASA, DIN, and GOST film speeds.

Common film speeds include ISO 25, 50, 64, 100, 160, 200, 400, 800, 1600 and 3200. Consumer print films are usually in the ISO 100 to ISO 800 range. Some films, like Kodak's Technical Pan, are not ISO rated and therefore careful examination of the film's properties must be made by the photographer before exposure and development. ISO 25 film is very "slow", as it requires much more exposure to produce a usable image than "fast" ISO 800 film. Films of ISO 800 and greater are thus better suited to low-light situations and action shots (where the short exposure time limits the total light received). The benefit of slower films is that it usually has finer grain and better color rendition than fast film. Professional photography with static subjects such as portraits or landscapes usually seek these qualities, and therefore require a tripod to stabilize the camera for a longer exposure. Photographing subjects such as rapidly moving sports or in low-light conditions, a professional will choose a faster film. Grain size refers to the size of the silver crystals in the emulsion. The smaller the crystals, the finer the detail in the photo and the slower the film.

A film with a particular ISO rating can be pushed to behave like a film with a higher ISO. In order to do this, the film must be developed for a longer amount of time or at a higher temperature than usual. This procedure is usually only performed by photographers who do their own development or professional-level photofinishers. More rarely, a film can be pulled to behave like a "slower" film.

History of Film

Hurter and Driffield began pioneering work on the light sensitivity of film in 1876 onwards. Their work enabled the first quantitative measure of film speed to be devised.

Early photography in the form of daguerreotypes did not use film at all. Eastman Kodak developed the first flexible photographic film in 1885. This original "film" was coated on paper. The first transparent plastic film was produced in 1889. Before this, glass photographic plates were used, which were far more expensive and cumbersome, albeit also of better quality. The first photographic film was made from highly flammable nitrocellulose with camphor as a plasticizer (celluloid). Beginning in the 1920s, nitrate film was replaced with cellulose acetate or "safety film". This changeover was not completed until 1933 for X-ray films (where its flammability hazard was most acute) and for motion picture film until 1951.

Spectral Sensitivity

The first films were sensitive to blue light only. Orthochromatic film sensitive to the spectral range from green to blue was introduced in 1879 and was dominant until the mod-1920s, when panchromatic film sensitive to the entire visual spectrum, became standard. All of these films were used to produce black and white images, regardless of spectral sensitivity.

Experiments with colour photography were first made in 1861, but generally usable emulsions only became available in the 1930s. After the Second World War much progress was made, and colour became used for the overwhelming majority of photographs.

Effect on Lens and Equipment Design

Photographic lenses and equipment are designed around the film to be used. The earliest lenses needed to focus blue light only. The introduction of orthochromatic film required the spectrum from green to blue to be brought to the same focus. A red window could be used to view frame numbers of rollfilm; any red light which leaked beyond the film backing would not fog the film; and red lighting could be used in darkrooms. With the introduction of panchromatic film the whole visual spectrum needed to be brought to the same focus. In all cases a colour cast in the lens glass or faint coloured reflections in the image were of no consequence as they would merely change the contrast a little. This was no longer acceptable with the introduction of colour film. More highly corrected lenses for newer emulsions could be used with older emulsion types, but the converse was not true.

The filters used were different for the different film types. The progression of lens design for later emulsions is of practical importance when considering the use of old lenses, still often used on large-format equipment; a lens designed for orthochromatic film may have visible defects with a colour emulsion; a lens for panchromatic film will be better but not as good as later designs.

While color processing is more complex and temperature-sensitive than for monochromatic film, the great popularity of colour and almost disappearance of monochrome prompted the design of monochromatic film which is processed in exactly the same way as a standard colour film.

Special Films

Instant photography, as popularised by Polaroid, uses a special type of camera and film that automates and integrates development, without the need of further equipment or chemicals. This process is carried out immediately after exposure, as opposed to regular film, which is developed afterwards and requires additional chemicals.

Films can be made to record non-visible ultraviolet (UV) and infrared (IR) radiation. These films generally require special equipment; for example, most photographic lenses are made of glass and will therefore filter out most ultraviolet light. Instead, expensive lenses made of quartz must be used. Infrared films may be shot in standard cameras using an infrared band-or long-pass filter, although the infrared focal point must be compensated for.

Exposure and focusing are difficult when using UV or IR film with a camera and lens designed for visible light. The ISO standard for film speed only applies to visible light, so visual-spectrum light meters are nearly useless. Film manufacturers can supply suggested equivalent film speeds under different conditions, and recommend heavy bracketing. e.g *with a certain filter, assume ISO 25 under daylight and ISO 64 under tungsten lighting*. This allows a light meter to be used to estimate an exposure. The focal point for IR is slightly father away from the camera than visible light, and UV slightly closer; this must be compensated for when focusing. Apochromatic lenses are sometimes recommended due to their improved focusing across the spectrum.

Film optimized for sensing X-ray radiation is commonly used for medical imaging by placing the subject between the film and a source of X-rays, without a lens, as if a translucent object were imaged by being placed between a light source and standard film. Film optimized for sensing X-rays and for gamma rays is sometimes used for radiation dosimetry and personal monitoring.

Film has a number of disadvantages as a scientific detector: it is difficult to calibrate for photometry, it is not re-usable, it requires careful handling (including temperature and humidity control) for best calibration, and the film must physically be returned to the laboratory and processed. Against this, photographic film can be made with a higher spatial resolution than any other type of imaging detector, and, because of its logarithmic response to light, has a wider dynamic range than most digital detectors. For example, Agfa 10E56 holographic film has a resolution of over 4,000 lines/mm—equivalent to a pixel size of 0.125 micrometres—and an active dynamic range of over five orders of magnitude in brightness, compared to typical scientific CCDs that might have pixels of about 10 micrometres and a dynamic range of 3-4 orders of magnitude.

Special films are used for the long exposures required by astrophotography.

Common Sizes of Film

- 135 (popularly known as "35 mm")
- APS (Advanced Photo System)
- 110
- 126
- 127
- 120/220 (for use in medium format photography)

- Sheet film (for use in large format photography)
- Disc film Obsolete format used in disc system cameras
- *Motion picture films*: 8 mm, 16 mm, 35 mm and 70 mm.

Companies that Manufacture Photographic Film

- Agfa-Gevaert*
- Bergger (European company composed of former Guilleminot employees.)
- Dai Nippon Printing
- Efke
- Foma
- Forte
- Ferrania
- Fujifilm
- Ilford
- Imation (Spin-off company of 3M has since sold the film business to Ferrania)
- Kodak
- Konica Minolta**
- Lucky
- Maco
- ORWO
- Perutz
- Polaroid
- ProClick
- Solaris (Ferrania)
- Svema
- Tasma
- Tura

Film manufacturers commonly make film that is branded by other companies. Modern films have bar codes on the edge of the film which can be read by a bar code reader. This is because film is sometimes processed differently according to specifications of the film, determined by its manufacturer; the bar code is entered into the computer printer before the film is printed.

To establish the OEM, read the bar code printed on the cassette. Divide the long number by 16 and record the number before the decimal, then multiply the number after the decimal by 16, this could give you a result such as 18 and 2.

The first number is known as the PRODUCT (film manufacturer) and the second number as the MULTIPLIER (speed of the film ISO). In the previous example, 18 identifies 3M as the manufacturer and 2 means it is 200 ISO:

- 3M = 18
- Agfa = 17 or 49
- Kodak = 80, 81, 82 or 88.

Note: *bankruptcy, **discontinued.

Notable Films

- Kodak Kodachrome is one of the oldest slide films still being produced and is known for its long archive stability.
- Fuji Velvia, also a slide film, is known for its high contrast and hyper-saturated colors. It is popular with landscape and nature photographers.
- Both *Kodak T-max p3200* and *Ilford Delta 3200* are B&W films with very wide exposure latitude. They are rated at roughly ISO 1000, but can be pushed to ISO 3200 or higher. Rated speeds of as high as ISO 25,000 have been obtained.
- Kodak Technical Pan, which has now been discontinued, is a widely acclaimed slow black and white film. With a speed of ISO 25, it gave clear, incredibly fine-grained results. It has now become somewhat of a commodity item among photographers as it is very limited, and very little if any stock remains at photographic suppliers.

CAMCORDER

A camcorder is a portable consumer electronics device for recording video and audio using a built-in recorder unit. The camcorder contains both a video camera and a video *recorder* in one unit, hence its compound name. This compares to previous technology where an acquisition and recording devices would be separate.

The earliest camcorders, developed by companies such as JVC, Sony, Canon, and Kodak, used analog videotape. Since the 1990s recording onto digital tape has become the norm. Starting from early 2000s tape as storage media is being gradually replaced with tape-free solutions like optical disks, hard disk drives and solid-state memory.

All tape-based camcorders have removable media in form of video cassettes. Solid-state camcorders can have either removable media in form of memory cards, or built-in memory, or both. HDD-based camcorders usually have non-removable media in form of a hard disk drive (HDD).

Camcorders that do not use magnetic tape are often called tapeless camcorders. Camcorders that use two different types of media, like built-in HDD and memory card, are often called hybrid camcorders. Some prosumer level tape and solid state camcorders can use compatible secondary media such as a hard drive or an optical drive that the camera's software will control, such as in the case of the Canon and Sony prosumer unit line.

History

Video cameras were originally designed for broadcasting television images. Cameras found in television broadcast centres were extremely large, mounted on special trolleys, and wired to remote recorders located in separate rooms. As technology advanced, miniaturization eventually enabled the construction of portable video-cameras and portable video-recorders.

Prior to the introduction of the camcorder, portable video-recording required two separate devices: a video-camera and a VCR. Specialized models were introduced by both JVC (VHS) and Sony (Umatic and Betamax) to be used for mobile work. The portable VCR consisted of the cassette player/recorder unit, and a television tuner unit. The cassette unit could be detached and carried with the user for video recording. While the camera itself could be quite compact, the fact that a separate VCR had to be carried generally made on-location shooting a two-man job, however the advent of these portable VCRs helped to eliminate the phrase "film at eleven". Rather than wait for the lengthy process of film developing, portable VCRs and video cameras allowed video to be shown during the 6 o'clock news.

In 1982, two events happened that eventually led to the home camcorder boom: JVC introduced the VHS-C format, and Sony released the first professional camcorder named Betacam. VHS-C was essentially VHS with a reduced-size cassette that had been designed for portable VCRs. Sony's Betacam was a standard developed for professional camcorders, which used component video to provide a superior picture. At first, cameramen did not welcome Betacam, because before it, carrying and operating the VCR unit was the work of a video engineer; after Betacam they came to be required to operate both video camera and VCR. However the cable between cameramen and video engineers was eliminated, the freedom of cameramen improved dramatically and Betacam quickly became the standard for both news-gathering and in-studio video editing.

In 1983, Sony released the Betamax-based Betamovie, the first consumer camcorder. A novel technique was used to reduce the size of the spinning video head drum, which was then used for many subsequent camcorders. The unit was bulky by today's standards, and since it could not be held in one hand, was typically used resting on a shoulder. Some later camcorders were even larger, because the Betamovie models had only optical viewfinders and no playback or rewind capability. Most camcorders were and still are designed for right-handed operation, though a few possessed ambidextrous ergonomics.

Within a short time JVC released its own camcorder using its pre-existing VHS-C format. The VHS-C cassette held enough tape to record 40 or 120 minutes of VHS video, while a mechanical adapter enabled playback of VHS-C videocassettes in home VCRs. This first model can be seen in the movie *Back to the Future*. After seeing the popularity of the small VHS-C "palmcorders", Sony redesigned its Betamax system to create the Video8 standard. Video8 eliminated the problem of short running time, by using an all-new metal composition video cassette. 8 mm video used a tape whose width is 33 per cent less than VHS/Betamax tape (~12.7 mm), allowing even further miniaturization in the recorder's tape-transport assembly and cassette media.

Both VHS-C and 8 mm video represented a trade-off for the consumer. Although the Video8 and Hi8 camcorders produced quality equal to VHS-C and Super VHS-C camcorders (250/420 lines horizontal), the standard 8 mm cassette had the advantage with up to two hours length (four hours in slow mode). On the down side, since the 8 mm format was incompatible with VHS, 8 mm recordings could not be played in consumers' VHS VCRs. Equally important entry-level VHS-C camcorders were priced less than 8 mm units, and thus neither "won" the war. It became a stalemate. (*Side note*: In 1986 companies like Panasonic began releasing full-sized VHS/S-VHS camcorders, which offered up to 3 or 9 hours record time, and thus found a niche with videophiles, industrial videographers, and college TV studios.)

In the mid-1990s, the camcorder reached the digital era with the introduction of DV and miniDV. Its cassette media was even smaller than 8 mm media, allowing another size reduction of the tape transport assembly. The digital nature of miniDV also improved audio and video quality over the best of the analog consumer camcorders (SVHS-C, Hi8), although some users still prefer the analog nature of Hi8 and Super VHS-C, since neither of these produce the "background blur" or "mosquito noise" of Digital compression. Variations on the DV camcorder include the Digital8 camcorder and the MPEG2-based DVD camcorder.

The evolution of the camcorder has seen the growth of the camcorder market as price reductions and size reductions make the technology more accessible to a wider audience. When camcorders were first introduced, they were bulky shoulder-operated luggables that cost over $ 1,500 US dollars. As of 2008, an entry-level camcorder fits in the palm of a person's hand and is sold at a retail price of approximately 100 US dollars.

Overview

Major Components

Camcorders contain 3 major components: lens, imager, and recorder. The lens gathers and focuses light on the imager. The imager (usually a CCD or CMOS sensor on modern camcorders; earlier examples often used vidicon tubes) converts incident light into an electrical (video) signal. Finally, the recorder encodes the video signal into a storable form. More commonly, the optics and imager are referred to as the camera section.

The lens is the first component in the camera-section's "light-path". The camcorder's optics generally have one or more of the following adjustments: aperture (to control the amount of light), zoom (to control the field-of-view), and shutter speed (to capture continuous motion.) In consumer units, these adjustments are automatically controlled by the camcorder's electronics, generally to maintain constant *exposure* onto the imager. Professional units offer direct user control of all major optical functions (aperture, shutter-speed, focus, etc.).

The imager section is the eye of the camcorder, housing a photosensitive device(s). The imager converts light into an electronic video-signal through an elaborate electronic process. The camera lens projects an image onto the imager surface, exposing the photosensitive array to light. The light exposure is converted into electrical charge. At the end of the timed exposure, the imager converts the accumulated charge into a continuous analog voltage at the imager's output terminals. After scan-out is complete, the photosites are reset to start the exposure-process for the next video frame. With the first (digital) camcorders, an analog-to-digital (ADC) converter digitized the imager (analog) waveform output into a discrete digital-video signal. The images in these cameras was a CCD which was analogue by nature. Modern cameras will generally have a CMOS chip in place of a CCD as a CMOS is completely digital in nature and there is no analogue voltage signal to digitize because the light is sampled directly by each pixel and converted to a binary digital signal per each pixel. CCD chips will generally see better in low light conditions because of the CCD's nature of capturing more light in the infrared range, but will severly lack in the human visibility spectrum, thus sacrificing color, on the other hand CMOS imagers do not have great low light capability but will capture the visible spectrum better and thus displaying color properly.

The third section, the recorder, is responsible for writing the video-signal onto a recording medium (such as magnetic videotape.) The record function involves many signal-processing steps, and historically, the recording-process introduced some distortion and noise into the stored video, such that playback of the stored-signal may not retain the same characteristics/detail as the live video feed.

All but the most primitive camcorders imaginable also need to have a recorder-controlling section which allows the user to control the camcorder, switch the recorder into playback mode for reviewing the recorded footage and an image control section which controls exposure, focus and white-balance.

The image recorded need not be limited to what appeared in the viewfinder. For documentation of events, such as used by police, the field of view overlays such things as the time and date of the recording along the top and bottom of the image. Such things as the police car or constable to which the recorder has been allotted may also appear; also the speed of the car at the time of recording. Compass direction at time of recording and geographical coordinates may also be possible. These are not kept to world-standard fields; "month/day/year" may be seen, as well as "day/month/year", besides the ISO standard "year-month-day". And the Danish police have the speed of the police car in the units "Km/t" *sic* (*time* being Danish for "hour").

Consumer Camcorders

Analog vs. Digital

Camcorders are often classified by their storage device: VHS, Betamax, Video8 are examples of older, videotape-based camcorders which record video in analog form. Newer camcorders include Digital8, miniDV, DVD, Hard drive and solid-state (flash) semiconductor memory, which all record video in digital form. (Please see the digital video page for details.) In older digital camcorders, the imager-chip, the CCD was considered an analog component, so the *digital* namesake is in reference to the camcorder's processing and recording of the video. Many next generation camcorders use a CMOS imager, which register photons as binary data as soon as the photons hit the imager and thus tightly marrying parts 2 and 3.

It should be noted that the take up of digital video storage in camcorders was an enormous milestone. MiniDV storage allows full resolution video (720×576 for PAL, 720×480 for NTSC), unlike previous analogue video standards. Digital video doesn't experience colour bleeding, jitter, or fade, although some users still prefer the analog nature of Hi8 and Super VHS-C, since neither of these produce the "background blur" or "mosquito noise" of Digital compression. In many cases, a high-quality analog recording shows more detail (such as rough textures on a wall) than a compressed digital recording (which would show the same wall as flat and featureless). Although, the low resolution of analogue camcorders may negate any such benefits.

The highest-quality digital formats, such as MiniDV and Digital Betacam, have the advantage over analog of suffering little generation loss in recording, dubbing, and editing (MPEG-2 and MPEG-4 do suffer from generation loss in the editing process only). Whereas noise and bandwidth issues relating to cables, amplifiers, and mixers can greatly affect analog recordings, such problems are minimal in digital formats using digital connections (generally IEEE 1394, SDI/SDTI, or HDMI).

Although both analog and digital can suffer from archival problems, digital is more prone to complete loss. Theoretically digital information can be stored indefinitely with zero deterioration on a digital storage device (such as a hard drive), however since some digital formats (like miniDV) often squeeze tracks only ~10 micrometers apart (versus ~500 um for VHS), a digital recording is more vulnerable to wrinkles or stretches in the tape that could permanently erase several scenes worth of digital data, but the additions tracking and error correction code on the tape will generally compensate for most defects. On analog media similar damage barely registers as "noise" in the video, still leaving a deteriorated but watchable video. The only limitation is that this video has to be played on a completely analogue viewing system, otherwise the tape will not display any video due to the damage and sync problems. Even digital recordings on DVD are known to suffer from DVD rot that permanently erase huge chunks of data. Thus the one advantage analog seems to have in this respect is that an analog recording may be "usable" even after the media it is stored on has suffered severe deterioration whereas it has been noticed that even slight media degradation in digital recordings may cause them to suffer from an "all or nothing" failure, *i.e.* the digital recording will end up being totally un-playable without very expensive restoration work.

Modern Recording Media

Some recent camcorders record video on flash memory devices, Microdrives, small hard disks, and size-reduced DVD-RAM or DVD-Rs using MPEG-1, MPEG-2 or MPEG-4 formats. However because these codecs use inter-frame compression, frame-specific-editing requires frame regeneration, which incurs additional processing and can cause loss of picture information. (In professional usage, it is common to use a codec that will store every frame inidividually. This provides easier and faster frame-specific editing of scenes.)

Most other digital consumer camcorders record in DV or HDV format on tape and transfer content over FireWire (some also use USB 2.0) to a computer, where the huge files (for DV, 1GB for 4 to 4.6 minutes in PAL/NTSC resolutions) can be edited, converted, and (with many camcorders) also recorded back to tape. The transfer is done in real time, so the complete transfer of a 60 minute tape needs one hour to transfer and about 13GB disk space for the raw footage only—excluding any space needed for render files, and other media. Time spent in post-production (editing) to select and cut the best shots varies from instantaneous "magic" movies to hours of tedious selection, arrangement and rendering.

Consumer Market

As the mainstream consumer market favors ease of use, portability, and price, consumer camcorders emphasize these features more than raw technical performance. For example, good low-light capabilities require large capturing chips, which affects price and size. Thus, consumer camcorders are often unable to shoot useful footage in dim light (though some units, particularly single-chip units by Sony, offer night vision capability) which utilizes the infrared sensitivity of the CCD imager, though this sacrifices color in well lit recording. Manual controls need space, either in menus or as buttons and make the use more complicated, which goes against the requirement of ease of use. Consumer units offer a plethora of I/O options (IEEE 1394/Firewire, USB 2.0, Composite and S-Video), but lack many manual settings, often excluding video exposure, gain control, or sound level management. For the beginner, entry-level camcorders offer basic recording and playback capability.

For the sophisticated hobbyist, high-end units offer improved optical and video performance through multi-CCD or multi-CMOS components and name-brand optics, manual control of camera exposure, removable optics, and more, but even consumer camcorders which are sold for $1000 such as the Panasonic GS250 are not well-suited for recording in dim light. When dimly-lit areas are brightened in-camera or in post-production, considerable noise distracts the viewer. Commercial special noise reduction algorithms are available to fix this as those available from Neat Image\Neat Video.

Before the 21st century, consumer video editing was a difficult task requiring a minimum of two recorders. Now, however, a contemporary Personal Computer of even modest power can perform digital video editing with editing software. Many consumer camcorders bundle a *light* (feature-limited) version of such software, as do some computers, and more advanced software is widely available at a variety of price points.

As of 2007, analog camcorders are still available but not widely marketed anymore; those that are still available are often less than US $250, but require special capture hardware for non-linear editing which may run into the thousands of dollars due to the plethora of sync and signal problems that may not be resolved with cheap capture equipement. In terms of sales, miniDV camcorders (and to a much lesser extent, Digital8) dominate most first world markets. Camcorders which record directly on DVD media are also on the rise, primarily among users with no plans to edit their footage. Nonetheless, software for editing video files created by DVD camcorders is available, including Womble DVD and VideoRedo. A user may also choose to recode the transport files of a dvd to that of an MPEG2 file which is supported by many other editing suites.

Hard disk based camcorders are appearing as well; JVC and Sony are the primary manufacturers of these units. Increased storage capacity over other types of media is the main advantage with these models; however, with this follows a slightly reduced image quality and loss of flexibility when compared to other formats such as MiniDV, making the ease of transferring the footage to a PC for quick editing the main attraction of Hard disk camcorders. Another downside Hard Drive based camcorders is the recording device itself which can be damaged irreparably by power failure or physical shock to the unit.

Other Devices with Video-Capture Capability

Video-capture capability is now available in selected models of cellphones, digicams, and other portable consumer electronic devices such as media players. Typically only digital cameras offer videos that are of useful quality for anything other than a novelty. The marketing approach is to claim 320 × 240 video is "VHS quality," and 640 × 480 video is "DVD quality." A few cameras can offer 800 × 600 resolution, and a recent development is High Definition (720p) in cameras such as the Sanyo Xacti HD1.

All are limited somewhat by having to serve as both cameras and camcorders. Compared to a dedicated camcorder they have poor low light performance, limited options, and many do not offer zoom during filming. (This is because the noise from the zooming motor is heard on the clip, only a few digicams have a manual zoom). Many either have fixed focus lenses, or autofocus lenses that are sluggish and noisy compared to a camcorder.

The quality varies widely depending on the compression format used and the type of device. Frame rates can range from 30 frame/s down to 10 frame/s, or can be variable, slowing down in dark settings. The length of clips can also vary from "unlimited" (up to the capacity of the storage media) down to as little as 30 seconds.

Low end MPEG-4 camcorders can often record unlimited length video clips at 320 × 240, but the quality is far below even a VHS-C camcorder. In addition, MPEG-4 is currently not widely supported in many video editing programmes. Cameras recording in Quicktime format produce videos of acceptable quality, but the compression appears as a grain or static in the video. Some cameras can offer exceptionally good video quality using the MJPEG codec, but because it is a lossless codec, the files are so large that the recording time at high quality with a 1GB card is up to ten minutes.

The use of digicams for recording video clips is limited mainly to circumstances where quality is not an issue. This is gradually being offset by the greater sophistication of the cameras, the increasing storage capacity of flash cards and microdrives, and the desire of consumers to carry only a single device.

Uses

Media

Camcorders have found use in nearly all corners of electronic media, from electronic news organizations to TV/current-affairs productions. In locations away from a distribution infrastructure, camcorders are invaluable for initial video acquisition. Subsequently, the video is transmitted electronically to a studio/production center for broadcast. Scheduled events such as official press conferences, where a video infrastructure is readily available or can be feasibly deployed in advance, are still covered by studio-type video cameras (tethered to "production trucks").

Home Video

For casual use, camcorders often cover weddings, birthdays, graduation ceremonies, and other personal events. The rise of the consumer camcorder in the mid to late '80s led to the creation of shows such as the long-running America's Funniest Home Videos, where people could showcase homemade video footage.

Politics

Political protestors who have capitalized on the value of media coverage use camcorders to film things they believe to be unjust. Animal rights protesters who break into factory farms and animal testing labs use camcorders to film the conditions the animals are living in. Anti-hunting protesters film fox hunts. Tax protesters provide live coverage of anti-tax demonstrations and protests. Anti-globalization protesters film the police to deter police brutality. If the police do use violence there will be evidence on video. Activist videos often appear on Indymedia.

The police use camcorders to film riots, protests and the crowds at sporting events. The film can be used to spot and pick out troublemakers, who can then be prosecuted in court.

Entertainment and Movies

Camcorders are often used in the production of low-budget TV shows where the production crew does not have access to more expensive equipment. There are even examples of movies shot entirely on consumer camcorder equipment (see *Blair Witch Project* and *28 Days Later*). In addition, many academic filmmaking programmes have switched from 16 mm film to digital video, due to the vastly reduced expense and ease of editing of the digital medium as well as the increasing scarcity of film stock and equipment. Some camcorder manufacturers cater to this market, particularly Canon and Panasonic, who both support "24p" (24 frame/s, progressive scan; same frame rate as standard cinema film) video in some of their high-end models for easy film conversion.

Even high-budget cinema is done using camcorders in some cases; George Lucas used Sony CineAlta camcorders in two of his three Star Wars prequel movies. This process is referred to as digital cinematography.

Formats

The following list covers consumer equipment only. (For other formats see Videotape)

Analog

Lo-Band: Approximately 3 megahertz bandwidth (250 lines EIA resolution or ~333x480 edge-to-edge)

- *BCE* (1954): First tape storage for video, manufactured by Bing Crosby Entertainment from Ampex equipment.
- *BCE Coloer* (1955): First colour tape storage for video, manufactured by Bing Crosby Entertainment from Ampex equipment.
- *Simplex* (1955): Developed commercially by RCA and used to record several live broadcasts by NBC.
- *Quadruplex* (1955): Developed formally by Ampex, and this became the recording standard for the next 20 years.
- *Vera* (1955): An experimental recording standard developed by the BBC, but was never used or sold commerically.
- *Umatic* (1971): The initial tape used by Sony to record video.
- *Umatics* (1974): A small sized version of Umatic used for portable recorders.
- *Betamax* (1975): Only used on very old Sony and Sanyo camcorders and portables; obsolete by the mid/late-80s in the consumer market.

- *Type B* (1976): Co-developed by Sony and Ampex and this became the broadcast standard in europe for most of the 1980s.
- *Type C* (1976): Co-developed by Sony and Ampex.
- *VHS* (1976): Compatible with VHS standard VCRs, though VHS camcorders are no longer made. Obsolete.
- *VHS-C* (1982): Originally designed for portable VCRs, this standard was later adapted for use in compact consumer camcorders; identical in quality to VHS; plays in standard home VCRs. Still available in the low-end consumer market (JVC model GR-AXM18 is VHS-C; see page 19 of the owner's manual). Relatively short running time compared to other formats.
- *Betacam* (1982): Introduced by Sony as a 1\2 inch tape for professional video recorders.
- *MUSE* (1983): Commercial system for analogue 1080i broadcasts developed
- *Video8* (1985): Small-format tape developed by Sony to combat VHS-C's compact palm-sized design; equivalent to VHS or Betamax in picture quality, but not compatible. High quality audio as standard. Obsolete.
- *Hi-Vision* (1985): MUSE renamed Hi-Vision and players started appearing on the market that could playback 1080i analogue video.

Hi-Band: Approximately 5 megahertz bandwidth (420 lines EIA resolution or ~550 x 480 edge-to-edge)

- *Laserdisk* (1978): Marketed originally as LaserVision.
- *Umatic BVU* (1982): Largely used in high-end consumer and professional equipment. The introduction of Umatic BVU spelled the end of 16 mm film recordings.
- *Umatic BVU-SP* (1985): Largely used in high-end consumer and professional equipment. The introduction of Umatic BVU spelled the end of 16 mm film recordings.
- *Betacam-SP* (1986): An minor upgrade to the Betacam format, but because of the upgrade, it became a broadcast standard.
- *MII* (1986): Panasonic's answers to Betacam-SP.
- *S-VHS* (1987): Largely used in medium-end consumer and prosumer equipment; rare among mainstream consumer equipment, and rendered obsolete by digital gear like DigiBetacam and DV.
- *S-VHS-C* (1987): An upgrade to provide near-laserdisc quality. Now limited to the low-end consumer market (example: JVC SXM38). As per VHS-C, relatively short running time compared to other formats.
- *Hi8* (1988): Enhanced-quality Video8; roughly equivalent to Super VHS in picture quality, but not compatible. High quality audio as standard. Now limited to low-end consumer market (example: Sony TRV138).
- *W-VHS* (1994): Shortlived 1080i tape format that had the ability to record.

Digital

- *Umatic* (1982): An experiments overhaul was made to umatic to record digital video, but this was impractical and the tapes were used as a trasport for digital audio only. This led to the D series of tapes about 4 years later.

- *D1_(Sony)* (1986): The first digital video recorder. It used digitized component video, encoded at Y'CbCr 4:2:2 using the CCIR 601 raster form and experimentally supported full HD broadcasts.
- *D2_(video_format)* (1988): This was a cheap alternative the D1 tape created by Ampex and this actually encoded video digitally instead of sampling composite video and experimentally supported full HD broadcasts.
- *D3* (1991): Created by panasonic to compete with the Ampex D2 and experimentally supported full HD broadcasts.
- *DCT (videocassette format)* (1992): This was the first compressed video tape format created by Ampex based on the D1 format. It used discrete cosine transform as its codec of choice. DST was a data-only standard introduced to the rapidly growing IT industry.
- *D5_HD* (1994): 1080i digital standard introduced by Sony based on the D1 tape.
- *Editcam* (1995): First drive recording standard introduced by Ikegami. FieldPak used a IDE hard and RAMPak used a set of flash ram modules. It can record in DV25, Avid JFIF, DV, MPEG IMX, DVCPRO50, and Avid DNxHD format, depending on generation.
- *Digital-s* (1995): JVC debuted a Digital Tape similar to VHS but had a different tape inside and supported digital HD broadcasts. Widely used by FOX broadcasting. Also called D-9.
- *MiniDV* (1995) was a smaller version of the DV standard released by Sony.
- *DVD* (1995): Uses either Mini DVD-R or DVD-RAM. This is a multi-manufacturer standard that uses 8 cm DVD discs for 30 minutes of video. DVD-R can be played on consumer DVD players but cannot be added to or recorded over once finalized for viewing. DVD-RAM can be added to and/or recorded over, but cannot be played on many consumer DVD players, and costs a lot more than other types of DVD recordable media. The DVD-RW is another option allowing the user to re-record, but only records sequentially and must be finalized for viewing. The discs do cost more than the DVD-R format, which only records once. DVD discs are also very vulnerable to scratches. DVD camcorders are generally not designed to connect to computers for editing purposes, though some high-end DVD units do record surround sound, a feature not standard with DV equipment.
- *DV* (1996): Sony debuted the DV format tape with DVCAM being professional and DVCPRO being a panasonic variant.
- *D-VHS* (1998): JVC debuted the digital standard of VHS tape and which supported 1080p HD. Many units also supported IEEE1394 recording.
- *Digital8* (1999), that uses Hi8 tapes (Sony is the only company currently producing D8 camcorders, though Hitachi used to). Most (but not quite all) models of Digital 8 cameras have the ability to read older Video8 and Hi8 analog format tapes. The format's technical specifications are of the same quality as MiniDV (both use the same DV codec), and although no professional-level Digital8 equipment exists, D8 has been used to make TV and movie productions (example: Hall of Mirrors).
- *MICROMV* (2001): Uses a matchbox-sized cassette. Sony was the only electronics manufacturer for this format, and editing software was proprietary

to Sony and only available on Microsoft Windows; however, open source programmers did manage to create capture software for Linux[2]. The hardware is no longer in production, though tapes are still available through Sony.

- *HD-DVD* (2003): Similar to blu-ray and based on the DVD standard. Offered more durable disks than BRD but sacrificed capacity in doing so. Codecs supported were MPEG-2, VC-1 and AVC.
- *XDCAM* (2003): A professional blu-ray standard introduced by Sony. This is similar to that of regular BRD but used different codecs, namely MPEG IMX, DV25 (DVCAM), MPEG-4, MPEG-2, and HD422.
- *BRD* (2003): Blu-ray disk was released by Sony as an optical recorder for full 1080p content. It can use a variety of codecs including MPEG-2, H.264/AVC, and SMPTE VC-1, though this was not formalized until 2004. The cartridge was also removed from the standard BRD so that it could compete effectively with HD-DVD, but lack of a cartridge make this disk susceptible to extremely easy damage.
- *P2* (2004): First solid state recording medium of professional quality, introduced by Panasonic. Recorded DVCPRO, DVCPRO50, DVCPRO-HD, or AVC-Intra stream onto the card.
- *HDV* (2004): Records up to an hour of HDTV MPEG-2 signal roughly equal to broadcast quality HD on a standard MiniDV cassette.

3× *DVD* (2005): Ability to record HD content on a DVD. HD Rec (2005): Ability to record HD content on a DVD.

- *CBHD* [2007]: The Chinese version of HD-DVD, free of any licensing agreement because the technology was licensed to the Chinese government. It uses the AVS codec. These are incompatible with any other player on the market.
- *S×S* (2007): Jointly developed by Sony and Sandisk. This is a solid state format of XDCAM and is known as XDCAM EX.
- *MPEG-2* codec based format, which records MPEG-2 programme stream or MPEG-2 transport stream to various kinds of tapeless media (hard disks, solid-state memory, etc). Used both for standard definition (JVC, Panasonic) and high definition (JVC) recording.
- *H.264* codec based (and derivative AVCHD) format, which records MPEG-4 AVC (H.264) compressed video to various kinds of tapeless media (recordable optical discs, flash memory, hard disks, etc.). Used mostly for high definition recording (Sony, Panasonic, Canon).

Digital Camcorders and Operating Systems

Since most manufacturers focus their support on Windows and Mac users, users of other operating systems often are unable to receive support for these devices. However, open source products such as Cinelerra and Kino (written for the Linux operating system) do allow full editing of some digital formats on alternative operating systems, and software to edit DV streams in particular is available on most platforms.

Many low-end tapeless camcorders, however, do not support any operating system but Windows, requiring either third-party software or a switch to a more standardized format such as DV.

CINEMATOGRAPHY

Cinematography (from Greek: *kinesis* (movement) and grapho (to record)), is the discipline of making lighting and camera choices when recording photographic images for the cinema. It is closely related to the art of still photography, though many additional issues arise when both the camera and elements of the scene may be in motion.

History

The first attempt at cinematography can be traced back to the world's first motion picture film, *Roundhay Garden Scene*. It was a sequence directed by Louis Le Prince, French inventor and showman, on October 14, 1888 in the garden at *Oakwood Grange* in Roundhay, Leeds, West Yorkshire, England. This groundbreaking event happened seven years before the Lumière Brothers' *Sortie de l'usine Lumière à Lyon* made the first paid exhibition on December 28, 1895 at Le Grand Café, in Paris, France. This date is known as the birth of cinema since it was the first time the cycle of production-distribution-exhibition happened. The European city soon became the motion picture capital of the world.

Cinematography is an art form unique to motion pictures. Although the exposing of images on light-sensitive elements dates back to the late 1600s, motion pictures demanded a new form of photography and new aesthetic techniques.

In the infancy of motion pictures, the cinematographer was usually also the director and the person physically handling the camera. As the art form and technology evolved, a separation between director and camera operator emerged. With the advent of artificial lighting and faster (more light sensitive) film stocks, in addition to technological advancements in optics and various techniques such as color film and widescreen, the technical aspects of cinematography necessitated a specialist in that area.

In 1919, in Hollywood, the new motion picture capital of the world, one of the first (and still existing) trade societies was formed: the American Society of Cinematographers (ASC), which stood to recognize the cinematographer's contribution to the art and science of motion picture making. Similar trade associations have been established in other countries, too.

The ASC defines cinematography as:

> A creative and interpretive process that culminates in the authorship of an original work of art rather than the simple recording of a physical event. Cinematography is not a subcategory of photography. Rather, photography is but one craft that the cinematographer uses in addition to other physical, organizational, managerial, interpretive and image-manipulating techniques to effect one coherent process.

Aspects of Cinematography

Numerous aspects contribute to the art of cinematography.

Film Stock

Cinematography can begin with rolls of film or a digital imaging sensor. Advancements in film emulsion and grain structure have led to a wide range of film stocks available to cinematographers. The selection of a film stock is one of the first decisions they must make during any film production.

Aside from the film gauge selection—8 mm (amateur), 16 mm (semi-professional), 35 mm (professional) and 65 mm (epic photography, rarely used except in special event venues)—the cinematographer has a selection of stocks in reversal (which, when developed, create a positive image) and negative formats along with a wide range of film speeds (varying sensitivity to light) from ISO 50 (slow, least sensitive to light) to 800 (very fast, extremely sensitive to light) and differing response to colour (low saturation, high saturation) and contrast (varying levels between pure black (no exposure) and pure white (complete overexposure)).

Advancements and adjustments to nearly all gauges of film created the "super" variety wherein the area of the film used to capture a single frame of an image is expanded, although the physical gauge of the film remains the same. Super 8 mm, Super 16 mm and Super 35 mm are all formats that utilize more of the overall film area for the image than their "regular" non-super counterparts.

The larger the film gauge, the higher the overall image resolution clarity and technical quality.

In the realm of digital imaging, various film stocks are no longer applicable, but the cameras themselves feature image adjustment capabilities that go far beyond the abilities of one particular film stock. The cameras can be adjusted to varying degrees of color sensitivity, image contrast, light sensitivity and so on. One camera can achieve all the various looks of different emulsions, although it is heavily argued as to which method of capturing an image is the "best" method. It should be mentioned that the digital method of image adjustments (ISO, contrast etc.) are executed by estimating the same adjustments that would take place if actual film were in use and are thus vulnerable to the cameras sensor designers perceptions of various film stocks and image adjustment parameters. Sensors generally have an optimal ISO rating past which faster speeds will result in noticeable increases in image noise, thus compromising the quality.

The Lab

Laboratory work can also offer a considerable variance in the image produced. By controlling the temperature and varying the duration in which the film is soaked in the development chemicals and by skipping certain chemical processes (or partially skipping them), cinematographers can achieve very different looks from a single film stock in the laboratory.

Filters

Filters, such as diffusion filters or colour-effect filters, are also widely used to enhance mood or dramatic effects. Most photographic filters are made up of two pieces of optical glass glued together with some form of image or light manipulation material between the glass. In the case of colour filters, there is often a translucent colour medium pressed between two planes of optical glass. Colour filters work by blocking out certain colour wavelengths of light from reaching the film. With colour film, this works very intuitively wherein a blue filter will cut down on the passage of red, orange and yellow light and create a blue tint on the film. In black and white photography, colour filters are used somewhat counter intuitively; for instance a yellow filter, which cuts down on blue wavelengths of light, can be used to darken a daylight sky (by eliminating blue light from hitting the film, thus greatly underexposing the mostly blue sky), while not biasing most human flesh tone. Certain cinematographers, such as Christopher Doyle, are well known for their innovative use of filters. Filters can be used in front of the lens or, in some cases, behind the lens for different effects.

Lens

Focal Length

The camera does what a human eye does. That is, it creates perspective and spatial relations with the rest of the world. However, unlike one's eye, a cinematographer can select different lenses for different purposes. Variation in focal length is one of the chief benefits of such an advantage. Cinematographers can choose between a range of wide angle lenses, "normal" lenses and telephoto lenses, as well as macro lenses and other special effect lens systems such as borescope lenses. Wide-angle lenses have short focal lengths and make spatial distances more obvious. A person in the distance is shown as much smaller while someone in the front will loom large. On the other hand, telephoto lenses reduce such exaggerations, depicting far-off objects as seemingly close together and flattening perspective. A Zoom lens allows a camera operator to change their focal length within a shot or quickly between setups for shots. As prime lenses offer greater optical quality and are "faster" (larger aperture openings, usable in less light) than zoom lenses, they are often employed in professional cinematography over zoom lenses. Certain scenes or even types of filmmaking, however, may require the use of zooms for speed or ease of use, as well as shots involving a zoom move.

Depth of Field and Focus

Focal length also affects the depth of field of a scene—that is, how much the background, mid-ground and foreground will be rendered in "acceptable focus" (only one exact plane of the image is in precise focus) on the film or video target. Depth of field (not to be confused with depth of focus) is determined by the aperture size and the focal distance. A large or deep depth of field is generated with a very small iris aperture and focusing on a point in the distance, whereas a shallow depth of field will be achieved with a large (open) iris aperture and focusing closer to the lens. Depth of field is also governed by the format size. 70 mm film has the least depth of field for the same focal length lens than does 35 mm. 16 mm has even more and most digital video cameras have more depth of field than 16 mm. As videographers try to emulate the look of 35 mm film with digital cameras, this is one issue of frustration—excessive depth of field with digital cameras and using additional optical devices to reduce that depth of field.

In *Citizen Kane*, cinematographer Gregg Toland used tighter apertures to create very large depth of field in the scenes, often rendering every detail of the foreground and background of the sets in sharp focus. This practice is known as deep focus. Deep focus became a popular cinematographic device from the 1940s onwards in Hollywood. Today, the trend is for more shallow focus.

To change the plane of focus from one object or character to another within a shot is commonly known as a *rack focus*.

Aspect Ratio and Framing

Aspect Ratio

The aspect ratio of an image is the ratio of its width to its height. Beginning in the 1910s, motion pictures settled on a ratio of four to three (four units wide to three units high). Often written as 4:3, this ratio may be reduced to 1.33:1 and this aspect ratio is commonly known as 1.33. The introduction of sound-on-film narrowed the aspect ratio briefly, before the Academy ratio of 1.37 was introduced in 1932 by means of thickening the frame line. For years, cinematographers were limited to this shape of image, but in the 1950s, thanks to the unanticipated popularity of Cinerama, widescreen ratios were introduced in an effort to pull audiences back into the theater and away from their home television sets. These new widescreen aspect ratios granted cinematographers a wider frame within which to compose their images. Many different proprietary photographic systems were invented and utilized in the 1950s to create widescreen movies, but one dominates today: the anamorphic process, which optically squeezes the image to photograph twice the horizontal area to the same size vertical as standard "spherical" lenses. The first commonly used anamorphic widescreen format was CinemaScope, which used a 2.35:1 aspect ratio, although it was originally 2.55:1. CinemaScope was used from 1953 to 1967, but due to technical flaws in the design and its ownership by Fox, several third-party companies, led by Panavision's technical improvements in the 1950s, now dominate the anamorphic cine lens market. Changes to SMPTE projection standards altered the projected ratio from 2.35:1 to 2.39:1 in 1970, although this did not change anything regarding the photographic anamorphic standards; all changes in respect to the aspect ratio of anamorphic 35 mm photography are specifically correlative to camera or projector gate sizes, not the optical system.

After the "widescreen wars" of the 1950s, the motion-picture industry settled into 1.85:1 (which is a cropped version of 1.37:1) as a standard for theatrical projection in the United States and the United Kingdom. Europe and Asia opted for 1.66:1 at first, although 1.85:1 has largely permeated these markets in recent decades. Certain "epic" or adventure movies utilized the anamorphic 2.39:1.

In the 1990s, with the advent of high-definition video, television engineers created the 1.78:1 (16:9) ratio as a mathematical compromise between the theatrical standard of 1.85:1 and television's 1.33:1, as it was not physically possible to safely create a television tube with a width of 1.85:1. Until that point, nothing had ever been originated in 1.78:1. Today, this is a standard for high-definition video and for widescreen television.

Lighting

Most likely the single most important aspect of cinematography is lighting. Light is necessary to create an image exposure on a frame of film or on a digital target (CCD, etc). The art of lighting for cinematography goes far beyond basic exposure, however, into the essence of visual storytelling. Lighting contributes considerably to the emotional response an audience has watching a motion picture. The control of light quality, color, direction and intensity is a major factor in the art and science of cinematography.

Camera Movement

One aspect of cinematography that strongly separates it from still photography (aside from having a moving subject) is the ability to move the camera, which represents the audience's viewpoint or perspective, during the course of filming. This movement plays a considerable role in the emotional language of film images and the audience's emotional reaction to the action on the screen. From the most basic movements of panning (horizontal shift in viewpoint from a fixed position; like turning your head side-to-side) and tilting (vertical shift in viewpoint from a fixed position; like tipping your head back to look at the sky or tilting your head down to look at the ground) to dollying (placing the camera on a moving platform to move it closer or farther from the subject), trucking (placing the camera on a moving platform to move it to the left or right), craning (moving the camera in a vertical position; being able to lift it off the ground as well as swing it side-to-side from a fixed base position), and a combination of all of the above.

Cameras have been mounted to nearly every imaginable form of transportation.

Most cameras can also be handheld, that is the camera operator literally holds the camera in their hands and moves from one position to another while filming the action. Personal stabilizing platforms came into being in the late 1970s through the invention of Garrett Brown, which became known as the Steadicam. The Steadicam is a body harness and stabilization arm that connects to the camera that allows the operator to move naturally while completely isolating the movements of their body from the movements of the camera. After the Steadicam patent expired in the early 1990s, many other companies began manufacturing their concept of the personal camera stabilizer.

Special Effects

The first special effects in the cinema were created while the film was being shot. These came to be known as "in-camera" effects. Later, optical and digital effects were developed so that editors and visual effects artists could more tightly control the process by manipulating the film in post-production.

For examples of many in-camera special effects, see the work of early filmmaker Georges Méliès.

Frame Rate Selection

Motion picture images are presented to an audience at a constant speed. In the theater, it is 24 frames per second, in NTSC (US) Television, it is 30 frames per second (29.97 to be exact), in PAL (Europe) television it is 25 frames per second. This speed of presentation does not vary.

However, by varying the speed at which the image is captured, various effects can be created knowing that the faster or slower recorded image will be played at a constant speed.

For instance, time-lapse photography is created by exposing an image at an extremely slow rate. If a cinematographer sets a camera to expose one frame every minute for four hours, and then that footage is projected at 24 frames per second, the event that took four hours to record will now take 10 seconds to present (1 frame per minute for 4 hours equals 240 frames, projected at 24 frames per second equals 10 seconds). This compresses the event that took place in four hours into just 10 seconds. At this speed, one can present the events of a whole day (24 hours) in just one minute. The inverse of this, if an image is captured at speeds above that at which they will be presented, the effect is to greatly slow down (slow motion) the image. If a cinematographer shoots a person diving into a pool at 96 frames per second, and that image is presented back at 24 frames per second, it will take 4 times as long to watch the dive as it did for it to actually happen.

In motion pictures the manipulation of time and space is a considerable contributing factor to the narrative storytelling tools. Film editing plays a much stronger role in this manipulation, but frame rate selection in the photography of the original action is also a contributing factor to altering time.

"Ramping" is a process whereby the capture frame rate of the camera changes over time. For example, if in the course of 10 seconds of capture, the capture frame rate is adjusted from 60 frames per second to 24 frames per second, when played back at the standard film rate of 24 frames per second, a unique time-manipulation effect is achieved. For example, someone pushing a door open and walking out into the street would appear to start off in slow-motion, but in a few seconds later within the same shot the person would appear to walk in "realtime" (normal speed). The opposite speed-ramping is done in *The Matrix* when Neo re-enters the Matrix for the first time to see the Oracle. As he comes out of the warehouse "load-point", the camera zooms into Neo at normal speed but as it gets closer to Neo's face time seems to slow down, perhaps visually accentuating Neo pausing and reflecting a moment, and perhaps alluding to future manipulation of time itself within the Matrix later on in the movie.

Role of the Cinematographer

In the film industry, the cinematographer is responsible for the technical aspects of the images (lighting, lens choices, composition, exposure, filtration, film selection), but works closely with the director to ensure that the artistic aesthetics are supporting the director's vision of the story being told. The cinematographers are the heads of the camera, grip and lighting crew on a set, and for this reason they are often called directors of photography or DPs.

Directors of photography make many creative and interpretive decisions during the course of their work, from pre-production to post-production, all of which affect the overall feel and look of the motion picture. Many of these decisions are similar to what a photographer needs to note when taking a picture: the cinematographer controls the film choice itself (from a range of available stocks with varying sensitivities to light and color), the selection of lens focal lengths, aperture exposure and focus. Cinematography, however, has a temporal aspect, unlike still photography, which is purely a single still image. It is also bulkier and more strenuous to deal with movie cameras, and it involves a more complex array of choices. As such a cinematographer often needs to work co-operatively with more people than does a photographer, who could frequently function as a single person. As a result, the cinematographer's job also includes personnel management and logistical organization.

Evolution of Technology: New Definitions

Traditionally the term "cinematography" referred to working with motion-picture film emulsion, but it is now largely synonymous with videography and digital video due to the popularity of digital cinematography.

Modern digital image processing has also made it possible to radically modify pictures from how they were originally captured. This has allowed new disciplines to encroach on some of the choices that were once the cinematographer's exclusive domain.

MANUAL OF STILLS PHOTOGRAPHY

Introduction

Stills photography involves taking photos of the film-making process. These are often used for promoting the film and as a documentary record. This area of film production is often overlooked on smaller budget films or some photographs are taken by members of the crew, but for promotional and documentary uses; good quality and professional images are a must. If the film budget can't stretch to a professional photographer, many photographers will do work to use in their portfolios, and for the experience.

Alternative Names

- ❑ Production stills
- ❑ Unit stills

Equipment

Both film and digital have their respective advantages and disadvantages. Digital photography provides instant results, and combining this with a notebook computer means the results can be viewed instantly by the photographer, crew and cast. The choice often comes down to personal preference, but is sometimes dictated by the stills photographer's brief. Medium and large format cameras are often used for a higher quality image although 35 mm is usually sufficient, and is often used for speed and ease of use. Large format cameras—considered superior in terms of image quality—is a slower medium, and often hard to use on a busy set. Generally the equipment will suit the type of shots required. If the shots are "reportage" style, then 35 mm is advantagous. High-quality cast/set shots can be taken on medium/large especially for very large poster/billboard reproductions.

Publishing Stills Photos Online

If you have your own webspace then it's very easy to install a free gallery package and publish your photos online. Some excellent free gallery packages include:

- Gallery
- Coppermine

MANUAL OF SHOOTING STYLES

Blair Witch Project

The Blair Witch Project is different in its shooting style in many ways.

- The whole film is presented as if it were an unedited documentary, filmed by the protagonists, and as such the shooting style resembles that of an amateur documentary or a home movie.
- This includes shaking shots when the characters are running and more or less useless or irrelevant shots when the characters are just fooling around with the cameras.
- A large part of the movie is in black and white, as one of the cameras that the protagonists carry with them only shoots in this format. This adds to the realism of the movie.

Ken Loach

The films of Ken Loach have an incredible authenticity and 'realness' to them. How does he achieve this?

Taken from "Loach on Loach"

- Never use ADR.
- Run the entire scene for every shot, don't break the scene down into little "shot length" segments.
- Light the entire scene so you're not artificially telling the audience "THIS is the lead actor for this scene, the others are less important".
- Don't give the actors marks (indeed, you don't have to because you're lighting the entire scene).
- Actors should have vulnerabilities.

Dogme/Dogma

From Bright Lights Film Journal: *Copyrights lawyers are out of luck. Anyone can obtain a Dogme certificate if he (or she) shoots a film in accordance with the ten rules known as "The Vow of Chastity."*

The Vow of Chastity

- Shooting on location (no imported props or sets),
- Sound and image produced together,
- A handheld camera,
- Natural light,
- No optical work or filters,
- No superficial action (murders, weapons),
- No temporal or geographic alienation,
- No genre films,
- Film format must be Academy 35 mm, and
- No signature; the director must not be credited.

Alfred Hitchcock

A man dedicated to suspense and intrigue: Emotion is the ultimate goal of each of his shots. Hitchcock believed that emotion came directly from the actor's eyes. By bringing us closer or tearing us away he used camera angles to jerk us into the feeling of his moments.

The camera should be just like a person looking around for something out of place in a room. This allows the audience to feel like they are involved the action. Scenes can often begin by panning a room showing close-ups of objects that explain plot elements.

Hitchcock also loved to keep us on our toes by throwing in shots fast and close after being slow and far…

PHOTO IMAGING

We're all surrounded by images every day, but working in this exciting industry isn't just about being a photographer.

The Skillset Cymru Training Framework for the audio visual industries has been developed to support Freelancers and production companies in Wales, and to maintain the standard of skills and training within our sector. Find out more and apply here!

Skillset Approved Training

If you are looking for the best digital skills training but don't know where to start, Skillset can help.

Photo Imaging News and Events

Find out what's happening in the in the Photo Imaging sector across the country: Get the latest information about opportunities, new training schemes, events, master classes and other new services to help support the Photo Imaging industries.

Photo Imaging Standards

The standards provide the most up to date description of the skills, knowledge and understanding necessary to perform the main roles and responsibilities for occupations within the photo imaging sector.

11

Lights: Process and Power Sources

MANUAL OF LIGHTING

Lighting Conventions

Broadcast, Video, and Film Productions share common lighting conventions. Due to the fact that most lighting tools were originally developed for film, with a few tools introduced for video, the equipment carries ratings and specifications standardized for film. All the lighting tools found in a decently equiped video production studio have direct relatives (usually just larger, brighter and more expensive) in a film production studio.

Electricity

Every lighting fixture uses electricty. How much it requires and in what form varies on the application of the light(s). The electrical description consists of Voltage, Amperage, and Wattage. Commonly studio lights use 115 ± 5 V or 225 ± 5 V. The amperages (ampres or amps) and wattages (Watts or W) vary depending on the fixture, bulb type, and light output. 115 V lights range from 10 W (LEDs) up to 2000 W-2500 W (Halogen-Quartz), 225 V range also from 10 W to 4500 W-5000 W.

Terminology

- *Bulbs*: Refers to the actual light source. Most bulbs consist of a filament, insulating gas, and a glass encasement.
- *Fixtures*: The case that holds the bulb, and often serves the purpose of directing the light. Fixtures range from bulb-holders, to elaborate mechanisms capable of all but picking one's nose.
- *Mounts*: A device that holds the light where you want it to be. Some clamp to overhead lighting grids, while others are stands.
- *Power*: Or power source/supply. Where is light getting its juice?

Lighting Equipment

Lighting equipment consists of a great deal more than just sockets with bulbs. Lighting equipment (briefly) consists of bulbs, fixtures, dimmers/power units, mounts, light control/quality.

Bulb Types

Video/Film recording lights use many different bulb types. Some are standards from Edison (tungsten) but others are cutting edge of the 2000s (LED). Most bulb types use a filament-ignition process to produce light. A wire of some electrically excitable material is put under voltage in a oxygen-depleted environment, causing it to 'burn' without lighting afire. Flourecent bulbs and LEDs function rather differently from filament bulbs.

Tungsten

A tungsten light is basically a more powerful version of a common household lightbulb. While a household light bulb may only take a few hundred watts at most, lights that are used to light film sets are easily 1000 watts (1 K) and often over 20,000 watts (20 K). The tungsten light bulb naturally produces an orange hue, similar to indoor lights. Tungsten lights have a colour temperature ranging from 3200 to 3400 Kelvin. One typically uses a CTB filter to balance the colour temperature with outdoor or HMI light.

Redheads

Redheads are a specific type of open-faced light made by Ianiro. They are very compact and come in 600 and 650 watt versions. They are also known as Mickey-Moles (when made by Mole-Richardson). The term is often used to loosely describe smaller, open-faced lights.

Blondes

Blondes are a 2k open-faced light. Because they are open-faced, they tend to put out more light than a 2k fresnel.

Halogen-Quartz

Halogen-Quartz bulbs, often known as 'Halogens' or 'Quartz' are a staple of lighting. Halogens rarely posses a colour temperature outside of 3200°K. These same bulbs are often used in car headlights, portable worklights, and recently in house-decor lighting. The bulbs come in wattages ranging from 15 W-3500 W. Additionally the are manufactured in a wide range of enclosures, bases, and connectors. Common are the "T", and bayonet base. Halogens emit significant amounts of heat during operation, so much so that oils on the glass surface of the bulb case lead to un-even heat distribution and rupturing (through thermal shock to the glass) or heat build-up and exploding gas within the bulb.

HMI

An HMI light is used very often to light film sets. One requires a ballast in order to power and creates a loud noise when turning on, so it is set protocol to yell "striking" in order to warn others on set to both ignore the noise and avoid looking at the light. The HMI light is a different type of light bulb than the more common tungsten. An

HMI emits ultra-violet lights and emits a blue hue. HMI lights produce a colour temperature around 5600 Kelvin. One typically use a CTO filter to balance the colour temperature with indoor or tungsten light.

Fluorescent

Fluorescent bulbs were not used for lighting film and video until recently. This was because of problems with flicker and a tendency to emit more of a greenish hue. The Fluorescent lights used in film now are made to be flicker-free and come in both daylight and tungsten balanced bulbs. "Kino-flo" is one of the major companies involved in making fluorescent bulbs and fixtures for film and video production. Fluorescent lights tend to be very soft, but do not put out much light in comparison to other lighting instruments.

LED

Until the last five to ten years Light Emitting Diodes (LEDs) have seen little implimentation. Recent advances in production costs and chemical advances used in the diode junctions have led to inexpensive led 'bulbs' as well as even colour temperatures in multiple bulbs. LEDs are manufactured in all colours, and white comes in many color temperatures; 3200 K being the most common, but ranging from 3000 K to 5600K+. Diodes, due to their engineered design tend to have a very directional light. The front lens is parabolic, focusing the light to a small dot even several meters away.

Light Control, Quality, and Appearance

Lighting Shape/Area

There are a number of tools used to control where light falls. Often these are used to prevent light falling where it is not needed. In other circumstances a pattern created by the light is desired.

Barn Doors

Perhaps the most common form of lighting area shaping, barn doors are found around the front outside of the fixture. Most commonly there are four barn doors forming a square around the fixture, but the numbers vary for specialty applications.

Basically, barn doors block the light from hitting an area of the set or frame you don't want them to. They swing towards and away from the fixture opening.

Gobos

Gobos shape the light. Many gobos appear to be shapes cut in a cookie sheet (and indeed many are) but they consist of a material able to withstand the heat put out by the fixture, with shapes cut out for the light to travel through.

Think of gobos as jack o' lanterns.

Blackwrap

Blackwrap is essentially aluminum foil, but covered in black paint. It is often used to block light and kill any spill from a light. Blackwrap can be shaped however you like to affect where the light falls. It is useful in narrowing larger lights to point lights or spots or making lights non-circular. It is very inexpensive, light weight and more flexible than barn doors. However, it will burn on too hot a light, so watch for smoke.

Lighting Intensity

Flags

A flag can be any item that blocks light. A standard flag on set can be of varying sizes. The standard flag is attached to a small metal handle and short rod that can be attached to a C-Stand to place it so that it blocks the light from hitting something in the shot. Flags can be used to help prevent certain shadows from hitting certain walls and also be used to mimic doors and the such.

Types of flags include singles and doubles to cut down hard light. Solids to block light. Silks to diffuse light.

Focus

Adjusting the focus on a focusable light changes the distance between the actual bulb and a lens at the end of the light. This affects how diffuse the light is. Closer to the lens spreads the light out more, whereas farther back makes it closer to a spot. Try to do this before the light gets too hot, so you can adjust it without burning yourself.

Neutral Density Filters

Neutral density filters are a variety of gel (or camera filter) which reduces all colours of light equally, making a light less intense without altering its colour. This can be added on top of colour gels or used on its own to make a light less intense.

Lighting Quality

Gels

Gels are thin and translucent. They come in rolls that can be cut into a more manageable size when needed. While a gel can be any colour, there are two main colours which are referred to as Colour Temperature Orange (CTO) and Colour Temperature Blue (CTB). These two types of gel are respectively orange and blue, with varying degrees of darkness broken up into 1/8, 1/4, 1/2, and Full. Full is the darkest and 1/8 is the lightest. When asking for a gel, one may say "I'd like a quarter CTO put on this light."

Gels are attached to a light in order to alter their colour temperature. Tungsten lights produce an orange hue, while HMI's produce a blue hue. If filming outside with tungsten lights, gels would be needed to match the colour temperature of the daylight if the DP wanted all the light to be the same colour temperature. Daylight produces a blue hue like an HMI light, so CTB would be needed to be placed on all the tungsten lights. Gels are attached to lights with clothespins, also called "C-47's."

Besides CTO and CTB, to work with fluorescent lights or a "kino flo", there are "plus green" and "minus green" gels. Since fluorescent lights produce a green hue, a minus green gell would remove the green hue from a fluorescent light and a plus green gel would help match a non-fluorescent light to a fluorescent.

Attaching

Some lights have clips for attaching gels, but the most common method of attaching them is via wooden clothespins (also referred to as C47s, pegs, or bullets). These clothespins will begin to smoke before the gels, so you can prevent your gels from being ruined, and they also don't conduct heat, so they can be manipulated even on a very hot light. They can also be reversed to give them a longer mouth, allowing you to use them to pull scrims from hot fixtures. Once reversed, they often go by C-74's or "scrim pullers".

General Lighting

Here is the nitty-gritty of the page. Although different formats have varying needs in both quantity and quality of light, the underlying yet critical concepts of lighting are fairly applicable to any medium.

Lighting Digital Video

Dynamic Range: There are many differençes between DV and film, but one that particularily stands out regarding lighting is dynamic range.

Most DV and video cameras have a relatively low dynamic range (*i.e.* the Sony PD150 has about 4-5 stops, and Kodak's 50D film has up to 11). This means the range between the completely black and the whitest white is very low. One therefore has to keep this in mind while lighting. This has been an integral part of cinematography since the beginning. Controlling so one can see details in the darkest area of an image, and also in the brightest. One can always adjust the contrast in post (Colourgrading). This style of working is called shooting for post. (The DV standard has an ok light intensity resolution, so adjusting contrast in post is not as difficult as adjusting colour.)

White balance. As the DV standard has a low colour-resolution, it is important to control and know how to filter and white balance the image on set. It has been proved difficult to adjust colour in post with a good result, although it has been done. Regarding lighting, be aware of the possibilities the white balance setting on the camera have, and use gels on the lamps, and sometimes on windows to create a neutral image.

In return for these shortcomings, DV-cameras can be more light-sensitive than most film stocks, and therefore require less light intensity, to give the same image. (PD150 is about 320ASA versus Kodak's 50D's 50ASA. One would need about 8 times more light, to get the same image at the same F-stop). Although high ASA film is available.

Lighting HD

Lighting Film within the Movie Making Manual

- ❑ Power Sources: Generators, tie-ins, batteries, inverters etc.

Lighting Equipment Manufacturers

- ❑ [Lee Filters] Gels, filters and accessories
- ❑ [Matthews Grip] Century Stands (C-stands), and other equipment
- ❑ [ARRI] Lights, cameras and other

LIGHTING TOOLS AND TECHNIQUES

The camera doesn't know what's important in the picture. It sets the iris in the lens according to the brightest light.

 If your background is brighter than your subject the subject gets dark.	White background with no added lighting	 Shadows are a big problem on the face.
 The subject is lighter than the background in this picture. The camera adjusts the iris for the best light level on the subject.	Background darker than subject with no added lighting	 Shadows are less but still there.
 In this picture we've added lights aimed at the subject and not on the background. This makes the subject brighter than the background.	White background with lighting added	 The added lighting has reduced the shadows on the face, but the subject doesn't really stand out from the background very well.

 The lights are aimed at the subject and do not hit the background. This makes the subject brighter than the background.	Background darker than subject with lighting added	 The added lighting has reduced the shadows on the face and the subject stands out from the darker background.

MANUAL OF POWER SOURCES

On a film set, the power source is usually managed by the Electrical Department. Depending on where you are shooting and the volume of power the production requires, many different power sources are used. Typically you are either using Stage Power, House Power, A Tie-In, or a Generator.

Stage Power

When filming on a sound-stage large amounts of power are typically provided as part of the facility, although this is not always the case. Typically, power is provided in the form of 3-phase 110v with Cam-Lock hook-ups.

House Power

House power refers to power that is already installed within a location. For example, if you are shooting in a apartment, House Power refers to exiting power installed in the apartment. House power is generally not preferred because: lighting equipment can require more power than is available, circuit-boxes can be difficult to locate in the event of a overload, a relatively large amount of power is usually used which increases the power-bill for that cycle.

Tie-Ins

A Tie-In is a method of tapping directly into the power that feeds a building from the city power-grid, thereby bypassing the limits of the circuits that are installed in the building.

A Tie-In is a dangerous activity which requires experience and skill. Improper methods can result in damage to city power-grids and death.

Generator

Generators are used in Motion Picture Production to provide power to all the departments of the production, the most demanding on which is the lighting department. Typically generators are used when filming on location, as power is normally provided when filming on a sound-stage.

TELEVISION LIGHTING

Television is a means of changing patterns of light into electrical signals for storage or transmission and then recreating those patterns on a screen. In order to do this well, the television camera must be presented with properly illuminated scenes. The three important considerations are overall level, contrast range, and color temperature.

Level

Lighting levels for television are generally set by adjusting the incident light, or the light striking the subject. The unit of measure for incident light is the foot candle, which is the amount of light produced by a standard candle at a distance of one foot. Lighting measurements are made using an incident light meter, which has a white plastic cover over the sensing element and a logarithmic scale calibrated in foot candles. To measure the useful incident light for television, the meter is held near the subject and pointed toward the camera.

The minimum acceptable level for color television depends on the ability of the lens to transmit light to the camera, the sensitivity of the pickup tube or chip, and the amount of depth of field you need. For high-quality pictures you need something between fifty and two hundred foot candles. Most cameras can be operated in light ranging from the minimum up to ten thousand foot candles, or fairly bright sunlight. Where lighting conditions fall outside this range, steps must be taken to bring the lighting level into line with the capabilities of the camera. With too little light, additional lighting must be added. With too much, special neutral density filters must be used on the camera.

Absolute Rock Bottom

You'll see cameras advertised as 2 LUX or 4 LUX cameras. 2 LUX is equal to .19 foot candles. 4 LUX is about .37 foot candles. I was suspicious, so a number of years ago I set up an ordinary candle one foot away from a white square on a black background. I tested two cameras. The first was a popular CCD camera requiring four LUX for minimum illumination. The second was a broadcast camera using Saticon pickup tubes. At a nominal one foot candle the CCD camera produced 40 IRE units of video, but the amount of noise in the picture was very objectionable. At four foot candles the CCD camera produced 100 IRE units with an acceptable noise level. The broadcast camera produced 20 IRE units at one foot candle with the "boost" set at 18 dB. At four foot candles, it produced 46 dB at 0 boost and 95 dB at 9 dB boost. At four foot candles the broadcast picture was obviously superior to the picture from the consumer camera.

The difference at one foot candle is essentially the willingness to tolerate more noise in the CCD camera, giving it more apparent sensitivity under extremely low light situations. To mask some of the noise at low light levels, consumer cameras often use a setup, or black level, of zero IRE, rather than the 7.5 IRE broadcast standard.

Some cameras that automatically boost the signal in low light situations can also be run in manual mode where you can control how much boost you want to use.

Lighting levels of five to fifteen foot candles are common in homes, while office settings tend to range from fifty to sixty foot candles. Keeping the reservations in the preceding paragraph in mind, consumer camcorders should have plenty of light for acceptable pictures in either setting.

Contrast

Contrast refers to the difference in brightness from the darkest parts of a scene to the brightest.

Useful contrast for NTSC television is determined by the amplitude of the video signal. The NTSC standard calls for a "peak to peak" amplitude of one volt at 75 ohms impedance. Only seven tenths of a volt is used for the luminance, or black and white part of the signal.

Common digital video signals are 24 bit colour, with eight bits each for red, green, and blue. This scheme allows for 256 individual shades from dark to light for each colour. Since 24 bit colour allows for over sixteen million colours, the limited number of shades available for each colour isn't usually a problem, although the luminance steps may be visible in monochromatic scenes.

If there's too little contrast many receivers will produce a flat, grayish picture. If there's too much contrast, details in the brightest and darkest parts of the picture will be lost and the picture will look too harsh.

Since contrast is actually light reflected from the subject, it's measured using a reflectance light meter. The meter is held near a variety of very light and very dark parts of the subject and pointed toward each part of the subject to be measured. The ideal contrast range for NTSC television is about twenty to one. This corresponds to a difference of about four and one half f-numbers between the darkest and brightest parts of the picture on a reflectance light meter. In practice, actual contrast ranges are rarely measured using a meter. A subjective analysis based on camera output is generally sufficient.

Colour Temperature

The third consideration is colour temperature. Every source of light has a characteristic colour. This colour is related to its "temperature." Lower colour temperatures tend to be red or orange while higher temperatures tend to be green or blue. Colour temperatures are measured in degrees Kelvin.

The eye "remembers" how things are supposed to look and interprets colour accordingly, regardless of the colour temperature of lighting sources. A white sheet of paper seems white whether viewed under an incandescent lamp or sunlight. The eye can even adjust for "correct colour" when two light sources of different colours are present in the same scene. Sunlight streaming into a room which is also lit by incandescent lamps doesn't make objects it strikes appear bluish.

Colour Temperature

Temperature	*Source*	*Colour*
1950	Candlelight	Orange
2870	Normal Incandescent	Orange
3200	Most Photo or TV Lights	Orange
3400	Some Photo Lamps	Orange
3500-4000	Fluorescent Lamps	Green
5500	Midday Sunlight	Blue

Television cameras aren't so versatile. They must be set up to render colour in a way that's pleasing to the eye. They can do this only if all of the important lighting sources within a scene have the same colour temperature. A combination of filters and electronic adjustments is used to adapt colour cameras to each new lighting situation. Most cameras can adjust automatically to typical colour temperatures. They cannot resolve conflicts when major picture elements are lit at different colour temperatures.

Bibliography

1954 Russian Raguda (Rainbow) Field Sequential Colour Set, Early Television Foundation.

501 *Ways to Use the Overhead Projector'* by Lee Green.

A brief info on Kodak DCS-Series Digital Still SLR cameras, Photography in Malaysia.

'A Day in Radio' from The University of Virginia's Department of American Studies.

A Description of the Braun Paxiscope unit.

A História da Rádio em Datas (1819-1997) (in Portuguese)—notes on etymology.

"A new tape transport system with digital control", Oscar Bonello, Journal of Audio Engineering Society, Vol. 31, # 12, December 1983.

A standard defining the NTSC system was published by the International Telecommunication Union in 1998 under the title "Recommendation ITU-R BT.470-7, Conventional Analog Television Systems." It isn't publicly available on the Internet, but it can be purchased from the ITU.

"A Third Method of Generation and Detection of Single-Sideband Signals" D.K. Weaver Jr. Proc. IRE, December 1956.

A. Bruce Carlson: "*Communication systems,* 2nd edition", McGraw-Hill, Inc, 1981.

ABC Radio National Radio Eye.

ABC The Night Air.

About.com: Colour Television History.

All India Radio website

American Wide Screen Museum.

An Appreciation of the Camera Obscura.

Analog TV shutoff will be finished in April 4 2010.

Ang, Ien. *Living Room Wars.* London: Routledge, 1995.

______. *Desperately Seeking The Audience.* London: Routledge, 1993.

______. *Watching Dallas.* London: Methuen, 1985.

Ang, Ien. *Living Room Wars.* London: Routledge, 1995.

______. *Desperately Seeking The Audience.* London: Routledge, 1993.

______. *Watching Dallas.* London: Methuen, 1985.

Another set of diy lcd/lighbulb projectors.

Armstrong, E.H. (May 1936). "*A Method of Reducing Disturbances in Radio Signaling by a System of Frequency Modulation.*" Proceedings of the IRE *(IRE)* 24(5): 689-740. doi: 10.1109/JRPROC.1936.227383.

AsterDomus Planetarium site (portuguese)—planetarium manufacturer.

Australian VHF/UHF PAL B/G Television System Datasheet.

AV Technology Use Growing, February 10, 2006.

Bahai, A.R.S., Saltzberg, B. R., Ergen, M. (2004), *Multi Carrier Digital Communications: Theory and Applications of OFDM*, Springer, 2004.

Beauchamp, G and Parkinson, J (2005) Beyond the wow factor: developing interactivity with the interactive whiteboard. School Science Review (86) 316: 97-103.

Black and White World's, Enlarger Guide http://www.photogs.com/bwworld/enlargerguide.html l Accessed 29/07/2008.

Bobo, Jacqueline, and Seiter, Ellen. "Black Feminism and Media Criticism." Screen (London), 1991; reprint in Brunsdon, Charlotte, J. D'Acci an L. Spigel, editors. *fem.tv.* Oxford: Oxford University Press, 1996.

Boddy, William. *Fifties Television: The Industry and Its Critics.* Urbana: The University of Illinois Press, 1990.

Boithais, Lucien, "*Radio Wave Propagation.*" McGraw-Hill Book Company, New York. 1987.

Brandt, George. *British Television Drama.* Cambridge: Cambridge University Press, 1981.

British Educational Communications and Technology Agency (BECTA), "What the Research Says About Interactive Whiteboards," ICT Research, Coventry, 2003.

Broadcasters and Writers for AIR Lucknow: Swapnil Bhartiya.

"Broadcasting Public Notice CRTC 2007-53" (HTML). *Sections 50 to 80.* Canadian Radio-television and Telecommunications Commission (2007-05-17).

Browne, Nick. "The Political Economy of the Television (Super) Text." *Quarterly Review of Film Studies* (Los Angeles), 1984.

Burns, Paul, The History of the Discovery of Cinematography An Illustrated Chronology.

Burns, Tom. *The BBC: Public Institution, Private World.* London: Macmillan, 1977.

"C.B.S. Colour Video Starts November 20; Adapters Needed by Present Sets", *New York Times*, October 12, 1950, p. 1.

Camerapedia a free-content encyclopedia of camera information. Camerapedia.org website.

Canadian Communications Foundation—The History on Canadian Broadcasting.

Canadian Radio-television and Telecommunications Commission (2007-05-17), "The Commission establishes a new approach for Canadian conventional television". Press release.

Carl Zeiss Jena GmbH, manufacturer and provider of optical-mechanical and digital planetarium systems.

CBS Field Sequential System: Advertisements, Early Television Foundation.

"CBS Says Confusion Now Bars Colour TV," *Washington Post*, March 26, 1953, p. 39.

"CBS Subsidiary Starts Mass Production of Colour Television Sets", *Wall Street Journal*, September 13, 1951, p. 18.

Chang, R.W. (1966). Synthesis of band-limited orthogonal signals for multi-channel data transmission, *Bell System Technical* Journal 46, 1775-1796.

Chang, R.W. and Gibbey, R.A. (1968). A theoretical study of performance of an orthogonal multiplexing data transmission scheme, *IEEE Transactions on Communications Technology* 16(4), 529-540.

Cinema and its Ancestors: The Magic of Motion Video interview with Tom Gunning.

Collection of restored cinema projectors and lighting by Regal Group, UK.

"Colour Television Achieves Realism", *New York Times*, September 5, 1940, p. 18. A colour 16 mm film was shown; live pick-ups were first demonstrated to the press in 1941. "Columbia Broadcasting Exhibits Colour Television", *Wall Street Journal*, January 10, 1941, p. 4. "CBS Makes Live Pick-up in Colour Television", *Radio & Television*, April 1941.

"Colour TV Shelved As a Defense Step," *New York Times*, October 20, 1951, p. 1. "Action of Defense Mobilizer in Postponing Colour TV Poses Many Question for the Industry," *New York Times*, October 22, 1951, p. 23. Ed Reitan, CBS Field Sequential Colour System, 1997.

"Colour Television: Baird Experimental System Described", *Wireless World*, August 17, 1939.

"Communication Systems" 4th Ed, Simon Haykin, 2001. "http://en.wikibooks.org/wiki/Movie_Making_Manual/Sound_Recording".

Community Broadcasting Association of Australia.

Crane, R. J. (1979). The Politics of International Standards: France and the Colour TV War, Ablex Publishing Corporation.

D'Acci, Julie. *Defining Women: Television and The Case of Cagney and Lacey*. Chapel Hill: University of North Carolina Press, 1994.

de Couasnon T., Monnier R. and Rault J.B. (1994) OFDM for digital TV broadcasting, Signal processing (ELSEVIER) 39 (1994), pp. 1-32.

Demystifying Digital Camera Types (9/21/2007).

Department of Transport (Canada)—Meteorological Branch — Ceiling Projectors and Associated Equipment—Manual 70.

Digital SLR Basics (9/21/2007).

Digitalis Education Solutions, Inc.: Manufacturers of digital planetarium systems and inflatable domes.

Discussion of recording SECAM vs PAL on VHS (in French).

DLP vs. LCD Technologies. Boxlight Corp.

dpreview.com (October 2, 2007). Live view from a distance with DSLR Remote Pro v1.5. Digital Photography Review.

Dr. Alexander Russell, *Nature*, 18 August 1928.

Dutch Magic Lantern Site "de Luikerwaal" [Dutch/English].

DVB Project—including data on digital TV deployments worldwide.

Early Television Foundation: Early Colour TV.

Eco, Umberto. *The Role of the Reader*. Bloomington: University of Indiana Press, 1979.

Ed Reitan (1997). CBS Field Sequential Colour System.

Ed Reitan, CBS Field Sequential Colour System, 1997.

Education Week's Digital Directions: Whiteboards Inc.

Ellis, John. *Visible Fictions*. London: Routledge and Kegan Paul, 1982.

Episcopes and epidiascopes, photographs of a collection.

Evaluation of the DCSF Primary Schools Whiteboard Expansion Project, DCSF and Becta (2007).

Explanatory Notes (section) of David Constantine's 1994 translation of Goethe's *Elective Affinities*, Oxford University Press.

Feuer, Jane, Paul Kerr, and Tise Vahimagi. MTM: "*Quality Television,*" London: British Film Institute, 1984.

Fiske, John and John Hartley. *Reading Television.* London: Methuen, 1978.

Fiske, John. *Television Culture.* London: Methuen, 1987.

Fujifilm FinePix IS Pro digital camera specifications: Digital Photography Review.

Gaisberg, Frederick W., "The Music Goes Round" [Andrew Farkas, editor.], New Haven, Ayer, 1977.

George H. Clark Radioana Collection, ca. 1880-1950—Archives Center, National Museum of American History, Smithsonian Institution.

Glen Houser's World Of Radio http://www.worldofradio.com/ .

Glover D., and Miller D., 2002, The Introduction of Interactive Whiteboards into Schools in the United Kingdom, http://www.keele.ac.uk/depts/ed/iaw/

Glover, D. and Miller, D., Averis, D. and Door, V. (2005) The interactive whiteboard: a literature survey. Technology, Pedagogy and Education (14) 2: 155-170.

Goldie, Grace Wyndham. *Facing The Nation: Television and Politics, 1936-1976.* London: The Bodley Head, 1978.

Gronow, Pekka, "The Record Industry: The Growth of a Mass Medium", Popular Music, Vol. 3, Producers and Markets (1983), pp. 53-75, Cambridge University Press.

Gronow, Pekka, and Saunio, Ilpo, "An International History of the Recording Industry", [translated from the Finnish by Christopher Moseley], London ; New York : Cassell, 1998.

Hall, Stuart, Dorothy Hobson, Andrew Lowe, and Paul Willis, editors. *Culture, Media, Language.* London and Birmingham: Hutchinson and the Centre for Contemporary Cultural Studies, 1980.

Hall, Stuart. *Early Writings on Television.* London: Routledge, 1997.

Halloran, James. *The Effects of Television.* London: Panther, 1970.

Hebdige, Dick. *Subculture and The Meaning of Style.* London: Methuen, 1978.

Henrico County School, Study of Promethean Interactive Whiteboards in Classrooms, 2007.

Herzog, Herta. "What Do We Really Know About Daytime Serial Listeners," In Lazersfeld, Paul and Frank Stanton, Editors. *Radio Research* 1942-43. New York: Duell, Sloan and Pearce, 1944.

Hill, Donald R. (1993), 'Islamic Science and Engineering', Edinburgh University Press, p. 70.

Hindi RadioWorld.

Historic Radios from Around the World at Kurrajong Radio Museum, Australia.

Historic Ross Epidiascope.

History of Undersea Cables (1927). http://massis.lcs.mit.edu/archives/history/underseas.cables

Horzepa, Stan, "*Surfin': Who Invented Radio?*" Arrl.org. 10 October 2003.

http://web.tiscali.it/magiadellaluce the site of an Italian collector.

http://www.barb.co.uk/viewingsummary weekreports.cfm?report=multichannel &requesttimeout=500&flag=viewingsummary viewing statistics in UK.

http://www.darkroomsource.net/enlargers.shtml#what I darkroomsource.net article on enlargers I Retrieved 29/07/2008

http://www.ilfordphoto.com/applications/page.asp?n=113 I Ilford Photo article 'Diffuser vs Condenser Enlargers'.

http://www.odyssey-sales.com/products/browse.asp?range=71 I De Vere 504 DS Digital Enlarger.

http://www.ofcom.org.uk/research/tv/reports/dtv/dtv_2007_q3/dtvq307.pdf OFCOM quarterly survey.

http://www.pembers.freeserve.co.uk/World-TV-Standards/Colour-Standards.html# SECAM-IV.

Hugh Richard Slotten (2000). *Radio and Television Regulation: Broadcast Technology in the United States 1920-60*. JHU Press.

"Hytron's Deal With CBS Seen TV Colour Aid", *The Washington Post*, April 12, 1951, p. 15. In June 1951, Philco offered 11 television models that could show CBS colour broadcasts in black and white. "Philco Offers 11 TV Sets To Receive CBS Colour TV in Black and White", *Wall Street Journal*, June 4, 1951, p. 9.

IAteacher: Interactive Explanation of Radio Receiver Construction.

ICT in Schools: Interactive Whiteboards and Teaching.

IEEE, Early History of Single-Sideband Transmission, *Oswald, A.A.* http://ieeexplore.ieee.org/xpl/freeabs_all.jsp?arnumber=4051940

Interactive Whiteboards: New tools, new pedagogies, new learning? MirandaNorth, MirandaNet, Promethean, 2003.

Internet Radio Broadcasting Directory.

Interview: Yoshiyuki Nada, Olympus' Technical Product Manager. Retrieved on 2006-01-06.

Jhally, Sut, and Justin Lewis. *Enlightened Racism: The Cosby Show and The Myth of The American Dream.* Boulder, Colorado: Westview Press, 1992.

John G. Proakis, *"Digital Communications, 3rd Edition"*, McGraw-Hill Book Co., 1995.

John Hora, *The American Cinematographer Manual*, 9th Edition.

John Logie Baird, U.S. patent for colour television, filed 1929.

Johnny Chung Lee - Projects - Wii.

Join TV and Radio Production Training at R.K. Films and Media Academy, New Delhi.

Jon Stewart of "The Daily Show" was mock-outraged at this, saying, "That's what we do!", and calling it a new form of television, "infoganda."

K. Fazel, and S. Kaiser (2003), *Multi-Carrier and Spread Spectrum Systems*, John Wiley & Sons, 2003.

Kaplan, E. Ann. *Regarding Television*. Los Angeles: American Film Institute, 1983.

Krishnan, Prabha, and Anita Dighe. *Affirmation and Denial: Construction of Femininity on Indian Television.* New Delhi: Sage, 1990.

L. de Forest, article in Electrical World 22 June 1270/1 (1907), early use of word "radio."

Larry D. Wolfgang etal (ed.), *The ARRL Handbook for Radio Amateurs, Sixty-Eighth Edition*, (1991), ARRL, Newington CT USA.

Latest snapshots—Freeview/DTT bitrates (Mendip transmitter, UK).

Leeper, David G (2007), "WiFi - The Nimble Musician in Your Laptop", *IEEE Computer Magazine—How Things Work*, April, 2007, pp. 108-110.

Leigh White, *Buck Fuller and the Dymaxion World* (refers to Waldo Warren as the inventor of the word *radio*), in: The *Saturday Evening Post*, 14 October 1944, cited in: Joachim Krausse and Claude Lichtenstein (eds.), *Your Private Sky*, Lars Müller Publishers, Baden/Switzerland, 1999, p. 132.

Leon W. Couch III, "*Digital and Analog Communication Systems*, 6th Edition", Prentice-Hall, Inc., 2001.

Liebes, Tamar, and Elihu Katz. *The Export of Meaning*. Oxford: Oxford University Press, 1990.

Lindberg, D.C. (1976), 'Theories of Vision from Al Kindi to Kepler', The University of Chicago Press, Chicago and London.

Lipman, Samuel,"The House of Music: Art in an Era of Institutions", 1984. See the chapter on "Getting on Record", pp. 62-75, about the early record industry and Fred Gaisberg and Walter Legge and FFRR (Full Frequency Range Recording).

Loch Ness Productions list of planetariums worldwide.

Lopez, Lighting the Flame of Learning for English Langauge Learners Through the use of Interactive Whiteboard Technology by The Corporation for Public School Education K16 (2006).

Lumens guide. ProjectorPeople.com.

Magic Lantern Slide collection at the University of Bristol Theatre Collection, University of Bristol

Mahon, Basil (2003). *The Man Who Changed Everything – the Life of James Clerk Maxwell*. Hoboken, NJ: Wiley.

Martel Electronics. *Terms Commonly used for Tape Recorder*. Tape Recorder Speed.

McRobbie, Angela. *Feminism and Youth Culture*. Basingstoke, England: Macmillan, 1991.

Microsoft Buys Digital TV Ad Provider.

Millard, Andre J., "America on Record: A History of Recorded Sound", Cambridge; New York : Cambridge University Press, 1995.

Millard, Andre J., "From Edison to the iPod", UAB Reporter, 2005, University of Alabama at Birmingham.

Morley, David. *Television, Audiences and Cultural Power*. London: Routledge, 1992.

_____. *The Nationwide Audience*. London: British Film Institute, 1980.

Moss G, Jewitt C, Levaãiç R, Armstrong V, Cardini A, Castle F (2007) The Interactive Whiteboards, Pedagogy and Pupil Performance Evaluation: An Evaluation of the Schools Whiteboard Expansion (SWE) Project: London Challenge http://www.dfes.gov.uk/research/data/uploadfiles/RR816.pdf.

Nazeef, Mustapha (1940), 'Ibn Al-Haitham As a Naturalist Scientist', in Arabic, published proceedings of the Memorial Gathering of Al-Hacan Ibn Al-Haitham, 21 December 1939, Egypt Printing.

Needham, Joseph (1986). *Science and Civilization in China: Volume 4, Physics and Physical Technology, Part 1, Physics*. Taipei: Caves Books Ltd.

Newcomb, Horace, and Paul Hirsch. "Television as a Cultural Forum: Implications for Research." In Newcomb, Horace, editor. *Television: The Critical View.* New York: Oxford, 1994.

Newcomb, Horace. *TV: The Most Popular Art.* New York: Doubleday, 1974.

Nicholas J. Wade, and Stanley Finger (2001), "The eye as an optical instrument: from camera obscura to Helmholtz's perspective", *Perception* 30(10), pp. 1157-1177.

Nikon D300, previewed. Digital Photography Review (Thursday, 23 August 2007, 04:00 GMT). Retrieved on 2007-12-07.

Nikon SLR-type digital cameras, Pierre Jarleton.

Nowell-Smith, Geoffrey (ed.) *The Oxford History of World Cinema*, pp. 446–449. Oxford University Press: Oxford, 1996.

O'Connor, Alan, editor. *Raymond Williams on Television.* London: Routledge, 1989.

Omar, S.B. (1977). 'Ibn al-Haitham's Optics', Bibliotheca Islamica, Chicago.

Orrery and planetarium cardboard kits (Germany).

Painter, D, Whiting, E and Wolters, B (2005) The Use of an Interactive Whiteboard in promoting interactive teaching and learning.

People's Union for Civil Liberties (July 1982). "Freedom of the Press." *PUCL Bulletin.*

Planetario I. Danti, Perugia, Italy.

PlanetariumsClub - German encyclopedia for any topic on planetaria.

Présentation officielle de la télévision couleur—Archives pour tous.

Purser, Philip. *Done Viewing.* London: Quartet, 1992.

Radio Broadcasting from Ghana West Africa.

Radio Today Daily News and Information about radio.

Representation of the NTSC refresh rate on a television and on a DVD.

REVIEW: Canon Powershot S3 IS (July, 2006).

REVIEW: Understanding Depth Of Field.

RSA Cosmos manufacturer of Digital and Optical Planetarium.

Saltzberg, B.R. (1967). Performance of an efficient parallel data transmission system, *IEEE Transactions on Communications Technology* 15(6), 805-811.

Schlesinger, Philip. *Putting "Reality" Together.* London: Constable, 1978.

Science & Society Picture Library: the collections of the Science Museum, the National Railway Museum and the National Museum of Photography, Film and Television.

Seashore, Carl Emil, *"Psychology of Music"*, New York, London, McGraw-Hill Book Company, Inc., 1938.

Seiter, Ellen, with others. *Remote Control.* London: Routledge, 1989.

Sigma Corporation of America. Retrieved on 2007-12-07.

Simon Joinson (July 2007). Fujifilm FinePix S5 Pro Review. Digital Photography Review. Retrieved on 2007-12-07.

Sky-Skan, Inc.—Digital planetarium system manufacturer.

Smith, H.J. , Higgins, S., Wall, K., and Miller, J. (2005) Interactive whiteboards: boon or bandwagon? A critical review of the literature, Journal of Computer Assisted Learning, 21(2), pp. 91–101.11.

South Downs Planetarium and Science Centre, Chichester, England.

Spigel, Lynn. *Make Room For TV.* Chicago: University of Chicago Press, 1993.

Tamron USA. Retrieved on 2007-12-09.

Territory FM (An Australian-based community radio station).

The Advantage of Digital SLR Cameras.

The British DX Club.

The Camera Obscura in San Francisco — The Giant Camera of San Francisco at Ocean Beach, added to the National Register of Historic Places in 2001.

The Canadian parameter, C/(N+I) of noise plus co-channel DTV interface should be 16.5 dB.

The FCC's U.S. consumer-oriented DTV website.

The History of Single Sideband Modulation, *Ing. Peter Weber*. http://dj4br.home.t-link.de/ssb1e.htm

"The how and why of COFDM" Jonathan Stott. EBU: *EBU Technical Review* 278 (winter 1998).

"The Rise of the Machines: A Review of Energy Using Products in the Home from the 1970s to Today" (PDF). Energy Saving Trust (July 3, 2006).

The standard that defines the PAL system was published by the International Telecommunications Union in 1998 and has the title *Recommendation ITU-R BT.470-6, Conventional Television Systems.*

The story of the DP70 - The Todd-AO Projector.

The Winterthur Library Overview of an archival collection on magic lanterns.

Thomas, Howard, editor. *The Armchair Theatre.* London: Weidenfeld and Nicolson, 1959.

Thurber, James. *The Beast In Me and Other Animals.* New York: Harcourt Brace, 1948.

TV Coverage maps and Signal Analysis.

U.S. Supreme Court, "*Marconi Wireless Telegraph Co. of America v. United States*". 320 U.S. 1. Nos. 369, 373. Argued 9 April-12, 1943. Decided 21 June 1943.

Understanding and Measuring Video TV-RF Signals by Glen Kropuenske, CET, Sencore Application Engineer.

Wade, Nicholas J. and Finger, Stanley (2001), "The eye as an optical instrument: from camera obscura to Helmholtz's perspective", *Perception* 30(10): 1157-77, doi:10.1068/p. 3210.

Washington Chosen for First Colour Showing; From Ages 4 to 90, Audience Amazed", *The Washington Post*, Jan. 13, 1950, p. B2.

Williams, Raymond. *Drama In Performance.* London: C.A. Watts, 1968.

______. *Television, Technology and Cultural Form.* London: Fontana, 1974.

Index

Academic filmmaking programmes, 387
Adjustment wheel, 149
Adult film, 24
Advertisement, 23, 27-28, 38, 41, 44, 48, 57, 62, 77, 107, 174, 295, 299, 324
Advertisers, 4, 173
Advertising Code, 23, 38, 54
Aeroplane scattering, 349
African independent broadcasting authority act, 13
Akashwani Bhavan, 334-335
American
  broadcasting system, 187
  radio network broadcasters, 2
  radio programmes, 2
  television, 103, 296
Amperages, 400
Ampex, 77, 85, 96, 389
  equipment, 387
  videotape recorder, 99
Amplifiers, 69, 79, 224, 231, 273, 283-384
  linear, 224, 231, 240
  switching, 224-225, 240
Amplitude, 64, 67, 71, 97, 103-104, 187, 222-223, 236, 244, 249, 263, 265, 329
Amplitude modulation, 88, 226-228, 232, 236, 240
  quadrature, 250, 257, 263, 276, 284, 332
Amplitude-shift keying, 227, 244-245, 266
Analog
  carrier signal, 221, 244
  colour systems, 203
  conversion, 72
  information signal, 220
  lowpass channel, 225
  lowpass signal, 220
  modulation, 220
  recording, 72, 384
  signals, 178, 181, 209, 254
  television, 93, 178, 180, 182, 217, 330
Analytic representation, 234
Anti-globalization protesters film, 387
Anti-hunting protesters film fox, 387
Aperture plate, 134
Applied Associate of Science, 7
APSC film frame, 367
APS-sensor camera, 368
Army Signal Corp, 292
Artifacts, 90, 352
Aspect ratio, 90-91, 100, 102, 115, 134, 178-179, 184, 216, 218, 394
Assembling, 32-33, 55-56
Atmospheric pressure, 72
Attainment, 162
Attenuation, 72, 223, 276, 282, 286, 345, 349
Audicy, 353
Audience seating, 71
Audio
  amplifier, 230, 232
  Broadcast System, 64
  controls, 83
  data, 141-142
  production, 4, 315
  programme signals, 188
  signal, 67, 69, 84, 98, 187-188, 220, 231, 239, 329
  subcarriers, 199
  tracks, 83, 110
Audiovisual, 118-119
Autofocus systems, 360, 364
Automatic Gain Control, 69, 223
Awe-provoking imagery, 124

Bandwidth, 3, 92, 179, 181, 205, 216, 218, 229, 232, 236-237, 252, 291, 293, 330
  conserve, 236, 239
  fixed, 92, 262-263
  luminance, 99
  pre-compression, 216
Baseband signals, 222, 232-234, 284
  composite, 189, 284

Baud, 222, 275-276
BBC, 9, 82, 106, 174-175, 199, 240, 289, 295, 297, 302, 320, 324, 350
Bell Telephone Laboratories, 75
Bessel functions, 237-238
Betamax video tape, 208
Binary data, 227, 251, 254-257, 259, 383
Bit errors, 281
Bit rate, 92, 243
Bit stream, 112, 220, 223-224, 244, 275, 282
Black-and-white, 188
Blackboard, 150
Blackwrap, 403
Blair Witch Project, 387, 398
Bridge Cameras, 371-372
British cultural studies, 323-324
Broadband internet access, 106, 276
Broadcast
  audio signals, 188
  bandwidth, 96, 191
  Bill, 15-16
  cameras, 98, 407
  high powered Short wave, 337
  image resolution, 184
  license, 6
  network, 3, 6
  NTSC, 200, 208
  prerecorded, 2
  programmes, 336
  radio commentary, 38, 57
  Regulatory Authority of India, 32, 41
  signal, 22, 38, 187, 208
  television, 3, 99, 138, 173, 213, 300-301, 322
  unauthorized, 339
Bulbs, 149, 156, 400-403
  fluorescent, 402
Buoyancy, 347-348
Bureau of Indian Standards, 21-22
Business awards, 341

Cable networks, 18, 299
Cable television, 9, 19, 21, 23, 176-177
Cable Television Network Rules, 26-28, 30, 38, 54
Camcorders, 95, 108, 208, 300, 380-387
  professional, 381
Camera
  angles, 399
  automatic, 360
  body, 359, 362, 366
  ciné, 359
  digicam-style, 367
  exposure, 385
  filter, 403
  fixed-lens, 371
  lens project, 382
  monochrome, 103
  movement, 395
  obscura, 152-155, 358
  operator, 391, 393, 395
  output, 360, 363, 408
  pinhole, 153-154
  positioning, leeway in, 115
  shoot, 83
  shots, 302
  special, 114
  viewfinder, 144, 363
  zooms, 396
Cathode ray tube, 96, 129, 172, 212
Cell phones, 330, 332-333
Central Board of Film Certification, 27-28
Channel
  analog bandpass, 220
  audio, 110, 214
  bandwidth, 189, 197, 281
  broadcast, 41
  cable TV network, 220
  capacity, 262-263
  coding, 281-282, 287
  communications, 251, 259
  encrypted, 22, 34, 180
  free-to-air, 21, 174
  information, 207
  right surround, 141-142
  sequences, 291
  surfing, 182, 323
  wireless, 280-281
Chroma keys, 105-106
Cinema sound processor, 141-142
Cinemascope, 144-145, 394
Cinematographers, 138, 391-394, 396-397
Cinematography, 391-392, 395, 397, 404
Clip culture, 107-108
Code of Civil Procedure, 50-51
Coding
  convolutional, 281
  error correction, 281
  signals, 1
Colour burst, 101, 187
  signal, 193
Colour cameras, 409
Colour encoding, 186
Colour film, 374, 377, 393

Colour filters, 211, 393
Colour images, 211
Colour information, 184, 187, 191, 196, 203-204
Colour NTSC signal, 98
Colour sequence, 101
Colour space, 91, 93, 204
Colour standards, 199, 203
Colour subcarrier, 104, 184, 187-188, 191, 195, 204, 207
Colour television, 96, 98, 184, 195, 197, 211, 328
Colour temperature, 363, 401-403, 408-409
Colour video sources, 104
Commercial arrangements, 39-40, 45
Commercial sound motion pictures, 112
Community
  broadcasting service, 13-14
  radio programmes, 16
  radio, 12, 14, 16
Comptroller and Auditor General, 46-47
Computer
  graphics, 106, 115-116, 125, 304
  monitors, 89, 91, 94
Condenser
  enlargers, 157
  lens, 133, 364
Conditional Access System, 18-22
Confiscation, 46
Constellation diagram, 222, 249, 251-253, 255, 265, 267-270
Consumer sound recordings, 74
Continuous wave operation, 244-245
Converter box, 94, 181
Copyright Act, 52
Cosine waves, 252-254
Counterprogramming, 5
Cyclic prefix, 280, 285

Decoders, 17, 34, 48, 142, 281
Decoding broadcast signals, 171
Demodulator, 220, 223, 248, 250-251, 262, 265-266
Deutsches Museum, 124
Devices
  receiving, 33-34, 55-56, 81
  responder, 165
  transmitting, 33, 36, 55
Diffuser enlargers, 157
Digital Audio Tape, 83
Digital cameras, 89, 107, 146, 363, 368-369, 371-372, 385, 393
  advanced, 371
  modern, 359
  ordinary, 363, 365
Digital images, 159, 372
  compressed, 182
Digital signal, 88, 94, 178-179, 218, 225, 333
  binary, 382
  finitely-valued, 273
  processing, 222, 333
  transmitting, 88
Digital SLR cameras, 368-369
Digital soundtracks, 139, 141
Digital star projectors, 129
Digital technology, 129, 300, 359
Digital Video Broadcasting, 287
Digital-to-analog conversion, 221-222
Directional microphones, 67
Direct-to-Home (DTH), 15, 17, 19, 33, 55-56
Disciplinary hybridity, 318-319
Display
  device, 91, 171-172
  images, 121, 148, 169
Distortion, 70, 82, 86, 98, 190, 231, 244, 250, 383
DLP video projector, 149
Document cameras, 150
Documentary records, 48, 51, 397
Dolby, 78, 86, 140-142, 217
Dome image, 129
Doppler shift, 267, 279, 281
Downlinking, 30, 34, 58-59, 61-62
  multi-channel, 34, 56
DSLR cameras, 366, 370, 372
DTV, 88-89, 171, 178-179, 181, 183, 287
Duo-binary signaling, 272

Electromagnetic
  radiation, 334, 343, 374
  waves, 32-34, 55-56, 325, 343
Electronic test signals, 101
Encoding, 93, 204, 215, 218, 244, 259, 273, 276, 323, 333
Epidiascope, 151-152
Episcope, 151-152
Error rates, 249-250, 257, 259, 261, 267, 269, 286
Euclidean distance, 269

Fading channels, 250, 281, 285
Fast cameral movements, 100
Feature film director, 361
FFT algorithm, 279-280
Film emulsion, 392
Film-making process, 397
Fixed focus cameras, 359, 374

Flash-OFDM service, 288-289
FM
broadcast radio, 329
modulation, 204, 216, 240
radio stations, 88, 188, 341
receivers, 235, 240, 329
signals, 208, 216, 237-238, 240, 329
sound carriers, 184, 199
sound system, 199
Focal length, 361-362, 368, 373-374, 393
Focus, 127, 148, 151, 158, 161, 322, 358-360, 362, 364, 377, 393-394, 403
Foot candles, 407-408
Foreign language radio programmes, 329
Formats
consumer audio, 78-79
digital, 106, 113, 142, 191, 383-384, 390
standard raw image, 370
Fourier transform, 228, 233-234, 265
Free-to-Air, 12, 20, 22-23, 173
Frequencies
audible, 64
audio subcarrier, 188
baseband, 235, 243
chrominance subcarrier, 187, 198
colour subcarrier, 97, 186, 198
given set of, 33, 56
higher, 182, 345-346, 348, 350
instantaneous, 236, 273
radio transmission, 233
resonant, 333
Frequency drift, 240
Frequency-hopping, 290-294
Fresnel lens, 149
FujiFilm, 369-370

Gain reduction, 352-353
Gaussian filter, 271-272
Graphic materials, 114
Gray coding, 252, 258

HDTV, 91-92, 171, 177-178
Hilbert transform, 233
Hitz Radio, 341
Hi-Vision, 215, 218
Holographic film, 378
Hue, 97, 101-102, 104-105
blue, 402-404
green, 404

Illegal broadcasting, 48, 338
offence of, 48
Illumination, 131, 149, 157
Image
adjustments, 392
quality, 129, 181, 183, 205, 366, 368-369, 397
sensors, 363, 366
assembling, 300
black-and-white, 184
blue television, 211
bright, 126, 129
broadcasting television, 380
broadcast-quality, 117
computer, 117
continuous, 373
dark, 375
discrete, 117
fast-moving, 150
flicker-free, 185
halftone, 172
hemispherical, 144
professional, 397
recorded, 358
static, 151
transparent, 152, 375
videotaped, 102
yellowed, 149
Image-manipulating techniques, 391
Imager-chip, 383
Imaging sensors, 369-370, 372
Impedance, 65-66, 70, 97, 104
Impluse generator, 266
In-camera, 395
brightened, 385
Indian Broadcasting Company, 335
Indian Broadcasting Federation, 18
Indian Broadcasting Foundation, 61
Indian broadcasting regulations, 12
Infrared films, 378
Interactive whiteboard surfaces, 168-169
Intermittent motion, 137, 140
Inter-symbol interference, 279, 281
Iron-oxide sound recording strip, 143
ISO, 250, 275-376, 378-379, 383, 392

JPEG compression, 117
Junction point, 5

Kamasutra, 24
Khan, Shahrukh, 335
Kodak, 138, 141, 143, 146, 369, 376, 380, 404

Lamp
arc, 149

incandescent, 127, 132, 408
integrated, 149
LCD, 129, 131, 149-150, 176, 365
Leaf shutters, 373
LEDs, 400, 402
Legal Resources and Regulatory Notifications, 8
Lens
angle, 144, 169, 361, 393
condensing, 145, 157, 364
fixed, 365, 371
interchangeable, 372-374
modern television, 360
telephoto, 393
wide-angle, 359, 393
Light
beam of, 156, 325
block, 374, 403
blue, 377, 393
film recording, 401
fluorescent, 402, 404
incident, 382, 407
minimum amount of, 375
open-faced, 401
projector, 169
reflected, 151-152
visible, 325, 334, 350, 378
yellow, 157, 393
Lighting
film, 402, 404
tools, 400, 405
scattering, 349
Line codes, 225
Line-of-sight, 345
Live broadcasts, 2
Local delivery system, 34-35, 56
Logarithm, 375
L-sound system, 199
LUX cameras, 407

Magic lantern, 121-122, 155
Magnetic
film, 77
materials, 79, 85-86
sound recording system, practical, 76
sound, 142-143
tape, 72, 76-78, 84, 89, 239, 380
wire recorders, 76
Mandatory Sharing, 55, 58
Matte screen, 373
Media
electronic, 13, 52, 316, 354, 386
removable, 380
tapeless, 390
traditional, 108
Message signal, 241, 273
discontinuous, 273
low-frequency, 221
Metadata, 108-109
Meteor scattering, 346
Mic level signal, 67
Microphones, 65-72, 74, 80-81, 83-84, 310, 329
dynamic, 67
Military radios, 291
Miniaturization, 340, 380-381
Ministry of Information and Broadcasting, 12, 18, 35, 50, 334-335
Modern digital image processing, 397
Modulated chroma signal, 192
Modulated signal, 222, 228-229, 241, 244, 254-255, 257, 259, 265, 273
Modulation
alphabet, 221-222
digital baseband, 225
digital, 220-221, 254, 270
indices, 229, 237-238, 242
schemes, 179, 225, 240, 257, 263, 274-276, 286
signal, 105, 187, 203-204
single-sideband, 227, 232
trellis, 275-276
Morse code, 227, 244-245
Motion picture cameras, 137, 360
Motion Picture Production, 374, 406
MPEG, 100, 109-113, 382, 385
MPEG-1 Layer, 217
MPEG-4, 89, 92, 383, 386
MTS signal, 188
Multi-channel sound, 79
Multipath interference, 193, 273-274, 280
Multiple access, 224, 282, 292, 294
Multiple Cameras and Projectors, 145
Multiplexed Analogue Components, 213
Multivibrators, 186
Murphy, 352-353
Music radio programmes, 351
Music recordings, 78-79

National Law School of India, 12, 14
National Production Authority, 212
National Television Network of India, 8
Neutral density filters, 403
Nikola Tesla, 325, 327, 334
Nikon, 366-370

Noise, 67, 69-70, 79, 81-82, 86, 88, 99, 182, 240, 246, 384, 401, 407
noticeable, 99
power, 238, 248
ratio, 67, 69, 99, 216, 292, 294
reduction system, 78
signal, 293
white, 260-261, 293
NTSC colour, 185, 212
camera, 213
signals, 102
system, 103
television, 184

Off-camera lines, 84
Olympus, 365, 369-370
On-off keying, 227, 244-245, 332
Opaque projectors, 151-152
Optical glass, 393
Orthogonal frequency-division multiplexing, 276
Output signals, 116, 235
modulated, 232
Overhead projectors, 148-152
Over-the-air HDTV signals, 177

PAL, 90, 186, 190, 192, 194-200, 204, 206-208
colour system, 195, 198-199
discs, 198
formats, 192
signal, 200
Panasonic, 369-370, 381, 387, 390
Panavision, 144, 394
Panoramas, 120, 155
Parametric equalizers, 72
Passband signal, 222
Pentaprism, 363-364, 366
Pentax, 366, 369-370
Personal camera stabilizer, 395
Phase
alternation, 196, 200
ambiguities, 259, 261
angle, 103-104
continuous, 270, 273
distortion, 223, 281
errors, 103, 196, 204
memory, 272
modulation, 226, 240-241, 263
negative, 81
positive, 81
shift, 233, 259, 280
trajectory, 272
Photo Imaging, 399
Photographic film, 359, 374-375, 377-378
black-and-white, 374
Photons, 334, 375-376, 383
Picture
area, 115
detail, 97, 112
elements, 217, 409
high quality, 182, 213
information, 183, 218, 384
moving, 98, 122, 131, 304, 306, 320
quality, 112, 215
sources, 97, 102, 104-105
Pinhole, 127, 152-154
Pirate station, 333, 338-339
Pitch, 81, 190, 243, 297
Pixels, 90-91, 94, 100, 102, 110-111, 115, 129, 146, 178-179, 187, 218, 382
Plan Coordination Cell, 59-60
Planetariums, 122-130
digital, 129-130
portable, 123, 125-126
Planning Commission, 59-60
Plastic fresnel lens, 151
Point-and-shoot, 372
Polarity, 66
Portable video-cameras, 380
Power density, 343
Prasar Bharti, 16, 18, 38, 52, 54-59, 61-62, 334
Programme assembly techniques, 316
Programme Code, 24, 38, 54
Projection systems, 118, 150, 169
Projectionist, 132, 135, 137, 143
Projectors, 127-130, 133, 135-141, 143, 149, 169
ceiling, 156
digital, 118, 129, 146
movie, 131
Propagation
modes, 345, 348-349
range, 346-347
Pseudorandom sequence, 290, 293
Public exhibition, unrestricted, 27-28
Public Service Broadcaster, 21, 35, 37-38
Pulse modulation schemes, 225
Pulse-position modulation, 273-275
Pulses, 97, 99, 216, 274-275, 331-332
electrical, 171-172
equalizing, 97, 103, 192
omnidirectional signal, 331
transmitted, 274

QPSK, 249-250, 252-255, 258-259, 268, 271, 286
  signal, 254
  systems, 253-254
  ordinary, 255, 257, 262
Quadraphonic sound, 79
Quadrature, 187, 263, 266-267
  axes, 249
  mixers, 233
  phase signal, 222
  phase-shift keying, 249, 252
Quality of service, 39, 44-45
Quicktime, 89, 100, 107, 109-110

Radar, 328, 331
Radio
  amateurs, 333
  aurora, 346
  broadcasters, 41, 334, 356
  broadcasting, 1, 6-7, 328, 350, 356
  Ceylon, 350
  channels, 37, 44, 214
  communication, 226, 236, 325-326, 328
  documentary, 355-356
  formats, 355
  Luxembourg, 339, 350
  pirate, 333, 338, 340-342
  propagation, 343-344, 350
  scattering, 349
  signals, 1, 325, 327, 331-333, 345, 349
  spectrum, 329–330, 333, 345
  stations, 2, 229, 327, 329, 331, 338-339, 343, 350, 352, 354-355
  studio techniques, 316, 354
  teletypes, 332
  transmitters, 68, 226, 242, 334
  waves, 325, 332-334, 343-346, 349
Rangefinder cameras, 360, 372
Rapidly-modulated wideband signal, 276
Rates
  baud, 222
  sample, 72
  standard film, 396
  subscription, 18-19, 22
  symbol-error, 269
Reality TV, 175, 295
Real-valued modulated physical signal, 222
Rear projection, 168
Receiver
  light-weight, 275
  multi-standard, 192
  optimal, 272
  reference clock signal, 223
  sets, 36, 57
Recording
  commercial, 73, 76, 78
  companies, 74-75
  devices, 316, 380, 385
  electrical, 74-76
  multitrack, 78-80
  wild, 84
Reed-Solomon coding, 281

Satellite
  channels, 12, 23
  radio broadcasting network, 33, 55
  television, 3, 19, 92, 177
Scattering, 1, 349
School of Broadcasting, 6-7, 357
Screen channels, 141
Screen films, 143
Screen orthographic system, 143
Screen programming, 8
SECAM, 90, 186, 188, 190, 192, 195, 197, 203-210
  analog signal, 209
  analog video format, 236
  countries, 208, 210
  signals, 97, 208
  system, 96, 190, 195
  television, 91
  video recorder, 208
Sensor Size and Image Quality, 366
Service providers
  broadcasting network, 32, 39-40, 55
  content broadcasting, 40
  licensed, 44-45
  licensee, 47, 49
Set Top Box, 20-23
Shooting styles, 398
Sidebands
  single, 233-235, 327
  upper, 188, 232, 234-236
  vestigial, 188, 236, 330
Signal
  amplitude, 104, 240
  analogue, 20, 86, 284
  analytic, 234
  balanced, 82
  bandwidth, 240
  blue, 101
  carriers, 271
  chain, 283
  chrominance, 184, 187-188, 208

competing, 329
components, 255-256
constant-amplitude, 240
constant-modulus, 270
constellation, 253, 259
cosine, 264
demodulated, 208
dimensional, 204
distortion, 87, 208
electric, 72, 89
encoded, 243
inphase, 222
levels, 225
losing, 182
lowpass, 222
luminance, 97, 99, 187, 196, 205, 208
modulation, 273
nearly-discontinuous, 273
pilot, 280
polarisation, 207
power, 238
propagation, 347
protocol, 93
quality, 179
reception, 182
recorded, 99, 171
sideband, 235
standards, 93
strengths, 226, 240, 348, 352
structure, 293
synchronization, 291
-to-noise ratio, 67
transitions, 257
travels, 283
Signal-space analysis, 254
Sine waves, 187, 222, 227, 249, 254, 266, 284, 293
Sinusoids, 249, 254, 263, 273
Slide projectors, 102, 118, 123, 132, 145-146, 148
Sliding wooden box camera, 358
SLR camera, 369
Soap opera, 318, 323-324
Sound recording, 64, 72-77, 81, 87, 315
digital, 80
electrical, 75
magnetic, 76
manual of, 81
practical, 73
revolutionised, 74
Sound reinforcement, 71
Sound signals, 69, 81, 184
electrical, 74
Sound systems
complete home, 79
digital, 141-142
domestic Surround, 79
electrical, 75
four-channel, 79
high-quality stereophonic, 79
optical, 141
Special effect lens systems, 393
Spectral efficiency, 271-272, 283
high, 271-272, 279
Spectral sensitivity, 377
Spectrum, 6, 72, 203-204, 222, 227, 235, 279, 282, 290, 292-294, 332, 334
electromagnetic, 334, 358
licences, 6
systems, 291-292
visual, 377
Sponsorships, 13, 343
Sports broadcasting signals, 54-55, 57-59
Sports channels, 61-62
Spread-spectrum signals, 290-291
Sprockets, 134, 137-138
holes, 137-138
Stereo sound
recording, 77
signals, 240, 329
Stills photography, 397
Storyboard Artwork Project, 311
Streaming video, 112
Stripes, 98-99
diagonal, 98
Studio Dominator, 352-353
Studios
equiped video production, 400
film production, 400
multi-camera, 315
Sub-channel programmes, 329
Symbol error rate, 251, 253
Sync signals, 98, 103
Synchronization, 77, 103, 185, 267, 273, 280
Synchronizing signals, 100
discrete, 103

Tape machines, 84, 87
Tape-recorders, 76, 79, 84-87
Teaching materials, 150
Telecasting programmes, 24
Telegraph Act, 36, 53, 57
Television
academic study of, 317, 319

analogue, 177, 195
audience, 320, 323-324
black-and-white, 184, 187
broadcasting, 1, 7-8, 176-177, 209, 211, 286, 295, 344
broadcasts, 26, 30-31, 236
cameras, 101, 360-361, 407, 409
channels, 30-31, 36, 58-59, 61-62
electronic, 171, 211
engineers, 103, 190, 394
high-definition, 171, 178, 190, 331
lighting, 407
networks, 6, 297
producer, 102, 305, 308, 318
programmes, 34, 56, 72, 106, 114, 295, 304, 306, 308, 318, 320, 322
receivers, 178, 360
scholars, 318, 324
screens, 115, 205
signals, 176-177, 345
stations, 1, 6-8, 116, 181, 308
text, 318, 320-322, 324
video, 89
widescreen, 394
Temporal redundancy, 92
Terrestrial
broadcast television, 177
television, 176-177
Theatre, 81, 120, 122, 124, 135, 137, 141, 145, 295, 317, 319, 394-395
Thunderstorm, 347-348
Tilted domes, 127
Timeslot, 283, 299
Timing diagram, 255-256, 259
Touch surface, 169
Traditional
cameras, 359
movies, 107
Transmission
schedules, 48, 51
signal, 284
Transmitter
land-based, 36, 57
mics, 68, 70
multiple, 293-294
output, 231-232
Transmitting programmes, 1
Tungsten lights, 401-404

Ultra-wideband, 288

VCRs, 98, 150, 181-182, 192, 198, 200, 208, 380-381
Vertical blanking interval lines, 193
Vertical interval reference, 192
Vertical resolution, 185, 205, 211, 217-218
VGA computer image, 100
VHF
channels, 177, 181, 207
frequencies, 287, 346
radio frequencies, 239
signals, 196
videotape, 109
Victor Talking Machine, 75-76
Video blogs, 106, 108-109
Video Broadcast System, 89
Video cameras
digital, 393
fixed, 152
studio-type, 386
Video colour representation, 91
Video editing programmes, 386
Videotape formats, 113
Videotape recorders, 96, 98, 102, 104
commercial, 96
Viewfinder, 115-116, 363, 365, 372-373, 383
electronic, 363, 365, 371
optical, 363, 365, 370, 372, 381
Vinyl records, 74, 77, 80-81
Vividh Bharti Service, 336-337
Voice tracks, 351-353
Voltage signal, analogue, 382

Webcams, 106-107
Whole-camera pans, 218
Wide screen systems, 145
Windscreen, 68
Wireless License, 339
Wireless Telegraphy Act, 53, 57
Wireless telegraphy, 3, 325-327
Wireless transmissions, 325, 327
World War, 2, 74-75, 119, 124, 149, 232, 292, 328, 350, 377

XERF, 339
X-ray films, 377

YouTube, 106-109

Zee TV, 9, 24
Zoom lenses, 361-362, 372, 393
Zoom TV, 24